NATIVE NATIONS

NATIVE NATIONS

A MILLENNIUM IN NORTH AMERICA

KATHLEEN DUVAL

RANDOM HOUSE
NEW YORK

Copyright © 2024 by Kathleen DuVal
Maps copyright © 2024 by David Lindroth Inc.

Published in the United States by Random House, an imprint and division
of Penguin Random House LLC, New York.

RANDOM HOUSE and the HOUSE colophon are registered trademarks of
Penguin Random House LLC.

LIBRARY OF CONGRESS CATALOGING-IN-PUBLICATION DATA
Names: DuVal, Kathleen, author.
Title: Native nations: a millennium of indigenous change and persistence /
Kathleen DuVal.
Other titles: Millennium of indigenous change and persistence
Description: First edition. | New York: Random House, [2024] |
Identifiers: LCCN 2023011941 (print) | LCCN 2023011942 (ebook) |
ISBN 9780525511038 (hardback) | ISBN 9780525511045 (ebook)
Subjects: LCSH: Indians of North America—History. |
Indians of North America—First contact with other peoples. |
Indians of North America—Politics and government.
Classification: LCC E77 .D887 2024 (print) | LCC E77 (ebook) |
DDC 970.004/97—dc23/eng/20231012
LC record available at https://lccn.loc.gov/2023011941
LC ebook record available at https://lccn.loc.gov/2023011942

Printed in Canada on acid-free paper

randomhousebooks.com

2 4 6 8 9 7 5 3 1

First Edition

Spot art by Adobe Stock/toriq

*For my students
in American Indian and Indigenous Studies at the
University of North Carolina, Chapel Hill,
past and present*

CONTENTS

LIST OF ILLUSTRATIONS
AND MAPS

ILLUSTRATIONS

MAPS

MANY NATIONS

I N THE FALL OF 2016, THE ROAD LEADING INTO THE CAMP WAS lined with flags. Lakotas and Dakotas of Standing Rock had been protesting the construction of the Dakota Access Pipeline since early that year, and recently the growing crowd of protesters had spread to this new and larger camp across the Cannonball River. Flying over the trucks, cars, horses, tents, tipis, newly constructed buildings, and demonstrators were more than three hundred flags, among them the red, white, and black stripes of the Arapaho Nation, the Northern Cheyenne Morning Star, the purple Hiawatha Belt with four white squares and a tree of peace representing the Haudenosaunee (Iroquois) Confederacy, and the sand-colored Navajo Nation flag, which shows the outlined shape of the Navajo reservation today between its four sacred mountains, under a rainbow representing its sovereignty. Some people brought American flags too, but the flagpoles flew the flags of Native nations.[1]

The flags and the people who gathered under them displayed not only the #NoDAPL protest's wide support among Native Americans but also the fact that Native nations are still here in North America, despite centuries of colonialism. Today, Indigenous North Americans are citizens of many hundreds of Native nations with sovereign rights within the United States, Canada, and Mexico. When Sharice Davids and Deb Haaland were elected to the U.S. Congress in 2018, they were described as the first Native American congresswomen but also as citizens of the Ho-Chunk Nation and Laguna Pueblo, respectively. Sierra Teller Ornelas, the first Native

#NoDAPL, 2016.

ROBYN BECK/AFP VIA GETTY IMAGES

American to be the showrunner of a television comedy series, introduces herself by naming her Navajo clans. Standing Rock tribal chairman Dave Archambault II explained during the #NoDAPL protests, "We're a nation, and we expect to be treated like a nation." The Standing Rock Sioux were demanding their sovereign rights as a recognized political entity with its own laws and land base. That land is Oceti Sakowin, Lakota for "Seven Council Fires," meaning the seven nations of that confederacy. Native supporters came to Oceti Sakowin not just as individuals but as citizens of Native nations.[2]

Yet the ways U.S. history has usually been told make it hard to understand how more than five hundred Native nations still exist within the United States today, from populous and well-known peoples such as the Navajo (Diné) and Cherokee nations to smaller ones, such as the Quapaw and Peoria nations. Until the late twentieth century, U.S. history books tended to portray precolonial Native peoples as being "so few in number and so little prepared to resist as to have relatively little effect upon the whites."[3] More recent U.S. history textbooks provide more coverage and rightly condemn the violence of European and U.S. colonialism but tend to emphasize victimization and decline. Howard Zinn's *A People's History of the United States* integrated Native history into American history but also taught generations of readers to see Native Americans as helpless victims, "naked, tawny, and full of wonder." Dee Brown's iconic 1970 *Bury My Heart at Wounded Knee* lamented that "the culture and civilization of the American Indian was destroyed." The geographer Jared Diamond's *Guns, Germs, and Steel* erroneously claimed that European military technology and disease caused Native Americans to enter into an almost immediate, precipitous, nearly inevitable decline. Charles Mann, after brilliantly surveying precolonial Native North America in his book *1491: New Revelations of the Americas Before Columbus,* succumbed to Zinn's and Diamond's mistakes in his next book. That book's title—*1493: Uncovering the New World Columbus Created*—sums up the flawed assumption that Europeans dominated North America virtually from the moment they arrived here.[4]

Books and classes about Native Americans have often portrayed them as people only of the past. Most states' social studies curricula include American Indians only in the pre-1900 period of history, and there mostly as generalized objects of U.S. colonization and westward migration with little or no differentiation, histories of their own, or connection to the modern world. Former New Mexico secretary of labor Conroy Chino, of Acoma Pueblo, reflects on the Native American history he got in school: Whether they were taught as savage enemies or victims, "it always served better to be white than to be Indian."[5]

In recent years, scholars of Indigenous studies have published articles and monographs stressing what Ojibwe professor Gerald Vizenor has termed "survivance," a combination of survival and resistance. As Vizenor explains, survivance implies "a sense of native presence over absence, nihility and victimry." Ojibwe historian David Treuer's 2019 *The Heartbeat of Wounded Knee* explains that Native American history did not end with tragedies such as the 1890 massacre at Wounded Knee but continues through the present.[6]

· · ·

THIS BOOK CONTRIBUTES to that change in emphasis by showing how Native nations existed in North America long before Europeans, Africans, and Asians arrived and continue to the present day. Indigenous civilizations did not come to a halt when a few wandering explorers or hungry settlers arrived in their homelands, even when the strangers came well armed. Native Americans made up the majority of the North American population through the mid-1700s and controlled most of the land and resources of the continent for another century after that. Before and during European colonization, Native North Americans lived in diverse civilizations with complex economies and commercial and diplomatic networks that spanned the continent. They live in history, adapting to changes in the Americas for at least twenty thousand years—and counting.[7]

For more than three hundred years after Europeans' arrival, most Native people believed that these newcomers were insignificant wanderers and that the people who mattered were the diverse Native peoples of the continent—nations that had a history with one another, who had seen individual powers rise and fall over centuries. Theirs was an entire world as complicated as those of the kingdoms of Asia, Africa, and Europe. The decisions and actions of Native people affected and shaped European colonialism and, north of central Mexico, restricted European colonies to the coasts and a few river posts for more than two hundred years. And for most Native nations until the nineteenth century, their alliances and wars with one another took up much more of their collective time and attention and had a much bigger impact on their lives than anything Europeans did. For most Native nations, the impacts of Europeans, including land loss and attacks on their cultural and religious practices, were felt much later, in the nineteenth and twentieth centuries. And, contrary to the standard U.S. national narrative, nothing was inevitable about the rise of the United States.[8]

European colonizers generally had no choice but to recognize Native sovereignty; it was only nineteenth-century white Americans who came to believe their triumph was inevitable and who then rewrote the continent's history to fit their assumptions. In a process that scholars call "settler colonialism," nineteenth-century

Americans took Native land and claimed that it had never really belonged to Indigenous people. In the words of an 1854 history of Woodbury, Connecticut, "our pioneer forefathers" encountered a "desert waste" where "roamed the savage wild beasts, and untutored men more savage still than they." Many later scholars who were less blatantly racist still unquestioningly repeated myths of disappearance. As White Earth Ojibwe historian Jean O'Brien explains, these false histories "created a narrative of Indian extinction that has stubbornly remained in the consciousness and unconsciousness of Americans." Native history was pushed into archaeology and anthropology, where Indigenous people were portrayed as having "cultures" more than history, essential and timeless ways of being rather than, like all humanity, changing over time. Mohawk scholar Scott Manning Stevens points out that natural history museums used to put dinosaurs and early primates next to figures of Native Americans, implying that they were all relics of the past.[9]

To stress the survival of Native nations is not to suggest that colonists' intentions were benign or that Native people have not suffered from colonialism. Sometimes Europeans wanted to trade with Native people, sometimes they wanted to take their resources and labor without their consent, and sometimes they tried to get rid of them entirely, but in every case, one of the points of colonialism has been taking the resources of others. Among countless official and unofficial calls for genocide, here's just one example: In the 1750s, the British lieutenant governor of Massachusetts issued a proclamation urging "his Majesty's Subjects of this Province to embrace all opportunities of pursuing, captivating, killing, and destroying all" Penobscot Indians. Penobscots and their allies died in large numbers, and the survivors suffered terribly. Yet, more than 250 years later, you can read about this proclamation on the website of the Cultural and Historic Preservation Department of the Penobscot Nation. It is important to know that the British attempted genocide against the Penobscots. It is even more important to know that they did not succeed.[10]

Countless Native individuals, families, towns, and nations experienced terrible effects from colonialism. Some nations did not survive as independent sovereignties, and their people merged into other Native nations or colonial communities, as refugees or as captives and slaves. Indeed, the inclusive social and political structures of some Native nations allowed them to combine peoples and become some of the largest Native nations today. Telling Native American history for any time after 1492 requires balancing the seemingly contradictory themes of genocide and survival.

American Indians are still here, as individuals and as nations, and they have had a renaissance in the late twentieth and twenty-first centuries. Even as Native communities continue to struggle with poverty, healthcare crises, and the weight of historical loss, they are reinvigorating language and traditions and exercising new political and cultural power. Western Shoshone historian Ned Blackhawk points out "the rising power of American Indians over the past two generations." David Treuer describes Native nations as "surging," and Mississippi Choctaw and Cherokee artist Jeffrey Gibson uses the word "thriving." Osage scholar Robert Warrior writes of this renaissance as "a burst of energy—revitalized languages, profitable business enterprises, the reclamation of lost land and resources." Yet, as these scholars warn, Native nations still are fighting a form of genocide today from people who think they would be better off if they would cease their claims of nationhood and land rights. States and municipalities repeatedly try to bring Native nations under their jurisdiction, attempts that Native nations have to fight in U.S. and state courts. Sovereignty was at the heart of *Haaland v. Brackeen,* the 2023 case in which the U.S. Supreme Court found constitutional the Indian Child Welfare Act, which declared that tribal governments have jurisdiction over the foster care and adoption placements of Native children. The 2016 book *The New Trail of Tears: How Washington Is Destroying American Indians* argued that ending Native sovereignty would be the best solution for American Indians. There is work for all of us to do in what U.S. Secretary of the Interior Deb Haaland calls a "new era" of "truth, healing and growth."[11]

By spanning a millennium-long Native American history, this book connects the past and the present to illuminate both. Rather than give a comprehensive overview, it presents examples and trends of Native North American sovereignty, politics, economics, diplomacy, and war by devoting entire chapters, in most cases, to a single Native nation. The book moves forward chronologically while touching down in different parts of the continent. For the most part, I have chosen not to focus on histories of Native nations when they were subject to overwhelming European or U.S. power. History books, classes, documentaries, and feature films tend to overemphasize the periods of catastrophe, so the history of Jamestown's defeat of Pocahontas's people and the Cherokee Trail of Tears get told again and again, with little attention paid to Cherokees in the seventeenth and eighteenth centuries, or to twenty-first-century Pamunkeys—one of the nations that descends from Pocahontas's people and remains in Virginia. Histories of Native power are part of the large and complicated answer to the question of how Native nations survived to the present.

But as we move toward the nineteenth and twentieth centuries, we will also see the damage that European empires and the United States have done to Native nations. The goals of colonialism were always exploitative, and colonists early on revealed what they might do when they had the numbers to overpower Indigenous people. Some Native nations faced this crisis sooner than others, and all eventually lost land, resources, and autonomy to colonialism. When the demographics were in their favor, Native Americans wielded great power in their relationships with colonizers and often benefited from trade and military alliances, in which they usually set the terms. It was in no way inevitable that Europeans and their descendants would have the chance to actually colonize the vast continents of the Americas. This book won't look away from the damage done by white settlers even as it uncovers the ways that Native nations shaped their own destinies and continue to do so today.

While the book's chapters focus on Native nations in periods of relative strength, their histories also reveal that the nature of Native power changed over this long period. At the start, Native nations had the raw strength of numbers. In the nineteenth century—and earlier for peoples who were locally outnumbered by colonists, mostly near British colonies on the Atlantic coast—as the European

American population grew, Native demographic and military power decreased. Indigenous people had to adjust to a world in which U.S. citizens and their state and federal governments often set the rules. Native Americans learned to use the political and judicial systems as well as the language of colonizers to survive. At the same time, as invasive polities became too powerful to control or ignore, good relations with other Indigenous people became more important, whether in the form of military alliances in the late-eighteenth-century Ohio Valley, nineteenth-century peace negotiations among eastern and western Native nations, the Society of American Indians and the Inter-American Indian Institute in the twentieth century, or the coordination of Indigenous peoples' representatives and institutions in the United Nations. Today, Native nations have rights based on treaties, the laws of the United States and other countries, and international law, as well as a moral and cultural power as the continent's first peoples, with the longest connection to this place.[12]

This book mostly takes place in what is now the United States but will also reveal connections across the hemisphere and around the world. Both in the past and today, Native conceptions of space have often crossed borders drawn by Europeans and their descendants, as the Mohawk and Tohono O'odham nations still do today across the U.S.–Canada and U.S.–Mexico borders, respectively. And although the Spanish established control over central Mexico and islands in the Caribbean in the sixteenth century, scholarship on Latin America has revealed similar continuing Native power for centuries in many parts of what the Spanish considered their empire—a startling contrast to the long assumption of near total Spanish conquest.[13]

One of the goals of this book is to reinsert Native American history into world history. In the centuries before 1492, the place that is now the United States, Canada, and northern Mexico had much in common with the grand changes of the rest of the world: global climate changes, agricultural revolutions, the rise of cities, continent-wide trade, workshop-style manufacturing, and civilizations growing in size. But because of the purposeful erasures that came later, too often people imagine Native Americans as historically more

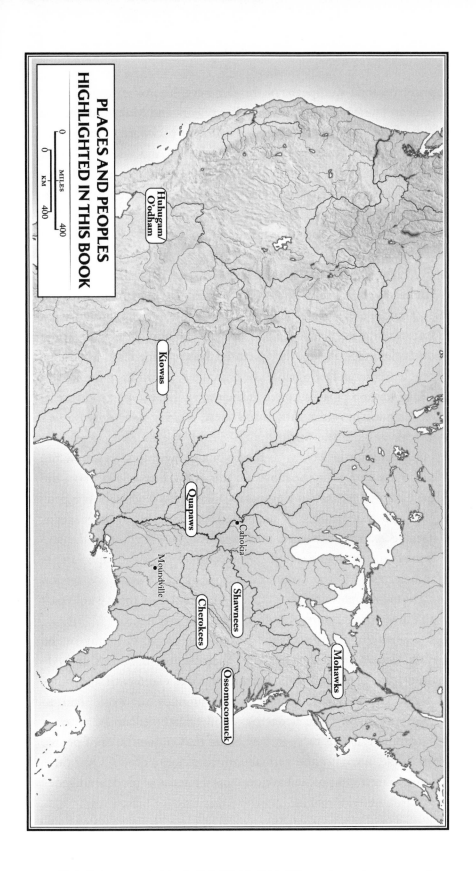

PLACES AND PEOPLES
HIGHLIGHTED IN THIS BOOK

0   MILES   400

0   KM   400

Huhugam/
O'odham

Kiowas

Quapaws

Cahokia

Moundville

Shawnees

Cherokees

Mohawks

Ossomocomuck

primitive than Europeans of the same era. Cherokee women spinning and weaving fabric from mulberry bark and Makahs doing the same from cedar fibers can sound exotic or backward, until you remember that cotton and flax are plants, too. And we will see how that misconception of Native Americans as primitive resulted from Europeans' misunderstandings of the quite complex polities (egalitarian democracies, we might call them) that Native Americans had created to prevent the concentration of power and wealth after the fall of North America's medieval-era cities.

When my sons were young, they learned at summer camp that "Indians started fires with flint and stone." As the campers hunched over piles of dry grass under the North Carolina pines and oaks, striking flint against stone and desperately hoping a spark would catch the grass on fire, they pictured Native Americans as strange people of the past who had to work insanely hard, out in the woods, just to warm themselves or cook their food. The campers didn't realize that when Native Americans were cooking over fires, so was everyone else in the world, and, like everyone else, they kept coals smoldering in the hearth so they wouldn't have to start a new fire each time. People on the move, for war or hunting, might start a fire the hard way, but so did Europeans. Like everyone else, Native people stopped depending on premodern processes when other means became available. They adopted steel to use with flint in the sixteenth century, matches in the nineteenth century, and piped-in gas and electricity in the twentieth. Europeans came upon one version of Native peoples and took it as representative of their whole past and their whole future. A snapshot became eternity.[14]

Native Americans became part of the global economy in the early modern era at the same time that Europeans, Asians, and Africans did. Three centuries later, in the late eighteenth and nineteenth centuries, Indigenous people around the world had to confront a new, more dangerous kind of nationalism based on a hardening sense of race—a new belief that certain races of people were fundamentally and permanently superior to others. Over time, some Indigenous people have developed a sense of global Indigeneity that is forged, in part, by their parallel experiences with colonialism, even as they have maintained their more local identities.[15]

Comparing Native American history with the rest of the world also modifies some of the biggest claims about the impact of "old-world" diseases on the Americas. Smallpox, measles, influenza, and many other diseases that developed in the eastern hemisphere were unknown in the Americas until Europeans crossed the Atlantic, and they were devastating. But some scholars have inadvertently perpetuated the victimization-and-decline model by implying that disease uniquely and universally destroyed Native communities and their way of life, even before Europeans had much population or military strength in the Americas. These scholars used very thin evidence to create the highest possible estimates for the 1491 population of the Americas—as much as 120 million—while understating later population numbers to reach a conclusion that, within 150 years, the Native population of the Americas fell by around 90 percent. Scholars who don't study Native America then have picked up on those estimates to make completely unfounded assertions such as this one from a 2021 book: "The Native population collapsed upon contact with the front edge of white settlements." This overgeneralizing gives the impression that Native Americans were quickly and completely, if sadly, destroyed.[16]

In recent years, scholars have revised these numbers and realized how weak the demographic evidence is. When Chief Powhatan told English captain John Smith, "I have seen the death of all my people thrice," high counters assumed he meant three huge epidemics, but archaeologists have found no evidence of mass burials. Powhatan probably meant he had seen three generations before him die, meaning he had lived a long time. Archaeologists have found no mass graves or other evidence of anything close to a 90 percent death rate anywhere. When a European explorer recorded fewer people in a place than the previous European had, scholars tended to assume that the population had declined from disease spread by the previous explorer, yet explorers' accounts are spotty and often confused. They frequently missed towns, and they seldom understood that large numbers of people regularly left for extended periods of hunting, trading, gathering, or visiting family. And avoiding hungry and demanding Europeans was something Native people learned to do. Disease did spread from European settlements and through Native trading networks, and some of the new diseases killed in horrifying numbers in some times and places. Urban places such as the Aztec cities of central Mexico and the Inca cities of Peru were especially vulnerable. But comparative history reminds us that Europeans did not have much protection either. People everywhere died in huge numbers from diseases that today are prevented by vaccines or cured by antibiotics. The plague known as the Black Death killed perhaps a hundred million people in Europe and the Middle East in the 1300s. In the late eighteenth century, five thousand Philadelphians died of yellow fever in a single summer, some of them rushed to their graves by bloodletting and leeches. They were buried in mass graves in public parks. And, of course, in our own time millions of people—a number that kept rising as I wrote this book—around the world have died of Covid-19. Native Americans practiced quarantine and basic nursing (fluids and rest), which were the best defenses against disease in the past, and, as we learned in 2020, with new diseases even today. In 1793, when a Chickasaw delegation on its way to see President George Washington learned about the yellow fever outbreak in Philadelphia, they turned back.[17]

Relative to Europeans and Africans, North America's Native population did decrease dramatically, changing the balance of power on the continent. But this change happened over centuries, and the violence and dispossession of colonialism bears most of the blame. In places where Europeans settled in large numbers, pushing Native Americans from their land and resources, disrupting food and water supplies, and exposing them to multiple diseases year after year, Indigenous people were vulnerable to the worst effects of disease. And slave raids directly reduced the populations of some communities. Where Native people were still in their own communities, with good access to food, water, shelter, nursing care, and traditional quarantine methods, they died in smaller numbers and recovered faster, and on their own terms. Slavery, dispossession, and colonialism were greater dangers to Native nations than germs alone.[18]

THIS BOOK WILL cover a lot of ground as we move through the centuries, back and forth across the continent, into the histories of several Native nations as well as Native and non-Native neighboring populations, and occasionally around the globe for connections and comparisons. It is the culmination of my quarter-century career as a historian of early North America and draws on documents in Spanish, French, and English archives, as well as translations from Cherokee and Dutch. I have learned from the work of other historians and archaeologists, especially Native scholars, both in academic institutions and Native American governments and communities. Their work and their willingness to share and to collaborate on projects have transformed the fields of Native American and U.S. history and made this book possible. I have tried to live up to the call of Shawnee Tribe Chief Benjamin J. Barnes for scholars to "work *with* not *on* indigenous communities."[19]

This book begins with peoples who lived a millennium ago, a foundation for the long story of how we got to where we are today. Throughout the book, I'll discuss ways in which this history has been mistold and what kinds of sources we have, including written documents, archaeology, oral history-keeping traditions, visual art, and the languages and customs that Native Americans have today, whose roots stretch deep into the past. In each chapter, we'll also hear from descendants today who help with the central purpose of this book: connecting the Native past with the Native present. Most surveys of Native American history foreground war and violence, and there will be both in this book, but I have learned from the work of historians Brooke Bauer (Catawba), Brenda J. Child (Ojibwe), and Susan Sleeper-Smith how Native women were particularly essential to maintaining their peoples' identities, beliefs, and practices through changing times, so there will also be quite a bit on farming, crafts, town governance, and other realms of women.[20]

At the back of the book, I include a list of suggested readings, most of them written by Native scholars about their own nations. Tribal cultural centers and tribal museums are excellent places to learn about the past and present of particular nations—you can probably find one near you with a quick search on the internet. If you haven't visited the National Museum of the American Indian in Washington, D.C., or New York City, I hope you will—these are evolving, living museums curated by Native Americans to tell their own stories. I draw on exhibits from the NMAI and tribal cultural centers throughout this book.

B EFORE WE GET started, a few notes on language. There is no ideal term for the peoples native to the Americas. "Indians" reflects Christopher Columbus's geographic confusion, while both "American Indians" and "Native Americans" oddly include the first name of a minor Italian navigator as well as implying their incorporation into the United States of America (reinforcing the sense of inevitable U.S. dominance). I mostly use "Native," but also "American Indian," "Native American," and "Indigenous" when I need an overarching term. More important, I refer to specific peoples wherever possible. As historians Brooke Bauer (Catawba) and Elizabeth Ellis (Peoria) explain, in contrast to general terms like "Native American," "our identities as Peoria and Catawba are the product of our ongoing and historical relationships to our nations, our peoples' homelands, our cultural practices and ontologies, and the communities that claim and recognize us through citizenship and kinship." The inexactness in any catchall name is a good reminder that there is no single Native American history or culture.[21]

To be an American Indian (as opposed to having some Native American ancestry, which many more Americans do) is to be a citizen of a Native nation, someone who formally belongs to a Native community, meaning both that the Native community recognizes that person as belonging and that the person accepts the responsibilities as well as the rights that belonging to that particular community entails. Native Americans have long lived in nations, even as definitions of that word have changed over time. Europeans called Native polities "nations" in English and French and "provincias" in Spanish—"tribes" is a word that comes later—because many of them fit pre-nineteenth-century European definitions of that kind of polity. A nation was "a people, or country," from the Latin for "to be born," the same root as in the word "native." Before the late eighteenth century, Europeans used "nation" to mean both a polity and a people who shared attributes that united them: language, history, religion, creation stories, geography, kinds of work they did and products they made, and various ways of doing things.[22]

Still, the term "nation" is originally a European one. There are many Native words to describe polities similar to but not quite the same as "nation," such as the Muscogean word "okla." And the nation has never been Native Americans' only identity. People have often identified more by family, band, clan, town, or language, or as the followers of particular leaders. But the term "nation" is useful for understanding what outsiders have often ignored: Native peoples have always organized themselves into sovereign, self-governing polities with their own political structures, laws, economic systems, and foreign policies. They are specific peoples with specific places that are their homelands, whether they still live on them or not. Despite stereotypes that Native Americans all shared the land or that their lands were only lightly used (and therefore available for others to take), Native nations had their own lands, often with clear borders between them. The ways in which Native people used and thought about land differed from one nation to another, and differed from the concepts of Europeans, and they changed over time, but certain places belonged to certain peoples.[23]

It is important to note that "nation" is a label and concept that many Native Americans today embrace as the English word that best embodies the political status of their communities. The Quapaw Nation and the Oneida Nation of Wisconsin are among many who in recent years have voted to change their official name from "Tribe" to "Nation." As Quapaw businesswoman and leader Barbara Collier wrote in an op-ed in the Quapaw newspaper during the election, the word "tribe" is associated with an "unsophisticated, and

unrefined condition," while "nation" connotes "a politically organized community of people possessing a more or less definite territory and government" and is compatible with Quapaw concepts of
people, clan, family, and camp. I try to follow the nations' own naming practices, so you will see "Haudenosaunee" instead of "Iroquois
Confederacy," "Muscogee" instead of "Creek," and "O'odham" instead of "Pima" and "Papago." And in each of the chapters, I introduce Native terms and concepts to aid in understanding. I am
grateful to Native linguists for their translations and explanations.[24]

Understanding this deep past is essential for making sense of
today's headlines, from protests against the Dakota Access Pipeline
at Standing Rock to cases before the U.S. Supreme Court to tribal
governments' roles in Covid aid. At the heart of Native American
struggles and triumphs today is national sovereignty, and that sovereignty exists because of this long history of Native women and men
protecting and promoting it before and throughout the centuries in
which people of European descent attempted to colonize the continent.

PART I

THE INDIGENOUS PEOPLES
OF NORTH AMERICA,
1000S TO 1750

NATIVE NORTH AMERICANS MADE HISTORY FOR TENS OF thousands of years before 1492. As the title of a history program on the Chickasaw Nation's television network puts it, "Our History Is World History." Because the ancient Romans and the ancient Chinese left written records, historians have traditionally found the details of their histories easier to access than those of Native Americans who lived at the same time, generally assuming that eras without written records are the realm of archaeologists. Yet writing is really the exception—most societies around the world did not write until the nineteenth century. Increasingly, historians are crossing disciplines and using archaeology, oral tradition, and evidence from descendants as sources to understand the histories of the distant past. With this broader evidence in hand, comparisons with other places in the world at the same time reveal that societies with written records did not have any more dynamic or exciting a history than those without them.[1]

In the very broadest terms, Native North Americans lived much like everyone else in the 1100s through 1500s. Most human beings kept their records orally, lived in kin groups, stayed close to home, shared buildings that had no heat or light except from fire and sunlight, and feared death from wounds and diseases that today would yield to modern medicine. Most people believed that the spiritual and physical worlds were not separate and that supernatural forces intervened in daily life, for good and for evil. Agriculture began in central Mexico and South America about ten thousand years ago, around the same time as in Mesopotamia, and gradually spread throughout the Americas, as it did to the rest of the world. People built cities and established continent-wide trade networks to exchange food, textiles, pottery, art, jewelry, and raw materials. People everywhere saw the same stars and adapted to the same environmental changes as the planet warmed starting in the ninth century and cooled again four centuries later, as we shall see in chapters 1 and 2.[2]

While people in the Americas in this era were more like their contemporaries around the world than like us today, they were also highly diverse. They lived in thousands of independent polities and spoke hundreds of languages. They didn't think of themselves as one people or one race. Many were members of loosely affiliated nations or confederacies but also identified with smaller family groups or with one town or group of towns.

There were, of course, differences between North America and other parts of the world. People's beliefs, traditions, and languages were their own, forged in common experience and particular to them. And the history of the Americas before 1492 would shape how these peoples interacted with the rest of the world in the centuries to come. In some ways, they moved in parallel with the rest of the world, developing agriculture and building cities, while in others they diverged, creating relatively more egalitarian economies and polities than those of Europeans by the late 1400s. Europeans would overstate these distinctions and underestimate the complexity of Indigenous societies, mistakes that snowballed into histories full of similar assumptions.

In the late nineteenth and twentieth centuries, white Americans convinced themselves that the people here before Europeans had been merely scattered opposition, quickly overrun, but Europeans who came to North America in earlier centuries had no such illusions. They encountered powerful and populous Native nations everywhere they went, and even when they brought well-armed militaries, they fared better when they found Native allies than when they sought to dominate alone, as we shall see in chapters 3 through 6. And although Europeans were ethnocentric in the same way that people all over the world were—believing they were more important, the center of history—they didn't yet assume they were innately and permanently superior to other races, as people would in later centuries. Indeed, the droughts, famines, and pandemics of the medieval era gave Europeans little room for illusions of superiority. In the Crusades, they battled Islamic states whose architecture, art, and learning would help to shape their own standards of civilization. They knew that China and India were ancient civilizations with many products far superior to anything made or grown in Europe. They adopted and responded to ideas from around the world, including North America, as they became less parochial and more cosmopolitan in the fifteenth century and beyond. Only in religion—being Christian—were Europeans sure they were in the right.[3]

Europeans did pose dangers to Native Americans. The fertile lands of North America could produce crops to feed Europe's growing population and make profits for monarchs and lords, and colonization attempts would change the history of North America forever. In some places, European numbers and technology allowed them to gain the upper hand quickly, but in most cases, for centuries after 1492, American Indians held more local knowledge and power. Europeans who wanted land or trade had to negotiate on Native terms, terms that had been shaped by the earlier history of North America. The chapters in this book's first part show the development of North American peoples before 1492 as they responded to local and global forces, and how they confronted and in many cases welcomed and made use of the newcomers who came to their shores in the following centuries.[4]

CHAPTER 1

ANCIENT CITIES IN ARIZONA, ILLINOIS, AND ALABAMA

I T IS RARE THAT EVERYONE IN THE WORLD HAS THE SAME THING on their minds at once, but we know one thing that everyone was talking about in the spring of 1006: the star. It had always been in the sky, but now it was sixteen times as bright as the planet we call Venus. In some places it was visible during the day for an entire month and startlingly bright at night for several years. Scientists today say it was the brightest supernova ever recorded. A chronicler in Baghdad recorded that "its rays on the earth were like those of the Moon." A Benedictine monk in Switzerland wrote that "a new star of unusual size appeared; it was glittering in appearance and dazzling the eyes, causing alarm." Alarm was a common reaction. Egyptian scholar Ali ibn Ridwan wrote about wars and famines that followed the star's appearance. Chinese astronomers worried about whether what they called "guest stars" were auspicious or, as the scholar Li Shunfeng put it, a sign that "presages military action, death, and countrywide famine." Court astronomers worked to assure Emperor Zhenzong that, despite recent invasions, "it presages great prosperity to the state over which it appears."[1]

In our age of electric lights, it is hard to grasp how important the stars were to everyone before the twentieth century. People all around the world used the sky to keep track of time. They could see countless more stars than we can today, and many cultures believed that a change in the sky meant something significant was happening. When another supernova appeared in 1054, less than fifty years later, some people believed the skies were telling them to make a change. They moved to new places and adjusted their religious beliefs and practices. Leaders used the skies for guidance and sometimes pointed to them as evidence that people should follow whatever path they advised. The capital of the Ghana Empire fell to the Islamic Almoravids around the time of the 1054 supernova, and its call to change may have assisted in persuading Ghanaians to convert to Islam. Both the Normans and their English adversaries saw the appearance of Halley's Comet in 1066 as presaging the Norman conquest of England; it is woven into the Bayeux Tapestry.[2]

The people of North America watched the sky, too. Their calendars were based on changes in the moon and in the sun's position relative to Earth. Archaeologists speculate that the second supernova, in 1054, inspired people who had lived in small farming towns in what's now Illinois to tear one of them down and build Cahokia, a large and influential city that would set off a trend of grand civilizations called "Mississippian" that spread all across the Mississippi Valley and the American Southeast in the following centuries. Cahokians clearly saw the sky as important—near its central city was a huge outdoor calendar made of tall red cedar posts, carefully placed to mark solstices and equinoxes. Cahokia was just one of a constellation of city-states across the continent. Also around 1054, the already sprawling civilization of the Huhugam, in what's now Arizona, began its greatest period of growth and centralization.[3]

Around the world, a combination of portentous signs, agricultural expansion, and human decisions sparked the growth of cities. They became crossroads of economic and cultural exchange on a phenomenal scale. They grew and distributed food for thousands, even tens of thousands, of people; they were bursting with artists and craftworkers; and they had fighters capable of defending them and conquering surrounding territory. North America followed this global pattern, but Europeans and white Americans couldn't square this urban past with their assumption that Indians were primitive and nomadic, people whose use and ownership of the land were so light that it really didn't belong to them. By overlooking the continent's history of powerful, sophisticated cities in this self-serving way, Europeans and their descendants would justify taking a continent. This chapter starts by looking at those myths at their height, in the late nineteenth century, and Native Americans' attempts to correct those myths with their own historical and cultural memories. After that we'll look at the realities of that ancient past in three places: Cahokia, the cities of the Huhugam, and Moundville, in present-day Alabama.

MYTHS

In the 1880s, William McAdams, a member of the St. Louis Academy of Science, stood in a cellar in southern Illinois looking for evidence that the huge earthen pyramids that dotted the Mississippi Valley were human-made. Only a few decades earlier, the United States had forced the Chickasaws from their homelands, yet by McAdams's time, archaeologists puzzled over the places that the ancestors of Chickasaws and neighboring Native peoples had built. Indeed, after they removed Native Americans, nineteenth-century white Americans tried to forget they had ever been there at all. The aptly named Mr. and Mrs. Hill had built this house—and the cellar in which McAdams stood—on the highest place on their farm, the flat top of a pyramid ten stories above the prairie below. The walls of the cellar were black, carved out of rich soil that was easy to dig and fertile for the corn and pumpkins the Hills were growing on the flat surfaces of the multitiered hill. But interspersed in the black dirt of the walls here and there, McAdams could see patches of yellow clay and gray silty dirt. If these variations had been natural, they would have come in stratified layers, but these were patches, McAdams noted, "about such size as a man could easily carry."[4]

Humans had built this hill, one bucketful at a time. McAdams's certainty grew when Mr. and Mrs. Hill showed him artifacts they had found on their property, including pottery and axes. Mr. Hill explained that he had dug a well starting at the top of the mound, deep into the soft soil. At the depth of sixty-five feet, he had pulled up broken pieces of pottery and decayed ears of corn, perhaps the lunch remains of an ancient worker building the hill up from the prairie's surface.[5]

Cahokia's largest mound, and the short-lived site of the Hills' farm.
CAHOKIA MOUNDS STATE HISTORIC SITE

McAdams was contributing to a vigorous late-nineteenth-century debate about the origins of hills like this one that people could see rising abruptly from the flatlands of the Midwest, the floodplains of the Southeast, and the deserts of the Southwest. A few years later, exploring the place that had become the city of Phoenix, anthropologist Frank Cushing was astounded to see "the remains of the most extensive ancient settlement we had yet seen, or I had ever dreamed would be possible for us to find within the limits of the United States," a long series of flat-topped pyramids that "lay stretched out in seemingly endless succession," with "the yellow, almost angular slopes of the great central temple-mound" above them. All across the United States, many of these mounds still exist today, after centuries of erosion, although most were destroyed to make room for new towns and cities that Americans built on Native American land.[6]

McAdams had been drawn to the particularly dense ruins of a great Native city that archaeologists called Cahokia (after the Illinois-speaking Cahokia Indians living nearby in the eighteenth century). In his day, two hundred mounds rose up out of the tall prairie grass on both sides of the Mississippi River, so striking that one of St. Louis's early nicknames was "Mound City." McAdams and other scientists in the late nineteenth century were worried that the main city of Cahokia would be bulldozed before they had a chance to understand what they were—just as Cahokia's outlying cities already had been leveled to make room for St. Louis and East St. Louis. Developers were putting pressure on landowners like the Hill family to sell so they could build steel mills at this place near the confluence of the Mississippi River and the Missouri, Ohio, and Illinois rivers, as much a crossroads of the continent then as it had been in Cahokia's time.[7]

Nineteenth- and early-twentieth-century geologists, though, argued that the mounds were natural occurrences, raised up by a deep glacier passing through in a previous millennium or carved out of bluffs by erosion. Many Americans found the geological explanation for the mounds easier to believe than the idea that Native Americans had built cities on a grand scale centuries before the founding of the United States. In the Southwest, because the great civilizations had elaborate irrigation systems apparent to the untrained eye and, in some places, towering stone and adobe buildings, it was harder to claim that there was no human design there. In fact, all across the continent, flat-topped pyramids like the one the Hills had built upon were human-made and once had palaces and temples on top and cities all around.

By the late nineteenth century, explicit theories of white supremacy were at their height, and their proponents' fervor to prove that people of European descent had always been superior led them on a cockeyed search for alternative human builders. Historian Thomas Maxwell, using white supremacist circular logic, told the Alabama Historical Society in 1876 that "the high grade of military engineering skill" required to build one of the earthworks in Alabama "proves beyond a doubt that a more civilized race than the Indians" must have "occupied this continent in the ages that are gone."[8] In the 1780s, the prominent educator and later dictionary author Noah Webster hypothesized that Spanish explorer Hernando de Soto and his men had built the mounds of the South and the Midwest on their journey through North America in 1539–42. Recognizing that building thousands of mounds in less than four years was a bit much even for Spanish conquistadors, Webster and others argued that the Spanish had at the least given Indians the idea—although their motive wasn't quite clear. More damning to this theory were the accounts written by members of the de Soto expedition that mention North American cities built on and around pyramid mounds. Later scientific evidence revealed that the earliest examples of these pyramids were built centuries before de Soto.

People reached for other theories: a Welsh prince, a lost tribe of Israel, Phoenicians, Carthaginians, Egyptians, Greeks, Persians, Romans, Celts, Anglo-Saxons, Vikings, giants, or the survivors of Atlantis—people ancient, impressive-sounding, and definitely not American Indians. Indeed, in many of these theories, the supposedly savage ancestors of Native Americans had killed off these more civilized ancient "Mound Builders." President Andrew Jackson explicitly called them "memorials of a once powerful race, which was exterminated or has disappeared to make room for the existing savage tribes."[9] White Americans called the steep, sharp-sided structures "mounds" instead of "pyramids" and gave the ruins of a great city-state in what is now Alabama the mundane name Moundville. They plowed over them, covering up the continent's ancient past with new towns and cities and promulgating the myth that there had never been Native cities there at all.[10]

But Native people had never forgotten their connections to this urban past. In the seventeenth century, the O'odham told Spanish explorers that their ancestors had built the canals and cities. In 1909, the O'odham said the same to ethnologist Edward Curtis, who nonetheless concluded, "There is, however, little to encourage this claim."[11] As late as 2002, O'odham elders listened as members of the Arizona Archaeological Council discussed theories about what had happened to the people who built the pyramids, cities, and vast irrigation systems. Finally, one of the elders told them to stop asking what had happened to those people: "We are still here." When they toured the ruins, they showed the archaeologists that the roasting pits there looked very much like the ones in which their families had roasted agave hearts when they were young.[12] Huhugam is an

O'odham word that means "those who are no longer with us," a reference to the past generations who built the cities and canals that once covered the Phoenix and Tucson basins. Archaeologists had misapplied the term to mean a vanished civilization with no obvious connection to later Native Americans. For too long, most Americans didn't take oral history seriously, creating a mystery where there never was one. The question of who built these places and where they went are no mystery, O'odham elders and historians repeat: "We've always lived here."[13]

As in the Southwest, Native Americans living near Mississippi Valley pyramids in the eighteenth century told French travelers that they were "the tombs of their fathers."[14] In the early nineteenth century, Kaskaskia Chief Jean Baptiste DuCoigne (the Kaskaskias are one of the Illinois nations, along with the Cahokias) told American military officer George Rogers Clark that Cahokia "was the palace of his forefathers, when they covered the whole [country] and had large towns," and that from the top of the pyramid "they could defend the king's house with their arrows."[15] But Native Americans have also at times refrained from talking to outsiders about their sacred places. A man who grew up in Choctaw country in the nineteenth century recalled that Choctaws "possessed many traditions in regard to the memorial mounds" but "were utterly silent before the whites in regard to the manners, customs and traditions of their tribes, and would only converse upon these subjects with those whites in whom they had the most implicit confidence."[16]

Today, descendants are studying and teaching this long history as one of continuity. On a windy day in 2014, David Martínez, an Arizona State University professor and citizen of the Gila River Indian Community, stood on one of the paths of the S'edav Va'aki Museum (then called the Pueblo Grande Museum), in Phoenix, talking to an Indigenous Tours Project film crew. He gestured to the ruins of this Huhugam city: "All of this is part of our oral tradition. When we contemplate the boundaries of our historical homeland, the boundaries aren't limited to the reservation," a line drawn by treaties with the United States. As he spoke, tourists were peering at the signs and looking down into the excavations, just as I had when I visited here on my own. Professor Martínez explained, "For the tourists who are milling about here right now, this is just an archaeological museum. They are here to learn some history, they're here to learn about the Indians who vanished long ago." He smiled. "They have no idea that one of their descendants is standing right here filming this project."[17]

Rather than assume that Native Americans today have few connections to ancient North America, archaeologists are now required to look for them. The 1990 Native American Graves Protection and Repatriation Act (NAGPRA) requires museums and archaeology departments that hold Native American skeletal remains and sacred burial objects to inform the most likely descendants and give them the opportunity to reclaim them. Some archaeologists resisted the law, but many cooperative relationships have resulted, some of which are true collaborations, with Native nations assessing what's acceptable to study and providing context and meaning. Many archaeologists (and historians) now work from a "premise of continuity," a recognition that Native nations today are descended from the civilizations of the past and have not only knowledge about them but the primary stake in their interpretation.[18]

One example of combining knowledge is a program run jointly by the Chickasaw Nation and archaeologists at the University of Mississippi and the University of Florida in which Chickasaw students from all around the United States spend part of their summer in Mississippi excavating sixteenth-century Mississippian sites. In the summer of 2018, they excavated a flatland where houses had been, learning about how their ancestors lived and worked. The students described their experience as "coming to the homeland." Afterward, they had stories to tell their Chickasaw families and friends and might in turn learn from a grandparent or parent stories that their elders had passed down about their history. The Chickasaw Nation's history television series succinctly explains: "Much of our Chickasaw culture, as well as that of dozens of other southern and eastern tribes, descends from the Mississippian Civilization."[19]

THE RISE OF CITIES

Cities arise only when people are able to live apart from the locations of food production—when agriculture allows their lives to no longer be intimately entwined with the labor of growing food. By definition, urban people don't produce all of their own food. They take on other jobs: priests, artists, manufacturers, teachers, scholars, poets. Urbanization requires agriculture, but the adoption of agriculture did not automatically lead to urbanization and centralized states. For example, the civilization of Jenne-jeno, on the Niger River in West Africa, existed for seventeen centuries as many connected cities specializing in the production of various goods but did not build a large central city or establish a political or social elite. Mesopotamia farmed for four thousand years before developing a centralized state based on an agricultural economy.[20]

Still, over the millennia, some civilizations used the opportunities created by large-scale farming to build cities: in Mesopotamia, Egypt, South Asia, and China thousands of years ago; in the Mediterranean, Southeast Asia, central Mexico, and South America in the last millennium B.C.E.; and in Western Europe, Mongolia, North America (north of central Mexico), and the Sahel region of West Africa in the late first millennium C.E., at the start of what climatologists call the Medieval Warm Period. Temperatures during this period rose on average a few degrees. Frost started later in the fall, and ground thawed sooner in the spring, bringing a longer growing season farther north in Europe and North America. The weather also became more predictable than in the previous era (or the subsequent one). Even farther north, previously uninhabitable places such as Greenland could now support herding or fishing economies. In dry regions, including Mongolia, the West African Sahel, and the American Southwest, increased rainfall turned deserts into places where large-scale agriculture could exist in the river valleys, with the help of irrigation.[21]

There had been small-scale farming in the part of North America that is now the United States for thousands of years, but now the

Artist's conception of life in Cahokia, by Michael Hampshire.
CAHOKIA MOUNDS STATE HISTORIC SITE

changed climate meant that crops that had been developed in central Mexico—most importantly, corn—could be grown much farther north and on a scale never before imagined. Large-scale farming spread north from Mexico first to what is now the American Southwest and then, starting around the year 900, throughout most of the present-day United States. Similarly, in Western Europe agricultural expansion facilitated population growth, urbanization, and participation in the already established trading system that stretched from North Africa through the Middle East along the Silk Road to China, trade that would eventually propel Christopher Columbus across the Atlantic in search of a shortcut to Asia.[22]

People were drawn to cities for a variety of reasons. Cities are built on central access points for trade by water or land, so they have more access to material goods. They provide grand spaces for religious ceremonies and civic and cultural engagement. They can offer safety against human conflict and some natural disasters. Around the globe in the medieval era (to use the terminology of European history), cities, towns, and family groups provided people's primary identities. No one thought of themselves as European, African, Asian, or Native American. From Singapore to Genoa to Cahokia, the great cities were all what we might call city-states: a city, its outlying rural region, and perhaps satellite towns or suburban neighborhoods. Each city-state might trade and ally with others but governed itself, unless it was conquered by another one. Cities came with downsides, too, as we shall see. Urban environments are conducive to disease and inequality, and a strong identification with one city-state could pull people into war.[23]

Archaeologists in the past defined "city" so tightly that it didn't include even Cahokia or the Mayan cities, much less the more spread-out civilizations of other Mississippian places or the Huhugam in the Southwest. Only the great Aztec city of Tenochtitlán, with its population of 250,000, seemed enough like the nineteenth-century European idea of a city to qualify. But when we compare Native North American urbanization within its own period with preindustrial cities around the world, we see that these elaborate and cosmopolitan urban civilizations had a great deal in common in their scale and infrastructure. They depended on agriculture, boasted edifices that impressed visitors coming from miles away, and had economies that included long trade networks. Like the Silk Road or the trans-Saharan routes of the same period, North American trade routes stretched from the Great Lakes to the Mississippian city-states in the Southeast and the Midwest to Chaco, in today's New Mexico, and the Huhugam of Arizona, south to Mexico, and north to Canada. The cities were built at strategic river locations, like ancient Memphis on the Nile, Ctesiphon on the Tigris in the second century B.C.E., and London on the Thames, built by the Romans in the first century C.E.

North American cities' size alone puts them on a global map of the era. Thirteenth-century Moundville, with around one thousand people living in the city and perhaps another ten thousand in its surrounding neighborhoods and farms, was comparable to European cathedral towns of the same period, such as Oxford or Montpellier. Cahokia was bigger, with a central city perhaps the size of thirteenth-century London, Barcelona, or Timbuktu, plus outlying towns and farms, which are hard to estimate because so few have been excavated. The sprawling civilization of the Huhugam by the twelfth century had several cities of more than ten thousand people in the Phoenix and Tucson basins and a total population of perhaps fifty thousand—much smaller than the couple of million living there today but about the size of contemporaneous Delhi, Chichén Itzá, or Florence—and its castles approached the size of those in medieval France or the Benin Empire of West Africa.[24]

THE HUHUGAM WAY OF LIFE

In 1694, when Jesuit priest Eusebio Kino explored what's now the southwestern United States, the O'odham took him to see one of these castles, south of present-day Phoenix. They called it the "hottai ki" or "siwan wa'a ki"—Kino called it "casa grande" ("great house"). Nearby were a dozen smaller houses and the ruins of countless more. It was clear to Kino that "there once must have been a city here," and the O'odham told him that there were more ruined cities throughout their country. By the 1970s, Europeans and their descendants had been marveling at Casa Grande for nearly three centuries, but when archaeologists started to dig broadly around southern Arizona, they were still surprised to find that almost every place they dug yielded evidence of urban life.[25]

It might be a surprise to outsiders that the Sonoran Desert was home to the largest agricultural system of twelfth-century North America. Today, Phoenix averages only seven inches of rain per year and more than ninety days of temperatures above one hundred degrees. Across much of the landscape, giant saguaro cacti stand like sentries, dwarfed only by the buttes and mesas that rise up against the big blue sky and the mountains in the distance. Yet the Gila River and its tributaries have long rippled through this desert landscape, carrying water to the Colorado River near where it empties into the Gulf of California. Before the rivers were dammed in the early twentieth century, their bright green riverbanks colorfully contrasted with the desert sands. The Salt River, a tributary of the Gila, was why Americans in the 1860s built a town they called Phoenix, in hopes that it would rise from the ashes of the ancient civilization of the Huhugam.[26]

The O'odham today stress the relationships they have always had with the Sonoran Desert. Native people were already farming the valleys of the Gila River's southern tributaries in the Tucson basin by 2000 B.C.E. and those of the Phoenix basin soon thereafter. They planted seeds shallowly in the floodplain, and when the rains came hard after months of dry weather, water rushed down the rivers and arroyos (creek beds that are dry much of the year) and sprouted the plants. Their wells and reservoirs captured some of the rain so they could water the plants as they grew. Most deserts, including the neighboring Mojave, have only one annual rainy season, but this part of the Sonoran Desert gets one in the winter and one in the summer, so arroyos and wells filled more often.[27] When corn and ideas about the transformative power of large-scale agriculture and urbanization came north from Mexico in the last millennia B.C.E., the Gila and Salt river valleys were as promising a place as any.[28]

Mesoamerican ideas about urbanization and agriculture seem to have spread from central Mexico west to the present-day Mexican states of Michoacán and Jalisco and up the Pacific coast. Two cities of northern Mexico that were contemporaneous with the Huhugam were Paquimé, in Chihuahua, several hundred miles to the southeast, and a large civilization that archaeologists call Las Trincheras (the Trenches), for its irrigation system along the Altar and Magdalena rivers in what's now the state of Sonora. Along with the Huhugam, the people of Las Trincheras were ancestors of today's O'odham, as we shall see in chapter 5.[29]

Over generations, farmers in the Sonoran Desert expanded their irrigation system. O'odham oral tradition describes how the people "gathered to plan how they would make canals in order to irrigate their crops." After some false starts, they asked I'itoi, the "Elder Brother," to help them, and he directed them to a woman who had the power of fog and wind. As O'odham scholar David Martínez explains, the woman went to a point along the Salt River where they were trying to dig, and the fog and wind that followed her cut channels into the rock "that would enable the people to create the canals that would form the basis of their culture, their civilization."[30] Over time, they expanded the canals and, in an impressive engineering feat, redirected much of the rivers' flow to farms on the terraces above the riverbed, many miles away. At the river, a partial dam diverted flow into a main canal. A headgate there and other gates down the canal allowed for regulation of the amount. Using a combination of gravity and decreasing width, the elaborately designed canals pushed water to the fields. Regular watering allowed for the expansion of corn and other crops, eventually including several varieties of beans, squash, tobacco, and cotton, which weavers spun and wove into cloth. Capturing water from rivers and bringing it to the fields made farmers less dependent on rain and created a longer growing season. The same logic created irrigation systems around the world. The irrigation of rice, for example, allowed China's population to double between the eighth and twelfth centuries.[31]

The investment in irrigation required year-round habitation, so the Huhugam built more permanent houses, set into the ground so they would be cooler in summer and warmer in winter. Their agricultural success drew some people to migrate to their towns and others to borrow the idea. What once were separate bands with their own planting, harvesting, and gathering cycles combined into much larger towns of hundreds of people. They connected single canals with town irrigation systems and then combined these with neighboring systems. Eventually, the main arteries into which water flowed were more than sixty feet wide and fifteen feet deep. Some climbed five stories in the air in order to harness gravity's power to push water into subsidiary canals and smaller channels. By the year 1000, the Huhugam had built the largest irrigation system in the Americas outside of Peru, with well over one thousand miles of canals, irrigating thousands of acres and feeding more than a hundred thousand people. Shell bracelets, rings, and pendants were so ubiquitous that archaeologists suspect people wore them to signal that they were Huhugam when they traveled elsewhere, perhaps even after death. And all of the Huhugam used the same kinds of sparkling everyday ceramic dishes and fancy buff-colored pottery with red Huhugam designs.[32]

Planning, building, and maintaining the canals required increased centralization. Every stone or ounce of dirt was moved by human hands in this era before trucks and bulldozers, a feat as unimaginable to most Americans today as Egypt's ancient pyramids.

Archaeologists estimate that just one canal system would have taken a million days' worth of labor to build, not counting the effort needed to construct the smaller lines to the fields and the continuous work of maintaining, cleaning, and repairing the canals.[33]

Evidence from archaeology and O'odham history allows us to glimpse what life might have been like for a child born in the year 1000, on terraces above the Gila River in the place that the O'odham call Skoaquick, or "Snaketown," just south of present-day Phoenix. Children grew up in their family courtyard. In the morning, some of the men and women from the family went to work in the fields or on the canals, while the children played outside, perhaps sticking their heads into the houses of their grandparents or aunts or uncles, which formed the courtyard's perimeter. All day, the family slow-cooked meals in the shared roasting oven, and some of the family members made jewelry out of seashells imported from coastal Mexico or turquoise or jet from the East. Skoaquick was the major pottery producer for all of the Huhugam, so a girl was likely to train to become a potter, learning to roll clay into fat ropes and coil them into the shape she wanted, maybe a large storage container or a delicate incense burner. Then she thinned and shaped the pot by firmly pressing it from the outside with a paddle while holding a mushroom-shaped tool against the inside, and finally she smoothed it by hand or with a rounded stone. As she grew older and more skillful, she would make finer pottery and use a red iron oxide to decorate it with birds or geometric swirls or people carrying baskets.[34]

In the heart of Skoaquick was a plaza for very large gatherings, an earthen platform raised three feet above the ground for public dances, and a stadium—a sunken oval more than eighty yards long and about half as wide. Five hundred spectators could occupy the seating, made of piled earthen embankments, that encircled the court. If the game was played as it was in Mexico, each team tried to get a hard rubber ball through a hoop set high on a pole at one end of the court, without touching the ball with their hands. Some versions allowed kicking the ball, while others restricted players to their shoulders, hips, and backsides. Points were earned by getting the ball

Artist's conception of a Huhugam stadium, by Michael Hampshire.
S'EDAV VA'AKI MUSEUM, CITY OF PHOENIX

through the hoop or forcing the other team to foul by hitting the ball with their hands. Teams and fans would come to town for ball games, which were occasions for feasting, courtship, trade, and sharing news. The Huhugam eventually had at least two hundred stadiums. Their teams may have also traveled to play in the cities of northern Mexico and in Chaco Canyon, to the northeast.[35]

When people left Skoaquick to go to a game or on a longer trading expedition, they saw the densely packed world of the Huhugam. The feeling might be similar to driving on many streets of the United States today, along which the pizza places, gas stations, fast food restaurants, and tire stores don't change much as you leave one town and enter the next. The Huhugam in the eleventh century lived in a fairly undifferentiated procession of green fields and busy courtyards. Every few miles—within a day's round-trip journey—there would be a considerably larger town with a central plaza and stadium. Like Skoaquick, it served the nearby towns and farms as a center for commerce and culture. These larger towns functioned similarly to a county seat that holds the county courthouse, larger churches and stores and hosts the county fair. Irrigation for neighboring towns was probably coordinated by leaders or officials at the main towns. Hundreds—maybe thousands—of towns lined both sides of the rivers across the vast region, from the upper tributaries of the Gila and the Salt near present-day Flagstaff and Prescott, through the Phoenix basin, and along the Santa Cruz and San Pedro rivers near present-day Tucson and the U.S.–Mexico border. There were probably regional political bodies responsible for negotiating the management of resources, especially water, but there do not seem to have been highly centralized states or leaders in the early centuries of this civilization.[36]

But then the Huhugam dramatically centralized and urbanized. The 1006 and 1054 supernovas may have been a spark, and there was an urgent earthly reason: the Gila River. In the eleventh century, it began to expand its banks. Previously a predictable, fairly narrow channel, ideal for funneling water into irrigation canals, the Gila spread wider and dug into the floodplain on both sides, in a process that geomorphologists call downcutting. The widening river destroyed the original headgates and required new planning and new gates and canals. Evidence also suggests that rain became less dependable in this era, making irrigation even more essential. People became more dependent on large-scale irrigation building and maintenance, which required more central planning and authority.[37]

The rebuilding and centralization resulted in the multistory adobe castles like Casa Grande that would so amaze Father Kino in the seventeenth century and many more observers thereafter— places that looked more like Europeans' ideas of great cities than the earlier sprawl. In the frantic effort to replace headgates, Huhugam engineers made fewer of them, each serving a longer channel, in the hope that combined canal systems would maintain better flow. Having fewer canals meant that larger groups of towns needed to cooperate, and some merged as their populations grew. Most of the population of Skoaquick abandoned it and moved upstream on the Gila River or to population centers on the Salt. At the same time, immigrants from the upland border regions moved down into the river valleys, displaced by some combination of war and environmental crisis. New neighborhoods grew on the edges of the old cities, especially on the Salt River.[38]

Some of the growing towns became great cities with new kinds of public architecture: first pyramids and then, in some, castles or palaces. Townspeople built up the old low, rounded platforms formerly used as public stages and made them higher and wider, twice as high as a person, with sheer sides, sharp edges, and broad, flat surfaces on top. Perhaps the supernovas pulled their focus—like that of other civilizations around the world—up to the skies. Perhaps they intended the height to raise their religious and political leaders closer to the source of precious rain. Whatever the reason, the va'aki (in the O'odham language) marked a major change in public spaces. Stadiums—the center of Huhugam public life for several hundred years—were abandoned, no longer used for games or other activities but simply left to deteriorate. In their place, these new pyramids stood out against the sky. Historian Daniel K. Richter compares this kind of Native North American public architecture to cathedrals of Europe built in the same period, "soaring spaces focusing human attention on the spirit world" as "monuments to a new kind of agricultural civilization."[39]

The differences between the previous open, public stadiums and the new pyramids were striking. From the plaza below, a spectator could see an announcer or a leader standing at the edge of the pyramid's top but not what was going on at the center of the platform. And soon the view was even more obscured by buildings on top of the pyramids, at first an adobe structure or two and then, by 1300, as many as thirty attached rooms, interspaced with private walled courtyards and large spaces for feasting. More buildings were on the ground level near the pyramid, with a thick wall encircling the whole pyramid complex. Small buildings just outside these walls may have been guardhouses to prevent unauthorized entry. Quartz crystals and whistles made of bird bones found on top of the pyramids imply that religious ceremonies were conducted in the private rooms. The architectural changes reflect a more hierarchical political and probably social and economic structure.[40]

This major urbanization required a lot of labor, in addition to the canal repairs. The pyramid at the site known as Cline Terrace had a sixteen-thousand-square-foot base and was constructed of tens of thousands of cobblestones (carried from a creek bed several hundred yards away) layered with literally tons of adobe. Whereas the old stadium at Skoaquick had taken around a thousand days' worth of labor to build, a medium-size pyramid and compound would require three or four times that, and the largest cities—including the new cities on the Salt River known today as S'edav Va'aki (or Pueblo Grande) and Mesa Grande—fifty thousand person-days. Scores of cities of one thousand to ten thousand people rose above the valley, each with at least one pyramid as well as towers and grand decorated buildings of adobe and stone.[41]

People came into the cities to trade their produce and for religious rituals and festivals. All thirteenth-century cities wrestled with sanitation problems caused by unprecedentedly large numbers of people living in close proximity. Because of domestic animals, Europe's cities tended to smell even worse and harbor more disease—the Black Death would kill nearly half of Europe's population in the coming century—and it's possible that Huhugam skills in controlling water flow enabled them to dispose of sewage more efficiently and thus reduce disease.[42]

Even in this period, as inequality increased, there is no evidence of forced labor or Huhugam leaders who ruled through fear, as in much of Western Europe, in Montezuma's empire in central Mexico, and, as we shall see, in Cahokia. As centers of religious life, the cities inspired devotion, labor, and resources from a large number of followers, and they built a great civilization in the desert that could rival any of its time.

THE GREAT CITY OF CAHOKIA

Often when I am in St. Louis, I drive across the Mississippi River and a few miles into Illinois to visit the ruins of Cahokia, the greatest of the Mississippian civilizations. Human-made mountains with amazingly flat, broad tops rise steeply out of the prairie, still dramatic after centuries of erosion. It's hard to understand how anyone could have imagined that they were made by glaciers or could give them the underwhelming label "mounds." I run out of breath climb-

Artist's conception of Cahokia's plaza, by L. K. Townsend.
CAHOKIA MOUNDS STATE HISTORIC SITE

ing the 154 steps to the top of the highest one. From its ten-story height, Cahokia's leaders could see the sweeping prairie, the silvery lake and meandering streams, the distant bluffs with their own pyramids, and another city across the broad Mississippi River, where St. Louis sits today. A lookout could warn the people if a fleet of longboats or a marching army came into sight. I see only occasional cars passing on the nearby roads.

Cahokia began abruptly, around the same time as the 1054 supernova and when the Huhugam began to centralize, abandon stadiums, and build pyramids. Through the early eleventh century, most people in the middle Mississippi Valley lived in towns of less than one hundred to one thousand people, each with its own fields, houses, and perhaps a council house. People had been building pyramid mounds in the Mississippi and Ohio valleys for thousands of years before Cahokia and used them both for burials and as platforms on which to conduct ceremonies and feasts. Building and rebuilding them and conducting rituals upon them were ways for a community to come together.[43]

But in the middle of the eleventh century, people razed one of these old towns and built a dramatic new city. Cahokia was on the Mississippi, built above the floodplain so as to access its fertile land without flooding its homes, and near the Mississippi's major tributaries: the Missouri, Ohio, and Illinois rivers. Workers dismantled the old houses and covered the ground with a new layer of earth to build a higher, perfectly flat plaza, the size of thirty football fields. They built new houses fast, with steep gabled roofs covered in golden-yellow thatch, as identical to one another as homes in the most highly planned suburb today.[44]

Around the main plaza, they built platform pyramids out of river-bottom clay from nearby, laid in thin layers of alternating light and dark colors. They compacted the layers with tools and the pressure of human feet and covered them with a final layer of dark clay. A Choctaw tale recorded in the early twentieth century describes how their ancestors built this kind of pyramid. A group of men selected the site, onto which the Choctaws first laid sacks filled with the bones of their ancestors. As those men directed the work, other men, women, and children "carried earth continually" and built up the structure "until every heart is satisfied." Then they made it level.[45]

On top of the pyramids, Cahokia's builders erected large houses, halls, temples, and council chambers. The largest platform pyramid (upon which Mr. Hill would dig his well eight centuries later) was ten stories high, with three huge, flat terraces, each one crowded with buildings, including a large palace. As with the Huhugam, and like cathedrals and castles in Europe, Cahokia's pyramids connected the world of humans to the spirit world, with a holy elite guarding a majestic sacred space. And like the construction of the Huhugam cities, building Cahokia was a major feat, requiring unprecedented labor and resources. People literally moved mountains by hand. The central pyramid alone was made of more than twenty-one million cubic feet of dirt. Cahokia's laborers built with startling rapidity. They dug up dirt in one place, loaded it into baskets, carried them to the site, dumped them on top, and brought the baskets back down to do it again and again, making the designers' dreams a physical reality.[46]

The rapid building of Cahokia displaced thousands, and perhaps tens of thousands, of people from near and far. Immigrants came by foot and in huge canoes, lured by Cahokia's prosperity and prominence. Others may have been forced to come and labor. The city's population grew to more than ten thousand people—ten times its population just a generation earlier. A major road and river system connected the city to its outlying pyramids, towns, and farms.[47]

Unlike the many cities of the Huhugam, Cahokia had one main city, which housed its leaders and the bulk of its population. This grand city was built to align with the night sky. Its grid and central causeway, a sixty-foot-wide elevated boulevard that led from the city to pyramids on the bluffs beyond town, were set in line with the "lunar standstill," where the moon rises at its southernmost point. If you stood in Cahokia's Grand Plaza on the right evening and looked straight down the causeway, the moon would rise right over the pyramid where archaeologists made their most dramatic findings.[48]

In most of their sites, Cahokia's archaeologists have found many of the same artifacts that their colleagues have in the pyramids of the Huhugam: arrowheads, jewelry, stone tools, and lots of pottery. But in the 1920s, archaeologists digging into an elongated pyramid at Cahokia that they called Rattlesnake Mound discovered more than 150 bundles of bones, representing at least three hundred buried people. Today, NAGPRA protects Indigenous burial sites, and archaeologists would not rummage through Native American graves any more than they would ransack the ossuaries of a medieval European church. But there were no such protections then. Later, archaeologist Melvin Fowler and his team found the remains of two people, faceup, one on top of the other, lying among some twenty thousand shell beads, some as big as two inches across, probably symbolizing water, fertility, and the underworld. Fowler thought these were two male leaders, but more recent testing suggests they are a man and a woman, both in their twenties, perhaps symbolizing the complementarity of women and men and reiterating the fertility theme. Nearby were more young adult men and women buried at the same time and therefore perhaps sacrificed to die with a buried leader. Around them was a treasure trove of more than a thousand arrows, a three-foot-long sheet of copper from the Great Lakes, mica imported from the Appalachian Mountains, and stones for the popular game of chunkey. One very large pit contained more than fifty people.[49]

Archaeologists have found four people missing their heads and hands, and others lie in positions that suggest they were thrown into the pit while still alive, part of a ritual human sacrifice. The victims may have been foreign enemies taken in war or raids, or they may have come from Cahokia's large immigrant population, perhaps forced to surrender some of their youth in sacrifice. Requiring subordinates to give up children for sacrifice was not unknown in the Americas: It was the main reason the Aztec peoples under the rule of Montezuma rose up against him. The young people in Cahokia's pyramids lie near others who are clearly elite, buried in elaborate clothes with jewelry and grave goods.[50]

It appears that Cahokia's rulers had become a hereditary nobility with brutal techniques for enforcing loyalty and mustering the labor to build great edifices and form large armies. They provided well for an elite class but required people in tributary villages to supply crops, labor, and soldiers. Public sacrifice and its connection to the spiritual world seems to have been central to the power of Cahokia's leaders. The positioning of the main burial pyramids at the end of Cahokia's causeway suggests that the human sacrifices that took place at that pyramid, just half a mile outside the city, were no secret. Public ceremonies may have displayed rulers' spiritual power and connections to the weather, the rain, the river's flooding, the sun, the moon, and the stars.[51]

But Cahokia's leaders did not rule through fear alone; they offered prosperity and protection, especially to people who lived in the main city and its outlying neighborhoods. Death rituals were only part of the ceremonial importance of the city of Cahokia. The center of the Grand Plaza, in the middle of the city, was reserved for games and ceremonies, including annual planting and harvesting celebrations that reminded people of their leaders' combined religious, economic, and political power and the importance of agriculture to their cities. Mississippian games, like ball games among the Huhugam, may have helped to spread Mississippian culture. In the game of chunkey, one person rolls the round chunkey stone while two other players run after it, aiming to hit it with their spears. Basically, it's a gambling game. Children learned to play with smaller sets, and a family or town might have its own lucky stone. Stickball, played with rounded wooden and leather rackets and a ball, may have been even more popular, although its imprint in the archaeological record is not as ubiquitous as that of chunkey stones.[52]

Warfare declined in the region after Cahokia rose to power, in part because Cahokia's rulers established a monopoly on violence within their realm but also perhaps because organized stickball substituted for war between peoples under Cahokia's rule. Eighteenth- and nineteenth-century southeastern Native Americans called stickball the "younger brother of war" and sometimes used it to settle disputes. Archaeologists have compared Cahokia's peacekeeping influence to the Pax Romana, when imperial Roman rule and a focus on wars at the edges of the empire brought about a decline in warfare within the empire. Cahokia's leaders may have similarly combined public displays of power with a general sense that life was safer under their rule.[53]

As a powerful, hereditary elite, Cahokia's leaders established and maintained power in ways similar to hierarchies in other places around the world. In Western Europe, the feudal system developed in the late years of the Roman Empire as a system of personal patronage in which a lord provided protection for peasants, in return for which the peasants gave the lord a share of their crops. Above feudal lords, the king or overlord exacted military support from his subordinate lords when he went to war. In India, the zamindari system worked similarly, with a landowning nobility and peasants working the land, while in Japan daimyo landholders wielded more direct power than even the emperor. Hereditary rulers also reigned in central Mexico and Peru. As at Cahokia, leaders at the top of these socioeconomic hierarchies used ceremonies and rituals to persuade the people that their rule was legitimate, sanctioned by the natural order of things and the god or gods who oversaw it all. Farmers under Cahokia's rule gave their produce to Cahokia's rulers, who in turn distributed it along with manufactured goods, using that distribution to boost their own economic, religious, and political power. In return, farmers received military protection against foreign enemies. In times of trouble, peasants could take refuge in the city. Whether great lords, minor nobility, artisans, or peasants, people were born to a class and generally stayed there. Cahokia's laborers, farmers, artisans, bureaucrats, priests, lords, and ladies wore fabrics in particular styles and colors that displayed their rank and occupation. Cahokia's commoners wore fairly simple skirts and breechcloths, while its elite added vibrantly dyed capes, belts, sashes, fringe, headgear, and footwear and apparently were the only ones allowed to wear red (what Europeans would call a sumptuary law). Cahokia's realm saw an increase in militarization and glorification of war as leaders amassed and armed young men loyal to them. Warriors and severed body parts form a strikingly large part of the art of Cahokia, as they do in medieval Europe.[54]

Towns in the hills about a day's walk southeast of Cahokia reveal how the region changed to support Cahokia's economy. Diverse immigrants from the Illinois and lower Ohio and Arkansas river valleys settled there at around the same time that the city of Cahokia was built. In this densely populated region, some towns were intensive farming communities, while others specialized in manufacturing, including a town that made textiles and another that made beads from shells. Although they may have brought some of these skills with them from their former homes, labor was far more specialized in Cahokia's orbit. They still practiced some older ways. In most places, gathering and farming plants was a woman's role, and women were the farmers in Cahokia and other Mississippian civilizations. In the Mississippi Valley, over the course of a year, women planted a series of different crops in the floodplains along the rivers and streams. They planted traditional grains, greens, sunflowers, and squashes alongside corn, and they built their new houses like their old ones, around family courtyards rather than in the centralized style of Cahokia and its towns in the floodplain. Some evidence suggests that the people in some of these subordinate towns had diets inferior to those of Cahokia and perhaps sent any available meat, fish, and nuts to the city.[55]

By the late eleventh century, Cahokia had built a great civilization. People living within its realm saw benefits, and some of them became evangelists, ready to spread the word of this new way to live. They conquered other peoples and made them into tributary states. Farther afield, the word spread of Cahokia's new beliefs and practices. It was a weighty message, and it would dramatically change the eastern half of North America. Yet people would adapt Cahokian ways to their own circumstances and histories—in many ways Cahokia would remain unique in its extreme centralization and hierarchy.[56]

EMULATING CAHOKIA IN THE BLACK WARRIOR RIVER VALLEY

One of the many places where the news from Cahokia met a receptive audience was five hundred miles to the south along the Black Warrior River, where people would build the city today called Moundville. Starting in the Appalachians, the river twists and turns southwest to the Fall Line at present-day Tuscaloosa, Alabama, where the rocky piedmont soils end and the more fertile soils of the Gulf Coastal Plain begin. From there it runs south to become the Tombigbee River, which flows to Mobile Bay. Not coincidentally, nineteenth-century Americans would establish cotton plantations on the rich lands along the lower Black Warrior River. As in the pre-Cahokia middle Mississippi Valley and the pre-Huhugam Gila River Valley, people here lived mostly in small villages, farming corn, sunflowers, and greens in the floodplain.[57]

By the late eleventh century, the villages on the Black Warrior River had become crowded. Successful corn agriculture had improved health and allowed the population to grow. As their towns, fields, and hunting grounds expanded to feed their growing populations, they clashed with the people of other towns, which also were expanding.[58]

Cahokia offered an answer. Archaeologists know that Cahokia influenced changes in other places, including here, but we can only speculate about how the word spread. Emissaries may have visited and described the grandeur of Cahokia and claimed that its religion and economy—including specialization of labor—had given it the ability to feed and house an unprecedented number of people in peace, while also bringing its leaders new wealth and prestige. Perhaps they showed local leaders a great copper mask or an intricately carved conch shell. Or people in the Black Warrior Valley may have heard of Cahokia and made pilgrimages there to see how it worked. Or perhaps intermediaries described what they had seen and heard.

However they learned about Cahokia, starting in the second half of the eleventh century, people of the Black Warrior Valley began building a city after its model. They chose a high natural terrace, fifty feet above the river and therefore, like Cahokia, both prominent and safe from flooding. They started with two small platform pyramids, where archaeologists have found goods imported from other places—the beginning of the trading center the city would become. They could have taken another path—another group of farmers less than two hundred miles west in what's now Mississippi built small centers with pyramids but no major city.[59]

As in Arizona and Cahokia, once the leaders of the Black Warrior Valley started building, their ambitions grew. Around 1200, they replanned the city and began construction of more than a dozen pyramids at once, encircling a large rectangular central plaza much like Cahokia's. The tallest pyramid, on the north side of the plaza, was nearly six stories high. The people of Moundville built a strong palisade around their city, perhaps because warfare continued in its early years. The palisade alone required thousands of logs, and it continually needed reinforcing and rebuilding. Accounts from Hernando de Soto's expedition in the sixteenth century describe how Moundville's palisade might have looked: three stories high, "made of logs . . . driven into the ground so close together that they touched one another," with smaller beams "placed crosswise on the outside and inside and attached with split canes and strong cords" and mud and straw packed into all of the cracks "in such a manner that it really looked like a wall finished with a mason's trowel." De Soto observed defensive towers (bastions) every fifty paces, from which seven or eight archers could shoot, and there were holes in the wall below for shooting from ground level.[60]

People moved to Moundville from the surrounding region, and its population grew to between one and three thousand—nowhere near as large as Cahokia's main city but bigger than anything the

Black Warrior Valley had seen before. They grew corn and other crops in nearby fields and tended orchards for nuts. Some of what they planted remains today at the site, including yaupon, a holly bush native to the coastal South and presumably brought and raised here because the leaves and shoots make a caffeinated tea and, when steeped very strong, the ritual beverage later known as "black drink." "Yaupon" is a Catawba word meaning "small tree," and indeed the bushes can be as tall as trees. The homes of the town's elite sat on some of the flat-topped pyramids, while Moundville's other residents lived in neighborhoods between the pyramids. In workshops at Moundville or in outlying towns they made axe blades, from greenstone they mined locally, and sandstone palettes—large, flat disks probably used as portable altars.[61]

Like Cahokians, the people of the Black Warrior Valley shared their new ideas and technologies. Smaller communities near and far would send promising young people—male and female—to train to become priests. They learned songs, chants, dances, and secret ceremonies. They smoked Moundville's tobacco. Some saw visions, which they interpreted with the help of Moundville's priests. Once the training was complete, the newly minted priest would return home with a bag of sacred objects and one of the sandstone palettes used for religious ceremonies. Thus the wisdom and practices of Moundville—and Cahokia before it—spread throughout eastern North America.[62]

The pyramid mounds were sites of great activity, not just residences for the elite. On the flat platform on top of one, archaeologists have found evidence of religious ceremonies and related manufacturing. People mixed paints, painted figurines and pipes, and made red and green stone pendants, copper jewelry, and elaborate feather costumes. The spaces were grand: One large building was 2,400 square feet, and it opened onto an expansive walled courtyard of six thousand square feet, high above the river below. These open spaces hosted large feasts where banqueters ate lots of corn and venison. There are also remains of an astonishing array of other animals: bobcats, cougars, bears, gray foxes, minks, passenger pigeons, hawks, skunks, bison, sandhill cranes, peregrine falcons, and

Moundville today.
AUTHOR'S PHOTOGRAPH

sharks. Whether people were eating all of those animals or using them for ceremonies (or both), this was a special place, symbolizing and projecting political and social power.[63]

As in Cahokia, Moundville's elite had more elaborate burials than most, and pyramids on the northern edge of the city were specifically constructed for their graves. Yet there is no evidence of human sacrifice at Moundville, despite its many other similarities to Cahokia.[64]

Although Cahokia inspired people throughout the Southeast and the Mississippi Valley, it was unique. No other place had as large a central city—Moundville and all of the later Mississippian complexes had more spread-out living arrangements—and no other Mississippian city-states seem to have had as powerful an elite as Cahokia. Although the city of Moundville was a major public works project that required central planning, archaeologists have found no signs of coerced labor, internal violence, or even centralized economic control. The Museum of the Cherokee Indian, designed and run by the Eastern Band of Cherokee Indians, notes that pyramid building could have been done through community projects where people took pride in their contribution to building a great city.[65]

People in the small towns and farms ate pretty much the same things as people in the city. Whereas some American cities of the same period show tuberculosis taking hold in populations made vulnerable by inadequate nutrition and overcrowding, the people of the Black Warrior Valley—well fed and relatively dispersed across the land rather than highly urban—escaped heavy disease outbreaks. In the Black Warrior Valley, you didn't have to live in the city to have a feast. A town a few miles north of Moundville, for example, held feasts where fine serving platters came piled high with corn, venison, shellfish, rabbit, squirrel, raccoon, fruit, catfish, and redfish. Small clay jars held drinks to wash it all down.[66]

The earliest archaeologists at Moundville focused on the eponymous mounds, but it turned out that a big part of the history lay in the outlying farms and villages. The first inkling of their importance came in 1976, when archaeologist John Walthall surveyed a small patch of just over two square miles in the Black Warrior River's floodplain, hoping to find a long-lost farm or two. As he and his crew sampled, they discovered at least twenty farms in just this small space, all dating to the era of Moundville. Subsequent investigations found many, many more in the surrounding lands. Now we know that the floodplain for nearly fifty miles up and down the river from the city was populated with rural settlements and small towns. It's hard to date them precisely enough to know if they all were occupied at the same time, but it is clear that, even as some people moved to the city, many stayed behind.[67]

People who remained in the countryside adopted some new architectural and ceramic styles, clearly sharing ideas with the city. People in some of the towns built pyramid mounds after the Cahokia-Moundville model, and some of these towns started to get a little bigger, attracting immigrants from other towns or farms. They built more houses around a central open plaza. Eventually there were at least ten of these towns with one or more pyramid mounds strung along the Black Warrior River, a few miles apart so that most people lived within walking distance of one, where they would presumably go to trade and participate in ceremonies and other gatherings.[68]

The reigning theory among scholars today for how Moundville arose is that the towns sent some people to live and work in the new city, along with providing much of its food. This plan was vastly different from Cahokia's disruptive growth. An immigrant to Moundville would have found much to ease her transition and make her feel at home. She would come with her family through the gates of the palisade and be led to the neighborhood affiliated with her clan, nestled between its own two pyramids. Walking its small streets, past rows of houses, she would hear her own language and see familiar faces. As she stepped down into her new wood-framed house, the small space—perhaps three hundred square feet, about the size of today's "tiny houses"—with its central hearth felt familiar. As she had back home, she would spend most of her time out in the courtyard with neighbors, going indoors to sleep at night and when it rained. Walking outside the palisade to the fields was a new experience, as was passing by strangers on the way, but she would do it in the company of women like herself.[69]

Archaeologists now see Moundville less as a city ruled by political leaders and more as a "ceremonial ground," which is what Choctaws and other Mississippian descendants call the place where people of various towns gather for ceremonies that involve the entire nation. Different clans are responsible for different ceremonies, and at the ceremonial grounds people traditionally camp near fellow clan members, even if they come from different towns. The neighborhoods at Moundville may have been designed in a similar way, and its elite leaders seem mostly to have had religious functions, even if the founders of Moundville may have originally hoped to be as politically and economically powerful as their Cahokia models. The city's neighborhoods were decidedly separate, with unoccupied areas dividing them. Perhaps keeping them separate assured residents that they could continue to have the identities and families and local leaders they'd had in their hometowns, even as they became part of a great new city. People back home sent crops and meat for their relatives living at Moundville, maybe even bringing them at celebration times and joining in the feast.[70]

And it worked. There was peace and prosperity where there had been conflict and food shortages. Because of their continuing and apparently willing relationship with Moundville, its outlying communities were not subordinate ones, like those that fed Cahokia. They were prosperous, and they had a full religious and political life connected to the city but not entirely dependent on it. Cahokia and Moundville—even though fairly close in place and time and both part of the Mississippian world—display the diversity of North America. The Black Warrior Valley had its own unique history among the great cities of North America, and its people built on and preserved older traditions even as they added new ideas, architecture, and ways of living on the land.[71]

CONCLUSION

The Cherokee linguist Ben Frey and I visited Moundville Archaeological Park during its thirtieth annual Native American Festival, surrounded by groups of schoolchildren set free for the day to romp in the park's open spaces, eat chili dogs, and raise their voices above what's allowed at school. Professor Frey grew up in a suburb of Birmingham, just over an hour's drive from Moundville, so he was one of these schoolkids twenty-five years ago, and he attended Indian camp here once or twice. He remembers thinking it was strange to learn about Indians from park rangers rather than—as he usually did—from his Cherokee mom and her relatives, but he doesn't remember much else. He was a kid, after all, surrounded by non-Indian kids and not likely to call attention to himself and have to explain, as he so often did in Alabama, what his mother had told him: that he was a citizen of the Eastern Band of Cherokee Indians, that being Cherokee meant something more than his childhood self could quite put into words.

On this day, though, Professor Frey did call attention to himself, without quite meaning to. Having finished our fry bread and Indian tacos from the Choctaw Kitchen food stand, we walked into the living history exhibits. As a dressed deerskin caught my eye, Professor Frey leaned toward several women and men dressed in the vivid cottons and white beads of Cherokee regalia and said, "Siyo digali'i, osigwotsu?"[72] They looked up in surprise, and then Sandy Brown, who leads the dance and living history group Touch the Earth Dancers, replied, "Vv, osda, nihina?"[73] Her daughter recognized his name when he introduced himself, and she explained to the group that not only is he a fellow Eastern Band Cherokee, but he is a professor who teaches Cherokee language and is a leader in efforts to bring it back into daily use.

Sandy Brown put Professor Frey to use that day—her Touch the Earth Dancers were just about to start a demonstration of Cherokee social dancing on Moundville's Native American Stage, and they pulled him into all four of their dances in the blazing Alabama sun of that unseasonable ninety-two-degree October day. At the end of each dance, he would head toward the bleachers to try to take a break, but she would call over her microphone, "Don't go anywhere, Ben," wielding his name like a lasso. But she also explained to the audience, "Ben's a language speaker and a teacher; he teaches at UNC–Chapel Hill. He does a lot of great things for our people." By the last dance, the Friendship Dance, she was telling us all to follow his lead in the call-and-response singing, and we snaked around in formation to their strong voices and the beat of the drum in time with our feet.

The old myths that giants or Vikings built these mounds make no appearance at Moundville's Native American Festival. The Cherokee, Choctaw, Chickasaw, Muscogee (Creek), Houma, and Alabama-Coushatta performers, living history presenters, and craftspeople, along with Moundville's rich archaeology museum and the informational signs around the park, leave no doubt that this is an Indigenous place and that southeastern Native nations are its descendants. Native people lost most of these sacred places in the nineteenth century along with their other lands. They no longer control how their meanings are presented. There are still schoolkids who struggle to understand how their families and communities fit with non-Indians' ideas of what Indians should be. But there are also many Native people who know and teach the enduring legacy of these ancient places and how they are tied to their lives today. Many of the dances performed at Moundville these days have roots in stories told in common by people who descend from Mississippian societies. As Professor Frey explains, "We are linked through a common thread of history, rooted in these places."

The myth that Native Americans were primitive people too uncivilized to have developed cities was a convenient way for Europeans and European Americans to assert territorial claims and cultural superiority. In reality, Native America had a long and complex urban history that had been changing and growing for centuries before Europeans arrived. It was true that, by the seventeenth and eighteenth centuries, most of Native North America looked nothing like the cities that Europeans came from, but that was not because they were primitive or never had cities. Instead, by the time Europeans arrived, most Native Americans had rejected cities' centralized power. As we shall see in the next chapter, the cities' fall would create a new world in North America, long before Europeans claimed to have discovered one, and would prompt the development of some of the most egalitarian societies in the early modern world.

CHAPTER 2

THE "FALL" OF CITIES AND THE RISE OF A MORE EGALITARIAN ORDER

AROUND THE YEAR 1300, THE HUHUGAM GREAT CHIEF SI-
wani ruled over a mighty city, with many pyramids, an irrigation system that watered fifteen thousand acres of
crops for five large cities, and a great castle (what the Spanish would
call Casa Grande). By Siwani's time, the Huhugam had thrived in
the desert for nearly a thousand years. Modern Phoenix will have
lasted that long only if it is still around seven hundred years from
now. The O'odham descendants of the Huhugam tell in their oral
history that Siwani had "reaped very large harvests with his two
servants, the Wind and the Storm-cloud," but he had grown angry
with them and sent them away. It was a bad decision. As he should
have known, without Wind and Storm-cloud, "he could no longer
harvest any crops." The people ate the food they had stored from
past harvests "and came near dying of hunger" until he called Wind
and Storm-cloud home. But then more trouble came. So much rain
fell "that the whole country was covered in water." This oral history
suggests that the power of Huhugam leaders rested on their ability
to provide, in part by controlling the elements. When the weather
refused to cooperate, Siwani lost his awesome power. One day, as he
looked out from one of his city's towers, he could see a mass of
people coming to overthrow him. They mocked him as they approached: "Yonder stands the doomed habitation. About the pueblo
runs its frightened chieftain."[1]

The great chief Siwani was one of many North American leaders
between the late twelfth and late fourteenth centuries who faced

environmental and political disaster and the destruction of the civilizations they ruled. It was a time of dramatic change. By 1400, the cities of Cahokia, Moundville, and the Huhugam were abandoned. People continued to live nearby and, in many cases, continued to use the ruins as part of their ceremonies, but they no longer lived in the cities. Trade, religion, and politics became democratized, more the domain of the people. North America changed dramatically between 1200 and 1400, and the causes had nothing to do with Europeans. Christopher Columbus would not cross the Atlantic for another century.

One of the reasons for the dramatic alteration of cities was climate change. The warmth and less volatile weather of the Medieval Warm Period that had started in the ninth century and allowed large-scale agriculture to spread north into the present-day United States from central Mexico reversed itself, becoming colder and less predictable. First, year after year of drought battered the globe in the final century of the Medieval Warm Period (in the late 1100s and early 1200s). In the Khmer Empire of Southeast Asia, for example, monsoon rains that had supported large-scale rice production and a centralized empire with giant temples where thousands of people worked became less dependable and added to existing religious and political problems. A couple of thousand miles to the north, Genghis Khan capitalized on the troubles caused by drought to conquer much of Central Asia starting in the 1220s.[2]

Then, starting around 1250, the global climate began to cool, while weather volatility persisted. A bit like what we've experienced in our own early years of climate change (though with temperatures cooling rather than warming), one winter might come earlier and cause a harvest dramatically smaller than the previous one. But the next year's winter might return to normal, and people would assure themselves that the bad year had been a fluke—until the following year proved rough again. Over time, summers shortened and winters lengthened. Climatologists call the period starting around 1250 the Little Ice Age, an era of colder and more unstable weather that would last six centuries, not lifting until the mid-nineteenth century.

In the depths of the Little Ice Age, the annual global temperature was five degrees lower than in the Medieval Warm Period. The Thames River froze. Glaciers advanced down the Alps and covered whole towns in ice. In North America, it snowed in Alabama and south Texas. In the seventeenth century, the coldest and driest decades of the Little Ice Age, drought and the resulting famine brought down the three-hundred-year-old Ming Dynasty. In the same decades, famine and disease killed many thousands in Japan and Korea, and drought led to three million deaths in Gujarat, in western India.[3]

The Little Ice Age was particularly hard on large, centralized agriculture-based cities around the world, including those of Cahokia, Moundville, and the Huhugam. In times of hardship and famine, leaders struggled to maintain their positions, especially if they had claimed special powers over natural forces that were out of their control: rain, rivers, and temperature. The urbanized settlements of North America were unable to deliver the health and prosperity that people had enjoyed for generations. Now people saw conditions getting worse in their lifetimes: less food, more poverty, a declining future for their children.

A changing environment may require adjustments in how people live, but how they adjust—what they give up and what they hold on to, what they stop believing in and where they put their faith— depends on human decisions. It's easy to look at the archaeological record of abandoned cities and assume that societies declined, but in O'odham history, the fall of the Huhugam is part of their *creation* story, the history of how the O'odham rejected a less sustainable civilization and became who they are as a people. Oral, archaeological, and written evidence shows that large populations survived in all of these places by adjusting how they lived, by creating smaller-scale societies that in many ways worked better for people and their environments.[4]

Gradually, across Native North America, people developed a deep distrust of centralization, hierarchy, and inequality. The former residents of North America's great cities reversed course, turning away from urbanization and political and economic centralization to build new ways of living, more similar in scale to how their distant ancestors had lived and how some peoples had continued to live even during the height of the large civilizations. Smaller-scale communities allowed for both more sustainable economies and more widespread political participation. Peoples instituted a variety of political checks and balances to prevent dictatorial leaders from taking power and to ensure that citizens had a say. These changes did not all happen at once or in the same way everywhere. Many places had never established the hierarchical structures of Cahokia or the Huhugam, and some of the leveling trend continued in later years as societies adjusted to population declines resulting from European diseases or dispersed to get away from European settlements.[5]

Western Europe took a different path in the Little Ice Age. For Europeans, the city became the marker of civilization—indeed, they share the same root, "civis." They doubled down on hierarchy and centralization as means of dealing with the difficult times. Europeans' resulting beliefs have shaped subsequent notions of what civilization is. Their assumptions informed later anthropological models, still taught in schools today, of how societies develop along an imagined progression, from the hunter-gatherer "Paleolithic era" to the agricultural and urbanizing "Neolithic era," before they can truly be part of "history" once they invent writing, then passing through an age of absolute monarchs to eventually arrive at democracy. Europeans interpreted these steps as universal rules. Centuries later, in the Age of Revolutions, Europeans would call for the rights of man and curb (or guillotine) their monarchs. In some ways, Native Americans took a shortcut to democracy, developing participatory politics rapidly after rejecting the hierarchies of the twelfth century.

BRINGING DOWN THE CITIES

Urbanization is not a necessary condition for civilization, or for a good life. Smaller-scale societies that include hunting and gathering in their economies can provide their people with a better diet and more leisure time. Judging civilizations by their elaborate structures surely is less useful than asking what kinds of structures and ways of life made sense for people in a given place and time. In fact, people have had mixed opinions about cities for as long as they have existed. Those who live in and benefit from them often believe that urban life is the only life worth living. In the first large cities— ancient Rome and the cities of Han Dynasty China—urban thinkers and writers saw themselves as more rational, sophisticated, and advanced than rural dwellers.[6]

But there has always been an opposing view, held by those on farms and in small towns and even shared by some urban dwellers: that cities are corrupt places, whose residents are willing to trade autonomy for material comforts under autocratic rulers. In the last century B.C.E., the Roman poet Horace described the country mouse who traveled to the city. He enjoyed feasting in a wealthy home, but when he saw the city mice run in fear from the household's barking hounds, he was glad to get home to his simple "woodland hole."[7] A Chinese writer noted of early-seventeenth-century Beijing that

> the houses in the capital are so closely crowded together that there is no spare space, and in the markets there is much excrement and filth. People . . . live together in disorderly confusion, and there are many flies and gnats. Whenever it becomes hot it is almost intolerable. A little steady rain has only to fall and there is trouble from flooding. Therefore malarial fevers, diarrhea and epidemics follow each other without stopping.

A German doctor in 1796 called cities the "open graves of humankind."[8] One need only glance at global history to see that urbanization tends to be accompanied by centralized power and an increasingly rigid class structure, in which wealth and power concentrate among a few families. Diseases spread faster in urban populations, and even though the Americas did not suffer from smallpox or influenza before the late 1400s, they did have some kinds of tuberculosis and infections caused by bacteria, fungi, and parasitic worms, all of which thrive in dense host environments. Cities can also become less livable as they grow. A generation ago, Bengalaru (Bangalore), India, was known as "the Garden City," but now that it has doubled in population, it takes hours in terrible traffic to cross. In some urban areas in the United States, it can be difficult to find affordable fresh produce and other healthy foods.

What happens when dominant rulers fail in their omnipotence, when the security or prosperity they promise erodes? Throughout North America, the benefits of belonging to centralized civilizations declined, and the awe and loyalty that leaders inspired declined as well, as they proved incapable or corrupt. Some of these problems were internal, not clearly related to the Little Ice Age. Cahokians could see inequality increase in the late 1100s as elite Cahokia families built increasingly grander houses and had more elaborate jewelry and housewares. New walls surrounding the main city indicate that warfare increased, that Cahokia's leaders were less able to protect the people. And a wooden palisade built in the late 1100s around the central plaza and pyramid, with its temples and elite homes, heightened the distinctions between the elite and the city's commoners, as with the Forbidden City in China.[9]

North America's cities were built for the conditions of the Medieval Warm Period, even stretching the limits of their resources then. When rain became less consistent, cities' corn consumption increased. Whereas Cahokia's people ate a wide variety of foods in its early years, after 1200 corn made up a higher and higher percentage of their diet, causing a number of health problems, including anemia and general malnutrition. Droughts at the beginning of the Little Ice Age were an even bigger problem in the arid Southwest, where there was less room for error. As we saw in chapter 1, the Huhugam were able to respond to the widening Gila River in the late eleventh century by building bigger irrigation infrastructure, but that kind of problem multiplied in the subsequent century. It must have been horrifying when the Salt River also underwent downcutting, resulting in the same kind of widening. In the vagaries that climate change can bring, the Huhugam would suffer both drought and flooding. In the past, a major flood usually came once in a generation, but in the fifteen years from 1298 to 1313 the Salt River flooded five times. Powerful seasonal surges of the Salt and Gila rivers destroyed canal lines and flooded fields, ruining crops and requiring huge efforts to repair and realign the canals in hopes the next year would be calmer.[10]

In the preceding two centuries, as the populations of the cities on the Salt and Gila rivers doubled, they had stretched the limits of not only their irrigated fields but also nearby nonirrigated food, including mesquite beans and wild game. Making matters worse, people in the uplands had previously been important trading partners for the cities, providing wild foods and crops that did not require irrigation, but their migration to the river valley cities had dried up that food source. As in Mississippian cities, corn began to make up a higher proportion of the Huhugam diet, but flooding and drought prevented farmers from increasing corn production, so they simply had less food to eat. In the late years of the Huhugam, many women died in childbirth, and perhaps half of the infants born died before their first birthday. Deaths came so often that funerals were a steady fact of life. For those who survived past childhood, life spans decreased, and people were less healthy during their short lifetimes.[11]

As in Cahokia, Huhugam families walled themselves in. By the early fourteenth century, Huhugam cities and towns were fortified by adobe walls, and the desert areas beyond them, which once had nonirrigated farms, were unpopulated. Within the urban complexes that sprawled out beyond the central cities, the old family courtyards became gated compounds surrounded by thick walls over six feet high. Elite families now lived in their own walled compounds with their own stores of food. Perhaps longtime residents feared immigrants and wanted to protect their food. As they built walls, the Huhugam also withdrew from connections to the outside world. They had already stopped having the ball games that once brought in visitors, and now they ended the widespread regional trade they had engaged in for centuries.[12]

Inequality grew between the religious and political elite and most of the population. The pyramids reflected the rise of a Huhugam leadership that restricted access to ritual spaces and knowledge and claimed the exclusive power and right to mediate with the supernatural, as Siwani's relationship with Wind and Storm-cloud depicts. The Huhugam elite had more in life and in death: Rather than being cremated like everyone else, their bodies were placed into adobe sarcophagi and either put on display or buried in the new compounds on or near the pyramids. A few were buried with not just the shell jewelry and tools that accompanied the burials of ashes in family cemeteries but also symbols of power such as a trumpet made of a conch shell, presumably used in life to call the people together. These super-elite burials were rare, but when they occurred in all their glory they reminded everyone of the increasing distances between the elite and the commoners.[13]

As the crises grew and leaders seemed less deserving of their positions, people made changes. In Cahokia, residents began to move away. At first some moved out of the main city into its tributary cities, perhaps at the lords' direction as an attempt to reduce the city's crowding or risks of unrest. But as conditions worsened, huge numbers left Cahokia's realm entirely. The farming towns that supplied Cahokia were abandoned beginning around 1150. Over time, family groups left and tried farming in new places, beyond the reach of Cahokia's leaders, in places that still had woods full of trees for firewood and building and game to hunt, both of which had declined near Cahokia due to its rapid growth. Cahokia had grown fast and with some measure of force, and the decision to leave may have been facilitated by oral histories of ancestors forced to come to Cahokia from a former, more independent way of life.[14]

As Cahokia's leaders struggled to keep their power, they apparently grew more tyrannical: They beheaded people who opposed them, and rebellion and war broke out, prompting more to flee. Rough estimates for the population of the central city of Cahokia are sixteen to twenty thousand people at the height of its power in 1100, perhaps five thousand in the year 1200, and only three thousand by 1275. At some point the elite left as well, maybe fleeing rebellion or unable to sustain their city's economy and public works on their own. By the late fifteenth century, the cities of Cahokia's realm were completely gone, their palisades and buildings burned or fallen in, their pyramids, plazas, and fields overgrown with vines. The region around Cahokia was so emptied that archaeologists call it "the Vacant Quarter." All of the river valley towns were evacuated, and

Ruins of Casa Grande, photograph taken 1892.
PHOTCL 215 (112), THE HUNTINGTON LIBRARY, SAN MARINO, CALIFORNIA

the few people who remained in the region lived in the uplands and stopped building cities and pyramids.[15]

In the O'odham creation story—the oral history of how the Huhugam leaders fell and the O'odham came to be—the ancestors were divided into two peoples: the Huhugam and the Wooshkam. I'itoi, the Elder Brother, had helped the Huhugam make their way of life, but Huhugam leaders had become unhappy with him and tried to kill him. I'itoi summoned the Wooshkam to fight the in-flated Huhugam elite. The Wooshkam brought down the great houses one by one, starting with Siwani's Casa Grande. To restore a better balance with the land, they needed to destroy the misused powers forever, including making sure each formerly powerful leader was dead and that "the understandings that he had were gone." The Wooshkam may have been a separate people, or they may have been an offshoot of the Huhugam who started a revolution. They might have come from Las Trincheras, on the Altar and Magdalena rivers in what's now Sonora, Mexico, whose people farmed on a large scale but had not created large cities. In any case, by destroying the too powerful leaders, the Huhugam and the Wooshkam together found peace and built a more sustainable future in the O'odham home-land.[16]

Climate change and environmental destruction seem to have been triggers in the fall of North American cities, but each place had its own political, economic, and social factors, most of which are hard to see in the archaeological record alone. Looking at other city-states around the world of similar size that fell during the Little Ice Age reveals many reasons for dissent. In thirteenth-century China, harvests fell to cold and drought, frozen rivers and canals prevented food from reaching places in famine, and occasional monsoon years washed out fields and irrigation systems. But the Yuan Dynasty might have survived these climate-related disasters were it not for internal political rivalries and local rebellions by people who did not feel loyal to the empire.[17]

So, too, did Moundville carve its own path forward, based on a combination of older local traditions and the changes the previous era had brought. Like Cahokia, Moundville had rapidly grown into a bustling city, and as dramatically as it had risen, it too was evacu-ated. But in contrast to Cahokia and the Huhugam, it does not seem that the people of Moundville overthrew or abandoned their leaders when crops failed, perhaps because they hadn't consolidated their power to the same extent or asked the same sacrifices of their peo-ple. There's no evidence that they controlled the manufacture and distribution of goods, used force to compel submission, or unequally distributed resources.[18]

Hierarchy declined in the Black Warrior Valley, but without a dramatic fall along the lines of Cahokia or the Huhugam. Mound-ville continued to be a sacred place, perhaps more than ever. Most of the residents and activity moved out of the city of Moundville, but people continued to come from the surrounding areas by canoe and on foot for religious rituals and to bury their dead in the city's cem-eteries. Religious leaders continued to live on the pyramids of Moundville as it became a holy city, important and sacred to people in outlying regions, who sent corn and venison to the priests. Whereas those who left Cahokia did not return, Moundville's peo-ple maintained their connections to particular clan-based pyramids and priests there through the early sixteenth century. Moundville's palisade fell into disrepair, indicating a more peaceful and more open time. There is no sign of violent political or social change. Some towns in the Black Warrior Valley grew larger by building a pyramid mound or two and attracting immigration. Larger towns served as regional centers, and their importance increased when people no longer lived in Moundville. None came close to the previous size of Moundville, though, and most people lived on farms and in small towns.[19]

Similar change happened all across the Mississippian region. In the Ohio Valley and the Cumberland Valley of Tennessee, where Cahokia's influence had inspired cities, those who had swiftly converted to Cahokia's way of life now rejected it and moved back to smaller towns. Archaeologists discovered that in the Piedmont region of what's now North Carolina and Georgia, around 1450, people also abandoned the cities and towns. Some places still had towns with pyramid mounds where perhaps leaders and their families lived, but by the fifteenth century most people lived on farms— archaeologists have found tens of thousands of them in the north Georgia Piedmont alone. All across North America, the old era of hierarchy and centralization was ending. People were slowly building more sustainable ways of living that could more predictably feed and shelter people in an unpredictable climate. And they were creating more equitable ways of living together, in hopes of preventing leaders from accumulating too much power.[20]

A CHANGED WAY OF LIVING

Cherokee oral history tells that there once was a priestly caste called the Ani-Kutani, "of whom the people stood in great awe." The Ani-Kutani built pyramids and controlled the religious ceremonies. As the Museum of the Cherokee Indian, in Cherokee, North Carolina, explains, "No one knows how they came to power, or how long they maintained it, but over a period of time, they became haughty, insolent, overbearing and licentious to an intolerable degree." In the words of another version, "The people long brooded in silence over the oppressions and outrages of this high caste, whom they deeply hated but greatly feared." The exact spark that started the Cherokee revolution against the Ani-Kutani varies in different versions, and in some the mound builders are "cannibals" who misled the Cherokees, but all tell that "at last their power was annihilated by the nation," because "the people rose up" and destroyed "a hereditary secret society, since which time, no hereditary privileges have ever been tolerated among the Cherokees."[21] A character in the Cherokee novelist Sequoyah Guess's 1992 *Kholvn* explains that long ago his ancestors had "traded authority for security but wound up with coercion and fear." The revolution succeeded, and "it was a horrible and bloody lesson that needed to be passed down." If they were wise and lucky enough to remember their history, "they would never have to learn it again."[22]

Lessons told by the descendants of Chaco Canyon, in New Mexico, similarly tell of a rejected hierarchy. Wizards had misled some leaders, who became corrupt and hoarded wealth and power. According to the origin tale of Acoma Pueblo, in the time of Chaco, men accused of mocking the kachina—a religious figure—would be clubbed to death. But "some people did not approve" of this extreme punishment. They fought against the leaders; others simply left. A large group traveled to a new home, where "they went through the ceremony of forgetting . . . and left their sickness and trouble behind."[23] In a Navajo version of Chaco's history, "the Great Gambler" was a stranger who tricked people into building Chaco, but they eventually rebelled against him. The smaller-scale Pueblo communities of later centuries, with more public religion and shared governance, represented a conscious, deliberate reaction to and rejection of Chaco's centralized rule and religion.[24]

Ruins like those at Chaco Canyon and Casa Grande and vacant mounds like those at Cahokia and Moundville tend to conjure images of collapse and tragic loss of a golden age, but the generations that followed the cities' fall generally described what came later as better. Smaller communities were easier to keep clean and free of human waste. Most allied with neighboring towns but resisted raising an urban elite or committing to the requirements of building and maintaining large public works. Families lived in fairly uniform houses and received the same rituals after death. Cities' walls fell into ruin, and pyramids and palaces were abandoned, although descendants would continue to visit them because they carried an important connection to the past.[25]

All across North America, the process of decentralization continued over several centuries. In most places, people first moved out of the large cities into smaller cities, and in subsequent generations they decentralized further, into towns of a few hundred along rivers and streams. Descendants of the Huhugam spread out into towns in southern Arizona and northwestern Mexico. Descendants of Cahokia, Moundville, and other Mississippian cities built towns along the Mississippi, Missouri, Illinois, and Ohio rivers, and across a large expanse of the Southeast, from the Carolina Piedmont to northern Florida. West of the Mississippi, oral tradition says that the Quapaws, Osages, Kaws, Poncas, and Omahas moved from the east, perhaps fleeing the chaos of Cahokia's fall. Cahokia had combined different peoples, and after its fall they separated again.

The first European explorers who crossed North America got a glimpse of this changing world. Looking for gold, Hernando de Soto and his army wandered through the Southeast and the Mississippi Valley from 1539 to 1542, while right around the same time, other Spanish explorers in the West recorded some information about Huhugam descendants. In river valleys where the Huhugam had farmed, Spanish explorers found large populations, fertile fields, and no great cities. Friar Marcos de Niza marveled in 1539 at fields "so stocked with food that there is enough to supply more than three hundred horsemen" and "so well irrigated that it is like a garden."[26] De Soto's expedition described the Black Warrior Valley (which they called the province of Apafalaya) as "a very populous and fertile land" with "some large enclosed towns and a considerable population" spread out across the countryside. They found many a "good town" with "plenty of food." Instead of the concentrated city that Moundville once had been, de Soto saw in the Black Warrior Valley a set of towns, each with a pyramid mound or two serving as a ceremonial center for the people in farms and small towns within walking distance. All across the Southeast, de Soto saw small cities and large towns, some with leaders still ruling from pyramid mounds. Yet none of the cities was nearly as large as Cahokia or had its influence, and many places that had been cities in the past were no longer.[27]

Sixteenth-century Spanish explorers expected to find cities in the North because they had found them in central Mexico and Peru, where extreme centralization and hierarchy remained. The cities and towns that they found were much smaller than they had been in the twelfth century, but Spanish explorers didn't realize they were visiting a late stage of decreasing urbanism. After all, a town of a few thousand still constituted a city in early modern Europe. It was the later English and U.S. colonizers who would imagine that Native North Americans were too primitive to be urban.[28]

A DIVERSIFIED ECONOMY

In the seventeenth and eighteenth centuries, Europeans and white Americans would assume that North America's societies were primitive, simple, and timeless, but in fact societies that discourage the accumulation of authoritative power and wealth require complicated structures to encourage and maintain those values. As one anthropologist puts it, "Egalitarian societies do not just happen." Native North Americans developed complicated political, economic, social, and religious structures that encouraged shared prosperity and shared decision making. Anishinaabe historian Cary Miller explains that Native American nonhierarchical political systems "were neither weak nor random but highly organized and deliberate."[29]

Sixteenth-century Spanish explorers were able to find plenty of food because Native North Americans had put a high priority on diversifying food sources in the aftermath of the droughts of the twelfth and early thirteenth centuries and the continuing colder and unpredictable weather of the Little Ice Age. In the East, women grew beans and squash in the same field as corn so that the beans grew up the cornstalks and the squash vines covered the mounds to discourage weeds. To Europeans, this kind of field looked messy, but these methods were more efficient than European row planting, because the beans replaced the nitrogen that corn took from the soil and reduced the need for crop rotation, which requires leaving vast acreage lying fallow. They developed multiple varieties of corn for different conditions, providing more security against crop failures. Modern studies have found that seventeenth-century Haudenosaunee farmers produced three to five times more grain than European farmers did on the same amount of land. Part of the reason is that corn naturally has a higher yield than wheat, but also Haudenosaunee planting methods were highly efficient, and they didn't use plows, which were necessary to farm Western Europe's heavy soil but tended to degrade the land.[30]

Determined not to depend on one source of sustenance, people built a variety of foods into their lives. They hunted, fished, and gathered more, in order to be less dependent on farming. "Gathering" is a term that can conjure images of people randomly searching for food, but in fact women planted and nurtured particular plants in particular spots that they returned to seasonally, including nuts, fruits, and greens. Trade expanded, with goods carried all across the continent in dugout canoes and on trading roads, and provided a variety of products in good times and a safety net when drought or other disasters stressed supplies. If one year's crop failed, people still had plenty to eat.[31]

In 2019, I met with Arizona State University professor David Martínez in his office in Tempe to ask about connections between the Huhugam and their O'odham descendants. Professor Martínez is a citizen of the Gila River Indian Community and is of Akimel O'odham and Hia-Ced O'odham descent. We signed copies of our books for each other, and he explained that, according to O'odham oral tradition, "we had this great civilization" that suffered environmental catastrophe. Huhugam's descendants temporarily migrated away from the Gila River and its tributaries—the Salt, Santa Cruz, and San Pedro—"largely to let the land heal," and then slowly returned.[32] Martínez and other O'odham historians tell their history as one of continuity as well as change. When the land had healed, the Akimel O'odham moved back. Within two centuries of their abandonment of the cities, descendants of the Huhugam were again farming along the Gila and its tributaries, but on smaller farms, with a diversified economy that had reserve sources of sustenance for times when the rains might not come or the rivers might overflow. After all, Martínez explains, "We know it is in the nature of things to grow and to fall." In the aftermath, "we carried that historical trauma back with us, and we didn't forget."[33]

RECIPROCITY AND BALANCE

As Professor Martínez's words reveal, there is a deeper ideology to this multiplicity of food sources and trade. For the O'odham, it is their himdag, their way of life. The Tohono O'odham Nation Cultural Center and Museum—which they call the Himdag Ki, the Way of Life House—explains that himdag "involves relations between people, the land, and all creation."[34] It is a practical way of living in balance with the Sonoran Desert environment, which was neglected during the height of the Huhugam, and it's a value that the O'odham strive to live by today. People are supposed to share with one another according to what they have, especially the necessities of food and water. Giving away a surplus is an investment. As the Tohono O'odham history textbook *Sharing the Desert* explains, "This sharing of goods and food then created a debt that was expected to be repaid whenever the others had a surplus. ... When one family or village helped another, they did so knowing that when they needed help, they would receive it from their neighbors."[35] Trading was not only economically and socially important; it was what I'itoi, the Elder Brother, instructed the O'odham to do after the cities of the Huhugam fell. Whatever side they had been on in that war, I'itoi said, from now on they "must love each other and work together."[36]

"O'odham" means "people," and different O'odham groups identify themselves based on their particular himdag, their particular way of doing things. After they brought down the Huhugam leaders, I'itoi let each O'odham group choose which part of the land and himdag they wanted. The River O'odham—the Akimel O'odham (which literally means "River People") and O'odham in other river valleys of what's now southern Arizona and northern Sonora—rebuilt smaller-scale irrigated farms, where they grew and processed the food that would sustain them and create surplus to trade. They grew cotton, and women separated and spun the fibers and wove them into cloth, blankets, skirts, and shawls.[37]

In contrast to the farming River O'odham, the Tohono O'odham (Desert People) and Hia-Ced O'odham (Sand Dune People) built a different kind of himdag, away from rivers and without elaborate irrigation systems. Reciprocal ties among different O'odham groups supported the stability and sustainability of all O'odham. The River O'odham traded crops and cloth to the more migratory O'odham, in exchange for products they gathered, such as the sweet fruit of the saguaro cactus, salt from the Gulf of California, and medicinal plants like creosote—which was used to treat pain, colds, and stomachaches. Ethnobotanists who did a study of wild food plants in the Sonoran Desert counted more than 375 species, about forty of which were major staples of the O'odham well into the twentieth century. The study pointed out that most of the world depends on just a few domesticated species such as wheat, corn, soybeans, and potatoes, which are "genetically vulnerable to long-associated diseases and pests" and "depend on costly supplements of water and energy-intensive technology." By contrast, the Tohono O'odham got an estimated 20 percent of their food from agriculture, and the Hia-Ced even less. Even the River O'odham probably got only 50 to 60 percent of their food from their agricultural fields, the rest coming from foods they either collected or acquired from the Desert O'odham groups.[38]

In the aftermath of the fall of cities, communities and nations throughout North America developed their own unique egalitarian structures as they also shared ideas and developed some common values. One of the most broadly shared values was the philosophy of reciprocity, an ideal of sharing and balance that undergirded economics, politics, and religion across much of the continent. Lumbee legal scholar Robert A. Williams Jr. explains that people "lived in a complex web of connective, reciprocating relationships. Connection to others improved the chances of overcoming some calamity or disaster that might befall the individual or group. Peaceful relations with other tribes could provide inestimable benefits: trade and subsistence goods that were unavailable or in short supply in the territory, military alliances that extended power and influence, and protection from feared enemies."[39] Historian Daniel K. Richter calls this system "a sort of upside-down capitalism, in which the aim was, not to accumulate goods, but to be in a position to provide them to others."[40]

Reciprocity embeds exchange within permanent relationships of mutual obligation. It requires generosity and obligates the partner who has more to give more. In economies that depend on reciprocity, individuals have an obligation to other people's interests. This practice is distinct from market economies that emerged in other parts of the world at the same time. In a market economy, trade ideally benefits both sides as well, when individuals look out for their own best interest and tell the truth about their products. But obligations in a reciprocal economy go beyond acting in good faith: Individuals need to know that the exchange benefits their trading partners as well as themselves. Kiowa anthropologist Gus Palmer explains, "When you give somebody something that you supposedly own, say a song, that person has to make a return gift of some kind. . . . It is not the payment that is so important here as it is the recognition of something significant happening: the exchange."[41]

Reciprocity was important within as well as between societies. Men and women were assigned separate but equally important and interdependent roles in feeding and caring for their people. In most Native societies, women did the farming and gathering, while men did the hunting and fishing. In the spirit of reciprocity, women and men might help with each other's tasks, but they had different and equally essential responsibilities for sustaining their families. Many eastern North American societies were matrilineal and matrilocal, so a woman and her sisters lived and worked in the household of their mother and raised their children there. O'odham families were patrilineal and patrilocal, so a wife joined her husband's family, and the mother of a household managed the female work of her daughters-in-law and granddaughters. Some societies practiced polygamy, bringing more female labor into the household.[42]

Sometimes people who don't quite fit a society's gender structure can help us understand that structure. Many Native societies allowed individuals to abandon the gender they had been assigned at birth in favor of the other one, without stigma. Some had additional gendered categories beyond male and female for those who fit neither, but usually someone was expected to adopt all of the responsibilities of the other gender if they crossed over. In general, gender was not as radically exclusionary and hierarchical as it was becoming in Europe. In the nineteenth century, one of the siblings of Tohono O'odham Maria Chona's husband was what Chona called "a man-woman," whom Chona said was born a boy but performed the work of and wore the clothes of women. In this case, at least, the crossing over assisted the family. Chona appreciated that her brother-sister was strong and could carry more than the other women on their seasonal migrations. Reciprocal relationships required everyone to do their part, even if occasionally someone took on the opposite-gendered role.[43]

POLITICAL AND RELIGIOUS LEADERSHIP

As reciprocal economies emerged, the nature of leadership and expectations of leaders changed all across the continent. Probably drawing on oral traditions of pre-urban eras, when power was less centralized, and also conferring with one another on new political and religious ideas, Native North Americans almost universally created political structures designed to balance power, to provide all members with a say in governance, and to prevent the rise of dictatorial leaders.

Whereas previously some powerful rulers who made decisions for others had reaped wealth as a result, now people rejected such concentrations of wealth and power. Power and prestige lay not in amassing wealth but in assuring that it was shared wisely, and leaders earned support in part by being good providers. Rather than requiring tribute, they were responsible for public food supplies to be used in diplomacy and for those in need. Prestige goods declined, even as trade generally accelerated. People were honored in more equitable ways after death. Among the descendants of the Huhugam, for example, no one had adobe sarcophagi anymore; they returned to their older practice of cremation for everyone who died. "Siwañ"—the O'odham word for "chief" and the name of the Huhugam great chief from this chapter's opening—means "bitter." That is, the O'odham word for "leader" is rooted in the concept of bitterness. The Huhugam Siwani upset the balanced and reciprocal himdag required to live in the Sonoran Desert. Going forward, leaders all over North America were supposed to work to balance the "bitter" part of power with generosity for the good of their people.[44]

Many polities established councils of elders and balanced power through paired types of leaders, such as war chiefs and peace chiefs, or male and female councils. For example, Osage oral history records that they once had one great chief who was a military leader, but their council of elder spiritual leaders, known as the "Little Old Men," decided to balance that chief's authority with another hereditary chief, responsible for keeping peace. By the eighteenth century, each town in the Cherokee Nation had a war chief and a peace chief, who was in charge of diplomacy, mediating trade disputes, and resource use within the town. Each town also had a council of male advisers, a council of women in charge of providing food and shelter, and its own priests. Family-based clans had members in multiple towns, balancing the power of the chiefs and councils. We will see more on balanced leadership in various nations in later chapters.[45]

In most societies, all the people—women as well as men—had some say in important decisions such as choosing a new leader or going to war or making peace. Many had a requirement to convene all of the people for major political, military, diplomatic, and land use decisions. Hundreds or even thousands might show up, depending on how momentous the decision was. They strove for consensus, even though they didn't always achieve it. In some societies, it was customary for the losing side to quietly leave the meeting if they couldn't bring themselves to agree with the others, thus allowing consensus. Leaders generally governed by gaining consent. They facilitated consensus decision making in council meetings and public gatherings. They might need to persuade others by speaking wisely and well, so they needed to be skilled orators and quick thinkers. They gave gifts to encourage cooperation. They had to display generosity and provide for their people in the spirit of reciprocity. They heard disputes between neighbors over land and resources and helped to resolve them.[46]

Wider political participation is evident in public architecture that emerged after cities. There were no more ten-story-high pyramids or walled compounds. Southeastern descendants of Mississippians built large public meeting buildings, sometimes large enough that a whole town could fit inside, upon much smaller mounds than those of their Mississippian ancestors. Towns continued to form the center of politics in post-Mississippian societies—they were called talwa in Muscogee (Creek), okla in Chickasaw, and tamaha in Choctaw. The town square was a central and sacred space, like the plaza had been for their ancestors. The O'odham descendants of the Huhugam began building stadiums again and developed a new ball game played by women, while stickball continued or even increased in popularity in the Southeast. From Muscogee towns to the Osages west of the Mississippi, people still played chunkey.[47]

The decline of hierarchy doesn't mean there was no inequality or that everyone lived in peace with one another and with nature—those are stereotypes as wrong in their own ways as the belief that North America never had cities. In many Native societies, political and religious leaders had to come from a certain family, clan, town, or division, but within those requirements individual leaders usually were also chosen for bravery, oratory, and wisdom. Most of the societies that descended from Mississippians had clan systems in which only certain families were eligible for certain positions. Shawnees were born into one of five patrilineal divisions, and each division was responsible for a different aspect of Shawnee life. Peace chiefs for the nation came from two of the divisions, and war chiefs from a third, while the other divisions had responsibility for religious ceremonies and medicine. The Kiowas had a ranked hierarchy from ondei (best or most distinguished) to dapóm (helpless), but they were not inherited, and individuals were judged on their performance of their roles in society. Kiowa men were supposed to distinguish themselves in war. A political leader should be generous as well as wise, while a healer was judged on success at healing. Kiowa women could distinguish themselves with tipi making, leather tanning, and beadwork. A person could lose rank by lying or other moral failings. And even the helpless could find a place in the household of an ondei.[48]

Gender was as stark a dividing line in politics as it was in economic realms. Diplomatic and military leaders were usually male, while women's control of the land and responsibility for farming were central to the checks and balances of Native politics and economics. Women often held the power over the fields and towns, where their main responsibilities lay. Because they could withhold food for war parties or diplomatic efforts, women had a reciprocal responsibility for men's actions within those realms and the power to affect decisions about war and peace.

Haudenosaunee governance illustrates one form of balancing power. People belonged to matrilineal clans—inherited from their mothers—that worked within and across each of the five Haudenosaunee nations. Women ran the clans, which were responsible for local governance, while men were the representatives of their clans and nations in the Haudenosaunee council. Each council member—called a royaner—was chosen by a clan mother. Generally, she chose from among a set of cousins within a matrilineage, so it was an office that was both inherited and merit-based.[49]

Early modern European observers had trouble understanding leadership like this. They inaccurately translated royaner as "lord" or "noble," to acknowledge the office's lineal descent, but couldn't understand the checks and balances, so unlike those in their own emerging monarchies. Similarly, Europeans translated the Muscogean word "mico" as "king," even while realizing that Muscogean councils had many micos, so "king" couldn't be right. The word "chief" reflects this European confusion, reaching back to their premonarchical past with the hypothesis that Indians had primitive politics rather than highly developed nonhierarchical ones. And European observers completely failed to notice women's power to govern clans, towns, and fields.[50]

Like politics, religion now involved more public participation. To diffuse the power of dominant leaders, many societies cut or weakened the link between religion and political and economic power. Among the O'odham descendants of the Huhugam, male and female healers and spiritual leaders cared for the sick, advised about going to battle, and ceremonially chose baby names for infants and mature names for adolescents, but their religious importance no longer gave them political or economic power.[51] Cherokee oral tradition notes that, after the fall of the Mississippian Ani-Kutani leaders, "thereafter, the priestly functions were assumed by individual Medicine Men and conjurers." Priests no longer ruled towns.[52] Other peoples who didn't go as far as completely separating religion and politics still eliminated the combined religious-political hierarchy of the past.

All across North America, societies continued many of the religious beliefs and practices of the past but in a less hierarchical way. Priests were responsible to the people rather than being part of an unimpeachable elite, and they rarely maintained a monopoly on religious knowledge. Religious practices were generally public and participatory.[53]

If people from a twelfth-century Mississippian city-state had been able to visit a seventeenth- or eighteenth-century Muscogee town, they would have seen much that was familiar, yet it would have been clear that something fundamental had changed. Tukabatchee, for example, had several mounds, but they were much shorter and more accessible than in Mississippian days, only a few feet high. Everyone from the nearby Muscogee towns came to Tukabatchee for the annual Green Corn Ceremony to celebrate the harvest. As part of the annual ritual of renewal, Muscogee men prepared the plaza or "square ground" by scraping it flat and carrying the dirt scrapings to add to the mound. No longer a job reserved for the elite, these annual rites were performed together as a community, reinforcing a sense of shared purpose and identity within and between towns. The week of ceremonies included dances that took place on top of the mound, which would not have been allowed in earlier times. At the end of the ceremony, everyone tasted the new corn and then celebrated with a communal feast. When the United States forced the Muscogees to move to Oklahoma in the nineteenth century, they carried soil with them from their mounds so they could restart the rites in their new home.[54]

Still today, centuries after Cahokia fell, many Choctaws, Cherokees, Muscogees, and members of other Southeastern nations travel from wherever they live, all across the United States and beyond, to gather at their nations' ceremonial grounds and represent their people and their clans. The shape and meaning of those ceremonial grounds still reflect the town squares of their ancient cities. The modern building housing the Muscogee National Council and the nation's courts is set within a mound. The Choctaws consider the ancient pyramid Nanih Waiya, in what's now Mississippi, their "Mother Mound" and the "Heart of the Choctaw People." Built in the eleventh century, it still stands twenty-five feet tall, with a base of three-quarters of an acre. When Choctaws were forced west in the 1830s, one of their many objections was that they would have to "abandon their mother." In Indian Territory, they named the site of their new council house Nanih Waiya, and some Choctaws pilgrimaged back to the homeland and visited the original Nanih Waiya. Today it belongs to the Mississippi Band of Choctaws, a part of the nation that managed to stay in their homeland. Similarly, the Eastern Band of Cherokee Indians has bought back the Cherokee mother mound, Kituwah (ᏕᏍᎬ in the Cherokee syllabary).[55]

Because European cities are famous for their art museums, we sometimes conflate urbanism and art, but in fact great art flourished in this era, heightened by democratization. Art helped the descendants of cities to articulate their nationhood, religious beliefs, and adaptation to a changing world. In the eighteenth-century Muscogee town of Atasi, for example, the buildings around the square were decorated with Mississippian iconography, including human figures with the heads of ducks, turkeys, bears, foxes, wolves, and deer. These were symbols from the Mississippian past, but rather than being within sacred removed spaces, they were publicly displayed. Religious iconography of earlier eras spread to more and more people as religion democratized and became a force encouraging shared values. For example, as people spread out of Moundville and across the Black Warrior Valley in the thirteenth century, they took with them their methods of making pottery vessels engraved with representational figures. The Horned Serpent, a powerful underwater snake with wings and a bowed body stretched between a long tail and a forked tongue, which had previously been used only for ceremonial and elite purposes, became part of the everyday lives of ordinary people. People now had previously elite symbols like the Horned Serpent in their homes and saw them every day on pottery bowls and bottles, copper and shell necklaces, and stone pendants and platters.[56]

My UNC colleague Professor Ben Frey compared the democratized iconography that spread after the fall of the cities to wearing, say, a Detroit Red Wings jersey. You go to a game and bring it home and wear it because it reminds you of how you felt in the arena, part of something unifying and powerful, and in public its easily recognized insignia signals to other fans that you all are part of this meaningful collective identity. While Professor Frey was talking, I could readily picture the iconic logo of the Detroit Red

Horned Serpent and Crested Bird.
DRAWINGS COURTESY OF VINCAS P. STEPONAITIS AND VERNON J. KNIGHT, JR.

Wings, the stark red-winged wheel that has stood for Detroit in good times and bad. Similarly, the rarefied Mississippian images now belonged to the people, like the red-on-buff Huhugam designs, so common today that they are etched on highway overpasses in southern Arizona, still signaling a southwestern identity a millennium later.

Parallel to reciprocity, Native North Americans developed a religious philosophy of inclusivism, a value placed on the incorporation of new religious ideas and practices into those they already had. By contrast, Christianity, Judaism, and Islam are exclusivist religions. When people convert to those religions, they are supposed to renounce all other beliefs and practices. In practice, Christianity and Islam have not been as rigidly exclusivist as their theologies suggest. Christmas, for example, merged commemorations of the birth of Jesus with older European winter solstice celebrations. Yet Christianity's theological exclusivism meant that Christians tended to respond to other faiths with intolerance and evangelism rather than incorporation. Inclusivism, on the other hand, holds that spiritual knowledge and power grow with the incorporation of new ideas and practices. Inclusivism didn't mean that Native Americans unquestioningly adopted every new religious belief that came along. What it meant was that religious leaders would study and discuss new ideas and decide whether or not they had value. If so, they would be incorporated according to traditions already in place. In addition, if someone decided that a current religious belief or practice wasn't right, discarding that part wouldn't necessitate a break with the religion or denomination, as it often has with Christianity.[57]

WAR AND DIPLOMACY

Reciprocity, inclusivism, and broad political and religious participation were values, common general beliefs about the right way to live. Values are guidelines and aspirations, not necessarily descriptions of how people actually act. And certainly people disagree about how general values apply in specific situations. Ideally a leader would guide people to make wise decisions, but of course people differed over what course was wise. The transition from the urban period was not uniform or always smooth. In the fifteenth and sixteenth centuries, some rulers still held centralized power and ruled from pyramids. In some places, large armies clashed, and people sheltered in palisaded towns. And even in societies with structures designed to prevent dictatorial power, some individual leaders amassed a great deal of power and sometimes expanded their influence through warfare on other societies.[58]

In fact, without large and powerful centers to maintain a monopoly on violence, war increased in some places. Now individual clans or towns could decide to go to war on their own or to raid a neighboring people or take revenge for a slight, because decision making was less centralized and the ceremonies related to war were not restricted to an elite. Public town squares were ideal places to display scalps and other symbols of victory.[59]

Native North Americans went to war for all kinds of reasons. Two peoples might view the obligations of reciprocity differently enough to fight, as we shall see in chapter 4 with the Mohawks and the Mahicans in the 1620s. Enemies were generally defined as outside the system of reciprocal obligations. When newcomers arrived in a region, they might be incorporated in equal or unequal ways— or they might fight for their position. Some towns and nations went to war because their allies were at war. As elsewhere, if two groups had a history of enmity, disagreements were more likely to turn into violence, whereas a history of alliance made it more likely—though not guaranteed—that methods of diplomacy would work. Confederacies of towns were created in part to prevent violence between them. These confederacies became some of the nations still around today. The Choctaws probably descend partly from towns built in the Black Warrior Valley after the fall of Moundville. By the eighteenth century, they were living in more than forty allied towns clustered into three divisions, each with its own town leaders and councils. Confederacies, in turn, could wage warfare against people outside the confederacy. Indeed, often they were created as defensive alliances, a strategy that also proved useful against the United States, as we shall see in later chapters.[60]

Like politics and religion, war seems to have become more democratized after the fall of cities. Smaller groups were able to initiate or respond to a violent raid or attack, but in addition, Native armed forces were not regular armies. It's not clear whether earlier Native polities had ever developed anything like a standing army or the kind of class system that provided regular soldiers, as in Europe and Asia, but army size and centralization do seem to have declined in this era. In these relatively egalitarian societies, all young men were expected to serve as warriors, and war was sustainable only if deaths were few. If the death toll rose, people at home might start to question the war, and without popular support (or a standing army or military class), war could not continue. Early-seventeenth-century Native methods of warfare reflected this reluctance to risk life. Warriors chose battles they could win with few casualties on their side: a surprise raid on a poorly defended town or on a few women tending their crops, or an ambush of a small hunting or trading party. The raiders would shoot arrows from a distance, come in closer to club the men and capture women and children, then quickly withdraw and hope not to be followed. If attacked, they would stand their ground long enough to save face and perhaps gain honors of war for some individual men. But there was no shame in retreating. They would evacuate if high casualties were likely. None of this is to say that warfare wasn't brutal—clubbing someone to death is a nasty business—or that warriors tried to minimize *enemy* casualties. But attackers avoided battles that were risky to their own fighters, so even battles with large numbers of warriors might have very few casualties.[61]

To make peace and forge alliances, Native North Americans developed elaborate methods of diplomacy. With smaller centers of power competing for followers and trade—and more of them—leaders needed to cultivate external allies and their own people through gift giving and bonds of reciprocity. Diplomacy made strangers into kin, enveloping them in family-like webs of reciprocal obligations. Often, polities would use kin metaphors to describe their relationships. One town might be the mother town to others, or a stronger nation might be the elder brother to a weaker one.[62]

Native North Americans gradually developed methods of diplomacy understood broadly across polities, languages, and cultures. As perhaps in all societies, gift giving between leaders, feasting, and speeches were part of diplomacy. Coming out of town to greet travelers on the road was a common practice. In the desert of the Southwest, the O'odham brought water and arches or bowers made of tree branches—desert travelers clearly recognized water and shade as signs of welcome (and O'odham processions continue to use welcoming arches of branches and flowers). Caddoan communities in present-day Texas and Arkansas were performing the calumet (peace pipe) ceremony by the late 1200s. The highly recognizable calumet, with its decorated stem, was something a diplomatic party could hold out to show peaceful intent before anyone took a shot, and leaving it behind with a newly allied people served as a powerful reminder of their reciprocal obligations to one another. By the eighteenth century, the calumet ceremony dominated diplomacy from Texas to the upper Mississippi Valley. Participants would smoke the pipe together, perform ceremonial dances, and forge a kin-like relationship.[63]

In the Northeast, strings of shell beads became essential tools of diplomacy. Since at least the sixteenth century, nations there used them for opening and closing diplomatic and trade negotiations, to propose that allies join a battle, to make peace among enemies, and to console the bereaved both beyond and within their nations. Strings of beads helped an orator remember the intricacies of a complicated speech and the people to recall the pledges they had made in the past. The words most often used for these beads, "wampum" and "sewant," are Algonquian, reflecting the fact that the beads were made by Algonquian Native communities on the northern shore of Long Island Sound. They collected and processed periwinkle shells to make the white beads and used quahog clamshells to make the contrasting beads that were such a dark purple that they were often called black. The bead makers cut and polished each shell and drilled a hole through the middle for stringing. The white beads signified peace; the dark purple beads, war. Not simply memory devices, wampum strings embody messages, becoming the words themselves. Recipients who accepted the wampum were agreeing to the relationship and reciprocal responsibilities it conveyed.[64]

Diplomacy required elaborate rituals to put participants in the appropriate state of mind. In northeastern diplomacy, an Edge of the Woods Ceremony had to precede diplomatic meetings. As in the Southwest, the people would greet the diplomats at the edge of town and exchange gifts. An elder would recount some of the two peoples' shared history. A Condolence Ceremony would wipe the tears and clear the mind for negotiations, which was especially important if war between the two peoples had caused deaths.[65]

Throughout North America, trade, diplomacy, military alliances—none of these were possible alone. All had to be part of a deeper relationship among peoples, embodied by wampum, a calumet, or a sheltering structure and welcoming food and drink, as well as ceremonies, gifts, and speeches. Diplomacy didn't always work, and there was often war, but it was part of a widely understood set of values that shaped Native North Americans' interactions with one another and would shape how they approached the European newcomers who later came to their shores.

CONCLUSION

Future historians may call the early-twenty-first-century United States a golden age, pointing to extraordinary wealth, cures and illness preventions never before possible, overdue reckonings with past injustice, unprecedented diversity of foods for billions of people, and amazing technologies (85 percent of Americans owned a handheld supercomputer!). Or they may describe our era the way a book on the Huhugam entitled *Centuries of Decline* categorizes the late decades of that civilization: a time of "overpopulation, environmental degradation, resource shortages, poor health, social fragmentation, diffuse and ineffective leadership and a struggle to cope."[66] I hope future historians will understand that both versions have their truth.

The height of the great cities of Cahokia, Moundville, and the Huhugam can be seen as a golden age, but their descendants came to see it as a misguided era. The replacement of hierarchy with diversified economies, decentralized power structures, democratized religion, art, and war, and diplomacy expressed in beads, pipes, arbors, and ceremonies would look to seventeenth-century Europeans like evidence that Indians were and always had been primitive. In the 1880s, archaeologist Adolph Bandelier, fully steeped in the myth of primitive American Indians, observed the ruins of the Huhugam and decided that

> nowhere have they been able to raise their general culture or ideas of social organization above a very modest level. Their architectural remains, traditions, mythology, customs, arts, and industries all show that the sedentary natives have not attained a conception beyond that of the tribe or a tribal confederacy. . . . [They] never rose above their descendants of today, whose organization has been within documentary time that of a communistic democracy, with prominent military features, and with a controlling element of religion.

Bandelier's prejudices here are stark: To him, "communistic" democracies, tribal confederacies, and life-guiding religion are primitive, whereas the European-derived United States that sought to replace them with a society based on private property and an individual-centered economy, government, and religion would make better use of this land, building its own glory from the ashes of the Huhugam.[67]

But the descendants of North American cities told a different story, one of a wrongheaded period and a better way of life—the very life that Europeans called primitive. People in the following centuries told cautionary stories of leaders who had seized too much power. In the coming centuries, retelling the history of taking down powerful leaders, letting the land heal, and building a more sustainable life reminded people of why they lived as they did. At the same time, in the process of de-urbanizing, creating relatively more egalitarian societies, and, in some places in the coming centuries, facing destruction wrought by Europeans, Native people retained both a memory of the past and some of its attributes, from plazas (now as smaller town squares) to sacred iconography.[68]

By the late 1400s, North American civilizations (north of the Aztecs) were more different from Western Europe than one would have predicted when the second millennium began. From Russia to England, Europe moved in the opposite direction in response to similar troubles. During the Medieval Warm Period, large-scale agriculture had allowed Europe's population to grow dramatically. Between 1100 and 1300, Northern Europe's population rose from around 1.4 million to five million people, many of whom were farming marginal lands. When the droughts of the late Medieval Warm Period and then the Little Ice Age hit, hundreds of thousands of Europeans starved to death. Then the Black Death wreaked unimaginable havoc, especially in the cities. During the pandemic of 1347–51, between twenty and twenty-five million Europeans died, out of a population of around eighty million.

Facing the Little Ice Age and the shocking devastation of the Black Death, Western Europeans, like North Americans, sought more secure ways of living and questioned what kind of ruling system could best keep the people safe. In both places, there were diverse answers and different experiments over the centuries of adaptation. But in general, as Europe recovered, it became more centralized under the rule of hereditary absolute monarchs. Lords and monarchs in Europe amassed military power at home and abroad, building large armies and investing in new military technologies, including firearms. Through mercantilism and colonization, they sought global trade and sources of natural resources abroad in order to increase their power at home and in the world. Women's status declined as militarization increased, and men came to rule almost all religious and secular institutions, including marriage. Unlike the complementary gender structures of North America, patriarchy structured power in Western Europe, from the pope and kings through lords and priests, down to husbands within a household.[69]

While labor shortages in some parts of Europe allowed peasants to establish hereditary rights and even, in some cases, to become a class of small property owners, rulers for the most part emphasized centralization, hierarchy, and bureaucracy. These values were the lens through which Europeans viewed Native Americans, making it difficult for them to understand North American history or recognize the intentionality of the decentralized systems of governance Native nations had developed. While European texts of the era give lessons about what makes a good king and what makes a bad one, North American stories explain why people are better off without a king.[70]

Native Americans who visited European cities or even colonial towns were shocked at the inequality and lack of freedom, and Europeans wondered at societies with strikingly fewer strictures and less poverty than their own. Human choices had created these striking contrasts—after all, the climate had changed similarly in the two places—yet Europeans sought to naturalize and universalize their own history. They persuaded themselves that the smaller-scale polities they observed north of the Aztecs—"tribes" and "bands," as anthropologists would later call them—were simply backward, the only kind of civilization that Indians had ever had, perhaps the only kind they were capable of at all.[71]

There were hard times to come in North America, for sure. Recent scholarship suggests that early European expeditions such as Hernando de Soto's didn't spread epidemic diseases, as scholars once had thought—after all, sick explorers were unlikely to make it far into the continent—but newcomers in the seventeenth and especially the eighteenth, nineteenth, and twentieth centuries would bring tremendous disruptions. Yet the political structures founded in the centuries after the cities fell were probably better protection than more centralized structures would have been. Smaller, more spread-out towns and the buffer zones between them allowed for better responses to disease. Fewer hierarchies of tributary states meant there was no central leader or city that Europeans could conquer to gain an empire. Loose confederacies proved remarkably able to incorporate refugees, even entire towns, and to tolerate and benefit from linguistic and cultural diversity, abilities that helped to maintain and rebuild nations in the face of colonialism. For a com-

parison, one need only look to central Mexico, where Native resentment of the Mexica (Aztec) leaders helped the Spanish to put
themselves on top of a powerful empire, aided by a devastating
smallpox epidemic that hit the main city of Tenochtitlán as it was
under siege. And some of the changes brought by Europeans, including their diseases and weapons, encouraged even further decen-
tralizing. As Europeans came in the coming centuries, Native
nations would need every advantage they could muster.[72]

CHAPTER 3

OSSOMOCOMUCK AND ROANOKE ISLAND

IN THE SUMMER OF 1584, THREE MEN WENT TO MEET THE strange party that had come to Roanoke Island, off the coast of what today is North Carolina. They beckoned the visitors to come to shore, and one of the locals spoke in his Algonquian language. The English visitors could not understand him, but he didn't seem to be angry or fearful, so they assumed these were words of welcome. Through signs, they invited him to tour their two ships. He agreed, and they gave him food to eat and wine to drink, as well as a shirt and a hat. Then the man got into his canoe and, as one of the Englishmen recorded, "fell to fishing." Within half an hour he had filled his boat with as much as it could hold, and then he signaled to the Englishmen that each ship should take half of the catch.[1]

Like those Englishmen, we don't need to understand an Algonquian language in order to infer what the man was saying. He welcomed them with friendly words and gestures and, following standard sixteenth-century North American reciprocal customs, sampled what the newcomers had brought and, in return, provided them with a resource that he had to give. European goods had come to the region before. When Giovanni da Verrazzano landed to the south, at the mouth of the Cape Fear River in 1524, Native people there hosted him and encouraged trade. It's likely that even then, sixty years earlier, they already knew of Europeans and their goods because of Native networks of trade and information. Uncounted shipwrecks tossed waterlogged goods and sailors onto the shore. In 1570, fourteen years before the Englishmen appeared at Roanoke, a ship had wrecked just a few miles to the south, and local people still had some of the tools they had collected there.

The 1584 interactions at Roanoke seemed to bode well. Both sides apparently wanted trade and alliance. The people on Roanoke Island knew that men who came in sailing ships were the kinds of foreigners who had metal that was harder than North American copper. The people who met the English were at war with a coalition to the north and had only recently ended a war against people to the south that had been particularly fierce. And so trade with the English could bring metal weapons and armor for fighting enemies still armed with only clubs, bows and arrows, and wooden armor. In a subsequent meeting, a leader on Roanoke named Granganimeo hung an English tin plate around his neck as a breastplate and made signs to the Englishmen that they took to mean it "would defend him against his enemies' arrows."[2] War was also an English motivation. They had crossed the ocean to challenge Spain. Starting in the 1490s, Spain had taken the lead in colonizing the Americas, and now the English were desperately trying to catch up and use American wealth to fight Spain and other enemies in Europe. English privateers began targeting Spanish ships carrying silver and other treasures home across the Atlantic. In 1565, Spain had founded St. Augustine, Florida, to defend its North American claims and ships against the French and English. One goal of the current English expedition was to find a site to establish England's own post from which to attack Spanish ships.[3]

It may not be giving too much away to say that, despite early promise, this relationship did not go well. Violence would break out and, within a few years, English settlers on Roanoke would become the famous "lost colonists." In fact, not only was the Roanoke colony "lost," but nearly every other colonial venture north of central Mexico in the sixteenth century also failed. In 1567, Spanish explorer Juan Pardo built a fort three hundred miles inland, in the foothills of the Appalachians near present-day Hickory, North Carolina, which lasted until the residents of the Native city of Joara—ancestors of the Catawbas—burned it down and kicked the Spaniards out. In 1571, Algonquian speakers to the north in the Chesapeake Bay, whom the English would later know as Powhatans, killed Spanish Jesuits who tried to establish a mission there. Others did the same with Spanish missions in Florida. And England's Roanoke venture lost not just the famous "lost colonists" of 1587 but several other groups of people in 1586, as we shall see.[4]

Colonists, whether successfully founding a permanent colony or not, are usually portrayed from their first arrival as either the main story of North America or the harbinger of doom in stories that do center Native Americans, while Native people too often are seen as a sideshow—a primitive people whose losing streak starts the minute Europeans land. In reality, Native Americans had clear ideas about how Europeans could fit into their world, and in the early centuries they often persuaded Europeans to follow their customs and forward their goals.

They also learned that Europeans could be dangerous. While a major theme of this book is that Europeans for a long time had less power over North America than they claimed, their belief that the Christian god had given them the right to run the world both justified violence and accelerated it. By the time the Algonquian-speaking man toured the two ships, the English had already planted a flag in the soil of Roanoke, "to take possession of the [island], in the right of the Queen's most excellent Majesty."[5] When they ran up against the realities of their own limited power—the reality that Native peoples, not Europeans, had possession of the Americas—Europeans often unleashed violence far beyond most societies' norms, including their own. In the short history of the failed English attempt at Roanoke, we see both the hollowness of colonial claims and the self-justifying panicky violence of colonialism, both of which are part of the history of North America in the 1500s and beyond.

HOSTING STRANGERS

If you look across the shallow sound from the east side of Roanoke Island, you can see the barrier island where the Wright brothers took their first flight. From the west side, you can see the mainland. In 1584, this was all part of a place called Ossomocomuck. The name Roanoke is more likely to be familiar to readers than Ossomocomuck. Both are from the local language, part of the huge Algonquian family, which includes languages from south of the Carolinas through eastern Canada. Ossomocomuck spanned North Carolina's Outer Banks and the lands these barrier islands protect along Albemarle and Pamlico sounds. Roanoke was a small island in Ossomocomuck, an important place for gathering resources. The Algonquian name Roanoke means "people who polish," a reference to making shells into beads.[6]

On Roanoke Island and other parts of the Outer Banks, women gathered shells on the beach and, under the tall loblolly pines of the lush maritime forest, picked berries, roots, plants for medicinal uses, and yaupon holly leaves for caffeinated tea. Men hunted deer and other game, collected oysters, and rowed their large, finely crafted dugout canoes into the wetlands and sounds to shoot birds and net or spear horseshoe crabs, catfish, rays, small sharks, and sturgeon. They made their task easier by building fish weirs, traps into which the fish swam, as you can see in the image on page 80.[7]

The landscape of Ossomocomuck has changed less than many other parts of North America in the centuries since the 1500s. Its twenty-first-century towns have larger populations and modern buildings and roads, but they are similarly spread out. In between is the same mix of islands, waterways, and wetlands that confound outsiders and are deeply familiar to those who live there. To me, the landscape looks unvarying, and I have trouble distinguishing wetlands from channels. The first time I took a motorboat out in the sound between the Outer Banks and the North Carolina mainland, my friends and I got completely turned around, and another time my boat was grounded trying to cut through the banks of the Rachel Carson Reserve. Locals today, as in the sixteenth century, understand this environment's intricacies and how a heavy storm or just the wear of time can make a channel unnavigable or submerge part of an island. It is not an easy place for foreigners to navigate, as the English would learn.

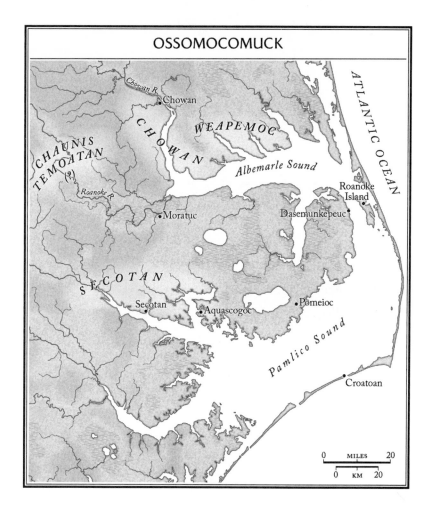

OSSOMOCOMUCK

The seven thousand or so people of Ossomocomuck lived on the mainland, which included arable land near rivers and along ridges that allowed the farming of corn, squashes, beans, sunflowers, and tobacco. Even mainland Ossomocomuck was mostly wetlands, though, and had never allowed for large-scale agriculture. There had been Mississippian cities farther inland, and in the 1580s a few of them remained. But most people in and near Ossomocomuck, as throughout the continent, lived in towns of a few hundred to a few thousand, connected by trade networks that brought goods from near and far. Most towns were confederated with others for purposes of defense and trade.[8]

The Method of Fishing of the Inhabitants of Virginia,
engraving by Theodor de Bry, plate XIII
of Thomas Harriot's 1590 *Admiranda narration.*
MARINERS' MUSEUM, NEWPORT NEWS, VIRGINIA

The people of Ossomocomuck traded beads, pearls, turtle shells, pottery, and fish for products from inland, including copper, flint, game, and plants that did not grow near the coast. They lived in towns of ten to thirty longhouses, with rounded roofs made of bent poles and covered with bark or rush mats, which were rolled up when they wanted to catch a breeze or let in more light. Their near neighbors spoke related Algonquian languages, while just inland, others spoke Iroquoian languages, more different from Algonquian tongues than Romance languages are from Germanic ones.

The Englishmen who came in 1584—Philip Amadas and Arthur Barlowe, sent as the first scouts for Sir Walter Raleigh—landed on Roanoke Island, at the edge of Ossomocomuck. Granganimeo was the werowance (the Algonquian term for a political leader) in charge of the Roanoke post. His brother, Wingina, was the chief werowance for most of Ossomocomuck. Believing the English could be useful, Granganimeo went to meet the two English ships as soon as

he heard the report from the man who had visited them. Granganimeo explained who he and Wingina were. He welcomed the English to their land, "striking on his head and his breast and afterwards
on ours to show we were all one, smiling and making show the best
he could of all love and familiarity." He gave a long speech, and they
exchanged gifts. Hinting at ongoing war in the region, he said that
Wingina could not come to meet them because he had recently
been wounded and was recovering at one of his towns on the mainland. A day or two later, Granganimeo returned to the ships, this
time with a diplomatic party that included his wife and children.
Granganimeo's wife had a name, of course, but the Englishmen
didn't catch it, so it is lost to us. She was clearly an important woman.
She dressed the part of a leader, in a leather dress and fur cloak, long
strings of pearls on her ears, and a band of white coral on her head
that matched Granganimeo's own.[9]

A few days later, Barlowe and Amadas ventured onto the island
and to its main town. Granganimeo's wife ran out of the palisade,
made of tall wooden stakes, to the edge of the water, where the eight
men sat in their rowboats. She smiled and beckoned them in. The
Englishmen had happened to visit on a day when Granganimeo was
away, gone to consult with Wingina on the mainland. If Granganimeo had been there, he would have led the negotiations, but Native women had a vital role in diplomacy as well. Diplomacy required
elaborate hosting, including feasts and specially prepared housing,
so women's work was often the most important part of a first visit.
In any case, it was what she had to offer, and there was plenty of
food at hand.

Granganimeo's wife appointed some men to pull the visitors'
rowboats to the shore and others to carry the men on their backs
through the surf so they wouldn't get drenched. She led them
through the palisade to her home, a spacious five-room longhouse
built of the fragrant red cedar that grew abundantly on Roanoke
Island. She gestured to them to sit beside the fire in the outer room
while she laid their clothes out to dry and went into the next room
to prepare a meal. Other women washed and dried the men's sandy
stockings and brought them bowls of warm water to soak their

chilled feet. When she led the strangers to her table, they were impressed with the meal they saw before them: a large pot of savory venison stew and another of fish stew and, on wooden platters, a venison roast, grilled fish, melons, and many grains, vegetables, and fruits they did not recognize, including her people's main staple, pagatowr (corn).[10]

Their Way of Eating Food, engraving by Theodor de Bry, plate XVI of Thomas Harriot's 1590 *Admiranda narration*.
MARINERS' MUSEUM, NEWPORT NEWS, VIRGINIA

Suddenly, some men returning from the hunt threatened the welcoming atmosphere she had created. They sauntered into town, talking in loud masculine voices and armed with bows and arrows. The nervous visitors rushed to look out, reaching for their own weapons. Quickly, she sent some men to make a show of breaking the hunters' arrows and ushering them back out of the palisade, averting a crisis. She calmed the visitors and, when she could not persuade them to stay the night, accompanied them to their boats with more pots of food. As it began to rain, the Englishmen realized that they should have accepted the offer to sleep in the warm, dry house and have a hot breakfast in the morning. Her efforts had paid off. Barlowe wrote enthusiastically of her hospitality in his report and concluded, "I think in all the world the like abundance is not to be found." Barlowe and Amadas would encourage Raleigh to send his colonists here.

Far from the stereotype of naive savages, the people who welcomed the English to Roanoke were savvy diplomats. They recognized that these visitors could be economically and militarily useful. When Europeans appeared, Native people nearly everywhere saw them as Ossomocomuck's diplomats did: not as omnipotent enemies but as people whose goods and powers they could use.

SIXTEENTH-CENTURY PEOPLE

Though their societies had grown further apart in the previous century, the sixteenth-century people of Ossomocomuck and England still lived more like each other than like twenty-first-century people. They all lived in a slower world than ours. Neither people nor communication traveled any faster than a canoe floating downstream or a ship sailing with a strong wind behind it. Both cultures were largely oral. Protestantism's emphasis on everyday people reading the Bible was only just introducing to Europe the idea that common people should learn how to read and write. Infant and childhood mortality were high, as was the birth rate. In the early summer, before the crops came in, food was in short supply, and hunger was not unusual, although North America's diversified economies tended to provide more food security. People's primary ways of identifying themselves were through kinship ties, extended family, and local communities. The wealthiest Europeans lived in grand (though drafty) castles and mansions, but most European and Algonquian villagers lived in similar thatched longhouses, with a central hearth, smoke holes in the ceiling rather than chimneys, and common rooms that had all kinds of uses, including work and sleep. What would have surprised Indians was the cattle living at one end of European longhouses. Coastal Algonquians' plates held an assortment of foods that would satisfy a modern nutritionist: corn, beans, squash, melons, and fish, probably the world's healthiest animal protein. Fresh water was more abundant in Ossomocomuck's towns than in English ones, where people mostly hydrated with beer, which was safer to drink than urban water sources.[11]

Sixteenth-century people tended to believe that everything happened for a reason and that nothing was random, even if the logic was beyond the ability of human beings to understand. Like many other Native North Americans, the people of Ossomocomuck believed that spiritual power was at work in the world and could prove to be either good or evil. The trick was to figure out which one. If good and useful, it could be incorporated, in keeping with their inclusivist approach. If evil, it should be overpowered or avoided. When Wingina's people saw the English compasses and clocks and the wounds that a gun could make in the flesh of an animal or a person, they quickly set about trying to put these tools to use.[12]

In Europe, as in North America, the sacred and the secular weren't separate realms. It's easy for us today to assume that Sir Walter Raleigh's desire for America's natural resources was purely economic: How to make a profit? But in fact, Raleigh, like many Europeans, believed that because the Bible's book of Revelation called 666 "the number of the beast," the year 1666 might be the end of the world, and it was Christians' responsibility to reunite all the world's knowledge and languages, which had been scattered in the biblical era after Adam's fall from Eden. One theory held that the people of the Americas were one of the Ten Lost Tribes of Israel, and many Europeans believed that their god had revealed the Americas—two previously unknown continents—because the end of the world was near. Christopher Columbus wrote in his *Book of Prophecies* that "the Lord opened my mind to the fact that it would be possible to sail from here to the Indies" in order to fulfill the Bible's prophecy that "the Gospel must now be proclaimed" for "the conversion of all the nations," which would help to bring about Jesus's second coming.[13]

Europeans marveled at what they found in the Americas, much as Native Americans were impressed with European technologies. Explorers were impressed with Native fish weirs as well as seeing people successfully spear fish with sharp poles. Barlowe gushed about Granganimeo's wife's earrings "of pearls hanging down to her middle," the size of "good peas." But Europeans tended to see the bounty of the Americas as natural rather than created by Native men and women. Despite the fact that it was the labor and design of Native farmers, hunters, and fishers that fed Ossomocomuck, Barlowe described it as Eden-like: "The earth bringeth forth all things in abundance, as in the first creation, without toil or labor."[14]

The long distance that the English had traveled was part of the appeal of the relationship on both sides. Indeed, the power of both Native and European political leaders was underpinned by long-distance connections. In Ossomocomuck, a leader was supposed to be a conduit to the larger world, who shared the benefits from outside with his people. When Englishmen tried to give some goods directly to several of Granganimeo's men, he put the goods in his own basket and made sure the Englishmen saw him do so. Their axes, knives, and kettles were his to redistribute and in turn increase his own power, especially so because they were exotic goods, useful and interesting but also carrying spiritually important connections to knowledge from the world far beyond Ossomocomuck. Granganimeo would provide for his town and pass goods and information on to Wingina, who in turn would provide for his people and his allies, who would see him as a wise leader and a good provider. On the other hand, if everyone in Ossomocomuck were able to trade and speak directly with the English, the leaders would lose their exclusive access to this powerful and useful foreign source. Reciprocity had its rules and customs; it had its own hierarchy.[15]

Europeans understood this kind of leadership. In both places, leaders built prestige and power by redistributing resources and creating a sense of loyalty and obligation. In this era before standardized currencies, competitive gift-giving was common throughout the world. For European nobility, as for Wingina and Granganimeo, gifts bound families, ensured the loyalty of military retainers, and brought favor from God. In the French *Song of Roland,* the king of Saragossa (Spain) sends the French king Charlemagne gifts of "lions, bears, dogs of good breed, . . . a thousand molted hawks, . . . and seven hundred camels, too, and teams of mules to draw four hundred carts, all heaped with silver and gold and other finery."[16]

English kings were referred to as beah-gifa ("ring giver"), in recognition of the treasure a king distributed to his lords after victory in battle. The best way to guarantee loyalty, Europeans understood, was via the strategic distribution of goods and gifts.[17]

Europeans recognized Native leaders as people with power. Artist John White drew a werowance, possibly Wingina, in a traditional posture with his hand on his hip and his elbow pointed out, a posture that in sixteenth-century Europe denoted an aristocrat or military leader. Self-commanding and socially assured, the man in White's portrait parallels White's patron, Sir Walter Raleigh, painted here in a similar posture.[18]

A Weroan or Great Lord of Virginia, engraving by Theodor de Bry, plate III of Thomas Harriot's 1590 *Admiranda narration,* and portrait of Sir Walter Raleigh, 1593.

MARINERS' MUSEUM, NEWPORT NEWS, VIRGINIA; NORTH CAROLINA COLLECTION, LOUIS ROUND WILSON SPECIAL COLLECTIONS LIBRARY, UNIVERSITY OF NORTH CAROLINA AT CHAPEL HILL

But the democratization of religion and politics in Native North America meant that Native political power involved more people than in either sixteenth-century Europe or the long-gone civilizations of Cahokia, Moundville, and the Huhugam. "Werowance" may literally mean something like "he who is rich," but being rich meant having plenty to give away, so it's sometimes instead translated as "he who is wise."[19] Although werowances were treated with special respect, being a werowance would not put you in a big house on top of a pyramid, as in Cahokia. Leaders were supposed to distribute wisely, and the people would reciprocate with their support. By contrast, European leaders generally gave gifts only to religious figures or to other nobles. In late-sixteenth-century North America, persuasion, reciprocity, consensus, kinship, and hospitality spanned everyone.[20]

Women's authority in Native America made politics and economics there look particularly chaotic to Europeans, whose highly patriarchal systems had no recognized role for women (with the occasional huge exception of an individual, such as Elizabeth I). In England, the legal system of coverture subsumed a married woman's legal identity under that of her husband, as symbolized by a wife's taking her husband's name—Barlowe called his host "Mrs. Granganimeo." Indeed, the absence of Granganimeo on the day that the Englishmen visited their town was what required Barlowe to give us a rare insight into Native women's lives and responsibilities. European men usually noted only the male leaders, leading to the exaggeration of men's power and prominence in both European accounts and histories ever since.[21]

Yet European women also contributed to their societies' economies and had informal jurisdiction over many parts of life. In European and North American societies, women were responsible for most of the food preparation and care of the home and children, while men—like Granganimeo and Arthur Barlowe—traveled for diplomacy and trade. In both, a woman's position depended in part on the status of her male relatives. When the English referred to Granganimeo's wife by her marital status rather than by her name, they didn't mean it as an insult. They were glad for the hospitality and a hot meal of a quality that any Englishwoman would be proud to serve.

The sixteenth-century people of England and Ossomocomuck shared a belief that gender was a fundamental category of human difference, what feminist theorists call an "essentialist" view of gender. Although in many Native societies individuals could cross genders, gender roles were starkly separate. This common belief made for important shared assumptions, such as warfare being a male realm. In other cases, when they saw differing gender practices, they tended to think they were wrong, not just different. The common Native acceptance of divorce shocked Europeans, while European explorers who came without women seemed to their Native hosts to be both warlike and incapable of feeding themselves.[22]

Europeans' notion of land as the kind of property that could be owned by one person and sold to another didn't exist within American Indian societies before the nineteenth century, but American Indians did have concrete ideas about ownership. Farmland and houses, for example, belonged to particular women's families. And there were clear borders between societies, as Roanoke colonists would soon learn the hard way. A French explorer was typical in noting that Native nations' "borders are regulated. Each Nation knows the boundaries of its Country."[23]

Perhaps the most important commonality between Ossomoco-muck and England—the reason most responsible for bringing their societies together and pushing them into alliance with each other—was that both were at war. Ossomocomuck's geography was split into regional alliances. While the origins of Ossomocomuck's wars aren't clear, its divisions are. Men proudly displayed tattoos unique to their particular towns, representing their distinct identities and violent rivalries.[24]

Yet there were already key differences between Europeans and Native Americans that would have a tremendous impact in the centuries to come. Beginning with the Crusades and continuing in wars between Catholics and Protestants, Europeans had developed new meanings and justifications for war, which would eventually wreak havoc on the world. The pope's 1494 grant of the Americas to Spain reflects the growing Christian European assumption that they had a literally god-given right to dominate the world—this belief is fundamental to colonialism. The distinction between individual property and the collective forms of ownership practiced in Native America was growing more stark, too. For instance, the custom of gift-giving by individual lords was evolving into a broader monarchical exertion of power. The Englishmen who came to Roanoke were from a country where class was becoming more extreme and less was held in common.[25]

In 1534, English king Henry VIII had separated the Church of England from the pope's Catholicism, but Protestant and Catholic monarchs alike assumed that Europeans could claim the lands of other people simply by saying so. A 1584 bill passed by the English House of Commons declared that Queen Elizabeth I's grant of Ossomocomuck to Raleigh passed legal muster because it was "not inhabited by any Christian Prince or Christian people."[26] If a Christian didn't have it already, it was effectively unowned, in European eyes. Barlowe, despite describing the Algonquians he met as a "goodly people, and in their behavior as mannerly, and civil as any of Europe," claimed to have established Queen Elizabeth's possession of their land.[27] His small party of men could not actually take possession of Ossomocomuck, or even Roanoke Island, but their claimed "doctrine of discovery" would serve Europeans and their descendants as a justification for centuries to come and a foundation, however shaky, of American Indian law to this day.[28]

Starting in the twelfth century and escalating in the sixteenth century, Englishmen used brutal tactics to colonize Ireland, which they subsequently brought across the Atlantic. Like many men who would become involved in England's colonial efforts in the Americas, Walter Raleigh and his half brother, Humphrey Gilbert, had both served in Ireland. After one siege, Raleigh carried out his superior's orders to execute several hundred Irish troops who had surrendered. Gilbert acquired a bloody reputation for having Irishmen beheaded and putting their heads on posts all along the path leading to his command tent, as a warning to others. The new kind of siege warfare, with artillery, muskets, and defensive fortresses, had led to larger armies and huge military budgets. Late medieval and early modern European history is an important reminder that, as Dakota scholar Philip Deloria puts it, despite images of pilgrims from "pious, civilized England," these men came from "a land that delighted in displaying heads on poles and letting bodies rot in cages suspended above the roads. They were a warrior tribe."[29]

NATIVE EXPLORERS

Yet at Roanoke in 1584, it seemed that both sides' aims might be compatible. When the English sailed back home that September, Wingina took the opportunity to send explorers of his own with them. Usually historical narratives follow Europeans into the Americas, but in fact hundreds of American Indians from the late fifteenth through nineteenth centuries traveled to see Europe for themselves, to formalize their people's alliances with Europeans, and to report back on their findings. Wingina sent two men with skills of observation and language: a young warrior from Granganimeo's post on Roanoke Island whom they called Wanchese and Manteo, a young man from Wingina's allies on Croatoan Island whose mother was a werowance. Croatoan seems to have served a similar function as Roanoke Island, as a seasonal fishing camp, with its main town near the southern end of the island near today's Cape Hatteras Lighthouse.[30]

Manteo and Wanchese could not have predicted how miserable the voyage would be: more than two months of being tossed on the open seas, sleeping in close quarters with strangers, and eating hard, dry food. They spent much of the voyage talking with Arthur Barlowe in order to learn English, hear about the country they were traveling toward, and explain to Barlowe the geography, history, politics, and religion of Ossomocomuck, as best they could with their new language skills. Because the English and the people of Ossomocomuck had thus far communicated only through gestures and actions, there was a lot left to explain.[31]

London must have been a shock, with its crowds and traffic. When the Mississippian and Huhugam cities fell and their descendants spread out into smaller towns, London had done the opposite—becoming denser in population and more of a national metropolis than ever. By the 1580s London had rebounded from the population decline caused by crop failures and the Black Death, and around 150,000 people lived within its medieval city walls and the new suburban slums right outside. The city's unemployment and

poverty would have been completely alien to Wanchese and Manteo's experience and extreme even to the older world of Cahokia and
the Huhugam. With a total urban area of at most two square miles,
London had a population density greater than Manhattan's today.
Wanchese and Manteo saw sights such as the Tower of London and
London Bridge, where mounted heads revealed Queen Elizabeth's
brutality toward those who would oppose her. They stayed in Durham House, Walter Raleigh's mansion outside the city walls, where
Anne Boleyn had lived when in good graces with Henry VIII. After
receiving the estate from her father, Elizabeth granted it to Raleigh
for his loyalty. The lack of trees in England would also have been
strange. Four hundred years earlier, most of the landscape would
have been as wooded as Ossomocomuck, but during the agricultural
expansion of the Medieval Warm Period, the English had cut down
half of their forests. Wanchese and Manteo didn't record what they
thought, but the contrast between poverty and wealth may have
struck them as it did Muscogee leader Tomochichi, who in 1734 expressed surprise that the British king lived in a palace with an un-
necessarily large number of rooms. An Englishman recorded that
Tomochichi observed that the English "knew many things his
Country men did not" but "live worse than they."[32]

On a sunny winter day in 2018, I walked from my office, on the
campus of the University of North Carolina at Chapel Hill, to Wilson Library to view the closest approximation I could find to Durham House, which was leveled in the eighteenth century. I stood
outside the library's "Raleigh Rooms," trying to imagine myself as
Wanchese or Manteo, and then walked in. These two rooms are re-
creations of the kinds of rooms that Wanchese and Manteo would
have seen in Durham House, with furniture and oak paneling collected from similarly fine sixteenth-century English buildings. Even
with overhead electric lighting, the rooms are dark. The paneling,
oak doors, and heavy furniture are dark wood, and the small window
lets little light in through its tiny panes, crossed with dark wooden
grilles, which were needed before the production of large panes of
glass. Native American longhouses could be dark as well, usually lit
only by central fires, but the walls of Raleigh's house could not be

rolled up to let in light and breezes, and England's weather did not permit people to spend most of their time outside, as they did back home in Ossomocomuck. I suspect that Manteo and Wanchese spent much of their time looking out windows on the mansion's south side at the wide, muddy Thames River and its sailing ships, like the ones they had traveled in, and countless boats and canoes, or by the fire, avoiding the outside cold and the drafty edges of the rooms. They had arrived in London in wintertime, and their primary impression of the place may have been how cold it was.

A view of the River Thames, with Durham House, Salisbury House, and Worcester House as they were circa 1630, c. 1808 engraving.
THE PRINT COLLECTOR/GETTY IMAGES

At Durham House, Manteo and Wanchese worked with Thomas Harriot, a scientist and mathematician whom Raleigh had chosen to accompany the next expedition. They helped him compile an orthography of their language—a systematized way of spelling the words using roman letters—at the bottom of which one of them wrote, in the script they created, MATEOROIDN, which may mean "done [DN] by Manteo the king [ROI]."[33]

Manteo and Wanchese also visited the House of Commons and

Hampton Court, where Queen Elizabeth lived. Like an ambitious tech entrepreneur today, Raleigh introduced the visitors to potential investors for a permanent colony, hoping the friendly diplomacy and descriptions of their country's resources would display the colony's potential and its high chance of success. Raleigh's half brother, Humphrey Gilbert, had died not long before in a failed attempt to colonize Newfoundland, and Raleigh needed to persuade people that Ossomocomuck was a more promising location.

Raleigh found enough backing to send another voyage to Osso-mocomuck in April 1585, and Manteo and Wanchese set sail for home. After stopping in the Canary Islands to take on more provisions, the ships crossed the Atlantic. They landed at a remote spot on the island of Puerto Rico to collect water, make repairs, and build a small sailboat that they would use to explore Carolina's shallow coastal waterways. After setting sail again, they captured a couple of Spanish frigates they came across and stopped on the coast of Hispaniola (present-day Haiti and the Dominican Republic), where the local Spanish governor treated them to a banquet, a bullfight, and an exchange of gifts. The stops in the Spanish colonies give a few independent impressions of Wanchese and Manteo. Spanish officials reported that they saw "two tall Indians, whom [the Englishmen] treated well, and who spoke English" and were "well-attired." These accounts also include the only mention of a fascinating part of the cargo: On board ship were many musical instruments, including clarion trumpets and organs, being brought back to Ossomoco-muck, the English sailors told the Spaniards, because "the Indians like music."[34]

After more than three months at sea, Manteo and Wanchese sighted the barrier islands of home in late July 1585, having been gone for nine months. They returned in a far more impressive fleet than the one that had brought them to England: seven sailing ships, including the queen's own 140-ton, thirteen-gun ship *Tiger*, with a crew of eighty sailors. Also in the ships were considerable armaments and provisions and six hundred men, some of whom were to form the first Roanoke colony under the command of Sir Richard Grenville and Governor Ralph Lane. As they caught sight of home,

John White's watercolor of the flagship *Tiger* from his "Plan of a
fortified encampment at Mosquetal (Tallaboa Bay, Puerto Rico)."

Manteo and Wanchese may have stood on deck reflecting that this
fleet and cargo might make them heroes for sealing the alliance and
bringing useful goods and knowledge.[35]

DRAMAS OF 1585

The 1585 ships were not bringing the famous "Lost Colony," the
name given to a subsequent attempt a few years later, although these
colonists would also lose plenty. Because of their earlier interactions,
the people of Ossomocumuck and the Englishmen arriving there
knew enough about each other to imagine that they could achieve
what they wanted from trade and diplomacy. And each believed
their side had the power to control the relationship. Both were
wrong.

Perhaps it was a bad sign that the flagship *Tiger* grounded trying
to enter the inlet and took on enough water that, despite the crew's

desperate efforts, its goods were ruined. Yet there were other ships, and lots of armaments left. Another alarming sign was that these English had not brought women to do the farming and other essential tasks that the people of Ossomocomuck considered women's work. It had been strange enough that the exploratory party led by Amadas and Barlowe was all men—women were a traditional sign that a party came in peace—but that group had shown by its small size and obvious fear and weakness that it posed little threat. By contrast, this army could be dangerous, yet it might also be a vital asset to Wingina in the region's wars.

Over the next few weeks, Manteo and Wanchese briefed Wingina, Granganimeo, and the other werowances. They had a lot to tell about interest in the goods that Ossomocomuck's people wanted to trade and what they could get in return. They probably reported that England was a larger and wealthier country than the small first expedition had led them to believe, albeit one with many enemies, including the Spanish.

Soon these heavily armed men went exploring beyond Roanoke Island. Grenville took sixty Englishmen across the sound in three rowboats and his small sailboat to Pomeioc, a town directly across the sound from Croatoan. Manteo and Wanchese had told the English that Pomeioc had been at war against Wingina and his allies until they made peace two years earlier. According to Barlowe, Manteo and Wanchese had repeatedly suggested that the English could launch a surprise attack on Pomeioc "and assured us, that there will be found in it great store of commodities." It's not clear from the English records whether Manteo or Wanchese was with Grenville's expedition to the mainland or if Harriot was serving as interpreter, using the Algonquian they had taught him. If Manteo or Wanchese led Grenville's party to Pomeioc, they either hoped to start a fight or to impress Pomeioc with Wingina's new allies.[36]

What we do know is that John White, enlisted by Raleigh to be the expedition's artist, was with Grenville and that he left us with striking watercolor pictures of Ossomocomuck, almost the only visual images of sixteenth-century America north of Mexico. Theodor de Bry made engravings (which print more clearly) for the books that Harriot published about Ossomocomuck, based on White's watercolors and details from what they read in the accounts of Harriot and others who had been there. The images of Pomeioc give us a sense of life there when White visited. It is July, and the houses are open to the breeze. The artist has set the poles of the palisade far enough apart that the viewer can see through them, although in reality they would have been set tightly together for protection in case of attack. The engraving shows the town's integration with its environment, including natural resources from the forest and lakes nearby and a small reservoir they had built, shown at the top right.[37]

The Town of Pomeioc, engraving by Theodor de Bry,
plate XIX of Thomas Harriot's 1590 *Admiranda narration.*
MARINERS' MUSEUM, NEWPORT NEWS, VIRGINIA

The meeting at Pomeioc was as peaceful as the scene in the pictures, so Grenville's men continued down the coast for about thirty miles and into the mouth of the Pamlico River. They visited the town of Aquascogoc on July 13 and Secotan, to the southwest on the Pamlico River, on July 15. The English "were well entertained" with a feast similar to what Granganimeo's wife had served Barlowe and Amadas a year earlier.[38] As at Pomeioc, White's pictures of Secotan depict people busy with a variety of activities, including farming and hunting. There's also a depiction of a green corn harvest ceremony that the English witnessed during their time in Ossomocomuck. Secotan was not surrounded by a palisade, perhaps because it was firmly allied with Wingina, whereas Pomeioc had recently been at war.

Trouble was about to break out between the English and Aquascogoc, and when it did, the entire region learned of the English proclivity for violence. A silver cup went missing, and somehow Grenville became convinced that a man at Aquascogoc had stolen it, so upon their return to Roanoke he sent Phillip Amadas back to Aquascogoc to demand its return. The people of Aquascogoc, seeing trouble coming, left the town, so the Englishmen, turning to the kind of terror tactics they had used when outnumbered against the

The Town of Secota, engraving by Theodor de Bry,
plate XX of Thomas Harriot's 1590 *Admiranda narration*.

Irish, burned it down and destroyed the town's corn. Perhaps this new relationship would not be easy after all.

TAMING NEWCOMERS

It's not clear whether Aquascogoc was an ally of Wingina or in alliance with Pomeioc, but in either case, Wingina and his fellow werowances had a lot to discuss when they learned that the English had burned it down. Realizing it would be essential to keep these dangerous men and their armaments subordinate to Wingina's rule, they hurried Manteo and Granganimeo to the ships to invite the English to build their own town on Roanoke Island, where Granganimeo could keep an eye on them and prevent any further rogue exploration. Wingina probably envisioned the English post as serving a function like Granganimeo's fishing outpost on Roanoke Island: to provide resources, under his authority.

The English were lucky to have Wingina's support. Because the water damage to the *Tiger* had destroyed almost all the provisions that were supposed to sustain the colony for the coming year, Grenville took most of the men home with him when he sailed back to England to report to Raleigh and collect more supplies. Just over one hundred men, mostly soldiers, stayed behind, while there were thousands of Ossomocomuck Natives living within fifty miles. It was one thing for Raleigh to claim the region as "Virginia" back in England, but if the English wanted to stay, they needed local patrons to support them.

With Grenville's departure, the command fell to Ralph Lane, a military officer who had served in England's bloody wars in Ireland. At Roanoke, Lane's men built a very small fort and, between it and the town of Granganimeo and his wife, a few wooden houses with thatched roofs. Only Manteo and Wanchese's descriptions of London's architecture could counter the impression that the English knew only primitive building techniques. On the other hand, considering that Algonquian women were usually in charge of building houses, they might have viewed the Roanoke colony as forgivably rustic because the men had brought no knowledgeable female home builders with them.[39]

Over the coming months, with Manteo interpreting, Wingina began spending more time with the English at Roanoke, getting to know this new asset he had added to his domain. He asked the men questions about themselves and their ambitions. He escorted English parties to towns within his alliance, showing off his powerful new allies and likely gathering opinions from other werowances and Native priests.

The newcomers' obvious militarism was an enticement but was also dangerous. English matchlock muskets, developed during the incessant series of wars in Europe in the sixteenth century, were inaccurate and slow to load. They were nearly useless in the rain, except as clubs, because of the need to keep the rope-like fuse lit at all times. Still, they made impressive noise, smoke, and bloody holes in bodies—against which wooden armor was no protection. Warriors who knew how to use them would be useful allies, if they could be controlled.[40]

The English also seemed to have the deadly power of making people ill. According to Thomas Harriot's account, Wingina observed a startling pattern in the fall of 1585: In every town that did not welcome the English or sought to betray them in some way, a few days after the English left, Indians there started to fall ill, and some of them died. Harriot believed that 120 people died in one of these outbreaks, although he may have overestimated the death rate, because Indians often evacuated towns when there was trouble, quarantining in small camps until they were confident it was safe to return home. Yet even if Harriot's numbers were exaggerated, Wingina could see that European disease was a powerful force. A comet that appeared in mid-October 1585, around the time the sickness began, added celestial evidence for the power of the English god.[41]

Wingina and the werowances assumed rightly that the English had brought the disease, but the English had no control over it. In fact, Europeans had no more idea of how disease spread or how to prevent it than American Indians did. Horrific disease outbreaks would still regularly sweep through Europe in the coming centuries, with a particularly vicious outbreak of the plague in 1665–66 killing tens of thousands in London alone. No one in the world knew what bacteria or viruses were. The best defense for all medieval and early modern peoples was living outside of cities. Every year until 1800, the city of London had more deaths than births and kept existing only because new people moved in. Like the people of Ossomocomuck, their English visitors assumed that their survival was god's doing and perhaps that he had indeed sent the disease to punish their opposition and impress their allies.[42]

That the English did not die had nothing to do with any special medicine: European practices of closing windows, bloodletting, and inducing vomiting did more harm than good for most maladies. Europeans would not adopt inoculation—which China was practicing at the time—until three centuries later. The health of the English at Roanoke was, in part, the result of acquired immunity from childhood or from their mothers, and also owed to the healthy diet, climate, and water on Roanoke Island and simple luck. Their survival was a distinct anomaly. At most European settlements, the death rate among early colonists was startlingly high, not least at Jamestown two decades later, where disease, starvation, and violence would kill all but sixty of five hundred colonists in one winter alone.[43]

Nevertheless, English disease made an impression in Ossomocomuck, and there were rumors that they might be not only immune but immortal. Wingina himself was deathly ill twice and, his own priests being unable to heal him, sent for the English to pray to their god. His recovery seemed to validate English control of disease. Wingina then asked the English if they could cast the disease upon his enemies. For sixteenth-century Christians, that kind of prayer was taboo, so the men said that their god would not answer requests like that. Rather, they should pray for disease to subside. When people from other towns kept dying, however, Wingina's people inferred that this Christian god had granted their wish and thanked the English for their assistance.[44]

Being inclusivist, the people of Ossomocomuck saw the Christian religion as something they could selectively incorporate into their own beliefs and practices. Perhaps they could learn to cast disease where they wanted it to go. On tours of his own town as well as others, Wingina asked the English to lead them in prayer and singing psalms. He recognized Christian prayer for what it is: asking for blessings on the people praying. By joining in the Englishmen's prayers and introducing them to his allies, Wingina harnessed their spiritual power and shared it—exactly what a Native leader was supposed to do.[45]

But the dangers that the English posed prompted discussions about whether they brought greater harm than benefit. Harriot heard that some werowances hypothesized that these were only the weak advance scouts for what would come next: supernatural Englishmen who were "invisible and without bodies" and would come from the sky and kill them "by shooting invisible bullets." Opponents of this theory accused Ossomocomuck's doctors of making up the idea of invisible bullets as an excuse for not being able to cure the new diseases.[46]

By late 1585, some had decided that the English were too barbarous to tame. When the English first came, Wingina had accepted them as a community under his rule and therefore part of his redistribution commitment. But if the English failed to be pliable subordinates, the demands of reciprocity would end. The exact sequence of events is impossible to reconstruct from the English accounts, which were written by confused and defensive men after they had fled. It seems that the English killed people in some of the towns they visited, although it's not clear whether these were towns affiliated with Wingina or enemies to him. According to Harriot, the violence made an impression on Wingina's people in any case, leading to "the alteration of their opinions . . . concerning us."[47] If the killings happened as they usually did in Ireland, the English struck without warning, and they beheaded their victims. Beheading was not common in North America, and it may have seemed as shockingly barbarous in Ossomocomuck then as it would today.

During this period, in late 1585 or early 1586, Granganimeo died, perhaps from European disease. He had been a great advocate of allying with the English, and his death probably added to arguments that the English were too dangerous, even to allies. Without

Granganimeo, Wingina certainly lost one of his main negotiators with the tricky visitors. In the wake of his deputy's death, Wingina changed his name to Pemisapan.[48]

It's a reminder of how little we understand the internal dynamics of Ossomocomuck that we don't know why Wingina changed his name to Pemisapan and whether it had anything to do with the English or with Granganimeo's death. It was common for American Indians to take on new names at different stages of life, so perhaps the change reflected a change in station after Granganimeo's death. It's also possible that the English were confused about his name the whole time. I'll call him Pemisapan from now on.

Going to England had given Manteo and Wanchese the skills and knowledge to be ideal interpreters and negotiators, but Manteo stayed in Roanoke, whereas Wanchese left. The English believed Wanchese had turned against them, and both popular accounts and scholarly histories of Roanoke have portrayed Manteo and Wanchese as opposites: Manteo as steadfastly loyal and Wanchese as, in the words of one fictionalized account, "the deadly enemy of the white man."[49] In this common interpretation, Manteo turns against his own people in favor of the English, dazzled by the supposedly superior English culture. Yet the real Manteo and Wanchese acted as they did for their own reasons, based in the history, politics, and culture of Ossomocomuck.

The Manteo–Wanchese dichotomy reflects English ignorance of Native politics and an attempt to simplify a situation that the English didn't quite understand. These attempts often labeled one person, town, or entire people good and another bad. Manteo and Wanchese, before he left, often served as interpreters, so English views of nearly everything were filtered through them. Manteo was from Croatoan, which was an ally of Wanchese's people but independently governed, with perhaps its own motivations for English alliance.

Pemisapan (Wingina) and the other elders may have assigned Manteo to his diplomatic role at Roanoke in order to learn about the people of the Roanoke outpost and help maintain good relations with them. It's possible that they assigned Wanchese the opposition role in council—the role of arguing against alliance with the English. Rather than actually reaching opposite conclusions about the good or evil of the English, Manteo and Wanchese may have been performing designated roles in the elaborate consensus politics of sixteenth-century North America.[50]

When spring came, Pemisapan decided it was time to test whether the English could be put to use. Could Pemisapan use English arms and numbers against his enemies to the north, the coalition of peoples ruled by a man named Menatonon and his Chowan Nation? Pemisapan had previously described Ossomocomuck's borders and his enemies within and beyond them, and now he told Roanoke commander Ralph Lane that he had received intelligence that Menatonon was organizing an assembly at his town. According to Pemisapan, Menatonon had invited all of his allies to bring their soldiers, to prepare to attack Roanoke. Pemisapan told Lane that Menatonon's close allies could raise three thousand men, plus perhaps that many more if he rallied his neighbors as well. He urged Lane to strike first.

Lane was very interested in the north, but for his own motives. By this point he knew that the coast of Ossomocomuck consisted of complicated shallows and islands with no deepwater harbors. A century and a half later, the English would establish ports at Wilmington on the Cape Fear River and at Charleston Harbor, but in 1586 the English knew the Cape Fear River as the place their ships nearly ran aground whenever they came that way, and any location farther south was considered dangerously close to Spanish Florida. By contrast, earlier initial exploration to the north had brought news of the Chesapeake Bay, a deep bay that sounded exactly like the port that Raleigh wanted and might be just the right distance from the Spanish. So, encouraged by Pemisapan and by his own desires, Lane prepared a heavily armed force to go north.[51]

Pemisapan gave Lane provisions for the journey north and sent Manteo and two other men and a woman to accompany him. In March 1586, they took the sailboat and several other boats across the Albemarle Sound and up its interior source, the Chowan River, controlled by Menatonon's Chowan Nation. This was an obviously prosperous place, its fields planted with corn, beans, squash, and other crops. Older fields, no longer planted and beginning to fill with second-growth plants, attracted small game and birds, while forests were lush, and streams and wetlands provided fish and aquatic birds for those who could catch them.[52]

Apparently Menatonon had not been assembling a war party or planning to attack Roanoke. The town of Chowan was completely surprised when Lane's men entered with their guns and swords drawn and their two large mastiffs (war dogs) baring their teeth. Taking advantage of the confusion, Lane's men captured Menatonon, who apparently had a physical disability: Lane describes him as "impotent in his limbs."

Yet what might have been a complete success by the English ultimately reveals how thoroughly dependent they were on Native people. For two days Lane and Menatonon talked, and even though Menatonon was the prisoner, he controlled the conversation. The Chowan leader easily discerned what Lane was looking for; his frantic questions about pearls, metals, and deep water revealed all his wants. Taking advantage of the Englishman's desire and ignorance, Menatonon told Lane that everything he wanted was in reach—Lane just needed to listen to him. Lane was impressed. He concluded that this man had deep knowledge of "his neighbors round about him ... and of the commodities that each country yieldeth."[53] By the end of the second day, Menatonon had completely changed Lane's perceptions. Rather than fight Menatonon's Chowans, Lane now considered them his most trustworthy allies and suspected Pemisapan of plotting against him all along.

Menatonon was a powerful werowance with a larger realm than Pemisapan's, but he had his own problems, bigger than these gullible English. In addition to his conflict with Pemisapan, Menatonon was fighting a powerful polity farther to the north around the Chesapeake Bay, whose werowance was often referred to by his title: "the Powhatan." Powhatan ruled over the land of Tsenacomoco, which consisted of several districts that he had inherited near today's Richmond, Virginia. In 1586, Powhatan was in the process of expanding his realm through war and diplomacy, including marrying women in subordinate towns and giving their children positions of privilege, one of whom would be the girl called Matoaka or Pocahontas. Eventually Powhatan's realm would include tens of thousands of people in several hundred towns.

English captain John Smith would later call Powhatan's realm an empire, and many archaeologists and historians call it a "chiefdom." Indeed, Powhatan's power seems closer to the hierarchies of the Mississippian era than is true of most of his contemporaries. It was still possible to amass a considerable amount of power even in post-Mississippian Native America through a combination of threats and promises.[54]

Powhatan was a direct threat to Menatonon's power. To Menatonon, sending Lane's party into Tsenacomoco had obvious appeal. Perhaps Lane's soldiers would overpower Powhatan or at least persuade him that Menatonon had powerful allies and that he should not try to expand south. More likely, Powhatan would defeat Lane and end the English problem in the region. Either way would work out fine for Menatonon and the Chowans.

Menatonon knew what to say to make Tsenacomoco enticing to Lane. He described how a three days' journey up the Chowan River and then four more days of walking north led to the land of a king "whose Province lyeth upon the sea," a "very deep" bay, out of which his people gathered "so great quantity of pearl" that they used them to decorate not only their clothes but also beds and houses. Menatonon gave Lane a string of black pearls from there and, when Lane asked if there were white pearls too, assured him that the king "had great store of Pearl that were white, great, and round." Menatonon offered guides to lead Lane there but also advised him that he would need a large force, because "that king would be loath to suffer any strangers to enter into his country, and especially to meddle with the fishing for any pearl there," and would defend his land and resources with large numbers of men who "fight very well."[55]

With this advice from his new ally, Lane realized that a mission against Powhatan was too ambitious. In his report to Walter Raleigh, Lane spent several pages imagining a future in which he would build a chain of small forts from the Chowan River to Chesapeake Bay, where he would build a large one, leaving the trouble-some Roanoke behind. But for now, with only forty men and a few boats, Lane set his sights on another place Menatonon described, which he called Chaunis Temoatan, about twenty days' journey west.[56]

Lane focused on Chaunis Temoatan because Menatonon de-scribed it as a source of a precious metal he called wassador. Manteo translated wassador as "copper" but also explained to Lane that there was no word in local languages for gold, silver, or the other metals he had seen in England. To Lane's eager ears, the wassador of Chau-nis Temoatan did not sound like the copper he had seen in Ossomo-comuck, but instead like "a marvelous and most strange mineral," perhaps gold or an unknown metal with new and valuable proper-ties. Menatonon's son Skiko reported that, although "he had not been at Chaunis Temoatan himself," he had seen the metal used in large plates decorating the homes of a neighboring people on the Roanoke River. Lane was eager to have his metallurgist, Joachim Ganz (probably the first Jewish English colonist), "try the metals that may be discovered."[57]

The Chowans also hinted that there was a very large body of water at the western end of the Roanoke River, which Lane inferred must be either the Gulf of Mexico or the fabled "South Sea," which led to the Pacific. If these hypotheses seem crazy, that is because we tend to underestimate sixteenth-century European ignorance of North American geography. They had no idea how wide North America was, even after Spaniards had explored the Gulf Coast and northern Mexico. To them, the Pacific might be just over the Ap-palachians. Technology of the time was quite accurate for measuring latitude, but the sun's position is no help in determining longitude; it would take until the eighteenth century before there was an ac-curate, portable method for that. Therefore, east–west distances were more complicated for sixteenth-century people to judge than north–south ones. Lane decided to follow Menatonon's guides west.[58]

The trip did not go well for the English. As Lane put it, "I will-ingly yielded to their resolution: But it fell out very contrary to all expectation."[59] According to Menatonon's instructions, at sundown of the first day they should have arrived at the town with the metal plates, but they did not reach it. The supposedly friendly people who lived in between did not feed them, as Lane had counted on, but instead packed up their food supplies and disappeared, reappearing occasionally to shoot at them from a safe distance.

Town after town was emptied of people and food, and the corn in the fields was not far enough along to eat. Lane's men ate the last of the small supply of food they had brought from Chowan and lay frightened on the bank of the Roanoke River the first night. All the next day they traveled upriver, not seeing a single person, although they could occasionally glimpse fires in the distance. Then, in the afternoon of the second day, tired, hungry, and confused, they heard a call that sounded friendly: "Manteo." Manteo called back to the voice, and singing came from the woods. The English interpreted the song as a "token of our welcome," but Manteo could understand the words and told Lane the bad news: "They meant to fight with us." As soon as Manteo said this, a volley of arrows rained down. The arrows missed the men, and the bowmen ran into the woods. By then the sun was starting to set again, so the English settled in for another sleepless night. It is difficult to imagine a scene more revealing of English failure than these confused men, who soon had to resort to eating what Lane called "Dogs porridge." They killed their own mastiffs and stewed the meat with leaves from the only plant they recognized as not poisonous: sassafras. Called "winauk" in Ossomocomuck, sassafras roots make a tasty tea, but the sticky leaves aren't much good for eating.[60]

Meanwhile, back at Roanoke, everyone was sure that Lane and his men had either starved or been killed. They knew he had survived his initial foray into Chowan, because he had sent his sailboat back to Roanoke with news that he was bound for Chaunis Temoatan. Among those disembarking was Menatonon's son Skiko, who told Pemisapan that the English had captured his father, freed him in exchange for Skiko, and sent Skiko to be kept as a hostage at Roanoke. So Pemisapan had sent Lane against Menatonon and then Menatonon had sent Lane against Chaunis Temoatan. All hoped never to see him again.

UNTRAINABLE?

Pemisapan's experiment seemed to prove that the English were neither as powerful as he had feared nor as reliable as he had hoped. According to the few English who had stayed back at Roanoke, Pemisapan and others began "flatly to say, that our Lord God was not God." The evidence of English weakness seemed to invalidate their claims of divine favor.

Imagine, then, how quickly Pemisapan and his people revised their opinion when Lane's boats appeared one morning. Manteo and the other Native people Pemisapan had sent with Lane reported that they had faced great perils and survived, despite the odds. Everyone knew that the north was full of dangers; therefore, for two boatloads of Englishmen to return alive (if starving) seemed miraculous. It was also striking that they returned the morning after Easter, when the Englishmen at Roanoke had celebrated their savior's rising from the dead.[61]

The English later learned that in council, one of the elders, a man named Ensenore (who may have been the father of Pemisapan and Granganimeo) had argued that the English were too powerful to fight against. Ensenore declared that the English "were not subject to be destroyed" by them and that anyone who sought their destruction "should find their own." The theory of English immortality arose again in light of the Easter resurrection story, and many elders argued that if the English were killed, they would return more powerful than ever. Other werowances in the region seemed to agree. Menatonon and Okisco, a werowance from Weapemeoc (north of Roanoke and east of Chowan), sent conciliatory delegations to Lane.[62]

Lane's return to Roanoke may have seemed to the people of Ossomocomuck to be proof of his power, but he must have realized that it mostly reflected his weakness. Lane knew that many at Roanoke opposed him—he considered Ensenore "the only friend to our nation that we had amongst them"—and he now believed that Pemisapan had sent him north to die. Yet his only choice was to direct his tired and starving men back to Roanoke, where he had left his other men and where he hoped that Pemisapan's people would fill their empty bellies and that English ships would relieve him.

Luckily for the English, Pemisapan's council decided to be careful. At Ensenore's urging, they had men build weirs for the English to catch fish and had women plant crops for them, in the sandy soil of Roanoke Island and on the much more fertile mainland near Pemisapan's town of Dasemunkepeuc. When several weeks passed without rain in the crucial weeks after planting, they asked the English to pray to their god to preserve the growing corn. The subsequent rain appeared to be a sign that the English god wanted his people to be fed and had the power to make it happen. But then Ensenore died. His admonition that anyone who sought English destruction "should find their own" now seemed to have things exactly backward. Two men who had argued in council for English alliance—Ensenore and Granganimeo—were dead. In council, Wanchese argued that the English must be destroyed. But directly attacking them seemed too dangerous.[63]

After much debate, the council decided to starve them out. With the corn not ready to reap, the English were dependent on corn from Pemisapan's stores and fish from the weirs. So Pemisapan's people destroyed the weirs and stopped providing corn. He returned to his mainland town of Dasemunkepeuc to avoid Lane's constant requests for food. Not knowing how to repair weirs, Lane's men had no fish and not "one grain of corn." As Pemisapan foresaw, Lane had to disperse his men to keep them from starving. Some set out to collect oysters on other islands, and some men abandoned the settlement to live at Croatoan and elsewhere along the Outer Banks.[64]

In the midst of all this trouble, Lane heard a rumor that, in a plan worthy of Shakespeare or *Game of Thrones*, Pemisapan had invited all of his allies and enemies to attend Ensenore's upcoming funeral, instructing them to bring their bows and arrows and be ready to fight the English. This rumor had it that fighters would cross over to Roanoke Island at night, set fire to the thatched roofs of the English buildings, and kill the men as they ran outside in a panic. It would then be easy to pick off the rest of the English who were seeking food on the Outer Banks.

You may have found yourself at times in this chapter confused about the various people in and around Ossomocomuck. Imagine Lane, then, not reading all this in a book but instead lying awake at night, knowing his life depended on keeping these alliances and enmities straight. He had no idea who was lying to him and who was telling the truth. He was completely dependent on information from the very people he didn't trust. What all this complexity reveals—and what Pemisapan's supposed plan counted on—was that Roanoke Island was a trap for the English. In fact, its isolation was probably one of the reasons Pemisapan had settled them there. The only thing we know for sure is that Lane was desperate and confused and worried that his men would starve to death.

Trained in the lessons of Ireland—*Don't trust anyone and, when outnumbered, use extreme violence*—Lane decided to act first. On the morning of June 1, the people of Dasemunkepeuc saw a canoe approaching holding twenty-five men, including Lane and Manteo. Lane asked the people who came to greet the boat to tell Pemisapan that they were bound for Croatoan. Pemisapan agreed to see him, as he had so many times before. But once in Pemisapan's presence, Lane gave his men the secret signal to open fire: "Christ our victory!" Pemisapan fell, perhaps wounded, but then ran out of the building and into the woods as another shot hit him. Lane's men ran after him, and one of them emerged from the woods holding Pemisapan's head in his hand.[65]

News of these shocking events quickly reached Croatoan Island, including word that some people from Croatoan had been among those whom Lane's men had killed at Dasemunkepeuc, despite Manteo's insistence that Lane look out for them. Still, the Croatoans didn't turn against the score of starving Englishmen they were hosting. Instead they allowed them to keep a fire going to attract the attention of ships, and only a week later, two dozen sailing ships appeared on the horizon. The English hoped that the ships were bringing supplies from Grenville and Raleigh but feared they bore Spaniards coming to kill them. In fact, this was the fleet of English privateer Francis Drake, stopping by the English post on his way from sacking Cartagena and St. Augustine. If Drake hoped for a respite from seafaring and eating hardtack, he was disappointed by the sorry scene that confronted him. After conferring with the English at Croatoan, Drake's fleet anchored closer to Roanoke, where Lane had holed up after the battle at Dasemunkepeuc. Lane briefly considered staying at Roanoke with reinforcements and supplies from Drake, but a hurricane blew in. The English and the Algonquians alike saw hurricanes as supernaturally powerful, bringing days of rain, hail, high winds, storm surges, choppy seas, and even waterspouts near the ships. To the English, this was an alien kind of power: The word "hurricane" was only just coming into European use, adopted by the Spanish from a word used by the Native Taino people of the Caribbean. The hurricane was a sign to give up.[66]

Native scouts watched as the English loaded their baggage onto Drake's boats and evacuated Roanoke. Manteo and another Native man went with them, perhaps because they feared violence at home or because they planned to continue diplomacy with the English, even at the risk of never returning home. Wanchese, on the other hand, had no desire to cross the Atlantic again. The Englishmen, for their part, hoped never to return to Ossomocomuck. Drake wrote of them, "They were so hard-pressed and broken by the scarcity of all things, that they wanted nothing more than to return to their native country with us as soon as possible."[67] On June 19, 1586, they set sail in a hurry, abandoning their Roanoke buildings and accidentally leaving three of their men behind. Writing the history of the events back in England, Richard Hakluyt would infer that "the hand of God came upon them for the cruelty, and outrages committed by some of them against the native inhabitants of that country."[68] The people of Ossomocomuck surely would have agreed.

THE TRAP OF ROANOKE

The English were gone, but they had left damage in their wake. Pemisapan was dead, as were several other leaders. Roanoke and Dasemunkepeuc had both been damaged by violence and possibly contaminated by English disease. The people of Ossomocomuck soon abandoned Roanoke, perhaps as a form of quarantine, and only a few warriors, led by Wanchese, remained at Dasemunkepeuc. Most of the men and all of the women and children left, likely moving south and inland from Dasemunkepeuc into parts of Ossomocomuck that the English knew less well.

They did keep watch on Roanoke Island and, strangely enough, within a few weeks of Lane's departure, ships began arriving. Unlike in the past, no diplomatic party went to meet them. Most of the guards returned to the mainland or Croatoan to report, but the English captured one of them and took him on board to meet with the fleet's leader, none other than Richard Grenville. He had finally come with supplies and men for his colony. The captured Ossomocomuck man told Grenville that Lane and his men had left with Drake. Disgusted, Grenville departed, leaving only around fifteen men with provisions and artillery to guard the remaining English buildings and fort at Roanoke.[69]

There's not much mystery about what happened to those fifteen men. There was no chance the people of Ossomocomuck would allow this tiny force to remain after what Lane had done at Dasemunkepeuc. People on Croatoan Island would later tell the English that Wanchese had led thirty men across to Roanoke Island. Two approached the English fort and greeted the two Englishmen who came out to meet them with an embrace. But it was a ruse: One of Wanchese's men drew his wooden sword out from under his cloak and struck one of the Englishmen on the head, killing him. Then more men emerged from hiding, their bows drawn. After casualties on both sides, the surviving English soldiers fled. Some of them managed to get into a boat and row out toward the Outer Banks, along the way picking up four of their comrades who had been out fetching oysters.[70]

Although we don't know if the version told on Croatoan is exactly what happened, the next English expedition found only "the bones of one" man, and not even the remains of any of the rest. If some survived, it was because they persuaded some other Native people to take pity on them. Pemisapan had failed to persuade Lane's colony to be subordinate to his rule, but isolated foreigners could more easily be incorporated. If any of them were spared, they were probably divided up and sent to live in separate towns, where they may have married and had children and become part of Native Ossomocomuck.

A similar fate may have met a large group of West Africans and Native South Americans whom Drake had seized from the Spanish. Drake's records don't say where along his journey these women and men disembarked, but they weren't with his ships when they returned to England, so it's possible he left them in Ossomocomuck to make room for Lane's men. Not at all the threat that Lane posed, they would have been good candidates for adoption, the common practice of incorporating outsiders.[71]

I'm probably not the only person in North Carolina who has imagined that, if I abandoned my home, deer and vines would quickly take it over. Plants grow fast in this wet, subtropical climate, and the growing deer population in the eastern United States now lives in close proximity to expanding towns and suburbs. That's what happened to the English colony on Roanoke Island. Vines curled into the buildings and thrived in the cleared dirt of the cabin floors. Melons grew on some of the vines and enticed deer to make the houses part of their rounds so they could venture inside for a sweet treat.[72]

It must have been a surprise to the people of Ossomocomuck when, in July 1587, a year after they had killed or dispersed Grenville's men, two ships anchored off the Outer Banks. A sailboat left the ships and landed at Roanoke; on board were Manteo and the other Native man who had left Ossomocomuck with Drake, along with a group of Englishmen, a few boys, and, for the first time, some women, two of them visibly pregnant. These were the aspiring settlers who would become known as the Lost Colony.[73]

The people of Ossomocomuck surely wondered why this vulnerable group had come to the same place where Englishmen had fled after killing Pemisapan just a year earlier. And indeed, the English planners had meant for these colonists to land in the deep harbor of the Chesapeake Bay, where they would have a new start with different

Native communities. This time, they were supposed to be a permanent colony. They brought families rather than troublemaking soldiers, with enough food to last a full year, in an attempt to get along better with and learn from local Indians how to work the land. The fleet's captain had advised them that the powerful Powhatan people of the Chesapeake were unlikely to welcome them, either, and he might have been right that the Chesapeake would prove even more dangerous. So here they were, set down in the very place where their predecessors had made so much trouble. Another problem was that the planners had promised each colonist five hundred acres. Finding fifty thousand available acres on Roanoke Island was impossible—it was probably slightly bigger than the ten thousand acres it is today—and at any rate it is poor agricultural land. This colony was not going to work, not in this place. Still, the colonists gamely walked to the north end of Roanoke Island and set about repairing the cabins and building new ones in the eerie absence of any Native people.[74]

Lane's attack on Dasemunkepeuc had shown the danger the English posed to anyone who got close to them. Scouts watched the latest foreigners closely, and when one was unwise enough to go out alone to catch crabs, a group of men, probably from Dasemunkepeuc, shot him with arrows, hitting him sixteen times, then rushed to club him and beat his head to pieces. His mangled body was a powerful image of the likely fate of these unwanted colonists.[75]

When Manteo learned of the killing, he recognized it as a sign that there was no use trying to make peace between the English and Dasemunkepeuc. Instead, on July 30, he led a group to confer with his mother at Croatoan. When they landed at Croatoan, Manteo quickly called out in the local language to avoid being attacked. To his relief and that of the English, the Croatoans welcomed them. The Croatoans already knew at least two of the English. One was Master Edward Stafford, who as captain of one of Lane's military companies had spent time at Croatoan gathering food and keeping watch for ships after Pemisapan stopped feeding them. The other was the new colony's governor, John White, the artist who had been with Lane's group. The contrast between a colony led by White and the one under Lane the military man suggested different aims and perhaps a new start, as did the female colonists, including White's own daughter, Eleanor Dare. Still, the Croatoans strictly warned their visitors not to take any of their corn. It was July, and the previous year's stores were mostly gone, while the new crop was still in the field. They were relieved to hear that these English had brought plenty of provisions and that they intended "to live with them as brethren and friends." At that, the Croatoans invited the English party up to their town for a traditional welcoming feast.[76]

The Croatoan leaders told the English that keeping the peace would not be easy. Men from Dasemunkepeuc had killed or dispersed the men Grenville left in 1586, and they recalled the tragedy of how Lane's attack on Dasemunkepeuc had resulted in the death of some Croatoans, despite Manteo's effort to protect them. Through Manteo, Croatoan's leaders asked Stafford if "there might be some token or badge" the English could give them in order to identify them as friends when they met them anywhere beyond Croatoan. At the English request, the Croatoan werowances agreed to "do the best they could" to help make peace between the English and the various werowances of Ossomocomuck by telling them that the English hoped "that all unfriendly dealings past on both parts, should be utterly forgiven and forgotten."[77]

After Manteo, White, and Stafford left, Croatoan's werowances needed to decide how to act. They presumably did go to talk with neighboring werowances, although they may also have discussed doubts as to actual English intentions. In any case, most people in Ossomocomuck probably had little interest in English peace offers.

And they were right to doubt. About a week later, around midnight on August 8, a group of Croatoan men and women was sitting around an outdoor fire at Dasemunkepeuc—Pemisapan's old, now abandoned town—when they were ambushed. A group of about twenty men started shooting at them. One of the Croatoans was killed, but the rest fled into some thick reeds nearby. As the attackers pursued them into the reeds, one of the Croatoans recognized Stafford and called out his name. Like Lane, White had felt trapped on Roanoke Island. Having heard no news from anyone, not even the Croatoans, he had decided to go on the offensive. But to the dismay of everyone present, his men had fired on their only allies: visiting Croatoan men and women who explained that they were there to gather corn, tobacco, and pumpkins left behind when Dasemun-kepeuc was evacuated.[78]

The fresh start that Manteo and White had envisioned died with the violence. According to White's account, Manteo deflected blame by saying to the Croatoans that "if their werowances had kept their promise in coming to the Governor [White] at the day appointed, they had not known that mischance."[79] The English formally declared Manteo "lord" of the now emptied Roanoke and Dasemunke-peuc, and he converted to Christianity in a christening ceremony. It's easy to know what this all meant to the English—they had alienated just about everyone and were entirely dependent on Manteo—but what did Manteo think? He was certainly not lord of the region in the way the English meant that word, but he may still have believed he could harness some English spiritual power by being baptized. He also may have been acting on the instructions of his mother and the other werowances at Croatoan.

Manteo and the other Croatoans could see the ships departing on August 27, 1587. John White was on board, hoping that if he went back to England in person he could hurry the next shipment of colonists and supplies. He left behind approximately ninety-seven men and boys, seventeen women, and two babies, born since their mothers landed. Yet war with Spain had restarted, and Queen Elizabeth required all ships to defend England. During the war, the Spanish considered attacking Roanoke from St. Augustine but had higher priorities. For three years, White could only wonder what was happening at Roanoke, including to his daughter and infant granddaughter. Lane's violence and his own had doomed both England's and Ossomocomuck's hopes for their relationship.[80]

NOT LOST

During those three years, Ossomocomuck would recover from the troubles with the English. Drought put pressure on farming, making their diversified economy more necessary than ever. Powhatan continued expanding and threatening war from the north. If the people of Ossomocomuck could stay out of war, they could concentrate on food production and trade and tending to everyday life, with its marriages and births, its modest human joys and sorrows. If conflict broke out, though, life would be a lot harder.[81]

They would have only a little to do with Europeans for generations. Much has been made in popular memory of the mystery of where the English lost colonists disappeared to, but White himself wasn't puzzled. Before he left in 1587, they had all agreed that if the colonists left Roanoke Island, they would "write or carve on the trees or doorposts the name of the place where they should be." If they were fleeing danger, they would add a "distress symbol, which was to be a cross over the name of the place they were going." When he finally returned in 1590, White saw C R O and CROATOAN written in two places, both without the distress symbol and therefore signifying an unhurried, considered move to Croatoan. White's men landed on the north end of the Croatoans' island, walked aimlessly around, capsized some boats on the shore, and lost several men in the heavy surf. When they finally reached Roanoke Island, their trumpet blasts and English songs went unanswered. And then they left. The storms had broken the cables to most of the anchors and convinced the sailors that it was too dangerous to stay. The people of Ossomocomuck were surely glad to see them sail away, taking their perils with them.[82]

The colonists, with their small children, poor agricultural prospects on Roanoke Island, and little hope of relief from England as the months and years wore on, would have been wise to accept the safety and bounty of Croatoan, where Manteo and his mother were likely to ease their reception. But Croatoan Island was not a place where some one hundred hungry visitors could stay for long. It is likely that they went to the mainland with the Croatoans. They might have built their own town under a werowance's domain, much as Pemisapan had envisioned at Roanoke Island, or dispersed as refugees into Native towns. Perhaps someone killed the men to rid themselves of danger, but it is likely that the women and children, and certainly the two babies, were adopted into Native families somewhere in Ossomocomuck or its neighboring regions. Whatever happened, John White never found out.[83]

The Lost Colony of Roanoke gets a lot of attention in North Carolina for something that happened more than four hundred years ago. Virginia has Jamestown and Colonial Williamsburg, Philadelphia and Boston have the sites of the American Revolution, California has Spanish missions, and coastal North Carolina has the first English attempt to found a colony in what's now the United States. And it has the advantage of being a mystery story.

Every theory of what happened to the lost colonists necessarily involves the Native people of Ossomocomuck, who lived in this place long before English people set foot here and whose descendants live here still. Nonetheless, Native Americans have played decidedly supporting roles in most tellings of the Lost Colony, including the outdoor drama *The Lost Colony*, written by University of North Carolina professor Paul Green in the 1930s and staged on Roanoke Island nearly every summer since 1937. In Green's play, the English characters, in seeking a better life in a new place, begin what will become the United States—quite a stretch, given that they disappeared, their colony failed, and the United States would not come into being for another two hundred years. As the colonists prepare to leave England, Sir Walter Raleigh (who was played in the 1950s by a young Andy Griffith) calls them "pioneers of a new nation soon to be." As Red Cliff Ojibwe historian Katrina M. Phillips puts it, in dramas like *The Lost Colony*, "regardless of the plot line, America was the star."[84]

As a New Deal progressive, Green wrote the play as part of a new movement in outdoor historical drama. He wanted to counter the explicit white supremacy of the previous decades and reckon more honestly with America's history. He recognized that American Indians were part of that history, and, as a result, Native characters are important to his drama. Yet in his script, the Native characters seem to have no motivation, no depth of humanity or culture or history. For the most part, they simply live in "the wilderness that swallowed [the colonists] up." In the first few decades that *The Lost*

Colony was performed, the Native characters spoke their lines in broken English, which made them seem as if they were the foreigners instead of the colonists.[85]

I saw *The Lost Colony* in the summer of 2018 with my friend and colleague Malinda Maynor Lowery and our kids. Professor Lowery and her daughter are Lumbee Indians whose ancestors lived in what's now eastern North Carolina when the English tried to establish a colony at Roanoke. Lowery's daughter liked the play but had some questions about its portrayal of her ancestors—basically, she wanted to know if she and her mother should be on their side or not. During their opening dance, she leaned over and asked her mother, "Are these real Indians?" As some of them attacked the English settlement, she questioned, "Why are they burning down the house? Is that good?" The show's historically inaccurate insistence that these doomed 1580s English people somehow laid the foundations for the United States makes her want to root for them as well as the Native characters. She is, after all, an American girl as well as a Lumbee girl.

As a historian and a Lumbee, Malinda Maynor Lowery of course recognized the shortcomings of *The Lost Colony*. But she is also a film and theater producer, and she explained to me that one of the points of outdoor historical drama is that it takes place at the site of the original events. As we watched the play, the sun went down and the stars came out, and that was when the power of the setting and its real history hit her. She and her daughter were in the place of their ancestors, looking up at the same stars they saw in the 1580s and that Lumbees and other Native North Carolinians still see. As Professor Lowery put it, "even if the story wasn't told right, I knew this is where it had happened." Some English men and women had been "lost," but its Indigenous people had not. They were sitting right here, looking up at the stars.

This wasn't the first time Professor Lowery had seen *The Lost Colony*. Fifteen years earlier, she and her husband, the late Willie French Lowery, went as part of their research for the Lumbees' own outdoor drama, *Strike at the Wind!* In the early 2000s, they were revitalizing this Lumbee play, first written in the 1970s, with music by Willie Lowery, inspired by the success of *The Lost Colony* as well as the outdoor drama *Unto These Hills* in Cherokee, North Carolina. The Lumbee play *Strike at the Wind!* tells the nineteenth-century story of Henry Berry Lowry, who fought against former Confederates who were trying to maintain white supremacy in the aftermath of the Civil War. The fact that it is set nearly three centuries after *The Lost Colony* directly counters that play's implication that Indigenous people would soon disappear to make way for English America. In their play, as its narrator puts it, Lumbees "celebrate the past lest we forget and are in turn forgotten."[86]

Outdoor drama is powerful storytelling, and *Strike at the Wind!* celebrates and remembers. Robin Cummings, chancellor of the University of North Carolina at Pembroke, recalled seeing the play as a Lumbee boy on "summer evenings under the stars with my family."[87] Like *The Lost Colony*, its performance in the place where its events happened is essential. When my son and I saw it in the summer of 2019, we drove through the Lumbees' flat and lush rural country, past fields of corn and sweet potatoes and the kind of second-growth woods you can see all across the South, to get to the Lumbee Cultural Center's amphitheater. We parked and walked past a Lumbee Tribal Security car, both patrolling the lot and signaling that we were on Lumbee land. We took our seats as Charly Lowry and her band played Willie Lowery's "Streets of Gold." The excitement of the crowd getting settled in their seats was similar to that at *The Lost Colony*—in a beautiful outdoor place, anticipating a special experience—but here there were also community members greeting one another, one of the older cast members circling through the audience to talk to friends while the younger cast members, self-conscious in their nineteenth-century dress, greeted people more shyly as they came in. We could see behind the amphitheater a narrow stand of pines and a vast green wetland—a quintessentially eastern North Carolina landscape. In the first scene, one of the characters leaned against one of the pine trees inside the wall that creates the stage, making the woods part of the scenery.

There is a lot more moral ambiguity in *Strike at the Wind!* than in *The Lost Colony*. The characters struggle and argue with one another about the moral way to fight injustice—there isn't always a simple or righteous answer. Throughout the play, Lumbee characters defend their right to self-determination, including the right to not be conscripted into fighting for the Confederate Army, and they are Americans as well as Lumbees—truer Americans than the Confederates. They are fighting in part for their right to vote in North Carolina and U.S. elections. And simply performing the play, from the very start of the Native renaissance through today, as Willie Lowery explained, "raised awareness about things that people in Lumberton didn't even want to talk about. Our culture. Our existence. Our presence and our being there, period, was a fight and a struggle."[88] Ultimately, it is the place and the people that matter. As Henry Berry Lowry sang "In the Pines," a traditional song in Willie Lowery's haunting arrangement, the sun set, the clouds flamed pink behind the stage, and the cicadas and a chorus of frogs joined in.

And for its eighty-fourth season, in 2021, Lumbees helped to remake *The Lost Colony*. In a partnership with the Lumbee Tribe, director Jeff Whiting worked with Kaya Littleturtle and other Lumbee artists as well as choreographer Jerad Todacheenie (Navajo/Tlingit) to write new songs and dances and Algonquian-language lines for the Native characters. They redesigned costumes and props based in part on John White's drawings. For the first time, the Native characters were all played by citizens of North Carolina and Virginia tribes—Lumbee, Coharie, Haliwa-Saponi, and Chickahominy. Some of Paul Green's outdated lines have been changed or deleted. (In a similar change, the Eastern Band of Cherokee Indians has rewritten and produced *Unto These Hills*, adding Cherokee language and perspectives.)[89]

CONCLUSION

People whose ancestors lived in or near Ossomocomuck in the sixteenth century—including Lumbees, Coharies, Haliwa-Saponis, Meherrins, Occaneechis, and smaller Native communities in North Carolina and Virginia—have by no means disappeared or lost their history. As descendants of coastal Carolina Algonquians, Iroquoians, and Siouans, many of them see the history of Roanoke as less about the fate of a few English people and more as one of many events that tie them to the long past, present, and future of this place, a place that is no more lost than its Native people. Today North Carolina has eight state-recognized tribes, nearly 100,000 enrolled tribal members, and more than 160,000 North Carolinians self-reporting Native American as their primary race in the 2020 census. Even the permanent English colony of Jamestown did not succeed in destroying the Native peoples whose land Virginia ultimately took—eleven Virginia state-recognized tribes still exist today on the lands of their ancestors. Clearly, rumors of the demise of Indians, even on the Atlantic coast, where they bore the brunt of seventeenth-century English settler colonialism, have been greatly exaggerated.

Like the continuing memory and use of sacred spaces and images from Cahokia, Moundville, and the Huhugam, the history of the Carolina coast is still alive in contemporary Native nations. Native communities survived within the same region where they lived in previous centuries, and they neither forgot their past nor surrendered their identities. Nevertheless, as we shall see in later chapters, surviving and maintaining sovereignty would become much harder when Europeans came in greater numbers and stayed.

The beheading of Pemisapan and John White's blundering attack on the group of Croatoans at Dasemunkepeuc demonstrate the brutality that Europeans could inflict, a brutality that is not surprising, given the central tenet of colonialism—that Europeans had the right to seize and rule the land and resources of others. This belief served to justify appalling violence.

Yet the panic and fear that motivated that brutality reveals the ignorance and weakness of the Europeans as they reacted rashly to a disadvantaged position. It also points to Native rejection of colonialism's empty claims of dominion over sixteenth-century Ossomocomuck. Throughout the short history of the Roanoke colony, the people of Ossomocomuck held most of the power and almost all of the information, and their greater concerns were about Native rivals. At the end of that short history, Native peoples still dominated the region politically and economically, whereas the English had only a lost colony and an increasing sense that colonizing or even understanding North America would be harder than they had thought.[90]

Europeans' sixteenth-century attempts to colonize regions north of central Mexico all failed. By the end of the century, Spain clung weakly to only St. Augustine and Santa Fe, their presence barely tolerated by local Natives, while all of their other attempts had been destroyed. The English and the French had nothing to show for a century of exploring and attempting to colonize the north since John Cabot in 1497 and Jacques Cartier in 1534. Still, Europeans would keep trying to pull profits out of North America by settling colonies on Native land. They would try again in the early decades of the 1600s, but for a long time they would be able to establish only isolated outposts that either were useful to surrounding Native communities, like the trading posts of Quebec and New Amsterdam, or that were so aggressively defended that they militarily defeated the Native nations on whose land they settled, like Massachusetts and Jamestown, or that reached a compromise with one Native people that included mutual defense against another more powerful one, including Santa Fe. Over time, English, Spanish, French, and Dutch traders and settlers would slowly establish themselves in North America, most often by being of use to local Native people, as we shall see in the next chapter.[91]

The people of Ossomocomuck did change in the centuries that followed, but there is little reason to think that those changes resulted from the few years English people spent at Roanoke. Thomas Harriot heard a rumor of disease devastation in 1585–86, but there is no evidence that Ossomocomuck's population declined dramatically in the 1500s. Experience with the Roanoke colony and European piracy might have discouraged living right on the coast, although archaeology shows that people continued to spend time harvesting resources on the Outer Banks. It would be another hundred years before English settlers came in large enough numbers to do serious damage.[92]

CHAPTER 4

MOHAWK PEACE AND WAR

T HE HIAWATHA BELT HAS A BACKGROUND OF DEEP PURPLE wampum (shell beads) interwoven with symbols made of white wampum representing the five Haudenosaunee nations, also known as the Iroquois Confederacy or the Iroquois League. The Mohawk nation is the white square on the right, signifying the easternmost Haudenosaunee nation. The others, moving from right to left, are the Oneida, Onondaga (in the middle, represented by a white Tree of Peace), Cayuga, and Seneca nations, connected in a row on the belt. Since the eighteenth century, the Haudenosaunee have included a sixth nation, the Tuscaroras.[1]

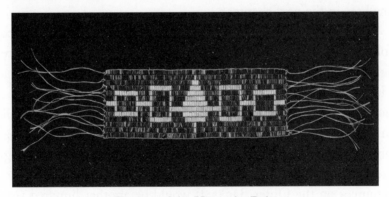

Replica of the Hiawatha Belt.

As we saw in chapter 2, wampum has long held great significance for the Native peoples of the Northeast. Because white beads signify peace and dark purple beads war, the Hiawatha Belt shows both how the Mohawks and other Haudenosaunee nations created peace out of war and how balance can come from intermingling. When Europeans—French, Dutch, and English—came to the region starting in the late sixteenth century, they quickly adopted wampum as both a diplomatic tool and a currency. To defend themselves from attack, to buy food from Native neighbors, and to trade for furs for profit, Europeans needed wampum. Wampum's description doesn't make it sound precious, and a purely Eurocentric view of value might lead us to think that Europeans tricked Indians into accepting as legal tender something that had no value.[2]

But it's important to remember that there's no absolute value to gold or silver any more than there is to shell. Currency has to be recognized as valued and be in scarce supply. Because of the combination of having to find shells and to process them with skill, shell beads fit the bill as well as gold did then and specially marked paper does for us today. People in the colonies also used deerskins as currency—thus the term "bucks." But pelts and skins vary greatly in value depending on their size and thickness and the skill of the men who killed the animals and the women who processed them, and supplies vary seasonally. By contrast, wampum beads were remarkably consistent, and the arrival of Europeans and their iron tools made drilling easier and even more uniform. Rather than leading to a decline in value, increased production allowed for large pieces like the Hiawatha Belt, made up of many strings.[3]

Colonists used wampum not only in the Indian trade but when trading with one another. It became an accepted currency of New Netherland and New England. A couple of centuries later, world currencies would be set to the gold standard, and China was already using paper money, but in the seventeenth century shell was still a common currency around the world. The Dutch were already familiar with wampum from their experience with West Africans who traded with shell beads. To facilitate their participation in trade, the

Dutch even began producing glass beads in the Netherlands, adopting glass technology from Venice, but they also continued to depend on Algonquian manufacturers and dealers.[4]

Wampum is just one example of how seventeenth-century Native people set the terms of their relationships with Europeans. If Europeans wanted to live in North America and trade with Mohawks and other Native people, they had to follow local practices. They had to pay in products that their diplomatic and trading partners wanted. But they also had to understand that wampum wasn't just a currency. Just as the Hiawatha Belt symbolizes the deep and sacred connections among the Haudenosaunee nations, wampum exchanged between Europeans and Native peoples embodied the creation of a similarly sacred relationship. Rather than mere practical agreements that might be broken when interests changed, trade relationships were familial and intended to be permanent—breaking these bonds would be like betraying family. Through trade, Europeans accidentally agreed to reciprocal obligations that embedded them in local politics and wars, even when they would have rather stayed safely neutral.

Yet the most well-known story about wampum is that in 1626 the Dutch bought Manhattan Island from Munsees (Algonquian-speaking groups, most of whom in the early 1700s merged with Lenapes to become the Delawares) for a paltry $24 worth of beads. It is true that representatives of the Dutch West India Company got permission from local Munsees to establish a post at the mouth of the Hudson River and gave sixty guilders' worth of wampum as part of the agreement. The exchange seems ridiculously one-sided only if you don't understand wampum's value and meaning, Native people's recruitment of European trading posts, and the fact that Munsees didn't vacate the island but instead continued to live in a patchwork of communities surrounding the Dutch. As Abenaki scholar Lisa Brooks explains, exchanging wampum and other goods "sealed a pledge to share space, creating a negotiated relationship as much as an economic transaction."[5] Both they and the Dutch envisioned sharing the island and its resources as trading partners and allies.

The wampum both confirmed the arrangement and embodied their new relationship with the Dutch.

The presence of Europeans changed eastern North America, but mostly through Native decisions and actions. Mohawks raided enemies for furs to trade to the Dutch, which increased Mohawk access to guns, gunpowder, and musket balls, in turn facilitating Mohawk warfare. Their enemies then went in search of their own European trading partners, including the French at Quebec and the English in Massachusetts and the Chesapeake Bay. Native peoples took advantage of opportunities as the fur trade developed and populations shifted because of war or disease. European pressure shifted the Indigenous balance of power, but Europeans' impact was often indirect and almost never what they intended.

For the time being, colonization would be just a sideshow in the real drama of seventeenth-century northeastern North America: the rise of the Mohawks, Oneidas, Onondagas, Cayugas, and Senecas, as represented by the Hiawatha Belt. In the 1600s, these Native nations came to dominate a region far beyond their homeland between Lake Erie and the Hudson River: Their expansive reach stretched from the western Great Lakes to the Atlantic and from the St. Lawrence River Valley, in present-day Canada, to the Carolinas. They used wampum and other diplomatic methods to create and maintain peace among the Five Nations, while bending other Indians and Europeans alike to their will, by diplomacy and by force. Together they controlled Native and European trade routes. They remade a vast region and shaped the histories of all the Native and European people in their reach.

MOHAWKS AND THE GREAT PEACE

There was a time before the Haudenosaunee when the Mohawks, Oneidas, Onondagas, Cayugas, and Senecas fought against one another and could not prevent violence even within their own towns. Their descendants would later tell how "even in his own town a warrior's own neighbor might be his enemy and it was not safe to roam about at night.... Everywhere there was peril and everywhere mourning."[6] Mohawk historian Tom Sakokweniónkwas Porter writes that "this period of time was perhaps the darkest, most violent and hopeless time of our entire history."[7] That's quite a statement, given the dark and violent times that the Mohawks and other American Indians have lived through in the centuries between these long-ago conflicts and today. It's not in the nature of oral history to give exact dates, but tribal historians estimate that this period of chaos was between the ninth and sixteenth centuries, so possibly during the aftermath of the fall of the continent's centralized, hierarchical societies, as explored in chapter 2. Perhaps the violence resulted from the absence of old governing structures that had not yet been replaced.[8]

The Five Nations turned their history around with the principle of Gayanashagowa, the Great Law of Peace, the requirement to be in harmony with one another and the world around them. Gayanashagowa became the formal law that the Haudenosaunee would follow to get along within their nations and with one another. Through it, they would work as a confederacy in their foreign policy, war, and trade. Yet they would remain independent in their domestic governance, and each would retain its own territory and identity as a nation: the Mohawks (the Kanyen'kehaka, or People of the Flint), the Oneidas (the Onyota'a:ka, or People of the Standing Stone), the Onondagas (the Onönda'gega', or People of the Hills), the Cayugas (the Gayogohono, or People of the Marsh), and the Senecas (the Onöndowága', or People of the Great Hills).[9]

Oral history tells that Dekanawida, the Peacemaker, came to the Five Nations to spread Gayanashagowa. Knowing that war would end and peace prevail only if women stopped supporting war expeditions, he persuaded Clan Mother Jikonsaseh to join him, in part by agreeing to her demand that women and farming should have a central position in the new era. Another of the Peacemaker's converts was Hiawatha, the namesake of the Hiawatha Belt, a man who was grieving for family members lost to the violence. Together with the Peacemaker and Jikonsaseh, Hiawatha traveled to each of the

Five Nations to spread the word of Gayanashagowa and its power "to abolish war and robbery between brothers and bring peace and quietness."[10]

One fierce Onondaga war leader named Tadodaho represented all that the Peacemaker was trying to change. This man loved war and conflict and fought to destroy women's agriculture. There were "rattlesnakes that nested in his hair.... And if you came too close they would lunge at you and they would bite you." But the Peacemaker combed the snakes out of his hair and replaced them with strings of wampum, taming his mind with Gayanashagowa. The Peacemaker and Jikonsaseh offered him and his nation a key role: The council would meet at Onondaga, which was geographically in the middle of the Five Nations. He would open the councils, and in the future that office would be called by his name, Tadodaho, while all future head clan mothers would be known by the title Jikonsaseh.[11]

The enemies of the Five Nations called them the Iroquois, a pejorative term that may have meant something like "snakes." They call themselves the Haudenosaunee, which means "people of the longhouse."[12] Their families lived in longhouses, much like in Ossomocomuck in chapter 3. In a longhouse, many people had to live together and share space without letting any minor disputes escalate into violence. They might not all agree all the time, but their purpose in living together was mutual support. A Haudenosaunee speaker explained the symbol to a Frenchman in the 1650s: "We make up just one house, ... we have but one fire, and we have always lived under the same roof."[13] Like an extended family sharing a longhouse, the Haudenosaunee nations would have to "discuss issues until they are resolved." The Mohawks were the "keepers of the eastern door," responsible for security and trade on their eastern border.[14]

In fact, the Haudenosaunee nations would still argue and sometimes fight, but confederating gave them a structure and an ideological commitment to getting along, as their elaborate symbolism reveals. Besides the longhouse, another symbol of the Haudenosaunee was five arrows "strongly bound," signifying "that all the lands and all the warriors and all the women of the Confederacy have become united" in a bundle that "no one can bend or break." Yet they were still five arrows—they did not meld into one nation. On occasion they might even fight separate wars, but they were strongest when united. Another symbol was the advice to "eat together from one bowl the feast of cooked beaver's tail. While they are eating they are to use no sharp utensils for if they should they might accidentally cut one another and bloodshed would follow." Their shared hunting grounds were to be a "dish with one spoon" to feed and provide for everyone, not to fight over.[15]

As we saw in chapter 2, replacing hierarchical governments with more egalitarian ones does not mean a society became simpler or primitive; participatory governance requires quite elaborate rules so that everyone feels heard and respects the final decision, whatever their original opinions were. We don't know exactly what was in the original law, because it has been amended over time. Like the British constitution, the Five Nations Great Law is not one written document. It was kept orally using wampum until versions were written down in the late 1800s. The word for a member of the Confederate Council, "royaner," has the same root as Gayanashagowa (the root can be spelled roya or gowa), which means "good" or "great." The word "gayanasha" can be translated as "peace" or "law," while the root roya/gowa brings them together in a sense of "goodness" or "good-mindedness."[16]

The Haudenosaunee held a royaner to a high standard: "The thickness of their skin shall be seven spans—which is to say that they shall be proof against anger, offensive actions and criticism. Their hearts shall be full of peace and good will and their minds filled with a yearning for the welfare of the people of the Confederacy . . . all their words and actions shall be marked by calm deliberation." The ideal royaner should always "look and listen for the welfare of the whole people and have always in view not only the present but also the coming generations, even those whose faces are yet beneath the surface of the ground—the unborn of the future Nation."[17] Consensus is a tricky form of governance. Gayanashagowa required that nothing be decided unless everyone agreed, but it also valued getting along and bending toward a decision rather than in-

sisting on one's own way. At the heart of Gayanashagowa, Haudenosaunee scholar Kayanesenh Paul Williams explains, "is a
fundamental idea that human beings of good mind would naturally
seek and maintain peace."[18]

Of course, these repeated instructions reflect the awareness that
Gayanashagowa was aspirational; representatives would not always
be selfless and patient. The people had a responsibility to not pull a
royaner into "trivial affairs" but to encourage them in broad-
mindedness.[19] As in most Native American polities by this era, great
numbers of people often came to councils to witness and be consulted by their representatives. Apparently, the ideal was also often
the reality. In 1678, Frenchman René-Robert Cavelier, Sieur de La
Salle, noted with admiration of the Haudenosaunee that "in important meetings, they discuss without raising their voices and without
getting angry." All of the men and women, he observed, "listen to
the one who is speaking, even when he speaks for an hour, and they
content themselves with saying from time to time: You speak well,
you are right . . . and they give these indications of consent to all the
speeches which they consider equally, whether they believe them or
not."[20] Before gatherings, a Haudenosaunee spiritual leader would
give a Thanksgiving Address to praise everything in creation for
maintaining its responsibility and remind the listeners to maintain
their own responsibilities.

Ceremonies like the Thanksgiving Address and the Condolence
Ceremony (the pre-peacemaking ritual discussed in chapter 2) are
still important to the Haudenosaunee. At the start of the 2021 Native American and Indigenous Studies Association conference, Mohawk scholar Ryan DeCaire spoke (in the Mohawk language and an
English translation) words similar to those said in ceremonies by his
ancestors for centuries to help establish "clear thinking" among the
conference goers. Each of us, Professor DeCaire explained, "brings
different challenges and burdens, things that might distract you." In
that year of Covid-19, we all needed the Condolence Ceremony's
components: to wipe away tears "so that you can see everything
around you more clearly and make good decisions," its eagle feathers
to clear our ears "so you can hear everything," and "the cleanest

water from the other side of the sky to clear your throat so you are comfortable to talk."[21]

Because each royaner represented a clan that already existed within the Haudenosaunee nations, the new system was based on older forms of order, including the central role of women in Haudenosaunee families. The Haudenosaunee nations are matrilineal, meaning that they trace their family lines through, and inherit their clans from, their mothers. Being a royaner was a male role, while the electors would be women, reflecting ideals of balance and reciprocity. From among the men of the correct lineage within their clan, the clan mothers had the discretion to determine "one who is trustworthy, of good character, of honest disposition, one who manages his own affairs, supports his own family, if any, and who has proven a faithful man to his Nation." The men of the clan then would consider the choice. If they objected, the women reconvened and nominated someone else. If, while serving, a royaner proved unworthy, the clan mothers could reprimand or, if necessary, depose him.[22]

Building women's power into the political and economic system was not a concept seventeenth-century Europeans understood. The Dutch minister Johannes Megapolensis believed that Mohawk women "are obliged to prepare the land, to mow, to plant, and do everything; the men do nothing, but hunt, fish, and make war upon their enemies."[23] Anyone who has killed and butchered a deer, caught enough fish to feed a family, or been to war knows those are hardly leisure activities, but Europeans who saw women working in the fields often believed they were taken advantage of by lazy husbands, fathers, and brothers. And European men usually did not notice women's political power at all. But for the Mohawks and other Haudenosaunee, all power needed to be balanced, and dividing it up by gender was a transparent way to do so.

Haudenosaunee women's power was equal to men's, yet, like European societies at the time, Haudenosaunee society was strictly divided into roles and responsibilities based on two genders. As in Ossomocomuck, women generally were the farmers and town builders and were responsible for the fields and towns, impressive enough in their size and fortifications that Dutch explorers who came across them called them "kastelen" ("castles"). Haudenosaunee women explained to U.S. officials in the eighteenth century that they could not negotiate land deals with only Haudenosaunee men: "We women ... are *the owners of this land*—and it is ours; for it is we that plant it for our and their use."[24] Nor did the political role of women end once they chose their royaner. As Seneca scholar Barbara Mann explains, "Clans operate as the local level of government," and "women ran the clans, that is, they ran the local level of government." And clan mothers sent speakers to the council to convey their decisions and advice. Female and male Faithkeepers within each clan were responsible for spiritual and ceremonial affairs.[25]

The principles of consensus building and the structures of the clans and the council allowed the Haudenosaunee to achieve a remarkable peace within and among their nations. Megapolensis, the Dutch pastor, despite looking down on Indigenous people in most respects, could not help but "think with astonishment upon all the murders committed in" his homeland of the Netherlands, "notwithstanding their severe laws and heavy penalties," in contrast to the Haudenosaunee, who seldom if ever murdered one another.[26] Today, even after the defeats and extreme displacements of the late eighteenth, nineteenth, and twentieth centuries, the Mohawks, Oneidas, Onondagas, Cayugas, Senecas, and Tuscaroras still exist as nations scattered across the United States and Canada, the Haudenosaunee Confederacy survives, and Gayanashagowa is still the way of peace that many Haudenosaunee people strive to follow. A Mohawk greeting remains "Shé:kon ken skennen'kó:wa?" ("Is the Great Peace still among you?"). Or, for those who know it well, the first person will simply ask, "Shé:kon?" ("Still?") and the responder, if all is well, will say, "Shé:kon."[27]

ENEMIES WITH GUNS

The Mohawk woman pulled her long hair back to keep it out of her way, then set the big clay pot of water onto the fire. As the water began to bubble, she added ground hominy—cornmeal that had been prepared by soaking it along with ashes from the fire. The lye from the ashes had softened the corn, released more of its nutrients, and removed toxins. She stirred as the mixture cooked into a thick porridge. When it was done, she spread it out on a flat clay surface to dry near the fire, producing the seventeenth-century version of quick grits. When it was completely dry, she mixed in some ground dried venison and a bit of salt and maple sugar crystals and packed it into small leather bags. When men left their town, they would carry these bags along with a cooking pot, a wooden bowl, and a spoon, so they would only have to heat up some water to make a hot meal, or if they were in enemy territory and didn't want to light a fire, they could hydrate their dinner with just a little water.[28]

Women made these packs for hunting expeditions and war parties, and in the 1600s there were many war parties to supply. The success of the Haudenosaunee in bringing peace within the Five Nations had not ended war against people outside the confederacy.

Haudenosaunee fighters with prisoner, French drawing
based on Haudenosaunee original, c. 1666.
ARCHIVES NATIONALES D'OUTRE-MER, AIX EN PROVENCE, FRANCE,
COL CII A2, FOLIO 263

In the summer of 1609, a group of around two hundred Mohawk men packed their food bags and weapons and walked out of their towns.[29] They followed the road downhill into the river valley that lay under the snowcapped Ratirón:tak (Adirondack) Mountains. When they reached the crystal-clear Mohawk River, they launched their canoes and floated past what even their enemies conceded to

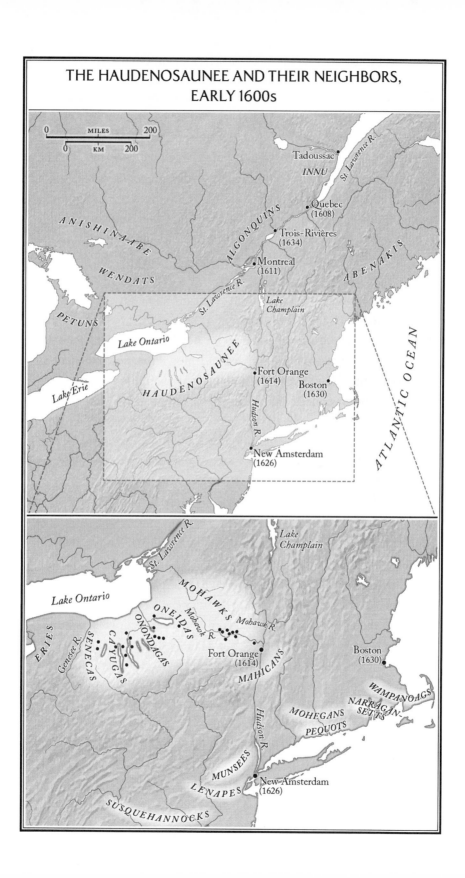

THE HAUDENOSAUNEE AND THEIR NEIGHBORS, EARLY 1600s

MILES 0 — 200

KM 0 — 200

Tadoussac

INNU

St. Lawrence R.

ANISHINAABE

ALGONQUINS

Quebec (1608)

Trois-Rivières (1634)

WENDATS

Montreal (1611)

ABENAKIS

PETUNS

St. Lawrence R.

Lake Champlain

Lake Ontario

HAUDENOSAUNEE

Fort Orange (1614)

Boston (1630)

Lake Erie

Hudson R.

ATLANTIC OCEAN

New Amsterdam (1626)

St. Lawrence R.

Lake Champlain

Lake Ontario

MOHAWKS

ONEIDAS

Mohawk R.

ERIES

Genesee R.

SENECAS

ONONDAGAS

CAYUGAS

Mohawk R.

Fort Orange (1614)

MAHICANS

Boston (1630)

WAMPANOAGS

NARRAGAN-SETTS

MOHEGANS

Hudson R.

PEQUOTS

MUNSEES

New Amsterdam (1626)

LENAPES

SUSQUEHANNOCKS

be "beautiful valleys, and fertile fields of corn." Some were meadows prepared and maintained through the use of controlled fires to cultivate habitat for berry bushes and for deer and other game. In the fall, the trees would turn red and gold. In winter, pine trees would stand out green against the other trees, all above a carpet of snow, and the river would be packed with ice. By then the longhouses would hold hundreds of bushels of corn and other food, and people would stay warm with big fires and thick bearskins. But now, in the summer sun, the trees were their deepest green, and the corn was nearly ripe.

The Mohawk River flows into the great Skaunataty, the river the Dutch would call the North River and the English would name the Hudson. But these men wanted to go north, so they lifted the canoes onto their shoulders and walked along the portage road to Kaniá:taro'kte, the long, thin lake that empties north into Kaniatarakwà:ronte, the lake Europeans would name after Samuel de Champlain. The water of that lake flows north, eventually reaching the St. Lawrence River, which flows northeast out to the Atlantic. If, like me, you grew up where rivers all flow in one direction, let me say that again: The Hudson River flows south, while the rivers north of the Adirondack Mountains flow north.[30]

The Mohawks were on a raiding mission. They rowed into Lake Kaniatarakwà:ronte, past shores without crops, longhouses, or towns. People had lived there in the past, but they had fled the violence between the Mohawks and their enemies to the north and east. The Mohawks were fighting against the Wendats (whom the French called the Hurons), a rival confederacy of peoples who spoke Iroquoian languages related to the Haudenosaunee languages, as well as a coalition of several nations of the large Algonquian language and culture group. That group included the Innu (Montagnais), who lived close to the mouth of the St. Lawrence; the Abenakis, on the eastern shore of Lake Kaniatarakwà:ronte and farther east and north; and the peoples just north of the St. Lawrence and along the Ottawa River, known as Algonquins. (Note the difference between the name "Algonquin," which signifies one particular people, and "Algonquian," which describes a much larger linguistic and cultural grouping —similar to "Germans" versus "Germanic.")[31]

The Mohawks hoped to launch a surprise raid on a town or trading and hunting party, but just after nightfall, they were spotted by a group of Wendats, Algonquins, and Innu, who had waited on shore hoping to head off approaching Mohawk raiders. Their wait was rewarded. They climbed into their canoes and rowed out into the lake. The Mohawks decided to pull onto shore to set up a defensive position. Quickly, some men chopped down trees while others piled them into barricades. When the opposing canoes came close to the shore, one Mohawk called out to them to ask if they were looking for a fight. To no one's surprise, they yelled back that they "wanted nothing else."[32]

But neither side actually wanted to fight just then, when it was so dark that they might accidentally shoot people on their own side, so they returned to their camps to wait for dawn. All night, each side danced and sang and prepared for battle as they taunted their adversaries. One of the men yelled out that the others were cowards and that soon "they would feel the day of their ruin coming." The enemy called back in similar terms. There was little sleeping that night.[33]

As the sky began to lighten, the enemy came ashore, and the Mohawk warriors came out of their barricade. The Mohawks were an impressive sight—nearly two hundred of them, painted for war, with wooden armor and helmets to protect them from their enemies' arrows and wearing their distinctive Haudenosaunee short-feathered headdresses, which inspired terror in their enemies. One of the men on the opposing side described them as "strong and robust . . . solid and confident."[34]

The approaching Wendat, Algonquin, and Innu warriors let out a cry and then did something unusual. When they were about thirty steps away from the Mohawks, they parted into two groups, leaving in the middle one man, covered in metal from his hat to his knees. As the Mohawks pulled back their bows, preparing to shoot their first round of arrows, they heard an enormous cracking boom, as if thunder and the sound of a waterfall had combined and struck for

Engraving of the 1609 battle in Samuel de Champlain's *Les Voyages faits au grand fleuve Saint Laurens.*

THE LOUIS ROUND WILSON SPECIAL COLLECTIONS LIBRARY,
UNIVERSITY OF NORTH CAROLINA AT CHAPEL HILL

just a moment right in front of them. One of the Mohawks standing near the front fell down dead, shot right through his wooden armor. The enemy force shouted in delight. Another bang. Another man fell. The Mohawks had never yet seen guns, and it was astonishing to see people fall without being hit by an arrow. The Mohawks had hoped to be surprise raiders, and then, when their enemy spotted them, they assumed they would engage in a battle where both sides showed their bravery but didn't do much damage to the other side. This battle had suddenly turned lethal and unpredictable. The Mohawks retreated rapidly into the woods, some of them falling as arrows and more of the strange new shots pursued them.[35]

European-manufactured guns were not entirely better than bows and arrows, but they were different. The kind of musket fired in this battle by the man in metal, Samuel de Champlain, was similar to what the English had in sixteenth-century Ossomocomuck: not particularly accurate and tedious to reload but with some psychological advantage over people who did not have their own guns. Usually, warriors would pull an arrow out of the victim and try to stop the bleeding, but here there was no arrow to remove.

The Mohawks practiced a kind of warfare similar to that common across North America after the fall of large cities. They preferred raids, ambushes, and quick victories, and they would make a hasty retreat rather than risk high casualties. If Haudenosaunee enemies had a new weapon, one that could pierce wooden armor, everything could change. That fall, word probably spread to Mohawk towns that Henry Hudson's ship had fired similar weapons on the Skaunataty (Hudson) River, and another engagement of Mohawks against Algonquins and Innu the following June repeated the 1609 battle and, for the first time, allowed the Mohawks to see the weapons causing the damage.[36]

Guns were not the first European goods Mohawks had seen. Long before Christopher Columbus crossed the Atlantic, perhaps as early as the tenth century, Native North Americans on the northern Atlantic coast obtained goods from Norse explorers. By the late 1400s, glass beads and pieces of wrought iron and brass were arriving by way of trade with European fishing boats or as detritus washed ashore from shipwrecks. Mohawk towns acquired some of those goods, either through trade or by raiding. Although Europeans were the most direct source of European manufactured products, most Native communities got these goods through Native traders. Initially the Mohawks used European goods as raw materials. Strips cut from a copper kettle made lovely pendants and rings that could demonstrate the wearers' or givers' connections beyond their towns and region. Pieces of an iron knife could be made into needles for many people to use in sewing and tattooing. Years before the 1609 battle with muskets, Algonquians began placing bits of iron and brass on the tips of their arrows, increasing their chances of shooting through Mohawks' wooden armor, and Mohawk warriors, when they could get metal, did the same.[37]

If we rush too fast through the seventeenth century, we might interpret the arrival of guns and metal-tipped arrows as the start of Native dependence and European dominance. But we would be wrong. Local rivalries, customs, and geography continued to be the most important factors in Native decisions and determined the opportunities and limits for Europeans. There had been new weapons here before, and new ways of defending against them. When your enemy gained some advantage, you adapted, and that is what the Mohawks did.

Native Americans wanted European trade, but almost all European efforts in the sixteenth century had failed, as we saw in chapter 3. All sixteenth-century French attempts to found permanent mainland North American colonies failed, as did trading posts if the Europeans did not abide by local rules. In 1542, residents of a short-lived colony unknowingly sent a shipload of fool's gold (pyrite) to France, to their great embarrassment. In 1580, when a Frenchman attempted to trade directly with a Penobscot town on the Gulf of Maine rather than through Mi'kmaqs who had set up the trade as intermediaries, the Mi'kmaqs drove him off. In 1599, French merchants tried to found a colony at Tadoussac, an Innu trading post where Basque whalers had been stopping to trade for at least a generation, but the French abandoned that effort after eleven of the sixteen colonists died the first winter, the others surviving only because the Innu fed and sheltered them. Tadoussac remained an Innu post, where ships of several European nationalities stopped to trade with the Innu and their Algonquin allies.[38]

By the early years of the seventeenth century, Europeans had established a handful of North American posts that lasted. In addition to Spain's St. Augustine and Santa Fe, the English began Jamestown in 1607, and the French established the town of Quebec in 1608. Closer to the Mohawks, in 1609, Henry Hudson, hired by the Dutch to look for a northwest passage between the Atlantic and Pacific oceans, sailed partway up the Hudson River, and Dutch ships subsequently began coming annually, with metal and beads and jewelry to trade for furs and food.[39]

When the French established Quebec in 1608, it was on Innu land and because Innu leaders invited them. Like many Native Americans, they drew Europeans and their weapons into preexisting North American conflicts. The Innu and their Algonquin and Wendat allies wanted a steadier source of French goods and hoped to lure French soldiers into fighting with them against the Mohawks.

In preparation to fight the Mohawks in 1609, Wendats and Algonquins traveled down the St. Lawrence River to Innu country to join them in persuading Quebec commander Champlain to join their fight. The Innu, Algonquin, and Wendat delegation explained that they were "wanting vengeance" against the Mohawks and other Haudenosaunee, whom they had "fought for a long time, because of the many cruelties that they have committed." They proposed to Champlain that they all "go to war together."[40] When Champlain hesitated, his new allies insulted the French with the gender stereotypes they shared, saying the French had "the heart of women, and didn't know how to make any kind of war except on their furs."[41] It was ultimately Native politics and economics that pulled the French into the 1609 and 1610 battles and that killed both Mohawk and French men on the shores of the lake that would eventually bear his name.

Fighting the powerful Haudenosaunee was really the opposite of what Champlain wanted. He was in North America to obtain beaver pelts to sell at a profit in Europe, where they would be made into fashionable felt hats. Europeans had long imported beaver pelts from Russia, but overhunting had dried up the supply. For Champlain, trading peacefully with all Native American nations would have been ideal. He knew that peace "would be a great benefit," because of "the increase in business, greater ease of exploring, and the safety in hunting for our Indians . . . who don't dare to go to certain places, where beavers abound," because of warfare. But those people, the first people Champlain met along the St. Lawrence River—Innu and Algonquins—did not give him that choice. They set their own foreign policies, not Champlain, and if he was going to be their trading partner, he had to fight their enemy.[42]

From their first interactions with the French, Algonquin and Innu diplomats shaped French relationships in North America, including defining the Haudenosaunee as the enemy. Two Algonquins had traveled to France in 1602, and on their return one of them made a speech to a group of Innu, whose leader was a man named Anadabijou. The Algonquin speaker told them that in France he had met King Henry IV, who had declared that he "wanted to send people to their country, and to make peace with their enemies (who are the Iroquois [Haudenosaunee]) or to send them forces to vanquish them."[43] Anadabijou's response made it clear that the latter was his preference. He responded that he was "very glad" for the king to build Quebec on Innu land, "to send people to his country, and to make war on their enemies." He did not mention the option of peace. To build Quebec and profit from the fur trade, the French had to make enemies of the most powerful people in the region.[44]

This kind of recruitment happened everywhere Europeans went. In June 1615, Champlain traveled southwest up the St. Lawrence River from Quebec, to what's now metropolitan Montreal. There, a group of Wendats expressed their delight to see the Frenchmen and their hope that the French would send soldiers "to assist them in their wars against their enemies." They told Champlain that it was very hard for them to travel to Quebec to trade, because "the Iroquois, their old enemies, always held the path that blocked their passage." And they pointedly reminded Champlain that he "had always promised them to help them in their wars." They persuaded Champlain to join another expedition against the Haudenosaunee, this time an attack on a palisaded Onondaga post. Although that military expedition failed, and Champlain was wounded, the Wendats and Algonquins succeeded in persuading the French to establish two new posts closer to them: Montreal and Trois-Rivières, halfway between Quebec and Montreal.[45]

Not only were the French unable to direct their allies' foreign policy; they could hardly feed themselves. In 1628, Champlain imprisoned an Innu man who he believed had killed two Frenchmen. It was a big mistake. The Innu stopped selling food to Quebec, so Champlain and his men, much like the English at Roanoke, could only wait desperately for supply ships from France, hoping they would arrive before they starved to death, as "we counted out our peas to eat." The lack of food "greatly diminished our forces, and most of our men became weak and feeble." An attempt at growing crops yielded only "a little barley, peas and corn each week ... and we had to go through a miserable time." Their Innu neighbors agreed to sell them some eels but "gave us only a little bit, and sold them to us for very high prices." To get even the eels, the French had to sell their own clothing and the beaver skins they had bought earlier in the year and had planned to ship to France. Champlain freed the prisoner.[46]

The Frenchman knew that his Native allies were using him. He reflected that, alongside many qualities he admired in the Innu, they had "a wickedness" as well, "which is taking vengeance and being big liars. . . . They promise much and do little." But he recognized that his ambitions "seem to be possible only through their means."[47] Everywhere the French, Dutch, Spanish, and English went in early-seventeenth-century North America, they depended on Indigenous locals. Nothing was possible except through Native means.

THE MOHAWKS COURT NEW WEAPONS AND ALLIES

In many ways, the Mohawk Valley was the perfect place to live. Sheltered by the mountains and well watered by rain and rivers, it offered extremely fertile soil, while the woods and meadows hosted plentiful game and natural resources. Another advantage was that all rivers flow away from Haudenosaunee country—the Mohawk River flows east into the Hudson, and the rivers of the other four Haudenosaunee nations run west to Lake Erie or south into the Susquehanna and Allegheny watersheds—making it hard for enemies to get to.[48]

But when European trade came to the Atlantic coast, suddenly Native communities downstream had an advantage, because they were closer to the ports. As the "keepers of the eastern door," the Mohawks would be responsible for European diplomacy and trade for the Haudenosaunee. Lake Champlain and the St. Lawrence River had long been part of Mohawk travels, and soon after the first enemy hit a Haudenosaunee target with a metal-tipped arrow, Mohawk warriors began waylaying Algonquin and Wendat traders returning home up the St. Lawrence with kettles and other European goods. Yet the French, vastly outnumbered, preferred not to give even their allies guns. As a result, Mohawk raids seldom put guns in Haudenosaunee hands, and Wendats, Algonquins, and Innu made it hard for the Mohawks to reach French posts. Enemies to the south also blocked Haudenosaunee traders from the English at Jamestown.[49]

But a closer opportunity arose in the 1610s, and the Mohawks did everything they could to develop it. An old history textbook, if it includes New Netherland at all, might say that colony was founded by Dutch traders boldly going inland in search of furs. In fact, Native people—the Munsees and related Lenape/Delaware groups on the lower Hudson and Delaware rivers and Mohawks and Mahicans up the Hudson—actively encouraged Dutch trade and settlement.

The Mohawks took advantage of their good relations with the Mahicans to establish Dutch trade. The Mahicans lived near the confluence of the Mohawk and Hudson rivers, and they were the people whom Henry Hudson met at the northernmost point of his 1609 exploration. So the Mahicans would be key to Mohawk interests—another blocked port would not do them any good. The Algonquian-speaking Mahicans were not part of the Haudenosaunee, but their interests in attracting Dutch trade up the Hudson River coincided. The Haudenosaunee had a wider hunting range than the Mahicans and could keep the Dutch coming back upriver to collect a large supply of furs, and they may have initially paid tribute in furs to the Mahicans for the right to trade in their country.[50]

At first, the Mahican/Mohawk plan worked. In 1614, the Dutch established a small trading post on an island in the Hudson River, and ten years later the Dutch West India Company built a permanent post on Mahican land, Fort Orange (later renamed Albany by the English). Fort Orange would be the first permanent Dutch trading post in North America, despite its inland position, 150 miles up the Hudson River. Mohawks and Mahicans persuaded Dutch traders that this spot—their spot—was where the Dutch could buy the most and best beaver pelts.[51]

Beaver pelts provided the sellable good that Dutch traders were looking for in North America as they established their early-seventeenth-century global trading empire. In 1602, the Dutch chartered the Dutch East India Company to trade in Indonesia and south and east Asia. To build on its success, the Dutch chartered the *West* India Company in 1621 to trade in Africa and the Americas. Private Dutch traders had been operating on the Hudson River since Henry Hudson's explorations, but the West India Company would intensify those efforts, providing the Mohawks and Mahicans with a permanent and reliable source of European goods.[52]

But in the 1620s, the formerly good relations between the Mohawks and the Mahicans descended into war. The reason war broke out may have been that Mohawks discovered that Mahicans had invited other Algonquian-speaking nations to the post to trade directly with the Dutch, increasing competition without Mohawk permission. Or perhaps Mahicans had started importing furs from people who lived farther north and hunted beaver in colder climes, which had thicker fur and fetched a higher price. Or maybe Mohawks had been paying tribute to the Mahicans for the right to trade in their country and instead wanted to extend Haudenosaunee dominion over Fort Orange. Whatever the spark, Mahicans clearly did not want to be subordinate to the Haudenosaunee and wanted to keep their jurisdiction over Fort Orange. The Mohawks temporarily made peace with the Innu, French, and Algonquins on the St. Lawrence in 1624 and 1625 so that they could direct their military force toward the Mahicans.[53]

Because the Mahicans now demanded that their Dutch allies and guests protect them against Mohawk aggression, the Dutch at Fort Orange, like Champlain, found themselves pulled into a war that was not in their interest. In 1626, most of the small Dutch force at Fort Orange accompanied a Mahican force marching west toward the Mohawks. They had ventured only a couple of miles from Fort Orange when a Mohawk war party "fell so boldly on them with a discharge of arrows, that they were forced to fly, and many were killed," including the Dutch party's leader.[54] The Dutch realized that the Mohawks could destroy New Netherland. The "wretched little fort," as one French visitor described Fort Orange, could not withstand a Mohawk attack, and this early fighting sent the few Dutch colonists living around Fort Orange packing.[55]

Fortunately for the Dutch, a Dutch–Mohawk war was not in Mohawk interests either. A few days after that battle, a Dutch delegation went to the Mohawk towns to reestablish peace, at the risk of meeting the bloody fate of the last Dutch to travel west. To the relief of the Dutch emissaries, the Mohawks happily accepted their peace offerings. The Mohawks explained that when the Dutch men joined the Mahican war party, they "had meddled" in matters that were not their business. "Otherwise, they would not have shot them."[56] The Dutch took those words to heart and never again sent a war party against the Haudenosaunee, despite Mahican entreaties.

The Mohawk–Mahican War went on for more than a year, and the Mohawks eventually prevailed. The Mahicans abandoned their towns on the west side of the Hudson River in 1628 and built new towns on the east side. They still had close relations with Fort Orange, but now the Mohawks controlled trade there. The Mahicans no longer invited competition into Fort Orange and instead developed a role as intermediaries between Hudson River trade and fur and wampum production in the east.[57]

The Dutch were greatly relieved when the war ended. The Mahicans and Mohawks were both vital to trade at Fort Orange, and their war had temporarily dried up the beaver supply. Now that the Mohawk–Mahican War was over, the fur trade on the Hudson was back, bigger and more profitable than ever, and Mohawks were raiding on the St. Lawrence again.[58]

It turned out that the early-seventeenth-century Dutch were the best possible trading partner for Mohawk purposes. Their shipping was on the cutting edge of European technology, and Dutch weapons manufacturing was the most advanced in Europe because of their war against Spain. Dutch innovators developed the mass-produced flintlock musket in the 1620s. Flintlocks fired using the friction of a flint, making them more dependable than matchlocks (which ignited the charge with a cord that had to be kept lit) and easier to produce than wheel-lock muskets (which employed friction through a more intricate mechanism). Dutch mass production of weapons would supply both North America and the Thirty Years' War in Europe, which started in 1618.[59]

Mohawks kept rivals from trading with the Dutch, even if they were Haudenosaunee. They traded goods on to the Haudenosaunee to their west but did not invite them to come to Fort Orange themselves. Indeed, when Oneida or Onondaga traders tried to cross Mohawk country to reach the Dutch, the Mohawks waylaid them. To them, their role as the keepers of the eastern door included being the providers of Dutch goods to the rest of the Haudenosaunee.[60]

As the Dutch colony of New Netherland grew, a great many Dutch guns would end up in Mohawk and other Haudenosaunee hands. Mohawks would return home from the Dutch post at Fort Orange bearing goods from Europe, which came up the Hudson River from the post that the Dutch had founded on Manhattan Island: New Amsterdam. West India Company restrictions on selling munitions and liquor to Indians proved impossible to enforce, because Indians demanded them. Repeatedly, Dutch colonists were called before the Fort Orange Court on charges of selling alcohol to Mohawks or Mahicans. Innkeeper Egbertjen Egberts admitted that she had sold beer to Indians "in contempt and disregard of the ordinances and placards of the director general and council." The court officer requested that she be fined five hundred guilders, receive corporal punishment, and be banished from New Netherland, but the court levied a smaller fine and no other punishment.[61]

In August 1657, a Mohawk man named Kanigeragae, accused of drunkenly committing "many acts of insolence" one Sunday morning, offered to lead Fort Orange authorities to a place where Indians bought brandy, if they gave him a beaver pelt to pretend to buy it with. He led them to the house of Marten Bierkaecker and Susanna Janssen. Kanigeragae took an empty kettle into the house while the Dutchmen stayed out of sight. They waited. And waited. He came back out of the house a suspicious forty-five minutes later—plenty of time for a few drinks. His kettle now held three pints of brandy, beer, and wine, mixed together with sugar, so the Dutch investigators rushed inside to investigate. Although Bierkaecker denied any knowledge, Janssen admitted that she had sold liquor, blaming "extreme poverty" and fear that their three children would starve. The court sentenced her to pay a fine but didn't record an amount, so she probably didn't pay anything. Dutch people had to sell the goods that Native customers wanted.[62]

Native leaders themselves sometimes worried that the liquor trade was too big. Mohawk leaders occasionally asked New Netherland officials to stop the alcohol trade because they worried that the "nation drinks so much brandy" that "if we drink ourselves drunk, we cannot fight." Yet alcohol is hard to refuse once one has a taste for it. At a 1659 meeting in which Mohawk leaders asked for better enforcement of the liquor trade, they themselves closed their statement commenting that "when we leave now, we shall just take some brandy with us, and then no more after this time."[63]

Dutch and English traders would take advantage of alcohol's addictive properties to sell massive quantities of rum—produced from sugar by enslaved men and women on Caribbean plantations—to Native communities. Alcohol brought considerable profits to European traders, and pleasure but trouble to Indigenous people. Sixteenth-century Mohawk leaders would hardly be the last Native voices calling for regulation of the liquor trade and personal temperance. But, at least for the time being, Mohawk hunters had the economic power to ensure that liquor sales continued.[64]

Unlike with alcohol, Mohawk leaders were not ambivalent about munitions sales. Like the French, West India Company officials tried to stop the trade, even passing an ordinance levying the death penalty for arms sales, yet the Mohawks wanted to buy guns, gunpowder, and musket balls, and these goods were the only way Dutch traders could buy enough beaver pelts to make New Netherland worth having at all. Selling guns earned them huge profits. For one gun a Dutch trader might get twenty beaver pelts. He could trade those twenty pelts in Europe for ten guns to take back to Mohawk country and trade them for more furs. Everyone ignored the prohibition on arms sales, all the way up to the colony's highest officials. Some of Albany's most prominent families made their wealth from dealing in guns or related industries. Philip Pieterse Schuyler—the great-great-grandfather of Eliza Schuyler, the future wife of Alexander Hamilton—moved from Amsterdam to New Netherland as a gunstock maker around 1650 and also traded in furs and brandy.[65]

Before long, it became clear that if the Mohawks couldn't purchase weapons from the Dutch, they would buy them from someone else. New Netherland governor Peter Stuyvesant in 1654 justified violating company policy by explaining that "Mohawks, now our good friends," had told him that they "have been out of necessity forced to seek munitions" from the English. Starting in the 1630s, English traders in the Connecticut Valley paid better prices for their beaver pelts and gave them "substantial presents and gifts." If the Dutch refused the Mohawks, Stuyvesant continued, "it might well follow that we would also lose the Mohawks' friendship and consequently burden our people and nation with more misfortune." Therefore, he and the New Netherland Council "deemed it proper and highly necessary" to provide the Mohawks with "a moderate trade in munitions."[66] Haudenosaunee men eventually began making their own musket balls out of bars of lead, and a craftsperson who could make an arrowhead could replace the flint in a flintlock musket, but Mohawks kept coming to Fort Orange for new guns, significant gun repairs, and gunpowder. If New Netherland hadn't provided goods and services that the Mohawks wanted, it would have ceased to exist.[67]

To Europeans, this was not how colonialism was supposed to work. The European designers of colonies believed in what economists call mercantilism: Nations derived their power from trade, and the uneven trade relationship between a nation and its colonies enhanced the nation's power. The point of colonialism was not reciprocity. It was taking the resources of other places to enrich Europeans at home and assist their conflicts in the "Old World." Colonies were supposed to provide cheap natural resources the nation could process into manufactured goods, some of which would be sold back to the colony at a high profit.

The Mohawks' furs and hides were imported into the Netherlands and used for leather, but Mohawks set such high prices for them that it was hard for the Dutch West India Company to make a profit selling anything to them but guns. Mohawks were hardly the passive consumers that colonial planners hoped for. In the late 1630s, because the West India Company's attempts to attract colonists had failed, it lost the monopoly on the fur trade that the Netherlands government had granted. In its place came a system of relatively unregulated trade designed to attract colonists. A New Netherland resident recalled in 1647 that there had been very little Dutch settlement anywhere in the colony "until every one had liberty to trade with the Indians."[68] With lots of competition, goods flowed in for Native customers.

The West India Company made rules as if it were in charge, but Native people determined which rules would hold. They approved of New Netherland's Freedoms and Exemptions Act of 1629, which forbade taking land from Indians without approval from both sides. Mahicans granted the Dutch the land for Fort Orange and a nearby settlement named Rensselaerswijck in return for benefits and payments. With these agreements, the West India Company gained jurisdiction over a few places, but the vast majority of what European maps labeled "New Netherland" remained Mahican, Munsee, Lenape, and Mohawk land. The same was true for "New France," "Florida," and, for a while, until their settler populations grew large, "New England" and "Virginia."[69]

SHOPPING

Mohawks came to Fort Orange for the guns, but they stayed for the cake. When they visited Fort Orange and Rensselaerswijck, they sampled Dutch cakes, cookies, and bread and took some home for others to try. The excellence of Dutch baking was universally recognized. The English word "cookie" comes from the Dutch koekje. Mohawk women made cornbread, but it may have seemed dense and mundane when compared with the treat of an airy yeasted white bread, fine cake, or cookie after making the trip to Fort Orange with a load of beaver furs and baskets of corn. To the frustration of many colonists, Mohawks' proceeds from the fur trade allowed them to pay high prices. The Dutch colonists who introduced white bread and cakes to the region soon could not afford them.[70]

Colonists repeatedly complained to the New Netherland Council that bakers sifted whole wheat flour and sold the white flour "greatly to their profit to the Indians for the baking of sweet cake, white bread, cookies, and pretzels," leaving "largely bran" to sell to the townspeople. The petition concluded in horror: "The Christians must eat the bran while the Indians eat the flour." In an effort to appease colonists, the council outlawed the sale of white bread and cake to Native customers, but, as with liquor and guns, Native demand prevailed. Bakers continued selling baked goods made from white flour to their best customers.[71]

Selling products that Mohawks wanted made the Dutch fur trade thrive. By the 1630s, New Netherland was exporting tens of thousands of furs every year, mostly from Mohawk sources. Trade worked in Native reciprocal fashion: Mohawks profited, and the Dutch profited, even if some of them had to eat heavy whole wheat bread while Mohawks ate cake. Dutch colonial life was shaped by the rhythms of the fur trade. Every spring, once the ice on the Hudson River had broken up, Rensselaerswijck's colonists knew that ships would be coming up from Manhattan with goods to stock for the beaver trade and that soon after that, in May or early June, Mohawk men and women would start arriving. They canoed down the Mohawk River with loads of furs from the winter's hunt, plus corn and other products. The Mohawk River goes over a seven-story waterfall right before it meets the Hudson, so they carried their goods on their backs for the last portion of the journey, walking down what colonists called the Mohawk Road or the Woods Path, what's now Route 5 and Albany's State Street. Property values were highest just on the edge of town along the Mohawk Road, where Dutch people might persuade Mohawks not to go any farther with their packs and instead stop there for good prices, food, drink, and a comfortable place to sleep. In 1661, trying to attract Mohawks even sooner, some Dutch traders established the post of Schenectady at the place where Mohawks disembarked from their boats.[72]

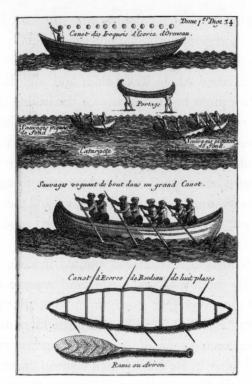

Haudenosaunee (Iroquois) canoe technology and use in
Nouveaux voyages de Mr. Le Baron de Lahontan.
THE LOUIS ROUND WILSON SPECIAL COLLECTIONS LIBRARY,
UNIVERSITY OF NORTH CAROLINA AT CHAPEL HILL

By high summer, hundreds of Mohawks—some years as many as a thousand—lived in Rensselaerswijck for weeks at a time, sometimes outnumbering the few hundred colonists. Some camped in fields and around town, and others stayed with Dutch or Mahican hosts. Some Dutch men and women built houses specifically for trading with and lodging customers—you can see them on colonial maps, marked as "little house" or "Indian house." Others reserved space in their front rooms for trading and socializing with Native men and women, selling them homemade beer, milk, butter, and cheese and letting them sleep on the floor. One Dutch colonist observed with disdain that, "not being satisfied with merely taking them into their houses in the customary manner," some had tried to attract "them by extraordinary attention, such as admitting them to the table, laying napkins before them, presenting wine to them and more of that kind of thing."[73]

While this kind of hospitality seemed excessive to European observers who saw Indians as dangerous and perhaps savage, it was necessary for anyone who wanted Mohawk customers. Despite the efforts of the colonists waylaying them on the road in, Mohawks generally would go farther into Rensselaerswijck to enjoy the hospitality of individual houses and farms. In addition to cake and bread, men chose gunpowder, iron tools, shirts, and fishhooks, and women picked out hoes, awls, fabric, ribbons, and buttons. Mohawks and Dutch colonists alike carried wampum around town in elaborately decorated bags made by Mohawk women.[74]

Dutch trading posts became international sites. The ferry across the Hudson River, operated by an African ferryman, might have Mohawks sitting next to Dutch farmers and soldiers; Mahicans; Munsees; French speakers from Belgium; immigrants from England and its colonies and from Scotland, Scandinavia, and the German states; and people of African descent, mostly held in bondage by the West India Company or by individual European colonists. In the early years, this mixed population mostly communicated in a simplified trade jargon that mixed Dutch with Mohawk and Mahican words, although over time their conversations allowed Dutch and Mohawk traders to learn each other's language. For diplomatic negotiations, where misunderstandings would be more costly, the best interpreters were people like Agheroense, a Mohawk man who knew all the neighboring Native languages in addition to Dutch. He negotiated a peace in 1645 on the lower Hudson between the Dutch and several Munsee and Lenape peoples, and he interpreted for countless multilateral conversations.[75]

In Rensselaerswijck, Mohawks also observed aspects of Dutch life that impressed them less than muskets and cake. One Sunday morning, a group of Mohawks went into the church to hear Dutch minister Johannes Megapolensis preach. As they listened, they smoked their long tobacco pipes, catching a few Dutch words here and there. At the end of the service, they asked the pastor why he wanted to "stand there alone and make so many words, while none of the rest may speak." It was the opposite of Haudenosaunee meetings, where each had the chance to talk. Megapolensis explained that he was "admonishing the Christians, that they must not steal, nor commit lewdness, nor get drunk, nor commit murder." Having observed all of this behavior in New Netherland's posts, and probably Dutch drunkenness just the previous night, the Mohawks replied that the admonishments didn't seem to be working.[76]

Because Mohawk and Dutch women both had public roles in the economy, Native and European women interacted in Rensselaerswijck to a greater extent than was usually the case in colonial relationships. Like many Native women, Mohawk women traded the corn and other food they produced and bought the goods they wanted, and they probably also had some say in the sale of the furs they had processed. In this respect Dutch settlers were more similar to Mohawks than other Europeans were. While most European societies undervalued women's economic contributions and kept them out of international trade, the Dutch were somewhat less patriarchal, at least when it came to business.

The Netherlands and the Dutch colonies practiced civil law, which, in contrast to coverture in the common law of England and its colonies, allowed married women to own property and have standing in court. In New Netherland, women could own property and sue and be sued, rights that were essential for managing a business. Single and married Dutch women owned and ran a great many of New Netherland's businesses and sold food and drink to Mohawk and Mahican customers, both men and women. With all of the drinking and sleeping in close proximity, surely sexual encounters sometimes happened between Mohawks and Dutch people, but no one seems to have complained about it. Any children of a Mohawk woman and a Dutch man inherited a Mohawk national and clan identity, and any children of Dutch mothers and Mohawk fathers apparently were tacitly accepted as Dutch.[77]

By the 1660s, New Netherland was a fairly stable colony, with between seven and eight thousand colonists, but its stability resulted from people's adopting one another's ways when useful and otherwise rejecting them without much conflict—as in the case of the

Mohawks listening to the sermon. Many of the Mohawks' relationships with their neighbors did not go this smoothly, so the Dutch were lucky. And Mohawks were lucky that they faced colonization not in the unruly times before the forming of the Haudenosaunee Confederacy but with a large and reasonably united population on their homeland. The Dutch could be dangerous and brutal, as evidenced by their involvement in the Atlantic slave trade and plantation slavery in the Caribbean, as well as occasional violence against Munsees and Lenapes along the lower Hudson River.

By the mid-1600s, if you visited a Mohawk town, you could see how they had incorporated European consumer goods into their material culture, alongside older goods and customs. At first glance, the town would have looked like Mohawk towns in the previous century, with several dozen longhouses built of local materials and covered in bark. But a closer look would reveal signs of the new economy as well. Parts of the buildings were held together with iron nails, and the interior doors were made of imported split planks of wood and hung on iron hinges. Iron simply worked better for some things than stone or copper. Indeed, iron was such an important addition that Mohawks sometimes called the Dutch Kristoni, meaning "I am a metal worker."[78] In among the bearskins you could also see wool blankets. If it was winter or early spring, beaver pelts were stacked in the corners by the hundreds, ready to take to Rensselaerswijck. Mohawk men often wore linen shirts imported from Europe, because they were breathable and comfortable. But they didn't wear them the way European men did, tucked into pants under a coat. They wore the shirts basically like slickers, untucked over leggings, and they greased the linen to make it waterproof. They rejected European pants as much less practical than their deerskin leggings. In parallel, Europeans, including soldiers and officers, adopted moccasins because they were superior footwear. By late in the seventeenth century, every Haudenosaunee warrior had a musket and often a pistol as well, while their enemies still were lucky if they had one for every two warriors.[79]

If you could peek inside a mid-1600s imported brass or copper kettle simmering over a Mohawk fire, you would see the same foods that the mothers and grandmothers of the cooks once made in ceramic pots: corn, beans, pumpkins, venison. Kettles made of metal conduct heat better than pottery, so water boiled faster, a particularly important quality when women were making large quantities of food in their communal kitchens. Before acquiring European trade, North American Indians used copper for jewelry and ceremonial objects, but not for pots, because copper by itself causes a toxic chemical reaction with food. Europeans lined their copper kettles with tin or alloyed them with brass. Still, despite the new kettles, Haudenosaunee women continued to use pottery and probably made even more than before, to sell to Dutch consumers for storing and serving food and drink.[80]

Mohawks changed their consumption and production patterns, while at the same time continuing many of the practices and beliefs of their ancestors. They increased their production of beaver pelts by adding to their usual summer hunt an additional hunting and raiding season in early winter, when beavers' pelts were thickest and when women did not need the men for the labor-intensive work of preparing fields in the spring or harvesting crops in the fall. Then Mohawk women could scrape and process the furs in the heart of the winter, when they had no work in the fields. Mohawks even wore the new furs for warmth that winter so that by spring they were broken in and softer and thus more valuable on the market.[81]

Haudenosaunee production supplied the European market, while

European pipe tomahawk made for Mohawks, c. 1750.
NATIONAL MUSEUM OF THE AMERICAN INDIAN, SMITHSONIAN
INSTITUTION (22/7211). PHOTOGRAPH BY NMAI PHOTO SERVICES

Haudenosaunee demand also had global consequences. Mohawk scholar Scott Manning Stevens points out that, while the tomahawk became the quintessential symbol of Indians, in fact tomahawks were manufactured from metal and wood in Europe, specifically for Native markets. European factories made goods to Indian specifications, including heavy woolen cloth in a variety of specific sizes and colors for different Native nations. Early on, Dutch traders learned that red cloth wouldn't sell, "because the Indians say that it hinders them in hunting, being visible too far off."[82] Dutch flintlock muskets destined for the Haudenosaunee were made half as heavy as other muskets, at their request, because lighter guns were better for hunting and raiding. Some French-made guns featured a serpent-shaped side plate (the metal opposite the lock plate), signaling that they were designed and made for American Indians. To their buyers, they advertised the fearsome power of the serpent. The Dutch began manufacturing kettles specifically for the Native American market as early as the 1610s.[83]

It is only stereotypes of Indians as primitive that make their power to transform markets surprising. Mohawks could hunt and process furs and hides efficiently, and in return they got products they needed or wanted. Manufacturing on both sides responded to demand. European traders complied with Native requirements to embed trade within relationships of alliance, renewed regularly with ceremonies and speeches. Colonists in seventeenth-century North America were seldom able to achieve colonialism's exploitative goals, though not for lack of trying. Instead, Mohawks and most others who established commercial relations with Europeans in this era had the power to control the terms of trade and to draw Europeans into their alliances and wars.

WAR AND PEACE

In the seventeenth century, Haudenosaunee warfare grew, drawing in everyone around them. Perhaps surprisingly, the Haudenosaunee explain the wars of this era in terms of Gayanashagowa—that they were seeking to bring balance to the region by enveloping everyone within the Great Law of Peace. The Great Law instructed the Haudenosaunee to "endeavor to persuade other nations to accept the Great Peace." They believed that the philosophy and methods that had moved the Five Nations from chaos to peaceful respect for one another might transform the violent and chaotic world beyond. In this view, bringing more people under Gayanashagowa would both be good for those people and enhance Haudenosaunee spiritual and political power. Other communities, nations, and confederacies, understandably, did not share this view and resisted being incorporated. Whatever the combination of original motivations, it is clear that the violence spiraled out of control in the 1640s.[84]

In the version of the Great Law written down in the late 1800s, there is a clear method for incorporating foreign nations. It's not clear whether this exact procedure was already in place in the seventeenth century, but it does convey the promise and the threat that accompanied the Haudenosaunee attempt to spread Gayanashagowa and turned it into war. At a joint council, "the foreign nation is to be persuaded by reason and urged to come into the Great Peace." Haudenosaunee emissaries would present wampum and speeches conveying the wisdom and benefits of joining the Haudenosaunee Great Peace. Should those speeches not immediately persuade the foreign nation, its representatives could go home and discuss the offer and return for a second and, if necessary, a third council, where more speeches would attempt to assuage the foreigners' doubts. If they still refused by the end of the third council, a Haudenosaunee representative was to drop the white wampum strings he had been holding and, at least according to one version of the Great Law, "bound quickly forward and club the offending chief to death," and "war shall thereby be declared."[85] Members of the Five Nations saw extending Gayanashagowa as a generous and inclusive offer; however, as this sudden move to violence reveals, the offer included no provisions for other nations to politely decline. The Great Law says that if an invited nation "refuses to accept the Great Peace, then by such refusal they bring a declaration of war upon themselves from the Five Nations. Then shall the Five Nations seek to establish the Great Peace by a conquest of the rebellious Nation."[86]

The Haudenosaunee effort to absorb neighboring populations into Gayanashagowa would shape the history of everyone around them, Native and European. In addition to their battles against the Mahicans on the Hudson River and the Algonquins and Innu in the St. Lawrence Valley, they would repeatedly push the colony of New France to the brink of destruction, steer the course of wars among the English and the Algonquian-speaking groups to the east, and send Wendats and other non-Haudenosaunee Iroquoians fleeing into exile. They would bring thousands of people into their domain, some as nations, towns, or families that accepted Gayanashagowa and Haudenosaunee protection and some as captives and refugees of the wars they waged.

The ideal way to spread Gayanashagowa was for an entire nation to agree to join. The Great Law said that any nations that accepted the offer and agreed to "obey the laws of the Great Peace" could keep "their own system of internal governance" and be a recognized nation within the confederacy, as long as they adhered generally to Gayanashagowa.[87] In the early eighteenth century, the Tuscarora Nation would join as a full and equal Haudenosaunee nation, turning the Five Nations into the Six Nations. Some others, as we shall see, after suffering violence at the hands of the Haudenosaunee, would accede to some degree of Haudenosaunee dominance over their external affairs, in return for peace. But most nations would resist the Haudenosaunee.

Much of the incorporation occurred on an individual level, sometimes in the form of unwilling captives. Adoptees were supposed to assimilate into an existing clan and nation and forget their previous identities. Once adopted, a person "ceased forever to bear their birth nation's name." No one was ever to "mention the original name or nation of their birth. To do so will hasten the end of our peace."[88] In battles and raids, Haudenosaunee warriors would torture and kill most of their defeated male enemies, but they would capture women and children. Back home, Haudenosaunee women would decide whether each captive would die or live. Those spared might be adopted into a family that had suffered the death of a child or a wife or husband, or they might be passed on to another Haudenosaunee town. The adoptee would help to assuage grief and maintain families through the work they added and any children they might bear. Adult female captives might become Haudesaunnakéhte, "they carry the name," because they had not been born into a clan but were assigned a Haudenosaunee clan at their adoption. As a result, their children would belong to Haudenosaunee clans and be full members of their fathers' Haudenosaunee nations.[89]

There are some obvious parallels between Haudenosaunee expansion and European empires. Both used war to expand their influence, including religion, across a growing territory, where they acquired resources that they used in part to buy the weapons that, in turn, allowed them even more expansion. The Haudenosaunee drive to pull other people into Gayanashagowa, with force if necessary, was an evangelical one, and many of their targets found them more formidable and threatening than any Europeans were to them.

Still, there were significant differences between the Haudenosaunee and the empires that were pushing out of Europe at the same time. The Haudenosaunee religious ideological underpinning was inclusivist rather than exclusivist. Unlike in Christianity, accepting it did not require rejecting existing beliefs and practices. And there was nothing like early modern European empires' assumed divine right to territorial expansion and resource extraction.[90]

When the Haudenosaunee faced losses from war and disease, captives could provide recompense. When people died, not only did their loved ones grieve, but their absence weakened their lineage, clan, and nation and the confederacy as a whole. A captured enemy could relieve the situation by being adopted in place of the deceased, or sometimes the bereaved would take out their grief by torturing and killing the captive. Adopting a captive into the lost person's place restored demographic and spiritual power.[91]

In a vicious cycle, losses from war and disease prompted more fighting to replace the losses, but that fighting, in turn, caused more population losses and more need for adoptees. Epidemics had not caused significant damage to the region in the sixteenth century, and there's evidence that the Mohawk population had actually increased. When only small groups of European men briefly raided, traded, or traveled in North America, they were not likely to spread sickness. But those conditions changed starting in the 1620s. The fledgling colonies of New Netherland, New France, Virginia, and New England all grew in population, and they now included children, the most likely age group to catch and spread many kinds of disease. A smallpox pandemic in 1633–34 caused disastrous loss of life among Narragansetts, Pequots, and Mohegans near New England and then moved to Mohawk and Wendat towns, where many died. In 1634, the family of Adriochten, one of the leaders of the Mohawk town farthest downstream, moved out of town to stay in a cabin a quarter mile away. Adriochten explained to a Dutch traveler that "many Indians here in the castle had died of smallpox." Devastating outbreaks continued to hit the Mohawks after the initial one in 1633.[92]

War accelerated to assuage grief, bring in captives, and restore populations. Despite disease and war, the Haudenosaunee were able to maintain their political, economic, and social structures. It helped that their methods of choosing leaders and representatives allowed for flexibility. In rigidly patrilineal medieval and early modern Europe, if there were no surviving sons in a generation, coups and civil wars often followed. Miscarriages, infant deaths, and smallpox created succession crises in Europe through the eighteenth century. The Haudenosaunee ability to choose political leaders from among various men of a lineage allowed some flexibility. And grieving and adoption ceremonies allowed the Haudenosaunee to rebuild families, give relatives to motherless children, sustain clans, and maintain Haudenosaunee religious, political, and economic structures. As Kayanesenh Paul Williams explains, "adoption was crucial to the survival of the Haudenosaunee."[93]

The need for both captives to adopt and furs to trade for guns and other goods at Fort Orange accelerated Mohawk raids in the St. Lawrence River Valley in the 1640s. Whereas Mohawk parties had previously raided Algonquin and Wendat traders on their way home from Quebec with French goods, now that the Mohawks had a market at Fort Orange for as many furs as they could collect, they added new targets. They began raiding Algonquin and Wendat hunting parties just south of the St. Lawrence and even in Algonquin territory to the north, sometimes with the help of Oneida and Mahican fighters. They targeted canoes going downriver toward French posts, full of furs to sell. Bands of twenty to a hundred well-armed Mohawks patrolled and ambushed along the river, with new bands coming to replace those that returned home with captives and furs. They would station small parties at key points along the St. Lawrence and Ottawa rivers to attack any canoes passing by. The previously sporadic raids grew into a blockade.[94]

A 1642 Mohawk attack on a Wendat convoy was typical. Forty Mohawk fighters canoed up Lake Champlain and across the St. Lawrence River. They disembarked and built a small fort in the woods overlooking the river. From this vantage point they could watch for canoes bound for the new French post of Montreal, just a mile downriver, or Trois-Rivières and Quebec, farther downstream. After a few days, they saw what they were waiting for: sixty canoes floating downriver, piled high with beaver furs and guarded by Wendats armed with bows and arrows, but no guns because of French trade restrictions. As the canoes passed close to the riverbank, the Mohawks rushed out from the woods, firing their muskets and letting out a fearsome war cry. They overtook the canoes, swinging clubs and tomahawks. Those Wendats who could escape ran along the bank toward the French fort. The Mohawks clubbed to death and scalped some French men who got in their way.

Knowing that the surviving French and Wendats would be too intimidated to counterattack, the Mohawks returned to their camp to celebrate and count their winnings: twenty-three Wendat and two French captives, and furs that a Frenchman described as "without number"—so many that they had to leave thirty behind. There wasn't enough room for all the people, either, so they killed thirteen of the Wendat captives before returning home with the furs and the remaining captives, "triumphant with joy, and loaded down with valuable spoils."[95] Back in Mohawk country, the captives would be killed, ransomed, or adopted into bereaved families. The furs would be sold to the Dutch.[96]

The economy of New France came to a screeching halt in these years as the furs intended for France went south in Mohawk canoes and landed in Dutch hands. French officials, merchants, and priests could only rail against the Haudenosaunee and the Dutch. The Jesuit report for 1642–43 lamented that "the Iroquois have spread themselves so much along the great river of the St. Lawrence" and its tributaries "that there is no safety" above the post of Trois-Rivières. "Those Barbarians hide sometimes in one place, sometimes in another, and throw themselves unexpectedly on the French, on the Hurons [Wendats], and on the Algonquins, whenever they see an opportunity: so much so that we dare not navigate these beautiful rivers for the whole Summer, unless we had Caravans, as in Arabia, which we cannot do because of our small numbers."[97]

The Dutch also had "small numbers," but their fur trade grew with the influx of thick northern pelts in large quantities—as long as they conformed to Mohawk rules. In 1633, the Dutch patroon Kiliaen van Rensselaer wanted to invite other Native hunters to bring furs to Fort Orange. He pleaded with the West India Company to send more troops to the colony, explaining that the Mohawks, "who are now stronger than ourselves, will not allow others who are hostile and live farther away and have many furs to pass through their territory."[98] But the Dutch had no power to change the situation, and the Mohawks continued to trade furs for weapons that in turn reinforced their power.

THE PEQUOT WAR AND KIEFT'S WAR

The 1636 Pequot War that enveloped New England and all the surrounding Algonquian-speaking nations is often told as New England's defeat of the Pequot Indians, who stood in the way of English expansion into present-day Connecticut. That story is true—the English had killed or enslaved hundreds of Pequots by the end of the war—but the war makes little sense without its larger Native context, which includes the Mohawks. By the early 1630s, Pequots had established something of a monopoly over wampum distribution from the lower Connecticut River, where it empties into Long Island Sound. The Pequots forced Algonquian-speaking nations there who manufactured wampum to sell it to Pequot intermediaries, who then sold it to others, including New England colonists in the east and Mahicans in the west, who in turn sold it to the Dutch, Mohawks, and Munsees. The conflict broke out when some Algonquian wampum makers attempted to bypass the Pequots. As this conflict erupted into a regional trade war in 1636, Narragansetts and Mohegans (an Algonquian-speaking people in what's now Connecticut, not to be confused with the Mahicans, near Fort Orange) pulled their English allies into fighting against the Pequots. Ultimately, the Mohawks would use the war to expand their influence east of the Hudson River to the parts of Long Island Sound where the Mahicans had been acquiring furs and wampum.[99]

Knowing that the Mohawks could swing the balance of this war and that if they joined the war it would be to access wampum, competing Pequot and Narragansett delegations traveled to Mohawk country to try to recruit them. The delegation led by Pequot leader Sassacus gave the Mohawks an astounding amount of wampum, estimated at three or four bushels, or £500 worth—the equivalent of perhaps eighty horses or ninety cows, an amount a skilled tradesman in England might take twenty years to earn. Hearing the news, English colonist Roger Williams shuddered that "if the Lord please to let loose these mad dogs," the Mohawks and the Pequots together would destroy the Connecticut settlements. The Narragansetts also brought wampum and presented their counterargument while Sassacus's Pequots were still in Mohawk country. The Mohawks chose to accept the Narragansett proposal, executed the Pequot emissaries, and sent Sassacus's scalp to the English.[100]

Because the Mohawks sided against the Pequots, the Pequots lost the war. They were enslaved in the homes of New England colonists, shipped to distant colonies, or absorbed into other Algonquian-speaking communities. The Mohawks retained and improved their wampum access through the Narragansetts and had plenty to pass on to the rest of the Haudenosaunee. And they began to sell beaver pelts through Mahican traders to the English market in the Connecticut River Valley.[101]

After the Pequot War, New Netherland officials worried about the expansion of the growing English population, so they recruited immigrants from France, Scandinavia, the German states, and even from England and New England itself to settle in places near Manhattan. Hundreds of them began establishing farms in what later would be the outer boroughs of New York City and nearby New Jersey. Many of them settled without Native permission and brought pigs and cattle that damaged Munsee women's crops. As the West India Company spent more and more money building forts and staffing them with soldiers to guard against enemies, the New Netherland Council decided to require allied Munsees and Lenapes to pay tribute to maintain the forts rather than be paid rent for the land to put them on. In 1639, tensions escalated into Kieft's War, between New Netherland and nearby Munsee and Lenape communities. New Netherland governor Willem Kieft was just as willing to use brutal violence against Indians as the English were, but whereas the English had firm anti-Pequot allies, the Dutch attacks encouraged Munsees and other Algonquian groups to unite against them. The war killed more Native people, but also enough settlers that many survivors fled for safer Dutch places, and the war dissuaded more from coming. In the short run, at least, fighting close Native neighbors was more dangerous to colonists than appeasing them.[102]

The English were able to expand their settlements and the extent of their trade because of losses by the Pequots and the Dutch, but they worried that the Mohawks would prove even more dangerous to New England. Three years after the Pequot War ended, Plymouth governor William Bradford wrote a frightened letter to Massachusetts Bay Colony governor John Winthrop, spreading a rumor that Narragansett leader Miantonomi was recruiting the Mohawks to attack Massachusetts. The Indians might prevail, Bradford feared, because they were "well furnished" with muskets. Winthrop increased his colony's watches and sent a commission to the Narragansetts, who reassured him that they were plotting no war and intended "to continue friendship" with the English.[103] Yet, repeatedly in the 1640s, rumors raced through the English settlements that the Mohawks were considering attacking, once that they had even "come within a day's journey of the English" with a thousand men.[104] New England's colonial population had grown dramatically during the 1630s and as a result was much larger than New Netherland or New France. Yet civil war in England stopped the flow of immigrants in 1642, and the English colonies knew that they were vulnerable to the still far more powerful Mohawks.[105]

The Mohawks never attacked Massachusetts, and probably never intended to. Indeed, they may not even have known about the rumors, which were spread by others trying to frighten and control New England. In one instance, Narragansett diplomats warned the English that they should stop trying to interfere in Narragansett affairs, or else they "would procure the Mohawks against them," who "would lay the English cattle on heaps as high as their houses" and leave every Englishman unable to "stir out of his door to piss, but he should be killed."[106] Native allies of the Dutch similarly spread rumors that the Mohawks were considering attacking New Netherland and were distributing wampum to try to persuade others to join the fight. Dutch leaders at Fort Orange who heard such a rumor in 1650 reflected on their vulnerable position, "living as we do under the unrestrained domination of inhuman people and cruel heathen." The Mohawks had real power, and both Native and European people around them not only respected it but also invoked their powerful reputation in their own disputes.[107]

"ONE PEOPLE AND ONE LAND"

By 1640 the Mohawks, by fighting against Algonquins, Innu, Wendats, and French in the north and Mahicans and then Pequots in the east, had enriched themselves with captives and goods. Haudenosaunee towns adopted individual captives and refugees, strengthening their populations. They controlled the trade at Fort Orange. The Dutch were managed, and the Mohawk–Mahican War had persuaded the Mahicans to move away from Fort Orange and to become useful intermediaries with Native and English people to the east.[108]

Throughout their wars, the Haudenosaunee made peace overtures. Having too many enemies was both dangerous and not in the spirit of the Great Peace. On several occasions in the 1630s and '40s, the Mohawks tried to peel the French or the Wendats from their alliance with each other and the Algonquins and Innu. But those Mohawk enemies were on their guard. In 1641, some Haudenosaunee came to Trois-Rivières proposing peace with the Innu, Algonquins, and Wendats. An Algonquin there responded, "I represent all of the nations that you named, in their absence, and I say to you on their behalf, that you are a liar." He told the French that the offer was fake, a cover while other Haudenosaunee attacked. So the French governor decided to stick with his existing allies, noting that "otherwise, we would enter into a more dangerous war than the one that we avoid: because if these peoples among whom we live every day, and who surround us on all sides were to attack us, as they might do if we abandon them, they would give us much more trouble than the Iroquois."[109] Other peace attempts sometimes worked for a while then faltered, usually because of disputes about returning captives or disagreements among the Haudenosaunee about whether to make peace with a particular enemy.[110]

In the second half of the 1640s, the Haudenosaunee launched full-scale wars against non-Haudenosaunee Iroquoian nations—the Wendats and, to their west, the Petuns, Eries, and Neutrals (a confederacy of the Chonnonton Nation and others who had tried to be neutral in the war between the Wendats and the Haudenosaunee). Generally, this war was led by the western Haudenosaunee, but Mohawk war parties joined them and brought back captives, and the war was armed by Mohawk–Dutch trade. Iroquoian speakers all shared not only similar languages but also ways of dress and many other customs. As a result, the Haudenosaunee saw them as perfect for incorporation and adoption. They first targeted the Wendats,

whose location, to the north on Lake Ontario, made them the closest and was ideal for trapping thick-furred beaver. In at least one
version of the Haudenosaunee creation story, the Peacemaker was
born among the Wendats but they rejected his message, so bringing
the nations of the Wendat Confederacy into the Haudenosaunee
may have long been a goal. These wars were far more than raids. A
French captive observed in 1643 that "the aim of the Iroquois
[Haudenosaunee], as far as I can tell, is to take all of the Wendats if
they can and, having killed their leaders, and a lot of the others, to
make both into only one people and one land."[111] As one Oneida
explained to several Wendats at Trois-Rivières in 1656, "I am taking
you by the arm to lead you away. You know, you Huron [Wendat],
that in the past we made up but one longhouse and one country. I
don't know by what accident we were separated. It is time that we
reunite."[112]

The war went badly for the Wendats. Repeated Haudenosaunee
attacks forced them to begin living inside their fortified towns,
which brought trouble when food supplies ran low. Wendats also
were unable to send out patrols that could warn them when a large
Haudenosaunee army invaded, as it did in 1648. Haudenosaunee
forces brought down the Wendat palisades, probably using the very
effective iron hatchets acquired in European trade. They destroyed
Wendat towns, killed hundreds of people, and took hundreds more
home to adopt. The remaining Wendats either fled west or agreed to
resettle their towns in Haudenosaunee country under Haudenosaunee protection.[113]

After defeating the Wendats, Haudenosaunee forces in the 1650s
attacked Iroquoian Petuns, Neutrals, and Eries to the west in the
eastern Great Lakes, many of whose towns had taken in Wendat
refugees. The Haudenosaunee used the same tactics here, driving
them into fortified towns and then invading with thousands of warriors. People who weren't killed or adopted fled. Eries went south
and became known as the Westos, taking patterns of firearms warfare and captivity from the North to wreak havoc on the Southeast.
Petuns and Wendats regrouped to the west on the lands of their
Anishinaabe allies.[114]

Thousands of captives from these wars flowed into Haudenosaunee towns, where their descendants would become part of Haudenosaunee life and lineages. Some Erie and Neutral towns accepted resettlement on Seneca lands. Some towns just remained where they were once they accepted Haudenosaunee victory. As a result, not only did the Haudenosaunee population expand, but so did their territory. French observers in the late 1650s and '60s estimated that Haudenosaunee towns had "more foreigners than natives of the country" and that the majority of Haudenosaunee were "just a bunch of different peoples whom they have conquered." Nearly three centuries later, Seneca historian Arthur Parker explained, "Tribes of the Iroquoian stock were broken up and the scattered bands or survivors settled in the numerous Iroquois towns to forget in time their birth nation and to be known forever after only as Iroquois." [115]

"THE MOST PERVERSE AND WICKED NATION"

It is difficult to disentangle the reality of Haudenosaunee might from their reputation. The Haudenosaunee wars were real—they are recorded in the archaeology of destroyed towns, firsthand accounts of French prisoners, and the oral histories of the Native nations that fought and fled. Wendats today refer to fleeing the "murderous onslaught of their cousins, the Iroquois Confederacy." [116] Native enemies of the Haudenosaunee told Europeans startling tales of their prowess at war and penchant for torture, and the French had their own losses as evidence, as hundreds of French people were killed or captured by the Haudenosaunee over the course of the seventeenth century. [117]

Still, much of the story comes from European documents reporting second- or thirdhand news told by Native people who wanted Europeans to help them fight against the Haudenosaunee. One Frenchman's report noted that "countless Indian Nations in Canada tremble at the mere name *Iroquois*," which was both true and a propaganda effort to urge the French to loosen their restrictions on the sale of guns and gunpowder.[118] And European writers repeated and inflated one another's rumors in an echo chamber of Haudenosaunee horror stories.

Demographically, the Haudenosaunee couldn't have actually been responsible for all they were blamed (or credited) for. When Quapaws west of the Mississippi River, more than a thousand miles from Mohawk country, told a Jesuit missionary that war had pushed them and the Osages west from the Ohio River in an earlier generation, the priest assumed that "the Iroquois drove them out by cruel wars."[119] It is possible—the Haudenosaunee did have a long reach—but more likely it was unrelated, probably part of the much earlier conflict surrounding the fall of Cahokia.

But the reputation of the Haudenosaunee tended to convince French people that they were responsible for just about everything, and the Haudenosaunee encouraged this reputation. And, as Scott Manning Stevens points out, Haudenosaunee people were "willing to play it up," in what became a self-fulfilling prophecy of their power.[120] Mohawk warriors wanted you to recognize them. Their short-feathered headdresses could be seen from a distance, as could their namesake hairstyle: a two- or three-inch-wide strip of hair they cut and shaped with bear's grease to make it stand straight up, with the hair on both sides cut very short.[121]

Tales of torture were a major component of both French and Indigenous portrayals of the supposedly brutal and dangerous Haudenosaunee. The damaged fingers of a captured French Jesuit attested to the rumor that Mohawks "bite off the nails of the fingers of their captives, and cut off some joints, and sometimes even whole fingers." Stories abounded of captives forced to sing and dance while being taunted, having their beards plucked out, and being roasted and eaten.[122] A Native ally of the French named Erouachy told Champlain a tale of how a Haudenosaunee town had pretended to welcome a delegation of one Frenchman and several Indians, one of whom the Mohawks suspected of treachery. The hosts asked their guests to sit down by the fire while they put on a kettle. The Mohawks kindly asked them if they were hungry, and the guests replied that they were—they had walked all day without eating. In a scene right out of a horror story or an urban legend, one of the Mohawks pulled out a knife, cut some flesh from a guest's arm, and put it in the kettle. Then "he gave him some of his own half raw flesh." They did the same with "morsels from his thighs and other parts of his body" before the man finally died. They burned the Frenchman "with firewood and birch bark torches, making him feel intolerable pain before he died." After telling his tale, Erouachy got to his purpose: Champlain should fight the Haudenosaunee, "the most perverse and wicked nation of all those in this country." Surely after hearing of these atrocities against their allies and their countryman, the French commander would be, as he himself put it, "amenable to this legitimate war, which in destroying these people, would make the countryside and the rivers free for commerce."[123]

English colonists learned the name Mohawk long before they had met any. A 1634 book described Mohawks as "a cruel bloody people, which were wont to come down upon their poor neighbours with more than brutish savageness, spoiling of their corn, burning their houses, slaying men, ravishing women, yet very Cannibals they were, sometimes eating on a man one part after another before his face, and while yet living; in so much that the very name of a *Mohawk* would strike the heart of a poor Aborigine dead."[124]

The familiar wording here suggests that the English writer was just echoing the same tales that the French had recorded. Algonquian speakers encouraged (and likely invented) the rumors of cannibalism. "Mohawk" comes from an Algonquian word meaning "man-eaters." Similarly, the accusation of "ravishing women" comes from European assumptions about war atrocities. Sexual violation was rarely, if ever, part of Native warfare in this era, perhaps because captives could become kin—a warrior's new sister or daughter—and because sex with women was seen as the opposite of war. In any case, these exaggerations reveal one thing for certain: Native people feared the Mohawks more than they did any Europeans.[125]

Mohawk tortures were horrific—and designed to instill horror—but they were not abnormal in their seventeenth-century context. Haudenosaunee enemies practiced fairly similar forms of torture, including burning captives to death. And it's important to remember that the Geneva Conventions would hardly approve of medieval and early modern European tactics of violence and torture either. European explorers tortured both Native captives and their own men so routinely that accounts cavalierly note that commanders such as Francisco de Coronado used dogs to try to get information from a captive. You can hardly read a page of the medieval French *Song of Roland* without one soldier cleaving another's head in two. Dutch histories told that at the 1567 Siege of Valenciennes, during the wars against Spain, Catholic forces fired muskets into the Protestant church where their adversaries had taken refuge and then set fire to the church "and kept up till all were roasted or suffocated."[126] Elaborate torture devices in museums all across Europe still preserve physical evidence of societies that thought a lot about how to torture.

The Haudenosaunee aimed to increase their numbers and power through warfare and the forced incorporation of foreigners. To their enemies, of course, the prospect was frightful.

"MASTERS OF ALL"

Mohawk tactics were exaggerated, but their violence was real. It inflicted serious damage on the Wendats and other nations, and it kept New Netherland and New England in check and New France from doing much more than just hanging on. Jesuit missionary Father Barthelemy Vimont wrote that "this country is just a picture of massacres." The Mohawks "ravage everything and make themselves masters of all."[127] The official Jesuit journal kept for 1650 judged that Trois-Rivières "has been able to exist only through a miracle."[128]

The Dutch, French, and English were powerless to stop the Haudenosaunee, as much as their Native allies pressured them to try. The main reason was Haudenosaunee power, but other conflicts also tied up Europeans' military means. New Netherland fought a series of wars, including Kieft's War, against Munsees and Lenapes as well as Susquehannocks. The colony would have been destroyed at several points if others had not joined the Dutch side or, in the Mohawk case, at least refrained from fighting against them. Similarly, the English in Virginia and New England were engaged in wars against several Algonquian-speaking nations in each place, wars that at times pushed those colonies to the brink of destruction. In the Americas and in Europe, the Catholic French fought the Protestant Dutch and English, and the Dutch and English regularly clashed with each other. None of these Europeans could risk conflict with the Haudenosaunee.[129]

During their many wars, Haudenosaunee representatives regularly traveled to see the Dutch at Fort Orange to make sure they would keep supplying trade. Since the Haudenosaunee were in the midst of their heaviest fighting against the Wendats and the Eries, a Mohawk delegation pointedly instructed the Dutch to keep "quiet and show neutrality." The Dutch assented, agreeing that "we should not meddle or concern ourselves" with their wars.[130] Mohawk representatives explicitly asked the rhetorical question "Who of the three nations are to be the masters, the *Mohawks,* the *Senecas*" (a term the Dutch used for all four of the other Haudenosaunee nations), "or the Dutch?"[131]

In the 1650s, the Haudenosaunee continued to battle Abenakis and other Algonquian speakers in what's now northern New England and northeastern Canada; their Iroquoian enemies who had fled west to the Great Lakes, the upper Mississippi Valley, and the Ohio Valley; and the Iroquoian Susquehannocks and others to the south in the Delaware Valley, the Chesapeake region, and even as far as the Carolinas. By 1660, the French priest in charge of missions in New France called the Haudenosaunee "victorious over all the Nations" and certain "that their destruction could never happen, without it dragging the whole world down with it."[132]

Nonetheless, some of their enemies proved better able to defend themselves than earlier Haudenosaunee targets. Like the Mohawks with the Dutch at Fort Orange, Susquehannocks persuaded Dutch and Swedish traders on the Delaware River, as well as English traders in Maryland and Virginia, to sell them weapons and were able to hold their ground. In the 1660s, the French finally gave in to their Native allies' demands for guns, and raids on the St. Lawrence became riskier for the Haudenosaunee. In the west, Anishinaabe peoples, the Iroquoian refugees they had taken in, and their French allies together launched a counterstrike, using French weapons, that put the Haudenosaunee on the defensive. When the English seized New Netherland from the Dutch in 1664, the Haudenosaunee had to work to train them to continue supplying weapons and other goods.[133]

At the same time, Jesuit missionaries from New France had made some converts in select Haudenosaunee towns, resulting in an exodus of mostly adoptees to Jesuit mission villages, where they formed new communities with non-Haudenosaunee. Internal divisions grew among the Haudenosaunee about how much to accept or reject these new teachings and whether to tolerate Haudenosaunee people who wanted to practice them. After all, inclusivism was selective, and the conversion of some people to a theoretically exclusivist religion posed problems.[134]

Afraid of both losing at war and losing adoptees they had sacrificed to get, the Haudenosaunee changed their strategy. Starting in the late 1660s, they shifted to slightly more modest ambitions for Gayanashagowa. Rather than expect to incorporate outsiders, they built a relatively more equal "Covenant Chain" of alliances. This was a diplomatic network wherein the Haudenosaunee would serve a central role in a chain of allies from the English, at the eastern end— and the French, after making peace with the Haudenosaunee at the start of the 1700s—to an interior network of Native allies. The Covenant Chain was in effect an extension of the Hiawatha Belt, with the Mohawks and other Haudenosaunee nations in the center, the English and the French as eastern links in the chain, and Native nations in all directions linked through the Haudenosaunee.

Within the Covenant Chain, Native nations could continue to govern themselves internally but should conduct diplomacy and war under the auspices of the Haudenosaunee. The Haudenosaunee had previously established relationships like this with the Mahicans and some Munsees. In 1649, a Munsee leader named Pennekeck told New Netherland governor Peter Stuyvesant that "it is the wish of the Mohawks, that we and you should be and remain friends." Adopted captives could help with the peace negotiations that established the relationship between their birth nation and their adopted one. The Haudenosaunee and the Munsees and Lenapes on their southern border (who later became the Delawares) set up a relationship in which the Haudenosaunee spoke for all of them—acting as their "uncle" or "elder brother" nation—in diplomatic relations, and the Susquehannocks assented to a similar relationship. As we shall see in chapter 7, some of these nations would look to the Haudenosaunee to protect them in the eighteenth century, when the settler population on the Atlantic coast grew and tried to take their lands, but they would not always agree with the Haudenosaunee about their respective roles within the Covenant Chain.[135]

The Haudenosaunee relationship with European groups in the Covenant Chain was represented by a Two-Row Wampum belt. Two parallel deep purple rows represent two boats traveling side by side on the white background. This is how the Onondaga Nation today explains the meaning of the Two-Row Wampum belt: "One boat is the canoe with the Haudenosaunee way of life, laws, and people." Europeans sail in parallel in their own ship, and "each nation will respect the ways of each other and will not interfere with the other." As the wampum belt illustrates, "neither will attempt to steer the other's vessel."[136]

The Covenant Chain did not limit Haudenosaunee alliance making. When the English tried to persuade the Haudenosaunee that allying with the English required being enemies of the French (much as France's Native allies had done against the Haudenosaunee), the Mohawks' answer, as Kayanesenh Paul Williams describes it, was that "we are a free people and will go to either fire, as we will."[137] In the meantime, despite new peace agreements, war did not end. The Covenant Chain and the peace it brought to the north and the east allowed the Haudenosaunee to continue their wars farther south and west.[138]

CONCLUSION

Native nations made peace and war based on factors that had little to do with Europeans. In these early centuries, Native Americans continued to control almost all of North America. When they lost ground, it was almost always to Native enemies, not European ones. And yet historians have long told this story exactly wrong, rushing to backdate late-eighteenth and nineteenth-century Native losses to more than a century earlier. An otherwise quite up-to-date book in 2003 repeated the absurd conclusion that, with the coming of the Dutch and the French, "ancient Indian communities had entered a process through which, slowly but surely, they would be destroyed."[139]

In fact, after the arrival of the Dutch, seventeenth-century Mohawks expanded their commercial connections across the Atlantic. They became major exporters of animal furs and skins that they produced or acquired from other Indigenous producers by trade or by force, and they used their market power in furs to set Europeans' prices. As consumers, they demanded European products and changed European production. They were not duped or forced into the commercial marketplace—they actively worked to define their place within it, helping to shape the Atlantic economy in the process. Europeans became important players, but the Mohawks and other Native people continued to dominate the region.

About a century ago, the New York State Museum bought the Hiawatha Belt for its collections. But in 1989, after much effort, the Haudenosaunee persuaded the State of New York to return it and other historic wampum belts to the Onondagas. Although Americans and Canadians took most of their land and tried to destroy them in the late eighteenth, nineteenth, and twentieth centuries, today the Mohawks still survive, as does their Haudenosaunee Confederacy. They are still an influential force in their region and in the world, even though they lost most of their homeland and today live in dispersed communities across the United States and Canada. As Scott Manning Stevens puts it, the Haudenosaunee were "left with little in the way of our historical territory," but the "constellation that makes up Iroquoia" is very powerful. "We are at the place of our sacred spaces. We know that when we are in the place called New York State we are in our homeland."[140]

CHAPTER 5

THE O'ODHAM HIMDAG

I N EARLY 1691, A GROUP OF O'ODHAM LED TWO SPANISH PRIESTS
to the lands that in the 1200s had been home to the Huhugam.
The priests, Father Eusebio Kino and Juan María Salvatierra, had
been visiting the Himuri O'odham, in what's now the Mexican state
of Sonora, and intended to turn back at the northernmost Himuri
town, Tucubavia, at the headwaters of the Altar River, today about
twenty miles south of the U.S.–Mexico border. But an embassy of
Sobaipuri O'odham arrived, carrying wooden crosses, symbols that
the bearers knew were signs of peace for European travelers. The
priests accepted their invitation to come another fifty miles north to
their town of Tumacácori, in what's now southern Arizona.

By the time they arrived in Tumacácori, a town of around forty
closely clustered houses, representatives from throughout Sobaipuri
country had assembled there to meet them. Tumacácori's women
had already built for their guests three new open-air structures made
of poles and roofed with saguaro cactus ribs, including one to shelter
the priest who said mass. The Spanish called these structures "ramadas," derived from the Spanish word for "branches" (Ramada Inns
took their name from them, as a symbol of an inviting shelter for
welcome guests). The people of Tumacácori fed the guests under one
of the ramadas and allowed them to baptize a few infants, as they
had at previous towns. Kino and Salvatierra were impressed by the
"docile" and "friendly" people they met in their "fertile and pleasant
valleys" and determined to ask their superiors to station priests there
permanently.[1]

In the coming years, the Sobaipuri O'odham would escort Father Kino ever farther north, to the town of Tucson (meaning "at the foot of the black mountain"), to Akimel O'odham towns on the Gila River, where Phoenix is today, and into Tohono and Hia-Ced O'odham country, in the desert between the river valleys. They all would welcome the priests as enthusiastically as the people of Tucubavia and Tumacácori had.[2]

The River O'odham (Himuri, Sobaipuri, and Akimel), Desert O'odham (Tohono), and Sand Dune O'odham (Hia-Ced) whom Kino saw in the seventeenth century were living the himdag—the way of life—established (or reestablished) in the aftermath of the fall of the Huhugam, as explained in chapter 2. By the 1690s they practiced a centuries-old way of life that protected them against the hazards of centralization that had proved so dangerous in the distant past, and reciprocal connections among the different O'odham stabilized life after the crises of the era of the Huhugam.

Still, living in the desert remained precarious, and the O'odham were alert to ways they could further ensure their livelihood. When newcomers arrived, the O'odham would work to fit them into networks of reciprocity. They would be remarkably successful doing so with Spaniards, adding Spanish crops and livestock, elements of Catholicism, and Spanish military assistance where it was useful to their himdag, while rejecting and at times violently expelling things and people that were not. The O'odham shaped the Spanish into aligning with their himdag. In turn, the Spanish were able to maintain a presence in the region only because the O'odham assented.

Meeting Native needs was no more what the Spanish wanted than the English, French, or Dutch, but, like them, when the Spanish wanted to set up a permanent presence in a foreign country where they were vastly outnumbered by their hosts, they usually had to play by local rules. By the time Father Kino was in O'odham country, Spain had spent two centuries trying to make good on its claim to nearly all of the Americas. The Spanish crown would rather have colonized the north with armies and settlers than a few priests, but they had little choice, as they now competed against other Europeans wanting to seize as much as they could of the overextended

Spanish Empire. Priests, too, had to live with Native peoples' inclusivist adoption of Christianity and refusal to reject their old lives in favor of complete conversion. Like would-be colonists throughout North America, the Spanish had to accept all kinds of relationships antithetical to the aims of colonialism.

SEVENTEENTH-CENTURY O'ODHAM HIMDAG

In September, O'odham river towns would prepare to host their Tohono and Hia-Ced O'odham cousins. They cleared the road to town of any brush and other debris that had built up, and they prepared water and food, as well as torches to take out along the road if their visitors arrived at night. Once the visitors reached the town, they unpacked the foods they had cultivated and processed in the desert, the most anticipated being sweet saguaro syrup. In return, their hosts shared their corn, tortillas, squashes, and tobacco. They ate and drank together and shared news of the year apart.[3]

Ramadas sheltering O'odham taco making beside
Mission San Xavier del Bac, 2019.
AUTHOR'S PHOTOGRAPH

This kind of fall celebration happened in hundreds of towns in the three regions where River O'odham lived. The Akimel O'odham farmed (and still farm today) formerly Huhugam lands in the Gila River Valley just south of present-day Phoenix. The Sobaipuri farmed formerly Huhugam lands to the south along the Santa Cruz and San Pedro rivers, which flow north from Sonora past Tucson to empty into the Gila in Akimel O'odham country. The people whom this chapter will call the Himuri O'odham (their seventeenth-century towns seem not to have called themselves by one name) farmed along the Magdalena and Altar rivers of Sonora, which start from springs in the mountains and flow in parallel before the Magdalena curves to meet the Altar. The Himuri O'odham were descendants of Las Trincheras, a civilization that was contemporaneous with the Huhugam and similarly farmed large irrigated fields but did not build the cities and hierarchy they did. When Spaniards came across seventeenth-century River O'odham, they struggled to name the sprawling farm towns near their fields, a kind of social organization they didn't really understand. They settled on the label rancherias, to distinguish them from more urban pueblos or ciudades. Archaeologists and colonial-era Spanish writers agree that the river valleys were heavily populated, with scores of rancherias and many thousands of people in each of the valleys of the Gila, Santa Cruz, San Pedro, Altar, and Magdalena rivers.[4]

Meanwhile, the Tohono O'odham, the "Desert People," migrated seasonally between their hillside winter homes and their summer farms near arroyos (seasonally dry creeks). Thus they are sometimes called "the two-village people," in contrast to the "one village" River O'odham groups. In addition to their winter and summer homes, the Tohono O'odham had shorter-term camps at gathering places in between and spent time in the towns of the River O'odham. In the far west, the Hia-Ced O'odham, the "Sand Dune People," also migrated seasonally, in their case along the northern shore of the Gulf of California in a region today called the Gran Desierto de Altar (the Great Altar Desert), which is the largest sand dune system in the Americas. Sometimes the Hia-Ced O'odham were called the "no-village people" because they were the closest to a truly nomadic people among the O'odham. In reality, the Hia-Ced did have settlements clustered near water sources, and River O'odham did go out on gathering excursions, yet "one village," "two village," and "no village" are useful shorthand terms for the River, Tohono, and Hia-Ced economies, respectively.[5]

The River O'odham groups are sometimes known as Pimas and the Tohono and Hia-Ced O'odham as Papagos, both names that the Spanish called them. When Spaniards met their first O'odham-speaking people, the Spanish asked a question to which the O'odham replied, "Pim-maic," which means "I don't know" or "I don't understand." Pretty soon, Spaniards realized that these people in fact called themselves O'odham, but the name Pima stuck for a long time. The name Papago may come from *bawi o'odham,* meaning "tepary bean eaters," in recognition of a major Tohono crop.[6] Today the Tohono O'odham have their own nation, and the Akimel O'odham are citizens of the Gila River Indian Community, the Salt River Pima-Maricopa Indian Community, and the Ak-Chin Indian Community. Other River O'odham and Hia-Ced O'odham are members of those four nations or the O'odham de Mexico.[7]

The diversity of the O'odham diet was central to their himdag after rejecting dependence on centralized irrigated agriculture. Although outsiders tended to describe the Hia-Ced and Tohono O'odham life as one of unsettled scavenging, they had to admit, in the words of an early-eighteenth-century priest, that all of the O'odham "live, nonetheless, content." Indeed, "they are generous and liberal as far as they can be in their poverty, and no one who arrives at their rancherias and houses, be they locals or foreigners, will lack for anything."[8]

The complementary nature of the River and Desert O'odham economies is still apparent if you travel south from Phoenix through the high-tech irrigation systems and green fields of the Gila River Indian Community and Ak-Chin Indian Community into the Tohono O'odham Nation. The first time I drove into the homeland of the Tohono, I expected to see the land become dry and barren. I was wrong. The desert is lush in its own way. It was March—wildflower season—and I kept pulling over to marvel at the dense patches of

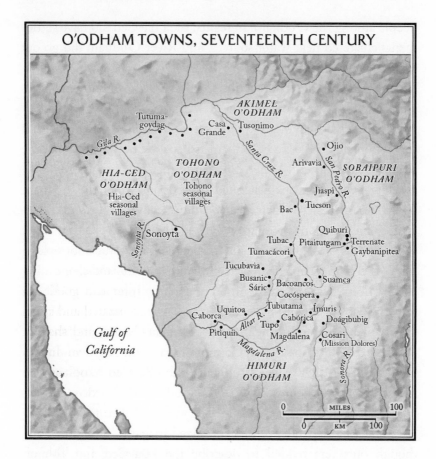

O'ODHAM TOWNS, SEVENTEENTH CENTURY

bright orange, purple, and yellow wildflowers, shockingly vivid against a background of desert plants in every shade of green and the towering saguaro cacti spaced so evenly across the landscape it seemed as if they had been planted (as perhaps they were). The Sonoran Desert is a bounteous place, and the O'odham have long known how to benefit from it.

River O'odham irrigated their fields by transporting river water in well-designed canal systems built on top of the ancient Huhugam ones. They were less centralized than their ancestors, though, and depended on reciprocity with other O'odham. River O'odham women processed and stored the food that would sustain them and create surplus to trade with the Tohono and Hia-Ced O'odham and other friendly neighbors. They roasted and ground the corn into pinole and made tortillas and tamales. They were known for their skill and artistry in making baskets to hold the bounty, large enough to fit two and a half bushels of corn. The baskets were functional but, with their intricate designs, were art as well. In the hot summer months, women and girls would gather and dry supplies: cattails, light-colored willow shoots, and the hook-shaped devil's claw that provided the basket's black contrast. All through the winter months, women would make baskets from these supplies they had stored. They made a cattail base for the basket size they wanted and then used an awl to make holes in the base where they could push through light-colored willow or black devil's claw. They created coils so tight that people sometimes describe their pieces as sewing more than basket-weaving. They would fill their storehouses and outdoor platforms with large baskets full of surplus, ready to use and share.

Other crops also provided work for the winter and goods to trade. River O'odham grew cotton, and women separated and spun the fibers and wove them into cloth, blankets, skirts, and shawls, which they painted in red and yellow patterns. Agave grown on the edges of cornfields provided not only tasty hearts to roast and eat but also long leaves that the men processed and twisted into rope. The Sobaipuri O'odham raised macaws for their scarlet feathers.[9]

Beyond the irrigated fields, River O'odham, like Desert O'odham, harvested a spectrum of semi-wild, semi-cultivated plants. One of the most important of these foods was mesquite bean pods. River O'odham women managed multiple groves of mesquite trees, whose varieties produce at different times of the year and under various conditions and have different tastes, all valued characteristics in this diversified economy. Mesquite trees have deep roots that can extend more than thirty feet to find water, and they produce even in drought years. Dried pods can be soaked and strained to make juice or ground into protein-rich mesquite flour. The flour can be added to soup or made into cakes by mixing it with water and drying it in the hot desert sun, an efficient way to bake without a fuel-consuming fire. O'odham compare their taste to cinnamon, dark chocolate, or graham crackers. Mesquite sap can also be used as a glue, and, as backyard barbecuers know, cooking over a fire of mesquite wood gives food a rich smoky flavor.[10]

The River O'odham were host to family groups of Tohono O'odham for much of the fall. The visitors spread across many river towns, helping to harvest crops and maintain the canals alongside their hosts. In late fall, as the hot temperatures eased, Tohono men and women packed the dried corn and other products they had acquired and went into the foothills, meeting others along the way, to go together to their compact winter villages near wells built on natural springs. Once they arrived, they cleaned out their winter roundhouses, slightly set into the ground, with a domed roof and entered through a small door, the smoke from the fire escaping between the branches of the roof. They stored the provisions they had brought and inventoried the tools, water jars, grindstones, and other heavy items they had left behind the previous winter. In the winter houses, the older women made baskets and nets, while the older men made tools, rope, and weapons. They ate from their stores, adding rabbit, venison, and antelope hunted by the men and wild greens and nopales (prickly pear pads) gathered by the women. There were also important products to collect here for the rest of the year, including groves of medicinal plants. Anthropologist Ruth Underhill noticed in the 1930s what she described as a creosote "plantation," where the bushes were "as evenly spaced as a checkerboard" to allow each one enough groundwater.[11]

When spring came, the Tohono O'odham spread out into smaller family groups again, this time for the serious harvesting that was central to their economies. As men kept them supplied with meat, women harvested cholla buds and the fruit of the barrel cactus in April and May, saguaro fruit in June, and different varieties of prickly pear all summer long. They slept outside under the stars, because there was virtually no chance of rain, and at night they might hear singing from other camps not far away. Picking was only the start of the work. Cholla buds were roasted overnight in pits lined with lava rocks, where the spines were burned off and they gained a smoky taste in addition to their natural tangy flavor, similar to asparagus or artichoke hearts. Roasted and dried cholla buds were light to carry and would keep all year for cooks either to rehydrate in boiling water and fry or to grind into powder and use in soup as a thickener that added calcium and other nutrients as well as flavor.[12]

The saguaro was the most important product of the desert spring. Tohono O'odham women knocked the plump ripe fruit down with cactus poles, and the children rushed to break into the muted orange-colored outside to get to the bright red pulp, sweet and wet. They also picked up the saguaro fruit that had dried in the sun and fallen to the ground, where it became candy-like with its intense, caramelized flavor. The pulp that wasn't eaten right away was boiled over a fire in a big pot and then strained into a deep red syrup. Tohono O'odham cooks today say that, "naturally sweet, ripened by the heat of the sun and tinged with mesquite smoke, the smooth, molasses-thick syrup tastes like nothing else." They set some aside to ferment for the annual nawait ceremony, in which families who had been at separate camps came together with the others of their village to celebrate the saguaro harvest and encourage the rains of the coming monsoon season. They also ground the tiny dark black seeds that remained from straining the pulp into a spread, rich in protein, fiber, and healthy fat, to flavor and enrich tortillas. Stored in stoppered clay jars, the saguaro syrup can last up to a year, and the candy and seeds keep indefinitely.[13]

The giant saguaro cacti grow slowly, but the semiannual rains—heavy storms in summer and light rainfall in winter—of this part of the Sonoran Desert mean they grow faster here than elsewhere, and they bear fruit for a hundred years. In drought years they still produce, providing not only food but also necessary liquid nourishment. Tohono O'odham poet and linguist Ofelia Zepeda describes how, during gentle winter rains, "the saguaro cactus quietly pulls in the moisture and stands plump, holding the moisture, ready for the next inevitable dry period."[14] When an old saguaro finally stopped bearing fruit, it was still useful. Its ribs would become roofs for ramadas, tongs to seize and twist cholla buds and prickly pears, sticks for reaching the tops of other saguaros to knock down fruit, and calendar sticks on which they marked important events of each year.[15]

If all went well, soon after the saguaro harvest and the nawait

Tohono O'odham women harvesting saguaro fruit, 1854, painting by Arthur Schott in *Report of the United States and Mexican Boundary Survey*.

DAVIS LIBRARY, UNIVERSITY OF NORTH CAROLINA AT CHAPEL HILL

ceremony, the sky would darken over the Sonoran Desert, lightning would appear in the distance, and huge drops of rain would begin to fall, all indicating that it was time to plant. Families packed up their stores of spring produce and headed for their arroyos. In the dry creek bed, women and men used brush and rocks to build small temporary dams that would direct rainwater toward their crops. They needed to be ready by the time the monsoons came in walls of rain to fill the arroyos with several feet of water. Today these floods still come fast; in the Tohono O'odham Nation, signs at every dip in the road warn people to stop if they see water. This floodwater farming is called "ak-chin," meaning "at the mouth of the wash or arroyo." Tohono O'odham Community Action Farm manager Noland Johnson recalled, "I've heard stories about my mother having to sleep out in the fields to be ready when the rains come. . . . If you can see the clouds and know that it's raining, you know that wash is gonna be coming; so they'd have to go in the field to get ready." Once the rain fell, the men and women dug holes in the wet ground with their planting sticks and placed a few seeds in each hole: squash, corn, tobacco, and tepary beans.[16]

The Tohono O'odham had chosen and developed crops that germinated quickly with sudden rain and thrived in the desert sun. O'odham corn matures in only sixty days after a heavy soaking. Tepary beans are the only bean native to the present-day United States, and they were developed by the O'odham and their ancestors. If well watered in their first few days, they shoot up fast and, unlike all other bean varieties, their scraggly plants don't need much more water to become covered with small white flowers and then hundreds of dangling green pods. Some people say they actually bear more if they get less water as they grow. Modern-day estimates say that one acre can yield one thousand pounds of beans. Johnson reflects that tepary beans "remind me of my people; we as desert people want to have the same characteristics—be able to go for a long time without water and live in the desert environment."[17]

When the harvest was complete and the dry season began, Tohono O'odham families left their summer villages and once again spread out to the towns of the River O'odham, carrying dried tepary beans, cholla buds, dried meat and skins, medicines, and saguaro products to exchange in their reciprocal economy. Maria Chona, a Tohono O'odham woman who came of age in the second half of the nineteenth century, recalled her family preparing to leave for towns on the Altar River. By then the Tohono O'odham had horses, so the children, bedding, and heavy grinding stone rode while the women, carrying nets full of pots with dried food, some with a baby secured on top, ran beside the walking horses. "Far up in the hills," she recalled, "our husbands went running with their bows and arrows, looking for deer, and sometimes they met us with loads of meat on their backs. At night we camped and my mother-in-law cooked a big pot of gruel. Next day I carried it among the pots so we could stop and eat it midday." When the Tohono O'odham arrived at the river towns, there were feasts and celebrations once again.[18]

Unlike the green agricultural fields of the River O'odham and the dense, if dry, vegetation of the Tohono O'odham desert, the Hia-Ced homeland does look barren. Here, where the U.S. states of Arizona and California and the Mexican states of Sonora and Baja California meet, the Colorado River deposited tremendous amounts of sediment on its way to the Gulf of California more than one hundred thousand years ago. When the Colorado River shifted northwest, the sand remained, in sheets and in dunes some thirty stories high and bright rusty red. Within this dune field or "sand sea," as some people call it, are equally desolate-looking lava fields, left by volcanoes that erupted long ago in the nearby mountains. Cinder cones and huge craters give the place an otherworldly appearance. Astronauts trained here in the 1960s to prepare for walking on the moon. Spanish explorers called the lava fields malpaís—badlands.[19] According to one priest, "all of this vast space is . . . incapable of supporting life because of the great lack of water and the sterility of the land." David Martínez (Hia-Ced/Akimel) notes that "from the earliest contact with Spanish explorers and missionaries the Hia-Ced O'odham were portrayed as a marginal people on the verge of extinction." Outsiders were "amazed that any group, however loosely organized, could sustain an existence in such a barren region."[20]

But there is bounty even here. The Hia-Ced O'odham were known for the root they gathered called "hia-tatk," meaning "sand root" or "sand dune root." In fact, this food may be the origin of the Hia-Ced name, rather than the sand dunes themselves. Found only in the Sonoran Desert, the root (whose scientific name is *Ammobroma sonorae* or *Pholisma sonorae*) is also called the "sand food of Sonora." All year round, Hia-Ced women looked for the tops sticking up from the sand. The roots could be roasted in their bark on hot coals, peeled and boiled, or sun-dried for easier transportation, sometimes ground with mesquite beans as a dried soup mix. Their taste has been compared to "the finest sweet potato only far more delicate."[21] Hia-Ced men hunted jackrabbits, deer, muskrats, mountain sheep, and reptiles, from the tiny side-blotched lizard to the desert iguana. In the Gulf of California, men caught crabs and fish, which could be salt-cured and sun-dried. They provided fish as well as salt and seashell ornaments to other O'odham, and they also hosted men and boys who made summer pilgrimages to the Gulf of California to gather salt and conduct rites of passage.[22]

Even at the one place where they had a permanent stream, the Sonoyta River, which flows into the Gulf of California, the Hia-Ced O'odham didn't depend much on agriculture. They built some permanent irrigation canals here and grew some corn, beans, and squash, yet Spanish observers were shocked to see that here, where there actually were "fertile lands, with irrigation canals," the residents didn't even pick all of the corn that grew. In fact, it was their insurance and what they used if they needed extra for hospitality.[23]

Living in these lava and sand fields required knowing how to find potable water. Hia-Ced people knew where there were natural springs, and they established settlements nearby and built roads for traveling among them. The Hia-Ced traveled in small family groups that didn't require a large water source. Both the Hia-Ced and Tohono O'odham maintained pools and reservoirs (often called "tinajas") to collect water. Some were shallow, wet only from the morning dew and dry by afternoon, while others were permanent small reservoirs. A traveling Spaniard admired these "reservoirs made by hand and with great skill."[24] Some of them had formed from seasonal waterfalls as rainwater plummeted down the sides of the mountains and, over time, eroded the rock, some creating long runs of multiple pools. The O'odham kept the pools cleared of debris and went farther uphill to get water as the downhill pools ran dry. They also knew where there might be groundwater running under dry arroyos. To the Spaniards' perpetual surprise, no matter how desolate the landscape looked, as they traveled the sand dunes and the barren-looking landscape, their hosts always knew where to find a spring or a pool.[25]

The daily need for water made both Hia-Ced and Tohono O'odham children great runners. At times of the year when they did not live beside a water source, girls ran—literally—every morning to get water from pools or springs, returning with stoppered water jugs in their net backpacks. These daily runs conditioned them for their migrations, for fleeing enemy attack, and for races that they had against children in the river towns. Looking back on her youth, Maria Chona remembered, "Ah, how we could run, we Desert People."[26]

Having built a himdag upon reciprocity among O'odham groups, they also drew non-O'odham in. One important group was the Piipaash (also called Maricopa), who had long lived to the west of the Akimel O'odham on the Gila River, near its juncture with the Colorado. The Akimel O'odham enhanced their own stability by allying with the Piipaash. In contrast to Tohono and Hia-Ced O'odham families' seasonal visits, many Piipaash moved in permanently with the Akimel O'odham. Whereas O'odham is an Uto-Aztecan language, the Piipaash are Yuman-speaking and culturally and linguistically had more in common with the Yavapai, Quechan, and Mohave Yumas to their north and east. Visitors familiar with the O'odham called the Piipaash "a people with very different clothes, features, and language."[27] The Piipaash sometimes warred against other Yuman speakers, so joining defenses with the Akimel O'odham provided them protection. The Piipaash not only farmed but also complemented Akimel O'odham production with their famous pottery, made of clay with a red slip, hand-rubbed to a brilliant shine, and decorated in jet black.[28]

This Piipaash–Akimel O'odham relationship is a striking example of two separate peoples who formed a political and economic life together without either assimilating into the other's identity. By the seventeenth century, they were already closely associated and living side by side. Yet visitors always noted that they were different peoples, and the Piipaash retained their customs of painting or tattooing their bodies, keeping their hair short, and piercing their ears. Today, more than three centuries later, the Gila River Indian Community, the Salt River Pima-Maricopa Indian Community, and the Ak-Chin Indian Community all include both Akimel O'odham and Piipaash people. An official description of the Salt River Pima-Maricopa Indian Community states that it "is composed of two distinct Native American tribes," and a sign in the Gila River Community tells that, "while these two Tribes have completely different languages, cultures and genetics, they have lived in harmony for hundreds of years." Both languages are still spoken by tribal members today, and signs are in both languages as well as English.[29]

Neither the Sobaipuri nor the Himuri river towns had a resident ally like the Piipaash, but they did establish important trading connections with others. The Sobaipuri traded occasionally with the Pueblo peoples of New Mexico, far to the east, for bison products and turquoise. Wide, well-traveled roads connected the Sobaipuri to the Himuri, who in turn traded with other O'odham to the south and west.

VISITS FROM FATHER KINO

When Jesuit priest Eusebio Kino followed O'odham guides up those roads to the Himuri towns and then on to the Sobaipuri town of Tumacácori, he was seeking to convert the region to Christianity, and if you look at the vast number of Spanish names on the detailed maps that he made of the region, you might think he had succeeded. On the 1696 map below, that's the Gila River running east–west across the top of the map, with the ruins of the Huhugam Casa Grande where the Santa Cruz River joins it from the south, as does the San Pedro River, farther east. The Altar and Magdalena rivers start at the word PIMERIA and run southwest toward the kneeling priest about to be shot with arrows (more on him in a moment). The tiny boxes topped by crosses indicate missions, while the circles mark rancherias where Kino planned to place missions.

Some historians in the centuries since have believed this map's message: that Jesuit missions had begun to cover the land of northern Sonora and southern Arizona. Kino's accompanying reports detailed tens of thousands of O'odham and Piipaash people living in these Spanish-named towns. Histories of the region that don't look any deeper end up with sentences like these: "Father Eusebio Kino arrived in 1687 and began gathering the Pimas Altos into pueblos"

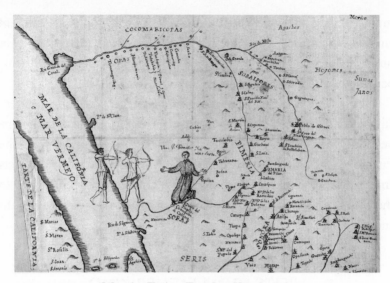

Map by Father Eusebio Kino, 1696.
© ARCHIVUM ROMANUM SOCIETATIS IESU, ROME

and "Within this vast region the Spanish organized the amenable Pima around the missions, to which the Pima were to donate three days of agricultural labor weekly."[30]

Yet here is how the Huhugam Ki Museum, run by the Salt River Pima-Maricopa Indian Community, summarizes the period from the seventeenth through the early nineteenth centuries: "Spanish missionaries and subsequent Mexican settlers arrive in small numbers. Relations with them remain friendly, as they seemingly pose little threat."[31] This version is considerably more accurate than those that mistake Spanish aspiration for reality. Like most maps, Kino's serves the purposes of its maker. It shows his desire to persuade his superiors to support his efforts. Renaming places was what colonizers did, often the first thing. So, for example, the Sobaipuri rancheria that Kino first visited, Tumacácori, is marked on his map toward the southern part of the Santa Cruz River with a church symbol and the name S. CAYETANO, short for San Cayetano. On the map and in his writings, Kino renamed the town for Saint Cayetano, a sixteenth-century Italian priest who had been canonized two decades before Kino's visit. Kino merely tacked the saint's name in front of the town's existing name. So Tumacácori—whose inhabitants continued to call it by that name—in Spanish records became San Cayetano del Tumacácori, Saint Cayetano of the Tumacácori. Similarly, the Himuri town of Ímuris (still called by that name today) appears on the map as S. JOSEPH. The map's S. FRANCISCO XAVIER DEL BAC sounds like a Spanish Catholic mission, but in fact not a thing had changed at the rancheria of Bac. In fact, not a single Spaniard lived in the O'odham country of what's now the United States until the eighteenth century, and even in that century, most were there for only a few years. Spanish names on a map did nothing to change Native reality.

Kino did the same in-name-only labeling with local leaders in his written accounts, adding Spanish titles to their Native names and, for the very few whom he baptized, giving them Spanish names, when in fact the O'odham continued to call them by their original names. Thus, a Sobaipuri leader named Coro became "Captain Coro" in Kino's reports and later "Antonio Leal" when he accepted baptism and was christened with the name of a Jesuit leader. But even Kino continued to refer to him as Captain Coro. Kino awarded local leaders these titles as well as staffs and other physical signs of leadership, reflecting the desire to impose Spanish rule over whatever local hierarchy existed. So when Kino recorded that he had given Coro of Quiburi the title Captain Coro, the priest was inserting Coro into the Spanish hierarchy, above the other people of Quiburi but below the Viceroy of New Spain, with King Carlos II above him and the pope and God above the king. Of course, Coro was not agreeing to Spanish rule, and he and men in other rancherias whom Kino called "captain" or "governor" may have been diplomats and assigned representatives to the Spanish rather than the main political leaders.[32]

By Kino's time, the Spanish crown had given up most of its ambitions for this northern imperial frontier more than a thousand miles from Mexico City. A hundred and fifty years earlier, O'odham had welcomed the Spanish expeditions, but the lack of gold and the obvious unsuitability of the desert for sugar plantations meant it attracted little subsequent attention. The Spanish had too few soldiers and settlers for all of the places they were trying to colonize. The heart of Aztec and Inca lands and other places where gold and silver were discovered got the most attention, not the edges of Spain's vast claims. So Spanish officials invited Jesuit missionaries to try to establish a Spanish presence in O'odham country. When priests heard about this heavily populated region with tens of thousands of souls to save, they jumped at the chance. In the early 1600s, Jesuit priests began to establish some missions and presidios in southern Sonora, including among some southern O'odham-speaking peoples.[33]

Most priests who ventured to the Americas in this period wanted not just to introduce Christianity but to change Indians' whole way of life. Priests wanted the O'odham to become Christian Spanish subjects living in concentrated mission towns, no longer living in spread-out rancherias or seasonally migrating. They called their missions "reducciones," places where they aimed to "reduce" Native people from what they saw as their barbarous nomadic way of life into concentrated and permanent towns like those of Spain. In these missions, they wanted everyone to live closely together near the church, convert to Christianity, attend mass, work the fields to grow food for themselves and the priests, and pay tribute to the crown. In time, as a 1513 Spanish law put it, these Native towns would become "so civilized and educated, that they will be capable of governing themselves" as functionally independent vassal towns within the Spanish Empire.[34]

It is no surprise that Native people—who were already governing themselves—rejected priests' radical demands for spiritual, social, and economic change. In a pattern that repeated over and over, Native communities at first welcomed priests and then realized the extent of their goals and decided they were more trouble than they were worth. In the 1680s, the Pueblo peoples of New Mexico united to expel the Spanish entirely, in what historians call the Pueblo Revolt. All across northern Mexico, similar conflicts left priests dead and missions in ruins.[35]

Where missionaries learned to compromise, they were more likely to be allowed to stay. To the south of the O'odham in the 1680s, priests in Opata country learned to become less demanding, and Opatas in large numbers lived near missions seasonally, coordinating with them for mutual benefit while not being "reduced."

Kino compromised in O'odham river towns in hopes of reaping a large harvest of souls. Born in northern Italy, Kino claimed to be from Spain because the Spanish crown was trying to limit the number of non-Spanish missionaries in its colonies. In the early 1680s, Kino had begun a mission in what's now the Mexican state of Baja California, but after more than a year there he had managed to baptize only five people, all of whom were "in articulo mortis," just about to die. Priests weren't supposed to baptize converts until they demonstrated a full understanding of the Christian catechism—the basic beliefs of the faith—although exceptions could be made for the dangerously ill and for babies. Baptizing those near death was hardly the way to build a self-sustaining mission, so Kino decided to try a new approach, this time in the O'odham homeland.[36]

Rather than try to build one mission, as he had in California, Kino went abroad among the O'odham, introducing huge numbers of people to Christianity. He hoped that if he demonstrated Native interest in Christianity to his superiors, they would send a flock of priests to help. He received permission to try this approach in Pímeria Alta, the name that Kino gave to O'odham country in the northern region of Sonora and the southern part of Arizona, the lands of the Tohono, Hia-Ced, Himuri, Sobaipuri, and Akimel O'odham. (Pímeria Baja was the name for the lands of other O'odham speakers to the south.) He traveled throughout the region giving away cattle, sheep, goats, and seeds while preaching Christianity. He accepted lodging and hospitality in keeping with O'odham ways of reciprocity. Standard reducción practices required Native towns to pay tribute to the Spanish, an obvious source of conflict, so he persuaded the king to exempt his converts for the first twenty-five years.[37]

I followed Kino's path into Himuri O'odham country in the spring of 2022, and it was easy to imagine his delight in arriving here. The Magdalena and Altar rivers lie in valleys surrounded by undulating land, with mountains visible in the distance on all sides.

Today the valleys have grazing cows, railroad tracks, electric lines, and a highway, and Magdalena is a midsize sprawling city, radiating out from its central plaza onto the surrounding rolling hills. Still, for long stretches, the mesquite and cottonwood trees and the occasional prickly pear, organ pipe, or saguaro cactus standing out against the rolling hills of yellow grass and desert scrub still make the landscape look much as it did to Kino on horseback or an O'odham runner bringing news from one town to another.

On his first visit, in 1687, Kino declared the Himuri O'odham perfect for his mission. He recorded that the fertile Magdalena Valley had "many docile and domesticated people." He was confident he could fix the scattered nature of the rancherias by "reducing them to good new pueblos." Kino had learned some of the O'odham language from communities in the south, so they could understand at least some of what he said. At every new encounter, he showed a map of Spain's known world and described how the Spanish had come in ships across the Atlantic, then traveled by land into central Mexico and up through Sinaloa and Sonora. His O'odham hosts, in turn, gave him information for the map he was making of their region. At each place, Kino described the mission he hoped to build for them, with a "church, lots of provisions, wheat and corn, many cattle and horses."[38]

The Himuri and other O'odham river towns sought out Spanish contact and ultimately incorporated Spanish crops and animals into their economy, because they complemented their existing himdag. Metal tools work well, horses and mules can carry heavy loads, and sheep and new crops added to river towns' production. Wheat and barley fit River O'odham cycles: planted during winter rains and harvested in late spring before the corn crop. When a priest later was stationed at one Himuri rancheria and a neighboring rancheria learned of the decision, its people protested that it was unfair that the other receive "so many worldly and spiritual good things: vestments and clothes, large and small livestock, horses and mules, a farm and cow-hands, pack animals, and mule-drivers."[39]

As that rancheria's protest mentions, religion was part of the Spanish appeal. Being inclusivist, the O'odham could add parts of

Christianity judged useful and true by O'odham religious leaders. The statues, paintings, vessels, and vestments for the mass that Kino brought with him were clearly sacred, as were the mesmerizing chants. Unlike today, priests in Kino's time said the mass in Latin and faced away from the people, heightening the sense that they were holy men different from other people. If baptism helped keep a child healthy, that was a blessing worth repeating. But if the child died or the priest proved incompetent or heavy-handed, they could cast him out.[40]

Kino seemed more useful than dangerous as he rode through the countryside, usually accompanied by only one other priest or official and a few Native Christians from the south. But the O'odham would never accept the Spanish as the kinds of rulers that the Spanish wanted to be, especially given their rejection of the rule of the Huhugam. Kino established a base mission at the town of Cosari, in the upper Sonora Valley, from which he could get supplies from Spanish missions and mining towns to the south. From Cosari, which he called Nuestra Señora de los Dolores de Cosari (Our Lady of the Sorrows of Cosari), Kino traveled almost constantly for the next two decades.[41]

Speaking in Himuri rancherias, and in those of the Sobaipuri and Akimel O'odham in subsequent journeys, Kino advised everyone to move into a few mission towns to achieve his plan of reducción (which they did not do). In 1689, the Jesuit superiors, persuaded by Kino, assigned four priests to Himuri rancherias, where the O'odham built small adobe churches for them. After his 1691 trip to Sobaipuri country, Kino returned the following year with fifty pack animals loaded with goods. At the Sobaipuri rancheria of Bac, eight hundred people gathered to hear what he had to say. Because it was September, some were probably Tohono O'odham who hadn't yet left for their winter towns. They crossed the plain to the San Pedro Valley and visited a large rancheria of several hundred people (whose name, Quiburi, means "many houses"), where Kino met Coro, who would serve as a Sobaipuri diplomat to the Spanish for the next two decades.[42]

When Kino met the more migratory Tohono and Hia-Ced

O'odham, he imagined that they would abandon their way of life to move permanently to the Himuri, Sobaipuri, and Akimel river towns. The mobile Hia-Ced O'odham struck Kino as the most desperately in need of dramatic reducción. Because he didn't understand their many sources of subsistence and their symbiosis with river towns, Kino believed the Hia-Ced lived miserable lives. Over the coming years, he repeatedly urged them to "move to one of the rivers and fertile lands." Each time, he thought they agreed, but either they didn't understand his presumptuous suggestion or they just wanted to appear agreeable. In any case, none of them changed their himdag.[43]

CHOOSING ENEMIES

In the final two decades of the 1600s, the O'odham considered their options as two new forces came into the region: the Spanish from the south and armed bands of Apaches, Janos, and Jocomes who began raiding on horseback from the east. Both posed dangers, but ultimately the O'odham deemed their relationship with Spanish priests and soldiers easier to control. As with the Mohawks armed with Dutch guns, the Apache, Jano, and Jocome raids were an indirect result of colonialism. In the early sixteenth century, following the Spanish conquest of Mexico City, Spanish raiders had ridden north to capture people and force them into slavery. The pope and the Spanish crown outlawed Indian slavery in the 1530s and '40s, but the Spanish had created a lasting enmity among their victims in the north, who would use Spain's horses against them for more than two centuries to come.

When the Spanish fled from the Pueblo Revolt in 1680, they left horses behind, and Pueblo communities began breeding and selling horses to Native people who came to trade. After the revolt, some Apache bands used horses to live more of the year on the plains. Whereas the O'odham built a diversified economy with agricultural river towns that traded with seminomadic Desert O'odham, Western Apaches based their livelihood on a combination of raiding, gathering, and small-scale seasonal agriculture. Permanent O'odham, Opata, and Spanish towns were ideal targets for accessing surplus food.[44]

Apaches allied with Janos and Jocomes, fellow former victims of Spanish raids who lived in the river valleys of what is now southwestern New Mexico and northwestern Chihuahua. Together they turned the tables on the former Spanish slave raiders. Janos, Jocomes, and Western Apaches became the terror of the Spanish, swooping in on horseback to steal horses, cows, corn, beans, and captives. They also took Spanish weapons, including swords they made into long lances, which were especially dangerous when wielded by a warrior on horseback. Yet bows and arrows remained their greatest weapons. As one Spaniard recorded of Apaches, they "are incomparable archers, and seldom miss; their arrows, when let fly by a strong arm, have more power and effectiveness than a bullet from the best musket."[45]

Much of the time the Spanish would call them all Apaches, a word that the Spanish generally used to mean mobile people who rode in on horseback to raid and otherwise lived far from Spanish control or understanding. The O'odham viewed them much the same, calling them simply the obga (or 'O:h)—"the enemy."[46]

These new enemies created some mutual interests between the Spanish and people like the O'odham and Opatas, who were targeted by horseback raiders by the late seventeenth century. The Spanish sent a few troops in addition to priests and eventually built a few forts in that region, south of the present U.S.–Mexico border. The one closest to O'odham country was Fronteras, more than a hundred miles southwest of today's town of Nogales, built in 1692. The Spanish staffed Fronteras with around fifty soldiers who were given the nearly impossible task of protecting the mines and cattle ranches that Spaniards tried to build to the south but were perpetually "on the verge of being lost."[47]

Like the English at Roanoke, Spanish soldiers whose orders were to control Native people who vastly outnumbered them could be brutal. In 1688, Spanish soldiers, frustrated in their losing war against Western Apaches and their allies, believed an Opata rumor that southern O'odham were assisting the Apaches. Spanish soldiers captured several O'odham from the town of Mototícachi, on a tributary of the Sonora River southeast of the Himuris. Under torture, the O'odham captives acceded to the soldiers' suggestions that their town was helping the Apaches. The soldiers rode into Mototícachi, rounded up the people, put them in chains, and burned the town. The soldiers executed forty-two men and marched the women, the children, and the elderly four hundred miles south to the Sinaloa presidio. News of the atrocity spread throughout O'odham country, and Spanish priests and officers rushed to assure the O'odham that it had been the work of ruffian Sinaloa soldiers who didn't represent the Spanish Empire.[48]

Yet violence was an inherent component of colonialism, not just the work of a few bad apples. Not only soldiers but also entrepreneurs and priests could be violent when Native people did not comply with their expectations. Events of 1695 gave the northern O'odham more information on whether or not the Spanish were really worth inviting to live nearby. First, a Spanish military officer named Antonio Solís brought violence to the Sobaipuri rancheria of Bac. His superiors in Mexico had sent him north to fight Apache, Jano, and Jocome raiders who had been attacking the northernmost Spanish settlements in Mexico. But raiders can be hard to track, and frustrated soldiers looking for a fight usually find one. Solís and his men rode into Bac and saw some Sobaipuri with what he believed was horsemeat. He inferred that they had stolen horses from the Spanish. In fact, the meat was venison, hunted by the O'odham. But, persuaded that he had caught some horse thieves red-handed, Solís killed three of them and had the other two whipped. This was shocking, unprovoked violence within their own town. And soon more trouble broke out with the new priests among the Himuri O'odham.[49]

The Himuri townspeople of Tubutama had requested and welcomed Father Daniel Januske in 1694, but they soon found themselves surprised at the demands he made of them, which fitted neither their understanding of their agreement with the Spanish nor the realities of power. At the time, there were four priests and no soldiers stationed in northern O'odham country, home to more than sixteen thousand O'odham. Yet Father Januske tried to implement reducción: He ordered the residents of Tubutama to stay at the mission, to go to mass, and to grow food to feed him, his livestock, and eventually more O'odham he hoped would move into the mission in the spirit of reducción. Tubutamans had expected to provide food— that made sense, as it was their obligation under the rules of reciprocity—but according to those same rules, the priest should either work alongside them or give them substantial meat from the herd of animals he had brought. As one Spaniard explained reciprocity, both "giving and receiving are for them signs of firm friendship."[50] When he failed to do so, some O'odham shot and ate Januske's animals. The Tubutamans would decide when and whether to go to church and to go out gathering and hunting, and their intimate lives—whom they married and had sex with—were none of his business. Many of Tubutama's families moved out of town to avoid him, exactly the opposite of the reducción he was trying to draw them into.[51]

Another problem was that Januske brought with him an Opata man, christened Antonio, to teach O'odham men how to take care of the mission's livestock. The name Opata may come from the same O'odham root (obga) as their word for Apaches and therefore also indicate enmity.[52] The Jesuits knew that Opatas were historic O'odham enemies, but because some of the earliest converts in northern Mexico were Opatas, there really was no other choice when it came to deciding who would help the tiny number of priests to run the new missions.[53]

According to later testimony, as disputes over work and authority grew in Tubutama, Antonio beat local O'odham men whom he expected to work as he ordered. One received more than one hundred lashes as punishment for eating some of the priest's wheat, although the accused insisted that the horses had eaten it. Apparently, one of the whipped men encouraged others to fight back. During Holy Week in 1695, while Januske was gone, some men from Tubutama killed Antonio along with an Opata boy who was his assistant, stripped the bodies, burned down the small church and the priest's house (both of which they had built), and destroyed the vessels for saying mass. A large crowd gathered to feast on the cattle and listen to the leaders speak of the need "to be rid of this ill-treatment by foreigners."[54] Some of the men then traveled throughout Himuri country, spreading the word of what they had done and why. They gathered forty or so men and decided to proceed to Caborca, the westernmost town that had gotten a priest. Soon that priest, Francisco Javier Saeta, lay dead. Father Saeta is the martyr portrayed on Kino's map. To ensure that his martyrdom was not in vain, Kino argued, the Jesuits should continue his work.[55]

In the conflict that followed, the O'odham would both see the violence that colonizers were capable of and enforce their own norms in the relationship. Several hundred Spanish, Opata, and allied Comcaac (Seri) fighters arrived. When the people of Tubutama and Caborca heard of their approach, they fled, and Spanish soldiers killed and wounded adults and children they came across in other towns and destroyed the whole corn crop of a rancheria next to Tubutama, even though its people had not been part of the violence at Tubutama. The violence enraged all of the Himuri towns and encouraged more to join the fight on Tubutama's side.[56]

In June, in an attempt to make peace, Kino and some O'odham peacemakers invited Himuri O'odham leaders from Tubutama and other towns who were in hiding to meet with the Spanish, "in peace and without weapons." Eventually they agreed, and more than a hundred of them came, unarmed and carrying crosses, to the meeting spot at a marsh between the Altar and Magdalena rivers.[57] The Spanish insisted that the O'odham perpetrators of the original violence at Tubutama be surrendered, so one of the O'odham pointed out a man who he said was the leader. Captain Antonio Solís, always too quick with his sword, rose up and chopped off the accused man's head. Chaos broke out, and all the O'odham tried to escape. But Solís had said that any soldier who allowed an Indian to get away would have to take his place and die, so, as a brokenhearted Kino had to report, the guards indiscriminately killed nearly fifty people, including their host, the leader of a nearby rancheria who, "with much care, had worked to bring these people, who came in peace."

The O'odham still remember this shocking betrayal as La Matanza (the Massacre).[58]

After La Matanza, war broke out in full force, with hundreds of O'odham men raiding and killing whatever Spanish, Opata, and Comcaac fighters they could find. Knowing that its soldiers had been in the wrong and that their presence only increased the violence, the Spanish army retreated. The O'odham forces burned the small churches that they had built in Himuri rancherias and took the sheep, goats, and horses. The Spanish had overreached, and the Himuri O'odham had cast them out.[59]

But continuing raids by Janos and Jocomes from the east helped to bring the Spanish and O'odham back together. These raids tended to target Sobaipuri O'odham river rancherias. The Sobaipuri O'odham wanted Spanish assistance in fighting those enemies, so they led the effort to deescalate the war that had just broken out between the Himuri O'odham and the Spanish. War really was in none of their interests. The Himuri O'odham wanted to get back home to tend to their crops. Spanish officers stationed on the northern front of New Spain wanted to get back to defending against the Apache, Jano, and Jocome raiders who, as one soldier wrote in frustration, were riding down in large numbers from their homes in the "rugged sierras" and "are able to do whatever they wish" to the vulnerable northern colonial towns and mines that the soldiers were supposed to protect.[60]

So the Sobaipuri O'odham decided to broker peace between the Himuris and the Spanish. When a squadron of fifty soldiers passed through a Sobaipuri rancheria, diverted from the Apache front and on their way "to wage war" on Himuri O'odham, Sobaipuri leaders worked to stop the assault on their Himuri relations.[61] They told the Spanish that they would spread the message to the Himuris that La Matanza had been a mistake and that if they surrendered the men who had started the violence, the Spanish would agree to peace. Sobaipuri leaders traveled with Kino and the Spanish soldiers, along with many Himuris, to the site of the massacre. Men and women went back and forth between the two sides for several days with information and messages. They agreed to meet in that deeply meaningful spot and make peace. The Spanish accepted the explanation that there were only two men left alive who were responsible for killing the priest and that they could not be surrendered to Spanish justice because they had "run away to the naked ones" (presumably meaning the Hia-Ced O'odham).[62]

The Himuri O'odham had to decide whether to keep fighting to avenge La Matanza or accept Spanish peace overtures. Maybe it was true that just a few individuals were to blame. Perhaps the fault lay with Antonio the overzealous Opata, Solís the quick-to-violence Spaniard, the two Tubutamans who had taken refuge with "the naked ones," or even the devil that the priests talked so much about. Plus there were advantages to having a potential enemy live among you, where you could watch him and keep him on your side. Material benefits came from contact with the Spanish, including new crops and animals. In fact, when Himuri O'odham fled to Sobaipuri towns, they brought animals they had seized from the incipient missions: an astounding five hundred sheep and goats plus a herd of mares.[63]

Weighing their options, the O'odham preferred the relative benefits and risks of the Spanish to the dangerous Native raiders. In the future, when priests, soldiers, or settlers overstepped, locals would sometimes kill them. Because there were so few Spaniards in the north, it rarely came to that. After the violence of 1695, Himuri towns almost immediately began inviting the Spanish back. In May 1696, Father Agustin de Campos reestablished the mission of San Ignacio, on the Magdalena River, that he had fled during the violence. His longevity and their mutual ability to get along made it the only church that continuously had a priest from 1696 until 1737.[64]

Although individual O'odham rancherias and regions governed themselves separately, the interdependent reciprocity of their himdag meant that decisions by each community had repercussions far beyond it. The Himuri and Sobaipuri now brought the northernmost O'odham—the Akimel—into the Spanish alliance. In the spring of 1697, Akimel O'odham leaders from rancherias along the Gila River—within today's Gila met with leaders from all across Sobaipuri country. Representing Ojio, a large Sobaipuri rancheria on the San Pedro River with around 350 residents, fifty miles north of Coro's Quiburi, was a man named Humari, whom Spaniards described as "an old man, much admired, the principal Captain of all the rancherias on his part of the river," and "the Indian with the most followers of all this Sobaipuri nation."[65]

The Akimel and Sobaipuri O'odham decided to send a joint delegation of twenty-five representatives south to meet with other O'odham and recruit more Spanish. They had arrived at Kino's Mission Dolores de Cosari, in southern O'odham territory, by Easter and were joined by Himuri O'odham leaders from the Altar and Magdalena valleys. From there, with Kino and some of his assistants, the Himuri, Akimel, and Sobaipuri representatives walked a hundred more miles into Sonora to meet with Kino's Jesuit superior, Horatio Polici. Along the way, they met both Native leaders and Spanish missionaries. They told Father Polici of their desire to have missions and good relations with the Spanish. Humari and his sons were baptized, all with Christian names honoring Spanish priests or saints: Francisco Eusebio, Francisco Xavier, and Horatio Polici. A Himuri O'odham leader was baptized as Don Marcos, and an Akimel O'odham leader was baptized as Don Juan de Palacios, after the highest official in the Mexican church.[66]

Spaniards interpreted this 1697 expedition as focused on them, but the O'odham likely went because they valued the renewal and forging of O'odham ties. This kind of expedition of leaders to other parts of O'odham country and gatherings of multiple O'odham groups surely had a precedent in an era before the Spanish, and it continues even today. O'odham leaders had plenty to talk about, from trade and resource use to defense against Apaches, Janos, and Jocomes. The Spanish certainly were one topic, and it seems that the O'odham solidified a joint strategy going forward: They would welcome the Spanish and try to avoid conflict. Despite the violence of La Matanza, the Spanish seemed on the whole to be controllable and worth working with.

After the 1697 diplomacy, the Himuri, Sobaipuri, and Akimel river towns consistently welcomed Spanish visits, and the Tohono established good relations with Spaniards in the river towns. Kino brought sheep and other animals to distribute, and Spanish soldiers often came along to strategize defense. At every place, residents cleared the roads, prepared ramadas, and came out to welcome the travelers with food and water. Kino recorded, "There was always enough food, even more than enough."[67] It would be easy to suspect Kino's accounts of being merely propaganda designed to impress his superiors so they would give him more resources, which he certainly wanted, but the soldiers who accompanied him recorded the very same accounts of joyous welcome in every O'odham town. A Spanish soldier wrote that the people of one rancheria "gave the soldiers so many cooked beans and cornmeal, that they ran out of bags (those being all that they had brought) in which to fill and load for the trip."[68]

The Sobaipuri O'odham, with their vulnerable location, built a strong military alliance with Spanish soldiers. The Spanish quickly realized that, "being on the frontier and closer to the Apaches, Jocomes and Janos," the Sobaipuri were the "greatest sworn enemies" of those peoples.[69] When the Spanish visited in the fall of 1697, Coro's men had recently killed thirteen Jocomes who had tried to attack a town on the San Pedro River. They were eager to go on the offensive, as one of the officers recorded, "offering to leave for the campaigns at all times."[70] The Sobaipuri showed their visitors six scalps they had taken recently and two boys who had been captured by warriors of Bac. The Spanish were so delighted at the O'odham victories and the prospect of powerful allies against the hated Apaches that, when Kino sent word of the victories to Sonora, priests dedicated masses and fiestas to celebrate. Missions "rang the bells in joy." Sonora's military governor praised the victory as being "for the entire benefit of all the Province." The residents of one district sent five hundred pesos' worth of clothing to thank the victorious O'odham.[71]

On his travels, Kino and the small detail of soldiers with him were always vulnerable. Any of the O'odham rancherias could have killed them all, either directly or by sending them off into the desert to die. But instead the O'odham recruited the Spanish, with all of their potential as a diplomatic and military ally, trading partner, and spiritual asset. A flurry of church building over the next few years attests to this decision. Several Himuri rancherias began building adobe churches at the end of the 1600s. In April 1700, Himuri, Akimel, and Tohono O'odham families traveled to Bac along with Humari and one of his sons to help Kino "start the foundations of a very large and spacious church" and priest's house, "all of the many people working with great pleasure and fervor, some in digging the foundations and others in carrying many fine stones" and using water from the irrigation canals to make the mortar.[72] Afterward, one of Bac's leaders sent his twelve-year-old son home with Kino, "to teach him the prayers and the Christian doctrine and to assist at mass."[73] It seems clear that Kino's spiritual offerings were part of his appeal and that the people of Bac, at least, saw the mission as a valuable source of religious and material support for their himdag.

For now, the Spanish did not hold the power in O'odham country, but in the late nineteenth century people of European descent would disrupt the economy of the O'odham and steal much of their land and most of their water, transforming the landscape and gravely threatening the O'odham ability to control their own himdag. Still, in the 1680s and for another two centuries, the O'odham controlled the movement and ambition of Europeans, and when it was in their interest, they banded with the Spanish to fight Apaches and other enemies much more powerful than the few Spaniards who came to their lands. The O'odham valued neighbors who abided by the rules of reciprocity and contributed to their himdag, but those who mistook generosity for submission and tried to extract goods and labor without reciprocating were not welcome.

SANTO HIMDAG

Over time, many O'odham began to integrate some Christianity into their religious beliefs and practices, creating a santo himdag, or "the saint's way." Priests were such a sporadic presence from the 1600s until the late 1800s that the O'odham largely shaped their Christianity in their own inclusivist way. In the late twentieth century, Tohono O'odham elder Frances Manuel recalled how her family went to both O'odham healers and white men's doctors and said prayers both to the sun and earth and to the Creator. As she put it, "my people . . . are true Catholics and respect the Church. My people believed in God and the Church in their own way."[74]

From priests' first visits to O'odham country, of course, they talked about Christianity. Kino said there was "one true God, who created the heavens, its light, land, birds, animals and fish of the ocean and freshwater, trees, plants and fruits to serve and sustain the man Adam . . . and his consort Eve whom He made of his own flesh and rib." Adam and Eve had broken God's law, Kino explained, and "fell into disgrace, condemning all of humanity; from whose tree we descend from original sin." He described "the eternal fire of the inferno" but also told them the good news that God, "in his infinite mercy," had sent Jesus, born to "the ever Virgin Mary, to redeem us from the devil." If the O'odham accepted Christianity, he promised, they would be saved from the fires of hell. He showed them how to make the sign of the cross, and he said the Our Father and the Ave Maria with them. He described the sacrament of baptism and offered it to their children and anyone who was sick.[75]

Like most Native North Americans, the inclusivist O'odham believed—in contrast to Kino's exclusivist Catholicism—that new beliefs and symbols could be added to existing ones. They experienced the world as full of mystery and the human condition as full of questions—they were unlikely to reject potential answers that might help make sense of the world and one's place within it. Of course, most of Kino's message on his first visit would have been lost in translation—both literally, because neither he nor the O'odham spoke each other's language particularly well, and more abstractly, because "un solo Dios verdadero" and "el fuego eterno del infierno" were not concepts that made sense in seventeenth-century O'odham religion, which was neither monotheistic nor punitive. Yet even at this first visit, his hosts seem to have recognized Kino as bringing new information and ideas. All but the most isolationist societies would appreciate his vivid tale of his journey and the places he knew that no O'odham had visited. The iconography of crosses and saints was easy to incorporate. Baptism and the story Kino told of a great flood probably had particular resonance—it should come as no surprise that water and flooding would hold tremendous significance in the desert, and indeed a flood plays a part in some versions of the O'odham creation story.[76]

Even if an eternal hell made little sense, Jesus might have been seen as a parallel to I'itoi—both of them beings somewhere between a common human and a creator or god. Sin and forgiveness could be translated into the O'odham concept of bringing things back into balance. Twenty-first-century O'odham elders have hypothesized that traditional O'odham values of respect and the obligation to share with outsiders were part of the reason that they welcomed Kino, as well as perhaps complementarities they saw between their own religious beliefs and Christian teachings. The O'odham certainly would have rejected European Christians' "great chain of being," which placed the Christian god on top of a hierarchical structure of the Catholic pope and European monarchs, below which sat multiple European classes and Native peoples who were to be their vassals, with enslaved people at the bottom. But inclusivist religions allow for picking and choosing. The fact that the missionaries relied on O'odham translators meant that Christianity was always interpreted through O'odham understandings. Seventeenth-century Jesuits talked a lot about the devil as a force active in daily life, trying to lure people away from God. Over time the O'odham developed a concept of the devil, jiawul (an O'odham pronunciation of the Spanish word "diablo"). Like other O'odham spirits, a jiawul was not evil. It represented things out of balance, and its presence ideally reminded people to return to their himdag.[77]

It's easy to understand why Spanish missionaries and administrators were delighted at much that they saw developing in Himuri and Sobaipuri towns—at the church building, at the houses that locals made for the priests, at the growing fields of sheep and the baptisms, at the lack of conflict after the violence of 1695 and the diplomacy of 1697. In Spanish eyes, all these things were preparation for reducción, which, to their annoyance, had not started but now seemed close at hand. Yet when one Spanish army officer met people who lived beside their agricultural fields outside the rancheria, he asked his O'odham guide, "Why they did not take these people into the village?" The guide's answer reveals that he thought the officer was a bit slow: "They had their lands there where they sowed and harvested their crops." When that was done, "they would withdraw to the pueblo." Between growing seasons, one's winter house might be more tightly clustered with others, but having to commute every day out to the fields would be a waste of time. Over and over, Spaniards told the spread-out River O'odham and the migrating Tohono and Hia-Ced O'odham to move permanently to a few central pueblos, but these few wandering Spaniards were hardly in a position to do any ordering. The people continued to live as they had before. They used the Spanish and Christianity to help their himdag, not change it.

A CONTINUING HIMDAG

Reading the accounts of travelers who passed through Himuri, Sobaipuri, Akimel, Tohono, and Hia-Ced O'odham country, from the earliest sixteenth-century Spanish explorations through U.S. expeditions in the nineteenth century, can give a historian a sense of déjà vu: *Haven't I read this account already?* Explorers enter a town and are greeted by jubilant crowds and abundant feasts. They sleep in hospitable guest accommodations and talk about religion and war deep into the night. They write about the potential of the region, imagining that its people will change to be more like them.

To the countless Spaniards who visited this region over the centuries, the O'odham river towns were always on the *verge* of change. In 1706, for example, Kino called Don Marcos's Himuri O'odham rancheria a "pueblo or incipient mission" with "a little church with its altar in which to say mass, and a large church begun, wheat, corn, beans, cattle, sheep, goats, more than 200 head, and droves of mares, all of which the natives are tending very well for the father whom they ask and hope to receive."[78] Reducción seemed so achievable in every place like this: There was food and space for many more families, especially if they would build the multistory adobe buildings of their Huhugam ancestors, so evident in the ruins along the Gila. Tohono O'odham families already visited Himuri rancherias like this one. Surely they would recognize the wisdom of moving in permanently. Surely reducción was imminent.

But it wasn't. The existing himdag worked just fine. The supplements of wheat and sheep added to the diversity of their economy and their culture but did not overturn them. Wheat and small domestic livestock fit well into the O'odham himdag, just as corn and potatoes from the Americas enriched but did not upend European ways of agriculture. Planting a winter crop of wheat gave River O'odham an additional harvest season. Horses made the Tohono O'odham trips to river towns easier. By the 1700s, alongside the corn, beans, and cotton growing in the river valleys of the Akimel, Sobaipuri, and Himuri O'odham rancherias, there were fields of wheat and, in many places, barley, black-eyed peas, and watermelons. Later in the eighteenth century, some farmers added garbanzos, oats, lentils, and onions as well as new crops from other parts of the Americas, including kidney beans and chile peppers. Grapevines and fig and pomegranate trees thrived in the dry conditions. Closer to the river, some people planted peach, apricot, and apple orchards. Some of the rancherias raised and bred not only sheep and goats but also chickens, donkeys, mules, and horses. Some developed herds of hundreds of cattle. These economies have lasted. Still today, the formerly Himuri O'odham town of Caborca is one of the breadbaskets of northern Mexico, growing wheat, corn, grapes, peaches, melons, cotton, and olives.[79]

Yet they repeatedly rejected nonsensical Spanish recommendations. Why not live close to fields when there was work to be done there? Why swelter in an adobe house all summer rather than enjoy the nighttime breeze that an open-air ramada allowed? Why wear heavy clothes all year round rather than what fit each season, which in summer was breechcloths held by a belt for men, cotton skirts for women, and nothing at all for children? Why shouldn't O'odham live in different, complementary ways? People worked at what they were supposed to do, and they tried to be generous—values that they learned in childhood. When they erred, as humans do, their community pressured them, but not with physical punishment.[80]

More significant changes came as a result of the war against the Jocomes, Janos, and Apaches. In retaliation for the victories that O'odham forces had over Jocomes in the fall of 1697, in February 1698 a large force of around three hundred Jocomes attacked a Himuri town while most of the men were off on a trading expedition, as they often were in February. The enemies killed two Himuri women, sacked the town, burned the houses and the small church, and carried off horses, food, and all the small livestock before retiring to the hills.[81]

Therefore, the Sobaipuri were on alert when, a month later, in the early morning of March 30, 1698, the southernmost rancheria on the San Pedro River was attacked by a similar force. The men rushed out with their bows and arrows to fight. Sobaipuri in nearby rancherias saw smoke rising from the scene of the fighting and quickly put together a large force of five hundred men, including Coro and some Tohono O'odham men who were visiting. By the time the Sobaipuri and Tohono O'odham force arrived, the townspeople had fled, and the raiders had settled in to have a meal before riding away. Jocome women had come with the force to feed the fighters and process food from the town to take home. They were roasting and drying the meat from the cows and horses they had killed and parching corn to make more transportable cornmeal. As the raiders ate and worked, the O'odham force surrounded the rancheria, and Coro went to parley with the leader of the Jocome party, Capotiari. According to Coro's later account, Capotiari called Coro and his people "not men but women" and scoffed at them for allying themselves with the Spaniards, who "were not brave," saying that "frequently he had killed many of them." In the fighting that ensued, Coro killed Capotiari, and the attackers fled. The O'odham fell upon them as they tried to get away, killing more than fifty men and women.[82]

Despite this victory, the Sobaipuri of the upper San Pedro River decided not to tempt fate and risk another attack. For the O'odham, this war had no higher purpose, the way spreading the Great Peace did for the Mohawks or conquests did for crusading conquistadors. It was a defensive war, to protect against destructive raiding. Instead of rebuilding the destroyed rancheria, all of the O'odham on the southern half of the San Pedro moved to the relative safety of the Santa Cruz River, to the west. In moving, they could have settled into the kind of compact mission towns the Spanish had in mind by either moving in with an existing rancheria or building such a town from the population of the evacuated rancherias. Instead they chose an unoccupied spot to build spread-out rancherias just like they had before. By September, at least five hundred former San Pedro River residents, including Coro and his family, were living and farming along Sonoita Creek, a tributary of the Santa Cruz River. As Kino recorded, along this stretch now, "everywhere there were many more people and more houses than six months before," not concentrated but instead almost contiguous, with newly planted irrigated fields.[83]

Humari and the Sobaipuri who lived on the northern end of the San Pedro, nearer to the Gila, remained there for a time and continued to fight Jocomes and Apaches in coordination with the other O'odham. In 1699, Humari used the Spanish to try to make peace with some of the raiders. Kino had given him a cross and some gifts to take to the Hopi towns in the north, who Kino believed were ripe for conversion, but he didn't have any priests to send that far—nearly five hundred miles north of Mission Dolores de Cosari. But to the Sobaipuri, carrying Kino's message and gifts more than three hundred miles, where raiders were known to ride, seemed a low priority and a dangerous mission. Instead, Humari used the Spanish gifts to attempt peace with an Apache band. News of a secret O'odham–Apache peace would have thrown Spanish settlements in Sonora into terror—might their close neighbors and best allies have switched sides?—but Humari, after the deal, wisely had his messengers to Kino describe it as a joint O'odham–Spanish–Apache peace that would bring security to Sonora. Kino saw the sense in the plan and wrote to his superior, portraying the news as a prize for Kino's efforts and an opening of the entire region to mission work. Bells rang in churches throughout New Mexico and Sonora to celebrate the peace and the prospect that, as his Jesuit superior wrote back to Kino, "it appears that the prophecy . . . is fulfilled that the Apaches were to be reduced and embrace our holy faith."[84]

That judgment was a bit hasty. The peace did not hold, and in any case, the Apaches had certainly not agreed to move into Spanish missions, a suggestion Humari would not have made to them anyway. Humari was pursuing his own people's interests, not spreading Christianity. Ultimately, Humari's Ojio and the surrounding rancherias also moved west, in their case farther north on the San Pedro to the Gila, to combine defenses with the Akimel O'odham and the Piipaash. These moves left the San Pedro Valley as a buffer zone where no one lived but where O'odham women and men still gathered resources. The Spanish did not build a fort there, despite Sobaipuri requests, until 1772, seventy-five years after Kino's first visit, and even then its feeble size didn't do much good, and raids continued.[85]

In the following years, raids increased on the Sobaipuri and Akimel O'odham, Himuris and other O'odham to the south, and Spanish settlements in Sonora. A military officer wrote to Kino in 1703 that the enemies "are now becoming so bold, that there is no hope of any remedy, if God Our Lord doesn't provide it through our friends the Pimas." The Spanish forces "want to do something but we cannot for lack of equipment, etc."[86] Spanish forces were nearly impotent against the raiders, often merely riding around, Don Quixote–like, unable to find a target. They needed O'odham assistance more than the O'odham needed them. Losing could drive the Spanish from the north entirely, undermining Spain's imperial claims. As a Spanish soldier summarized, if it hadn't been for the O'odham, raiders "would have burned and annihilated everything, not leaving even a memory of Spanish missions, churches, mines or inhabitants."[87] Decades later, in the late 1700s, a missionary reflected that occasional O'odham success over the Apaches and their allies "is the only thing which to some extent restrains them and has kept them from destroying Sonora completely."[88] Spain never was able to end the warfare on its northern frontier.

Defending, moving, adding what was useful—all served the goal of maintaining O'odham himdag. For example, at Bac around 1700,

Kino remarked on the rancheria's hundreds of bushels of stored wheat, sheep, goats, and cattle that "had a lot of tallow and fat because of the excellent pastures." Bac's "fields and farmlands were so numerous and watered by so many irrigation canals ... that they would be enough for another city like Mexico City."[89] Every fall, Bac and neighboring rancherias were packed with Tohono O'odham families there for the season.[90] In 1701, Kino did note that more than two hundred of Bac's cattle had wandered away while the people were off gathering saguaro. Bac's priorities had not changed: Saguaro season was saguaro season, and they could collect the cattle in their own good time.[91]

An interaction between the Akimel O'odham and foreign rancherias to their northwest in what's now California reveals how Native people used Spaniards to expand their networks of reciprocity. In 1701, it hadn't rained in the Gila Valley as much as usual, and the crops had suffered. The Akimel O'odham and the Piipaash had heard that a people to the northwest "had an abundance of provisions, corn, beans, squash." These people were not part of the regular O'odham network of allies and trading partners, and the Akimel O'odham had no history of reciprocity to draw on with them or anything much at the moment to trade, except the novelty of their Spanish connections. So around three hundred Akimel O'odham and Piipaash persuaded Kino to venture with them across the Gila River to make contact. The people there had never heard of horses or mules, so when the O'odham and Piipaash told them that "our horses ran faster than the fastest Natives," they didn't believe it, and "it was necessary to prove it to them." An O'odham who had come with Kino saddled a horse and raced several local runners. He let them get a little ahead, "and they were very pleased, until he left them far behind, marveling and amazed." These initial interactions went well, and the Akimel O'odham and Piipaash "returned well loaded with all kinds of provisions" and with new connections for the future.[92]

Like the River O'odham, the Tohono O'odham incorporated selected Spanish products, some as part of their seasonal trips to river towns and some at home. They began growing some Spanish crops and animals, especially sheep, whose wool gave them a more direct source of material for clothing than cotton bought from the river towns. But the Hia-Ced O'odham seem to have found hardly anything worth adopting from the Spanish. They greeted Spanish visitors with friendly reciprocity and accepted gifts of metal knives and needles, but raising livestock and wheat would be useless to the Hia-Ced economy, and the idea of moving permanently to the river towns was laughable. As David Martínez suggests, the Hia-Ced "found the Spanish to be simply ignorant about the land in which they have lived for countless generations and regarded their suggestion about moving to be nothing short of foolishness."[93]

Even the Spanish—blind to how well the O'odham himdag worked—could see that the mandate of reducción around a mission was a farce. For most of the years when Kino was supervising church building at a dozen rancherias, he and Campos were the only priests in all of northern O'odham country. In June 1698, a new priest, Father Gaspar de las Barillas, was stationed at Caborca, where Father Saeta had been killed three years before. Despite an initial welcome, Barillas started to feel nervous and left after only a month and didn't return. In the coming decades, additional priests arrived but soon died or left because they were sick, frightened, or recalled for a mission elsewhere in Mexico. Kino, Campos, and any other priests who were around traveled circuits to say mass at multiple churches, yet the numbers and the distances meant that most of these churches had no priest the vast majority of the time.[94]

When Kino died, in 1711, he was replaced at Mission Dolores de Cosari, and Campos continued to make regular expeditions around O'odham country and to put pressure on his superiors to send more priests. Only in 1731—twenty years after Kino's death—did another set of priests come to Sobaipuri country. They tried to impose stricter mission requirements than Kino ever had, and they had no success at all. By 1734 all but one of them had died or left, and even in Himuri country only three priests remained.[95]

When larger numbers of Spaniards came in the mid-eighteenth century and attempted to institute control, the O'odham struck back to keep them in line. First, in southern Sonora, Spanish colonists began to establish mines and farms, angering the O'odham there, who spread news of these new Spanish threats to the northern O'odham. Spanish officials hoped that large numbers of colonists (who were usually of mixed European and Native descent) might provide protection against Apaches, but they also endangered relations with the O'odham by squatting and letting their livestock graze on lands that belonged to the O'odham. (Spaniards declared the lands owned by no one, because they were not populated year-round.) Then a new group of missionaries came north in the 1730s and '40s who assumed that the O'odham, after four decades of Christianization, must be far down the road to reducción. As at Tubutama and Caborca earlier, these new priests overstepped, demanding compliance with their terms and punishing with violence.[96]

All this pressure led to conflict first in the south and then, in 1751, among the few missions in northern O'odham country. At a small rancheria at the top of the Altar River, a man named Oacpicagigua urged all of the Himuri rancherias to expel missionaries and other Spaniards who lived among them. He recalled from his own experience in fighting alongside Spanish soldiers against the Comcaac that the Spanish had few forces and were too weak to enforce the demands that the new missionaries were making. The Hia-Ced O'odham at Sonoyta had recently accepted a missionary to live with them. With Oacpicagigua's encouragement they killed the missionary and never again allowed a mission. Throughout northern O'odham country, churches were brought down, lands were reclaimed, and more than a hundred people lay dead. Not everyone rallied to the cause, and Oacpicagigua died in one of the skirmishes with the Spanish, but the Spanish ended up backing down. The Spanish governor of Sonora and Sinaloa knew he had only about 140 soldiers and militia with which to counter what he estimated were three thousand O'odham fighters, so he retreated, and the missions were largely abandoned.[97]

Another reason many O'odham rejected missions was that by the mid-eighteenth century they had a reputation as places of sickness. As epidemics increased over the course of that century, smallpox in particular hit missions and the towns around them hard, because of their more crowded conditions and closer contact with foreigners. Missionary Ignaz Pfefferkorn noted that, "although many Spaniards die also, smallpox kills incomparably more Indians."[98] Other diseases, though, seemed to hit the Spaniards harder, probably because O'odham practices of quarantine were reasonably effective, while reducción facilitated disease transmission. Spreading out into smaller groups away from the towns was the best protection. Over time, the populations of mission towns throughout Sonora declined, some because of deaths from disease and war, but perhaps even more because people left for safer places. Some missions became basically residences to care for—and often bury—elderly and sick people who could not safely or comfortably travel. It is easy to see how scholars could misinterpret these events from a purely Spanish point of view to conclude wrongly that disease wiped out the mission populations.[99]

When raids made it hard for rancherias on the frontier to farm safely, they called on other O'odham to augment their security and economic stability, as they had since the cities of the Huhugam had fallen. Sobaipuri and Himuri O'odham coordinated expeditions against their common enemies, and they invited groups of Tohono O'odham to live with them for longer seasons, some eventually moving in more or less permanently. Some Tohono O'odham young people married Sobaipuri or Himuri men or women. Most Tohono families continued to migrate seasonally, now sometimes joined by Sobaipuri or Himuri families. In the few places where missions actually existed, they served as useful guardians over the agricultural fields between planting and harvesting, freeing large numbers of O'odham either to go on the traditional Tohono O'odham seasonal migrations or make shorter resource-gathering trips.[100]

Gradually, the Sobaipuri who had moved to the Gila were incorporated into the Akimel O'odham. Some Sobaipuri and Himuri families became part of the larger nation known as Tohono O'odham. Other Himuri O'odham remained on the Altar and other rivers as the O'odham de Mexico. In the twentieth century, U.S. newspapers occasionally dramatically declared the extinction of the Sobaipuri. The Tucson *Arizona Citizen* declared Toribio Aragon, at his death in

1930, "the last survivor of the Sobaipuri braves," despite the fact that his grandchildren, great-grandchildren, and sister's descendants lived nearby, as did a woman who would die the following year, and whom the paper would also deem the last of the Sobaipuri. In fact, the people lived on among other O'odham, living the himdag of their ancestors.[101]

The Spanish could hardly complain that the Himuri, Sobaipuri, Akimel, Tohono, and Hia-Ced O'odham were not colonized—Spanish forces had their hands full to the south, east, and west. Even with O'odham and Opata military efforts against common enemies and with the few forts that the Spanish built, colonial settlements were always being besieged and often abandoned. The Spanish fought the Comcaac on the Gulf of California coast in the 1720s and battled on the Baja California Peninsula in the 1730s and '40s. In 1740, Yaquis and Mayos threw Spanish settlers out of the large region along Mexico's west coast south of the Sonora River, and southern O'odham people did the same, expelling Spaniards from mines and farms. Apache raids on Spanish settlements in northern Mexico only increased as more Apache bands moved south in the mid-1700s, pushed by Wichitas, Caddos, and Comanches.[102]

Facing these various sources of violence, the Spanish considered abandoning the region entirely. Even in southern Sonora, where substantial ranching had begun, Apache and Comcaac raids sent the colonists fleeing back to central Mexico or huddling close to the few Spanish forts. By the 1790s, a priest wrote, the former ranchers were refugees, "forced to get along wretchedly on a small farm and with the little stock remaining to them, or to exist on earnings from gold and silver mines or from trade." In southern Sonora, many relied on food from Native allies.[103]

Yet Spanish officials and missionaries continued to imagine that the northern O'odham might condense their lives into a few mission towns, preferably on the Apache frontier so they could protect Spanish mines and ranches. In a typical response, Sobaipuri leader Chachalaca of Tucson responded that his people would stay in the place they had chosen. He told Sonora's governor that during the 1751 violence against the missions, "I and my kinsmen were good, and anywhere we live we will continue to be loyal." The governor could only accept Chachalaca's answer. He blamed the "wandering spirit" of the Sobaipuri, even though, of course, they were insisting on doing the opposite of wandering: staying where they had built their rancherias. The Spanish had no power to make them do anything they didn't decide for themselves.[104]

CONCLUSION

In 1776, as colonists on the Atlantic coast were declaring their independence from the British empire, Spanish official Juan Bautista de Anza was warning the Spanish Empire not to make ambitious plans for the regions of northern Mexico. Nothing would work in Sonora, New Mexico, Texas, or California if colonists tried to take local people's crops or demanded too much of them. These colonies could exist only by serving Indigenous people. In the 1770s, Native people were as in control of this region as they had been a century before. Changes would come, including the building of an actual church at San Xavier del Bac in the 1780s and '90s, but the O'odham himdag would remain much the same until after the U.S. invasion, another seventy years later.[105]

Looking back from the 1970s, Anna Moore Shaw of the Gila River Indian Community reflected that Spanish, Mexican, and even early U.S. settlers "had little effect on the ... Pima [Akimel O'odham] way of life. It is true that many Indians now had a Spanish name as well as an Indian name, but the Pimas clung to their ancient values and legends." As much as the Spanish had tried to change how the O'odham lived, there had been nothing like the upheaval when the Huhugam fell.[106]

Well into the nineteenth century, the O'odham adopted what they found useful out of what outsiders brought. As the Western Apaches increased their range and power in the 1700s, the O'odham coordinated with one another and with the Spanish military. Some made Christian missions and priests part of their spiritual lives; sometimes they threw them out. They all rejected reducción.[107]

Today Christianity is part of himdag for most O'odham. There are churches throughout O'odham country. San Xavier del Bac has a large church complex, yet the flag of the Tohono O'odham Nation flies there, and songs at the masses are sung in O'odham and English. In addition to statues of the Virgin Mary and Saint Xavier, one of the founders of the Jesuit order, there is a statue of Kateri Tekakwitha, the Mohawk saint canonized in 2012. Pilgrimages to Magdalena, Sonora—one of the old Himuri towns—are an important part of O'odham Christianity. In Tohono O'odham elder Frances Manuel's youth, the people of Magdalena still prepared ramadas and houses for the pilgrims and fields for the horses to graze. In the twenty-first century, the town of Magdalena provides space for people to camp and park their cars and trucks every October. For those pilgrims who walk from Arizona and across the U.S.– Mexico border, local people all along the route give them water and food, continuing the centuries-old tradition of hospitality that the seventeenth-century O'odham gave to travelers.[108]

Writing in 1959, Akimel O'odham author George Webb titled his chapter on the time up to the early twentieth century "A Peaceful Life." He recalled that reciprocity continued to be essential to the O'odham himdag. "If you came to the home of another Pima, no matter what time of day, the first thing placed before you would be some kind of food. When you had travelled a long distance, your team was taken care of with water and feed. When Pimas visit among each other, when the visiting party leaves, they are given beans, corn, cactus syrup or melons to take home." In the summer, Tohono O'odham families took saguaro syrup and salt to the Akimel O'odham, "and we would give them beans and corn in exchange," Webb wrote, and "they would stay with us for a few days and help us harvest our wheat." Like their ancestors, Webb's grandmother made mesquite cakes, and his grandfather hunted for rabbits, quail, and deer with a bow and arrow. Most of the men and women went out to the fields in the morning to plant and tend corn, melons, wheat, tobacco, and cotton. A few women and children stayed home and brought lunch out to everyone, maybe "a little cactus syrup with whole wheat bread." Webb's history shows products the Akimel

O'odham had incorporated since the coming of the Spanish: melons, wheat, horses, and oxen to pull the plows they made. Yet, "up to the time I am remembering there had been no white people in our part of the country, except some Spanish explorers who passed through but never stayed." The River People "knew their seasons and planted their crops accordingly and they prospered." On wheat bread, the saguaro syrup still tasted as sweet.[109]

CHAPTER 6

QUAPAW DIPLOMACY

I N 2017, I SAT IN THE CLINTON PRESIDENTIAL LIBRARY AUDITO-
rium in Little Rock, Arkansas, watching Quapaw dancers and
listening to Tribal Historic Preservation Officer Everett Bandy
explain the origins of their traditional attire to an audience of middle school teachers. The single eagle feather and roach headdress
were what his ancestors had worn long ago for ceremonies and
feasts. The sleigh bells jingling around his knees were a nineteenth-
century replacement for the rings of clicking deer toes the men
once used. The women's ribboned blouses and skirts combined ancient skills with finely printed calico, first cut by Quapaws in the
late nineteenth century from flour sacks (the same kind of sacks
that my rural white foremothers also sewed into dresses and quilts).
Bandy explained that the men with huge feathered bustles who
danced fast and furious were the Quapaw fancy dancers, a style that
Quapaws adopted in the twentieth century as part of going to powwows, where many tribes meet and share their dances and styles of
dress.

The next dance, Bandy announced, would be the "Indian two-
step." As the name implies, eighteenth-century Quapaws and other
Native nations saw colonial French couples dancing and incorporated their style into their own repertoires. As the drumming and
singing resumed, the Quapaw dancers went out into the audience,
each inviting a partner to join the two-step. That was how I found
myself on Everett Bandy's arm at the head of a line of dancers. I was
there as a historian, speaking to the teachers about Quapaw history

in the eighteenth century, but I had a lot to learn too. As I concentrated on making my feet keep time to the Quapaw drums, I was feeling some of what French explorers, traders, and government officials had felt three centuries before me. The Quapaws were leading, and I was trying to keep up.

In 1673, the French explorers Louis Jolliet and Jacques Marquette and their Native guides rowed in canoes from Canada across the Great Lakes, through the country of the Illinois Indians, down the Mississippi River, past the ruins of Cahokia, to the Quapaws' home on the Arkansas River, a hundred miles downriver from where Little Rock is today. The two Frenchmen came along at an opportune time. The Quapaws had many enemies, and by the 1670s some of them were armed with guns. Jolliet and Marquette and the French people who came after them would be welcomed by the Quapaws, taught their dances, and pulled into helping them.[1]

With astounding diplomatic skill, the Quapaws leveraged their location at the confluence of two major rivers in the heart of North America, the Mississippi and the Arkansas, to connect their towns to the global economy. They gave Europeans permission to establish a small post on Quapaw land so they could trade for valuable European goods, including guns. In fact, they turned mercantilism around by establishing an uneven trade relationship in their favor. They would not agree to trade exclusively with the French but instead kept the French from trading with people they wanted to keep from getting European goods. Although European goods and markets would bring change to Native economies, for the Quapaws the alliance with Europeans didn't dramatically change their lives. The French Empire—and later the Spanish and British—made the Quapaw Nation stronger, but not because these newcomers meant to do so. The Quapaws were in charge: They chose what they wanted and made European imperialism work for them for more than a century.

There are around five thousand Quapaws today, about the same number as in the 1600s. Even if you know that the Mohawks, the Cherokees, and the Apaches wielded substantial power, you may be surprised to hear how the relatively small Quapaw Nation expertly dominated the officials, traders, missionaries, and colonists of France, Spain, Britain, and, for a while, the United States.

QUAPAW COUNTRY IN THE
SEVENTEENTH CENTURY

In 1673, the Quapaws lived in several towns. Tongigua (Tą́wą žíka, "Small Town") was on the east bank of the Mississippi River, and on the west bank were: Osotouy (Ozó tiowé, "Bottom Land with Trees"), Imaha (Imąha, "Up River"), Tourima (Ttíoádimą, no clear translation), and their main town of Kappa (Okáxpaxti, from their word for Quapaw, meaning "the people who went downstream"). Oral tradition and linguistic evidence show that, in a previous generation, they and other Dhegiha Siouan peoples (Osages, Omahas, Poncas, and Kaws) had migrated to the Mississippi River together. The Quapaws had settled on the Mississippi "downstream" from the others. Today the Quapaws speculate that either they came west as part of the migrations to join Cahokia's realm and moved downstream after its fall or came in the early 1600s, fleeing Haudenosaunee-related violence.[2]

In this verdant place, the Mississippi River flows wide and slow as tributaries—the Arkansas, White, and St. Francis rivers—join its course toward the Gulf of Mexico. Smaller creeks and oxbow lakes add to the richness of the lowlands of the Quapaw homeland, where women farmed two or three crops of corn each year, plus beans and squashes, on fields stretching for miles beyond their towns. On the edges of the fields were grapevines and orchards of persimmons, mulberries, and plums. Europeans and Africans had introduced peaches and watermelons to Florida, and Native travelers had brought their seeds inland, so by the late 1600s there were peach trees in Quapaw orchards and watermelons among the squashes. In the region's wetlands, women gathered wild rice and roots, and men hunted ducks and other birds and small game. During the spring and fall, when large flocks of birds migrated up and down the Mississippi Flyway, men would try to catch some alive and pluck their wing feathers so that they could keep the hobbled birds in town to kill for fresh meat when needed. In the summer, large groups of men and women went on long hunts up the Arkansas River. Along its north bank, the Grand Prairie was a vast grassland that men had long burned clear of brush in order to encourage the kinds of grasses that bison like to eat. They regularly burned the undergrowth at the edges of the nearby woods to make them good spots to gather berries and other edible plants, which in turn attracted deer and bears that they could hunt. A little farther up the Arkansas and other western tributaries, the blue-green Boston Mountains, a range of the Ozarks, and the rolling green Ouachita Mountains held hardwood forests of oak and hickory that provided wood and nuts for people and animals. At the end of the hunt, Quapaws would float the bison hides, meat, and gathered products downriver in canoes to their towns.[3]

In 1673, the Quapaws' home was contested as well as productive. In addition to raids from the Northeast that continued from the Haudenosaunee-related wars, the Quapaws were fighting Tunicas, Yazoos, and Koroas to the south and Caddoan and Wichita peoples to the west, all of whom contested the Quapaws' right to the lands at the juncture of the Mississippi and Arkansas rivers. And just recently, people from the Southeast, including the Chickasaws, had begun to raid Quapaw towns for captives.

Native North Americans had taken human captives in warfare for as long as anyone could remember, usually the women and children who survived a battle, but it was Europeans who introduced a slave economy to North America. The founding of Virginia and South Carolina in the 1600s dramatically increased the market for enslaved Native Americans. Native war parties began to sell captives into these markets, and some began to raid for the purpose of capturing people to sell. As in the past, they mostly took women and children and killed the men who got in their way. By 1720, tens of thousands of Native people from the Atlantic coast to the Mississippi Valley had been captured, traded to Europeans for guns and other goods, and enslaved in colonies on the mainland or in the Caribbean. The slave market increased warfare and left everyone on edge. Quapaw women working in the fields outside of town were afraid that raiders would sweep in on horseback and carry them off to unknown fates.[4]

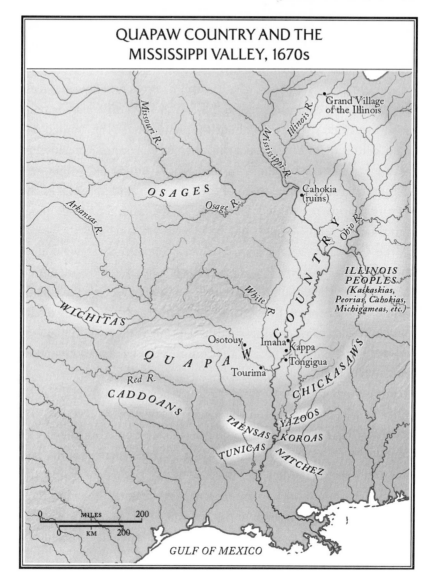

QUAPAW COUNTRY AND THE MISSISSIPPI VALLEY, 1670s

Surrounded by well-armed enemies and fearing raids, the Quapaws needed guns. However, like many other nations in the interior of the continent, they had no direct access to Europeans. Southeastern Native peoples armed with English guns cut the Quapaws off from English trade, while northeasterners prevented them from reaching out to Dutch, English, or French traders on the northern Atlantic coast. Apaches and hundreds of miles of prairie and plains lay between Quapaw country and Spanish New Mexico and Sonora. So when Jolliet and Marquette landed at their doorstep, the Quapaws were glad to see them, and they quickly moved to use the French to their own advantage.[5]

The Quapaws welcomed the handful of Frenchmen with a feast that the women had prepared, and afterward Quapaw leaders convened to decide what to do about the newcomers. The council debated killing them but, considering their need for arms, decided to make an alliance with them instead. They summoned Jolliet and Marquette and informed them of their decision, and the chief of the town of Kappa performed the dance of the calumet (peace pipe) with them.[6]

The Quapaws were specific with the French about what they wanted: guns, gunpowder, musket balls, metal goods including knives and needles, and French military support to secure their lands against their enemies. In return, they offered to be the allies of the French in the region, giving them a base on the Mississippi River and helping them to negotiate the complicated terrain and societies of the Mississippi Valley.

From the outset, the Quapaws proved they were in charge. When Jolliet and Marquette asked the Quapaws to provide them with a guide for the next leg of their journey down the Mississippi, the Quapaws refused and warned that the nations to the south "had guns and were their enemies." Because of the Quapaw warning, the Frenchmen turned back to Canada in 1673 without achieving their goal of tracing the Mississippi to the Gulf of Mexico. In the continent's interior, Europeans did not go where Native nations did not want them.[7]

After Jolliet and Marquette's visit, the Quapaws lost contact with their French allies and decided to seek them out again. In 1680, a Quapaw delegation traveled with some Osages and Chickasaws to the country of the Illinois Indians, where they knew some French missionaries were staying. They brought deerskins to trade and told the Frenchmen that they wanted to "establish a good relationship, and commerce with the French Nation." They offered to take the French farther than they had let Marquette and Jolliet go, so that "all the nations of the lower Mississippi would come to dance the Calumet of peace."[8] The Quapaws deliberately sought out Europeans as pliable and useful neighbors, so much so that they temporarily cooperated with their Chickasaw enemies in order to resume their dealings with the French.

Two years later, the French explorer René-Robert Cavelier, Sieur de La Salle, took the Quapaws up on their offer. As La Salle and his small contingent of Frenchmen and Illinois Indians floated down the Mississippi River toward the Quapaw town of Kappa, they heard drums and what sounded like war cries. As a precaution, they docked their canoes on an island in the Mississippi, where seven leaders from Kappa came across to meet them. One of the Illinois Indians translated into French the Quapaws' friendly invitation to come to Kappa.

To seal alliances, the Quapaws used ceremonies that were common in North America by the seventeenth century. They smoked the calumet with friendly visitors, regardless of whether the other party was European or Native, helping to envelop them in a kinlike relationship. And, like most Native peoples, the Quapaws practiced reciprocity. Each side in an alliance was supposed to give what it had. The women of Kappa prepared a feast and housing for the visitors, and the men introduced them to their neighbors. The French were to give guns and other goods that their people knew how to make. And it would all be confirmed by smoking the calumet and, of course, dancing. Though the French did not necessarily understand, the Quapaw dance incorporated them into the ways of the Quapaw Nation. They were teaching the French how to be allies.[9]

Of course, the French brought their own ceremonies and their own very different purpose: to colonize Quapaw country and the entire Mississippi Valley for the French Empire. After several days of Quapaw dances, feasts, and speeches, La Salle led the people of Kappa, along with his French and Indigenous contingent, to a hill outside town, where his men built and erected a cross and posted King Louis XIV's coat of arms. The Quapaws watched as the priest who had come with La Salle intoned, "O crux, ave, spes unica" ("Hail to the cross, our only hope"). The priest circled the cross three times as the Frenchmen shouted "Long live the king!" and discharged their muskets. Then La Salle spoke, with one of the Illinois interpreting into Quapaw and the French notary recording his words. We can only imagine the Quapaws' thoughts as they heard

> From the most high, invincible and victorious Prince Louis the Great, by the grace of God King of France and of Navarre, 14th of this name, this day 13 March 1682, with the assent of the nation of the Quapaws assembled at the town of Kappa and present in this place ... I take possession in the name of His Majesty and of his heirs and successors of his crown, of the country of Louisiana and of all its lands, provinces, countries, peoples, nations, mines, minerals, ports, harbors, seas, its streams and roads.

As the notary recorded, La Salle claimed the Mississippi Valley for King Louis XIV and named it Louisiana in his honor.[10]

The Quapaws recognized that La Salle was using ceremonial language and ritual to make a religious and political point, but if they understood the words "take possession" in Quapaw translation, they let them pass by without arguing. The idea that the French were taking possession of anything would have seemed absurd, given La Salle's small group of Frenchmen and the multiple villages of Quapaws surrounding them. The Quapaws were also eager to seal an alliance, and it made sense to do so with both their rituals and those of the French. La Salle had made it clear that his king was back in France, and he himself was just an emissary. The Quapaws extracted from La Salle a promise that "all those who would attack them would have to fight all the power of [the king] and of the French, his subjects, who would revenge the injury." La Salle handed out more goods and pledged that he and other Frenchmen would return with even more. As they joined their voices in one last round of "Long live the king!" the Quapaws were by no means surrendering sovereignty to this handful of visitors. On the contrary, they planned to use French alliance to bolster *Quapaw* sovereignty.

THE REAL LOUISIANA

If La Salle imagined that he was now in charge, he soon learned differently. Despite their previous promise that if a Frenchman came to them, the region's peoples would all come to "dance the Calumet of peace," in fact the Quapaws allowed La Salle to visit just those towns they wanted him to, exactly as they had with Marquette and Jolliet a decade earlier. The people of Kappa led La Salle and his men to each of the other Quapaw towns and then to the eight towns of the Taensas, allies who lived about two hundred miles down the Mississippi. On the way, the Quapaw guides literally steered La Salle away from the Chickasaws and Yazoos on the east bank of the Mississippi, explaining that they were "enemies of the Quapaws and Taensas."[11] As with the wars of Ossomocomuck and those between the Mohawks and their enemies, it's hard to know the historical reasons behind the enmity between the Quapaws and the Chickasaws and Yazoos, but, as in those other cases, what is clear is that La Salle's new friends were determined to shape his understanding of which people were his friends and which were his enemies.

When they reached the Taensas, the Quapaws led the French to peace ceremonies with seven hundred Taensas who assembled to meet them. But a group of Koroas who were visiting the Taensas joined in, which probably did not please the Quapaws. The Koroas were enemies of the Quapaws, who did not want to share their new French friends with them, but perhaps the Taensas were taking the opportunity to make peace, or perhaps the Taensas had never joined the Quapaw–Koroa conflict. In any case, this was Taensa territory, so the Quapaws did not have much choice.

A bit farther into their journey down the Mississippi, the French/Quapaw party reached a Tunica town. As they approached, the Quapaw guides informed La Salle that this was not a diplomatic stop. Instead, they said, he "had to get off there," and together they would "easily defeat them with our weapons." La Salle managed to persuade them that he did not have enough men with him to start a fight, and they reluctantly turned back toward Quapaw country, hoping the French would fight for them the next time.[12]

Although they could not persuade La Salle to fight a battle against the Tunicas for them, the Quapaws kept him from meeting them and possibly establishing an alliance with them. The act of introducing the French to their Taensa allies and to their Koroa enemies also probably heightened their diplomatic importance in the region—similar to when the Illinois guided La Salle to the towns of their Quapaw allies.

Although the Quapaws clearly were in charge, the French set about doing the kind of imperial naming and claiming possession that Europeans did everywhere they went. La Salle rewarded one of the lieutenants from his 1682 expedition, Henri de Tonti, with a land grant of Quapaw country and the exclusive French right to trade for furs at the mouth of the Arkansas River. Tonti returned to Quapaw country in the spring of 1686 with trade goods and an inflated sense of ownership, and he built a post he called the Fort and Mission of St. Étienne. Like Father Eusebio Kino in O'odham country, La Salle and Tonti laid a fictional foundation for European colonization, one that sent a meaningful signal to other Europeans that this place was French. Although these claims were meaningless to the Quapaws at the time, they foreshadowed how Europeans would exercise power once they had it here. They would take Native land and give it to themselves, along with the right to extract resources.

But for now Tonti's men referred to the post, more realistically, as "Aux Arcs," meaning "at the home of the Arkansas Indians"—the Quapaws. The French struggled to transliterate the sounds of the Quapaw language in their own alphabet; "Arkansas" was one of the ways they translated "Quapaw" (which Quapaws at the time pronounced more like "Okapa"). Thus the French called the river the Arkansas and used that word for the region and its Native people. The Quapaws called the ruddy river Ny-jitteh or Zhi-te, after the Quapaw word for "red."[13]

If the Quapaws had not wanted Tonti's post on their land, they would have destroyed it, a task that wouldn't have been difficult, since the post had only six men, surrounded by some five thousand

Quapaws and hundreds of thousands of their allies and enemies. Instead the Quapaws encouraged the French to establish a post. And why not? Like the Mohawks and the O'odham, they wanted trade. A permanent post would mean a steady supply of goods, and they had experience managing French ambition. By 1714 observers noted that Quapaw men were "almost all armed with guns," which they used "very skillfully."[14] But the supply line from Canada through the Great Lakes was tenuous, often cut off by Iroquoians and Algonquians in between. By the end of the 1680s, Tonti had failed to produce a profit and decided to abandon the post, and the Quapaws had to resort to traveling in order to purchase guns.

Of course, King Louis XIV of France had not sent emissaries around the globe to serve Indians. He wanted colonies to achieve the standard goals of empire: extract raw materials, sell manufactured goods for profit, bring non-Christians into the Christian faith, and ward off European rivals. But in the early years of Louisiana, the French were weak—so weak that they didn't even serve Quapaw

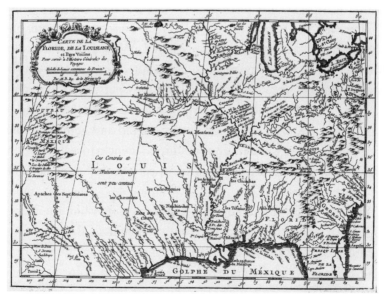

Carte de la Louisiane et pays voisins, pour servir a l'Histoire générale des voyages, by Jacques-Nicolas Bellin, 1757. The "Acansas" are the Quapaws.

LIBRARY OF CONGRESS, GEOGRAPHY AND MAP DIVISION

purposes well. The problem was not that the French lacked ambition. One look at any French map of North America from this period reveals the grandiose plans that the French had for Louisiana. On such maps, their imagined colony is enormous. It spans both sides of the Mississippi River, from the Appalachian Mountains to the Rockies and from the Gulf of Mexico to the Great Lakes.

Though the situation on the ground was nothing like the huge territorial coup envisioned on the maps, the French had ambitious plans for the region: plantations. In contrast to chilly French Canada, the lower Mississippi Valley had a climate that was ideal for growing sugar and indigo for the world market, and imperial planners knew that plantations could yield big profits. Using their plantation colonies in the Caribbean as a model, the French founded New Orleans in 1718. Situated near the mouth of the Mississippi, New Orleans was an ideal port for transporting goods in and out of Louisiana and connecting the French colony to the Gulf of Mexico, the Caribbean, and the Atlantic. The French began bringing enslaved Africans to build plantations in Louisiana—and Quapaw country was part of the plan.

However, the French crown lacked the funds to start this new colony on the scale that they envisioned. Wars against the Holy Roman Empire and England had bankrupted the country. In 1720, Scottish economist and speculator John Law persuaded the French crown to give him a monopoly over Louisiana trade. Law's Mississippi Company promised quick profits in gold and gems and long-term profits from plantation agriculture. French investors poured money into the Mississippi Company, certain that Louisiana was the next big thing.

Eventually, sugar and cotton plantations would line the Mississippi River and drive Quapaws from their homes. But that future was still a century away. For the time being, the Quapaws welcomed the French and happily granted them a plot of land for the French "Arkansas Post," near Kappa. They hoped it would finally establish the steady access to French trade they had been trying to secure for several decades.

Welcoming a contingent of outsiders and giving them a place to live was nothing new in North America generally or in Quapaw country specifically. Sometimes these were refugees fleeing trouble at home, and sometimes they were there for diplomatic purposes, somewhat like an embassy of a foreign nation today. A group of Michigameas (one of the Illinois peoples) had a village near the Quapaw town of Tourima, which helped to keep the peace between the Quapaws and the Illinois by providing steady communication between the two peoples. Living near an ally was traditionally a sign of good relations, so the Quapaws had no reason to resist a small European settlement on their land. And, for now, no one knew that European colonialism would grow into a population of more than five million by 1800—and twenty-three million by 1850—a neighbor so large and powerful that no enemy or ally was safe, even if Native peoples on the Atlantic had some early evidence of colonial numbers large enough to realize imperial ambitions. By 1720 the English colonial regions of New England and the Chesapeake were both large enough—each with populations of more than one hundred thousand—to push out or surround those regions' Native nations.[15]

John Law's Mississippi Company did have grand ambitions for its day. Its two purposes for Arkansas Post were to guard shipments going up and down the Mississippi and to transform Quapaw country into an agricultural colony, where Frenchmen and their slaves and servants would grow wheat and other food for themselves and to send to New Orleans. In the summer of 1721, the first commandant, Lieutenant Claude Guerin de La Boulaye, arrived with a dozen soldiers plus nearly a hundred laborers, both indentured Europeans and enslaved Africans. Their orders were to clear the land and prepare for the French colonists who would receive land grants.

These wheat farms foretold the nineteenth-century future of cotton plantations, and they might have begun to encroach on Quapaw sovereignty even in the eighteenth century had it not been for the fact that, by the time the slaves and servants arrived, news had spread in France that no gold or gems had been found in Louisiana. Investors sold their shares in a panic. John Law's company crashed, and he fled France. The French effort was so hopeless that it is possible the Quapaws never even knew of French plans to transform their nation into plantations. The Quapaws were just disappointed that the French post, staffed with a tiny number of French soldiers, had failed to provide them with any real protection or a steady supply of European products.[16]

SEEKING REFUGE WITH THE QUAPAWS

The Quapaws' world was changing in the early 1700s. In 1698, a devastating smallpox outbreak had killed several hundred people. The people of the Quapaw town of Tongigua decided to move from the east side of the Mississippi to the west, in order to be closer to the other towns of their nation. Once there, Tongigua eventually merged with the town of Tourima. In 1721, the people of Kappa moved away from their prominent but vulnerable location on the Mississippi and built a new town on the Arkansas River, closer to the other Quapaw towns. Around the same time, the town of Imaha also moved south to the Arkansas River, where it would eventually merge into the remaining Quapaw towns. As the Quapaws slowly drew closer together, they abandoned their land claims on the east side of the Mississippi, and the two previously separate towns that combined learned to live as one, probably governed by a form of joint leadership.[17]

Meanwhile, after John Law's Mississippi Company failed, it had withdrawn from the Arkansas River by 1722, taking its slaves and most of its indentured servants away but leaving behind about forty French men, women, and children, who were suddenly refugees in Quapaw territory. The Quapaws rescued them and allowed them to establish their own small village near Osotouy, the town whose name in Quapaw meant "bottom land with trees." Women from Osotouy had cleared some land on the banks of the Arkansas River, and the Quapaws offered the abandoned French settlers the chance to farm there. Those farming attempts were not particularly successful, so the Frenchmen started hunting with Quapaw men and selling furs to New Orleans.[18]

If the Quapaws pitied these French people, it was not because their situation was unusual. In this era, because of war and slave raiding, both Native and European individuals sometimes found themselves far from home, unable to return and unsure of how to build a new life. And it was not unusual for nations that had suffered population loss from disease and warfare to invite refugees to stay, as individual immigrants or sometimes as entire towns.[19]

Over the years, this French refugee town grew and prospered, on Quapaw terms. Visitors in the 1720s who traveled from the Mississippi River up the Arkansas River would first see Osotouy on the north bank. If it was late summer or fall, the water would be low, and Osotouy would appear on a high bluff, three stories above the river; but in the high waters of spring, the bluff would be much less imposing, only a few feet above the waterline. Osotouy's forty or so large houses were home to between three hundred and four hundred Quapaws. Osotouy protected the refugee village, which was just over a mile north-northwest and inland of Osotouy, from anyone approaching on the river. And the refugee village was much smaller: just under fifty men, women, and children. Although Europeans wanted to convert Indigenous people to their ways, in fact, the residents of the small French town became more like Quapaws. As the years went on, some married and had children with Quapaws and became part of Quapaw lineages, as well as their fictive ties of kinship. A Frenchman visiting in 1758 called the two communities "more like brothers than like neighbors."[20]

The refugee village became known throughout the region as a place where people running away from French authority could find help. If you could make your way to the main Quapaw religious house, you could ask for Quapaw protection and permission to live in the refugee village. A Quapaw religious leader would hear your case and decide whether to grant asylum. The refugee village grew as the Quapaws accepted Louisiana's deserting soldiers, accused criminals, and people escaping indentured servitude and slavery.

French officials called the refugee community voyageurs—unlicensed traders—and the British called them "the few Banditti at Arkansas."[21] They did not fit well with Europeans' imperial self-image. To the Quapaws, though, there was no contradiction between the vulnerable status of the refugee community and European empires—empires had proved weak and dependent throughout their history in the Mississippi Valley.

Other Native people also sought Quapaw protection. Some enslaved Native Americans escaped and moved into the voyageur town, and others may have been adopted into Quapaw families. Newcomers all gained security and access to French trade, as they added to Quapaw security and prosperity. Still, the Quapaws did not accept all refugees. When they went to war against the Natchez in the early 1730s, for example, and captured Native enemies or enslaved Africans in battle, they killed them or ransomed them to the French.[22]

Even the soldiers in Arkansas Post depended on Quapaw protection. Originally, Commandant La Boulaye had built Arkansas Post as a small fort near the Mississippi River to guard the company's commerce, which supposedly would soon clog the river. But as La Boulaye sat in his tiny post, understaffed because of desertion and illness, he thought about the well-armed Chickasaws and others who, in the absence of any actual convoys to attack, might raid his post for its armaments and provisions. After Kappa moved up the Arkansas River to be closer to the other Quapaw towns, La Boulaye followed a few months later. He and his men built a new fort close to Osotouy and the voyageur settlement, which was just getting started. The explanation was that there they could "live more conveniently," even though their mission was to guard the convoys on the Mississippi, a task that would be less "convenient" from the new location. But being near the Quapaws and the voyageur settlement was safer, even if it came at the expense of imperialism.[23]

The French eventually recalled La Boulaye and his small garrison, after which they could not supply Quapaw demands or come close to holding up their end of the bargain as allies and trading partners. Occasionally, a small group of traders would venture north from New Orleans, but their sporadic visits did not supply the weapons the Quapaws needed to defend themselves from their many enemies. By the mid-1720s the French were so weak in Louisiana that—far from colonizing the Quapaws, as their grand maps suggested—most had retreated to New Orleans. And those strag-glers left behind had been incorporated into the Quapaw Nation.

THE NATCHEZ WAR AND QUAPAW OPPORTUNITY

The French did continue to build plantations on the outskirts of New Orleans and in one other location: the lands of the Natchez Indians, on the Mississippi River halfway between Quapaw country and New Orleans (near today's Natchez, Mississippi). In contrast to the small Arkansas Post and the refugee voyageur settlement on Quapaw lands, large numbers of outsiders came to Natchez lands to grow tobacco as a cash crop. Over the course of the 1720s, these plantations grew to almost three hundred enslaved men, women, and children and more than four hundred French people. This pop-ulation and its use of the territory were not at all what the Natchez had in mind, but, with the arrogance of colonizers, the French per-suaded themselves that they could just take this land. They were dead wrong.[24]

Late in 1729, news arrived in the Quapaw Nation that the Natchez, along with their allied Koroas and Yazoos, had massacred the French who lived near them. The informant invited the Qua-paws to join the Natchez side and help expel the French from Lou-isiana. It was true that, on the morning of November 28, 1729, a group of Natchez warriors had arrived at the French fort near their towns. They sang and danced their calumet with the commandant while other groups went to the French houses and asked to borrow guns for a hunting expedition, promising to bring back deer meat to share. Others traded corn and chickens for gunpowder and musket balls. It was a deception: They used the guns to kill nearly all the Frenchmen, including the commandant and the Jesuit priest. They captured most of the French women and children, the indentured servants, and the enslaved Africans and proceeded to destroy the French houses, fort, and tobacco crop. The Koroas and Yazoos did the same with the small number of French near them.[25]

The Natchez had more in common with their Mississippian ancestors than most of their contemporaries did. Long after nearly everyone else in the Mississippi Valley had left behind the old hierarchical ways, the Natchez retained a fairly powerful nobility. These Natchez rulers were flabbergasted at the French arrogance. They had initially allowed French settlements, with the intention of making the French into a subordinate state, something they had done occasionally with Native settlements. When the French proved less subordinate than the Natchez expected, they used violence to try to bring the French in line, just as they had with other Indians in the past.

After that bloody day in November, the French retaliated, in what became known as the Natchez War. Both sides solicited the Quapaws' help. By the summer of 1730 the Chickasaws were supporting the Natchez, Yazoos, and Koroas, and they sent invitations to the Quapaws, Choctaws, Cherokees, Miamis, and several Illinois peoples to join with them against the French. The invitations promised that the Chickasaws would provide English military supplies for the war effort.[26]

But the Quapaws chose the French, as did most other Native nations in the Mississippi Valley. The Quapaws had fought against the Natchez, Koroas, and Chickasaws in the past, and they knew the French gave them the best chance of establishing a permanent supply of European goods. Some Quapaws may have advocated taking the Natchez side, but 1729 was long before Indians and Europeans divided along racial lines in the Mississippi Valley. The Quapaws, not surprisingly, chose their new and well-supplied friends over their longtime enemies.

Although the Quapaws declared to the French that "while there was a [Quapaw] in the world, the Natchez and the Yazoos would not be without an enemy," they did not actually fight much.[27] Upon hearing the first French call for help, a group of Quapaw warriors did quickly set off for Natchez country, but after waiting a couple of weeks while the French forces organized themselves in New Orleans, they sent word that, "tired of hearing no news of the French Army," they were going home.[28] Beginning early in 1730, Quapaw

Quapaw warriors in A. Antoine de Saint-Gervais,
Nouvel album des peuples, Paris, 1835.
LIBRARY OF CONGRESS

war parties sporadically attacked the Natchez as well as the Yazoos and Koroas. Occasionally they arrived in a French post to announce that they had captured, tortured, and killed a Natchez, and the French rewarded them each time. Whether the Quapaws really had captured a Natchez or not, the French were not in a position to judge.[29]

Despite their heated rhetoric, the Quapaws never made the Natchez War their highest priority. Even so, by combining their fighting power, the French, Quapaws, Tunicas, Choctaws, and other enemies of the Natchez won the Natchez War, killing many Natchez, selling hundreds of others into slavery, and driving them from their lands. Survivors took refuge with the Chickasaws, who were powerful enough to protect them.[30]

And then the French made a mistake. Seduced by their own self-importance and ignoring the fact that they owed the victory over the Natchez to allies who would not necessarily follow them into another war, the French called for a full-scale war against the powerful Chickasaws. After all, Louisiana was a French colony in their view.

The Quapaws would have been very glad to see the Chickasaws defeated. Chickasaw raids had been one of the earliest motivations for forming a French alliance and acquiring guns. But times had changed. By moving the town of Tourima west of the Mississippi, clustering all of their towns closer together, and acquiring French firearms, the Quapaws had already discouraged Chickasaw raiding. The market for Indigenous slaves had also declined in Virginia and the Carolinas, after the Yamasee War demonstrated to colonists the dangers of encouraging slave raids in their own backyard. With the decline of that market, the Chickasaws now were less likely to raid the Quapaws at all. To top it all off, reigniting the Chickasaw conflict would be much more dangerous for the Quapaws than fighting the Natchez, because the Chickasaws were more heavily armed from their steady trade with Charleston. With six hundred warriors, they were not the largest nation in the region, but they had a fearsome reputation, and the extra two hundred or so Natchez warriors who had survived their own war with the French added to their strength.

Even the French officials couldn't agree on whether fighting the Chickasaws was a good idea. Mobile Commandant Bernard Diron d'Artaguiette warned that the Chickasaws were strong enough to "bar the Mississippi to us for more than one hundred leagues."[31] But Louisiana's governor believed the French could take them on. With the arrogance of a colonizer who didn't truly understand the region, he decided that the best way to deal with the Chickasaws was "to destroy them without fail."[32]

When the French tried to increase their military presence on the Mississippi River, the Chickasaws proved that Commandant d'Artaguiette's fear was warranted. In the winter of 1735–36, a French convoy of six boats arrived in the Quapaw towns with a tale of their narrow escape from a Chickasaw attack on the Mississippi, and another French-led convoy heading north from Quapaw country with a boatload of gunpowder was fired on from the banks of the Mississippi by a group of Chickasaws. Unluckier than the other convoy, all but two of the men on board the boat were killed, and the Chickasaws captured those two along with the gunpowder. A Frenchman noted the irony: "The gunpowder that was supposed to be used for the war against the Chickasaws would go toward their own defense."[33]

The Quapaws tended to the first convoy's Frenchmen when they arrived, battered and terrified from their narrow escape, and they reasoned that a major French campaign against the Chickasaws might be of some benefit, so they hoped for French success but didn't offer more. The French didn't ask the Quapaws for military assistance at first, because the campaign's commander, the Sieur de Bienville, formerly governor of Louisiana, decided to attack the Chickasaws by pushing north from Mobile through Choctaw country—what is now Alabama and Mississippi. The large force that departed Mobile in April 1736 included French regular army troops, French white and Black colonists, enslaved Africans, and more than twelve hundred Choctaws. The Choctaws had some of the same reservations about the venture as the Quapaws, but they went along to see if it turned out to be a good opportunity to strike their Chickasaw enemies.

The force made camp seven leagues (about twenty-one miles) from the main Chickasaw town, which was heavily fortified with tall wooden palisades. The Chickasaws had needed strong defenses against many enemies in recent decades. If Bienville had been fighting in England or the Netherlands, at this point he would have begun a siege, starting with a zigzag trench from his base camp to a trench parallel to the target, upon which his men would mount the artillery. From there, they would gradually take more ground with more zigzag and parallel trenches until they were close enough to fire on the Chickasaw fort without being overly vulnerable to counterattack. But Bienville assumed that Native fortifications were unsophisticated, so he had not brought heavy artillery or enough supplies for a siege. His heart sank at the sight of the Chickasaw walled city.[34]

Still, Bienville decided to go on the offensive. At least if he acted quickly, he could strike before the Choctaws abandoned the effort, as they had threatened to do even while still on the march toward the Chickasaws. Bienville's regular troops would attack the Chickasaw fort head-on, and then the entire force would sweep into the town. But the initiative did not go as planned. A hail of bullets rained down from the fort, taking down French soldiers, whose own shots merely lodged in the palisade walls and their earthen protec-

tions. Out of ammunition, with a hundred casualties and the Choctaws calling for retreat, Bienville abandoned his effort. Having
learned that he needed better preparation against this formidable
enemy, he wrote to his superiors in France for reinforcements and
siege equipment.[35]

Bienville sent a French engineer, the Sieur de Vergés, in the fall
of 1737 to discuss the next campaign with the Quapaws and specifically to determine if it would be easier to get supplies and troops up
the Mississippi River and from there to the Chickasaws by land
rather than by the former route from Mobile. When the Quapaws
began to describe the route they knew well, Vergés realized that if
the French had asked the Quapaws first, they could have saved
themselves the trouble of the disastrous attempt from Mobile.

From their towns, a group of Quapaws escorted Vergés up and
across the Mississippi and into enemy territory. They showed him
the best landing place for a large force (just north of present-day
Memphis), with the shortest route to the Chickasaw towns, and
they began to lead him along it. After they had walked for a few
hours, they climbed to the top of some bluffs, halted, and told Vergés that they were only twelve leagues (thirty-six miles) from the
Chickasaws, about a day and a half's march for an army. They also
explained that, while the road was good this time of year, it flooded
from January to July, so it would not work as an attack route in those
months. There was one river to cross between there and the Chickasaw towns, a river that was "negligible" from the late summer through
fall but "floods all this part of the Chickasaw country" in the late
winter and early spring. Vergés would have to take their word for it,
though. The Quapaws "did not wish to go any farther forward" into
Chickasaw country. Vergés returned to New Orleans with the Quapaws' information, which seemed too good to be true. Surely the
Chickasaws were farther from the Mississippi than that. But when
he and Bienville cross-checked the math with their surveys from
Mobile, they saw that the Quapaws were right. The French decided
to take the Quapaw route and advice and come the following fall.[36]

The Quapaws did help the French build a fort on land north of
their towns, where the small St. Francis River empties into the Mis-

sissippi. It would be the gathering point for supplies from New Orleans and the force of French soldiers, enslaved Africans, and Quapaw, Choctaw, and other Native warriors. When the fighting force had gathered, they crossed the Mississippi together and built a second fort on a plain protected by a small rise. The road the Quapaws had shown the French was comfortable enough for people on foot or riding a horse, but wagons hauling heavy artillery were a different matter. Bienville ordered his men—enslaved and free—to widen the road. He knew that his Native allies would refuse to do this kind of manual labor for him, so he didn't ask. In the meantime, more people poured into camp, including Frenchmen from Canada and the French posts in Illinois country, along with their Native allies.[37]

All this hubbub worried the Quapaws, who believed a surprise attack would be far safer. As the weeks dragged on, the French soldiers started complaining, too, about the long wait and the inadequate provisions. One French writer would later conclude, "Never had anyone seen, and perhaps no one would ever see, in this country an Army so strong and composed of so many different Nations; however, it stayed in this camp without undertaking anything from the month of August 1739, until the following March." By then it was raining, and the Quapaw contingent and most of the Choctaws and other Native allies had given up and gone home. Those who remained, without Native men to hunt game, began eating the horses that were supposed to pull the wagons to the battlefield. Bienville had no choice but to accept a Chickasaw peace offer.[38]

When that peace did not last, the French let their Native allies take charge of the war effort. The Quapaws and others coordinated surprise raids on the Chickasaws using French weapons but persuaded the French not to attempt another large-scale attack. The French paid the Quapaws for Chickasaw scalps and had to acknowledge that harassing the Chickasaws was the best they could do. French officers wanted Indigenous subordinates who would labor and fight when and where they were ordered. The reality on the ground always seemed to go differently from what the French had imagined, and once again Quapaw leaders and warriors made up their own minds about when and how to fight.[39]

The Natchez War changed the direction of Louisiana history. Importing enslaved Africans to work stolen Native land had proved too dangerous and expensive for the French in this place where they were far outnumbered by multiple Indigenous nations. Instead, the crown took over administration of the colony from the failed Mississippi Company. Plantations survived near New Orleans, but the French stopped the importation of new enslaved people and scaled back their goals: Louisiana would be another fur trade colony, like Canada.

The Natchez had demonstrated with French blood that Europeans could not take Native land by force without consequences, although ultimately the Natchez paid the greater price. To the Quapaws, having a few Europeans as dependents was as appealing as it had been to Wingina in Ossomocomuck initially, to the Mohawks and Mahicans with Dutch traders, and to the O'odham with Spanish priests and soldiers, as long as the Europeans were pliant. Indeed, to the Natchez, the French had at first seemed fine. By fighting in the Natchez War alongside the French, the Quapaws ensured that the French reestablished an Arkansas Post in Quapaw country and would keep it and its small garrison there after the war, at the Quapaws' request.

QUAPAW DIPLOMACY

Arkansas Post was especially important to the Quapaws because they ultimately received more goods as gifts from French officials than they did by exchanging deer and bison skins or anything else they produced. Whereas the French had wanted to make fortunes from plantations and now hoped to at least reap some profits from the fur trade, instead they ended up paying huge amounts of goods to the Quapaws simply for the privilege of being there at all. Essentially, the French paid tribute to their Quapaw landlords. This kind of relationship was so common throughout North America that one historian has termed it "the diplomatic gift economy."[40] Native nations required European officials to give guns, gunpowder, shot, knives, needles, cloth, blankets, and other goods as a regular part of maintaining their diplomatic relationship and presence on Native land.

By the mid-1700s the Quapaws were receiving annual payments, plus additional gifts whenever a new French official arrived or needed a particular service, such as a guide, interpreter, or military escort. The practice had developed in the Iroquoian and Algonquian relationships with the Dutch and English in the late 1600s and had been adopted by France's Native allies in Canada and the Great Lakes. By 1716 the governor of Canada was writing to his superiors that he needed gifts of six hundred guns, forty thousand pounds of gunpowder, and sixty thousand pounds of musket balls yearly "to maintain peace with the Indians and to prevent them trading with the English." A South Carolina merchant represented many a frustrated European official when he wrote that "the Indians have been so used of late years to receive presents that they now expect it as a right belonging to them, and the English, French and Spaniards are in some measure become tributary to them."[41] Europeans wanted to believe that North America belonged to them, but in reality they were paying tribute or rent to have access to particular Native land and resources.

Over time, French gifts, food, and drink became part of some Quapaw rituals. When the Quapaws conducted diplomacy with allied Indigenous peoples, they included the French, but the French had to pay to play. Native diplomacy required countless feasts lasting many days, with gifts for everyone, all provided by the French government. By the 1750s, more losses from disease prompted more Quapaw consolidation. They established a new political position, that of great chief. It became the custom when the Quapaws chose a new great chief that the French provided presents. Often the new chief would travel to New Orleans with an entourage for a ceremony and more presents from the governor. Individual Quapaw leaders came to expect individual gifts. Across much of North America, Native leaders started wearing "peace medals" manufactured in Europe to signify their alliances with these makers of valuable things.

Historians in the past who overestimated European power

pointed to these medals as evidence that Europeans were influencing internal Native politics or that Native Americans were becoming dependent on European goods and officials. Some historians even believed that French commandants were choosing the Quapaws' great chief for them. It is true that, because most seventeenth- and eighteenth-century Native peoples required their leaders to provide for them, access to European trade became an expected part of Native leadership in many places. A chief who could not get European munitions and gunpowder could not guarantee his people's security, and a European medal signified the leader's individual connection to Europeans. But Europeans were important goods providers, not rulers. The medal conveyed the Native leader's power, not that of the Europeans.

King Louis XIV peace medal, c. 1693.
GILCREASE MUSEUM, TULSA, OKLAHOMA

Quapaw Chief Guedetonguay is a perfect example of how Native leaders used Europeans. In 1752, Arkansas Post commandant Paul Augustin Le Pelletier de La Houssaye reported that he had given Quapaw Great Chief Guedetonguay a medal. Other French officials interpreted this action as La Houssaye having made Guedetonguay great chief, and the Natchez commandant even suggested to the governor that they choose a different man to be chief. But Guedetonguay remained, and there is no reason to think he wasn't the Quapaws' choice, whose French medal confirmed him as their point person with the French. La Houssaye reported that he gave Guedetonguay "small presents occasionally" and in "many good ways" showed that the French recognized his importance. La Houssaye explained to the governor that these gifts were all part of his efforts in "managing" Guedetonguay.[42]

But "managing" merely meant persuading Guedetonguay to continue the Quapaw–French alliance. And the governor did not think the efforts were good enough. The following year, he was so afraid that the Quapaws might develop "an indifferent attitude toward us," which "gradually would have led them perhaps to abandon us," that he invited Guedetonguay and seventeen other leading Quapaw men to spend two weeks in New Orleans, where he "showed them great attention, and entertained them well."[43] The governor's superior in France warned him that "if on the one hand it is necessary, considering all the present circumstances, to humor the Indians," it was also essential not to "let them set a tone that accords neither with the king's authority nor the good of the colony." Still, with the approval of King Louis XV, the French ministry approved the decisions of the commandant and the governor.[44]

French interpreters translated Guedetonguay's title as "great chief of the Arkansas Nation," but the Quapaw towns still ruled themselves in daily matters, so he was probably more of a foreign minister or ambassador than a governing chief. He was in charge of diplomacy for the Quapaws and therefore was the most important Quapaw for the French to cultivate, yet he gave them little or no influence over his people's internal politics. Within the Quapaw towns and nation, other leaders balanced his power, including female chiefs with their own authority.[45]

The French government's payments to the Quapaws did not buy the French the right to tell the Quapaws what to do. Arkansas Post commandant La Houssaye gave as regularly as he could and still had to report to the governor of Louisiana that he had not been able to persuade the Quapaws to escort a convoy on the Mississippi "because they choose to occupy themselves with their corn harvest."[46]

The Quapaws and other Native allies of the French on the Mississippi usually prevented French traders from going any farther west to trade. Tens of thousands of Caddos, Wichitas, and Pawnees lived on the prairies, with easy access to bison on the Great Plains, but were unable to reach French posts because of the Quapaws, Osages, and other French allies in the Mississippi Valley. At the same time, the Apaches and the Comanches blocked the prairie peoples from reaching Spanish posts in New Mexico, Sonora, Chihuahua, and Coahuila. In 1719, one ambitious Frenchman, Jean-Baptiste Bénard de la Harpe, managed to travel up the Red River from southern Louisiana, then overland to the south bank of the Arkansas River, west of the Quapaws.

When they saw La Harpe's party approaching, Caddoans and Wichitas assembled a crowd of several thousand to tell him that they all wanted to ally with the French, who they hoped "would bring weapons for them to defend themselves against their enemies." In return, they promised bison hides, deerskins, salt, tobacco, horses, and Indigenous captives whom the French could enslave. They boasted that their country was "beautiful, full of domesticated bison, of horses and of deer." One chief even hinted at the prospect of gold, mentioning that upriver there was "some yellow metal," which "the Spanish value very highly." La Harpe enthusiastically promised to return.[47]

In a letter to investors, La Harpe gushed that the upper Arkansas Valley was so promising that it would become "one day the Peru of France." That is, it would provide to France the riches that the Incas' Peru had to Spain.[48] The French governor of Louisiana approved La Harpe's request to lead a return expedition along an easier route up the Mississippi to the Arkansas River. Along the way, he and his sixteen soldiers were to rest at Arkansas Post and buy provisions from the Quapaws. Their orders were to explore the route up the Arkansas River, carry goods to the Caddoans and Wichitas, and, "if he by chance encounters any Spaniards who are trying to settle on these rivers, he will oppose them, telling them that we discovered all this region before they did, and that in addition, all these rivers that flow into the Mississippi belong to the government of this province."[49]

Of course, no Europeans owned this place at all, and Spaniards were not the problem La Harpe encountered. When he got to the Arkansas River, his Quapaw allies refused to assist him with his expedition. When he asked them for information about going upriver, he "could not get any clarification from the Indians, who seemed displeased with his journey" and feared he "might make an alliance with nations that were their rivals." The women and old men began ostentatiously weeping, explaining through their tears that they were mourning his certain death, because Osage Indians would kill him if he canoed up the Arkansas. When he tried to trade for supplies, they would give no more provisions than a small amount of corn and beans, and they refused to sell him a canoe at any price, even though La Harpe could see more than thirty of them in their towns. In their frustration, the Frenchmen stole a canoe and began to paddle up the Arkansas River, but Quapaw runners caught up and told La Harpe, through an interpreter, that they were "hungry for killing Frenchmen." La Harpe returned the canoe and gave up on his mission. The Quapaws had ensured that Caddoan and Wichita country would not become France's Peru.[50]

French officials were frustrated with the power and independence of people they believed they had colonized. Louisiana governor Étienne Périer wrote in dismay that France's Native allies were "insolent," because "they think that they are necessary. Although they are very bad they make us pay them dearly." To a representative of France, it was tremendously frustrating that "the least little nation thinks itself our protector." Périer and every other French governor knew that France paid a great deal to Indians and did not get much in return, but they could not have been in the Mississippi Valley at all without the aid of the Quapaws and other Native allies.[51]

While they prevented unwanted French–Indigenous alliances, the Quapaws themselves would not be limited in which Europeans they traded with. They felt free to have friendly diplomatic relations with anyone they saw fit, including the British, France's archenemy for the entire eighteenth century. The Quapaws expertly used British overtures as leverage in their more established relationship with the French. In 1745, Quapaw leaders told the French commandant that the British "every day offer to establish themselves" at the Quapaw towns and that the Quapaws would invite them to take the place of the French if the commandant did not improve the supply of goods. The supply rapidly improved, even though the colony really couldn't afford such an increase.[52]

The Quapaws were skilled political strategists in all their relationships, not just with the French. Their diplomacy with the powerful Osage Nation, on the Missouri River, north of the Arkansas,
may have been the Quapaws' most important—and trickiest—
political relationship, because the Osages were by far the most powerful people in the region. Like the Quapaws, the Osages were using
trade and diplomacy with the French for security and economic
benefit, but unlike the Quapaws, the Osages developed a large trade
in furs and became an expansionist military power. Like the Mohawks a century earlier, the Osages used their access to guns to defeat their enemies and drive them away. They blockaded the Missouri
River, just as the Quapaws did with the Arkansas River, and they
expanded and eventually drove Caddoans and Wichitas off the
middle and upper Arkansas River entirely.

The Osages could be a far more dangerous enemy to the Quapaws than any Europeans. In the mid-1700s, the French had at most
a dozen soldiers on the lower Arkansas River, and the Quapaws had
a few hundred men of military age, while the Osages had around
two thousand skilled warriors. They didn't depend on the Quapaws
as guides and interpreters, as the French did. Osage power had been
growing just as other Native threats to the Quapaws subsided, with
the destruction of the Natchez, some cooperation with the Tunicas,
and less vulnerability to Chickasaw raids. And Osage expansion had
ended threats to the Quapaws from Caddoans and Wichitas to the
southwest, even if the Osages were a threat themselves. If the Quapaws could keep from becoming Osage victims, they could sustain
the relative peace and prosperity they had established in the late
1600s.

There were historical and cultural reasons for the Quapaws and
the Osages to be friends rather than enemies. Having migrated together from east of the Mississippi River in an earlier epoch, they
may have once been the same people or related peoples within the
same Mississippian chiefdom. They still spoke related Dhegiha
Siouan languages (similar to how French and Spanish are related
Romance languages) and had some cultural similarities in clan
structure, dance, and agriculture.

French documents don't record eighteenth-century Quapaw–Osage diplomacy, but evidence of Quapaw diplomatic practices suggests that they would have reminded the Osages of their shared history and interests and demonstrated that they weren't a threat. Perhaps their obligations of reciprocity included Osage protection of the Quapaws, while the Quapaws served as intermediaries for the Osages with the French. It worked. The Quapaws were one of the very few people the Osages did not fight in this era, and the two nations together managed to stop France's westward expansion.

ALLIED BUT NOT COLONIZED

In 1750, Europeans had been in the Americas for more than 250 years, and yet, in most of North America, Europeans' relationships with Native Americans were more likely to be based on Native customs and meeting Native needs than on those of the Europeans. For nearly eighty years, the Quapaws and the French had fought together, traded, and lived side by side, while at the same time the Quapaws and their Osage allies had held the French to an imperial standstill in their region. French priests had made few Native converts in the Mississippi Valley, French military strategists had more or less lost their war against the Chickasaws, and French profiteers and crown officials were despairing of ever making money from Louisiana. None of this was what the French had in mind when they set their sights on Louisiana.

The Quapaw diplomats who greeted Jolliet and Marquette in 1673 and traveled to see the French east of the Mississippi in 1680 would have been pleased with the situation in 1750. The Quapaws had established the "good relationship, and commerce" that they had proposed nearly a century earlier. While warfare and disease had brought trouble and sorrow, times were less volatile in many ways. The Osages were growing in power, and they were good friends to have, while other enemies had fled or were generally leaving the Quapaws alone.

If you visited the Quapaws in the 1750s, you would have seen them living securely in possession of their homeland. Their material lives had changed—had been enriched, most of them would probably say—by acquiring knives, needles, vermilion (red dye), cloth, wool blankets, shirts, and brandy. Of course, Europeans had brought destructive forces as well. Warfare was deadlier than in the past, and diseases carried from Europe had brought suffering and population loss. While Quapaw population numbers are nearly impossible to reconstruct, they almost certainly declined between 1680 and the end of the 1700s. As a result of a smaller population and the need for protection from enemies, the Quapaw towns had become less independent of one another than in the past. They lived closer to one another and conducted their foreign policy as one. They also now lived closer to non-Quapaws, including the village of voyageurs, refugees, and their families, the Michigamea Illinois town, and the small French military post. The support these outsiders gave to Quapaw security apparently outweighed any concerns the Quapaws had about inviting foreigners onto their lands.[53]

Everyday life and work remained much the same. In the fields outside their towns, Quapaw women grew most of the food that fed the people on the lower Arkansas River. Like the Mississippian peoples before them, they planted corn in raised, rounded beds. Beans grew up the cornstalks, and the vines and leaves of squashes, pumpkins, and melons diminished the need for weeding. On the edges of the fields, sunflowers raised their golden heads. Nearby were patches of greens and grapelike muscadine vines. Quapaw women planted, pruned, and nurtured fruit trees. Anyone passing through in the spring smelled the sweet blossoms and knew these were no ordinary woods. In summer, the plums and mulberries ripened, and in the fall women and children kept a close eye on the persimmons, to pick them in the short period after they became sweet enough to eat but had not yet become too soft or been stolen by birds. Along with peaches and watermelons, they added flavor to the Quapaws' standard fare of cornbread or grits stewed with bear oil.

Men from the Quapaw towns joined with men from the voyageur town to hunt deer and small game and to fish and hunt waterfowl in streams and wetlands. A few times each year, they packed food for several days, set off to the west with their guns and ammunition, and brought back bison, deer, and, if they were lucky, bear. The turkeys and geese in Quapaw towns provided meat more consistently.

On a small scale, Quapaws sold goods they produced to European, African, and Indigenous trading partners: smoked meats, pottery, wooden platters, and dugout canoes. In towns throughout the region, Native people and Europeans alike ate from vessels made by Quapaws or neighboring Indians, or made in France, England, Italy, or Mexico. The Quapaws lived in the same kinds of houses their ancestors had, made of a river-cane frame filled with plaster and roofed with thatch, while most of the French built wooden houses in the style of their ancestors. But the Quapaws had chosen not to hunt and trade in large volumes. One traveler noted in the 1760s, "They hunt little more than for their common subsistence."[54]

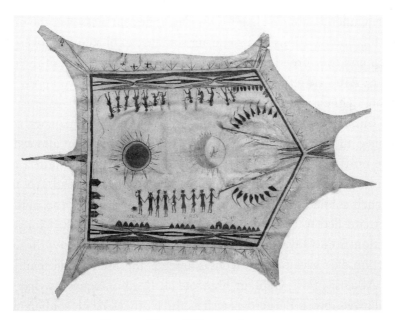

Quapaw Three Villages robe, c. 1740.
MUSÉE DU QUAI BRANLY—JACQUES CHIRAC, PARIS/ART RESOURCE, NY

There is a bison hide in a Paris museum, painted by a Quapaw around the 1730s, that serves as both a map of Quapaw towns and the French settlement and a window into the Quapaw view of their relationship with the French. In the scene, the Quapaws perform a ceremonial dance at their towns (the three sets of houses below the dancers), then Quapaw warriors follow the path to the left to the French voyageur town (you can see one of the men smoking a calumet just outside one of the French buildings), and then finally, the warriors follow the path to fight a battle, probably against the Chickasaws. The artist portrayed the French as a friendly neighbor with whom to consult and collect supplies before a battle against a common enemy, not a dominant imperial force.

French limitations extended to the spiritual. There was not a single church among the Quapaws, and most years there was no missionary around. The only one who stayed for several years failed to even keep the French soldiers and voyageur families in the faith and did not convert any Quapaws. The missionary had to say mass in the dining hall of the fort, because he could not persuade the Frenchmen to build a chapel. One day, as he said mass over the noise of food preparations and swearing soldiers, a chicken flew over the altar and overturned the chalice, to the great amusement of the soldiers. After he left, in the late 1750s, no other priest would do any more than pass through for the next forty years.[55]

Similarly, in matters of crime and justice, the Quapaws continued to rule their lands and protect the people they allowed to live on them. For example, in 1756 French soldiers fell into a disagreement over something, and a corporal ended up dead. Another French soldier, Jean Baptiste Bernard, was accused of the murder. Bernard fled to the Quapaw town of Osotouy and asked for protection from Ouyayonsas, the Quapaw religious leader with jurisdiction over asylum. Ouyayonsas agreed. The French commandant of Arkansas Post, Captain Francois de Reggio, requested that the Quapaws return Bernard as well as three other French soldiers who had previously deserted and were now living among the Quapaws. Ouyayonsas refused to hand over the Frenchmen, but he did eventually agree that the soldiers could go to New Orleans for trial in front of the French governor of Louisiana—Bernard for murder and the others for desertion, also a capital crime—as long as he could accompany them. Also making the trip would be several other Quapaw leaders, including Chief Guedetonguay, whom we met earlier.

In New Orleans, Guedetonguay argued for Quapaw sovereignty over the case to the French governor of Louisiana, Louis Billouart, Chevalier de Kerlérec. Standing on the sandy ground of the French Government House on the edge of town, Guedetonguay bowed his head and gravely explained that his "heart wept much." He knew that "these four men would have been put to death" if he had not accompanied them to New Orleans. He explained that anyone, "guilty of whatever crime, who finds a way to take refuge in their sacred cabin where they practice their religion, is regarded as washed clean of his crime." As their protector, he regarded the men as his "own children" and would feel their deaths as keenly as he would for his own sons and daughters. In fact, he told the Frenchmen, his son had been killed and a daughter wounded in a battle against their common Chickasaw enemy.[56]

Guedetonguay's words reflect how Quapaws saw their relationship with the French colonial government: as a military alliance whereby the Quapaws helped the French make and keep allies. Guedetonguay pledged that he "listens to the word of the French, and," exaggerating a bit, "at all times . . . carried it everywhere." In turn, Guedetonguay expected that French leaders "would listen to his [word], which is that of the nation in whose name he speaks."[57] When Kerlérec was appointed to the governorship of Louisiana, he expected to rule over Indians, not the other way around. He had served in the French navy for nearly five decades and had won his position by advancing through the ranks. He told Guedetonguay that, "in spite of all the friendship that the French had for him and his nation, these four men had deserved death."[58]

In Kerlérec's mind, his decision should have ended the matter, but Guedetonguay stayed silent for an awkwardly long time and then spoke, sounding sorry to have to say what he was saying. If the governor put the Frenchmen to death, Guedetonguay said, he "would not answer for the dangerous attacks and the rebellions that the chief of the sacred cabin [Ouyayonsas] could bring about and that would not fail to take place."[59] There would be war—did the governor want that?

He did not. Governor Kerlérec pardoned all four men. Guede-tonguay and Ouyayonsas agreed that in the future they would hand over any other refugees whom French officials requested. Nonetheless, more refugees came, and the Quapaws took them in. To the Quapaws, when people—whatever their ethnicity or race—wanted to leave the protection of one nation and seek that of another, they could do so. If the Quapaws agreed to take them in, that was that. They were a sovereign nation, just as much as France, and had their own rules about immigration and nationality.

Despite Quapaw power, the French rarely complained about them. Compared with the Chickasaws, the Natchez, and others who caused large war expenses and casualties—or the Osages and the Choctaws, who kept Europeans and Indians alike in fear of their power—the Quapaws were good allies. That alliance might cost the French, but it was worth it. In 1764, a Quapaw delegation told acting governor Jean-Jacques-Blaise d'Abbadie, "You are surrounded by tribes who do not observe the word of the French. It is not the same with us. We have always listened, and have never reddened our hands with the blood of the French."[60] While this was technically true—Quapaws listened and had killed no French—like any independent nation, they had always pursued their own goals, whether or not they conflicted with French ones.

QUAPAW SOVEREIGNTY

By 1750, people in Europe thought of the Mississippi Valley—if they thought of it at all—as the French colony of Louisiana. It had busy ports on the Gulf of Mexico, small but growing colonial towns at New Orleans and Mobile, and plantations and smaller farms stretching fifty miles or so northwest of New Orleans.

Beyond those places, though, the colony was a million square miles of Indian country dotted with fewer than a dozen places like

Arkansas Post—tiny posts that served local Native nations and housed a handful of soldiers, colonists, and indentured and enslaved laborers. The total number of French troops in Louisiana varied over the years, from fewer than two hundred to just shy of one thousand. The garrison at Arkansas Post was never more than fifty and usually closer to twelve.

In 1749, flooding damaged the fields of the Quapaw town of Osotouy, and the Quapaws built a new town with fields on higher ground. The move took Osotouy farther up the Arkansas River, and therefore farther from the French military post and the voyageur town. One might expect this distance to inconvenience the Quapaws, but it was the French who suffered dire consequences. Chickasaw Chief Paya Mataha led 150 warriors against the unprotected Arkansas Post and the voyageur town, to avenge French attacks on the Chickasaws. Before the Quapaws could arrive to help, the Chickasaw party killed six Frenchmen and captured and took away eight French women and children, a fairly large percentage of a town that was probably a couple dozen people. The Quapaws suggested that the French commandant move the fort and town closer to the new location of Osotouy, and he complied—not the first time the French moved because of a Quapaw decision.[61]

Given the small and weak French presence, we might ask why other Europeans considered the Mississippi Valley "French Louisiana." In fact, this state of affairs was not unusual for North American colonies. In 1750, the total European population north of central Mexico nearly matched the total Native population, but the vast majority of them—more than nine hundred thousand—lived in the British colonies on the Atlantic coast. Across the rest of the continent were more than a million Native Americans, who vastly outnumbered any Europeans living nearby. The large and growing British colonial population along the East Coast would mean trouble for everyone else in the coming decades, but for now it was no threat to Indigenous peoples in the vast majority of the continent.[62]

Whereas some Native nations, such as the Mohawks and the Osages, used trade to establish regional dominance, Quapaws wielded their political power as gatekeepers in a strategically important region. They were so good at it that for nearly a century they controlled relations with the imperialistic French without producing furs, slaves, or anything else for the world market. As Louisiana governor Pierre François de Rigaud, Marquis de Vaudreuil-Cavagnial, put it in 1750, "We can do nothing by ourselves."[63] The only goal the French crown achieved in the Mississippi Valley was simply keeping the British and the Spanish from getting it, and even that limited goal depended on Indigenous people.

Native power proved so great in Louisiana that the colony never made money for France. The French spent huge sums to keep up their alliances with Native nations, yet brought in little income. Against all expectations, plantation-capable Louisiana *lost* money, whereas Canada was actually slightly profitable because of the thriving fur trade. When wars broke out against Britain in the mid-1700s, France had to spend even more.

The Quapaws were particularly skilled diplomats, and their success in attracting European gifts and loyalty, given their small size and without increasing their hunting or warfare, is remarkable. But they were not unique. Their story was the norm throughout North America, not the exception. Many Native nations lost ground, but others expanded and grew stronger. People negotiated new boundaries and relations with allies and enemies, with or without European involvement. We know that there was a disaster brewing for Native nations in the rapidly growing British population a thousand miles to the east, but no one beyond the Atlantic coast at the time could see that future coming—although, as we shall see, in the late 1700s Shawnees and others came west with warnings that westerners would find hard to believe, given the weak Europeans they had long known.

CONCLUSION

It's easy to imagine that colonialism was a sweeping force that overwhelmed Native peoples as it moved inexorably across the North American continent. In fact, until the nineteenth century, colonialism came to most Native North Americans in the form of small and tenuous settlements like Arkansas Post in Quapaw country, Father Kino's mission attempts in O'odham country, and Fort Orange on the Hudson River. As just those three examples show, European settlements faced very different circumstances depending on where they were located, whom they allied with or fought against, and how many people they brought with them. In 1750, Europeans in most places in North America were more like those at Arkansas Post than the heavily populated colonies of New England and the Chesapeake.

But Europeans' intentions were different from their present reality. During the campaign against the Chickasaws, the French governor of Louisiana at the time, Étienne Périer, wrote to his superior, "The present would be the time to get rid of this wretched nation." The governor had no qualms about genocide and would have destroyed an entire nation if he had the power to do so. He knew he did not have that power. He did not even have enough boats to transport the few soldiers he had upriver in a crisis, and, as we know, he did not defeat the Chickasaws.[64]

Europeans like Governor Périer came to the Americas to conquer them, to bring their lands and resources under their rule and make them work in their ways, economic, political, and religious. Quapaws wielded power over the French (and, in the late eighteenth century, the Spanish and the British) to gain security and preserve their sovereignty in a contested place. Mohawk and Osage goals were more similar to those of Europeans. They expanded their reach over new territory and drove off or incorporated other peoples to enhance their power and prestige. Their victims may have seen little difference between them and European colonizers. Yet they would have been shocked to see the Spanish, Portuguese, British, French, and Dutch colonies of the Caribbean, with their plantations where hundreds of enslaved men and women were held against their will and forced to work under brutal conditions. They would have been shocked to read the genocidal aims in the letters of frustrated officials who carefully hid those ambitions from Native diplomats. Most still found the tales from the East Coast of thousands and thousands of armed Europeans squatting on Native hunting and gathering lands and even forcing people from their homes rather improbable.

When we flip the story of colonialism from European to Native perspectives, we see the long history of North America as it actually was, not as Europeans wished it to be, and perhaps what it might have continued to be. Most Native Americans fitted Europeans into their preexisting categories of others, and they shaped them to their own rules and needs. In the eighteenth century, from the Appalachians to the Pacific and between the European posts of Quebec and Montreal in the north and St. Augustine, New Orleans, and the New Mexican and Sonoran missions in the south, Native nations still controlled North America. The Quapaws were an important nation in a diverse and complicated continent, where civilizations rose and fell and newcomers came and went—often dancing local Indigenous dances, literally and figuratively. A hundred years after the first Europeans came to their country, Quapaw sovereignty was as strong as it ever had been.

PART II

CONFRONTING SETTLER POWER, 1750 AND BEYOND

I N 1784, MORE THAN 250 SHAWNEE, HAUDENOSAUNEE, DELAWARE, Cherokee, Chickasaw, and Choctaw representatives arrived at St. Louis, the trading post that French fur traders had built near the confluence of the Missouri and Mississippi rivers. St. Louis was four hundred miles upriver from the Quapaws and on the site of one of Cahokia's vacated satellite cities. The seven-hundred-year-old pyramid mounds still rose above the small trading post. At St. Louis, the delegation presented strings of wampum to Spanish officials, who had taken over the post from the French at the end of the Seven Years' War, two decades earlier. In a great council, the multinational Native delegation described the effects of British colonists' successful revolt against their empire in the American Revolution. These Americans, the delegates explained, were "a great deal more ambitious and numerous than the English." They had "put us out of our lands, forming therein great settlements, extending themselves like a plague of locusts in the territories of the Ohio River which we inhabit." These white settlers were heavily armed and believed that their victory against Britain had earned them most of North America east of the Mississippi River. In the face of this growing danger, these Native nations and the Spanish agreed to form an alliance based on Native North American traditions of reciprocity. They pledged to support one another against this "plague of locusts."[1]

One way of organizing U.S. history is dividing it into the "colonial period" before the American Revolution and the "early republic" that starts with the independence of the United States. As the 1784

St. Louis meeting shows, the creation of the United States did have unprecedented effects. Yet the colonization of North America was far from finished at the end of the American Revolution. Only thirteen of the British colonies became an independent country. The Spanish, French, and other British colonies in the Americas, including Canada, were still parts of empires dependent on Native allies. American Indians still controlled most of the land that today is the United States, and they were still the majority of the population west of the Appalachians.

That "west of the Appalachians" caveat matters a great deal, though. While the independence of the United States would not affect the O'odham, Apaches, or Kiowas for several more generations, Europeans had gradually taken over the East. It had taken a long time. While the Powhatans and most Algonquian-speaking peoples near New England lost their lands early, for a century English colonists were mainly confined to the coast and the lower reaches of eastward-flowing rivers. As late as 1730, British settlements still extended only about seventy-five miles west of the Atlantic Ocean. Everything to the west was controlled by what colonists recognized as "foreign nations." The place that would become Thomas Jefferson's Monticello was still Shawnee and Cherokee hunting land.[2]

But in the eighteenth century, British colonists flooded into the regions west of their coastal colonies. By 1750 their settlements were approaching the Appalachian Mountains. Only sixty years later, because of immigration and the large number of children born to farming families of European descent, the non-Indigenous population west of the Appalachians passed one million, far surpassing the hundred thousand Native Americans living between the Appalachians and the Mississippi River.[3]

British colonists could have lived side by side with Native nations, continuing to ally and trade in mutually beneficial ways. And some of them did, at times even marrying into Native communities. Sometimes British and even U.S. officials would try to balance the claims of Native allies and their own people. But generally their search for profits combined with their fear of Native power to create a desire to be free of Native nations, whether by assimilation, expulsion, or what they called "extinction." Once the American Revolution split the colonies from Britain and created the United States, settlers had a government that was responsible only to them and would support its constituents' efforts to make a country without Native nations more so than European empires ever had.[4]

Native nations in the 1700s and 1800s had to develop new sources of power as British colonists and their U.S. descendants came to possess the power of numbers that Native Americans had previously held. Many found power in collective action within and across Native nations, including former enemies. Those completely surrounded and outnumbered by non-Natives fled to take refuge in other Native nations or formed minority communities within colonies and states. They learned to use the tools of British and U.S. courts, legislatures, and newspapers to forward their individual and group rights.

Some of these communities became the basis for the idea of reservations, a greatly reduced but protected space where a Native community could still own some land communally, surrounded by farms individually owned by white families. Reservations had similarities to the reducciones that the Spanish had tried to impose on the O'odham, though usually without a missionary presence. In the United States, as well as Mexico and Canada, reservations were part of a gradual reversal in thinking about land. In previous centuries, all land had belonged to Native peoples if it hadn't been given or sold to foreign empires or the United States. The creation of reservations flipped this status, assuming that all land belonged to the United States and could be owned by U.S. citizens if not "reserved" for Indians. Some of these Native communities in the East were labeled by outsiders as either generically Indian or "free people of color," imagining away their Native identities and histories.[5]

Take North Carolina, for example. Descendants of Ossomocomuck and its neighbors continued to rule most of what would become eastern North Carolina for a century after the English failure at Roanoke. But the balance of power began to shift in the 1660s. The Weapemeocs, still living where Ralph Lane had met them north of Albemarle Sound, had to sell land to the increasing numbers of English surrounding them. In 1676, devastating attacks from Bacon's Rebellion, to the north in Virginia, began "a tragic period of increased warfare, forced migrations, social marginalization," in the words of Lawrence A. Dunmore III, tribal chairperson and council chief of the Occaneechi Band of the Saponi Nation. The Chowans and Meherrins along the Chowan River, at the northwest end of Albemarle Sound, had to accept "tributary status," an agreement that left them a reservation on their reduced homeland and semi-independent status. People in the southern part of Ossomocomuck held off substantial encroachment until the aftermath of the Tuscarora War in the 1710s, when they had to agree to a twenty-thousand-acre reservation near the old town of Pomeioc. Native people from Roanoke and Hatteras islands moved to join them on the reservation.[6]

Just to the west, the Occaneechis, on the Roanoke River upstream from Ossomocomuck, near what's now the North Carolina–Virginia state line, had fended off English encroachment on their lands by incorporating Native people from the coast and controlling the Great Trading Path that ran from Catawba towns and Charleston in the south to the descendants of the Powhatans and the English Virginia colony in the north (now traced by part of Interstate 85). After Bacon's Rebellion, though, the Occaneechis fled the Roanoke River and built a fortified town close to allies on the Eno River near what's now Hillsborough, North Carolina. In the early eighteenth century, most of the Occaneechis moved again, clustering with Saponis and Tutelos around Fort Christanna, near the North Carolina–Virginia state line on land "reserved" for Indians when Virginia took the rest. In the late eighteenth century, some moved back to their ancestral central North Carolina homelands as rural communities of related Native families. Other people from central North Carolina moved south to become part of the Catawba Nation, who maintained a rare independent national status in the midst of English colonies, in part by fighting on the side of North and South Carolina and Virginia in the Seven Years' War and the American Revolution. Over the course of the eighteenth century, the people who became the Lumbees concentrated in the wetlands between the coast and the piedmont. Europeans still generally ignored this space, because the geography could not support plantations. Yet, as Lumbee ecologist Ryan Emanuel observes, it had floodplain forests, sandy uplands suitable for small-scale farming, and riverine wildlife and plants familiar to southeastern coastal peoples—the kind of landscape that befuddled Ralph Lane and the English as they failed to establish their Roanoke colony.[7]

While coastal people were adjusting to dispossession and "reserved" lands, inland nations were growing as Native refugees from colonial wars fled to them. Some combined formerly independent peoples into new confederacies, most prominently the Muscogee (Creek) Confederacy, which by the mid-1700s had some thirteen thousand people and growing. In the second half of the eighteenth century, though, they would face settlers more determined than ever to replace Native nations, and now with the numbers to take advantage of any Native weakness.[8]

In this era, as we shall see in the coming chapters, the Shawnees and the Cherokees began to centralize their nations, in part so they could negotiate more effectively with Europeans, the United States, and their Native allies. Some allied nations forged tighter obligations to one another, pledging not to surrender any land without the agreement of all. The Shawnee brothers Tecumseh and Tenskwatawa went further and urged all Indians to join together as one Native American race with a centralized leadership, giving up their separate national identities. Yet as some people urged centralization or merging, others worried. Centralization might be a slippery slope toward the extreme hierarchy and inequality that their ancestors had long ago rejected. Winning might not be worth assimilation into someone else's identity, even a Native one.

As people from the United States flooded into their lands in the late eighteenth and early nineteenth centuries, Native men and women debated how to respond. Should they try to continue living on much reduced parts of their former homelands, move in with allies who still had land, or go west across the Mississippi River to get away from the United States entirely?

How far should they go in joining together for mutual interests, centralizing national governance, and allying with old enemies? How much independence should a family, clan, town, or nation give up in order to resist U.S. power? Could they find a cure that wasn't worse than the disease?

CHAPTER 7

SHAWNEE TOWNS AND FARMS IN THE OHIO VALLEY

T HE SHAWNEE TOWN OF CHILLICOTHE, ON THE SCIOTO RIVER, was well prepared for the winter. The women had harvested the last of the corn from their extensive fields south of town and stored it along with pumpkins and other squashes, beans, apples, hickory nuts, and bear oil. There would be plenty to feed the towns-people and their cattle, pigs, and chickens through the winter. Their log houses were well built, each according to the style of the women who designed and built it, and cozy with furs that the men had hunted. In case someone came home with frostbite at the end of a journey, there were sassafras roots ready to mix into a poultice with a little cornmeal. A lively trade meant they had clothing and cloth manufactured in Europe, as well as silver jewelry. The winter months would give time for making clothes and processing deerskins.[1]

If you know only one thing about Shawnee history, it probably has something to do with Tecumseh rather than with how the people of eighteenth-century Chillicothe prepared for the winter. Along with his brother, the prophet Tenskwatawa, Tecumseh fought the United States in the early nineteenth century. He is often remembered as a noble but tragic military leader, alongside Geronimo (Apache) and Crazy Horse (Lakota). The town of Chillicothe, Ohio—where the Shawnee town once was—has an annual summer outdoor drama inspired by North Carolina's *The Lost Colony*, entitled simply *Tecumseh!*[2]

Given Tecumseh's prominence in U.S. history, I was surprised when I visited the Shawnee Tribe Cultural Center, in Miami, Oklahoma, to see that Tecumseh wasn't mentioned in any of its exhibits and that none of the many published biographies about him was available in its gift shop. It's not that Shawnees don't see Tecumseh as important. He is prominently featured on the website and flag of the Eastern Shawnee Tribe of Oklahoma, one of the three federally recognized Shawnee tribes today, along with the Shawnee Tribe and the Absentee Shawnee Tribe of Indians of Oklahoma.[3]

But the Shawnee Tribe Cultural Center tells Shawnee history not as a sequence of great men and not as a tragedy. It is a narrative of continuity, of men and women being Shawnee in places like Chillicothe in the eighteenth century and northeastern Oklahoma in the twenty-first. Its mission is "to be the place for Shawnees to tell the story of the Shawnee past, how that informs and shapes Shawnees today, and who we see ourselves becoming tomorrow." The exhibits connect the Shawnee past, present, and future. A panel beside a gourd rattle (thee'kwane) made recently explains that "gourd rattles have been used at the White Oak ceremonial ground for over a hundred and fifty years" and are used today in the Native American Church. Another exhibit shows Shawnees working with archaeologists and a Wyandot (Wendat) potter to discover how their fifteenth-century Shawnee ancestors may have made pottery. Having experimented with different kinds of tempering and other techniques, they now teach the skills to Shawnee children at the cultural center.

During a panel of the American Society for Ethnohistory in 2020, Shawnee Tribe Chief Benjamin Barnes noted, "We don't really need another book on Tecumseh. Let's tell the stories of the days when there weren't bullets flying, of women and children in the villages."[4] While chapter 8 will delve into how Tecumseh and Tenskwatawa tried to persuade Native Americans to unite as one people, this chapter is one answer to Chief Barnes's call. Some bullets and arrows will fly, but Shawnee towns and families will be the center of this story, as they were the center of Shawnee life and identity. In the face of tremendous pressure from British colonists and then the United States, it was their decisions, as Chief Barnes explains, that "enabled the modern Shawnee tribes to survive."[5]

MANY TOWNS

"The Master of Life . . . made the Shawnees before any others of the human race," a Shawnee speaker noted in 1803, and "gave them all the knowledge which he himself possessed."[6] Until the late 1600s, Shawnee ancestors lived in the Ohio River Valley. They were likely part of a civilization that farmed corn and built large towns and mounds there at the same time as Cahokia. By the 1680s the Haudenosaunee wars of the seventeenth century (covered in chapter 4) had spread west along the south shore of Lake Erie and into the Ohio Valley. In addition, Chickasaws and other enemies of the Shawnees frequently raided in the region for captives to sell to the English as part of the same Indigenous slave trade that targeted the Quapaws. To protect themselves, Shawnee women made sure to go out to the fields in large groups, and children stayed close to home. Warfare cut off the Ohio Valley from its trading networks, leaving Shawnees hard-pressed to supply and defend themselves.[7]

So Shawnees picked up and left the Ohio Valley, seeking refuge with other people in other places. Some Shawnee towns relocated several hundred miles southeast to the Savannah River to access English trade at Charleston. Other towns moved onto lands of their Illinois and Miami allies near the Mississippi River, where French traders regularly visited. When warfare erupted there in the 1690s, those Shawnees accepted the invitation of the Delawares to move east to their lands along the Delaware and Susquehanna rivers. Here, the rolling hills and river valleys looked like home. The nearby colony of Pennsylvania provided a market for deerskins, and its Quaker-run government abided by its Indian treaties. The Munsee and Lenape peoples who together became the Delawares were joined in the early 1700s by Tutelos, Saponis, and Tuscaroras from the piedmont and lower river valleys of Virginia and North Carolina, peoples who had been inland neighbors of Ossomocomuck.[8]

The move to Delaware country changed the Shawnee relationship with the Haudenosaunee. As we saw in chapter 4, the Mohawks and the rest of the Haudenosaunee built a "Covenant Chain" of alli-

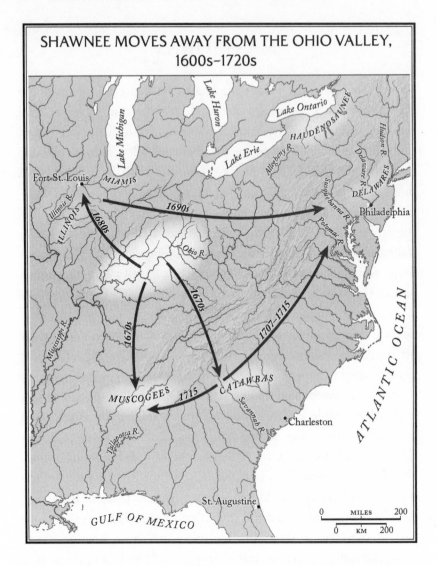

SHAWNEE MOVES AWAY FROM THE OHIO VALLEY,
1600s–1720s

ances with Native nations, which they extended to the English colonies of New York and Pennsylvania starting in the 1680s and to New France in 1701. The Delawares had become part of the Covenant Chain, and they extended it to the Shawnees in the early eighteenth century, thus bringing trade access to English towns in Pennsylvania, New York, and Maryland. Because the Delawares and now the Shawnees had accepted the invitation to join the Great Peace, Haudenosaunee diplomats believed those nations had given the Haudenosaunee the right to speak for them when negotiating alliances with other members of the Covenant Chain, including Britain and France. The Shawnees and Delawares lived between Haudenosaunee country and the Catawbas and Cherokees, with whom the Haudenosaunee were still at war, so they also provided a protective barrier and friendly territory through which Haudenosaunee warriors could travel with captives and other prizes taken from their southern enemies. Although the old Shawnee–Haudenosaunee animosity from the time of war in the Ohio Valley did not end entirely, this new situation, living with the Delawares and under Haudenosaunee protection, proved so beneficial that Shawnees who had not yet left the Ohio Valley now migrated to join the other Shawnees on Delaware lands.[9]

In the South, Charleston traders pressured the Shawnees who had moved to the Savannah River into becoming slave raiders themselves. In the 1680s, they began raiding for captives to sell to Charleston and as a result became ensnared in even worse violence than they had faced on the Ohio River. Seeking a more peaceful existence, in the early eighteenth century most of them came north to Delaware country too. The rest went southwest from the Savannah River and founded a Shawnee town in what today is Alabama, among the Upper Towns of the Muscogee Confederacy, who were welcoming many refugees and saw the Shawnees as especially wise negotiators and therefore particularly useful neighbors.[10]

Even as they left the Ohio Valley for safer places, Shawnees retained their identities as Shawnees as well as members of their specific Shawnee towns, divisions, and clans. Generally, a Shawnee town belonged to one of the five patrilineal divisions, and when a town moved, it usually moved intact. Each town had a bundle of sacred objects representing its division, and it brought it to the new place as a sign of its continuing identity. Retaining the decentralized structure of divisions and towns facilitated moving while remaining Shawnee.[11]

Another force that united Shawnees was a continuing connection to their Ohio Valley homeland. Shawnee ancestors had nurtured the grasslands on the Ohio River's south bank in what's now Kentucky, a name that probably comes from the Seneca word for "meadow," gëda:yë' (*k* and *g* make the same sound in Iroquoian languages). They had long burned woods and brush to encourage bison, elk, and deer, and now, with no people living there most of the year, Kentucky became a game park. Shawnees and their allies would travel there for their winter hunts, staying for two or three months at a time. The Ohio Valley's rivers and streams were home to waterfowl and fish, and its woods had bears and turkeys. Shawnees gathered for ceremonies in the Ohio Valley, and groups who lived apart would share the year's news and renew their sense of being one people. A continuing connection to a former homeland (whether that means actually returning there or simply keeping its memory alive) is a common attribute of peoples in diaspora, as the Shawnees were in the late 1600s and early 1700s.[12]

And then in the 1720s, when the Ohio Valley was at peace again, Shawnees began returning there to live, along with some of their Delaware allies. First, some moved to the river's headwaters, west of Pennsylvania's outer settlements, and then near a multiethnic settlement called Logstown, on the upper Ohio just downstream from where Pittsburgh is today. More Shawnees came, and they continued their move downriver. Those who had been children in the 1680s led their families back home, now that the slave raids were no longer happening there. The colony of South Carolina had stopped buying Indigenous captives after the Yamasee War killed hundreds of colonists, so the raiding of earlier decades had dramatically decreased. The Great Peace of 1701 between the Haudenosaunee and France and its Native allies had also helped to end warfare in the region. Even after varied travels and new alliances, Shawnee identity remained strong. When they moved back to the Ohio Valley, residents of different towns and divisions began holding Shawnee councils together. People moved as entire towns, but they spread out more than before, with houses and fields stretched out along a waterway.[13]

The lands between the Ohio River and the Great Lakes became a model for coexistence, for how Native people could be strong together without losing their individual national identities. Native to the Great Lakes were the Anishinaabe peoples: the Three Fires Confederacy, initially composed of Ojibwe, Ottawa, and Potawatomi peoples. By the 1640s, the Anishinaabe also included Algonquins, who had fled the Haudenosaunee. Iroquoian-speaking Wendats who also fled were living near Lakes Huron and Erie. Now, in the early eighteenth century, the Shawnees who returned to the Ohio Valley, along with their fellow Algonquian-speaking Delawares, shared hunting and gathering lands north of the Ohio River with the Anishinaabe and Wendats. With peace in the valley, and peace between England and France in the 1720s and '30s, British traders from Philadelphia and Albany and French traders from Quebec and Montreal followed the Shawnees and Delawares and set up shop in places like Lower Shawneetown, near where the Scioto River meets the Ohio. Shawnees also traveled to trade back in Pennsylvania and at posts that the French had established among the Illinois peoples and at Detroit.[14]

The Shawnees who returned to the Ohio Valley in the mid-1700s were pulled by the promise of reunification in their homeland near friendly allies, abundant game, convenient trade, and well-watered and fertile farmland that only needed to be re-cleared and planted; they also had reasons to leave the East, where they were being crowded by English, German, and Scots-Irish immigrants flooding in. Pennsylvania's colonial population more than quintupled in the forty years between 1690 and 1730, from 8,800 to 49,000, and would double again before 1750. Many of these settlers desired the Delawares' land to grow wheat for Philadelphia and ports beyond. In a series of treaties, the British seized lands belonging to the Delawares in what's now eastern Pennsylvania. The land loss, combined with anger at both the British for taking the land and the Haudenosaunee for failing to prevent it, increased the appeal of returning to the Ohio Valley.[15]

The lands between the Great Lakes and the Ohio River repopulated, with careful attention to living together as equals, rather than with the Haudenosaunee governing according to their Great Law of Peace. As Shawnee and Delaware towns moved in, some Wendats and groups of Anishinaabe moved south from the Great Lakes onto the northern tributaries of the Ohio, where they had long hunted but now lived year-round. Shawnees also renewed good relations with people living on the Wabash River, which flows into the Ohio. Sometimes called the Wabash Confederacy, they included the Miamis, Kickapoos, Mascoutens, Piankeshaws, and Weas.[16]

People who lived here were cosmopolitan and often could speak multiple languages, while retaining separate identities as Shawnees and other nations, in addition to their identities as members of families, towns, clans, bands, and divisions. Even some Haudenosaunee moved close by, establishing towns on the Allegheny River, one of the headwaters of the Ohio, on lands they had won in their war against the Eries and the Neutrals. These Haudenosaunee who settled in the upper Ohio Valley are usually called the Ohio Senecas or the Mingos (a Delaware word for Iroquoians).[17]

The resettlements required a tremendous amount of diplomacy and coordination among the newcomers and older residents. Shawnees and their neighbors knew the devastation of war, and they purposely avoided it in the Ohio Valley. In previous chapters I have stressed the fact that Native nations have territories and borders, but this region between the Ohio River and the Great Lakes was an unusually shared space. Each town in the Ohio Valley had a specific nationality, yet some individuals lived in towns of other nations, because they married into those towns, stayed as permanent diplomats or traders, or came as refugees, including some Mahicans and Meskwakis (Foxes). Towns tended to cluster by nation, but not entirely. A Shawnee town might be nearer to a Miami town than to another Shawnee town. Lands for hunting and gathering resources were shared among the region's many constituent groups. There surely were councils of women or men who helped to settle disputes that arose between towns and nations over valuable gathering, hunting, and fishing spots. Fighting on the same side also could seal bonds between peoples. Shawnee and Haudenosaunee men traveled south together to fight the Catawbas.[18]

While men were in charge of war and foreign relations, women built and maintained the farms and towns that made peace and prosperity possible in the Ohio Valley. If food had been scarce, it would have been much harder to live amicably without clearly defined borders and use rights, and malnutrition would have left them all vulnerable to damaging bouts of disease. Women kept everyone fed by farming the river valleys with the corn, beans, and squash that their ancestors had grown, and, like O'odham farmers, they added wheat and new vegetables, including cabbage, cucumbers, and turnips. They harvested nuts and fruit from orchards they cultivated and wild plants for food and medicine. They ate beef and chicken in addition to venison. If someone did get sick, conditions of peace and prosperity made quarantine and healing possible.[19]

Now that they were living closer to the abundant game south of the Ohio River and had access to British traders, Shawnees bought products from Europe in exchange for furs and deerskins that men hunted and women processed. England had industrialized its textile manufacturing, and Shawnees joined British colonists in buying cotton, linen, and silk fabric. Much like colonial women who made dresses from the latest silks and calicos (dyed, printed cottons), Shawnee women applied their skills of sewing, embroidery, and beading to these new materials to create a style of dress that displayed their prosperity and taste.[20]

If you go to a Shawnee stomp dance today, it is likely that your first impression will be color. Men's shirts and women's dresses stand out in deep red, brilliant orange, and many shades of blue, set off by ribbons in purple, yellow, white, and pink. Similarly, paintings of Shawnees from a hundred years ago are alive with colorful clothing. Shawnees developed these styles in the eighteenth century. They bought white linen shirts manufactured in Britain and dyed them dramatic colors with plant and mineral dyes. Like Mohawks, Shawnee women and men wore them untucked, hanging over leggings, for men, and skirts and leggings for women.[21]

Shawnees also wore silver—in large quantities. In the Mississippian era, shell had been an adornment that, in addition to its beauty, conveyed the wearer's connection to foreign places and sources of wealth. Silver now served the same function. Silversmiths in Montreal, Philadelphia, Boston, and New York made silver necklaces, armbands, wristbands, earrings, and all sizes of brooches for the Ohio Valley Indian market. Sometimes a woman would place hundreds of brooches all over her clothing or close together on a shawl to make a robe of flexible, reflective silver. And, like shell, silver could be taken off and used for currency if needed. Over the course of the eighteenth century, like British colonists from Kingston to Boston, Shawnees bought tea, china teapots and cups, and silver spoons. As with the Mohawks, their demand for certain products and styles, such as silver brooches, influenced production. British factories were producing goods, British ships were sailing the seas, and Shawnee consumers were producing furs and food to exchange.[22]

Shawnee silver brooches, 1830–1900.

NATIONAL MUSEUM OF THE AMERICAN INDIAN, SMITHSONIAN
INSTITUTION (2/4773). PHOTOGRAPH BY NMAI PHOTO SERVICES

If the goal of the fur trade had been individual or family accumulation or elevating one town or nation over another, it might have doomed the region's peaceful coexistence as surely as scarcity would. Yet cooperation and reciprocity held. If one town's crops or hunt failed, other towns shared what they had and leveled the wealth, even with families and towns of other nations. Perhaps the memory of Mississippian times echoed through the centuries. In any case, Shawnees and their neighbors valued mutual prosperity.[23]

The colorful garments, silver, ribbons, and beads of the Shawnees and their Native neighbors came to identify them as Ohio Valley Indians, the peoples who lived between the Ohio River and the Great Lakes in proximity, prosperity, and mutual protection. When a European trader or diplomat went into the region, he would change into a linen or calico outer shirt and wear some silver if he had any, to convey his friendly intentions. In parallel, Shawnees and other Ohio Valley Indians would put on European clothes when they went to conduct diplomacy and trade in Philadelphia or London. Shawnee Chief Blue Jacket kept a British red coat with gold epaulets and a King George medallion, which he would wear, along with red leggings and moccasins. A portrait of Shawnee Chief Black Hoof during a visit east depicts him in the European-style coat and cravat that he donned for meeting with U.S. officials. He wore a silk turban, light blue, like many Shawnee men.[24]

Ca-Ta-He-Cas-Sa, Black Hoof, Principal Chief
of the Shawanoes, in Thomas L. McKenney and James Hall's
1836 *The Indian Tribes of North America.*
NATIONAL PORTRAIT GALLERY, SMITHSONIAN INSTITUTION

Outsiders sometimes called them collectively the Ohio Indians or the Northern Indians, and their way of dress looked undifferentiated to those who did not spend much time there, but in fact they had subtle distinctions. Shawnees were known for being especially fond of printed calicos, and Shawnee women developed a particular style of wearing long woolen European men's coats that they belted at the waist. Different nations had specific ways of making and decorating moccasins, which families and individuals further differentiated according to personal style. They spoke Shawnee and conducted Shawnee ceremonies, and they cultivated strong ties among their towns based on a common identity as Shawnees. They consistently introduced themselves to outsiders as Shawnees, not by their divisions or towns, and not as Ohio Indians.[25]

The Shawnees didn't develop strong centralized political structures. One British visitor noted both the style of politics practiced by the Shawnees, which was common all across Native America, and the European tendency to misunderstand it: "Every town has its head men, some of which are by us called kings; but by what I can learn this appellation is by the Indians given to none. . . . The chief use of these head-men is to give counsel, especially in time of war; they are used also as most proper to speak with us on any occasion, especially if it be important." The headmen were counselors and diplomats but certainly not kings. Shawnees instead distrusted "civil power and authority: they look on it that God made them free—that one man has no natural right to rule over another . . . that a ruler's authority extends no further than the pleasure of the people."[26]

Shawnee women and men built new prosperity in this old and beloved place, and they shared its resources and peace with a diversity of others, integrated into the Atlantic and global economy—all of this was what it meant to be an eighteenth-century Shawnee. A visitor to one Shawnee town remarked that "they are the most cheerful and merry people that I ever saw . . . both men and women in laughing exceed any nation that ever came under my notice."[27]

THE SEVEN YEARS' WAR AND PONTIAC'S WAR

The Seven Years' War—the French and Indian War, as British colonists would call it—started at the forks of the Ohio River, near Logstown at the present-day location of Pittsburgh. In the preceding decades, the Shawnees and others in the region had developed ways of sharing this strategically important place peacefully, but Eu-

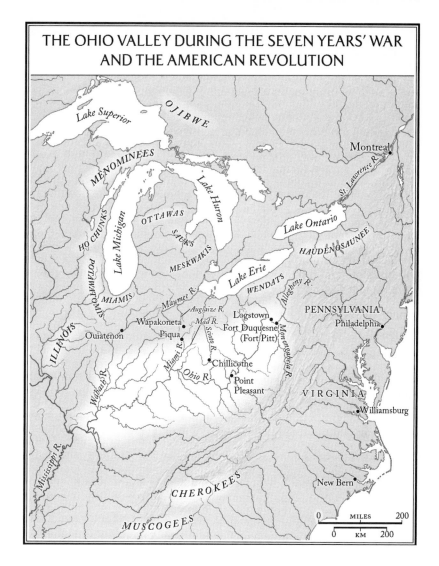

THE OHIO VALLEY DURING THE SEVEN YEARS' WAR
AND THE AMERICAN REVOLUTION

ropean claims proved harder to integrate. The French and the British—including separate claims by the colonies of Virginia and Pennsylvania—saw the region as under their dominion alone, and in the 1740s France and Britain began vying to take physical possession of it. Soon the Ohio Valley would be as threatened as the Delaware Valley and countless other places east of the Appalachians had been in earlier years.[28]

Though rooted in European conflict and eventually fought all around the globe, the Seven Years' War began with this North

American conflict. The French were worried that the British were taking over North America. Whereas in the mid-1700s the French had fewer than seventy-five thousand colonists spread from Quebec to New Orleans, the British mainland colonies—a smaller area—were home to a million and a half colonists. British settlers were expanding into contested regions, and British traders were traveling into Native nations, advertising their cheaper goods and lower prices. France feared that the economic competition would doom New France and that British expansion would cut it off from Louisiana. In 1753, the French began building forts in the contested region from Fort Presque Isle, on Lake Erie, down the Allegheny River, and in the spring of 1754 they established Fort Duquesne at the forks of the Ohio, only twenty miles from Logstown. They were building on a place that the British king had recently granted to a group of Virginians, including George Washington's older half brothers, Lawrence and Augustine. These men had incorporated as the Ohio Company of Virginia to speculate on those lands.

French fort building in the upper Ohio Valley alarmed not only Virginia speculators but also the Shawnees, Delawares, and Ohio Senecas. They protested against the French right to put forts there and, at first, hoped that the British and the Haudenosaunee would help them expel the French. And the British did take action. In May 1754, the colonial governor of Virginia, Robert Dinwiddie, also a shareholder in the Ohio Company, sent Virginia militia under the young colonel George Washington to try to scare off the French and make good on the Ohio Company's claims. When that plan didn't work, the British sent General Edward Braddock across the Atlantic with two thousand troops to enforce the British claim. The Shawnees assumed that Washington and Braddock were there to fulfill British and Haudenosaunee alliance obligations to defend the Ohio Valley together against the French.[29]

But Braddock was there to prepare the way for British expansion. When six Shawnee, Delaware, and Ohio Seneca leaders met with Braddock, Delaware Chief Shingas asked him "what he intended to do with the land if he could drive the French and their Indians away." Braddock replied, "The English should inhabit and inherit the land." Chief Shingas gave him a chance to revise his answer. Perhaps, Shingas suggested, "the Indians that were friends to the English might . . . be permitted to live and trade among the English and have hunting ground sufficient to support themselves and families." Braddock, a veteran of wars in Europe and overconfident about British military might, answered unequivocally that "no savage should inherit the land." Asking again the next day and getting the same reply, the Shawnee, Delaware, and Ohio Seneca leaders declared to Braddock that "if they might not have liberty to live on the land they would not fight for it." Braddock responded that he "did not need their help." The delegation's report back home made their people "much enraged," and some of them immediately went to meet with the French. Anishinaabe and Wendat fighters, allied with the French since the seventeenth-century anti-Haudenosaunee wars, had already joined the French force. Together, French, Anishinaabe, and Wendat fighters, along with a few Shawnees, Delawares, and Ohio Senecas, attacked Braddock near the Monongahela River. The Battle of the Monongahela was a rout. Braddock was killed. Washington had two horses shot out from under him and barely escaped with his life.[30]

In the past, when posts were established in the Ohio Valley, it had been at Native American request, much like Fort Orange for the Mohawks and Mahicans, Kino's missions for the O'odham and Opatas, and Arkansas Post for the Quapaws. But these French and British posts were clearly meant to stake a different kind of claim— the precursor to the settler colonialism that had already pushed the peoples of Ossomocomuck and other eastern places onto fragments of their former homelands. Shawnees and Delawares decided it was time to conduct their own war targeting British settlements that had already spread west from Pennsylvania, Virginia, and the Carolinas. Armed with French weapons and ammunition, in 1757 and 1758 they killed or captured hundreds of people and forced the rest to abandon their farms and settlements and take refuge in colonial towns as far east as Philadelphia. They also recruited in Muscogee and Cherokee country for the war against Britain.[31]

The victories over British settlers came at a price, as other Native nations made different decisions about their interests in the war. Rather than join the Shawnees, the Cherokees, along with the Catawbas and the Saponis, entered the war on the side of the British and, starting in 1756, attacked their old Shawnee enemies in the upper Ohio Valley and the French at Fort Duquesne. In 1758, hundreds of—perhaps more than a thousand—Cherokee, Catawba, and allied fighters mobilized to fight France and its allies. At the same time, French supplies were dwindling, and a devastating smallpox epidemic had begun to spread in 1757.[32]

Appealing to both the British desire to stop French-armed raids on its settlers and the Shawnee and Delaware desire to prevent British-armed raids on their towns, the Haudenosaunee stepped in and brokered the Treaty of Easton in October 1758. As part of the negotiations, British officials agreed to disavow their former claim that the Haudenosaunee had given them the upper Ohio Valley. The British and the Haudenosaunee confirmed that this region was still Delaware and Shawnee hunting land, and the British officials agreed to prevent colonial settlement there, presenting wampum belts to substantiate their promises. In return, Shawnee and Delaware delegates agreed to stop fighting the British. Shawnees and Delawares also extended peace efforts to the Cherokees and Catawbas. The following summer, the Shawnees and the Delawares brought their Wendat, Anishinaabe, Illinois, and Miami allies to join the peace. In accordance with Native tradition for affirming a serious negotiation, men, women, and children gathered on the upper Ohio River and agreed to the peace.[33]

In large part because of the loss of Native support, France lost the war. British victories on the Canadian border cut off French supply lines coming south, and the peace agreement between Britain and the Shawnees and their allies greatly decreased France's chances of winning in the Ohio Valley. In November 1758, French troops evacuated Fort Duquesne, where the war had started. British forces took Quebec in September 1759.

The British, who said outrageous things like "No savage should inherit the land," had pushed France off the continent. Though the Shawnees had never trusted the French, they had now lost that source of weapons and knew they would have to persuade the British to keep their promises from the 1758 Treaty of Easton. It did not bode well when, as soon as British forces occupied Fort Duquesne (renaming it Fort Pitt for the British prime minister), settlers quickly followed, setting up the homes and farms that would become Pittsburgh and hunting far down the Ohio, just as they had before the war. The Cherokees, long allies of the British, were astonished when British squatters killed Cherokee men crossing former shared hunting lands on their way home from fighting on the British side. Cherokees went to war against those settlers in 1759 and ended up fighting a devastating three-year war against British soldiers they had fought alongside not long before.[34]

With France's defeat, British colonists' ambitions grew. British officers sent troops to remove squatters west of the Appalachians, but they kept coming back. And with France having surrendered, the commander of British forces in North America, Jeffery Amherst, cut the budget both for enforcing the Treaty of Easton and for diplomatic gifts to Britain's Native allies. He did fund troops at the formerly French forts and even a large new fortification at Fort Pitt. During the war, the British had promised that these forts on Native land were there only to oppose the French, and Native Americans in the Ohio Valley and the Great Lakes expected British troops to leave their land after the war. Yet the war was over, and the very forts that had heightened tensions between Ohio Valley peoples and the French at the start of the war were still there, and the British were neither paying rent to the Native owners of the land nor effectively preventing illegal settlement.[35]

For some people in the Ohio Valley, French and British actions from before the war through the recent treaty violations were evidence that *all* Europeans were the enemy of *all* Native Americans. A Delaware prophet named Neolin began preaching to Delawares and Shawnees that Europeans were determined to take everything that belonged to Indians. It was time to reject them entirely. Earlier prophets had given similar warnings, starting at least as early as the 1730s, as Pennsylvania colonists had pushed west. Now Neolin preached that the Master of Life promised help. He would reverse the tide of Europeans and restore the game that had been declining if Native people would stop trading furs to Europeans, give up European goods and influences, cease fighting one another, and "drive from your lands those redcoat dogs who will do you nothing but harm." They were to send the British "back to the lands I made for them, and let them stay there."[36]

The message persuaded an Ottawa war leader named Pontiac. He modified Neolin's prophecies, directing them exclusively at the British, and carried them north to Ottawas and other Anishinaabe nations and Wendats around the Great Lakes. In May 1763, his followers attacked the British (previously French) fort at Detroit. When word spread of the attack, Native fighters besieged British forts all across the region, seizing nearly every one on the Great Lakes and the Ohio River. Shawnees and Delawares besieged Fort Pitt and attacked the settlements that had grown up around it and at the western edge of Virginia and North Carolina. They even targeted British settlements as far east as their former homes in the Susquehanna Valley.[37]

It was during the siege of Fort Pitt that British officials tried to infect their Native enemies with smallpox. In the past, Europeans had understood little about the diseases they brought with them, but this time making Indians sick was a deliberate tactic. They gave a Delaware diplomat blankets and a handkerchief from the smallpox hospital at Fort Pitt. A British trader and speculator who was present recorded in his diary, "Out of our regard to them we gave them two blankets and a handkerchief out of the small pox hospital. I hope it will have the desired effect." It's not clear whether it did, but biological warfare was certainly the British intent. Commander Jeffrey Amherst encouraged his officers to use every possible method "to Extirpate this Execrable Race."[38] The purposeful use of germs for genocide—this was new.

But British policymakers, deeply in debt from the war, knew they could not afford to keep fighting in the Ohio Valley. So in 1764 and early 1765 they made peace with the various Native peoples at war with them. The most important compromise was the Royal Proclamation of 1763. In it, the British crown declared the Appalachian

Mountains the dividing line between colonial settlements and Native land. From now on, no one but the crown could buy land from Indians, and the transactions had to be made through official treaties. No Europeans should settle in the protected lands, and any already there were to be removed by the British army. By 1765 the Shawnees and their allies had all agreed to peace.[39]

British colonists were appalled at the Proclamation of 1763. It, along with taxes that Parliament levied to pay off British war debt, would help to spark the American Revolution. British colonists believed that, in defeating the French, they had won the right to all of the mainland of North America that France had claimed. They were shocked that their own government had proclaimed that they could not settle those lands and in fact was devoting troops and tax revenue to defending the line. The greatest opponents would be land speculators like the Washington brothers.[40]

Shawnee, Delaware, and Ohio Seneca diplomats conducting peace negotiations with the British, October 1764. Ohio Seneca diplomat Kiyashuta holds a wampum belt. Engraving by Charles Grignion, after a sketch by Benjamin West, in William Smith's 1766
An Historical Account of the Expedition Against the Ohio Indians in the Year 1764.
LIBRARY COMPANY OF PHILADELPHIA

WILL THE SAME WORLD DO FOR THEM AND US?

Even with British assurances, the threat of colonial expansion loomed. As Shawnees worried about how they could best continue their way of life and preserve it for their children and grandchildren, they increasingly defined their interests as being in common with their Native neighbors and opposed to people of European descent. And British colonists would soon fight a war against Britain for the right to pursue liberty and opportunity in all of the places that those empires had claimed, including the lands of Native nations. It was hardly surprising that another fight was coming between Indians and colonists. Together with other Native peoples living between the Appalachians and the Mississippi, Shawnees built more formal military and diplomatic alliances than in the past, in order to more effectively fight white settlers. One of the debates would be over how much to combine together: whether simply as allied nations or as something more permanent and unified, even a Native American race.[41]

Still, at the end of Pontiac's War, the American Revolution was a decade off. Peace came to the Ohio Valley, and the Shawnee population grew. Because warfare killed more men than women, polygamy (specifically polygyny, one husband with multiple wives) helped Shawnee families to grow. Peace and prosperity encouraged more births and helped more babies and children live to adulthood. During and after the war, Shawnees who had not yet moved back to the Ohio Valley now did, and towns on the upper Ohio River near Fort Pitt moved west to rebuild near existing Shawnee towns in the central Ohio Valley. Other Shawnees built towns near the Miamis on the Wabash River and the Wendats on the south shore of Lake Erie.[42]

These places were all under Native control, but in some places to the east, leaks appeared in the Proclamation Line. By 1766, more than five hundred British families from the colonies of Virginia and Pennsylvania had pushed into the region around Fort Pitt. That fall, the fort's commander ordered them to leave and had his troops

encroachments on their eastern lands. They heard much that they approved of in the delegation's speeches, and they agreed that the Ohio Valley confederates could notify the Americans that the Muscogees had resolved to join what now would be a Grand Confederacy of Northern and Southern Nations, "to attack the Americans in every place wherever they shall pass over their own proper limits" and "never to grant them lands, nor suffer surveyors to roam about the country."[64]

Muscogee leader Alexander McGillivray tried to build the southern half of the confederacy, modeled on and in coordination with the Ohio Valley Confederacy. Son of a Scottish father and a Muscogee mother, from whom he inherited a Muscogee clan and full citizenship as a Muscogee, McGillivray believed that the way for his people to resist Georgia's aggressive post-Revolution expansion was with a unified Muscogee, Cherokee, Chickasaw, and Choctaw southern confederacy, parallel to the Ohio Valley Confederacy to the north. The allies armed themselves with weapons from the Spanish, through diplomacy like that in St. Louis in 1784. During the Revolutionary War, Spain had won British-claimed lands along the Gulf Coast in what's now Florida, Alabama, and Mississippi and added those claims to the colonies it already had in Louisiana, Texas, and most of the rest of the West. Like Muscogees and Shawnees, the Spanish were beginning to worry about growing U.S. power on the continent.[65]

A united Native confederacy from north to south along the long border of the United States was a huge crisis for President George Washington's new administration. Although the U.S. population was growing, it was not large enough and certainly not well enough supplied to fight all Native nations east of the Mississippi River. Unable to afford a massive war they might not win, Washington and Secretary of War Henry Knox backed down from post-Revolution claims that the United States had defeated all Indians by defeating the British. They formally recognized Native nations as independent and rewrote federal policy to be more like British and French policies before them. For now, at least, the United States declared that it would buy land, not just claim it as conquered. U.S. delegates traveled to the Ohio Valley to inform Indians of the new policy and negotiate a price for some land north of the Ohio.

But Indigenous people between the Appalachians and the Mississippi had come to see the United States as the embodiment of land-hungry settlers. Diplomacy and reciprocal alliance and trade with the French, the Spanish, and even the British were possible, but the United States apparently had goals incompatible with Native interests and seemed entirely untrustworthy. Not seeing this offer as a change of policy at all, Shawnees and Miamis declined the invitation. When a U.S. emissary went to a Shawnee town to try to get them to send delegates, Shawnee Chief Blue Jacket countered that he would take no part in their efforts "to take away, by degrees, their lands."[66] Delegates of confederated nations who did go to the negotiations insisted to the U.S. representatives that the permanent border was the Ohio River. With a combination of threats and promises, the U.S. negotiators persuaded a few present to sign what they called the Treaty of Fort Harmar, but the agreement was clearly invalid. Miami Chief Little Turtle blamed the Haudenosaunee, claiming that they had "seduced some of our young men to attend it, together with a few" Ojibwe, Wendats, Ottawas, Delawares, and Potawatomis. It was not signed by the Ohio Valley Confederacy according to its rules, and therefore it was invalid.[67]

Yet nothing the Native confederates or the U.S. government did stopped the flow of illegal immigrants. In 1788, an unauthorized band of about sixty Virginia militiamen joined forces with the men who had lingered at Vincennes. The U.S. commander at Vincennes objected, but he had only nine soldiers at his disposal. He couldn't stop the militiamen from plundering and killing Miamis nearby. One spring day in 1789, Shawnees discovered men surveying and laying out markers for streets that would one day be Cincinnati, at a site north of the Ohio River between the Great Miami and Little Miami rivers, smack in the center of Shawnee country. When the Shawnees asked what they were doing there, the leader replied that he represented the United States. He showed them the commission that proved it: a signed, written document marked with the seal of the United States, a bald eagle holding in its right talon an olive branch and in its left a bundle of thirteen arrows. When the man explained the commission and the symbolism of the seal—that the United States desired peace (the olive branch) but would fight if necessary (the arrows)—one of the Shawnees countered that he "could not perceive any intimations of peace from the attitude the Eagle was in; having her wings spread as in flight." As anyone familiar with birds and symbolism would know, he said, folded wings would show "rest and peace." To him, the eagle was "bearing a large whip in one claw, and such a number of arrows in the other, and in full career of flight," that it must be "wholly bent on war and mischief."[68]

Now based out of Miamitown and the Shawnee and Delaware towns clustered near it, the Ohio Valley Confederacy grew in size, strength, coordination, and determination to enforce the Ohio River as the border between themselves and the United States. Worried about the growing coordination, Secretary Knox explicitly instructed commissioners "to form separate contracts, or treaties, relative to boundaries, with the several tribes to whom the lands actually belong, avoiding, as much as possible, to confirm the idea of an union, or general confederacy of all the tribes."[69] For their part, British officials in nearby Detroit hoped that the confederacy would form and protect a sovereign multinational Native country allied with Britain as a friendly barrier between British Canada and the United States. Shawnee–British relations grew closer as several Shawnee women married British officers.[70]

The Haudenosaunee would have been a valuable ally in this fight, but the American Revolution had done great damage to them, and they generally had become reluctant to keep fighting the United States. The Revolutionary War had in part been fought on Haudenosaunee lands, and even between Haudenosaunee, with the Oneidas and the Tuscaroras taking the side of the Americans against the rest of the confederacy. In 1779, Continental Army general John Sullivan, on orders from George Washington, had marched several thousand men across Haudenosaunee country with the goal of destroying towns, crops, and storehouses. Haudenosaunee families fled, abandoning most of their towns, including all of the towns in the Mohawk Valley. Some Mohawks took refuge at Akwesasne and other towns that Mohawks had established in the late seventeenth century just up the St. Lawrence River from Montreal, and others went north of Niagara along the Grand River in what's now Ontario. In their new homes, Mohawks and other Haudenosaunee focused on renewing the confederacy, repairing the longhouse. When U.S. officials and the Ohio Valley Confederacy each tried to draw the Haudenosaunee into renewed conflict, their diplomats answered, "We are neither on the one side, or on the other . . . We desire to be still, and to be at peace with both."[71]

As the Ohio Valley confederates defended their border, President Washington in 1790 sent 320 regulars and more than a thousand Virginia and Pennsylvania militia under General Josiah Harmar to destroy Miamitown, which he saw as the heart of the confederated nations. A large force of confederates led by Shawnee Chief Blue Jacket and Miami Chief Little Turtle soundly defeated Harmar's force, killing or wounding more than 350 of his men. Native families had evacuated Miamitown and nearby towns when they heard of the invasion, so the U.S. force was able to burn and loot Miamitown and the Shawnee town of Pickaway. But the confederacy had won the battle, and their women and men rebuilt in the Auglaize and Maumee valleys, where more people joined them.[72]

Shawnee and other emissaries carried wampum belts and the news of the 1790 victory over Harmar's army north throughout the Great Lakes region as well as south to Muscogee and Cherokee towns. They gathered weapons and ammunition from British and Spanish officials and traders in preparation for more battles. Therefore, by the time they heard that Washington had mustered another army in the fall of 1791, under another Revolutionary War veteran, Arthur St. Clair, the Ohio Valley Confederacy had assembled its largest force yet. St. Clair had orders to defeat the confederacy and build U.S. forts in their country. But by the time St. Clair marched his two thousand men into the Ohio Valley, Blue Jacket and Little Turtle were waiting for him with a thousand Shawnee, Miami, Delaware, Wendat, Ottawa, Ojibwe, Potawatomi, Mohawk, Muscogee, and Cherokee men, as well as some French and British traders. Attacking just before dawn, they won another resounding victory. St. Clair's force had nearly one thousand casualties, with more than six hundred killed.[73]

In the fall of 1792, Shawnees, Miamis, and Delawares hosted a council for thousands of people at their towns in the Auglaize and Maumee valleys, including the Anishinaabe nations, Wendats, Sauks, Cherokees, and Muscogees. Shawnee Chief Painted Pole (sometimes translated Red Pole) was the principal speaker for the council, and he opened it with a condolence ceremony and passed the calumet among the delegates. The hosts hoped that the Haudenosaunee might agree to join the confederacy, and they delivered to the Haudenosaunee representatives a large bundle of wampum strings and belts from the many nations they were bringing together. But Haudenosaunee representatives urged the Ohio Valley delegates to make peace with the United States. Seneca leader Red Jacket told them, "We are very glad you have strengthened the Chain of friendship with all the distant Nations from whom you received these Belts" but recommended that they all "unite and consider what will be best for us, our women, and children, to lengthen our days, and be in Peace." Mohawk Joseph Brant told them of the Washington administration's decision to try to end the fighting by giving up the claim of having won all Indian lands in the Revolution, holding back illegal settlement, and negotiating with Native nations more in accordance with past British and French terms. Washington and Secretary Knox knew that the help of the Haudenosaunee was essential in getting what they wanted without fighting in the Ohio Valley, and Brant hoped to use the occasion of mediating for the United States to reinstate the Haudenosaunee as negotiators for the Shawnees and the Delawares.[74]

Brant recommended that Ohio Valley confederates accept a compromise line west of the Ohio River. But they were in no mood to take advice from the Haudenosaunee, and they refused to accept their wampum strings or the $50,000 in goods that the United States offered to exchange for land. Painted Pole picked up the wampum strings that Red Jacket had presented and threw them back at him, accusing the Haudenosaunee: "you are still talking to the Americans" when "all the Americans wanted was to divide us." He told them to tell the Americans "that the boundary line then fixed on is what we now want and that is the determination of all the Nations present, yours as well as ours. You say Washington will make us a compensation if our land was not purchased of the right owner, we do not want compensation, we want restitution of our Country which they hold under false pretenses."

The confederacy delegates listened with more sympathy to Mahican delegate Hendrick Aupaumut, who spoke to them in his Algonquian language about how much the Ohio Valley meant to all of them and how the Mahicans might eventually need to move there to escape the United States. They knew of the long history of conflict, as well as the alliance between Aupaumut's Mahicans and the Haudenosaunee and alliance and trade with the Delawares (Lenapes and Munsees), going back to their trade with the Dutch on the Hudson River. Since then, both the Mahicans and the Delawares had lost their homelands to the United States. In the seventeenth century, Aupaumut's Mahicans had moved with other refugees to a mission town in Massachusetts called Stockbridge. Facing settler encroachment after the Revolution (despite having fought as their own company on the colonists' side), they accepted an Oneida invitation to relocate on their lands as New Stockbridge. To confederacy delegates, land loss in the East was reason to take a stand north of the Ohio River, not to compromise.[75]

In August 1794, Washington tried a military invasion again, this time with more than three thousand regulars and militia under General Anthony Wayne. A much smaller number of confederated fighters than in 1791 assembled at a place strewn with dead trees, taken out by a tornado sometime in the past. At what became known as the Battle of Fallen Timbers, Wayne's force drove off the confederacy forces, who rushed for assistance to Fort Miami, built by the British on the Maumee River just over a year earlier as part of preparations to fight the United States together. But the confederated fighters were denied refuge at the fort, because Britain and the United States were technically not at war. Rather than pursue them,

Wayne settled his men into the evacuated Shawnee, Delaware, and Miami towns and fields along the Auglaize and Maumee rivers and ordered them to build two new forts to prevent rebuilding there: Fort Defiance and Fort Wayne (now Defiance, Ohio, and Fort Wayne, Indiana).

There was plenty of food for the army, because, as Wayne noted, "the very extensive and highly cultivated fields and gardens, show the work of many hands." The riverbanks "appear like one continued village for a number of miles . . . nor have I ever before beheld such immense fields of corn, in any part of America, from Canada to Florida." The men feasted on the corn and vegetables, sent them east by the wagonful, and destroyed the rest, along with most of the towns. William Clark (the brother of George Rogers Clark), who would later travel across the continent with Meriwether Lewis, recorded in his journal of the campaign that "for spite burnt all the Indian huts throughout the vicinity of the garrison and put the finishing stroke to the destruction of the cornfields, gardens, haystacks etc. etc." Another soldier estimated that "upon the smallest calculation we must have destroyed between three and four hundred thousand bushels of grain. It will therefore be impossible for the savages to live through the winter unless their friends the British, are remarkable kind to them."[76]

CONCLUSION

The lack of assistance from the British and the Haudenosaunee, combined with the devastation that Wayne's army inflicted—the fifth or sixth time in less than twenty years that some of their towns had been destroyed—were dispiriting blows for the Shawnees and other peoples of the Ohio Valley. When British and U.S. negotiators agreed in Jay's Treaty of 1794 that Britain would evacuate Detroit and other Great Lakes posts, British assistance looked even less likely. Because the loss of Kentucky lands now made it harder to replace destroyed crops with hunting, food shortages were dire. Some leaders began to negotiate a peace with Anthony Wayne.

Eventually most of the confederacy, represented by Shawnee chiefs Blue Jacket, Black Hoof, and Painted Pole, along with Little Turtle and other Miami, Delaware, Ohio Seneca, Wendat, Anishinaabe, and Kickapoo leaders, reluctantly signed the 1795 Treaty of Greenville. The treaty left them their towns and fields in exchange for ceding most of their remaining hunting lands and no longer defending the Ohio River as the border with the United States. In essence, they agreed, under duress, to earlier treaties that they had refused to sign or recognize. In addition, the United States gained much of what would become the state of Ohio, a couple of other settlement areas including Vincennes, and some spots for forts and trading posts. Besides those places, the United States would "relinquish their claims to all other Indian lands northward of the river Ohio, eastward of the Mississippi, and westward and southward of the Great Lakes." The confederated nations reserved their base, as well as the right to hunt in the ceded territory, and they were to receive $20,000 and annuities of $9,500 "forever," $1,000 of which was annually to go to the Shawnees.[77]

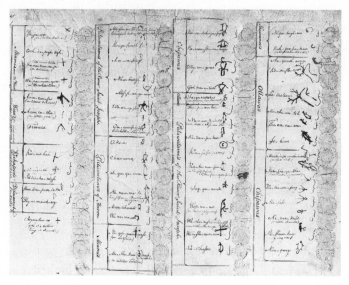

Signatures on the Treaty of Greenville.
U.S. NATIONAL ARCHIVES RG II, INDIAN TREATIES

The Treaty of Greenville was a major loss and a devastating fall from the promises of a mighty confederacy. If major coordinated military action armed with British and Spanish weapons was not a possibility, what was next? Two Shawnee brothers, Tecumseh and Tenskwatawa, had an answer.

CHAPTER 8

DEBATES OVER RACE
AND NATION

I N 1808, THE SHAWNEE PROPHET TENSKWATAWA DECLARED TO
U.S. officials that they were wrong to suspect him of rallying Indians to support the British against the United States. His only
goals, he assured them, were religious and cultural, not military. And
he declared success at those religious and cultural goals. "The religion which I have established for the last three years," he claimed,
"has been attended to by the different tribes of Indians in this part
of the world." Now "they are all determined to practice what I have
communicated to them, that has come immediately from the Great
Spirit through me." While "those Indians were once different people; they are now but one."[1]

Tenskwatawa was describing what white Americans called "race,"
the idea that Europeans, Africans, Asians, and Native Americans
have fundamental differences from one another based in biology.
Race is a human invention, something made up to describe what
Europeans wanted to believe about their place in the world, but its
falsity has not prevented race from having power.

European racial categories were designed to be hierarchical. In
the eighteenth century, the Enlightenment obsession with categories created our modern "races" based on continent of ancestry. Europeans placed themselves at the top of the hierarchy, with Black
Africans at the bottom and Asians and Native Americans somewhere in between. The nineteenth century hardened racial ideas—
combining them with long-standing European beliefs that men are
superior to women—into a philosophy that only white men had the

rationality and independence to be eligible for self-governance and citizenship. In the nineteenth and much of the twentieth century, U.S. policy would fluctuate between an older belief that Native Americans could become as "civilized" as white people if they would give up their nations and assimilate to European American ways and a more rigidly racist belief that Indians were permanently inferior.

Tenskwatawa and his brother Tecumseh responded to this kind of thinking with their own version of racial classifications. They were not the first. Since the mid-1700s, a theory of separate creations had been circulating among Native Americans—the idea that God had created Native Americans, Europeans, and Africans separately. Some versions implied a hierarchy. A Shawnee speechmaker explained, a few years before Tenskwatawa, how the Master of Life had formed the world's people: "After he had made the Shawnees, he made the French and English out of his breast, and the Dutch out of his feet; and for your Long-Knives kind," the Americans, "he made them out of his hands. All these inferior races of men he made white, and placed them beyond the great lake," the Atlantic Ocean. The Creator had made different continents for the different races and had meant for them to stay there. It was Europeans who had messed up the Creator's plan by stealing Africans from their homeland and coming to the land that the Creator had made for Native Americans.[2]

With the guidance of the Great Spirit, Tenskwatawa and Tecumseh aimed to lead Native Americans as a unified race. Their message was that Native Americans were all the same kind of people and different from everyone else in the world. The Great Spirit wanted them to discard their specific tribal traditions and religious practices and overthrow any of their leaders who refused to convert to Tenskwatawa's preaching. United, they would expel the descendants of Europe and reclaim North America for its Indigenous people. The brothers declared themselves the leaders of all Native Americans in these endeavors. Tecumseh reportedly claimed in 1810, "I am authorized by all the tribes" to speak for them, because "I am at the head of them all."[3]

It was not true. Although the brothers did attract many followers, Native Americans had not become "but one," and no nations had authorized Tecumseh to speak for them. Even most Shawnees—the brothers' own people—had little desire to follow their call to discard their Shawnee religious, political, and economic institutions. As we have seen, Shawnees were hardly isolationist. Just the opposite: They had a long and well-deserved reputation for making connections with people from the Atlantic coast to the Mississippi Valley and from the Great Lakes to the Gulf South. They knew that strong reciprocal Native alliances were the best hope for security and opportunity in a treacherous world. But connections and alliances had never required ceasing to be Shawnee, nor did they ask other nations to surrender their cultures, languages, or religious beliefs and practices.[4]

In the nineteenth century, Native Americans would largely reject defining themselves as a race. As the power and population of British colonies and then the United States had grown and threatened everyone in their path, Native Americans would live closer together and depend more deeply on their alliances, but they would remain their own nations. Many would work to strengthen and centralize their separate national political institutions, aiming to stand nation to nation with the United States and assert their rights to remain in their homelands as independent sovereignties. Others would move west to escape U.S. pressure, rebuilding sovereign communities alongside like-minded Native Americans from other nations. The calls of Tenskwatawa and Tecumseh to unite against the United States appealed to many people, but surrendering their distinct identities and practices as Shawnees or Quapaws, as Mohawks or Occaneechis, did not.[5]

TENSKWATAWA AND TECUMSEH

The family history of Tecumseh and Tenskwatawa reflected the moves that Shawnees had made in their recent history. Their mother, Methoataske, and father, Puckeshinwa, had moved from the Shawnee towns in Muscogee country back to the Ohio Valley as part of the return to their homeland around 1760. Tecumseh was born in 1768, in the peaceful years between Pontiac's War, in which their father fought, and the American Revolution. His little brother, who would become the prophet known as Tenskwatawa, was born in 1775 as war was raging once again. Puckeshinwa was Shawnee, so the children inherited a Shawnee patrilineal family and division. Methoataske may have been Muscogee by birth, perhaps born to a Muscogee mother and a Shawnee father, parents who would have given her citizenship in both the matrilineal Muscogees and the patrilineal Shawnees. If she was Muscogee through her mother's line, her children inherited a Muscogee clan as well as a Shawnee one. A few months before Tenskwatawa was born, his father and his oldest brother, Chiksika, fought at the Battle of Point Pleasant during Dunmore's War, and Puckeshinwa was killed.[6]

When war came to the Ohio Valley in the 1780s, the remaining family split up. Methoataske and one of her daughters moved west across the Mississippi River along with at least a thousand Shawnees. The west bank of the Mississippi River was part of the Spanish Empire in the late eighteenth century, and the Spanish, who were spread thin, welcomed the Shawnees along with groups of Delawares and Cherokees. The Shawnees built towns and farms just north of the small colonial town of Cape Girardeau, in what is now southeast Missouri, where they traded furs and skins for European goods.[7]

When their mother went west, four-year-old Tenskwatawa and eleven-year-old Tecumseh stayed in the Ohio Valley. One later account asserted that their mother had made Tecumseh promise that he "would never cease to make war upon the Americans." The brothers lived with their older sister Tecumpease and their brother Chiksika, who took the lead in teaching the younger boys how to hunt. Chiksika took Tecumseh along on raids with Cherokees and Muscogees against squatters south of the Ohio River, when Shawnees were still fighting there. Tecumseh was at one of these skirmishes, in 1788, when Chiksika was killed. Then, in 1794, both Tecumseh and Tenskwatawa were at the Battle of Fallen Timbers when their last remaining brother, Sauwauseekau, was killed. Tecumseh and Tenskwatawa were among the Shawnees and Delawares who strongly objected to the Treaty of Greenville. They moved away from the others and established new towns to the west, in what today is Indiana.[8]

It was ten years later, in the spring of 1805, that the younger of the two remaining brothers had a vision that would give him the name Tenskwatawa, "the Open Door." Around thirty, he was known by the name Lalawethika, "the Rattle" or "Noisemaker." He was living with his wife in one of the new towns, training to be a religious leader and healer, and struggling with alcohol. During his lifetime, the United States had taken the vast hunting lands south of the Ohio River, and now, astoundingly, well over two hundred thousand white Americans were living north of the Ohio, a boundary that his parents had hoped to defend forever. In a vision, the Master of Life told him to be a prophet, and to instruct his people to return to older ways. From then on, he would no longer be Lalawethika the Noisemaker, but Tenskwatawa the Open Door, through which the Master of Life spoke.[9]

TENS-QUA-TA-WA or The One Who Opens the Door,
portrait made in St. Louis, 1823, by James Otto Lewis.
SMITHSONIAN AMERICAN ART MUSEUM

Within a few months of his vision, people were coming to Tenskwatawa's town to hear him recount how the Master of Life had told him that the game had not disappeared, as it seemed. The deer were merely "half a tree's length under the ground." If they did as the Master of Life said, he would turn the earth over and the deer "would soon appear again." In parallel, the Master of Life promised the prophet, "If you Indians will do everything I tell you I will turn over the land so that the white people are covered and you alone shall possess the land." Tenskwatawa told Native Americans to give up alcohol and goods manufactured in Europe. And they were not to fight one another.[10]

Much of what Tenskwatawa preached had precedents in the words of previous prophets and leaders like Neolin and Pontiac, who urged both reform and unity among, as Shawnee leader Painted Pole said in 1792, "the people of one color." Yet Tenskwatawa took the admonition for Indians to become one unified people much further. Through him, the Master of Life instructed them to give up their identities as members of different nations and clans and live together under Tenskwatawa's guidance. They were to get rid of not only European influences but also their national political and religious practices and to renounce their national leaders.[11]

Tenskwatawa urged his followers to leave their Shawnee, Wendat, Miami, and Delaware towns and move to a location on Greenville Creek, a northern tributary of the Ohio River, where the hated Treaty of Greenville had been negotiated in 1795 and which, according to that treaty, now belonged to the United States. There Tenskwatawa and his followers, including his brother Tecumseh, built a new town. Tenskwatawa preached a universal message to the residents and to pilgrims who came to hear his charismatic speeches in a five-thousand-square-foot council house that his followers built. When he correctly predicted a solar eclipse that occurred on June 16, 1806, more people came to visit and to hear what he had to say. A U.S. official who spent two weeks with him in 1808 noted that Tenskwatawa was "possessed of considerable talents" and that "the art and address with which he manages the Indians is really astonishing." According to observers, Tenskwatawa preached that "the great spirit will in a few years destroy every white man in America."[12]

Shaker revivalists who toured the Greenville Creek town in the spring of 1807 concluded, "Surely the Lord is in this place!" Listening to Tenskwatawa's words, interpreted into English by George Bluejacket, who had moved to Greenville Creek with his father, the great war leader Blue Jacket, they heard parallels to their own Christian beliefs and saw in Tenskwatawa the work of the Holy Spirit. Tenskwatawa, in turn, admired much in the life and beliefs of the Shakers. Later, Tecumseh would cite white Americans' denial of the Shakers' prophecies as evidence of American wickedness, noting that "you have shaken among you and you laugh and make light of their worship." Denying their own prophets seemed a frequent reaction among "the white people," Tecumseh noted, saying, "When Jesus Christ came upon the earth you killed and nailed him on a cross."[13]

At Greenville Creek, Tenskwatawa won over an Ottawa man called the Trout, who went on to spread the message among the Ottawas and other Anishinaabe. At his home, near where Lake Michigan and Lake Huron meet, the Trout spoke to an open council of men, women, and children. He displayed eight strings of wampum, four white and four dark, that the prophet had sent. The Creator had told Tenskwatawa that "my White and Red Children were ... marked with different colours, that they might be a separate people." North America belonged to the Creator's Red Children. The Creator was "the Father of the English of the French of the Spaniards and of the Indians" and had meant for the Europeans to stay "on the other side of the Great Lake [the Atlantic], that they might be a separate people." The Creator made them different and intended for them to stay that way: "To them I gave different manners, customs, animals, vegetables etc for their own use ... To you I have given the Deer, the Bear, and all wild animals. And the fish that swim in the River, and the Corn that grows in the fields, for your own use." The "Red Children" could play ball against one another, but "you are however *never to go to War against each other*." Instead they should "cultivate peace between your different Tribes that they may become one great people." While the Europeans were part of the Creator's plan for Europe, "the Americans I did not make—They are not my Children. But the Children of the Evil Spirit—They grew from the Scum of the great water, when it was troubled by the Evil Spirit—They are numerous—But I hate them—They are unjust—They have taken away your Lands which were not made for them."[14]

There was much here that earlier prophets had preached, but what was radical was Tenskwatawa's claims that the Creator wished for all of the "Red Children" to "become one great people." Tecumseh told a U.S. official that "it was the object of his brother and himself from the commencement to form a combination of all the Indian Tribes in this quarter to put a stop to the encroachments of the white people." Past efforts had not worked, and "the Americans had driven them from the sea coast, and would shortly if not stopped, push them into the Lakes." Therefore, "they were determined to make a stand, where they were," to establish and defend the "principle that the lands should be considered common property and none sold without the consent of all."[15]

Tenskwatawa's brother Tecumseh became the greatest messenger of the prophecies. A British official, upon meeting Tecumseh, wrote that "a more sagacious or a more gallant warrior does not I believe exist. He was the admiration of every one who conversed with him."[16] Starting soon after the establishment at Greenville in 1805, Tecumseh traveled to the Potawatomi towns and to the towns of the Peorias on the Illinois River, Ho-Chunks on Rock River, and Menominee at Green Bay. He spoke to diverse people gathered at the post of Prairie du Chien and descended the Mississippi River to the Sauks and the Meskwakis. A U.S. official marveled in 1811 that "for four years he has been in constant motion. You see him today on the Wabash and in a short time you hear of him on the shores of Lake Erie or Michigan, on the banks of the Mississippi, and wherever he goes he makes an impression favorable to his purposes."[17]

Tecumseh called his listeners to leave their old nations and assemble at Tenskwatawa's new town on Greenville Creek. Part of the reason the prophet wanted his followers to live together was to get them away from Native leaders whom he called "very wicked," be-

Tecumseh in Benson J. Lossing's 1869
Pictorial Field Book of the War of 1812.

DAVIS LIBRARY, UNIVERSITY OF NORTH CAROLINA AT CHAPEL HILL

cause they "would not believe, and tried to keep the people from believing, and encouraged them on in their former wicked ways." Tenskwatawa told the Shaker visitors that "the Great Spirit told him to separate from these wicked chiefs and their people."[18] Tecumseh repeatedly declared that it was the movement's "intention to put to death all the chiefs who were parties to the late Treaty, and never more to suffer any village chiefs to manage the affairs of the Indians, but that everything should be put into the hands of the warriors." From now on, Tecumseh said, foreigners should negotiate through him.[19]

Tecumseh, the Trout, and other prophets carried Tenskwatawa's wampum belts and message of becoming "one great people" all around the Great Lakes. Interested listeners pilgrimaged to Tenskwatawa's town on Greenville Creek and returned home to spread the word further. U.S. missionaries, traders, and agents noted that Indians were refusing to buy alcohol, no longer wearing hats, killing their dogs, and purging other things that came from the realm of white people. The U.S. Indian agent at Chicago reported in 1807 that one thousand Indians were passing through on their way from Green Bay, two hundred miles to the north, "on their way as they say to see the Shawnee at Greenville."[20]

THREE PATHS

By the 1810s the Shawnees, like Native nations all across the eastern half of the continent, realized that they would have to make some changes to keep what they thought was most important. As they considered how to respond, they weighed what they were willing to change and what they would not compromise. Tenskwatawa and Tecumseh put the highest priority on restoring North America to Native Americans, at the cost of nationally specific political structures and religious practices. But ceasing to be Shawnees was a hard sell. Like most people, Shawnees saw themselves at the center of the world and the center of the Creator's designs. A Shawnee speaker in 1803 said that "all the other red people were descended from the Shawnees," and "the Shawnees for many ages continued to be masters of the continent, using the knowledge which they had received." Ultimately, a minority of the Shawnees chose the brothers' way. Others moved west of the Mississippi River to attempt a future farther from the United States. And many stayed put in the East, determined to remain their own nation where they were.[21]

Those who moved across the Mississippi built new towns, hunted game, farmed, and participated in the fur trade as their ancestors had, giving up their homelands to seek a good life in a safer place. Moving was a choice Shawnee ancestors had made many times and in many places. Tenskwatawa and Tecumseh's mother had moved west to what is now Missouri when it was claimed by the Spanish. But in 1800 the Spanish king surrendered his claims to the region to Napoleon, who then sold it to the United States in the Louisiana Purchase of 1803. Now the Shawnees, Delawares, Cherokees, Miamis, and Kickapoos who had moved west to escape the United

States found themselves back in it. Tenskwatawa and Tecumseh urged western Shawnees to join the fight and bring back the world that the United States threatened to end.

On at least two visits, Tecumseh tried to recruit western migrants, but they remained committed to building in their new home. Their diplomatic efforts were focused on a military alliance not against the United States but against the Osages, who were fighting to push out newcomers whom they saw as illegal squatters on their territory. Most troubling for Tenskwatawa's movement, Shawnees west of the Mississippi also forged good relations with French Louisianans, who themselves had been living in a foreign jurisdiction (Spanish and subsequently U.S.) hemmed in by the Osages. Just before a visit Tecumseh made in 1810, an Osage war party had killed two Shawnees. One of the dead was related to Tecumseh and Tenskwatawa, so his words urging unity and forgetting past offenses carried particular weight as a relative. Yet the Shawnees in the West were not persuaded. They had committed to an old life in a new place, and their fortunes now lay west of the Mississippi along with allies there.[22]

A third choice was to stay in the East as their own nations, shifting their economies away from hunting and the fur trade and striving to live in peace with U.S. as well as Native neighbors. For the Shawnees, the center for this alternative—an adapted Shawnee life without military conflict—lay at a new town called Wapakoneta, built after the Treaty of Greenville on the upper Auglaize River, as close to their lost towns as possible. There, Chief Black Hoof, a veteran of earlier wars against the United States, led between five and eight hundred Shawnees in economic changes on a reduced piece of their homeland. At Wapakoneta as well as at the neighboring towns of Hog Creek and Lewistown, whose chief was fellow war veteran Captain Lewis (Quatawapea), Shawnees started raising cattle and selling meat, butter, cheese, and cash crops. They built a blacksmith forge, a gristmill, and a sawmill and worked on a salt-processing business with a neighboring Delaware town. They leased out tribal land, thereby embedding their land title in the kind of paperwork that they hoped would hold up in U.S. courts. To finance these ef-

Qua-Ta-Wa-Pea or Col. Lewis, a Shawnee Chief, in
Thomas L. McKenney and James Hall's 1836
The Indian Tribes of North America.
DAVIS LIBRARY, UNIVERSITY OF NORTH CAROLINA AT CHAPEL HILL

forts, Black Hoof made use of U.S. resources, including inviting a
Quaker missionary to help them break into new markets and investing in these developments the annuities that the United States had
paid for land cessions in the 1795 Treaty of Greenville.[23]

Tenskwatawa and Tecumseh called western Shawnees to come
home and fight, but they reserved their condemnation for those who
raised cattle and ground flour for sale. Tenskwatawa claimed that
the Great Spirit had told him that "we ought to live agreeable to our
several customs, the red people after their mode and the white people after theirs."[24] He and Tecumseh charged that Black Hoof and
the other men who had signed the Treaty of Greenville and compromised with the United States had "abandoned the Interests of
their . . . nations and sold all the Indians Land to the United States."
Now, they claimed, these chiefs had "requested the President to . . .
appoint masters over" the Indians. Chiefs like Black Hoof were part
of the Shawnee political structure that Tecumseh and Tenskwatawa
hoped to destroy, in pursuit of a larger polity of all Native people.[25]

Tenskwatawa and Tecumseh were right that U.S. officials wanted
to destroy Native nations. In the U.S. "civilization policy" of the late
eighteenth and early nineteenth centuries, missionaries and U.S. of-

ficials advised Native people to stop being hunters and warriors and instead support themselves entirely with farming and household production. Men should run the households and own and manage any property. Women should stop farming and perform domestic tasks, subordinate to their husbands' direction. Moving women from farmlands into the house and men from wide-ranging hunting lands onto small farms was designed to reduce their need for hunting and gathering land, which could then be given to white farmers. This so-called civilization policy urged Indians to gradually dissolve their political and social structures—their nations.[26]

On the surface, the changes at Wapakoneta and its neighboring Shawnee towns had some commonalities with the U.S. civilization policy, but there were fundamental and significant differences. Shawnee women who planted wheat and cabbages alongside corn were not assimilating into white America. Shawnee men who butchered cattle for meat, used horses to plow fields for the women to plant, and ground corn and wheat in a mill were not blindly following the orders of U.S. politicians, agents, or missionaries. In fact, these Shawnees had exactly the opposite motive of the "civilization policy": preserving and strengthening the Shawnee Nation in their Ohio Valley home. Annuities did give federal authorities some power over Native beneficiaries because they could be withheld, yet they also served as a new kind of security, a way to preserve wealth for future generations. When U.S. officials offered annuities in perpetuity, they assumed Native nations would fade away and obligations would cease before long—permanent annuities would not really need to be permanent. But leaders like Black Hoof were determined that there would be future generations of Shawnees and that perpetual annuities would help them persist. As much as Tecumseh and Tenskwatawa accused Black Hoof of doing U.S. officials' bidding, in fact many U.S. officials worried that Black Hoof's entrepreneurial efforts would make it harder to expel Shawnees from the Ohio Valley. Like Tenskwatawa and Tecumseh and like the Shawnees who moved west, Shawnees at Wapakoneta, Lewistown, and Hog Creek were trying to choose the best path toward a sustainable Shawnee future.[27]

In fact, Tenskwatawa's plan called for even more dramatic changes to Shawnee social and economic patterns than the Wapakoneta model or moving west did. Asking Shawnees to give up European goods would mean removing themselves from a global economy that they had been part of for many generations. For instance, Tenskwatawa's plan also called for women continuing to farm, but to give up European goods would mean doing so without metal hoes or other tools that they had used for generations, tools that did not seem foreign to them by the early 1800s. Shawnee women had adopted new tools for certain jobs. When collecting maple sap, they still used locally made bark buckets, which were light and easy to carry, but when they got the sap home, they boiled it into sugar in large brass kettles.

The movement of Tenskwatawa and Tecumseh was aimed at converting men—men should move to Greenville Creek, men should give up alcohol, men should fight the United States and stop fighting other Native men—but it would succeed only with women's support. The new settlement required women to build the houses and grow the crops. Yet Tenskwatawa's prescriptions also called for women to give up much of what made them Shawnee. He attacked women's styles that combined European and Native materials, telling them to give all of their clothing, hats, dogs, and cats to the first white man they came across. They were to wear, as the Trout put it, only "Skins, or Leather of your own dressing."[28] To many Shawnees, the idea that they should or even could divide their clothing, tools, and foods into "Red" and "White" and discard the latter may have seemed as absurd as U.S. advice that they should abandon Shawnee sovereignty and assimilate entirely into white society.

Tenskwatawa also preached that Shawnees should become monogamous. Although it is easy to imagine that ending polygyny would be freeing for women, in fact having only one wife for each husband would have created more work for married women and left more women single. There were more women than men in the war-torn Ohio Valley, and widows and younger sisters often married into existing households and added to their agricultural production. It's not clear whether Tenskwatawa preached breaking up existing polygynous families or just not making new ones, but he did require that "all Indian women who were living with White men" be "brought home to their friends and relations, and their Children to be left with their Fathers, so that the Nations might become genuine Indians." Parting with a family dog or a favorite calico shirt might not be appealing, but requiring women to abandon their children was another thing altogether.[29]

Most Shawnee women declined and stayed where they were. That decision meant serious food shortages for the large number of mostly male pilgrims to Tenskwatawa's town. A visiting Shaker observed that "the only meal we saw them eat" in a day's visit "was a turkey divided among 30 or 40."[30]

It's important not to imagine a dichotomy of Tenskwatawa's Greenville Creek as a religious place and Black Hoof's Wapakoneta as secular. Religion, politics, and economics were deeply intertwined at both, as well as at the Shawnees' western towns. For all three, planting and harvesting ceremonies and other religious rituals were a vital part of life. Debates among Shawnees were as much about religion as politics. Some Shawnees saw Tenskwatawa as a false prophet. One of the major objections to joining his movement was his call on Native men to discard their sacred songs and medicine bags in exchange for his form of religion. "Medicine" is a clumsy translation for a complicated religious concept that combined sacred power and spiritual lineal connections. A medicine bag contains small sacred items specific to the man carrying it, some of the items passed down from his father and grandfather. They are too secret and sacred for outsiders to know much about, and responsible museums that have medicine bags in their collections have returned them to their owners' descendants or taken them out of public display.[31]

When Tenskwatawa called on men to give up their medicine bags, he was making a radical demand, and one that clashed with traditional inclusivism. Casting aside the old medicine bags would be a striking way to demonstrate devotion to and trust in Tenskwatawa's prophecies. Part of the power of medicine bags was protection in war, and Tenskwatawa preached that his protection was more powerful. He urged his followers on witch hunts against Native leaders who rejected him. The movement inspired a particularly bloody witch hunt among Delawares, as well as the killing of two Shawnee men for "bad Medicine." Tenskwatawa also targeted Native leaders who had converted to Christianity or who, like Black Hoof, had accepted help from Christian missionaries. He accused Black Hoof of being a witch.[32]

Later, some would identify Tenskwatawa's calls to discard tribally specific religion as the root of problems for the movement. A Sauk man named Wennebea told an American, "We always carry medicine bags about us . . . We take them when we go to war . . . We administer of their contents to our relations when sick . . . They have been transmitted to us by our forefathers, who received them at the hands of the Great Master of Life himself." And yet, Wennebea recalled in the 1820s, "some of us did, at one time, at the instigation of the Shawnee prophet, . . . throw them away." Wennebea remembered that Tenskwatawa and his emissaries had told them "that the medicine in our bags, which had been good in its time, had lost its efficacy," so "many of our chiefs cast away their bags." But, he said, "this proved to us the source of many heavy calamities, it brought on the death of all who parted with their bags."[33] Wennebea was looking back, after military defeats, and he blamed Tenskwatawa's advice to discard the religious beliefs and practices of Sauk forefathers.

Like Tecumseh and Tenskwatawa, Black Hoof and Miami leader Little Turtle believed that some centralization of foreign policy-making would enable their nations to better negotiate with the United States and European powers as fellow nations, but they didn't insist on such sweeping changes, and their vision was based on continuing national distinctions. Many leaders east of the Mississippi River in this era shared a vision of strengthening and centralizing Native nations while building strong alliances with other Native nations—we will see a similar process with the Cherokees in the following chapter. As in other societies after the fall of the great cities, Shawnee political structure was designed to encourage balance, reciprocity, and participatory governance. Each town had a council of elder men as well as a peace chief and, in time of war, one or more war chiefs. If there was a need for a war chief or peace chief to preside over multiple towns or speak for the towns with non-Shawnee diplomats, it was a temporary office and limited by town-based leaders. There were female councils as well, which oversaw women's realms, including agriculture and providing food for diplomacy and war. Councils could ask a peace woman to appeal to a war chief not to go to war. Dispersal, resettlement, and decades of near constant war had shifted towns and roles, including heightening the importance of war chiefs, and Black Hoof and Little Turtle were forging somewhat new roles as permanent negotiators with the United States and Britain who accepted annuities on behalf of their nations. Behind that diplomacy, though, there continued to be town councils that made their own decisions.[34]

Tecumseh and Tenskwatawa opposed even this limited nation-based centralization, because they thought separate tribes were part of the problem, not a solution. Tecumseh claimed that the United States wanted by its "distinctions of Indian tribes in allotting to each a particular track of land to make them to war with each other."[35] They charged that separate nations would always have difficulty, even if they tried to hold one another to agreements not to sell land. Indeed, multiple tribes sharing common land could lead to loss of lands, if one group under pressure signed away lands claimed or lived on by their confederates. Europeans and Euro-Americans had certainly shown that they could define one nation's agreement to a land cession as enough, as they had with the Haudenosaunee.

One of the reasons that Tenskwatawa made more converts among some nations than others may have been that prophets who carried his word to their own people downplayed his demands to surrender tribally specific religious beliefs and practices. That is certainly what the Potawatomi prophet Main Poc did. In 1807, Main Poc brought a modified version of Tenskwatawa's message to his town. Whereas Tenskwatawa declared that "all medicine bags, and all kind of medicine dances and songs were to exist no more" and that converts were to gather and publicly destroy their medicine bags, Main Poc encouraged his fellow Potawatomis to continue Potawatomi religious traditions and practices even as they stood up to the United States alongside Tenskwatawa.[36]

BUILDING PROPHETSTOWN

As Tenskwatawa's U.S. and Native opponents put pressure on his Greenville Creek settlement, his ally Main Poc proposed a solution: The brothers could build a new "Prophetstown" more than a hundred miles to the west, near the juncture of the Tippecanoe and Wabash rivers, where they would be farther from Black Hoof and the United States and closer to Potawatomi towns, from which Potawatomi women could feed them until their first harvest. It was also on the road to British Canadian trading posts and the potential Native converts Tecumseh was trying to reach in the North. The brothers heartily agreed.[37]

Tenskwatawa believed that he, as the prophet defending Native people, had every right to establish Prophetstown on the Tippecanoe River, but the Miamis considered the spot to be in Miami country. Tenskwatawa believed that defining land as belonging to one Native nation was not the Native way, and he accused the Miamis of being under foreign influence. It was the United States who "have taken upon themselves to say this tract belongs to the Miamis, this to the Delawares & so on. But the Great Spirit intended it as the common property of all the Tribes, nor can it be sold without the consent of all."[38] National leaders like Little Turtle of the Miamis advocated for pacts not to sell land to the United States, but to them these were, as in the past, agreements among Native nations that did not preclude continuing national rights to allow or forbid settlement by outsiders, even Native ones. There was bound to be trouble, as definitions of tribal and commonly owned property clashed, along with interpretations of the will of the Creator.

In the spring of 1808, a delegation of Shawnees opposed to Tenskwatawa and Tecumseh traveled to the Mississinewa River, south of the Wabash, to confer with other nations. They decided to send Miami Chief Little Turtle and several other leaders to try to stop Tenskwatawa from building Prophetstown on Miami land. The delegates discovered that Tenskwatawa and his followers had already left Greenville Creek and were now high up on the Mississinewa, "making canoes to descend that river" to their new location. In reply to the delegates' warning, Tenskwatawa declared that he would not change his plans, which "had been laid by all the Indians in America." His plans "had been sanctioned by the Great Spirit," and "it was not in the power of man to interrupt them." The Indians, he said, "had unanimously agreed to meet him and remove the cause of their poverty[;] to effect this it only required the Indians to be united—they would then be able to watch the Boundary Line between the Indians and white people—and if a white man put his foot over it that the warriors could Easily put him back."[39]

Tenskwatawa arrived at the new location with about eighty people, including Main Poc's Potawatomi followers, and began to build Prophetstown. By the fall of 1808, as Tecumseh recruited in northern towns, the population grew to several hundred, including Ho-Chunks, Ottawas, Sauks, and Wendats. Men helped with the farming, even though that work went against the return to traditional gender roles. Nevertheless, food supplies were far too short that winter. When they asked for more food from Potawatomi towns, those women refused, not wanting to risk starving their own people. Reportedly, more than one hundred people at Prophetstown died of starvation that first winter. In part because only a few Shawnees were among the dead, people from other nations blamed Tenskwatawa, and in the spring most left.[40]

But more reasons to join Tenskwatawa and Tecumseh came soon enough. In September 1809, in the Treaty of Fort Wayne, Delaware, Miami, and Potawatomi leaders ceded to the United States another large parcel of land north of the Ohio River, adjacent to lands ceded in the Treaty of Greenville fourteen years earlier. Tecumseh and other emissaries traveled from town to town to preach that the treaty was a violation of earlier agreements not to sell land without the consent of all, and they threatened to kill the chiefs who had signed it. Although no Shawnee leaders were part of the treaty, Tecumseh went to Wapakoneta in the spring of 1810 to try to persuade Shawnees to leave the towns of Black Hoof and Captain Lewis and come to Prophetstown. A few left with him, as well as larger groups of Wendat and Ojibwe men and women. Importantly, although men still outnumbered women at Prophetstown, there were now enough women to work together to establish a more reliable food supply. By this point, they had planted two hundred acres of corn. Some of the men had brought cattle, technically a violation of Tenskwatawa's prescription against livestock but an important guard against starvation. Apparently Tenskwatawa figured that this compromise was necessary at least for the time being, as Prophetstown grew. In the meantime, Tecumseh would go farther afield to persuade more people to follow Tenskwatawa.[41]

RECRUITING IN THE SOUTH

In August 1811, Tecumseh rode south with several supporters to invite people of the Southeast to Prophetstown. The Muscogees, Cherokees, Chickasaws, and Choctaws—descendants of Moundville and other Mississippian cities—together had well over ten thousand trained fighting men. With the exception of the Cherokees, they had not suffered any major defeats at the hands of the United States, yet most of them had seen squatters appear on their own land for a generation and knew that the United States was a threat. Some Muscogees and Cherokees had already traveled north to hear Tenskwatawa. Back home, they had reported not only about the prophet and his movement but also about the large new U.S. settlements they had seen south of the Ohio River and west of the Appalachians, on their formerly shared hunting lands. As people in the South gathered and listened to the increasingly famous Tecumseh, their reactions were shaped by their local history, conditions, needs, beliefs, and power structures.[42]

Tecumseh and Tenskwatawa were most optimistic about recruiting in Muscogee towns. This was where Shawnee families had moved in the eighteenth century. While most Shawnees had moved back to the Ohio Valley or west of the Mississippi by 1810, they maintained strong connections. Shawnees still regularly traveled to Muscogee country, and the brothers had kin there. Shawnees, including Tecumseh, had fought alongside Muscogees in raids and battles against the states from the 1770s to the 1790s, both in the Ohio Valley and along the long border that the Cherokees and Muscogees had with Georgia and the Carolinas.[43]

Complicating Tecumseh's efforts, though, was the memory of Muscogee Alexander McGillivray's heavy-handed efforts to organize a similar consolidation. In the 1780s, McGillivray had described himself to his Spanish and British contacts as "head of a Numerous brave Nation, and of a Confederacy of the other Nations," and claimed that the Muscogees were the "head and principal" of the southern branch of the "Nations in Confederacy against the Americans."[44] But for the Chickasaws and the Choctaws, the problem with McGillivray's proposed southern confederacy was that it threatened their sovereignty as well as the peace they had worked to build with each other after Chickasaw–Choctaw wars earlier in the eighteenth century (as we saw in chapter 6). In 1787, after Chickasaw leader Piomingo and his council granted the United States some of their more distant lands and approved a U.S. trading post on Chickasaw land, McGillivray accused Piomingo of ceding land "which belongs to my Nation," and a war party of Muscogees crossed the border into Chickasaw country and killed Americans who were building the trading post. The Chickasaws were shocked at this violation of their sovereignty.[45]

By the time Tenskwatawa had his vision, McGillivray was dead, and the southern confederacy with him, but Tecumseh hoped that the growing U.S. threat would convince southeastern Native nations of the wisdom of giving up some sovereignty to join the brothers' movement. Tecumseh and his entourage visited many Muscogee and Choctaw towns and, according to some accounts, at least one Chickasaw town. Among the party was Seekaboo, a man who, like Tecumseh and Tenskwatawa's parents, had lived in the Shawnee settlement in Muscogee country. By birth, Seekaboo was Shawnee, Muscogee, or both, and he was reportedly related to the brothers. He interpreted for the Shawnee speakers. They made quite an impression. Seventy years later, elderly Choctaw men could still describe what their fathers and uncles had told them about Tecumseh's visit. One of the men, Charley Hoentubbee, said that when Tecumseh and his men arrived at his father's town, they were all dressed alike, each in "a buckskin hunting shirt, a cloth flap, with buckskin leggings and moccasins profusely fringed and beaded." They wore silver bands at the wrist and above and below the elbow, and large silver necklaces. Each wore a red flannel bandanna around his head with a silver band holding it in place. Choctaws remembered that the visitors wore their hair in braids down their backs, with the sides of their heads shaved. Most of the men adorned their hair with hawk and eagle feathers, while Tecumseh wore "two long crane feathers, one white, the other dyed a brilliant red." To southeastern Indians, white symbolized peace, while red stood for war, so the white feather signified "peace among the various Indian tribes" and the red feather meant "war to their enemies, the Americans." They all wore red war paint and were armed with rifles and tomahawks and had scalping knives tucked into their belts.[46]

Tecumseh traveled through the three Choctaw districts, meeting with leaders, giving his religious, historical, and political speech, smoking the calumet, and teaching Tenskwatawa's new war songs and dances. Seekaboo interpreted Tecumseh's speech into Choctaw about "the bad conduct of the white people, how they were seizing the Indians' lands and reducing them to poverty." Tecumseh urged "the duty of living at peace with the other Indian tribes; and that all the tribes ought to quit their inter-tribal wars and unite in a general confederacy." According to a listener, Tecumseh promised that the Choctaws could both "keep their lands and preserve their nationalities," so he may have downplayed Tenskwatawa's call for all Indians to become one, or Seekaboo's interpretation into the Choctaw language may have left that impression. Seekaboo would follow up with a more explicitly religious message detailing Tenskwatawa's visions and prescriptions. Choctaw Chief Pushmataha, a national leader more in line with men like Black Hoof and Little Turtle, accompanied Tecumseh to Choctaw towns to give a formal rebuttal. At each town, he gave a speech forwarding a more Choctaw-centered view of nationhood and urged Choctaws "not to think of going to war."[47]

In his travels, Tecumseh urged everyone to come to the Musco-

gee town of Tukabatchee that fall for the annual Muscogee National Council, where he would give a great speech. Muscogees
from their Upper and Lower Towns, Alabamas and Seminoles
(both loosely part of the Muscogee Confederacy), Cherokees,
Choctaws, and Chickasaws showed up. There were hundreds, perhaps thousands, assembled by the time Tecumseh arrived, including
some U.S. observers who wrote down what they heard. Tecumseh
and his party strode into the square wearing almost nothing but
their silver jewelry. Their faces were painted black and their heads
adorned with plumes, while buffalo tails hung from bands around
their waists and arms. They circled the ground and then ceremonially greeted the leading men. "All ears were anxious to hear" Tecumseh's speech. Tecumseh talked briefly and informally of the
need to "unite in peace and friendship among themselves and cultivate the same with their white neighbors," but for two or three
days he put off formally addressing the crowd, letting each day go
by and then saying, "The sun has gone too far to-day—I will make
my talk tomorrow," until finally the U.S. representatives attending
the council went home.

The night after the U.S. observers departed, Tecumseh gave his
speech to a huge crowd in Tukabatchee's square ground, with Seekaboo interpreting. According to later accounts, Tecumseh "talked
much of conversations with God on Indian affairs." He detailed U.S.
aggression, warning that "after the whites had possessed the greater
part of their country, turned its beautiful forests into large fields, and
stained their clear rivers with the washings of the soil, they would
then subject them to African servitude." He urged men to reject the
ways and goods of this "grasping, unprincipled race" and "wear none
of their clothes, but dress in the skins of beasts, which the Great
Spirit had given his red children for food and raiment [clothing],
and to use the war-club, the scalping-knife and the bow." He spoke
of the long history of Shawnees fighting alongside southeastern Indians and outlined the plan "for all the Indian tribes on the continent to hold their lands in one common stock." He promised that if
they fought when he gave the sign, and if Native northerners and
southerners unified to expel white Americans and their ways and

overthrow any local leaders who stood in their way, they "could re-cover all the country that the whites had taken from them." Then Seekaboo rose and said that he "frequently communicated with the Great Spirit, who had sent Tecumseh to their country upon this mission," and that "those who would join the war party should be shielded from all harm—none would be killed in battle; that the Great Spirit would surround them with quagmires, which would swallow up the Americans as they approached; that they would fi-nally expel every Georgian from the soil . . . that they would see the arms of Tecumseh, stretched out in the heavens, at a certain time, and then they would know when to begin the war."[48]

Some Muscogees said that Tecumseh was a harjo (a crazy man), a liar, or both, and almost all Choctaws, Chickasaws, and Cherokees agreed. For many Indigenous southeasterners, adaptability was val-ued, rooted in the inclusivism of the past. And putting Muscogees at the center of his organizing efforts was logical because of his fam-ily connections with them, but it hurt Tecumseh's chances with the others, given their memories of past Muscogee efforts to speak for other southeastern nations.

Still, when they listened to Tecumseh speak, there was much that rang true. The United States posed a new threat that clearly required new solutions. Tecumseh's talk of declining game struck a chord. But there were also many ways to respond. Alexander McGillivray's 1780s vision of "one Nation" had threatened the regional peace that southern Native nations had worked to build, and this new Shawnee vision of "one people" could do the same. Choctaws listened and discussed, and Chickasaws did as well, to some extent, but almost universally they declined to join.[49]

Many more Muscogees agreed with Tecumseh on the need for revival, but they would take their own path rather than join Ten-skwatawa and Tecumseh in the Ohio Valley. In the coming years, Seekaboo combined efforts with Josiah Francis, an Alabama Indian who would become known as Francis the Prophet or Heles Harjo ("Crazy Medicine"). Together they would convert many people among the Muscogee Upper Towns and among the Alabamas to what would become the Red Stick movement, which combined specifically Muscogee religious traditions with Tenskwatawa's prophe-cies and prescriptions. They did not provide the military help that Tecumseh hoped for, because the Red Stick movement sparked a bloody civil war within the Muscogee Nation, known as the Red Stick War. As we shall see in the next chapter, Cherokees would also have a religious revival movement in 1811 and 1812, but theirs would generally not prescribe violence against either outsiders or Chero-kees who did not join them.[50]

Josiah Francis self-portrait in a British military uniform, 1816.
© THE TRUSTEES OF THE BRITISH MUSEUM

THE BATTLE OF TIPPECANOE

Despite their difficulties transforming interested crowds into active participants, Tecumseh and Tenskwatawa's movement panicked U.S. officials. They heard of large gatherings at Prophetstown and elsewhere. They feared that the British were arming Tecumseh and Main Poc, who, starting in the spring of 1811, led some twelve hun-dred Potawatomi, Sauk, and Kickapoo fighters against U.S. settle-ments that had sprouted up in their homelands. Indiana Territory governor William Henry Harrison marveled that Main Poc's forces felt free to take horses "in open day-light." He was certain that Ten-skwatawa "is again exciting the Indians to hostilities against the United States," and heard in June 1811 that hundreds had gathered at

Prophetstown and that Tecumseh was expected to bring many more from his recruiting efforts.[51]

On his way to his southern tour that August, Tecumseh stopped at Harrison's post. He said he "was to set out on a visit to the Southern Tribes to get them to unite with those of the North," having "at length brought all the northern Tribes to unite and place themselves under his direction." Tecumseh assured Harrison that the United States had no reason to oppose his efforts, which were much like their own in uniting their states. When Harrison asked Little Turtle and other chiefs for news, they distanced themselves from Prophetstown but also insisted that they would cede no more land without the agreement of not only their entire nation but also their allied nations.[52]

A veteran of the Battle of Fallen Timbers, Harrison believed it was time to display the power of the U.S. Army again. While Tecumseh was traveling in the fall of 1811, Harrison amassed a force of more than a thousand infantry, cavalry, and militia to march on Prophetstown. Tenskwatawa heard the Americans were coming and decided to attack first, and signs in the sky seemed to indicate that the time was at hand. A comet with an astonishing two tails appeared in late summer and brightened as fall came. The fact that Tecumseh's name can be translated as Shooting Star surely added to the effect. Then, on September 17, a total eclipse blotted out the sun. When Harrison's force approached, the comet still visible in the sky, it seemed time for a decisive battle, perhaps the first step in casting out Europe's descendants. According to reports, Tenskwatawa told his followers as they prepared to attack that victory would be quick and without casualties on their side, and that "half the army was already dead and the other half bewildered or in a state of distraction and they had nothing to do but rush into the camp and complete the work of destruction with the tomahawk." Others simply believed that "these white soldiers are not warriors. Their hands are soft. Their faces are white. One half of them are calico peddlers. The other half can only shoot squirrels. They cannot stand before men. They will all run."[53]

The women evacuated Prophetstown, and in the early-morning darkness of November 7, between 250 and 600 Shawnee, Potawatomi, Ho-Chunk, Piankeshaw, Wendat, and Kickapoo warriors rode out to confront Harrison's force in what became known as the Battle of Tippecanoe, after the nearby river.[54]

At first it seemed that Tenskwatawa had been right. His force took out the first defenses and surged toward the American soldiers. After two hours of heavy fire, more than sixty Americans, including a large number of Harrison's officers, had been killed and another 126 wounded, so many that the wounded filled all the wagons. Between twenty-five and forty of Tenskwatawa's men had died, and others were wounded. But Tenskwatawa's force was soon running low on arrows and ammunition, and a U.S. bayonet charge forced them to retreat. The U.S. forces took over Prophetstown and feasted on the food that Tenskwatawa's followers had stored there before retreating. Harrison counted the battle as a victory, despite suffering greater losses. Indeed, he would go on to win the U.S. presidency in 1840 as the hero of Tippecanoe.[55]

Tenskwatawa could have made a similar claim to partial victory, if he had not raised expectations. It was a shock to his followers when the Battle of Tippecanoe led to the death of some followers and the temporary loss of Prophetstown. Some converts began to doubt his prophecies, while existing opposition to him became more vocal. Kickapoos and Ho-Chunks who lost kinsmen at the battle threatened the prophet's life. Delawares in a council the following spring reasoned that "both the red and the white people had felt the bad effect of his [Tenskwatawa's] counsels" and merely wanted "peace through the land of the red people," including among Delawares themselves.[56]

But Tenskwatawa saw the Battle of Tippecanoe as only a temporary setback. By December he and some of his followers had reoccupied Prophetstown. Then one of Tenskwatawa's prophecies came true. Four years earlier, in the winter of 1807–8, Tenskwatawa had predicted that within four years, "if the different nations should not obey his commandments . . . then he shall cause the day of Judgement to come." Tenskwatawa would "change the course of nature" and "take down the sun and moon" and call out "great snakes under the earth," and "all the unbelievers shall be utterly destroyed," including "all the white people." At the time, Mahican leader Hendrick Aupaumut, who recorded the prophecy, called Tenskwatawa a blasphemous "false prophet."[57] But the eclipse and comet in the fall of 1811 lent credence to Tenskwatawa's warnings. And then on December 16, just over a month after the Battle of Tippecanoe, a major earthquake shook the continent, which seemed to reinforce the prophecy. It was centered at New Madrid, on the Mississippi River, 350 miles southwest of Prophetstown, and was felt from the Great Plains to Philadelphia. The Mississippi River temporarily flowed backward, echoing Tenskwatawa's prophecy, and aftershocks and more quakes shook the region for months. Newspapers reported eyewitness accounts, including that of one man who reported that he had been swallowed up by the earthquake and then spat out, declaring that "the Shawanoe Prophet has caused the earthquake, to destroy the whites."[58] Muscogees remembered that the comet had appeared at about the time Tecumseh arrived and disappeared when he left and that he had told them, "You do not believe the Great Spirit has sent me. You shall believe it. . . . I will stamp my foot upon the ground, and shake down every house in Tookabatcha [Tukabatchee]."[59]

Many interpreted the earthquakes and other events as signs that Tenskwatawa and Tecumseh did convey the words and intent of the Great Spirit. Some joined the movement at Prophetstown, while others turned inward to their own rituals and explanations. Many Muscogees joined the Red Stick movement at home, and Shawnees and Cherokees mostly recommitted themselves to their own ceremonies, to the ways that their ancestors had dealt with portents and difficulties.[60]

RECRUITING IN THE WEST

In November and December of 1811, when the comet was still in the sky and the earthquake struck, Tecumseh left Muscogee country with Francis the Prophet and a few other followers. They crossed the Mississippi River, presumably to meet with Shawnees and Delawares in the West. That December or early in 1812, they went to speak to the Osages. The Osages were a strong and militarily successful people, and their thousands of fighting men could make a significant difference if war came. Wars against the Osages were serious and long-standing, and truly being "one people" would require ending these old animosities. In turn, ending those animosities would reveal the rightness of their teachings. Tecumseh would be able to tell them, as he had told Harrison the previous summer, that he had "taken the tomahawks out of the hands of those who were ready to march against the Osages."[61]

So it was that a large Osage crowd gathered to listen to the invitation to take a new path. Tecumseh spoke of the earthquake and its urgent call to change. The much later recollections of John Dunn Hunter, who witnessed the speech as a young man, provide the only account of what was said that day, but his account seems in line with what Tecumseh said to other crowds:

> *Brothers*—We all belong to one family, we are all children of the Great Spirit; we walk in the same path; slake our thirst at the same spring; and now affairs of the greatest concern lead us to smoke the pipe around the same council fire!
>
> *Brothers*—We are friends; we must assist each other to bear our burdens. The blood of many of our fathers and brothers has run like water on the ground, to satisfy the avarice of the white men. We, ourselves, are threatened with a great evil; nothing will pacify them but the destruction of all the red men.
>
> *Brothers*—When the white men first set foot on our grounds, they were hungry; they had no place on which to spread their blankets, or to kindle their fires. They were feeble, they could do nothing for themselves. Our fathers commiserated their distress, and shared freely with them whatever the Great Spirit had given his red children. They gave them food when hungry, medicine when sick, spread skins for them to sleep on, and gave them grounds, that they might hunt and raise corn. Brothers, the white people are like poisonous serpents; when chilled, they are feeble and harmless, but invigorate them with warmth, and they sting their benefactors to death. . . .

Brothers—The white men are not friends to the Indians; at first they only asked for land sufficient for a wigwam; now nothing will satisfy them but the whole of our hunting grounds, from the rising to the setting sun. . . .

Brothers—My people are brave and numerous; but the white people are too strong for them alone. I wish you to take up the tomahawk with them. If we all unite, we will cause the rivers to stain the great waters with their blood.

Brothers—If you do not unite with us, they will first destroy us, and then you will fall an easy prey to them. They have destroyed many nations of red-men because they were not united, because they were not friends to each other. . . .

Brothers—The Great Spirit is angry with our enemies—he speaks in thunder, and the earth swallows up villages, and drinks up the Mississippi. The great waters will cover their lowlands; their corn cannot grow; and the Great Spirit will sweep those who escape to the hills from the earth with his terrible breath.

Brothers—We must be united; we must smoke the same pipe; we must fight each other's battles; and more than all, we must love the Great Spirit; he is for us; he will destroy our enemies, and make all his red children happy.[62]

To the Osages in 1811, though, these threats of destruction rang hollow. Osage history over the preceding century stood in stark contrast to Tecumseh's history lesson. The Osages had militarily expanded, conquering, expelling, or controlling everyone in their way, including Europeans. Of course, Tecumseh's history was right, and by the end of the nineteenth century the United States would dominate the continent. But for now the Osages still had the upper hand in interactions with outsiders. Europeans feared them, not the other way around. To exaggerate their commanding height, Osage men shaved most of their hair and wore a five-inch hair clip of tall, stiff porcupine quills or deer tail hair topped by a tall eagle feather, bringing their total height often to seven feet. Thomas Jefferson, no shorty at six foot two, referred to the Osages as "certainly the most gigantic men we have ever seen."[63]

To the Osages, it was the Shawnees, Delawares, and Cherokees who had moved west who were the problem. They were the ones squatting on Osage land. In 1805, a delegation of Osages had signed a peace treaty at St. Louis with some of these rivals, because the United States promised to keep the peace and provide the hosting and presents required for ongoing diplomacy. But the peace had not held, and Osages blamed the Potawatomis for breaking it and for capturing more than thirty Osage women and children who were still held captive in Kickapoo, Sauk, and Meskwaki towns east of the Mississippi, even as Tecumseh spoke.[64]

Still, it may have been the religious message of the visitors, even more than the political one, that the Osages rejected. In Hunter's recollection, even though Osage Chief Pawhuska and the other Osage leaders ultimately turned down the request, they were impressed by "Tecumseh's eloquence," and they did discuss his military and diplomatic advice in council. The Osage reaction to the more explicitly religious speech given by the prophet Francis was quite different. His sermon, Hunter recalled, "enlarged considerably more on the power and disposition of the Great Spirit." Hunter believed that Francis's words did "more injury than benefit, to the cause he undertook to espouse." In 1811, Osages may have been willing to start to consider new military and diplomatic alliances, but they were not at all interested in this movement's call to give up specifically Osage ways for beliefs and practices that to them probably seemed more Muscogee and Shawnee, and perhaps more Christian, inflected as they were with Shawnees' inclusivist interactions with Christianity for generations.[65]

Tecumseh and Francis went home disappointed and would fight their coming wars against the United States without the Osages, the neighboring Quapaws, or even the western Shawnees and Delawares. Even worse, conflicts between nations still arose. Tecumseh and Tenskwatawa couldn't persuade everyone to put aside these conflicts and band together. Francis would help lead the Red Sticks during the Muscogee civil war. Even Main Poc, who led some of the largest attacks in 1810 against U.S. settlements, insisted that the Osages were an exception to the unification of all Native people. He told Tenskwatawa that "the Great Spirit always told him that . . . he must war [upon other Indians], otherwise his medicine would become weak and of no effect, and would be inferior to many Indians of the Nation."[66] Things were even a little muddy at Prophetstown. Some Kickapoos there in 1810 told a Frenchman that they knew the prophet intended to lead them to war, but they were not quite sure "whether he designed to attack the United States or the Osage nation."[67]

While these wars posed practical problems—military effort was directed away from the common U.S. enemy and toward potential allies—they also completely undercut the message of being one people. Generic unity and opposition to U.S. expansion sounded good to a lot of people. Actually giving up autonomy and ceding some decision making to enemies was quite a different matter. Even when they were receptive to calls to unite, Native men and women set their own priorities and followed their own values.

THE WAR OF 1812

Despite the barriers to unity, Tecumseh predicted that if war came, "all this Island will rise as one man."[68] When the United States declared war on Britain in the War of 1812, the time seemed ripe. Many Native Americans would enthusiastically join Tecumseh in fighting the United States, but they were not necessarily converts to the brothers' religious movement and almost universally were fighting as their own families, towns, bands, and nations. Whatever Native fighters' motives, the United States rightly feared a united Native, British, and possibly Spanish war that could overwhelm its small military force. As fears of war with Britain grew, an infantry captain at Fort Wayne wrote in March 1812 that it was said that "if we have a British war we shall have an Indian war . . . I have every reason to believe we shall have an Indian war this spring, whether we have a British war or not." It was clear that the Battle of Tippecanoe was the beginning of the war, not the end.[69]

By the start of the war, Prophetstown had rebuilt from the Battle of Tippecanoe. Rumors of its size varied, and people came and went, but it's safe to say that several hundred people were living there. Tecumseh returned from the West with only a few converts, although he hoped more would follow. He used Prophetstown as a base from which he traveled more locally for the war that seemed to be brewing. U.S. Indian Agent William Wells was sure that "he has determined to raise all the Indians he can, immediately, with an intention, no doubt, to attack our frontiers" with military supplies from the British. There were attacks on U.S. citizens in the West. A party of Ho-Chunks who had fought at the Battle of Tippecanoe targeted American settlers near the Mississippi and Chicago rivers. U.S. officials heard, too, that Ottawa and Ojibwe towns around the Great Lakes "were hostilely inclined towards the whites." U.S. settlers around Vincennes and elsewhere, Harrison wrote his superior, "have abandoned their farms, and taken refuge in such temporary forts as they have been able to construct."[70]

As war loomed, a grand council assembled at the Miami town of Mississinewa to debate what to do. Delegates included Tecumseh and leaders who opposed him; an observer estimated that there were six hundred attendees from twelve nations. A Potawatomi delegate pointedly noted that "some of the foolish young men of our tribe . . . have for some winters past ceased to listen to the voice of their chiefs, and followed the council of the Shawnee, that pretended to be a prophet." Yet most Potawatomis, he said, "consider them not belonging to our nation; and will be thankful to any people that will put them to death, wherever they are found." A Wendat representative spoke for the larger group to those Wendats who had moved to Prophetstown: "We are sorry to see your path filled with thorns and briers, and your land covered with blood; our love for you has caused us to come and clean your paths and wipe the blood off your land, and take the weapons that have spilled this blood from you, and put them where you can never reach them again." Leaders opposed to Tecumseh declared to a U.S. official in attendance that they wanted to "secure and maintain peace." Tecumseh responded to his critics with a speech in which he blamed the United States for the unprovoked attack on Prophetstown. "Our hearts are good, they never were bad," he said, but "Governor Harrison made war on my people in my absence." His own people were for peace, he said, "except when they come to our village with the intention of destroying us."[71]

Neither U.S. officials nor Tecumseh's Native opponents were persuaded. At a council the following month, Ohio governor Return J. Meigs threatened an audience of Shawnees, Wendats, and Ohio Senecas that "if you harken to the deceiver called the Prophet, and the mad man, Tecumseh, his brother, your skies will be cloudy, your paths will be dark, and you will tread on thorns." Handing Meigs a string of white wampum, Black Hoof pointedly responded that he hoped the Great Spirit would persuade both "the white people and me and my people to shut their ears against liars and all bad men."[72]

Ultimately, most Shawnees would decide not to join the brothers' movement. Of the approximately eighteen hundred Shawnees, only a few families—perhaps forty fighting-age men—joined the brothers' war against the United States when it started in 1811. In fact, many more Anishinaabe, Ho-Chunk, and Kickapoo fighters than Shawnees would stand with the brothers against the United States.

When Britain and the United States went to war in June 1812, Tecumseh and Tenskwatawa declared war on the United States. The previous recruiting work allowed them to assemble a fighting force of some two thousand warriors by the fall of 1812, including some Shawnees and a large number of Potawatomis, Sauks, Ho-Chunks, Kickapoos, and Ottawas. The British needed them to keep the United States from successfully invading Canada. When U.S. forces did cross into Canada, Tecumseh's fighters drove them back.

Prospects looked bright. Sauk leader Black Hawk declared himself "pleased" to hear that the British were going to join the fight: "I now began to hope." They pushed the Americans back to Detroit and then took that post and pressed on against U.S. forces, while Potawatomis took Chicago and raided U.S. settlements in the Illinois country. The British armed their allied Native forces and imposed naval blockades to cut off U.S. supplies from Europe. In 1814, the British invaded the United States from the east and took Washington, D.C.[73]

Yet British Canada faced the same difficulties French Canada had during the Seven Years' War. Fighting in the Great Lakes and the Ohio Valley required bringing troops and supplies a thousand miles up the St. Lawrence River. When U.S. ships defeated the British fleet defending Lake Erie in September 1813, they cut off the supply line to Tecumseh's and the other Native and British forces fighting on the western front, just as the British had cut off French supplies on the St. Lawrence nearly sixty years earlier. Without supplies, the British army in the West began to retreat, and Tecumseh's force dwindled as men left to hunt or defend their towns and farms. Tecumseh urged the British to keep fighting in the West, but he feared they would choose other priorities. He recalled past British betrayals: in the American Revolution, when the British at the Treaty of Paris "took them [the Americans] by the hand without our knowledge," and at the 1794 Battle of Fallen Timbers, when Fort Miami's "gates were shut against us." In the current war, he reminded British officials, the king "stood up and gave us the tomahawk, and told us that he was then ready to strike the Americans; that he wanted our assistance and that he would certainly get us our lands back, which the Americans had taken from us."[74]

But the Americans were winning on the western front, in part because too few Native Americans rallied to the cause. Some Shawnees, including Black Hoof and Captain Lewis, even aided the U.S. side by scouting, interpreting, hunting, or fighting, either out of opposition to the brothers, lingering anger at past British betrayals, or fear that fighting the Americans would bring disaster to their own towns and families. Generally, Shawnees avoided shedding the blood of other Shawnees. Delawares largely stayed out of the war, refocusing on Delaware-specific revitalization in the aftermath of the destructive witch hunts. Delaware diplomats worked to try to keep the region at peace. To the west, most people ignored Tecumseh's circulated wampum. Up the Missouri River from the Osages, the Otoes were typical in answering that they "could make more by trapping beaver than making war against the Americans." Main Poc's Potawatomi force, in addition to fighting the Americans in Illinois and around Detroit, crossed the Mississippi to attack the Osages.[75]

In addition to the Osage–Potawatomi war, other wars continued, including between the Lakotas and the Potawatomis and their Ojibwe allies, another conflict that pulled potential recruits away from joining Tecumseh's force. Cherokees, Choctaws, and Chickasaws helped the anti–Red Stick Muscogees and General Andrew Jackson to defeat the Red Sticks. Like Tecumseh and Tenskwatawa, the Red Sticks had maintained that "the war was to be against the whites and not between Indians themselves." But it was not to be so, as that same Red Stick speaker's next words revealed: "All they wanted was to kill those who had taken the talk of the whites."[76] The Red Stick War was a Muscogee civil war, the worst possible outcome.

Tecumseh's fighters retreated with the British army back into Canada, with Harrison on their heels. The two sides faced off in October 1813 at the Battle of the Thames, just north of Lake Erie and east of Detroit. Outnumbered and having had to flee without their artillery, the British force surrendered, while Tecumseh's force fought longer. In the intense fighting, U.S. soldiers killed Tecumseh.[77]

The United States claimed victory in the War of 1812, and Tenskwatawa, Tecumseh, and the Red Stick Muscogees lost. But the war between the United States and Britain was a stalemate. The Treaty of Ghent, which ended the war in December 1814, declared that nothing had changed between those two countries. The U.S.–Canada border returned to what it had been before the war. The British negotiators at the treaty tried to persuade the United States to agree to a permanent independent multinational Native state between Canada and the United States as a buffer and as a reward Britain had promised to its Native allies. The U.S. negotiators refused, especially Congressman Henry Clay, who mocked the "absurdity" of the British proposal, which he saw as, "in all its enormity—a proposition to sever our Country—made under the guise of a generous and disinterested attention to the welfare of their allies . . . savage tribes, scattered over our acknowledged territory." The British negotiators had to relent, and they went home disgusted. One remarked that "I had till I came here no idea of the fixed determination which prevails in the breast of every American to extirpate the Indians and appropriate their territory." Native nations were left to resist the United States alone.[78]

In the short run, the United States, bankrupt from the war, was in no position to enact its ambitions for the Ohio Valley. But Prophetstown was no more, and the United States would soon rebound and begin demanding the Ohio Valley again. Tenskwatawa and his followers stayed in Canada after U.S. officials told him he could return only if he settled in Wapakoneta, under Black Hoof's authority. For a few years, from Seminole country in the Southeast to the Great Lakes, women planted and harvested, and men hunted or tended domestic livestock, and they hoped that the United States might leave them alone in the homelands that remained to them.[79]

CONCLUSION

The early nineteenth century was a critical time for many Native nations as the United States pushed west over the Appalachians and beyond. There were urgent and deadly serious debates about how to forge a future in this changed and changing world as Native nations lost so much power. Some people envisioned a united Native America, one people together against foreign invaders. Others focused on their family, clan, town, or division as their central concern. And some worked to strengthen and save the Native nations that today are the principal site of Native sovereignty and identity.

Native nations exist today in part because their ancestors rejected both the U.S. civilization policy and efforts like those of Tecumseh and Tenskwatawa to persuade them to identify and act as a unified race. With the benefit of hindsight, it is easy to see the brothers' point. A continent-wide militant pan-Indian movement might have lessened land losses and carved out some of the continent as a permanent Native country, independent of the United States. It certainly would have been a strong counter to the civilization policy's demand that Indians stop being Indians. While Tenskwatawa and Tecumseh were wrong about Native willingness to discard the religious practices and identities of their ancestors to follow a new way, they were right that white Americans' version of race—whether the assimilationist civilization policy or calls for Indian dispossession and deportation—threatened everything about Native American life.

On the other hand, even if a unified Native America could have fought off the United States, it was the insistence in the nineteenth and twentieth centuries by Shawnees, Mohawks, Lumbees, Saponis, O'odham, Quapaws, Kiowas, and hundreds of others that they were not and should not be all the same that enabled Native nations to survive repeated predictions of their demise, as well as concerted efforts to make those genocidal predictions come true.

As ardently as nineteenth-century Native Americans debated how to respond to unprecedented pressures, they shared some basic assumptions about the future. None—whether advocates of Tenskwatawa's plan or Black Hoof's kind of economic and political change, whether moving west or determined to stay in their homelands, whether centralizing their nations or living within others' Native or European-descended communities—accepted white Americans' categorization of them as subordinate, deficient, and doomed. In the 1810s, and still today, there have been non-Indians who saw no future for Native Americans, who believed that as individuals and as nations they would cease to exist. One belief that Tenskwatawa and Tecumseh shared with all of their Native audiences, even the most skeptical, was that there would be a Native future. And even Tenskwatawa could not quite see himself solely as a Native American. Historian Stephen Warren observes that when Black Hoof and Tenskwatawa were interviewed in the 1820s, both of them pointed to family and town as their primary allegiances.[80] Despite centuries of pressure to assimilate—to one another or to white America or to a general category of "people of color"—Native people throughout the Americas did something very different from that. They did not vanish, or blend into a single Native American identity, or fade into white Americanhood. They retained and in many cases strengthened their national identities, even as they increasingly found common cause in opposition to the United States.

CHAPTER 9

THE NINETEENTH-CENTURY CHEROKEE NATION

IN FEBRUARY 1816, A CHEROKEE DELEGATION MET WITH PRESI-
dent James Madison in Washington, but not in the White House,
which was still in ruins from the British occupation of the city
during the War of 1812. The Cherokee delegation reminded Madison that their nation had sided with his in that war. The Cherokee
Nation had fought on the same side as the United States, along with
the anti–Red Stick Muscogees and the anti-Tenskwatawa Shawnees, and their side had won. Madison assured the Cherokees that
he knew that they had "fought by the side of their white Brethren
and spilt their blood together" against "our Red Brethren who believed in the lying prophet," Tenskwatawa.[1]

The Cherokees were in Washington to insist that the United
States act like the ally it supposedly was. Andrew Jackson's militiamen had destroyed Cherokee farms and livestock on their way to
and from fighting the Red Sticks, and after the war he attempted
to seize lands from his Muscogee and Cherokee allies, even though
his victories against the British and the Red Sticks had come with
substantial Muscogee and Cherokee help. Jackson had succeeded
in forcing huge land cessions on the Muscogees in their 1814 treaty
ending the war. The Cherokee delegates informed the United States
that 2.2 million acres of those Muscogee cessions actually were on
the Cherokee side of the Muscogee–Cherokee border, and therefore were in the Cherokee Nation and not the Muscogees' to sign
away.[2]

Cherokee Principal Chief Pathkiller (Nunnehi Dihi) and the

CHEROKEE NATION, EARLY NINETEENTH CENTURY

Cherokee National Council appointed a delegation, composed mostly of veterans who had fought alongside Jackson, to go to Washington "in behalf of our nation" and negotiate "a just settlement of the boundary line between our nation & our younger Brothers the Creeks" (the Muscogees), as well as to complain about "the multiplied intrusions on our lands by disorderly men" from the United States.[3] Despite Madison's assurances that he remembered their alliance, for a month his secretary of war tried to persuade the delegates to cede the land in question. But they held out and managed to persuade Madison to relent and recognize nearly the entire 2.2 million acres as Cherokee land and order the removal of illegal settlers from it. The Cherokee delegation went home in triumph. But Jackson was not done. That fall, he traveled back and forth across the Cherokee Nation, threatening, cajoling, bribing, and confusing individual Cherokee men into signing an agreement ceding all the land in question, and he persuaded the U.S. Senate to ratify a new and clearly fraudulent treaty.[4]

Cherokee nationhood was in serious danger. As the white population of Georgia, North Carolina, Alabama, and Tennessee grew to outnumber and surround the Cherokee Nation, those state governments reflected and promoted their constituents' growing belief that there should no longer be Native nations in their midst. To them, Indians had two choices. They could dissolve their sovereignty and live within U.S. states, some as fully assimilated white people and most as "free people of color" with second-class citizenship. Or they could exchange their eastern lands for lands west of the Mississippi, within the Louisiana Purchase.[5]

In the past, when Cherokees or Shawnees had moved west of the Mississippi, those decisions had been made by individual families, in conjunction with their Native and European allies, but after the Louisiana Purchase of 1803, "Indian Removal" to lands west of the Mississippi became part of U.S. policy. Thomas Jefferson saw the vast Louisiana Purchase as a way to provide Indians with choices in the short run. While Louisiana itself—New Orleans and the plantations along the lower Mississippi River—would soon become a state in the union and fully part of the United States, he believed that the rest—what's now Arkansas, Missouri, and the states to their west and north—would for many generations be for Indians, both those already there and any who chose to move west. Jefferson wanted white families eventually to have access to the western Mississippi Valley but figured they wouldn't need it for several generations. In the meantime, Native Americans could have most of the West. By the time white Americans needed it, Jefferson asserted, Native people there either would be ready to be assimilated, would move farther west, or perhaps would simply be doomed to extinction.[6]

The early-nineteenth-century Cherokee Nation rejected these choices and determined to retain both its sovereignty and its homeland. Like the Shawnees, the Cherokees centralized what had been a town- and clan-centered government. They created a republic with parallels to the United States and other new republics in the era, with, as we shall see, legislative, executive, and judicial branches, and in 1827 adopted a written constitution. They defined clear borders for the Cherokee Nation and outlawed selling land to non-Cherokees. They developed and adopted a written form of their language and published a national newspaper. They made these changes in ways that fit both their and U.S. citizens' ideas of how modern nations should function. And they laid the groundwork for the Cherokee Nation to survive the era of Indian Removal.[7]

ALLIED TOWNS AND CLANS

Until the late eighteenth century, Cherokee towns had largely been autonomous, each following the post-Mississippian model with its own councils of male elders and female clan leaders. Cherokees spoke an Iroquoian language and lived in the Appalachian Mountains, among deep green forests and rushing mountain streams. The name Cherokee (in Cherokee spelled GWY or Tsalagi) is a Muscogean word that may mean "people who spoke a different language." Cherokees call themselves DhBƟᏯ (Aniyuwiya), meaning "the real people" or "the principal people." Another name Cherokees use is Anigiduwa, "the people of Giduwa," their mother town in the Smoky Mountain range of the Appalachians.[8]

Recognizing Cherokee governance as both ancient and changing over the centuries is vital for understanding nineteenth-century Cherokee history. In the 1700s, there were at least sixty Cherokee towns, each home to several hundred people. Each was organized around a town square with a council house. The towns sent representatives to meet together in council only when necessary for decisions of war and peace and other matters of general importance to Cherokees. Traditionally, towns had peace chiefs and war chiefs, and major decisions were made in town councils where everyone could participate. As we saw in chapter 2, after the fall of strong Mississippian leaders who combined political and religious power, Cherokees separated political and religious leadership. Unlike Shawnee leaders, Cherokee chiefs were not religious leaders and did not claim spiritual power.[9]

Seven matrilineal clans created and sustained kinship links among Cherokee towns. Kinship was (and continues to be) the basis of Cherokee nationhood—you know you are Cherokee because of who your parents are, your aunts and uncles, your grandparents, and the Cherokees who know that your family is Cherokee. As Cherokee historian Julie Reed explains, "Membership in a Cherokee clan made a person a Cherokee, so clan identity provided a national identity." Clans had both religious and political functions, including enforcing laws when necessary.[10]

Male clan members came together to form war parties, but women had a major say in questions of war and peace. In 1758, Cherokee women described some of these responsibilities: "It is our parts to furnish the warriors with provisions whenever they go upon any exploit, it being our duty to do so[,] they being our children and brought forth by us." On that occasion, Cherokee warriors had gone north to join a Haudenosaunee war party, so the Cherokee women sent a message to Haudenosaunee women asking them "to take good care of them your way as we shall do here." They knew that Haudenosaunee women had similar roles, and they expected them "to fit them out with such necessaries as warriors stand in need of, so that they mayn't want when they are on their march, and when you expect them home again you will have such victuals etc. ready for them as may refresh them after their fatigues."[11]

Cherokee women traveled with war parties to do the food preparation and other gendered labor that the warriors needed, and sometimes women joined the fighting. Women who had been to war might earn the title "war woman" and later be able to speak to councils with great authority. In the 1750s, Nanyehi (Nancy Ward) left her town of Chota to go to war against Muscogees along with her husband, Kingfisher. After he was killed in a 1755 battle, she fought in his place and urged on the rest of the warriors. After that, Nanyehi spoke in councils and treaty negotiations for peace. She earned the title Ghi-gau (beloved war woman). At a treaty conference with the United States in 1785, she presented wampum strings and a pipe with tobacco and reflected that "I have seen much trouble during the late war." But with the peace they were making, she said, "I hope yet to bear children, who will grow up and people our nation."[12]

By the late eighteenth century, most Cherokees agreed with Nanyehi that the time for war was over. During the Seven Years' War, British forces had destroyed Cherokee towns, and after the war officially ended, unauthorized bands of Virginians continued to raid Cherokee towns and attack Cherokees out on the hunt. Disease compounded the losses as the destruction and displacement caused by war left Cherokees vulnerable to diseases they had been able to weather in the past. Many Cherokees had immunity to smallpox from an epidemic earlier in the eighteenth century, but the British tactic of destroying fields and towns created refugees from some towns and overcrowding in others, all of which made quarantine and healing difficult. As a result of war and destruction during and after the Seven Years' War, Cherokees had to cede hunting lands in treaties in 1768, 1770, and 1773.[13]

When the American Revolution broke out, Cherokees had to decide whether to go to war again. As we saw in the previous chapter, Shawnee delegates presented the case for war against the rebelling British colonists in 1776 at Chota, the Cherokee mother town in the Overhill region, along the Hiwassee and Little Tennessee rivers. Older Cherokee leaders were reluctant because of their experience with Virginians' violence, but the younger war leader Dragging Canoe persuaded them to join the fight against the Virginians' western settlements. Yet, because the British army focused on the fight in the North in the early years of the war, the Cherokees had to fight without direct British support, while thousands of rebel militiamen from Virginia, the Carolinas, and Georgia, with no redcoats to fight, were free to target Cherokee towns and fields. By the time British forces came south, most Cherokee towns had made peace with the United States in a 1777 treaty that ceded another eight thousand square miles. Dragging Canoe and his followers continued fighting, in coordination with Shawnees and Muscogees, but even they made peace by the mid-1790s. The loss in lives and land was staggering. The Cherokees had to cede one hundred thousand square miles to the United States, and this time it was not just hunting land but also scores of towns and surrounding farmland, including Chota and other Overhill towns in what became eastern Tennessee. The Cherokees had lost the majority of their once vast lands.[14]

So, by the start of the 1800s, a few Cherokee families had moved west of the Mississippi, where they lived not far from the Quapaws and the Shawnees who had also moved west. The rest of the Cherokees generally lived in three regions: A small population remained in the oldest towns in the Smoky Mountains west of North Carolina; many now lived in the Lower Towns, in what's now northeastern Alabama (Dragging Canoe's old stronghold); and Cherokees who had been pushed out of Chota and other towns in present-day Tennessee established the Upper Towns, including Amohee, Hiwassee, and the future capital of New Echota, in present-day northern Georgia and southeastern Tennessee. Each region had its own council—the Smoky Mountain towns near today's town of Cherokee, the Lower Towns at Willstown, and the Upper Towns at Ustanali.[15]

Nearly a million U.S. citizens surrounded the fifteen to sixteen thousand people in the Cherokee Nation. As early as 1809, Turtle at Home, one of the Cherokee chiefs, reported that people from the United States were building two settlements a mile from his town. The need to speak with one voice against further loss was urgent.[16]

FORMING A NATIONAL GOVERNMENT

Cherokees determined to hold on to their remaining lands and sovereignty not through war but by way of strong and consistent diplomacy to insist on their right to continue as a neighboring nation to the United States. To do so, they would need to end the diffuse decision making that had allowed U.S. officials and even individual land speculators to persuade a few Cherokee men to sign agreements to sell off the Cherokee Nation piece by piece, as Andrew Jackson had. The most important function of the newly centralized national government would be to protect Cherokee land and sovereignty against their aggressive neighbor. Sometimes U.S.-focused histories assume these changes were motivated by a desire to imitate or impress the United States. In fact, early-nineteenth-century Cherokee political leaders wanted the Cherokee Nation to take its place among the nations of the world and have its sovereignty respected by other nations. Just as the fledgling United States claimed to be "among the powers of the earth" in its Declaration of Independence, the Cherokee Nation would assert itself as a global sovereign presence.[17]

Losses in previous wars turned most Cherokees against military solutions like those proposed by Tecumseh and the Red Sticks. Some Cherokees were drawn to prophets—whether Tenskwatawa, Francis, or Christian missionaries—while others attacked them as impostors. Some Cherokees did perform acts of purification and change their clothing styles, especially after the 1811–12 earthquakes, but Cherokee revivals remained mainly inward-looking religious movements rather than political or military ones, in part because religious and political authority were more separate among the Cherokees than the Muscogees or Shawnees and in part because Cherokees had firmly decided to centralize decision-making and avoid war. If anything, Cherokee religious revivals reflected and strengthened the people's determination to remain Cherokee in their homelands and added momentum to their nationalization movement.[18]

Cherokees had killed one another in political disputes in the past, including over ceding land to the United States (and they would again during the extreme crises of the 1830s), but in 1809 Cherokees made structural changes that allowed them to speak largely with one voice for more than two decades. The immediate impetus came when a rumor circulated that Principal Chief Black Fox was considering trading Cherokee land for land west of the Mississippi River. Because U.S. officials demanded land in the East in exchange for land in the Louisiana Purchase, moving west was highly controversial within the Cherokee Nation. Every family that

moved had the potential to further erode Cherokee territory. In reaction to this most recent threat, opponents of westward migration
deposed the principal chief.[19]

This new emergency easily could have led to more violence and
death and perhaps to civil war, but the Cherokees were determined
to stop the cycle of land cessions and retributions. In the fall of 1809,
men and women gathered at the Cherokee town of Willstown
(today called Fort Payne, Alabama), representing towns all across
Cherokee country. The council unanimously agreed to reinstate
Black Fox as principal chief but also appointed his opponents to
important offices, including second chief. They wrote together as a
full council to declare their newly unified message to the United
States: "It has now been a long time that we have been much confused and divided in our opinions but now we have settled our
affair[s] to the satisfaction of both parties and become as one. You
will now hear from us not from the lower towns nor the upper towns
but from the whole Cherokee nation."[20]

In addition to reinstating the deposed chief, they agreed to oppose all future land cessions, and they made changes to their governing structure, including written laws and a centralized national
government. They hoped that instituting what Europeans and their
descendants in the Americas saw as modern governance would give
them the legal power and status as a sovereign nation to resist the
United States. They also centralized governance to try to prevent
groups of chiefs from acting on their own. These changes were part
of a global pattern of redefining nationhood with written laws. A
particular version of nationalism was rising in Europe and other
parts of the world in the late eighteenth and early nineteenth centuries. Early definitions of "nation" had been looser, but now nationalism gained a sharper definition, as a scholar of European history
puts it: the "belief that people living in particular geographical
spaces share distinctive cultural and historical traditions and have
the right to live in an independent political state." Cherokees and
many others, including the founders of the United States and contemporaneous nationalizing leaders in France and later Germany
and Italy, hoped to create this kind of politically centralized sover-

eignty, recognized by people both within and outside the nation as binding a certain kind of people together.[21]

The new centralization of government also suited Cherokees' newly spread-out living patterns. With the displacements of the previous decades, towns had already ceased to be the focus of Cherokee politics and identity. Many towns had been lost entirely, and most families who rebuilt chose to spread out on family farms and small communities rather than concentrate in towns, which had proved vulnerable to military attack and disease. Clans remained strong, connecting extended kin spread over their various farms and small communities. People still gathered for ceremonies and ball games, and regional councils continued to meet, but for most Cherokees there was no longer a strong connection to a group of male town leaders.[22]

The 1809 reforms created a permanent National Council that would meet every fall, rather than sporadic councils. The nation would be led by a principal chief and a second chief, but neither would be empowered to make treaties without direction and involvement from the National Council at its annual meeting, whose representatives came from throughout Cherokee country. To prevent outsiders from negotiating with unauthorized groups between sessions of the National Council, the Cherokees created a standing committee of thirteen men, which at first functioned as an executive branch and later as an upper house of the legislature, along with the National Council as the lower house. The committee could make decisions throughout the year as was necessary, but no major decisions would go into effect without ratification by the National Council at its annual session. As a later law spelled out, "the affairs of the Cherokee Nation shall be committed to the care of the Standing Committee; but the acts of this body shall not be binding on the Nation in our common property and without the unanimous consent of the members and Chiefs of the Council." There could be no treaties and no land cessions without *unanimous* approval by the National Council. Because of the need to react quickly to fend off U.S. attempts to seize land, the committee was generally composed of men who did business with the United States, and several could speak, read, and write English. By contrast, the National Council and its speaker generally spoke only Cherokee and were respected leaders in their regions.[23]

The leadership of Pathkiller and Charles Hicks reflects how the Cherokee Nation balanced two kinds of leaders. Pathkiller, who served as principal chief for most of the 1810s and '20s, was a traditional kind of Cherokee leader, a wise Lower Town elder respected as a military hero. By contrast, Second Chief Charles Hicks was the son of a white trader and a Cherokee mother and could read and write in English. Hicks practiced Christianity and for a while had served as the interpreter for the U.S. agent to the Cherokees. It's important not to exaggerate the differences between these two men. Charles Hicks was fully Cherokee, having inherited his clan from his mother and grown up in the nation. Like Pathkiller, he had been a warrior and practiced polygamy. Hicks knew Cherokee oral traditions well and made sure that younger leaders also learned them as they rose in the government. And, perhaps most important, both Hicks and Pathkiller fully supported centralization for the common goal of protecting the Cherokee Nation.[24]

U.S. officials knew exactly what the Cherokee Nation was doing, and they did not like it. U.S. Agent Return J. Meigs lamented in 1816 that the Cherokees had developed "an erroneous idea of their sovereignty and independence." As he described it, they wanted the Cherokee Nation to be "an empire within an empire," such that the Cherokee Nation and the United States would have "a veto on the other" where land was concerned. Of course, that *was* what they wanted—to continue their sovereignty over their homeland and have the powers that a nation should.[25]

Cherokee sovereignty was not only a tool against the United States, though. Centralization served other purposes, and it held through other crises of the era. As evidenced by the Cherokee declaration of war on the Red Sticks, foreign relations between Native nations remained important in this era of rising U.S. power. In the past, U.S. negotiators, including Andrew Jackson after the War of 1812, had taken advantage of a lack of clarity about what land belonged to which Native nations in order to try to seize land, so in

1821 a council of Cherokees and Muscogees met at Muscogee Chief William McIntosh's place and made a treaty setting a boundary line between their nations. As often happens when creating borders, there were people living in places inconvenient for the border drawing. The treaty didn't require people to move but instead agreed that "all the Creeks [Muscogees] that are north of the said line above mentioned shall become subjects to the Cherokee Nation. . . . All Cherokees that are south of the said line shall become subjects of the Creek Nation." Cherokees could live in the Muscogee Nation, and Muscogees could live in the Cherokee Nation, but like any foreigners, they had to abide by the laws of the nation they were in.[26] As in the past, the two nations appointed ambassadors to the other. The ambassadors attended one another's national councils and had the right to speak there as diplomats. Cherokee–Muscogee relations were hardly new, but as both became more centralized nations and strove to avoid future civil war or wars between their nations, they used methods of nineteenth-century nationhood, including strong and representative legislatures and explicitly drawn borders.[27]

FARMS, FERRIES, AND PLANTATIONS

Some of the strongest voices for banding together as a nation came from women. Women's Councils in the 1810s repeatedly reminded Cherokee men that the land was women's realm and not theirs to give away. At one National Council meeting, Nancy Ward, by then holding the title of beloved war woman, and other representatives of the Women's Council advised the National Council to keep resisting land cessions. They explained, "We have raised all of you on the land which we now have, which God gave us to inhabit and raise provisions. We know that our country has once been extensive, but by repeated sales has become circumscribed to a small track." Moving west was no solution, because "we do not wish to go to an unknown country." Instead, "your mothers, your sisters ask and beg of you not to part with any more of our land. We say ours. You are our descendants; take pity on our request. But keep it for our growing children ... Keep your hands off of paper talks ... Children, don't part with any more of our lands but continue on it & enlarge your farms. Cultivate and raise corn & cotton and your mothers and sisters will make clothing for you."[28]

As we saw with the Shawnees, when Cherokees lost towns, women had to make new homes and farms. They had to replant orchards and find fresh water to carry to their homes. Men helped, as they always had, in the heavy work of clearing fields, as well as at times that needed all hands for harvesting and shucking the corn. Increasingly, when Cherokee families rebuilt, they made log cabins with wood floors and chimneys, in the latest styles. Cherokee women had long woven cloth from mulberry, nettle, and other plants but had done so less since beginning to trade leather and other deerskin products to Europeans for European cloth—indeed, Cherokees hunted a great deal more deer in the eighteenth century than before. But as Cherokees lost land at the end of the eighteenth century, the deerskin trade declined and Cherokee farming again made up a larger percentage of the Cherokee economy. They added a large production of sweet potatoes, as well as peanuts, okra, watermelons, and peaches from Africa and Europe, to their corn, beans, and squash. Women turned back to weaving plants, this time primarily cotton. By the early decades of the nineteenth century, Cherokee leader Charles Hicks noted that "there is scarcely a family but what understands the use of the card and spinning wheel; ... The arts of weaving and knitting have become a common part of the female attention of this nation."[29] By the 1820s Cherokees owned more than seven hundred looms and over two thousand spinning wheels.[30]

Rebuilding farms and homes was hard, but at least women knew what they had to do; men's traditional work was harder to re-create. The deerskin trade had been a pillar of the Cherokee economy for generations, but suddenly making a living by hunting was no longer possible. Men still hunted near home and went on long-distance hunting expeditions in the fall and winter, but only those who traveled hundreds of miles and crossed the Mississippi River to hunt found plentiful game. Warfare had also accounted for a fairly large proportion of men's work in the preceding generation or two, and that had changed as well.[31]

When the fighting ceased and hunting was unprofitable, many men began to raise livestock on their wives' and sisters' family farms, work that paralleled hunting by providing meat to their families and for export—indeed, most let their livestock graze free and went out to hunt them when they wanted meat. Along with his description of women's work, Charles Hicks noted that the vast majority of Cherokee families had "either horses or cattle; and perhaps there is none without a stock of hogs."[32]

Some Cherokee men took advantage of the changing economy all across the continent and found a place at the cutting edge of nineteenth-century economic development in North America with large-scale trade operations. They established ferries, taverns, and inns along the roads that had long connected Cherokee towns to one another and places beyond, which now had more traffic, both Cherokee and non-Cherokee. Like Black Hoof and the Shawnees at Wapakoneta, they built sawmills to process timber, grain mills to grind wheat flour and cornmeal, and cotton gins to remove seeds from cotton bolls. Some Cherokee men worked for pay as carpenters or blacksmiths, building or repairing spinning wheels, looms, saddles, shoes, and silver goods bought by Cherokees and non-Cherokees.[33]

And some established cotton plantations, enslaving people of African descent. As in the United States, Black captives became capital for nineteenth-century Cherokee development. In the 1780s and '90s, Cherokees had raided plantations as part of their attempt to undermine the colonists' economy on the frontier and force them out of Cherokee hunting lands. In their raids, they took captives of African descent and sold them to Spanish or British colonies or to white Americans, including some who lived in the Cherokee Nation. By the time those wars ended, some in the Cherokee Nation were using enslaved Black laborers to expand their own agriculture, and some bought more from slave markets in the United States as they established cotton plantations.[34]

People of African descent had long lived in the Cherokee Nation. Some had moved there in search of better opportunities, whether freedom, if they had escaped slavery, or relatively better economic, social, and political freedoms, if they were already free. Some of these early Black immigrants became Cherokee citizens and married into Cherokee families. Others had been captured by Cherokee fighters in wars against white settlers. Of those, some became free, but others remained enslaved.

Jack Civills was a free Black man who married a Cherokee woman in the 1780s and lived in the Cherokee Nation the rest of his life. He owned a tavern and store that had Cherokee, white, and Black customers. Like white husbands of Cherokee women, Civills became a "countryman," meaning he had some rights of a Cherokee citizen; any children these men had with Cherokee wives were fully Cherokee, inheriting their mother's clan. Civills's freedom and citizenship offended the white U.S. agent to the Cherokees. The agent admitted that Civills "has obtained property by dint of his industry" but, in the mounting racism that U.S. men of his generation had no shame in expressing, concluded that "he certain is a spoiled Negro." The agent blamed the Cherokee Nation for treating him with "equality," which "appears too much for him to bear." Underneath the agent's disdain lies a truth about Civills and about Cherokee society: In 1803, the extension of Cherokee citizenship to Civills meant he was subject to their laws and not those of the United States. The agent recognized that "his Indian connection creates an idea of Indian independence" and belief that he is "not subject to the laws of the U. States."[35]

Similarly, a Cherokee family around the 1780s adopted a girl of African descent named Molley who had been enslaved in Georgia. They gave her the Cherokee name Chickaua, and her adoption gave her and her future descendants membership in a family and the Deer clan. When a Cherokee tried to re-enslave Molley and her children, her clan protested to the National Council that she was a free Cherokee and that her children born in the Cherokee Nation "have ever been and considered native Cherokees."[36]

Yet as the deerskin trade declined and commercial farming became the obvious route to economic prosperity in the rural South, a few Cherokee families amassed great wealth using the forced labor of Black men and women to grow cotton and export it to textile factories in the northern United States and in England. If the idea of Native plantation owners seems shocking, it is a reminder that nineteenth-century Native Americans, like all human beings, were people of their times. The nineteenth-century U.S. South had created a dramatic way to build wealth through the legal ownership of other people.[37]

The numbers of enslaved people grew. Whereas in the late eighteenth century around one hundred people of African descent lived in the Cherokee Nation, with varying degrees of freedom, by 1809 Cherokees held nearly six hundred people in bondage. In the next two decades, the number of enslaved people would more than double, and the Cherokees would adopt a racist Black code, though without the brutal punishments in the codes of neighboring states. Cherokee law forbade marriage between "negro slaves" and Indians or whites, outlawed property ownership by enslaved people, and prevented free Black people from moving into the nation without a permit. This acceleration in slavery and the closing off of paths to citizenship would have terrible consequences for enslaved people and their descendants.[38]

In their economic lives, Cherokees resembled white families in neighboring states, most of whom also farmed a few acres, raised domestic animals, and practiced the religion of their ancestors. Even a generation later, the 1835 census recorded 7.4 percent of Cherokee households as having enslaved people, and 1.5 percent enslaved ten or more people—numbers roughly similar to those of the surrounding white population. Perhaps the most consequential difference was that a far higher percentage of non-slaveholding white men aspired to own cotton plantations or enable their sons to become planters—and they believed Cherokee land was the path to that dream.[39]

Still, the vast majority of Cherokees in the early nineteenth century lived not that differently from their grandparents. At least 85 percent of the population spoke no English, and all children in the nation learned to speak Cherokee. They thought of their identity in terms of clan and family, and considered land within the Cherokee Nation to belong to the nation as a whole, even if controlled and managed by particular families. They continued their ancestors' religion and ceremonies and played or gambled on the game of stickball. Nineteenth-century Cherokees' idea of a nation was not necessarily the same as that of their ancestors, but the Cherokee Nation was a Cherokee vision.[40]

As in the young United States, centralization was about the economy as well as sovereignty. Centralized governance helped Cherokees to cement their economic position in a global market. They knew that unity and centralization would fortify the Cherokees against the U.S. advances, but they also needed to regulate business interactions as part of the nineteenth-century market economy. Treaties previously made with the United States included annuities of $9,000—a payment each year in perpetuity—which Cherokee leaders believed would allow their nation to pursue more viable economic strategies: sawmills, grain mills, and plantation agriculture.[41]

As in the United States and in other Native nations, political centralization was controversial among the Cherokees. Many people weren't sure they trusted the new leaders who wanted to centralize power, and they worried that they would lose the widely participatory nature of their local councils and clans. Because only male Cherokees could vote in the new national elections or serve in the new National Council, women were in danger of losing power. It was an open secret that the men pushing for centralization and regulation also seemed to be benefiting the most from the economic change and wanting new laws and institutions to protect their plantations and other businesses.

Yet even as the National Council passed laws to protect these men's wealth, many traditional parts of Cherokee law and governance remained in place. Cherokees had long distinguished between property that could belong to an individual man or woman, family, or household—such as clothing, jewelry, houses, kettles, guns, and captives—and land, game (before it was killed), and natural resources that were held in common by Cherokees generally. To the category of individual family property were added livestock, ferries, and taverns, and the category of captives expanded to include large numbers of human beings enslaved on cotton plantations. But common property and traditional rules of inheritance persisted alongside the changes. When the wealthy plantation-owning Cherokee James Vann wanted to will his wealth to his son rather than to his sister's children, as was the tradition for Cherokee families, the National Council allowed most of it to pass to his son but intervened to reserve some property for matrilineal heirs.[42]

Under U.S. law and its system of coverture, inherited from Britain, when a woman married, her husband gained legal ownership of property she brought to the marriage. That was not the case under Cherokee law, and no husband—Cherokee or not—could sell his Cherokee wife's property. A Cherokee woman named Ocuma explained the law to U.S. Agent Meigs. Around 1780, she had married an American named John Melton, "according to the established customs of my nation." Having been married to her and lived in the Cherokee Nation for thirty-five years, Melton was "recognized as one of my nation." When he died, she and their children inherited the property under, as she explained, "the laws of the Cherokee nation and existing treaties" with the United States, in opposition to the claims of Melton's brother that he should inherit.[43] Historian Julie Reed points out that these protections of both women's and men's property rights provided Cherokee families with "double protection" for their daughters and their sons.[44] The emerging Cherokee national political system protected both personal property and the land generally as all being part of the Cherokee Nation.[45]

Even as Cherokee institutions changed, consensus decision-making remained their central value. Women's Councils continued to meet during the year before the National Council and present their opinions at the full meeting. Both the National Committee and the National Council worked by consensus, and the custom continued that all Cherokee men and women attended the council to hear the discussions and voice their opinions. Historians often note similarities between the early U.S. government and the changes the Cherokee Nation made to its national government, but similarities with the Haudenosaunee are just as striking, including the need for consensus and unity and the continuing importance of women's institutions.[46]

The reforms of 1809 helped the Cherokee Nation to stand against attempts to take Cherokee land, but Andrew Jackson found ways around them. In 1817, he again traveled to the Cherokee Nation, now with the support of newly elected president James Monroe. Jackson presented the Cherokees with a choice: They could move west of the Mississippi River, or each Cherokee man could have 640 acres of former Cherokee land and become a U.S. citizen. The National Council responded in writing that "we wish to remain on our land, and hold it fast." Again Jackson peeled off several Cherokee men, including representatives of those who had already moved west, to sign a vague treaty that they saw as merely recognizing that some Cherokees had moved west but that Jackson interpreted as the first step toward mass removal.[47] Disastrously for those trying to hold on to the nation in the East, at least fifteen hundred Cherokees decided to move west of the Mississippi River in the 1810s to join those already there in their pursuit of a life free from white intrusion. Their decision may have occurred in part because they couldn't bring themselves to agree with the political and economic changes happening in the nation and so, in adherence to the rules of consensus, they withdrew. The Seminole Nation was created under similar conditions when some people within the Muscogee Confederacy left it to create their own separate nation. And around three hundred households accepted the 1817 treaty's opposite offer of 640 acres in their individual names.[48]

The Cherokees who remained were more unified in their determination to stay in place as the Cherokee Nation, and they made the centralizing reforms work. The National Council reiterated its declaration that only its unanimous approval could cede lands, and in 1819 it declared that it would cede no more land at all. Anyone who moved west of the Mississippi River would lose any claim on the common property of the Cherokee Nation. The National Council also created a National Treasury to pull funds away from the U.S. agent, who had been using his control of the money to coerce removal. And, importantly, the families that had accepted 640-acre plots did not stop being Cherokee. On the contrary, they kept their identity, and ultimately they would use individual landownership to keep their lands and retain a Cherokee Nation in the East permanently, even when the United States forced most Cherokees west.[49]

LEADING A NATION

As the Cherokee Nation centralized, two men who were neighbors in the Upper Towns rose in prominence. Major Ridge and John Ross were in the delegation that persuaded Madison to reverse Jackson's claim to Cherokee lands in 1816, and both steadfastly refused to sign any of the agreements in the following few years that sometimes fooled or tempted other leaders. In the years to come, they would both lead their nation in its quest to stay in the Cherokee homeland, though their ultimate fates would be dramatically different.

Major Ridge was born around 1771 at Great Hiwassee, one of the towns that was lost to Tennessee in the American Revolution. As a young man, he got the name Ganundalegi (ᏍᎤᎡᎵᏱ), which means "he walks along a high ridge," because when he tracked deer, he liked to follow the ridgeline. The Ridge, as he was known in English, was the fourth son of a mother in the Deer Clan and a father who had fought in earlier Cherokee wars. All of his life he would remember his family's expulsion from their town, as he later told an interviewer, "by the invasions of the white people, who burned their villages, and killed their people." His parents, "wearied of these hostile incursions," decided to leave. The family canoed down the Hiwassee River to the Tennessee River and then hid out in the mountains above what's now Chattanooga, among the ridges that gave the young man his name. He joined war parties to fight against the squatters in his family's old home. Eventually he would be called Major Ridge, in recognition of his military leadership. He began his political career young, chosen at age twenty-one to be a member of the National Council. He later recalled that he arrived for his first council "in meagre attire" on a terrible horse. He listened closely to the speeches of men more experienced and articulate than he was, and soon he was known as one of the National Council's great orators and wise decision makers. He was one of the thirteen men chosen for the first standing committee in 1809.[50]

Major Ridge married a Cherokee woman named Sehoya (Susannah Wickett), and around 1819 they moved to the Oostanaula River (near today's Rome, Georgia) as part of the migration from the Hiwassee River region to form the new Upper Towns. Like other Cherokees, rather than rebuild towns surrounded by communal fields, they lived on separate family farms. Nearby, Major Ridge's brother Uwati and Uwati's Cherokee wife, Susanna Reece, also built a farm.

Younger than Major Ridge, John Ross (JᎣᎥᎫᎯ/Guwisguwi) was born in 1790 at Tahnoovayah (Turkeytown), on the Coosa River, one of the Lower Towns founded after the American Revolution. Through his Cherokee mother, Mollie McDonald, he inherited membership in the Bird Clan. His father, Daniel Ross, was a Scottish trader. Daniel Ross hired an English-speaking schoolmaster to teach his children to speak, read, and write English. Then he sent John and his brother Lewis 150 miles north to an academy in what had recently become Kingston, Tennessee (and not long before had been Cherokee country that Major Ridge had fought for). There, John and Lewis Ross continued their education in English and business. With their mother's family connections and access to land, their father's capital, and their education, the brothers returned to the Cherokee Nation and established a business at Ross's Landing (today's Chattanooga), on the Tennessee River, with a general store to sell calico fabric, shawls, and tools imported from U.S. ports in the Northeast for deerskins and other products Cherokees produced. Eventually they added a profitable ferry that crossed the Coosa River and a cotton plantation worked by almost twenty enslaved men and women. It was a nineteenth-century plantation much like those of white southerners, with cotton fields, slave quarters, outbuildings, and an orchard. John Ross and his wife, Quata, eventually moved from Ross's Landing to the Oostanaula River, only two miles from Major Ridge and his brother Uwati, a place that was becoming the center of Cherokee politics.[51]

In their 1816 trip to Washington, Ross and Ridge were praised by the U.S. press as "men of cultivated understandings." Major Ridge spoke no English, but Americans could easily see he fit their ideal of a military hero grown into a wise and prosperous leader. Ross's education in both English and Cherokee prepared him for easy conversation on such subjects as Cherokee–U.S. victories in the War of 1812 and the price of cotton. They were a good team.[52]

Major Ridge, 1820s. Copy of original portrait by Charles Bird King, probably made during Major Ridge's 1824 visit to Washington, in Thomas L. McKenney and James Hall's 1836 *The Indian Tribes of North America.*
NATIONAL PORTRAIT GALLERY, SMITHSONIAN INSTITUTION

By the fall of 1818, both men had advanced in politics. Major Ridge was speaker of the National Council, and John Ross was president of the National Committee. The vast majority of Cherokees had opposed the 1817 treaty that lured some Cherokees west, and the Women's Council petitioned the National Council at its annual meeting to resist the pressure to cede the land. The National Council decided to appoint a delegation to go to Washington, led by John Ross and Second Chief Charles Hicks, to settle claims that the United States had made based on Cherokees who had agreed to

John Ross, 1830s. Copy of original portrait by Charles Bird King, probably made during a visit to Washington (he is holding a paper dated 1836), in Thomas L. McKenney and James Hall's 1836 *The Indian Tribes of North America.*

NATIONAL PORTRAIT GALLERY, SMITHSONIAN INSTITUTION

move west. In Washington, Secretary of War John C. Calhoun demanded that they cede land without the guarantee they sought—that the remaining land would be permanently Cherokee. The treaty they eventually signed did give up some lands in proportion to the people who had moved west, but it also clearly stated that "the lands hereby ceded by the Cherokee nation, are in full satisfaction of all claims which the United States have on them, on account of the cession to a part of their nation who have or may hereafter emigrate." It recognized the nation's national communal ownership of the rest—some ten million acres—and the obligation of the United States to remove "all white people who have intruded, or may hereafter intrude, on the lands reserved for the Cherokees."[53]

It's easy to see each of the late-eighteenth- and early-nineteenth-century treaties as a slippery slope toward first a reservation and then removal, but in 1819 Cherokees believed that this treaty and land cession would keep them from having to move west, and they made it work for almost a generation. The Cherokees ceded no more land until 1835, and they stopped the flow of Cherokees giving up on their homeland and going west or becoming U.S. citizens. Centralizing the nation and speaking with one voice was working, and Ridge and Ross were determined to continue that strategy.

They also recognized that a modern nation needed elements of bureaucracy that had been unnecessary in the past. States ranging from ancient China to ancient Rome had developed bureaucratic tools to regulate commerce, enforce borders, raise revenue for state treasuries, and engage with an international economy, and these instruments are deeply enmeshed in the functioning of modern governments, from small towns to the federal government. In 1819, the Cherokee National Council passed a law that all non-Cherokee schoolmasters, blacksmiths, millers, saltpeter and gunpowder manufacturers, ferrymen, turnpike keepers, and mechanics who wanted to live and work in the Cherokee Nation were required to have a permit from the Cherokee Nation. All non-Cherokee peddlers who wanted to sell their wares in the Cherokee Nation would need to obtain a license from the U.S. agent to the Cherokee Nation and pay $80 each year to the Cherokee treasury. Any peddler found operating without a license stamped PAID on the back was to be fined $200.[54]

In 1820, the National Council moved to standardize local government within the nation. It created eight districts, each with a district council that would have spring and fall sessions to hear concerns and decide on local matters. Each district would elect four members to represent it in the National Council. A system of district and circuit judges and eventually a supreme court heard cases and ruled on matters of law, and marshals and the Light Horse Brigade (created in 1808) were the Nation's force to "collect all debts" and "execute such punishment on thieves as the Judges and Council shall decide, agreeable to law." To pay for government, the National Council placed a flat tax of fifty cents on each head of family or single man under sixty years old. With this tax and various fees for services going into the National Treasury, the nation would be less dependent on the annuity payments coming from the United States. Local land disputes between women continued to be resolved by matrilineal clan leaders, and when the courts heard cases that involved women's property, they continued to recognize that women owned and managed much of the Cherokee Nation's land. Still, the men who now owned businesses, plantations, and enslaved laborers trusted the new court system to protect these forms of property.[55]

These bureaucratic and centralizing efforts meant that Cherokees were prepared in 1822 when the U.S. Congress granted the request of Georgia's governor and legislature to appropriate money and appoint commissioners to negotiate with the Cherokees for more of their land. Cherokees who could read English and subscribed to state newspapers quickly reported the news. Principal Chief Pathkiller and Second Chief Charles Hicks asked the eight district judges to "ascertain the sentiments and disposition of citizens of their respective Districts." The judges reported to the fall session of the National Council that the people's will was "*unanimously,* with one voice and determination, to hold no treaties with any Commissioners of the United States to make any cession of lands, being resolved not to dispose of even one foot of ground." With this unanimity of the Cherokee people officially reported, the National Committee and the National Council issued a joint resolution "that the Chiefs of the Cherokee Nation, will not meet any Commissioners of the United States to hold a treaty with them on the subject of making cession of lands." If representatives of the United States wanted to discuss "any other business," the resolution stated, they were welcome to address the National Council whenever it was in session, where they would be received "with friendship and cordiality." To make the point of unanimity, not only Principal Chief Pathkiller, Second Chief Hicks, National Council Speaker Ridge, and National Committee President Ross signed it, but more than fifty other members of the National Committee and the National Council—which was probably all of the sitting members. Over and over, just about every year for the next decade, U.S. commissioners would ask the Cherokees for treaty negotiations, and every time, the Cherokees stuck by their policy.[56]

When the U.S. commissioners in 1822 found that no Cherokees would meet with them, they recruited the help of William McIntosh, the Muscogee ambassador to the Cherokees. The U.S. commissioners gave him individual payments to offer to prominent

English speakers among the Cherokee leaders: Charles Hicks, John Ross, and Alexander McCoy, the clerk of the National Committee. McCoy later recalled the arguments that McIntosh made to them: "The whites would have their country at all events, & this would be a good time to put money in their own pockets." In previous years, picking off individual Cherokees had sometimes worked, as it still was working among the Muscogees. But building a centralized system of governance with a cohesive policy against land cessions had changed the game. The Cherokee leaders asked McIntosh to put his offer in writing.[57]

As speaker of the National Council, Major Ridge opened the council's next meeting on October 24, 1823, with McIntosh in attendance in his role as ambassador. John Ross arose and announced that he had the sad duty to inform his colleagues "that a gross contempt is offered my character as well as that of the General Council." He handed the letter he had received from McIntosh to the clerk, who read it aloud as the delegates listened to the damning words. "As a friend," McIntosh had written to Ross, "I want you to give me your opinion about ... whether the chiefs will be willing or not" to sign a treaty. If so, "I will make the United States commissioners give you two thousand dollars." He promised that McCoy and Hicks would get similar amounts, and he would add another $5,000 that "you can divide among your friends." After the reading of the letter, Pathkiller stood and denounced McIntosh. As McIntosh rode away in disgrace, the council wrote to leaders of the Muscogee Nation to inform them of his actions and suggest that they "keep a strict watch over his conduct."[58] Indeed, a few years later, McIntosh signed a treaty agreeing to Muscogee removal, and the Muscogee National Council declared him a traitor and ordered his execution.[59]

Over and over, Cherokee leaders heard reports of U.S. commissioners offering incentives to individual Cherokees, so a delegation that included Major Ridge, John Ross, and Charles Hicks's son Elijah went to Washington in January 1824. Unlike in the past, they came without an invitation, and they paid their own way to avoid any conflicts of interest or appearance of such. They told Secretary

Cherokee leader George Lowery (Tsatsiagili),
one of the delegates to Washington in 1824.
GILCREASE MUSEUM, TULSA, OKLAHOMA

of War John Calhoun, "The Cherokees have come to a *decisive* and *unalterable* conclusion, *never* to *cede away* any more *lands*." They insisted that nations respect one another's borders.[60]

The eighteenth-century treaties that the Cherokees signed with Britain and the United States had eroded Cherokee land and disrupted the lives of Cherokees who hunted or lived in those places, but those same treaties now provided elements of recognizable sovereignty, including clear borders, that the Cherokee Nation leveraged against further attempts to take their land. Treaties are made between nations, and the treaty relationship with European empires and with the United States reflected Native nations' sovereignty. Treaty obligations were especially serious for the United States as a new nation not particularly respected on the world stage. The 1796 Indian Trade and Intercourse Act levied punishments against squatting, stating that any U.S. citizen or resident who "shall make a settlement on any lands belonging, or secured, or granted by treaty with the United States, to any Indian tribe," would be fined up to $1,000 and imprisoned for up to twelve months. And it gave the U.S. president the authority to use military force to remove squatters "from lands belonging, or secured by treaty . . . to any Indian tribe."[61]

As hard as it is to believe in light of later forced Indian Removal, the U.S. government actually did remove squatters, sometimes hundreds of families, from the wrong side of treaty lines in the late eighteenth and early nineteenth centuries. And the United States recognized the right of Native nations to remove squatters themselves. In 1820, President James Monroe approved a plan by the Cherokee Light Horse Brigade to warn off squatters from their northern and western borders. The Cherokee Nation hired rangers to warn U.S. citizens against "placing, keeping and feeding, their horses, cattle, hogs, sheep or goats on Cherokee lands" and to fine them if they persisted.[62] Yet clearing them out seemed only to bring more. A Cherokee leader wrote the U.S. agent after one such removal, saying that "they have returned as thick as ever, the same as crows that are startled from their food by a person passing on the road; but as soon as he is passed, they return again."[63] Squatters violated both Cherokee and U.S. law. Despite the risks, illegally occupying Native land could pay off, because if that Native nation ceded the land, the United States sometimes gave those squatters preemption rights in recognition that they were there before any other U.S. settlers.

U.S. citizens contested Cherokee sovereignty in additional ways. When the National Council passed the peddler's license fee in 1819, there were fourteen U.S. traders operating in the nation. Nine of them paid the fee. Cherokee courts fined the five who refused $200 each, which the Cherokee government collected by seizing the traders' goods. The fined traders complained to the U.S. agent, who quieted them by reimbursing the traders for their losses and deducting the amount from the Cherokee annuity. The Cherokees were astounded by this violation of a fundamental sovereign right. In response, U.S. Secretary Calhoun claimed that the late-eighteenth-century treaties gave the United States the right to regulate trade within the Cherokee Nation. Cherokee leaders countered that the treaties gave the United States the right to regulate trade between the Cherokee Nation and the U.S. states, but "we cannot see that the Cherokees conceded their own right of making municipal regulations for themselves." Imposing a tax on foreigners who did business within the nation was domestic policy. Like the United States, they explained, "the Cherokees have a government of their own to support and consequently they, as well as all others, must resort to legal means to raise a revenue for its support."[64]

Cherokees argued that U.S. law confirmed that Native nations could regulate trade within their own borders. The U.S. Constitution stated that "Congress shall have power to regulate commerce with foreign nations, and among the several states, and with the Indian tribes." Therefore, John Ross and Charles Hicks argued in an 1826 letter, "by this section we are placed precisely on the same footing with foreign nations and the several states. And by this power can Congress prevent Great Britain, France and the several states from adopting municipal regulations affecting trade within their own sovereign limits?" No, clearly the U.S. Constitution could not and did not aim to limit Britain's regulation of trade within Britain, and U.S. states levied taxes and fees on peddlers and merchants within their states just as the Cherokee Nation had. "In the name of common sense and equal justice," Ross and Hicks demanded, "why is the right of the Cherokee Nation in this respect disputed?" After all, Cherokee citizens, like Britons, were not represented in the U.S. Congress. Surely Congress would not "impose a tax upon the Cherokee? The American Government, we believe, never has advocated the doctrine that taxes can be imposed by a body where the people taxed are unrepresented. The Constitution of the U. States *prohibits* an enumeration of the Indians for the purposes of representation. They are therefore unrepresented in Congress." Cherokees living within the bounds of their nation could not vote in U.S. elections, and their population was not counted toward representation in the House of Representatives, unlike white Americans and even unlike enslaved people—under the three-fifths clause of the U.S. Constitution, every five enslaved people counted as three residents for figuring representation (though they also did not get to vote).

Cherokee leaders pointed out to the United States that whether it followed its own constitution and treated the Cherokees like a nation or tried to subordinate them to U.S. sovereignty and treat them like a state, in either case the Cherokees could internally tax and regulate. They argued on the basis of both their sovereignty as it had existed long before the creation of the United States and also their sovereignty under U.S. law, a dual argument that Native nations would use again in the twentieth century to rebuild some sovereignty. Essentially, they argued that they were following their own laws, which was all that really should matter, but also that they were entitled according to U.S. laws. U.S. officials could see the Cherokee Nation as a state, parallel to Georgia or Tennessee, Ross and Hicks offered, although, because it had not ratified the Constitution, it was more similar to all of the states in 1789, when each had to decide whether to rejoin the United States under the new constitution.[65]

A few years later, a model could have been the republics of Texas and California, temporarily sovereign states that decided for themselves whether to join in equal union with other states. Some Cherokees did envision a State of Cherokee as one of the U.S. states, with two U.S. senators and the appropriate number of representatives in the House. Indeed, the 1785 Treaty of Hopewell included a provision that the Cherokee Nation "shall have the right to send a deputy of their choice, whenever they think fit, to Congress"—which the Cherokee Nation of Oklahoma did in 2019. (As of 2023, Congress had yet to seat the Cherokee delegate.)[66]

The houses that Sehoya and Major Ridge and their neighbors Quata and John Ross built along the Oostanaula River were two-story frame houses with brick chimneys. Unlike the matrilineal households of the past, where sisters would raise their children together, these were single-family dwellings. The two households, like that of Major Ridge's brother Uwati nearby, each had two parents and many children. Their tables had wheat bread as well as cornbread, and both pork and venison. It's easy to imagine that nineteenth-century Cherokees who owned a ferry, wrote letters in English to U.S. officials, or attended a Christian church or school were giving up some of their Cherokee culture or heritage, but the Ridge and Ross families, like many other prominent Cherokees, saw no loss or contradiction. They embraced the emerging capitalist economy of the nineteenth century as part of Cherokee development. They saw Cherokees as part of the modern world and Cherokee nationhood as developing in parallel with other nineteenth-century nations.

MODERN CHEROKEE RELIGION, MEDICINE, AND WRITING

Cherokees did not stop being Cherokee just because they were modern people. In a variety of ways, they incorporated new ideas and practices to supplement and support Cherokee nationhood. The sons and daughters of the Ridge and Ross families grew up speaking Cherokee at home and went to the nearby Moravian mission school to learn English. Moravians had established a mission and school in Cherokee country in the early 1800s, and the Ridges and Rosses seem to have practiced moderate forms of both Christianity and more traditional Cherokee religion, in keeping with Native inclusivism.[67]

For the most part, Christian missionaries didn't cause the Cherokees much trouble. Their message appealed to some Cherokees, and the English literacy and other skills they taught seemed useful. It seemed necessary that some Cherokees learn English so they could interpret the treaties and business agreements of white men. Early Moravian missionaries were "always spoken of in the most affectionate manner by the old Cherokees," a white man who lived in the Cherokee Nation recalled. When a group of Protestant missionaries—from the American Board of Commissioners for Foreign Missions—established several missions and schools within the nation in the 1810s, the children of the missionaries apparently learned more Cherokee than Cherokee kids learned English, because there were so many more Cherokee speakers around them. In the 1820s, itinerant missionaries sometimes caused trouble by crisscrossing the nation without permission, insulting Cherokee religious leaders, and attacking polygamy, liquor, gambling, and stickball (which they correctly recognized as being partially religious in nature). But the earlier missions and schools required the permission of neighboring Cherokees and generally seemed more useful than troublesome.[68]

As with religion, Cherokees borrowed medical practices when they were useful, while continuing to use traditional methods that also helped to prevent or heal disease, as well as refining these methods and sharing them with outsiders. When Cherokees in 1824 learned that smallpox was once again circulating in the United States, they protected the nation by vaccinating. Missionaries brought the vaccine to Cherokee country and vaccinated some people, and then Cherokee healers extracted pus from the injection sites of those who had been immunized and used it to vaccinate more people. The vaccine was almost miraculously effective—a game changer for human health around the world, not unlike the Covid-19 vaccine in the 2020s. Still, Cherokee healers continued to practice their traditional medicine and rituals, including quarantine—easier now that most people lived on separate farms.[69]

Perhaps the most important way in which Cherokees employed foreign ideas for Cherokee uses was the development of a written form of the Cherokee language. Cherokee historian Julie Reed explains of the writing system, "On one hand it is a trapping of civilization—a written language—and on the other hand it contradicts the civilization policy of the United States because it is the *Cherokee* language and it enables literacy so quickly that it helps revitalize older pieces of Cherokee tradition."[70]

Sequoyah, the man who developed the writing system, was born into the Red Paint Clan toward the end of the 1760s, in the town of Tuskegee, on the Little Tennessee River, near present-day Knoxville. Like all Cherokees at the time, he grew up speaking Cherokee. His family fled during the American Revolution to the region around Willstown, from where the Lower Towns continued to fight the United States. He became a blacksmith and silversmith and fought the Red Sticks in the 1810s. He was one of the Lower Town leaders who moved west of the Mississippi River, believing that was the only way to remain Cherokee.[71]

At some point in the late 1810s or early 1820s, Sequoyah was sitting with a group of Cherokees when a young man started talking about how white men could communicate by "putting marks on paper." Sequoyah found himself disgusted by how the others cited this example as evidence that white men had talents that Cherokees did not. He declared, "The white man is no magician." To demon-

Sequoyah, portrait by Henry Inman, c. 1830. Copy after the Charles
Bird King original, destroyed in the 1865 Smithsonian Castle fire.
NATIONAL PORTRAIT GALLERY, SMITHSONIAN INSTITUTION

strate what he meant, he reached for a flat stone and made marks on
it with a pin. Then he told them that if they all agreed that each of
the marks stood for a specific word, they could communicate through
them. The others laughed, but Sequoyah got to work.[72]

Sequoyah at first tried making a character for each word but
soon realized that would require several thousand characters, far too
many for people to memorize. Then he had the idea of assigning a
character to each syllable, and devised a syllabary—for example, the
word "Cherokee" has three syllables, so it has three characters: ᏣᎳᎩ.
He and his young daughter Ayoka tried to think of all the syllables
in the Cherokee language, adding more as they listened to conversations and speeches. They invented most of the symbols, using roman
letters and symbols from a missionary spelling book for some of
their inspiration. Neighbors who saw him listening and scribbling
said he was crazy. But soon he and Ayoka were ready to demonstrate
how it worked. Sequoyah asked his friends to say any word to him,
out of the hearing of his daughter. He made a scribble, then she was
called in, looked at it, and said the word.[73]

Sequoyah taught Cherokees both west of the Mississippi and in
the East, and they began writing letters back and forth, now able to

Cherokee syllabary, in Sequoyah's writing.

communicate directly with family and friends in distant places. Cherokees like John Ross who were literate in English were relatively late to adopt Sequoyah's writing system. By the time they began learning it, a large number of men and women who spoke only Cherokee were fluent in its written form. At the National Council of 1824, many representatives who could read and write in English were surprised to see Cherokees reading and writing in their own language.[74]

By all accounts, the syllabary was easy for Cherokee speakers to learn—much easier than learning to read with an alphabet. Because there are different dialects in different parts of Cherokee country, some regional differences in writing developed, but the syllabary worked for all Cherokee speakers. By all accounts, people who started to learn it could read and write reasonably well in only a couple of weeks. Each person who learned it taught more people. A missionary noted in 1824 that the "alphabet is spreading through the nation like fire among the leaves." Pens, ink, and paper were in high demand in Cherokee stores, and it was also fairly easy to make the characters with a knife or a piece of charcoal. Yet it was not readable at all if you didn't already speak Cherokee. One of the printers later hired by the nation admitted that the syllabary was "more incomprehensible to us than Greek." By the 1830s, around half of Cherokee households included at least one person who could read and write in Cherokee, a higher literacy level than the rate of English literacy among their white neighbors at the time.[75]

Cherokee leaders felt that written records were necessary for running the bureaucracy that their national government was becoming. They used English at first, but Sequoyah's syllabary allowed them to keep the nation's written records and correspondence in Cherokee. In 1826, the National Council appropriated funds for translating and copying existing Cherokee laws and the New Testament. When the nation began publishing a newspaper in 1828, it printed the laws in both Cherokee and English. These developments broadened accountability among Cherokees, which was not only a long-held Cherokee value but also necessary for maintaining vigilance against U.S. attempts to erode their country.[76]

Cherokee scholars today have discovered vivid physical evidence of the syllabary's importance in the nineteenth century. About three hundred yards into a cave not far from Willstown, partially hidden by graffiti in English left later by tourists, is a large set of writings in Cherokee. The most readable are those, remarkably, on the cave's ceiling, forty feet above the main passage. The writings have religious significance, and there are a lot of them, indicating that the cave was used repeatedly for ceremonies. Eastern Band of Cherokee Indians Tribal Historic Preservation Officer and archaeologist Beau Carroll notes that "for you to be able to pick out actual syllabary, you have to be familiar with it. I think it's all over the place. It's just that nobody's been looking for it."[77]

Much deeper inside the same cave is writing that recorded the ceremonies surrounding a stickball game. As the "little brother of war," stickball required cleansing, preparation, and completion ceremonies parallel to those required of warriors. The ceremonies had to take place in private and needed sacred waters, such as the underground creek that runs through this cave. The players and their religious leader must have ventured deep into this cave, walking for nearly a mile along its creek, holding up river-cane torches for light. Stickball games lasted several days and required multiple rituals, so it was unusual for teams to go this far from public sight. Perhaps they were hiding these ceremonies from Christians, either white or Cherokee, or from Cherokee rivals. One of the inscriptions is the signature of Richard Guess, one of the sons of Sequoyah (who was also called George Guess). Cherokee scholars today figure that Richard Guess was the stickball team's religious leader. He also wrote the date: April 1828.

Cherokees developed a written form of their language to communicate and to discuss and preserve knowledge by written as well as oral means. It helped to preserve the language for future generations. The Cherokee linguist and University of North Carolina professor Ben Frey describes how learning the Cherokee language gave him words for Cherokee concepts he knew from childhood but that English words can't translate perfectly. For example, he explained one day in the weekly Cherokee Coffee Hour gatherings that he hosts on campus in Chapel Hill, when Cherokee speakers want to ask "How are you?" and answer "I'm fine," they say, "Osigwo tsu?" and reply, "Osigwo." "Osi" means "winter house," a structure that is set into the ground for warmth. It has a hearth within it, from which smoke rises out of a hole in the roof, connecting the lower world of the earth to the middle world where people live and to the upper world of the sky. An osi is built in line with the four directions, with everything in balance. So the question means "Are you in the place where everything is as it should be?" The answer is "Yes, I am— Osigwo." Of course, a person can be Cherokee without speaking the Cherokee language, yet speaking the language of one's people, the words and patterns of one's ancestors, can be a powerful part of continuing their ways of thinking, of being the same nation they were, even as times change, and Sequoyah's syllabary has helped preserve it.[78]

Other Native nations developed systems to write in their own languages. Sequoyah apparently worked with Choctaws on the beginnings of a syllabary for the Choctaw language, although it was never completed. Most nations used roman letters and English, Spanish, or French pronunciation of them to approximate the sounds of their languages in writing, systems that allowed them to record in their own languages—in the eighteenth and nineteenth centuries and today—to revitalize and teach new generations the language of their ancestors.[79]

THE CHEROKEE CONSTITUTION

"We, the Representatives of the people of the Cherokee Nation, in Convention assembled, in order to establish justice, ensure tranquility, promote our common welfare, and secure to ourselves and our posterity the blessings of liberty; acknowledging with humility and gratitude the goodness of the sovereign Ruler of the Universe, . . . do ordain and establish this Constitution for the Government of the Cherokee Nation." In echoing the U.S. Constitution, the preamble to the Cherokee Constitution spoke directly to citizens of the United States. The framers of the Cherokee Constitution chose to convene on July 4, 1827. It declared to the United States that the Cherokees were a sovereign, modern nation, founded on similar principles of liberty and self-governance. They were not primitive; they were not vanishing, either into the West or into the past. But the Cherokee Constitution was not only a message to outsiders. Its framers were, as they wrote, "Representatives of the people of the Cherokee Nation," who hoped to ensure justice, tranquility, and liberty and promote their *common* welfare. As they did in writing, economics, religion, and medicine, Cherokees adopted political ideas and rhetoric to fit their own values and needs.[80]

Written constitutions were new in the late eighteenth and early nineteenth centuries. As empires fell in the Americas and Europe, people had to create new governments, and in an age of rising literacy, a written document provided reassurance that politicians weren't just making up the rules as they went along. The Cherokee Constitution and the constitutions of other Native nations that followed were different, in that they were not creating a government from scratch. But previous years had seen the Cherokee National Council become stronger, and the written constitution—distributed in Cherokee and English—demonstrated the central government's legality.

The 1827 constitution was a statement of Cherokee unity, but it started in controversy. In its fall 1826 session, the National Council called a constitutional convention to consolidate the changes made to the Cherokee government over the preceding years. As it developed, the convention became an opportunity for Cherokees to consider whether changes had already gone too far, although that probably wasn't the intent when the National Council called the convention. Between the National Council's session and the constitutional convention, some Cherokees called their own council to express their worries over how their government was centralizing. They may also have been concerned about the future of Cherokee leadership, because in January 1827 Principal Chief Pathkiller and Second Chief Charles Hicks died within two weeks of each other.

This alternative council met at Ellijay, the town of a former National Council member named White Path (Nunnahitsunega), who had been expelled from the council two years earlier. There are no written records from the Ellijay council, but a missionary reported that Cherokees "have risen up against the laws of the Nation and appear to desire their old form of Government." Sixty years later, a Cherokee elder recalled that White Path had "preached the rejection of the new constitution, the discarding of Christianity and the white man's ways, and a return to the old tribal law and custom." People heard about ceremonies and dances lasting all night among the people gathered.[81]

At the Ellijay council, some Cherokees complained about the decline in power of town councils and town chiefs. When patrilineal inheritance was allowed, maternal uncles lost familial power. Some

Cherokees opposed an 1825 law that prohibited polygamy, although it doesn't seem to have been enforced. Some called for changes to the National Council's requirement that officeholders swear an oath that included a Christian reference. They pointed to Christianity as a wedge between Cherokees who believed in it and those who thought they were wrong to embrace a religion that condemned Cherokee religious beliefs and traditions.[82]

Yet the Ellijay council ultimately worked to bring Cherokees together rather than drive them further apart. It may have been designed from the beginning less as an oppositional political movement and more as a gathering to discuss concerns and interpret visions in preparation for working toward consensus at the constitutional convention. Cherokees who attended the Ellijay council participated in the subsequent elections of convention delegates in May 1827 and in the convention itself. In White Path's district, a man named Kelachulee, who had been part of the Ellijay council, won his election against the sons of Major Ridge and Uwati to become a delegate to the convention. Kelachulee was already an elected member of the National Council, so he was hardly a political outsider, but he was among those who wanted to slow or reverse political change.[83]

The consensus building worked: Cherokees came together and reached compromises on a constitution to promote and project unity. The convention's opening days, in July 1827, were spent paving the way for consensus. Several Cherokees who had attended the Ellijay council smoothed over the disagreements by signing a document regretting any actions that might have detracted from harmony and unanimity. They promised that if they objected to any laws in the future, they would petition the National Council. Past periods in Cherokee history had involved similar political and spiritual work to heal divisions and find consensus, and perhaps there had been similar statements in the past by factions after they were pulled back into consensus. Issuing a written statement, though, was something new, and it might have been directed at U.S. readers as much as Cherokees, preserving a unified stance resisting U.S. pressure for land cessions.[84]

The constitution that they wrote was a compromise document. It reversed the previous moves toward Christianity by separating church and state. The constitution guaranteed "the free exercise of religious worship" and forbade "any public preacher of any religious persuasion" from being principal chief or a member of the National Council. It did require that no one hold office who "denies the being of a God, or a future state of rewards and punishment." This requirement may have annoyed the non-Christian majority, but it was easy to ignore—the official oath that council members had to swear was to the Cherokee Nation, with no mention of religion.[85]

Other parts of the constitution reinforced recent political changes and expanded the size of the national government. The National Committee became an elected body that would act as the upper house of a bicameral legislature, with the National Council as the lower house. The principal chief and the second chief would now be chosen every four years, and they were given more explicit executive powers. The constitution formally established the judicial system, including a supreme court. It included some European and U.S. rights of criminal procedure, including the right to a speedy trial and protection from unreasonable searches and seizures.

However, the Cherokee Constitution's primary focus was not individual rights but instead community rights. As Professor Julie Reed puts it, the constitution "enabled the national emphasis to remain on the community's protection."[86] A major contrast with the U.S. Constitution is that the very first article specifically outlined the boundaries of the Cherokee Nation, including its borders with Tennessee, North Carolina, Georgia, and the Muscogee Nation. It declared in no uncertain terms that "the sovereignty and jurisdiction of this government shall extend over the country within the boundaries above described, and the lands therein are, and shall remain, the common property of the Nation." Individual Cherokee citizens and Cherokee families could own the "improvements"—houses, stores, farms, ferries, barns, plantations—but the land beneath was the Cherokee Nation, and Cherokees could no more sell it to the United States than U.S. citizens could sell Virginia or Vermont to Britain or France.[87]

The Cherokee Constitution established voting rights according to how early-nineteenth-century Cherokees saw citizenship. Cherokee women held defined political and economic rights within the Cherokee Nation, which did not include voting or being representatives in the national legislature. As in the United States and other nineteenth-century republics, only "free male citizens" could vote and hold office. But whereas in the United States and Great Britain only property owners could vote, a property requirement made no sense in a country whose lands were common property and managed by women, so the Cherokee Constitution included no property requirement.[88]

The Cherokee Constitution disfranchised Black men and the sons of Black mothers. In language similar to U.S. restrictions, Cherokee citizenship extended to "the descendants of Cherokee men by all free women, except the African race." The sons of Black mothers and Cherokee fathers were not citizens and could not vote. The children of Cherokee mothers (from whom they inherited a clan) and free Black fathers could be Cherokee citizens to some extent, but they could not hold office. When the Cherokee Constitution set the boundaries of citizenship, it declared that those with some white parentage were assimilable, while those with recent Black parentage were permanently unequal.[89]

In choosing racist exclusivism, the Cherokee Nation was in line with its U.S. neighbors, yet that was not the only choice. There were models of racial inclusion that Cherokees could have followed instead. Cherokees subscribed to international newspapers and would have read about the republics established in Haiti, France, and Mexico, all of which banned slavery and made some attempt at equal citizenship for all men. The Seminoles, who split off from the Muscogees to become their own nation to the south, fully incorporated the children of Black men and women into citizenship. And there were Cherokees who advocated citizenship for the children of Cherokee and Black parents. Shoe Boots, a respected Cherokee war veteran, and Doll, his Black slave, had three children, Elizabeth, John, and Polly. In 1824, Shoe Boots asked the National Council to acknowledge his children as free and as Cherokee citizens, even though they were not able to inherit a clan through their non-

Cherokee mother. The council agreed in his specific case but, in that same session, passed legislation outlawing marriage between Cherokees and enslaved Black people and generally excluding the children of Cherokee and enslaved Black parents from Cherokee citizenship, and the constitution continued that exclusion. Shoe Boots did not ask for freedom for Doll, and the children they subsequently had together ended up being sold after his death. Uwati's son Buck Watie (Elias Boudinot) would later write, reflecting on Georgia, that if it wanted to be as great a state as New York or Pennsylvania, "she will have to overcome one great obstacle before she becomes a great state—slavery." The same could be said for the Cherokee Nation.[90]

Cherokees had long considered captives (of any race) to be in a completely different category from Cherokees, unless they were adopted. In the eighteenth century, some Cherokees had come to believe in the theory of separate creations, held by many prophets including Tenskwatawa. Now they went further, toward a belief that Black captives were different from other kinds of captives—they were not adoptable and therefore could never be Cherokee citizens. The Cherokee constitutional convention included fairly elite representatives and patriots, many of whom were enslavers, not so different from the men who gathered in Philadelphia in 1787 to write the U.S. Constitution. Apparently the Cherokees at the convention who didn't own slaves did not push to end slavery or extend citizenship rights to Cherokees of African descent. In the kind of vicious cycle in which democracy often traps powerless people, Cherokees of African descent had no political power and therefore no ability to effect change.[91]

Even though most of the pieces of the constitution already existed in Cherokee law, the familiar preamble, the word "constitution," and the symbolism of convening on July 4 ensured that U.S. citizens would recognize it for what it was: a clear declaration of Cherokee sovereignty. The governor of Georgia got the message. He demanded that President John Quincy Adams and Congress denounce the Cherokee Constitution as illegal under U.S. law. Adams demurred, taking the position that the U.S.–Cherokee relationship remained unchanged. Before a gathering of Cherokees, the U.S. agent conveyed President Adams's position:

> The subject of your having formed a Constitution and Constitutional Government has raised a considerable clamor particularly in the adjoining states. It has been brought before the Congress of the United States, and the President has been officially notified of it, and directed me to convene the chiefs and inform them, that he wishes them distinctly to understand, that this act of theirs cannot be considered in any other light than as regulations of a purely municipal character.

Adams wanted them to know that their constitution "will not be recognized as changing any one of the relations under which they stood to the General [federal] Government."[92]

In the 1820s, Cherokees didn't so much need to change their relationship with the United States as to force their U.S. neighbors to live up to the U.S. Constitution and past treaties. They said that the U.S. government should abide by its obligations, and the Cherokee Nation should be in charge of its own "municipal" or domestic governance. It was Georgians who were trying to change Cherokee— U.S. relations by discarding how European and U.S. law had always regarded Native nations. As Cherokee leaders repeatedly explained, the U.S. Constitution clearly placed Indian affairs under the federal government's responsibilities, out of the jurisdiction of the states. To this point, both European and U.S. officials had seen Native nations as possibly inferior, at times as enemies who should be fought brutally, and often as people it was acceptable to try to trick or push around, but they were nonetheless sovereign polities. And in 1828, U.S. law and policy still defined them that way.[93]

NEW ECHOTA'S PRINTING HOUSE

The new wooden case that held type for the Cherokee printing press had to be specially designed. Standard cases available in the United

States had places for twenty-six lowercase and twenty-six uppercase letters, not the more than eighty of the Cherokee syllabary. The case had to be bigger and arranged in a way that allowed printers to grab the most common letters efficiently, and intuitive enough that they wouldn't waste time searching. The syllabary type—the actual letters—also had to be specially ordered, made in Boston of cast iron and commissioned with help from the American Board of Commissioners of Foreign Missions (ABCFM). Along with a set of roman letters and their case, the syllabary type was brought by ship to the port of Savannah, then by steamboat up the Savannah River to Augusta, where wagons brought them to the new Cherokee capital in the hills of what's now northwest Georgia, twenty-five miles upriver from the Ridge and Ross homes. In 1825, the Cherokee National Committee and National Council had resolved to design and build New Echota, named for the old mother town of Chota.[94]

The National Council hired Major Ridge's nephew Buck Watie (Elias Boudinot) as the nation's editor. His job, in the words of the legislation that created his position, was "to edit a weekly newspaper at New Echota, to be entitled, the 'Cherokee Phoenix,' 'ᎦᏩ Ꮷ ᏦᎮᎠᏋᏅᎠ.'"[95] He was perfect for the job. Born around 1804, he grew up in a Cherokee-speaking household, the son of Susanna Reece and Uwati, Major Ridge's brother. They gave him the name Galagina, the Cherokee word for "buck" (male deer). Buck and his siblings, including his brother Degataga (Cherokee for "He Stands"), born a year later, inherited their mother's clan and took Watie as their last name, from their father's name, a new Cherokee custom in this era when people who did business with the United States needed surnames. So the boys were Buck and Stand Watie. When he was six years old, Buck started school at the Moravian mission school along with his cousins John and Nancy Ridge. At school, they learned to speak, read, and write in English and were taught the basic doctrines of Christianity. Unlike most people in the Cherokee Nation or the United States at that time, Buck and his cousin John went on to school at an academy (the equivalent of high school).[96]

The academy was far from home, nearly one thousand miles

away in Cornwall, Connecticut. Buck traveled there in 1817 or 1818, accompanied by two other young Cherokee men and officials of the ABCFM, the Protestant organization that was working in the Cherokee Nation. It was a long trip, more than six weeks of rough traveling through strange new places. The first week of travel took them north through the still extensive Cherokee Nation. They probably spent a night at the large brick inn and tavern run by the McNairs, a white husband and Cherokee wife, and their last night in the nation at the house of John Ross's brother and National Council member Lewis Ross, whose ferry they took across the Hiwassee River into what was now Tennessee, where Buck's father and uncle were born. From the Blue Ridge Mountains, Buck could see far into the distance—south toward home and north to where he was bound. He later told of how they met former presidents Thomas Jefferson at Monticello and James Monroe at Montpelier. More impressive to Buck was meeting in New Jersey a man named Elias Boudinot, who was a devout supporter of the ABCFM. He had served in the Continental Army and been president of Congress under the Articles of Confederation. Following a common Cherokee tradition, the impressionable young man asked this elder if he could take on his name. From then on, when speaking or writing in English, Buck Watie called himself Elias Boudinot. What impressed Buck and persuaded him to adopt Boudinot as a mentor may have been the elder man's 1816 book arguing that American Indians were a lost tribe of Israel (part of a long line of such arguments, as we learned in chapter 1). Presumably unbeknownst to the younger man, he was also a land speculator, who made his wealth in the 1780s by buying huge tracts of Shawnee land north of the Ohio River in and around what became Cincinnati.[97]

The Cornwall academy was in a part of Connecticut that Mohawks had traveled past two hundred years earlier, on their way to and from meeting and trading with the Pequots and the English. The ABCFM had founded it to teach foreign young men who had done well in their missions around the world and could be given an American education and then sent back home as missionaries. Besides those from the Cherokee Nation, students came from other

Native nations as well as Tahiti, Hawaii, and China. There were also a few young white men studying to be missionaries. The newly named Elias Boudinot must have been glad to see his cousin John Ridge, who joined him at Cornwall not long after. As Major Ridge put it, each boy's task was to get a good education, "so that when he comes home he may be very useful to his Nation."[98] They learned English reading and writing, geography, rhetoric, history, surveying, trigonometry, Latin, and philosophy, and they read the Bible. Boudinot converted to Christianity after a few years at the school.[99]

If young Elias and John thought that white New Englanders would treat them as equals, they were soon disappointed. They tested the boundaries of New Englanders' tolerance by falling in love with two white women—John Ridge with Sarah Bird Northrup, the daughter of the school's steward, and Elias Boudinot with Harriett Gold, the daughter of a physician in Cornwall who was a benefactor of the school. When the townspeople of Cornwall learned that the couples were engaged to be married, they called mass meetings, and the town newspaper published scathing editorials against the marriages. Harriett's own brother led crowds in burning the couple in effigy. But they married anyway and left what Elias later called, tongue in cheek, "the land of intermarriages." Both couples headed for the safety of the Cherokee Nation. In the face of public outcry, the school closed permanently.[100]

Elias Boudinot and Harriett Gold Boudinot.

Elias Boudinot briefly returned to New England in 1826, on a tour sponsored by the Cherokee National Council to raise money for a printing press and an academy in the Cherokee Nation so boys like him could get an advanced English education at home, in a school overseen by the nation. In front of audience after audience, Boudinot stood in a tailored coat, high-collared shirt, and wide cravat, dressed just like the men who listened to him. "You here behold an *Indian*," he told them. "My kindred are *Indians,* and my fathers sleeping in the wilderness grave—they too were *Indians.* . . . I now stand before you delegated by my native country to seek her interest, to labour for her respectability, and by my public efforts to assist in raising her to an equal standing with other nations of the world." Missionaries, reformers, and donors could help his people, he told his audiences, not by forcing them to become part of the United States or by pushing them west, but by assisting in their goal of becoming a modern nation alongside their own.[101]

With money from donations and the Cherokee National Treasury, Boudinot set up the nation's print shop in a new log house in New Echota, and on February 21, 1828, the first issue of the *Cherokee Phoenix* came off the press. "Phoenix" evoked the rising of the Cherokee Nation from the devastation of previous decades of loss. In the months before that first issue, Boudinot's tasks must have seemed impossible. As he waited for the type to arrive from Boston, he and his printers belatedly realized that the shipment didn't include paper, so they placed a rush order from a mill in Knoxville. The printers he had hired didn't know Cherokee and therefore had to decipher the Cherokee writing one character at a time, slowly placing the characters they thought they saw onto the press. They would print a test copy and take it to Boudinot or their Cherokee apprentice, John Candy, to check, then return to laboriously fix all their mistakes. They got faster. By March, Boudinot could stand in the printing house and watch the printers quickly grab each letter and place it with reasonable accuracy the first time. Two hundred copies went out weekly to subscribers throughout the nation and as far as Mobile, New York, and Europe.[102]

The *Phoenix* printed the rest of the draft constitution as well as

First issue of the *Cherokee Phoenix*, February 21, 1828.
DAVID M. RUBENSTEIN RARE BOOK & MANUSCRIPT LIBRARY,
DUKE UNIVERSITY

past council business: the 1824 Cherokee census and laws that the council had passed going back to 1819, all in Cherokee and English. The paper printed treaties, speeches, and correspondence between the Cherokee Nation and U.S. officials, both past negotiations such as those with George Washington in the 1790s and more recent ones. Boudinot worked with other Cherokees and with ABCFM missionary Samuel Worcester to translate the book of Matthew into Cherokee, publishing it in the *Phoenix* a few chapters at a time. It was common for nineteenth-century newspapers to print stories from other papers, and Boudinot looked for Native American news in particular. In October 1828, for example, he reprinted articles from the *Buffalo Journal* on a treaty between the United States and the Ho-Chunks. At the council's fall sessions, the *Phoenix* printed speeches and laws as they happened.[103]

For Cherokee laws and reprinted articles, the Cherokee and English versions were generally direct translations, but some items differ. Boudinot worded his editorials differently for his Cherokee readers and his U.S. English-reading audience. In the very first issue, Boudinot's editorial declared to English-language readers that the newspaper was engaged in the same goals as "those who wish well to the Indian race ... and who pray that salvation, peace, and the comforts of civilized life may be extended to every Indian fire side on this continent." He pointed out that "sufficient and repeated evidence has been given, that Indians can be reclaimed from a savage state, and that with proper advantages, they are as capable of improvement in mind as any other people; and let it be remembered, notwithstanding the assertions of those who talk to the contrary, that this improvement can be made, not only by the Cherokees, but by all the Indians, *in their present locations*." The demand to stay in their homeland stated the Cherokee Nation's position in no uncertain terms, in English, in its official newspaper.[104]

To anyone who can read only English or Cherokee but not both, the two versions of the editorial look as if they are simply translations of each other, but the differences reveal the quite different audiences the editor was addressing. He signed the Cherokee one with his Cherokee name, Galagina (Buck). In a recent translation of the Cherokee-language editorial into English by Cherokee scholars Tom Belt and Wiggins Blackfox, the editor writes, "For a long time, . . . the leaders and national intellectuals . . . and the councils of our eight districts" have wanted to "print a paper of our place and that would be in our own language." In this version, there was no mention of "improvement." He did not categorize Cherokee ancestors as "savage" or Cherokees as in need of training in "the civilized life." On the contrary, he wrote in Cherokee that not long before, the white people "were not literate; they were wild, they dressed in buckskins, they were war-like." The printed word had given white people an advantage for a while, but now the Cherokees had that too. Cherokee readers knew that many nations and states had newspapers, and it was time for the Cherokee Nation to do so, a decision made by leaders throughout the nation. "You'll hear about things just like white people do," and "the news will go into Native homes all over," he promised. It would also be sent to white people to teach them about the Cherokee Nation and its difficulties with Georgians who "always want to take us out of our lands." The *Phoenix* would be an advertisement to white audiences and a source of information and rallying for Cherokees.[105]

Because far more Cherokees could read Cherokee than English, the primary way of reaching them was in the Cherokee-language articles, some of which were printed with no corresponding English version. The first issue included the Cherokee transcription of a speech a Cherokee headman had given to the Georgia governor. Cherokee scholars who have read the speech note that nineteenth-century Cherokees would have recognized its language as Cherokee formal oratory, the kind a leader would have used in council or in diplomacy. It was a simple message, eloquently explained: Georgians "are wrong about what they believe belongs to them." The *Phoenix* followed the speech with a commentary from that same headman directed at Cherokee readers, explaining his impression from the meeting that the governor "greatly wants our land; it is not possible for the people of Georgia to leave that thought alone it seems, they believe that the earth encircles them." How to deal with such a people? "We cannot win, if we separate our land," he warned from his experience. But "if we love each other, no leaders can make us leave. And the Governor that has seized us that lives in Georgia, we will play with him." Cherokee scholar Constance Owl explains that the word translated as "play," yidedanelodi, has its root in stickball, the little brother of war, somewhere between play and war—a message his Cherokee readers would certainly have understood.[106]

Most newspapers in the early nineteenth century were highly partisan, but because the *Phoenix* was owned by the Cherokee Nation, it didn't endorse specific candidates in its election coverage. For the National Council election of 1828, the paper printed statements from the candidates as well as letters to the editor expressing various viewpoints. By accepting letters in either Cherokee or English and in most cases printing them in both languages, the paper increased participation in national political conversations. Elijah Hicks, running for the National Committee from Coosawattee District, laid out in the *Phoenix* his positions on the structure of the government and regulation of mission schools as well as his belief that the principal chief should be "a learned man" who could communicate in speech and writing with English speakers in the United States.[107] One controversy over the office of the treasurer prompted written accusations of "categorical fire" and "annihilating sarcasms." One letter accused the opponent of having no greater platform than *"I live at Echota. I am without an office, therefore elect me Treasurer."*[108]

Some writers aimed their rhetoric higher when advising readers about the upcoming elections. In a May letter to the editor, a Cherokee called Utaletah wrote in English, "In about three months hence, you will be called upon by the constitution of your country, to exercise a privilege of great importance to yourselves, and to your country." Voting was a serious matter. Utaletah suggested that the National Committee, the upper house, "should be composed of men of education, and good knowledge in the affairs of our nation; while the Council," the lower house, "should be composed of full blooded Cherokees, known for love of their country, the land of their forefathers, and also celebrated for their good natural sense, justice, and firmness." This balance of a National Committee of men trained in English and a larger National Council more grounded in Cherokee communities and families throughout the nation would combine, "by one common interest, having one object, the preservation of ourselves as a free and sovereign people." Utaletah described a fairly new structural version of an old value: The heart of Cherokee governance should be balance and reciprocity, all in service to Cherokee independence and sovereignty.[109]

As with leadership within the national government, the *Phoenix* had space for competing positions, as long as they were pro-Cherokee. In a subsequent issue, the *Phoenix* printed a counterargument to Utaletah's suggestion by a man named John Huss, a Christian preacher who preached only in Cherokee and who would be appointed to the Cherokee Supreme Court by the National Council in its fall session. Writing in Cherokee, with an accompanying English translation, Huss said that it would be better that both houses "should be mixed." In his opinion, "it would be a great evil" to have the committee and council present different constituencies, "for it would appear like creating a division among the people." Because the constitution gave each house of the legislature veto power over the other, they could easily become opposing bodies if their members were dramatically different. Huss urged all to vote using the advice that "when you see a man who you think will labor well for the good of us Cherokees, then vote for him." Despite his disagreement with Utaletah, their goal was the same: "Our Chiefs and Legislators have made for us a Constitution. If we be of one mind in the support of this Constitution, the inhabitant of Georgia will not take away our land. But if we be divided into parties we shall be liable to lose our territory. Let us then be careful to preserve unanimity in attachment to our country and the Constitution."[110]

The election took place in August 1828, and despite John Huss's recommendations, National Committee members were mostly wealthy Cherokees with some education in English, while National Council representatives were mostly speakers of Cherokee only. As Utaletah hoped, they balanced one another out. A missionary estimated that one-fifth of those elected were churchgoing Christians, a larger percentage than the approximately one-ninth of Cherokees who were Christian. Yet White Path, the leader of the Ellijay council, won a council seat from the Coosawatee District, beating John Ridge and Elias Boudinot.[111]

In October 1828, the National Council and the National Committee convened in New Echota. Cherokee men and women rode their horses south from the Smoky Mountains or came from the east, having crossed Vann's Ferry, on the Chattahoochee River. Others came from Ross's Landing, in the northwest, or straight east from Willstown, or northeast from Turkeytown, on the Coosa River. People who lived closer walked to New Echota, while a few families rode from plantations in horse-drawn carriages driven by enslaved men.

New Echota's central public square had a town spring and the council house, where the National Committee and National Council met on separate floors. Accounts vary as to the building's appearance, but it may have had a conical roof to echo older Cherokee council houses. Both the council house and the two-story frame courthouse had plenty of windows to let in light during sessions. Elias and Harriett Boudinot's house was in the center of town, on the same street as the printing house. It was a large two-story frame house, with a separate kitchen, a stable, corn cribs, a large garden, apple and peach orchards, and plenty of room for their growing family. The Boudinots' daughters attended school in the nearby courthouse between court sessions, where they were taught by Sophia Sawyer, a missionary from New Hampshire. There were five or so other frame houses in town and several stores, although only one of them operated all year, the rest opening only for the council sessions.[112]

A Cherokee man named White Horse recalled walking through New Echota in its heyday: "That long house to our right with beautiful surroundings is the tavern of A. McCoy—clerk of the council, just over the hollow further on is the large beautiful residence of Elijah Hicks,—member of the Senate from Cooseewatah," reported to have cost $1,500. Nearby were Lewis Ross's stone house and other homes and stores. The printers John Wheeler and John Candy lived in town, not far from the printing office, and were married to Elias's sisters: Wheeler to Nancy Watie and Candy to Mary Watie. On the edge of town was a commons, and not far away were two more taverns, at least one stickball field, and Samuel Worcester's house and mission, which also operated as the U.S. post office. Many more Cherokees lived on farms nearby.[113]

Reconstructed early-eighteenth-century council house, Cherokee Heritage Center, Tahlequah, Cherokee Nation.
AUTHOR'S PHOTOGRAPH

Reconstructed courthouse, New Echota State Historic Site.
AUTHOR'S PHOTOGRAPH

The newly elected representatives who came to New Echota in October 1828 assembled in the council house and listened to an address by John Ross, who had been elected principal chief, on a platform strongly opposing emigration. He explained in Cherokee: "Occupying your seats by the free suffrage of the people, under the privileges guaranteed by the Constitution," the members had important subjects before them. They had to consider "the organization of the new Government" and "the revision and amendments of the old laws, so as to make them in unison with the principles of the Constitution." Ross recommended that they pass laws that were short and plain so that the people could understand them when they were circulated by the *Phoenix,* "an important vehicle in the diffusion of general information" and a "powerful auxiliary in asserting and supporting our political rights."[114]

The fall sessions were a time of coming together, when New Echota filled with several hundred people for many weeks. They shared food and news and visited with dispersed kin, meeting babies born since they last gathered. The political decisions were fraught in these troubled times but may have been exciting as well, as Cherokees worked on nation building.

CONCLUSION

Today, New Echota is a Georgia state park. Visitors can walk through the reconstructed Cherokee National Council House, tour the reconstructed print shop to see how the *Cherokee Phoenix* was printed, and stand on the site of Fort Wool, built by the U.S. Army in 1838 right in the middle of town—in the capital of the Cherokee Nation—to detain Cherokee men, women, and children before forcing them onto the Trail of Tears. Streams, woods of pines, oaks, walnuts, and maples, and the blue-green of the Smokies in the distance still evoke what this capital and its countryside looked like in 1828, although the fields of corn and cotton have been replaced by a golf course, and the ferries and taverns are now bridges and convenience stores. What the visitor won't see is many people, unless a busload of schoolkids happens to be dropped off. On my visits to the park, the park rangers have outnumbered the smattering of visitors. Occasionally a jogger passes through. New Echota State Historic Site is a site of commemoration, where visitors can feel the emptiness created by Indian Removal.

Yet the emptiness at the New Echota State Historic Site overstates Cherokee absence. It is simply not true that, as one tourist website phrased this common belief in the early 2000s, "with the Trail of Tears the only capital of the Cherokee Nation was silenced forever."[115] In fact, today there are two Cherokee capitals. Tahlequah, Oklahoma, the capital of the Cherokee Nation, has more than seventeen thousand residents. Cherokee, North Carolina, capital of the Eastern Band of Cherokee Indians (who, as we shall see in chapter 11, managed not to be removed in the 1830s), has a population of two thousand. The town center of each has parks, a courthouse, restaurants and coffeehouses, history museums, and an arts center with exhibitions of contemporary Native artists. People come and go from government buildings on tribal business. Both towns have casinos, and their street signs are written in Cherokee as well as English. Outdoor dramas at both places are run and staffed by Cherokees. Tahlequah has a university, with Native and non-Native students, and is in the midst of the kind of downtown revival common to many college towns these days, with a brewery, a bicycle shop, and a cannabis store. Two monuments to the Confederate dead sat on the Cherokee National Capitol grounds in Tahlequah until the summer of 2020, when the Cherokee Nation removed them around the time that many similar statues were pulled down all across the United States. Tahlequah and Cherokee are twenty-first-century southern towns, and they are also living Cherokee capitals, as Cherokee—and as Native—as New Echota was in 1830.

Cherokee National Capitol, Tahlequah,
Cherokee Nation, built in 1867.
AUTHOR'S PHOTOGRAPH

In the early nineteenth century, Cherokees developed a modern nation in ways that reinforced their Cherokee identity and sovereignty. They made these changes for their own benefit, but also to demonstrate to Americans that the Cherokees were a nation. Indeed, their success did demonstrate to white Americans that Cherokees intended to remain, and Georgians demanded that the U.S. government help them end the Cherokee Nation. In May 1830, the U.S. Congress passed, and President Jackson signed, the Indian Removal Act, authorizing and providing funds for the president to negotiate treaties to "remove" all Indians living east of the Mississippi to the west—some one hundred thousand people. Support from states in the South and the trans-Appalachian West passed the legislation over considerable northeastern opposition. The *Cherokee Phoenix* printed speeches by New Jersey Senator Theodore Frelinghuysen and Maine Senator Peleg Sprague, who made heated arguments against the act. The senators asserted Native sovereignty and asked, rhetorically, "Is it one of the prerogatives of the white man, that he may disregard the dictates of moral principles when an Indian shall be concerned?"[116]

The Indian Removal Act passed anyway, and Jackson's administration moved quickly to do what he had attempted in the wake of the War of 1812: expel the Cherokees, Muscogees, Shawnees, and all Native nations from places that the United States wanted. In the next chapters, we will move west of the Mississippi for the history of some of the places where the U.S. government would move Cherokees and others and the effects those newcomers would have on the peoples of the West.

CHAPTER 10

KIOWAS AND THE CREATION
OF THE PLAINS INDIANS

THE KIOWAS HAVE LONG KEPT CALENDARS AS RECORDS OF their history. Each winter and each summer gets one picture, so it needs to be recognizable and unique—an image that will trigger memories long into the future about the events that happened that season. Usually, elders decided what the featured event should be. Then one or more calendar keepers drew it on a leather calendar made from a bison hide. Recounting history was a group activity, with people gathering to look at the calendars for reference and discuss the history of each season. In future generations, new calendar keepers copied the pictures onto new hides, cloth, or paper, in their own styles, and added years as they passed. For the summer of 1833, Kiowa artist Little Bear drew a beheading. Kiowas called it the "Summer That They Cut Off Their Heads" or the "Osage Cutthroat Massacre." In full-color versions, the blood spurting from the severed head draws the eye. (That's blood at the end of the knife in the black-and-white drawing.)[1]

The Summer That They Cut Off Their Heads,
Little Bear's calendar, 1833, in James Mooney,
Calendar History of the Kiowa Indians.
DAVIS LIBRARY, UNIVERSITY OF NORTH CAROLINA
AT CHAPEL HILL

In the previous two chapters, Native nations in the East tried various means to remain nations in their homelands. In this chapter we move to the Plains, where Shawnees, Cherokees, and Quapaws will have to go in the nineteenth century—and where Mohawks, the O'odham, and the descendants of Ossomocomuck will successfully resist going. These were the homelands of people like the Kiowas who were still the dominant nations in the Plains in the mid-nineteenth century. Their history of putting European goods and animals to their own uses would shape how they received the newcomers forced into their homeland.

By the Summer That They Cut Off Their Heads, more than three centuries had passed since the first arrival of Spaniards on the Plains. Less than two centuries have passed between that summer and the writing of this book. By 1833 there were steamboats and railroads and a smallpox vaccine. Europeans and their descendants had claimed parts of the Plains for three centuries, but in reality, Plains nations like the Kiowas still ruled there. The United States had been its own country for only a generation. The president of the United States, Andrew Jackson, had been a teenager during the American Revolution. But in the years since the Revolution, the U.S. border had moved from the western edge of the thirteen original states over the Appalachians and past the Mississippi River. Yet the lands that the United States considered the Louisiana Purchase were still mostly populated by Native nations, and even the most ambitious U.S. claims did not yet encompass the whole continent. In 1833, its neighbors in North America included not only Native nations but also British Canada and the Republic of Mexico, which had won its independence from Spain in 1821 and included Texas, New Mexico, Arizona, and California.

To the Kiowas and other Native nations in the West, the few scattered, geographically isolated posts inhabited by Europeans and their descendants (though usefully connected to global trade) did not constitute the large geographies claimed by the United States, Mexico, and Canada on those polities' maps. Similarly, those posts had not added up to a meaningful New Spain or French Louisiana.

Instead, to the Kiowas in the nineteenth century, European and U.S. posts were basically stores, allowed to exist only because local Indians wanted them, as we have seen with other European posts in previous chapters. Some were recognizable villages like Santa Fe, where people of mixed Spanish and Native ancestry lived, allied with the Pueblo communities that surrounded them. St. Louis, San Antonio, Laredo, and Chihuahua were towns of a few hundred to a few thousand people that existed mainly for the purpose of Native trade and a little local agriculture or ranching.[2]

As the summer 1833 Kiowa calendar reveals, wars with other Native nations were still their focus. Pressure from the United States and eastern Native nations moving west had pushed Osages farther west on their hunts, onto Kiowa hunting lands, but these pressures mattered little to the Kiowas. Until the 1870s, the most important turning points in Kiowa history came because of foreign relations with other Native nations and because of one new arrival: the horse.

CENTAURS IN THEIR SPIRIT

On the first day of my class on Native North American history, I show George Catlin's *Comanche Feats of Horsemanship*, a vivid painting of men fighting on horseback. The central rider clings to the side of his horse as a shield against the enemy warriors, and from the shield on his back dangle scalps of enemies he has killed in battle. The sky stretches wide above the Plains grasses. These are iconic Indians, and every student recognizes them from western films, book covers, and images that come up in a Google search of "American Indian." But this scene is a product of history. As I tell my students that first day, there were no horses in North America before the Spanish brought them.

The Great Plains aren't suited to most kinds of living. Especially in the shortgrass High Plains at the base of the Rocky Mountains, stretching from Montana in the north to Texas in the south, there is

Comanche Feats of Horsemanship, by George Catlin, 1834–1835.
SMITHSONIAN AMERICAN ART MUSEUM

little rain—twelve to fifteen inches per year. The winds can be vicious, as can heat and cold. There are few trees to provide temporary shelter or building materials for permanent homes. Kiowa novelist and essayist N. Scott Momaday explains, "At times the plains are bright and calm and quiet; at times they are black with the sudden violence of weather. Always there are winds."[3] When Spanish explorers passed through in the early 1500s, they found the Plains confounding. The only landmarks, a few tree-lined rivers, were invisible until one was right upon them, and they immediately disappeared after one left them. One of the men with Francisco de Coronado explained that even determining the direction from which his party had come was difficult, as the fifteen hundred people, one thousand horses, and more than five thousand sheep "left no more trace than if no one had ever passed there."[4] Yet even outsiders could appreciate the bountiful Plains economy. A Frenchman wrote of Plains Indians that "their country abounds so much in Buffaloes and Deer that they find no difficulty in finding provision."[5] George Catlin described walking through "one of the most lovely and picturesque countries in the world . . . The whole country seemed at times to be alive with buffaloes, and bands of wild horses."[6]

The wild horses that Catlin observed in the nineteenth century were the descendants of Spanish horses that had arrived in the seventeenth and impressed Native nations with their potential. After all, you can't ride a bison or a deer. People first domesticated horses around the fourth century B.C.E. in the steppe of what is now Kazakhstan, vast grasslands similar to the North American Plains. By the time Spaniards crossed the Atlantic, horses were such a major part of Spanish culture that the Spanish brought them on their ships. Spaniards tried to keep horses to themselves by not giving or selling them, but Native people wanted them. Early on, people near Spain's posts and towns acquired horses through raiding. After the 1680 Pueblo Revolt ousted New Mexico's Spanish missionaries and soldiers, the Pueblo peoples kept their horses and developed a thriving horse-breeding business, mating those with characteristics they wanted to see in the next generations and selling them to their trading partners. Other horses escaped and became wild herds on the Plains, which people caught and tamed. Thus, in the late seventeenth and early eighteenth centuries, peoples around the Plains, including the Kiowas, acquired horses, out of the control or sight of the Spanish.[7]

Horses that had been bred for the hot, dry conditions of Eurasia and North Africa proved ideal for the North American Plains and for hunting the largest game of the Plains: bison. The Little Ice Age seems to have brought the Great Plains relatively more rainfall, which watered the grasses and provided more food for bison and eventually horses. Bison hunting was tough going on foot: The huge animals run fast, and their thick hides require a spear-carrying hunter to get closer than is safe. Hunters would take a large number of men, women, and children on the hunt to herd bison over a short cliff and shoot arrows to pick off those that survived the fall. This kind of bison hunting was a big and dangerous production, so bands would have only one or two hunts per year, living the rest of the time in towns in the river valleys and mountains on the edges of the

Plains, farming, fishing, and hunting for smaller game such as deer and rabbits.[8]

Horses allowed bison hunters to cover more ground, find herds faster, and maneuver in order to get a good shot at a bison at full gallop. As on the Eurasian steppe, horses could graze on the Plains grasses, which were useless as a human food source. When Kiowas first learned about horses in the late seventeenth or early eighteenth century, their reactions may have been similar to that of a Cree man who recalled enemies riding in on horseback, "swift as the deer." He remembered being astonished at the riders' skill in using the horses' momentum to put great force behind their stone clubs, wreaking havoc in battle and quickly riding away. When he heard that a horse had been killed in a battle, "numbers of us went to see him, and we all admired him." As people always do, they interpreted new things using what they already knew. The Cree man said that the horse "put us in mind of a stag that had lost his horns," yet the horse was not free like a stag but instead "was a slave to man, like the dog, which carried our things," so some people referred to the horse as "the big dog."[9]

People made different choices about how to integrate horses into their economies and ways of life. Within just a few decades, in a dramatic change, Kiowas, Crows, Cheyennes, Lakotas, and Comanches became fully nomadic and abandoned agriculture completely, still gathering wild plants but relying on trading partners for corn, beans, and tobacco. By contrast, Osage, Pawnee, and Wichita women kept farming in their permanent river valley towns. Their men went out on bison hunts more frequently than in the past but lived in the farming towns for the rest of the year. Apache bands made various choices: Some remained mostly farming people, and others became nomadic hunters and raiders, as the O'odham knew only too well. And some peoples did not become bison hunters at all, despite also living near the Plains. Pueblo communities hosted trade fairs where people with horses came to trade bison products for agricultural produce. Mandans, Hidatsas, and Arikaras on the upper Missouri River did the same, and these agricultural towns became great trading centers for a variety of peoples and goods.[10]

Indeed, it was the agricultural production of these towns that allowed year-round bison hunters to continue relying on multiple sources of sustenance—something that people in the era after the fall of cities had learned to value. Plains bison hunters developed a reciprocal economy with Mandan, Pueblo, Wichita, and other agricultural towns, which enhanced economic security for all, and new connections with European traders added their metal goods and cloth to the mix. People who stayed put were a vital part of the lives of nomadic people, and vice versa.[11]

The horse arrived at different times around the world, but wherever it went, it brought possibilities. Like Native North Americans who called horses big dogs, people elsewhere compared them at first sight to zebras or tapirs or kangaroos. Navajos, like Aboriginal Australians and Native peoples of the Pampas in present-day Argentina, used horses to develop a ranching economy. With the space and pasture available on the Plains, Kiowas used horses to expand their world.[12]

Kiowas moved out of the Rocky Mountains of what's now western Montana and onto the northern Plains in the late seventeenth or very early eighteenth century. Oral histories recount that they moved at the invitation of the Crow Indians, who had recently developed their own Plains life and identity. The Crows had been Hidatsas, but when the horse arrived, some migrated to the Plains, re-creating themselves as nomadic Crow people, while most Hidatsas stayed in their farming towns on the upper Missouri River. Having their Kiowa allies living near them was useful to the Crows as the northern Plains populated.[13]

The Kiowas learned how to travel on horseback in all seasons and to live in huge portable tipis made of bison leather. In the nineteenth century, observers described them as "expert on horseback to an extraordinary degree, leaping from one horse to another while at full speed, and performing many feats upon the prairies never undertaken even by the best equestrians of the circus." Visitors noted the "noble bearing and fine athletic figures of these people, which we partly attributed to their being continually on horseback." Catlin's painting portrays their ability to—in an image right out of a Hollywood western—hang on to one side of a horse as they rode, stay-ing invisible to an enemy on the other side, and "discharge their arrows directly under their horse's necks." Men and women were equally skilled riders, and children learned early, often so young that they needed to be roped into their saddles. Observers marveled at "the ease and air of security with which their equestrians preserved their equipoise on the naked backs of their horses."[14]

Ledger art by Bad Eye, Tan-na-ti, Bird Chief,
Fort Marion, Florida, 1870s.
FAIRBANKS MUSEUM AND PLANETARIUM, ST. JOHNSBURY, VERMONT

With horses, Kiowas developed a whole new worldview and came to identify themselves as swift riders over a vast range. The world looked different from horseback. N. Scott Momaday describes his Kiowa ancestors as having "become centaurs in their spirit." It was, as historian Elliott West puts it, "a full union between the human and the nonhuman." Kiowas came to know a grander space and to think about the world differently. They could pick up their tipis and leave a region entirely if relations with neighbors turned sour or they found more appealing resources elsewhere. Home had a different meaning when it was portable and when lots of horses shared it. Language changed as people developed whole new vo-cabularies to describe horses' age, worth, color, condition, and sex. Horses required pasture and accessible water, and the large herds shaped Kiowa decisions. Living on the move was not wandering. It required planning and organization. They had to move when the horses had eaten most of the grass in one place, and winter camps needed accessible cottonwood bark to gather for the horses to eat.[15]

Kiowas developed new ceremonies, songs, and dances that related to mounted adventures. A horse medicine society developed healing rituals involving spirit horses. Men made shorter bows and smaller shields for easier wielding by warriors and hunters on horseback. People were buried with accessories and symbols relating to the horse. Status in Kiowa society reflected one's horses. The Ôñgòp were a class of families that had dozens or even hundreds of horses. The Óñ:dégú:[bà class had perhaps a dozen. The Kóon class had none and had to depend on other people's generosity. Kiowas rode horses to get everywhere and became notably less swift runners than other peoples—they could never have won a running race against O'odham girls. Horses became the gifts that leaders gave to followers, diplomats gave to allies, and prospective in-laws gave to one another.[16]

Horse nations interacted with more people across greater distances, contacts that both widened the Kiowa world and solidified their sense of themselves as Kiowa, in similar ways to the Shawnees in their diaspora. More frequent contacts led to more raiding, war, and violent captive-taking. Plains people became both more powerful and more vulnerable. New international relationships included alliances like that between the Kiowas and the Crows and between the Kiowas and a people known as the Plains Apaches. The Plains Apaches were the northernmost of the many Apache groups, who probably fled Pawnee and Comanche warfare in the 1720s and '30s. Sometimes they are referred to as "Kiowa Apaches" because of the alliance that they forged. A relatively small nation, they needed strong allies. But, similar to the Piipaash and the Akimel O'odham, they didn't become Kiowas or merge with other Apaches, and today they still have their own language and nation. Alliance with the Kiowas enhanced their security and allowed them to protect their separate identity.[17]

National identities are reflected in particular symbols. Kiowa calendars depicted the agricultural Arikaras with a corn pictograph and the Pawnees with their distinctive scalp locks. Nations had their own signs in the Plains Indian Sign Language, the new language that Indians on the northern Plains developed for interactions between people who spoke no common language. Because many Kiowa men cut their hair on the right side of the face to ear level while leaving the left side long, often wrapped with a leather strip, a style that distinguished them from other men, the Plains sign for Kiowa was made by rotating the right hand close to the side of the face, palm up, indicating the length of Kiowa men's hair on that side. The sign for Crow Indians involves a flying-like motion, alluding to birds. The Kiowas' sign for the Mandans indicated a tattooed chin, and for the Hidatsas they gestured dipping water with a cupped hand, reflecting their identity as the Water People.[18]

Pawnee man, Dance over Slain Pawnee Winter,
Little Bear's calendar, 1849–50, in James Mooney,
Calendar History of the Kiowa Indians.
DAVIS LIBRARY, UNIVERSITY OF NORTH CAROLINA AT CHAPEL HILL

Sometimes societies change slowly without even realizing the shift; Plains Indians, on the other hand, knew they had chosen a dramatically new way of life, and they worried about whether it was the right decision. A Cheyenne oral tradition recalls that when Cheyennes saw their first horses, ridden by Comanches, the Creator gave them the choice of whether to accept them. "You may have horses," the Creator said. "You may even go with the Comanches and take them. But remember this: If you have horses everything will be changed for you forever. You will have to move around a lot to find pasture for your horses. You will have to give up gardening and live by hunting and gathering, like the Comanches. And you will have to come out of your earth houses and live in tents. . . . You will have to have fights with other tribes, who will want your pasture land or the places where you hunt." It was a decision that would affect generations to come, so they would need to "think, before you decide." The Cheyennes accepted the gift (which in other versions comes from the Kiowas and Crows) but remembered it as a choice and a turning point in Cheyenne history.[19]

Although being horse nations brought more warfare and new challenges, Plains people who looked back on this era from the twentieth century believed their ancestors had made the right choice. A Crow woman named Pretty Shield recalled, "Ahh, I came onto a happy world. There was always fat meat, glad singing, and much dancing in our villages. Our people's hearts were then as light as breath-feathers." Her grandmothers had told her stories about the days before horses, stories Kiowa grandmothers surely told as well. They had to walk and carry all of their belongings on their backs and on travois (wooden sleds designed for the Plains) pulled by dogs. But with horses, as an observer in 1805 noted, "the women ride and have no loads to carry on their backs as is common among other nations." With horses to haul their possessions, they could transport corn and other food they bought from farmers. Killing more bison, as well as elk, deer, and pronghorn (similar to an antelope), for a greater part of the year made people better fed, better clothed, and better housed.[20]

As with most revolutionary change, it became hard to understand the kind of people their ancestors had been before. Plains people tended to tell this history as one of improvement, looking down a bit on their pre-horse ancestors, whom they saw as living a duller and harder life. Momaday describes the era before horses as "a struggle for existence in the bleak northern mountains." After the move, though, "no longer were they slaves to the simple necessity of survival; they were a lordly and dangerous society of fighters and thieves, hunters and priests of the sun." It was "the golden age of the Kiowas."[21]

Kiowas and other Plains Indians decided to live the way they did. Even at the height of the Plains economy and culture in the eighteenth and nineteenth centuries, most Native North Americans did not ride in search of bison to kill and horses to take. Indeed, the ubiquity of images of Indians on horseback reflects a false assumption that all Native peoples were nomadic by nature. Plains peoples purposefully developed a nomadic way of life, a change that had dramatic effects on their lives and their view of themselves. Their ancestors had not lived this way, nor did Europeans force them to make these changes.

KILLING, PROCESSING, AND TRADING BISON

Just as the iconic image of a warrior on horseback falsely conveys the notion that all Indians were Plains Indians, it also implies that the Plains Indian is a man. In fact, horse culture transformed gender relations. Women had previously been the farmers and the managers of both the agricultural fields and the earthen lodges in their towns, so women's roles had to change when their people left behind that kind of living. While men now spent more time hunting and fighting than their fathers and grandfathers had, women did the equally important work of butchering and drying the meat, scraping and tanning large numbers of hides, and caring for huge herds of horses. As in their permanent towns in the days of their ancestors, women were in charge of the camps, both the organizational planning and the heavy labor required to set up and take down accommodations for hundreds to thousands of people as well as taking care of children and elderly on the move and making sure everyone had enough to eat and drink. While in camp, they managed the day-to-day business of feeding, clothing, and caring for their extended families. And they still gathered plants for food and medicine, including berries, greens, the tuber that is sometimes called the prairie potato or prairie turnip, and—like O'odham women—mesquite pods. They bought corn from farmers and made it into hominy by the same method as Mohawk women, though the ashes they cooked the corn with came from cottonwood trees. Among the Kiowas, very successful hunters married multiple women to keep up with the workload, a sign of the importance of women's labor.[22]

As with the O'odham, work seems to have been what mattered most in gender divisions. Plains Sign Language includes a sign for "man-woman" (a combination of the signs for "man" and "woman"). Someone born male might become gendered female, and vice versa. And there may have been some room for people in between. In some ways, gender became less binary when everyone rode and cared for horses.[23]

Camp of the Kioway Indians, by Balduin Möllhausen, 1858.
THE LOUIS ROUND WILSON SPECIAL COLLECTIONS LIBRARY,
UNIVERSITY OF NORTH CAROLINA AT CHAPEL HILL

A huge amount of skilled labor went into manufacturing bison hides, and part of the reason for living in portable camps on the hunting grounds was for women to skin and dress the bison as soon as possible. When bison were killed in the fall or winter, women staked each hide out flat and scraped off the meat from the inside with a bone or metal tool. Once it had dried completely, they scraped the inside again and rubbed it with cooked and mashed brains, dried it again, then removed it from the stakes and wet it down to leave bunched up overnight. The next morning, they hung and dried it again, this time on a vertical rack, rubbing the inside smooth with a stone and then a leather strip and brushing the fur on the outside. Warm and soft, these winter skins made heavy robes that fetched a high price.

In the summer, women processed bison for their leather. Much of the process was similar to making a robe, but in this case they scraped the hair from the outside, and the final steps of the tanning process included making the leather soft by twisting and knotting the entire skin and pulling the skin back and forth across a leather strip. Leather was sold in whole skins or made into tipis, clothes, drumheads, shields, or moccasins, which were stiffened and made waterproof by rubbing them with tallow. Women and men painted tipis and other leather goods in colorful designs, women in geometric patterns and men with images of feats in hunting or battle. Clothes were decorated with fur and rows of animal teeth, beads, or bells made from sheets of copper. Some women who were especially skilled were in charge of designing and making their huge tipis, which required a dozen bison hides and more than twenty poles. Tipis had to be repaired every year, with new leather from the summer hunt replacing worn parts and painters touching up the decorations or adding new ones. Women kept track of the tipis and dresses they made just as men accumulated a record of accomplishments in battle and hunting.[24]

The Kiowas' alliance with the Crows on the northern Plains brought them into trade with the still agricultural peoples from whom the Crows had separated: Hidatsas, Mandans, and Arikaras. These towns on the upper Missouri River had existed for centuries when the dramatic increase in people living nomadically on the Plains allowed them to develop into large and widely known year-round trade centers. After a major hunt, Kiowas and Crows paraded in on horseback and then set up their tipis in camps outside town. At the towns, they smoked the peace pipe and exchanged news and

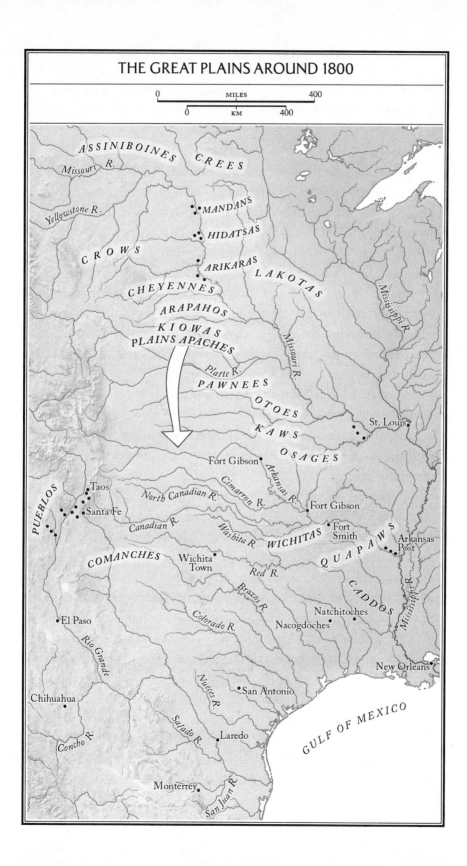

THE GREAT PLAINS AROUND 1800

0   MILES   400

0   KM   400

ASSINIBOINES   CREES

Missouri R.

Yellowstone R.

CROWS

MANDANS

HIDATSAS

ARIKARAS

CHEYENNES

LAKOTAS

ARAPAHOS

KIOWAS

PLAINS APACHES

Platte R.

Missouri R.

Mississippi R.

PAWNEES

OTOES

KAWS

OSAGES

St. Louis

Fort Gibson

Cimarron R.

Arkansas R.

PUEBLOS

Taos

North Canadian R.

Santa Fe

Fort Gibson

Canadian R.

Washita R.

WICHITAS

Fort
Smith

QUAPAWS

Arkansas
Post

COMANCHES

Wichita
Town

Red R.

CADDOS

Mississippi R.

El Paso

Brazos R.

Colorado R.

Nacogdoches

Natchitoches

Rio Grande

New Orleans

Chihuahua

Nueces R.

San Antonio

Concho R.

Salado R.

Laredo

GULF OF MEXICO

Monterrey

San Juan R.

gifts. Then Kiowas and Crows unloaded huge parcels of animal products: meat, leather hides, bison robes, pelts of wolves and smaller animals, and moccasins, leggings, shirts, and dresses made from leather.[25]

Kiowas and Crows also sold horses—lots of horses. Each year the Kiowas added to their large herds through their own breeding, trade, raids on the Spanish and Comanches to the south, and roping and taming wild horses. A Frenchman who witnessed Crows' arrival at the Arikara, Mandan, and Hidatsa towns in 1805 estimated that the men brought in ten to forty horses each. U.S. explorers Meriwether Lewis and William Clark first heard of the Kiowas when Mandans told them that the Kiowas "raise a great number of horses, which they barter" to the Mandans, Arikaras, and Hidatsas. They also traded human beings, captured in war and raids and brought to sell if they weren't kept by Kiowa families.[26]

In return, Kiowas bought hundreds of bushels of corn, plus beans, squash, and tobacco. They also purchased products that Arikaras, Mandans, and Hidatsas had bought from others, including shells and various kinds of stone and metal for making art, tools, and weapons. The towns sold goods made in Europe: metal knives, kettles, pans, and lances, as well as cotton and wool cloth, blankets, guns, gunpowder, and musket balls. Throughout the eighteenth and the first half of the nineteenth century, it was Native traders who provided the Kiowas with European goods, including guns, acquired originally at French Great Lakes posts, at English ports on Hudson Bay nine hundred miles to the northeast, or in St. Louis at the confluence of the Mississippi and Missouri rivers (although the powerful Osages blockaded this route and generally kept the St. Louis trade to themselves). By 1805 the Kiowas had enough guns that they were selling them to other Plains trading partners.[27]

European goods were only part of the vast trade economy of the Great Plains. Kiowas still wore leather clothes and moccasins. They still preferred bows and arrows for hunting and warfare—muzzle-loading muskets were far too hard to load on horseback. It was only horses that they adopted in ways that transformed them and helped them create a new—and still Kiowa—way of life.

A SUMMER PEOPLE

Every summer, the Kiowas gathered for the annual Medicine Lodge Ceremony, the Sun Dance, which renewed their bonds as a nation. It was an honoring and celebrating of life on the Plains together. Their closest allies, the Plains Apaches, joined the Kiowa Sun Dance, where they had their own reserved space, the same every year. Indeed, they trace their close alliance with the Kiowa to when they began joining the camp circle at the Kiowa Sun Dance. The Kiowa name for the Plains Apaches is Tàugûi, meaning "Seated Outside." Other Plains nations have similar ceremonies, and the Kiowas' probably began when they started living full-time on the Plains. According to oral history, the Táiñmé, a medicine bundle that served as the central sacred object of religious veneration in Kiowa and Plains Apache sun dances, came to the Kiowas when they lived on the northern Plains. The Kiowas may have initially had a space in the Crow Sun Dance circle before starting their own.[28]

The location and timing could not be decided until someone had a dream about when and where to go. Anyone who had such a dream would report it to the official keeper of the Táiñmé, who would then send messengers to the dispersed Kiowa bands and the Plains Apaches. People started expecting the messenger when the sun began to set later and later in the day as the year moved toward the summer solstice, the sage grass grew tall, the horses were putting on weight, and the white fluff from the cottonwood trees was blowing across the Plains, carrying the seeds of future trees. Although winter had its joys—when the rivers froze and kids played on the ice, the littlest ones pulled on hide sleds by the older ones— summer was the season everyone looked forward to. As Momaday explains, "The Kiowas are a summer people; they abide the cold and keep to themselves, but when the season turns and the land becomes warm and vital they cannot hold still."[29]

For much of the year, Kiowas lived in family bands usually composed of siblings and spouses and their children and grandchildren. Kiowas practice bilateral kinship rather than strict patrilineal or matrilineal descent, so when a couple married, they might live with either spouse's family band or even with different sets of family in different years. Sometimes several brothers married several sisters, forming a family band with multiple internal connections. Men who practiced polygamy often married sisters of their first wives, although wives could also enter families from diplomatic engagements or as captives. The adults in a band tended to treat the children as belonging to all of the adults of the generation above them rather than as the children of one couple. Most bands had twenty to thirty members, but a family leader who was known as a good provider and protector might amass a band of as many as eighty people—a "family of many tipis"—if he married multiple women or if his daughters and sons and their spouses all chose to remain with him. Successful leaders even attracted unrelated young men or poorer or very small families who wanted to join a successful band.[30]

For the Sun Dance, each band rode in and found its accustomed place in the large circular camp. The location was always near a river so the thousands of people would have plenty of water for themselves as well as water and grazing for their horses. Women set up the tipis and cut down cottonwood trees to build a medicine lodge at the camp's center for the Táiñmé keeper to display the Táiñmé. Kiowa George Hunt remembered the excitement of Sun Dances in the late nineteenth century as people visited friends and extended family they had not seen since the previous summer, much as Cherokees did at the annual National Council sessions.[31]

Once everyone arrived and the preparations were complete, the Sun Dance ceremony lasted four days, with dances, drumming, and songs of thanksgiving for success in war and hunting and of renewal and hope for the year ahead. Kiowas stayed in the Sun Dance camp for around a month as smaller groups conducted ceremonies of various sorts, men went out in small hunting parties, and women showed tipis and clothes they had made. Elders chose an event for the previous season's calendar and recited history to refresh their memories and teach new generations. Parents planned marriages for their children, and young women and men made their own plans, not always consistent with those of their parents. Any men who wanted to raise a war party to avenge a death or to raid an appealing target recruited from among the gathered bands. Leaders of the larger bands with more men and more horses considered many proposals before making a decision.[32]

Toward the end of the month, band leaders made plans for the late-summer hunt. Summer was bison mating season, when herds that spent the winter in small separate male and female groups came back together by the hundreds. After the Sun Dance, the whole Kiowa Nation went after one of the massive herds, continuing and reaffirming the spirit of the Sun Dance. Each season, the band leaders chose an older and respected man to conduct the movements, in consultation with other leaders. Under his direction, young men in Kiowa military societies were responsible for keeping the peace among the men in camp and making sure everyone got a fair chance at the hunt.[33]

Women managed the logistics of packing, moving, and setting up camps. When it was time to leave the Sun Dance camp, women took down the tipis and loaded everything onto horses. An observer of one move wrote that "we could not but admire the regularity with which the preparations for their journey seemed to be conducted, and the remarkable facility with which the lodges disappeared, and with all their cumbrous and various contents were secured to the backs of the numerous horses and mules." Everyone rode, with children riding behind an adult or three or four on a horse together, "the young warriors, with their lances and shields, galloping or racing along the line for caprice or amusement."[34] When they stopped, they set up camps, no longer in a circle but spread along a long stretch of river, sometimes on both sides. Men went out from camp to kill bison, and women butchered them, sometimes coming along on the hunt and dismounting to do their work as soon as a bison was killed. In camp, women dried the meat and did the first round of preparation of the hides.[35]

At the end of the summer hunt, the Kiowas dispersed, and many of the men joined the war party they had committed to. While small raiding parties could form at other times of the year, summer gathering allowed for much larger war parties. Sometimes women would go along, but usually they stayed in a camp with the children and any men who didn't go. For many years, the main target was the Lakotas, whom the Kiowas and Crows fought for space on the northern Plains. A Lakota calendar records that in the winter of 1814–15, a party of Lakotas visited a Kiowa camp on the North Platte River, in what's now western Nebraska, to discuss peace. The season's name, "Kiowa-Hit-on-Head-with-Axe Winter," reveals that the talks did not go well. Two men got into a fight, and the Lakota man ended up planting his tomahawk in the Kiowa man's head. Any chance of peace was ended.[36]

But by that winter Kiowas had already moved south of the Platte River toward the Arkansas River, in part to be farther from the Lakotas. This move brought new alliances and new enemies. The large Wichita trading town on the Red River, on the present-day Oklahoma–Texas state line (and within the bounds of today's Chickasaw reservation), was glad to add the Kiowas as valuable trading partners and allies. The Kiowas' name for the Wichitas was Evàun, meaning Pumpkin Braiders, Corn Braiders, or Food Braiders, reflecting the dried and prepared agricultural products that the Kiowas bought from them (or perhaps the baskets the food came in). For a while, some Kiowa bands remained in the North, and they kept up relations with their northern allies and still traded in Missouri River towns. Sometimes Kiowas left children there for a few years to learn the Crow language and preserve their alliance.[37]

If the South meant a new trading partner in the Wichitas, it also brought the Kiowas a formidable enemy, the Comanches. The headwaters of the Arkansas River and its tributaries were prime hunting land, and Kiowas clashed with Comanche hunters and raided Comanche bands for horses, many of which the Comanches had taken from Spanish ranches in the South. Comanches also blocked the Kiowas from trade with Spanish Santa Fe and the Pueblo communities. The Kiowa name for the Comanches was Câigù, meaning War or Enemy People. At first, the Kiowas tried to recruit help against the Comanches from Spanish Texas. In 1795, they joined a multinational delegation, led by Wichitas. They traveled together to San Antonio, which the Spanish had founded as a mission and presidio in 1718, to offer to ally with the Spanish against both the Comanches and the United States. But while Spain's colonial administration certainly wanted alliance and trade with these Native powers and would have liked to take advantage of this unprecedented opportunity, an alliance against the Comanches sounded dangerous, while fighting the United States would have been illegal, given that their countries were not at war. Turned away from Texas, the Kiowas would make peace with the Comanches instead, forging an alliance that would ultimately wreak havoc across northern New Spain and make Spanish officials wish they had jumped at the chance in 1795.[38]

PEACE ON THE SOUTHERN PLAINS

Sometime around the turn of the nineteenth century, a small Kiowa party riding south of the Arkansas River, near the present-day state line between Kansas and Colorado, stopped at a trading post run by a Spanish colonist. From the next room, the Kiowas heard voices speaking in Comanche and reached for their bows and arrows, but the proprietor, fearing the destruction of his post, suggested that if they ever wanted to make peace, this could be the opportunity. The Kiowas talked among themselves and, in a decision that would change the course of history, accepted the Spaniard's offer to mediate for them. The man went into the next room and told the Comanches that there was a group of Kiowas next door, but not to fear—they wanted to make peace. He assuaged the Comanches' fear that this might be a trap and brought out gifts and food for both parties to encourage them.

The leaders of the two groups, Wolf Lying Down for the Kiowas and Afraid of Water for the Comanches, began to talk. Wolf Lying Down was a prominent man in the Kiowa Nation and had enough authority to start real negotiations, but the Comanche nation was much larger than the Kiowas and composed of several fairly autonomous divisions. Afraid of Water made it clear that he was "just one war-party leader and that there were many other Comanche war-party leaders and chiefs who would have to be considered." Afraid of Water suggested that the Kiowa party travel home with the Comanches. Venturing into a Comanche camp was a frightening prospect, yet everyone knew that peace negotiations required broad support from both nations. The next step had to be discussions with either more Kiowas or more Comanches. Wolf Lying Down responded, "I am a chief. I am not afraid to die. I will go." He told the Kiowas with him to "go home and tell our tribe that I am gone to make peace with the Comanche. Return for me to this place when the leaves are yellow. If you do not find me here, know that I am dead and avenge my death."[39]

Wolf Lying Down rode south with the Comanches to one of their camps in what's now northwest Texas but at the time was decidedly Comanche country. Comanches in the camp rushed at Wolf Lying Down, calling for revenge for the people they had lost to the Kiowas. He stood bravely as Afraid of Water explained that the Kiowa had come to work for peace. The rest of the summer, Wolf Lying Down met with Comanches of various bands while the Kiowa party convened with more of their nation, including at that summer's Sun Dance. When fall approached, a large party of Kiowas rode to the meeting place, not knowing whether they would be making peace or avenging Wolf Lying Down's death. As they approached, Wolf Lying Down rode out to meet them, with Afraid of Water by his side. They had started a process by which the Kiowas and the Comanches forged a great alliance. Together they would dominate the southern Plains for the next eighty years.

Kiowa calendars for this era don't survive, but the Kiowa–Comanche peace appears as an important event in Kiowa and Comanche oral histories as well as in the written documents of the Spanish. Comanche history clarifies that this initial peace was with only one of the Comanche divisions, the Yamparikas, the division that the Kiowas probably had clashed most with in the upper Arkansas Valley. Not surprisingly, Afraid of Water is the hero in the Comanche version, and the emphasis on Wolf Lying Down's bravery is replaced with Afraid of Water's "patience and influence," which prevented the other Comanches from killing the Kiowas. In this Comanche version, Afraid of Water and Wolf Lying Down ride together on a single horse into the Comanche camp.[40]

Documents written at Santa Fe are helpful for establishing the time frame of the Kiowa–Comanche peace, though less informative about Kiowa and Comanche politics and motivations. Santa Fe trader and interpreter Juan Lucero reported in November 1805 that he was trading in the Kiowa winter camps when leaders there told him they wanted to be able to take their bison products to Santa Fe to sell but were blocked by the Comanches. In this version, they asked Lucero—who may have been the trading post proprietor in the Kiowa version—if the Spanish would help them make peace with the Comanches. Over the next few months, Lucero and the Spanish governor of New Mexico hosted Kiowa and Comanche delegations in Santa Fe as they negotiated.[41]

Because making peace with the Comanches required diplomacy with all of that nation's divisions, it makes sense that these negotiations occurred over several years, some taking place in Kiowa or Comanche camps and some in Santa Fe with feasts and gifts provided by the Spanish. Occasional clashes between Kiowas and Comanches continued in the early years of the nineteenth century, but the peace was complete by the 1820s and has lasted through the wars, forced removals, and other pressures of the two centuries since. In 1845, a U.S. observer noted the close reciprocal connection between the Kiowas and the Comanches, remarking that "they speak an entirely different language" from each other, and "their manners and customs are also quite different, yet they are firmly bound together by some unseen bond, and appear to feel a mutual desire to benefit each other."[42]

Alliance with the Comanches expanded Kiowa range and access to horses. At least one Comanche version of this history credits Comanches themselves with introducing horses to the Kiowas, calling them the "Foot Kiowas" or "Dog Kiowas" before the alliance, who became "a far-moving horse-culture people" only afterward.[43] Kiowas did have horses already, and Kiowas say it was Crows several generations earlier who helped them become a horse nation. Still, the histories agree that the Kiowa–Comanche alliance strengthened both peoples and changed the balance of power on the southern Plains, with ramifications for everyone around.

Sometimes war expands a nation's territory, but sometimes peace accomplishes the same goal. Expansion itself can have diverse motivations; for the early-nineteenth-century Kiowas, those motives were connected to their decisions in earlier generations to become nomadic. Kiowa scholar Gus Palmer writes that "although the Kiowas are noted for raiding, their real passion was to journey out on the land and take in the full breadth of that magical place."[44] After the Comanche peace, Kiowas were largely secure to live and work between the Arkansas and Red rivers in the vast southern Plains region, now made up of parts of Kansas, Oklahoma, Colorado, and Texas. The longer growing season in the South meant there was better grazing for horses. Kiowas could maintain larger herds, and there was less need to bring them cottonwood bark all winter. By 1821, an observer noted that the Comanches and the Kiowas "have great numbers of very fine horses—and equal to any I have ever known."[45]

The Kiowas and the Comanches helped each other forge useful relations with peoples on the edges of their space. The Plains Apache, allied with the Kiowas, had previously been separated from more western Apaches by the Comanches directly in between, but now the Plains Apaches were free to travel across the southern Plains because of their Kiowa and Comanche alliances. In the summer of 1818, some five to six hundred Plains Apache, Kiowa, and Arapaho families traveled south with Lipan Apache guides in a great homecoming celebration. The Kiowas brought the Arapahos into the Comanche peace and gave Comanches access to both the trade fairs on the Missouri River and the Wichita town on the Red River.[46]

In turn, Comanches brought Kiowas into trade at Spanish Santa Fe and the Pueblo towns. The Comanches had made peace with New Mexico in the mid-1780s, and in the summer of 1807 Yamparika Comanche leaders helped Santa Fe forge a military and trading alliance with the Kiowas. In a ceremony on August 3 in Santa Fe's Palace of the Governors, the governor gave silver medals to Chief Bule and two other Kiowas. The Kiowas had brought a delegation of their Arapaho allies, who also made peace with Santa Fe, the Pueblo peoples, and the Yamparika Comanches. Thereafter, Kiowas would travel annually to Santa Fe to renew their agreement and receive gifts from the governor, usually using the governor's hospitality to assist diplomacy with other Native nations there at the same time.[47]

The Spanish colonists and the people of the Pueblos were glad to have the Comanches, Kiowas, and Plains Apaches as trading partners rather than raiders. New Mexicans moved back out onto farms and ranches that had been abandoned because of raiding before the peace but now could safely grow corn and beans, some of which they sold to Plains Indians. During the year, New Mexican traders brought goods to the Kiowas to exchange for horses and bison products. Santa Fe and its allied Pueblo communities sent Plains products south on El Camino Real to Chihuahua and beyond, imported manufactured goods, and produced textiles and pottery to sell to all these trading partners. Peace between the Kiowas and the Comanches and now with the New Mexican Pueblos and settlers opened a truly global trade network.[48]

DEALING WITH THE T'Ó:T'ÁUKÂUI

The European Americans whom Kiowas began to meet in the early nineteenth century had a colonial map in their heads that was quite different from reality on the ground. Spain (and, after 1821, Mexico) claimed the vast region from California to Texas. After the 1803 Louisiana Purchase, President Thomas Jefferson sent four exploration parties to report about the place he had bought and to assert the most expansive possible interpretations of the U.S. borders with New Spain and British Canada. Meriwether Lewis and William Clark became the most famous of these expeditions, because they made it to the Pacific Ocean and back, whereas the others, all on more southern routes, failed. In 1806, the Zebulon Pike expedition traveled west to the headwaters of the Arkansas River in the Rocky Mountains, where Spanish troops found and arrested the party and marched them to Chihuahua. Osage dominance on the lower Arkansas River forced Jefferson to scale back his plans for William Dunbar and George Hunter and send them on only a short journey along the Ouachita River in what's now the state of Arkansas. Thomas Freeman and Peter Custis explored the Red River up to about today's Louisiana–Texas state line, where they were turned back by Spanish authorities. Trading expeditions that set out from St. Louis in the 1810s were routinely arrested by the Spanish and marched to Santa Fe and then to prison farther south.[49]

As Spain, the United States, and Britain tried to enforce borders against one another, the Kiowas saw the West as a place of many polities, dominated by powerful Native nations including themselves. There were smaller Native groups such as the Plains Apaches that allied with stronger ones. And there were permanent trading towns, some Native and some non-Native. Isolated colonial posts were inhabited mostly by people of some mixture of Native, French, Spanish, British, or African descent who were not citizens of Native nations but in most cases had lived in the region for generations and saw the Plains as the Kiowas did: a place that faraway empires might claim and even give away to one another without changing anything on the ground. The vast middle of North America was not a place colonized by Europe or the United States.

As with words and signs for different kinds of Native people, Kiowas tended to categorize people from the United States and European colonies by appearance and location more than the divisions of empires and republics. The Kiowa names for all of the European-related groups use the same stem, T'áukâui. This word's origins are unclear, but it seems to be related to the Kiowa words for "ear" and "skin" and sometimes is translated as "wrinkled," so Kiowa linguists suggest that it may have referred to the ears of the donkeys and mules that carried the possessions of Mexicans who came north into Kiowa country. Or it may have been a physical description trying to convey what European people looked like when they were out in the sun of the Plains all day. The Kiowa terms attach mostly regional descriptions to this stem, not national ones like "Spanish," "French," or "U.S." New Mexico's Spanish colonists were K'óp-T'áukâui, literally Mountain T'áukâui. The Spanish speakers of Texas and northern Nuevo León and Nuevo Santander (today the Mexican state of Tamaulipas and southern Texas) were the A:T'áukâui (Timber or Forest T'áukâui), although the Kiowas sometimes called Texans Dèhá:ñnòp (Tejano), from the Spanish name for that colony. The people around Chihuahua were Tóñ:hèñ:T'áukâui (T'áukâui of the Waterless Country). Colonists in northern Coahuila living near the range that the Kiowas called the Oak Bark Mountains were the Dótkáuiñ-T'áukâui, from the Kiowa word for "oak bark." Colonists living on the Río Grande northwest of Texas were called literally Río Grande T'áukâui, from the words for "river" (p'áu:) and "great" (êl): P'áu:êl-T'áukâui. Those right around Laredo were Tson-T'áukâui, from tsonda, "light-haired." Because Kiowas got silver from a community in southwestern New Mexico, they called those people Ts'ó:T'áukâui, using the word for "rock," ts'ó:. French traders and people from the United States got the same name, because both came south to Kiowa country from St. Louis or Canadian posts. Thus Kiowas called them T'ó:T'áukâui, from the word for "northern," sometimes translated as "cold."[50]

To the Kiowas, peace with the K'óp-T'áukâui of Santa Fe did not require peace with the A:T'áukâui or P'áu:êl-T'áukâui of Texas or the Dótkáuiñ-T'áukâui of Coahuila, because the Kiowas did not see individual colonies as part of global empires. The idea of one Spanish Empire was not only abstract but simply not true on the ground. Seven hundred miles separated Santa Fe and San Antonio, and both were hundreds more from Chihuahua, to say nothing of Mexico City. The Kiowa alliance with the Comanches and Santa Fe in fact freed Kiowas to raid other Spanish colonies. It was not unusual for them to take captives from El Paso, Laredo, or San Antonio and sell them in Santa Fe.[51]

These places continued to seem like separate polities after Mexico won its independence from Spain in 1821 and New Mexico, Texas, Coahuila, Nueva Vizcaya (later split into the states of Chihuahua and Durango), Nuevo León, and Nuevo Santander (renamed Tamaulipas) became part of the Republic of Mexico rather than the Spanish Empire. As an observer explained, "the Indians are at war" with Texas, "though at peace with New Mexico and the Spanish inhabitants there."[52] A Mexican official complained in 1833 that the Kiowas and the Comanches were free to "make war on the border towns of Chihuahua" yet "trade with the New Mexicans."[53] The Texas Revolution and the creation of an independent Republic of Texas in 1836 only reinforced Kiowas' impression that Texas was its own entity, and they did not change their minds when Texas became part of the United States in 1845 and New Mexico did in 1848. In U.S. and Mexican history, these are momentous continental changes, but to the Kiowas they were simply shifting alliances. Kiowas knew about the changes and adjusted their trading and raiding as new opportunities arose. Indeed, they dramatically expanded the range of their raiding campaigns after Texas independence. Their strength and autonomy continued undiminished.[54]

People who ventured onto the Plains from the United States in the decades after the Louisiana Purchase learned to see it as a place of many polities, the most powerful of which were Native. One U.S. expedition after another went west with grand plans and had to adjust to Native power. In July 1820, after the Sun Dance, Kiowas were camped with Cheyennes and Arapahos along both sides of the Arkansas River in present-day Kansas. Suddenly, horses that had been grazing at the edge of one of the camps bounded into the camp, clearly startled by something. Several people got up and ran in the direction from which the horses had come and discovered a dozen men. They seemed to be T'ó:T'áukâui, and, indeed, they were three French and nine U.S. men. They had been part of an expedition headed by Major Stephen Long that went west as a result of the 1819 Adams–Onís Treaty, which finally set a western border between the United States and Spain, making the Platte River Valley and most of the Arkansas Valley part of the United States. The expedition had made it as far as the foot of the Rockies along the South Platte River and turned south in a fruitless search for the Red River. Two days earlier, they had split into two groups, this one led by Captain John R. Bell heading downstream on the Arkansas River.[55]

The people who found Bell and his half of the Long expedition

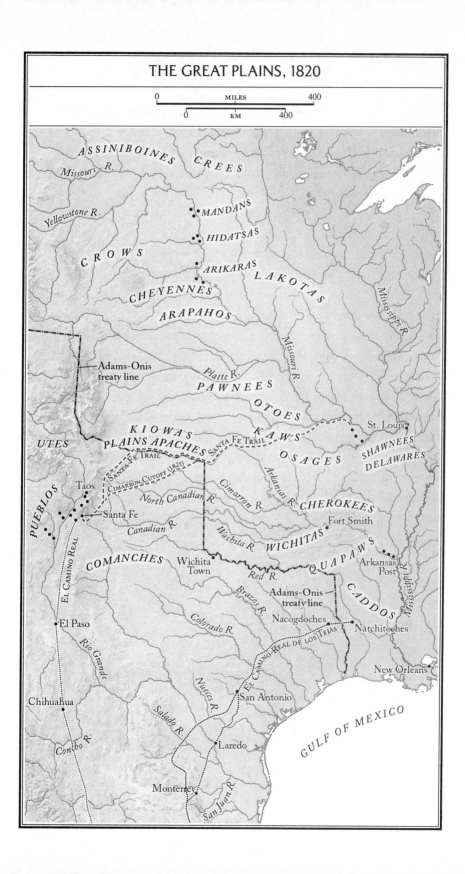

THE GREAT PLAINS, 1820

MILES
0   400

KM
0   400

ASSINIBOINES   CREES

Missouri R.

Yellowstone R.

MANDANS

HIDATSAS

CROWS

ARIKARAS

LAKOTAS

CHEYENNES

ARAPAHOS

Mississippi R.

Adams-Onis
treaty line

Platte R.

PAWNEES

Missouri R.

OTOES

St. Louis

KIOWAS

KAWS

PLAINS APACHES   SANTA FE TRAIL

SANTA FE TRAIL

SHAWNEES

UTES

OSAGES

DELAWARES

SANTA FE TRAIL

CIMARRON CUTOFF (1821)

PUEBLOS

Taos

North Canadian R.

Cimarron R.

Arkansas R.

CHEROKEES

Santa Fe

Canadian R.

Fort Smith

COMANCHES

Washita R.

WICHITAS

QUAPAWS

Wichita
Town

Red R.

Arkansas
Post

EL CAMINO REAL

Brazos R.

Adams-Onis
treaty line

CADDOS

Mississippi R.

El Paso

Colorado R.

Nacogdoches

Natchitoches

Rio Grande

EL CAMINO REAL DE LOS TEJAS

Chihuahua

New Orleans

Nueces R.

San Antonio

Salado R.

GULF OF MEXICO

Contho R.

Laredo

Monterrey

San Juan R.

welcomed them with friendly looks and gestures. As the visitors watered their horses, pitched their tents, and raised a U.S. flag over their camp, women brought them bison meat, freshly dried from a recent hunt. The next morning, some of the leading men came to smoke and speak with the visitors. One of the Kiowas spoke a common language (probably Wichita) with one of the Frenchmen, and through them Bell informed the assembled Kiowa, Cheyenne, and Arapaho leaders that his expedition "belonged to the numerous and powerful nation of Americans, that we had been sent by our great chief, who presides over all the country, to examine that part of his territories, that he might become acquainted with its features, its produce and population."[56]

These were strange claims. One of the Americans, Thomas Say, recorded that a Native leader "expressed his surprise that we had travelled so far, and assured us that they were happy to see us, and hoped that as a road was now open to our nation, traders would be sent amongst them." But he also corrected Bell's assertion that this land belonged to the president of the United States, noting that the T'ó:T'áukâui were "far" from their own nation and that T'ó:T'áukâui traders were welcome to travel the long road here. In Say's written description, it is clear that he, at least, understood the point. He

Kiowas crossing the Arkansas River to meet Stephen Long's expedition, in *James's Account of S. H. Long's expedition, 1819–1820*.
DAVIS LIBRARY, UNIVERSITY OF NORTH CAROLINA AT CHAPEL HILL

wrote that Bell had replied that they would report back saying they had been "hospitably treated while travelling through their country"—that is, the Kiowas' country. The Native leaders gave the visitors a few horses and received some knives, combs, and vermilion paint. Leaving the council, they grumbled to one another over the few gifts, not nearly enough to distribute among all the band leaders. If these men were a "numerous and powerful nation," they had not proved it today.

Although they did not receive much in the way of diplomatic gifts, the people did get a good look at these strangers. Under the pretense of bringing more meat and some leather, pretty much the entire Kiowa, Cheyenne, and Arapaho camps from both sides of the river, "of both sexes and of all ages, mounted and on foot," crowded into the tiny U.S. camp. Some of the children who came on horseback stood on top of their horses to get a better look. The women admired their tents, until it started to rain and they proved not waterproof and therefore far inferior to the tipis the women made.[57]

These remnants of Long and Bell's expedition, who eventually made it back to Fort Smith, on the Arkansas border, reinforced the Kiowa impression of T'ó:T'áukâui as unthreatening. When Kiowas spotted a similar group in November 1821 on the Plains in what's now southern Colorado, they thought these people might turn out to be useful after all. About a dozen men were trudging through the snow, walking beside horses piled so high with baggage that there wasn't room for the men to ride. Surely these were the goods that Captain Bell had promised that the U.S. president would send them. The U.S. men stopped to camp, not having spotted the Kiowas, so they were alarmed when thirty to fifty Kiowas rode in at full speed with their bows drawn and lances out as if they were going to strike. Having displayed their power and enjoyed a joke at the expense of these T'ó:T'áukâui, they came to a halt and welcomed the travelers with friendly gestures. They introduced themselves to the leader of the small group, Hugh Glenn. Glenn operated a trading post on the lower Arkansas River, which he had ascended with several French traders and men from the United States, including a member of the Lewis and Clark expedition, an enslaved man of African descent named Paul, and Jacob Fowler, who kept a journal of the expedition. The Kiowas accepted Glenn's offer of some cooked meat, although, as Fowler realized later, "they had plenty at their camp and ate with us out of pure friendship."

The next day, Kiowa men returned to lead the U.S. party to their camp. They put each of the men onto the back of one of their horses to cross the icy Arkansas River. According to the Adams–Onís Treaty, this stretch of the Arkansas River was the U.S. border, so Glenn and his men had just illegally crossed into Spanish territory. But to the Kiowas this was all their jurisdiction. At the Kiowa camp, the leader, whose name Fowler didn't catch, had them unload their horses and store their goods in his tipi, then he sent out word of their arrival to everyone around. All the rest of that day and the next, people rode in, and the camp became, as Fowler wrote, "a large town" with more than two hundred tipis "well filled with men women and children—with a great number of dogs and horses so that the whole country to a great distance was covered." The Kiowa leader escorted the visitors through the snow to meet other leaders, going into tipi after tipi to share tobacco and eat feasts of meat, corn, and beans that put the U.S. offerings to shame. If this felt like "a large town" of perhaps three thousand Kiowas, the next day, when some five thousand Comanche men, women, and children rode in, the camp "increased to a city."

The Comanches and the Kiowas assembled a joint council with Glenn, and one of the Comanche leaders spoke first, his words translated into Wichita for one of the Frenchmen to translate into English. The Comanche leader announced that they were "ready to receive the goods" that "the President had sent them." Glenn's party was flabbergasted. The goods his horses carried were on credit from St. Louis merchants and intended for sale, ideally in Santa Fe, where they could fetch Spanish silver. Glenn sheepishly responded that President James Monroe had not sent these particular goods. The Comanche leader, Fowler recorded, flew into "a great passion," accused Glenn of being "a liar and a thief" who had "stolen the goods" from the president, and threatened to kill Glenn and his men and take the goods. Glenn and his interpreter quickly withdrew from the council tent. Remaining in council the rest of the day, the Kiowas apparently persuaded the Comanches to let them take a different approach. The Kiowa leader told Glenn that they had talked the Comanche leader down, presumably arguing that the Americans could easily be managed. Glenn gave the Kiowa leader some gifts, including a medal with the likeness of General Andrew Jackson, apologizing that he didn't have one with President Monroe.

Perhaps to remind Glenn's party of who held the power here, or perhaps just to collect the expected goods or get a look at the strangers, an even larger crowd assembled over the next few days, including more Kiowas and Comanches, as well as Plains Apaches, Cheyennes, and Arapahos. Eventually Glenn's party estimated that there were ten thousand Indians surrounding thirteen Americans. The U.S. men were able to buy meat at reasonable prices, but their hosts absolutely forbade them from hunting, telling them that their inept methods "would drive the buffalo all off." Farcically, Glenn several times boldly declared that it was time for his men to be leaving and was told, in friendly enough voices, that the Indians would come with them.

They were still with the large group more than a month later when Spaniards rode into camp and, Glenn wrote, "all dismounted and embraced us with affection and friendship." Their friendliness (and Mexico's newly won independence) boded well for trade between St. Louis and Santa Fe along this road that Americans would call the Santa Fe Trail. Glenn was astonished, he claimed, at "the difference of treatment of the Indians to them and our party—the Indians commanded them as much as we command our negroes." The sharpness of his comment belies the fact that he and his men were basically imprisoned by the Kiowas and that Paul, one of "our negroes" held in actual slavery by one of Glenn's men, might have had a good deal to say about all of it. In fact, the Kiowas enforced hunting, boundary, and trade restrictions on all of these outsiders, whether U.S., Spanish, or Mexican and regardless of what white Americans saw as race.[58]

Being identified as T'ó:T'áukâui, who usually were traders, saved the lives of Bell's and Glenn's parties, whereas being misidentified when in the wrong place got other people killed. In the winter of 1832–33, a war party of several hundred Kiowas spotted a dozen men on the upper reaches of the Canadian River in what's now the Texas Panhandle. Like Glenn's party, they were traders from the United States who had traveled from St. Louis along the Santa Fe Trail. They made it to Santa Fe, where they sold their goods and loaded their mules with silver coins, choosing for their return trip a more southern route because they feared crossing the snowy central Plains in winter. The Kiowas who came upon them this far south assumed they were Texans, whom they had long fought as useless and unwelcome ranchers. Unlike the mock battle with Glenn, the Kiowas really shot their bows and arrows, killing two of the men. After the Kiowas pulled back safely out of rifle range, the U.S. party spent a frightening night and day as the Kiowas picked off mules and horses from the edge of the camp and the men in the camp "seldom ventured to raise their heads above the surface without being shot at." The second night, the Kiowas let the surviving men sneak away, leaving their horses, mules, and bags of Mexican silver—the survivors later claimed they had lost $10,000. The Kiowas used the silver to make jewelry, referring to the coins as "hair metal." The surviving U.S. men wandered, lost and hungry, arguing over the route back to the United States and eating roots and tree bark because they weren't able to hunt, having run out of ammunition and gunpowder. Of the dozen men, only seven made it back to St. Louis alive.[59]

THE KIOWA-OSAGE WAR

In the 1820s and '30s, the Kiowas and their allies saw an increasing threat, not from the United States but from the Osages. Yet the United States was the indirect cause of the conflict. After the Louisiana Purchase, the United States offered land in the West to Native Americans who agreed to move, and many did in the perilous early decades of the nineteenth century, joining Cherokee, Shawnee, and other Native immigrants who had crossed the Mississippi River starting in the 1790s. The Osages fought back against these intruders, and a full-blown Osage–Cherokee War resulted. That war, in turn, pushed Osage hunting into Kiowa country in the 1820s.

Native people who moved west at the invitation of the U.S. government demanded protection. To try to keep the peace in this mess it had created, in 1817 the United States had founded Fort Smith, between Osage and Cherokee towns on the lower Arkansas River. It sat not far from several Mississippian pyramid mounds, which the Osages used for observation and as a place to retreat to in times of defense.[60]

In the 1820s, the Cherokees and Shawnees who had moved west invited more and more Native peoples to join their alliance—an effort that would have tremendous implications for the Kiowas, the United States, and everyone in the western prairies and plains. Two of the leaders in the alliance were Captain Lewis (Quatawapea) of the Shawnees and Tolluntuskee of the Cherokees. Captain Lewis had led his Shawnee town west in the mid-1820s as pressure in Ohio had become unbearable. There they reunited with groups of Shawnees who had already moved west: the first ones from the 1790s, those who left at the end of the War of 1812, and a group whom Tenskwatawa had brought in 1826. In the West, Shawnees continued building alliances with fellow migrants from the East, circulating wampum, holding multinational councils, and now also circulating written letters. In part by building strong alliances with Shawnees and other immigrants while keeping peace with the Quapaws and the United States, the Cherokees prevailed in their war against the Osages, who traveled farther west to hunt in Kiowa country.[61]

The Osage–Kiowa War escalated as each side committed increasingly bloody raids. For the Kiowas, the worst came in 1833—represented in the calendar as the Summer That They Cut Off Their Heads. Most of the fighting-age men had gone raiding in the South, while a large Kiowa camp stayed near Rainy Mountain. One spring morning, some of the young men went out to look for horses and were startled when they saw an Osage in the distance. They came rushing back into camp in alarm. As a Kiowa later described, "thus rudely awakened, the Kiowa sprang up and fled to the mountain, the mothers seizing their children and the old men hurrying as best they could, with their bloodthirsty enemies close behind." Angry over past Kiowa attacks, the Osages caught up with one of the fleeing groups and killed a large number of men, women, and children. According to the Kiowas, the Osages beheaded the bodies and placed the heads in the Kiowas' brass kettles, leaving the decapitated bodies where they lay. The Osages rode back to their towns, three hundred miles away, with a hundred scalps, some of which were probably newly scalped from Kiowa victims' heads, while others were scalps Kiowas had taken in previous conflicts and had in their camp. The Osages also took more than four hundred horses as well as silver coins that Kiowas had taken from the traders the previous year.[62]

Most demoralizing, the Osages had killed the wife of the keeper of the Táiñmé—the Kiowas' most sacred object, central to the Sun Dance—and ridden off with it, along with two captives, a sister and brother around twelve and ten years old. Adding to the grief of mourning their dead and captured, the theft of the Táiñmé meant that the Kiowas could not perform that summer's Sun Dance, which was due to happen in a few months. To the Kiowas, "the loss was an almost unimaginable tragedy."[63]

This violence could have led to an escalated war between the Osages and the Kiowas, pulling in the allies of both, but instead the Osages would be at the center of a grand and highly unlikely peace between, on the one side, the Kiowas and their Comanche and Plains Apache allies and, on the other, the alliance just west of the Mississippi that Shawnees and Cherokees were building with Quapaws, Muscogees, Choctaws, Delawares, and Ohio Senecas. The sister and brother who were captured—as well as the captured Táiñmé—would be key to that peacemaking, as we shall see in the next chapter.

CONCLUSION

U.S. expeditions in the 1820s and early 1830s did nothing to persuade the Kiowas and other Plains Indians that the United States was a powerful country. Repeating a long-standing method of colonizers, including the English colonists at Roanoke, U.S. officials decided that the only way to persuade them was to show them the seat of U.S. power. As the commandant of Fort Smith somewhat desperately put it in 1818, the Plains Indians should be "taken on to Washington, that they may see the strength of our government, & enter into some treaty with it, as they at present do not acknowledge themselves under the protection of the U. States."[64] But the Kiowas weren't interested in visiting the TʼóːTʼáukâui or signing any papers. Over the coming decades, U.S. representatives insisted again and again that their country really was, as Bell put it in 1820, a "numerous and powerful nation." But despite what U.S. explorers claimed and Native people from the East warned, the Kiowas maintained their doubts.

The Summer That They Cut Off Their Heads, 1833, next to the Winter That the Stars Fell, Silver Horn's calendar, 1833–1834.
MANUSCRIPT 2531, NATIONAL ANTHROPOLOGICAL ARCHIVES, SMITHSONIAN INSTITUTION

Far more meaningful was a sight the winter after the Summer That They Cut Off Their Heads and the Kiowas' missed Sun Dance. People lay sleeping all across the midcontinent, in houses and tipis, when they slowly became aware that it was light outside, even though it was still the middle of the night. They cautiously emerged to see that the night sky was filled with flashes of light, stars streaking across the sky. Recorded in 1833 calendars as the "Winter That the Stars Fell," it was clearly a portent. Kiowas interpreted it in combination with the killings and the stolen Táiñmé. Quapaws, Shawnees, and Cherokees in the Mississippi Valley reflected on their recent history and their shocking loss of land and power. It was time to make a change. Perhaps they would lose the East, but strong, reciprocal Native alliances—some among former enemies—might still preserve the West as a Native land.[65]

CHAPTER 11

REMOVALS FROM THE EAST
TO A NATIVE WEST

I N DECEMBER 1830, PRESIDENT ANDREW JACKSON STOOD BEFORE Congress to give his annual message. "Humanity has often wept over the fate of the aborigines of this country," he acknowledged. Yet it was inevitable: "One by one have many powerful tribes disappeared from the earth." The Indians' disappearance was only natural, he claimed, like "the extinction of one generation to make room for another" and like the disappearance of the ancient Mississippians, who Jackson believed had been "exterminated." The changes were for the best, he asserted, for "what good man would prefer a country covered with forests and ranged by a few thousand savages to our extensive Republic, studded with cities, towns, and prosperous farms?" Under the provisions of the Indian Removal Act, which he had signed earlier that year, he encouraged the remaining Native Americans in the East to move to the wilds of the West to continue their "savage" life for as long as they could. But really, Jackson argued, their time had passed, and it was just as well.[1]

Of course, nineteenth-century Native North Americans were not doomed savages or relics of a past era, but real people living in history. They had not exterminated the ancient civilizations but were their descendants, changed from the past and still adapting to changing circumstances. The United States was not the first to build "cities, towns, and prosperous farms." Even with an aggressive nation in the East, most of the continent might have remained under Native rule. No one people had ever claimed, let alone controlled, this vast landmass, and in the early decades of the nineteenth century not even white Americans believed it was the U.S. "manifest destiny" to stretch "from sea to shining sea." Those concepts would come later in the century. More likely than U.S. dominance over the continent, most people believed, was a patchwork of European colonies and sovereign nations, which might include the United States as well as Spanish and British colonies, hundreds of Native nations, maybe a multinational Native confederacy in the Ohio Valley and Great Lakes region, and perhaps other independent former colonies modeled on but not part of the United States. The United States might simply have been one of many powers on the continent.

Yet the rapidly growing, land-hungry citizenry of the United States posed unprecedented challenges to everyone else on the continent. Throughout this book, population estimates of Native nations have usually been in the thousands or tens of thousands and European settlements in the dozens or hundreds. But the British colonies on the Atlantic coast that became the original thirteen states grew like no other place on the continent. Through immigration from Europe and natural increase, their population doubled every generation starting in the mid-eighteenth century. By 1830 the United States had an astounding 12.8 million people (two million of them enslaved), while around one hundred thousand Native Americans lived east of the Mississippi and there were fewer than a million total between the Pacific and the Atlantic. Thousands of Native Americans had already moved west under pressure before 1830.

The United States would forcibly remove the majority of Native Americans who had stayed in the East thus far—another eighty thousand people, of whom at least thirteen thousand died during or because of removal. Indian Removal started before the 1830 act and continued well into the nineteenth century, in all regions and in many forms. The United States forced some people to move and condense within a region, while tens of thousands, from east and west, north and south, were forced to the middle of the continent, most of them to what's now Oklahoma and Kansas. The deportations were all part of the long U.S. effort to transform Native homelands into a country belonging to the descendants of Europe.[2]

Native nations used many methods to resist white encroachment and dispossession. The Cherokee Nation fought Indian Removal in U.S. courts, the newspapers, and the halls of Congress. The Mohawks used the power of treaties and the proximity of the Canadian border. The descendants of Ossomocomuck hid from removal as families and small communities. The Shawnees and the Quapaws dispersed and reunited under great pressure. Farther west, the Kiowas and the O'odham were only just beginning to see the effects of U.S. growth and the need to use their strengths and alliances to keep it from destroying them.

Four years after the Indian Removal Act, in the summer of 1834, at the great Wichita town on the Red River, a gathering occurred that put the lie to Jackson's claims of Native decline and disappearance. Osages came 250 miles from their homes to the northeast, bringing Cherokees, Delawares, and Ohio Senecas to meet the Kiowas and Comanches. Some of their nations had fought in the past in wars that had done damage, most recently in the Osage attack on the Kiowas in the Summer That They Cut Off Their Heads. The peoples from the East knew that growing U.S. power made it imperative that they make a safe home in the West. At the Wichita town, the delegates agreed that now they had "hearts inclined for peace." More diplomatic meetings followed, adding Quapaws, Shawnees, Muscogees, and Choctaws to the alliance of "perpetual peace and friendship." As Quapaw Chief Heckaton put it, "there must not be any blood . . . unless it be the blood of the buffalo."[3] As the U.S. juggernaut pushed west across the continent, joint efforts among Native nations and the very act of resisting together, even when they lost to greater U.S. power, would ultimately allow Native nations to survive the upheaval and losses of the Removal era and beyond.

CREATING "INDIAN TERRITORY"

Thomas Jefferson's insistence in 1780 that the Shawnees move west or face "extermination" because "the same world will scarcely do for them and us" has much in common with Jackson's mock laments fifty years later.[4] But the 1830s United States was a more powerful and even less compromising neighbor. In theory at least, Jefferson's generation of U.S. leaders assumed that Native men could eventually become U.S. citizens (if they gave up their nations). And some part of the continent might continue to have sovereign Native nations for the foreseeable future, ideally allied with and somewhat subordinate to the United States.[5]

In contrast, by 1830 white Americans were imagining a much more limited "Indian Territory" west of the Mississippi where all surviving Native Americans would live. U.S. officials intended to deport Native nations from their existing territories and place them in this reservation surrounded by the United States. In one of the country's most extreme violations of sovereignty and human rights, it ultimately expelled tens of thousands of people from their homes and crowded them into Indian Territory. They included Cherokees, Choctaws, Chickasaws, Muscogees, Seminoles, Shawnees, Delawares, Kickapoos, Ottawas, Potawatomis, Miamis, Peorias, and Meskwakis from the East, as well as Quapaws, Osages, Kiowas, Comanches, Apaches, Cheyennes, and Arapahos from the West.[6]

The transition to acts of mass expulsion and removal marks the point when labels like "genocide," "ethnic cleansing," and "settler colonialism" began to fit undeniably well. White Americans persuaded themselves that only white men could be full U.S. citizens and that only white people could have territorially based nations that other nations had any obligation to respect. The federal government retained enough recognition of Native sovereignty for the Indian Removal Act to include a requirement of treaties for removal (albeit treaties that would be made under violent pressure and fraud). But the states of Georgia, Alabama, and Mississippi were already ignoring Native sovereignty and passing state laws intended to extend their jurisdictions over Native nations.[7]

Jefferson's initial plan to use much of the Louisiana Purchase as a place to send eastern American Indians put pressure on Quapaws and Osages just west of the Mississippi River to surrender land to make room. At first, U.S. officials expected to move Native nations onto formerly Quapaw and Osage land near the Mississippi River,

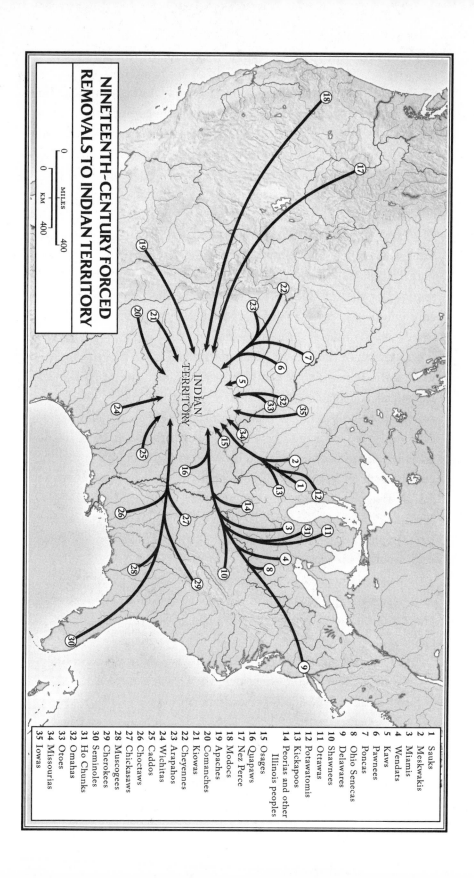

NINETEENTH-CENTURY FORCED
REMOVALS TO INDIAN TERRITORY

INDIAN TERRITORY

MILES
0   400
0   400
KM

1   Sauks
2   Meskwakis
3   Miamis
4   Wendats
5   Kaws
6   Pawnees
7   Poncas
8   Ohio Senecas
9   Delawares
10 Shawnees
11 Ottawas
12 Potawatomis
13 Kickapoos
14 Peorias and other
    Illinois peoples
15 Osages
16 Quapaws
17 Nez Perce
18 Modocs
19 Apaches
20 Comanches
21 Kiowas
22 Cheyennes
23 Arapahos
24 Wichitas
25 Caddos
26 Choctaws
27 Chickasaws
28 Muscogees
29 Cherokees
30 Seminoles
31 Ho Chunks
32 Omahas
33 Otoes
34 Missourias
35 Iowas

where Shawnees, Cherokees, and others had settled already. But white settlers—170,000 on Quapaw and Osage lands by 1830—also demanded those fertile lands, which became the states of Arkansas and Missouri. The Osages and the Quapaws had to surrender their easternmost lands in a series of treaties even before official Indian Removal created Indian Territory, which encompassed today's states of Oklahoma and Kansas and the Plains to the west.[8]

Reversing more than a century of close European–Quapaw relations, the United States took all of the Quapaws' land in just six years. After the Louisiana Purchase, the Quapaws became surrounded by thousands of U.S. settlers, while their population probably numbered less than five hundred. They offered to relinquish some land in order to secure their hold on the rest, hoping "that the powerful arm of the U.S. will defend us their children in the possession of the remainder of our hunting grounds." The resulting 1818 treaty ceded considerably more land than the Quapaws had proposed, about 90 percent of their country. They kept a small reservation along the lower Arkansas River, which included their towns, and the United States promised they could continue to hunt in the ceded territory. Yet white settlers squatted even on the Quapaws' greatly reduced lands and claimed that the treaty wasted good cotton land on "Savages" rather than giving it to "citizens." Just six years later, in 1824, the Arkansas governor strong-armed the Quapaws into ceding their remaining lands.[9]

That year, Quapaw leader Saracen told a French priest a version of Quapaw history that will sound familiar to anyone who has read chapter 6 of this book. Saracen remarked, in French, that

the French were good for the Arkansas [Quapaws], they taught us, they fed us and never mistreated us; the French and the Arkansas always walk side by side. My friends the Spanish came, the Arkansas received them; the Spanish were good to the Arkansas, they helped us and they walked together side by side. The Americans have come, the Arkansas received them and gave them everything that they could want, but the Americans are always pushing the Arkansas and driving us away.[10]

Initially, the United States didn't even provide the Quapaws with replacement land after the 1824 treaty took the last of their homeland. U.S. officials advised them to move in with the Caddos, one hundred miles away on the lower Red River. Quapaw Chief Heckaton resisted, declaring that (in the words of the English translation) "to leave my native soil, and go among red men who are aliens to our race, is throwing us like outcasts on the world. The lands you wish us to go to belong to strangers." When they tried that plan and found it entirely unworkable, Quapaw families tried settling in Texas and on lands reserved for the Choctaws and Muscogees in Indian Territory but kept advocating for their own land.[11]

CHEROKEE REMOVAL

Four and a half years after the passage of the Indian Removal Act, Jackson had to report to Congress, "I regret that the Cherokees east of the Mississippi have not yet determined as a community to remove."[12] It was not that Georgians weren't trying. Jackson's election had immediately given license to their worst ambitions. In December 1828, the Georgia legislature, inspired by Jackson's election to the presidency, had declared that a large region within the Cherokee Nation was now Georgia and therefore subject to Georgia's laws. In 1830, the Georgia legislature outlawed the Cherokee National Council and court system. The new law stated that "it shall not be lawful for any person, or persons, under colour or pretense, of authority from said Cherokee tribe, or as headmen, chiefs, or warriors of said tribe, to cause or procure by any means the assembling of any council, or other pretended Legislative body of the said Indians." The punishment was "confinement at hard labour in the Penitentiary for the space of four years." All white men living in the Cherokee Nation were required to swear allegiance to Georgia or also face prison time. Any turnpike tolls or other fees levied by Cherokees were outlawed.[13]

The State of Georgia told the Cherokee Nation that it no longer existed. It passed laws against its sovereign authority to tax and self-govern. Georgians figured, correctly, that their new president would support them in this action, even though it was clearly illegal under the U.S. Constitution and in violation of past practices of Indian affairs under the United States and European empires. Knowing that the Cherokees would not obey, the governor and the legislature created the Georgia Guard, a militia force whose purpose was to enforce Georgia's laws against the Cherokees. Surveyors began running lines within the Nation, and white settlers squatted on Cherokee land. People had recently discovered gold, and the Georgia governor declared that the State of Georgia owned any gold mines and that therefore Cherokees could not mine gold. The Georgia Guard arrested a man named George Corn Tassel for murder, even though both he and his alleged victim were Cherokee. Cherokee lawyers filed a motion in federal court asserting Cherokee Nation jurisdiction over the case, but Georgia officials executed him before the court could rule. The men who voted for Jackson in Georgia and other eastern states had had enough of the moderation of John Quincy Adams and trusted that their new president would put the raw power of the United States behind their ambitions, or at least not stand in their way.[14]

In February 1830, the *Cherokee Phoenix* printed the alarming headline "First Blood Shed by the Georgians!!" A group of Cherokees had attempted to enforce Cherokee law and property rights by ejecting seventeen U.S. families from Cherokee land. A band of Georgians fought back and killed one of the Cherokee men. It was reported "that a large company of Georgians were on their way to arrest Mr. Ross and Major Ridge" and that Cherokees were gathering at their houses to defend them.[15] The rumored attack didn't come, but illegal settlements kept cropping up, defended by armed white men. Harriett Boudinot wrote her sister that "the friends of the Indians seem sleeping while their enemies are diligently pursuing their work."[16]

With the Indian Removal Act before Congress that spring, Elias Boudinot wrote a blistering English-language editorial in the *Phoenix* against one of the arguments for the bill, that Indians could no longer live in the East because the game they lived off was almost gone: "We should like to see any person point to a single family in this nation who obtain their clothing and provisions by hunting. We know of no one.... Game has been nearly extinct for the last thirty years." The Cherokees did not need game. "They have plenty of corn, and domestic animals, and they raise their own cotton, and manufacture their own clothing." Indians were not "declining" in the East. On the contrary, "the common Indian among the Cherokees is not declining, but rising," like the phoenix their paper was named for.[17]

Bad news piled up locally. Georgians beat a Cherokee man for digging for gold. Intruders set fire to woods near a woman's home, and she had to run to put it out before it consumed her fence. The *Phoenix* reported that "it is said that during her efforts to save the fence the men who had done the mischief were within sight, and were laughing heartily at her!" A rumor circulated that the Georgia Guard had been ordered to "inflict corporeal punishment" on any Cherokee women who insulted them.[18] And a commander of the Georgia Guard summoned Elias Boudinot to meet with him.

Boudinot wrote subsequently in the *Phoenix* that the Georgia Guard commander had accused him of printing "a great many lies & abusive & libelous articles." Boudinot challenged him "to point to a particular part of the paper which was so offensive to him." Flummoxed, the commander continued merely complaining about its "general course and character" and let Boudinot go. It seems likely he had never read the paper and perhaps couldn't read at all. When the commander called Boudinot to come again, he refused to go, so the man sent seven armed men, who arrested him and threatened his family. Boudinot reported in the *Phoenix* that the guardsmen had threatened "to tie us to a tree and give us a sound whipping." Adding insult to injury, the commander called Boudinot "an ignorant man" who, as an Indian, couldn't possibly be a newspaper editor and pressured him to admit that the real editor of the *Phoenix* was missionary Samuel Worcester. The commander again let him go, perhaps really believing that a Cherokee wasn't capable of writing what he himself couldn't even read.[19]

For decades, the Cherokee Nation had successfully used political and religious rhetoric and moral suasion to argue for its sovereignty.

Cherokees persuaded white reformers including Jeremiah Evarts and Catharine Beecher to oppose removal in speeches and essays that persuaded a large public in New England. Hundreds of thousands of northern white women signed petitions. A substantial number of U.S. officeholders agreed that the Cherokee Nation had the right to exist in some form where it was and that Cherokee relations were a federal matter. Georgians were flouting precedent and law, and the current president seemed to support them, but the U.S. Congress was divided, courts had their own powers, and presidents lose office. The Cherokees did not yet despair of winning the day.[20]

In the 1830s, the Cherokee Nation continued its effort in two major ways. The first was suing Georgia in federal court on the basis of U.S. law, seeking to force the United States to play by its own rules. The second way was among the Cherokees themselves, as Cherokee leaders turned their attention from reforming the nation and demonstrating their sovereignty to outsiders to persuading all Cherokees to stick together. In an editorial published only in the Cherokee language on May 7, 1831, Boudinot promised that Cherokee leaders "will continue our commitment to the land that is ours." "Do not let your hearts weaken," he urged, but instead "strengthen our commitment to our homeland. Keep plowing and make your fields bigger, and keep building, and keep growing your food for your neighbors and for your children." To those who considered giving up, he asked, "Friend, where will you go? To the place where the forts are? The land for us there is not easy." The same troubles would find them there. "I see our only possible course," he concluded, "is to make clear to our beloved leaders our determination to hold on to our lands, to not lose our property, our homes, our fields."[21]

Under the U.S. Constitution, a foreign nation can take a case against a U.S. state directly to the U.S. Supreme Court. In June 1830, in *Cherokee Nation v. Georgia*, the Cherokees argued for an injunction from the U.S. Supreme Court to prevent the State of Georgia from enforcing state laws within the Cherokee Nation. Two of the justices agreed that the Cherokees could bring their case as a foreign nation, but the majority ruled that the court did not have jurisdiction, because the Cherokee Nation was not truly a foreign nation, but a "domestic dependent nation." The two dissenting justices wrote that the Cherokee Nation had an "unequal alliance" with the more powerful United States but had not thereby surrendered "the sovereignty or the right to govern its own body" and concluded that "they form a sovereign state. They have always been dealt with as such by the Government of the United States, both before and since the adoption of the present [U.S.] Constitution."[22]

Turned down in their attempt to go straight to the Supreme Court but heartened that both the majority and dissenting opinions recognized at least limited sovereignty, Cherokees brought a case to the lower U.S. courts, hoping it would make its way up to the Supreme Court. As part of Georgia's attempt to extend its jurisdiction in the Cherokee Nation, the state legislature had recently passed a law requiring any white men living in the Cherokee Nation to swear an oath to Georgia. Several of these men—including missionary Samuel Worcester and *Cherokee Phoenix* printer John Wheeler—refused to obey, on the grounds that as U.S. citizens living in the Cherokee Nation with its permission, they were not subject to the laws of Georgia. The Georgia Guard arrested them in New Echota and marched them to a Georgia court. After the court found that Worcester was exempt from the law because he was a U.S. postmaster, the U.S. agent stripped that office from him, and Georgians arrested him and tried him again. That September, a Georgia court convicted Worcester and ten other U.S. citizens living in the Cherokee Nation of having violated Georgia law by not taking the oath of allegiance. Nine of them relented and took the oath rather than serve the four-year sentence, but Worcester and another missionary refused and were carted off to prison. The Cherokees appealed on their behalf, knowing the weighty implications for Cherokee sovereignty if a U.S. state could regulate people within the Cherokee Nation. Elias Boudinot wrote that "very soon the virtue of the Republic will be put to the test."[23]

By the time the U.S. Supreme Court ruled in *Worcester v. Georgia* in the spring of 1832, Elias Boudinot and John Ridge were back in New England to raise money for the *Phoenix* and for the Cherokee Nation's legal bills. After the Indian Removal Act was passed, President Jackson had stopped sending the Cherokee annuity, the money that the U.S. government owed annually to the Cherokees for land they had already sold. With decreased revenues from turnpike tolls and other fees resulting from Georgia's illegal encroachment on Cherokee sovereignty, the nation was short on funds. When Boudinot heard that the U.S. Supreme Court had ruled in their favor, he wrote to his brother Stand Watie, "It is glorious news. The laws of the state are declared by the highest judicial tribunal in the country to be *null & void*. It is a great triumph on the part of the Cherokees so far as the question of their rights were concerned. The question is forever settled as to who is right & who is wrong." Friends started arriving to congratulate them. When Lyman Beecher—the father of Catharine Beecher and Harriet Beecher Stowe—dropped by, Boudinot asked him if he had heard the news from Washington. When Beecher said "No, what is it?" and Boudinot told him, "he jumped up, clapped his hands, took hold of my hand and said, 'God be praised,' and ran right out to tell his daughter" Catharine Beecher.[24]

The U.S. Supreme Court generally agreed with the Cherokee arguments. Using the same words as their opinion in *Cherokee Nation v. Georgia*, the court ruled that the Cherokees, as a "domestic dependent nation," were subject to U.S. federal law but not to that of Georgia or any other state. In the previous case, Cherokees had lost their attempt to be deemed a completely independent foreign nation, but *Worcester v. Georgia* nonetheless was a powerful ruling in favor of Cherokee sovereignty, along the lines of U.S. constitutional arguments that the Cherokees had been making for years. The court ruled that "the words 'treaty' and 'nation' are words of our language, selected in our diplomatic and legislative proceedings by ourselves, having each a definite and well understood meaning. We have applied them to Indians as we have applied them to the other nations of the earth." According to "the law of nations," simply being a "weaker power" did not mean that a nation had to "surrender its independence—its right to self-government," even if it had to seek the protection of a stronger ally. "The Cherokee nation, then, is a distinct community, occupying its own territory, with boundaries accurately described, in which the laws of Georgia can have no force, and which the citizens of Georgia have no right to enter but with the assent of the Cherokees themselves."[25]

In its English-language coverage, the *Phoenix* triumphantly proclaimed, GOOD NEWS. The paper printed the Supreme Court's order overturning Georgia's actions and explained that "the Court has sustained the right of the Cherokees to the utmost extent. They have declared the law of Georgia extending her jurisdiction over a portion of our territory unconstitutional. The question of Indian rights is now decided by the highest tribunal in the United States, and Georgia, as a member of the Union, will, we presume, yield to the mandate of the Supreme Court."[26]

Boudinot's Cherokee-language editorial in the same issue sounded a more cautionary note. He worried about enforcement of the decision. Cherokees were in the right according to both Cherokee and U.S. law, but "peace won't come quickly." Georgians would fight the decision, but the U.S. government should enforce it. "Friends," he urged, "let us be calm and not go against them. Now it is dangerous."[27] Boudinot's tone reflected mixed messages that he and John Ridge heard in Washington on their way home. Ridge met with Jackson at the White House, where the president told him he would not use the executive power of the United States against Georgia and that the Cherokees' only choice remained moving west. They met with Supreme Court Justice John McLean, who, despite his ruling, also urged them to make a treaty. Jackson's administration was intent on enforcing the Indian Removal Act and supporting the State of Georgia in ending the Cherokee presence on its border entirely. Congressmen who had supported the Cherokees also told them it might be time to give up. And on the ride into Cherokee country, only two days from New Echota, Boudinot saw a Georgia Guardsman building a public house on the road in anticipation of customers from Georgia. Boudinot read in a Georgia newspaper that the state legislature had passed a bill "authorizing the immediate survey and occupancy of the Cherokee country."[28]

Boudinot could see that Georgians were determined not only to make Cherokees into Georgians but to put them in the same racial category as people of African descent, whom nineteenth-century white Georgians enslaved, tortured, and oppressed with little restraint. Georgia had passed laws forbidding Indians from testifying in cases involving white people, suing a white person, or forming a legal contract with a white person, echoing both Georgia and Cherokee laws regarding Black men and women. Boudinot wrote in an 1832 editorial, "Think, for a moment, my countrymen, the danger to be apprehended from an overwhelming white population ... overbearing and impudent to those whom, in their sovereign pleasure, they consider as their inferiors." They would make "our sons and daughters" into "slaves." It was not a metaphor.[29]

What to do when slavery and genocide are on your doorstep? At some point, most people decide to run, to look for a safe place to survive and rebuild. Throughout the Cherokee Nation in 1832, Boudinot later recalled, "'What is to be done?' was a national inquiry, after we found that all our efforts to obtain redress from the General Government, *on the land of our fathers,* had been of no avail." Boudinot, along with his cousin John Ridge, Major Ridge, and some other Cherokees, decided that, "instead of contending uselessly against superior power, the only course left, was, to yield to circumstances over which they had no control."[30] As settlers streamed onto Cherokee lands and surveyors ventured into New Echota itself, Boudinot and the Ridges decided that the nation needed to exchange land and head west as a nation, before they all were killed.[31]

Most Cherokees disagreed. More than fifteen thousand Cherokees signed a statement objecting to anyone claiming the authority to sell land. Boudinot proposed to Ross that the *Phoenix* print debates over what to do, with statements from both those who wanted to stay and fight and those who thought it was time to escape to the West. But the *Phoenix* was the nation's paper, and the National Committee and the National Council both were still in firm opposition to removal. According to Cherokee norms of consensus, those who disagreed were supposed to bow out of the argument. Under pressure from Ross, Boudinot resigned from his position as editor later in 1832, and the National Council in 1834 expelled John Ridge and Major Ridge.[32]

One of the signature pages for the Aquohee District
from the Cherokee petition of 1834.
U.S. NATIONAL ARCHIVES. PHOTOGRAPH BY PATRICIA DAWSON

But rather than bow out, Boudinot, Major Ridge, John Ridge, and several others decided to go against Ross and the Cherokee government and negotiate with U.S. commissioners. In the Boudinots' house on December 29, 1835, they signed the Treaty of New Echota, which exchanged the Cherokee Nation lands in the East for lands in the West and $5 million. Boudinot and the other signatories decided that the only way for the Cherokee Nation to survive and individual Cherokees to retain their freedom was to flee. After signing the Treaty of New Echota, Boudinot wrote in anguish to Ross,

> What is the prospect in reference to *your* plan of relief, if you are understood at all to have any plan? It is dark and gloomy beyond description. Subject the Cherokees to the laws of the States.... Instead of remedying the evil you would only rivet the chains and fasten the manacles of their servitude and degradation. The final destiny of our race, under such circumstances, is too revolting to think of. Its course *must* be downward, until it finally becomes extinct or is merged in another race, more ignoble and more detested.[33]

Stay and become slaves or go west and remain the Cherokee Nation—to Boudinot, those were the only choices left. Harriett

Boudinot died of childbirth in New Echota early in 1836, so it was with their six children and his new wife, as well as Samuel Worcester and his family, that Elias went west, withdrawing from the Cherokee consensus against the Treaty of New Echota that he had signed. The rest of the Cherokee Nation was left to deal with the consequences.[34]

The Cherokee National Committee and National Council declared to U.S. officials that the Treaty of New Echota was invalid and that its signatories held no office in the Cherokee Nation, but white Americans pushed on with removal, now using the treaty as justification. In 1838, federal troops rounded up Cherokee families and placed them in stockades. They forced twenty thousand Cherokees, plus two thousand of their enslaved people, to leave their homes and travel hundreds of miles west to Indian Territory. Under terrible conditions, at least four thousand of them died along the way, from starvation, exposure, and disease. The town of New Echota would be renamed Calhoun, Georgia, for John Calhoun, who as secretary of war and a U.S. senator from South Carolina supported Cherokee Removal and eventually became a pro-slavery hero of Southern nationalists.

The Boudinot and Worcester families were working on building houses and a new mission a few miles south of where Tahlequah is today when the survivors of the Trail of Tears arrived. Cherokees who had completed the horrific journey executed Elias Boudinot, Major Ridge, and John Ridge for signing the Treaty of New Echota. In condemning and killing them, the Cherokees followed both traditional clan vengeance for the deaths caused by removal and the newer Cherokee law that made selling land a capital crime.[35]

On June 22, 2019, exactly 180 years after the execution of Elias Boudinot, Major Ridge, and John Ridge, University of Arkansas professor and Cherokee scholar Sean Kicummah Teuton led me on a walking tour of my hometown, Fayetteville, Arkansas. Professor Teuton met my family and me in front of the old post office on the town square, where merchants were packing up from the Saturday farmers' market. He pointed up at the second floor of one of the stately buildings that line the square. In that building, Elias and

Harriett Boudinot's son E. C. Boudinot had published a newspaper, following in the footsteps of his father. Professor Teuton told me about the route of the Trail of Tears that went through Fayetteville— Cherokees camped just south of what's now the University of Arkansas women's soccer field. And he showed me the house where John Ridge's widow, Sarah, lived after she fled with her five children and fourteen other Cherokee girls to get away from the conflict. She bought this house just off the square, a house I'd seen many times as a kid without knowing its Cherokee history. She helped start a school that became the Fayetteville Female Seminary, with day education for boys and a boarding school for girls. Cherokee and white children, including the mayor's daughter, went to school there together—one of the best schools and certainly the best girls' school in the region. In Fayetteville in the 1840s and '50s, you could see white and Cherokee girls riding around in carriages together, a living reality of the equality Georgians and the U.S. government had declared impossible.[36]

In the West, the Cherokee Nation rebuilt, again setting up legislative and court systems, schools, and other institutions. The Georgia Guard had seized the nation's printing press, so Cherokees bought a new one and had a new set of type made. The Cherokee Nation published the renamed *Cherokee Advocate* at Tahlequah in Cherokee and English from 1844 until 1906. Its motto was "Our Rights, Our Country, Our Race." Cherokees restarted the *Phoenix* in 1975 and still publish it today.[37]

SHAWNEE REMOVAL

While the Cherokee Trail of Tears is the most infamous Indian Removal, there were many more. Between the War of 1812 and the Indian Removal Act, white Americans had already forced Shawnees remaining in the Ohio Valley to cede all but three small reservations: Wapakoneta and the farms right around it, Lewistown, and Hog Creek.[38] In 1831, with the Indian Removal Act supporting them, U.S. negotiators headed to these small remaining reservations to

force them west too. According to a Quaker missionary who witnessed the proceedings, the negotiators threatened the Shawnees,
saying that the United States would let the State of Ohio "extend
her laws over them," force them to pay state taxes and labor on
Ohio's public roads for two days each year, and make laws "that
white men might turn horses and cattle in their grain-fields and
destroy it all . . . that they might be beaten or killed by white men."

It didn't matter how many Shawnees witnessed these crimes, the
negotiators told them; unless a white man corroborated their testimony, it counted for nothing. By contrast, if "they would *now* sell
their land and go west," President Jackson would give them "a good
rich country laid off for all the Indians to remove to, west of the
State of Missouri, purposely for them, which never would be within
any state or territory of the United States; where there was plenty of
buffalo, elk and deer; where they could live well without working at
all." One of the commissioners advised that "they ought always to
listen to the advices of the white people, because they were wiser
than the red people, as the red people were wiser than the blacks,"
and that "the Great Spirit created them so."

Wayweleapy, the Shawnees' speaker, replied that he did not think
that the commissioner "knew much about the Great Spirit." He said
he "believed that the Great Spirit created all men alike, of the same
blood, but if he did, as his friend had said, create them so very different that one race was so much superior to the others," it seemed
a bit suspicious "that it was his own race that was so much wiser
than the others were." If this was true, Wayweleapy reasoned, "it was
very likely that it was the Indians who had the most sense." The
treaty commissioners refused to let the Shawnees' French interpreter
participate or to read the treaty to the Shawnees. Some of the Shawnees reluctantly put their marks on the paper.[39]

Knowing that these negotiations were fraudulent even by U.S.
standards, the Shawnees sent a delegation to Washington that included Speaker Wayweleapy, Principal Chief John Perry, and Black
Hoof's son, along with their interpreter and the Quaker missionary.
In Washington, they told Secretary of War Lewis Cass what had
happened. When Cass had a clerk make them a copy of the treaty,

they were not surprised to learn that the payment the treaty stated was $115,000 less than what the U.S. commissioners had verbally offered in negotiations. Somewhat chagrined, Cass agreed to present to Jackson the Shawnees' request for renegotiation. But the president refused to consider changing the signed version. As the missionary recorded, Jackson "seemed to care very little for the Indians or their rights."[40]

Like the Cherokees, the Shawnees had to move. They sold their sawmill and gristmill and bought wagons, guns, and provisions. But the United States was slow in appropriating the funds for removal, and the Shawnees of Wapakoneta lingered for months. The women had not planted crops, because they had been told they would move in the spring, but they were still at Wapakoneta that fall, eating provisions they had bought for the eight-hundred-mile journey. When they finally left in September 1832, it was, the missionary wrote, "with heavy hearts ... They cast their last look at their favored spot—at old Wapaughkonnetta—where they had reared up dwellings with their own hands, planted orchards, and raised cattle, horses, and hogs—where they had good homes, and above all, were content." They "lamented most for having to leave the graves of fathers, mothers, brothers, sisters, and children, to the mercy of a people who, while living, cared little for them, and would care less for their dead." It was a sad and long journey. Hearing that there was cholera at St. Louis, they crossed the Mississippi higher up to avoid the town. When they arrived at their new reservation in what's now eastern Kansas, their annuities—the payments required by the treaty—took three years to begin arriving, so they did not have the plows, oxen, and seed they were promised to begin farming.[41]

The majority of Shawnees had already lived west of the Mississippi for decades, having left the Ohio Valley in multiple migrations before and after the War of 1812. The earliest had settled near the Mississippi River but had been forced from there onto lands along the Arkansas and White rivers near the Cherokee settlements. As settlers pushed into that region, Shawnees had split into smaller bands and spread out to the southwest. Others had moved to a reservation on the Kansas River in what's now eastern Kansas, including Tenskwatawa and his nephew, Tecumseh's son Paukeesaa. The groups had spent fifty years separated, governing themselves as separate polities. They were still not all back together, but they were in new clusters and had to decide what the new balance of power should be within and among the recombined Shawnee settlements.[42]

By the next summer, the newcomers had built new houses, cleared fields, planted corn and beans, and bought some livestock. Shawnees had built in new places before, and they did it again. And they forged strong alliances, with old and new neighbors, as Shawnees always had. The roughly fourteen thousand Shawnees, Delawares, and Kickapoos and their Cherokee neighbors in Indian Territory continued the Ohio Valley and Great Lakes practice of establishing towns near allies and sharing hunting and gathering land, ignoring the borders the United States tried to draw around reservations. The reunited Shawnees generally chose diplomats to the United States from among those who had lived in the East longer and chose leaders for the nation from multiple towns and divisions. Another group of more than a thousand Shawnees and Delawares, though, chose to leave the United States for Mexico. They joined settlements of Cherokees, Choctaws, and Chickasaws who also sought a new life beyond the United States. They farmed and ranched and traded with Caddos and with Mexican settlers, all of whom they joined to defend against Kiowa and Comanche raids.[43]

REMAINING NATIVE IN THE EAST

Indian Removal was a systematic expulsion designed to eliminate all Native nations east of the Mississippi, yet tens of thousands of Native Americans managed to remain in their homelands. Some Native communities used the support of white neighbors with whom they did business or went to church. Some held on to land by gaining individual title to it or retreated onto parts of their lands less desired by white Americans.

Hundreds of Cherokees in enclaves in western North Carolina managed to avoid capture. Indeed, some had moved there as Geor-

gia was increasing its intrusions on Cherokee sovereignty in the preceding decades. Some declared U.S. citizenship from the treaties of
1817 and 1819; some owned private property or had accepted reservations; some simply hid in the Snowbird Mountains. Many Cherokees died in hiding, but survivors rebuilt. An observer in 1840 noted
of the Cherokees that they "are forming settlements, building town
houses, and show every disposition to keep up their former manners
and customs of councils, dances, ballplays and other practices."
Today they are the Eastern Band of Cherokee Indians. Groups of
Choctaws and Muscogees similarly remained in Mississippi and
Alabama.[44]

The Haudenosaunee held on to a small portion of the land they
had left, including Seneca towns on Buffalo Creek, by using the
moral leverage of having signed the Treaty of Canandaigua with
George Washington in 1794, which acknowledged their sovereignty
and guaranteed their "reservations." In negotiations in the nineteenth century, Haudenosaunee diplomats brought out wampum
and used speeches and writing to remind their allies of their long
history together, the obligations of reciprocity, and the relationship
embodied by the Two-Row Wampum belt. The Haudenosaunee
also retained lands on the British Canadian side of the U.S. border,
although there, too, white settlers exacted land cessions.[45]

Even as most Shawnees were expelled, some, along with other
Native people of the Ohio Valley and Great Lakes, retreated onto
small family farms near wetlands unattractive to U.S. farmers because they had no navigable rivers for transporting crops to market
but where women could harvest wild rice and men could hunt small
game and fish. In the Great Lakes region, well over ten thousand
Anishinaabe, Ho-Chunks, and other Native Americans stayed on
reduced lands in the United States and Canada.[46]

In states all along the East Coast, Native communities—many of
them peoples who had accepted tributary status to colonies and
states—continued to exist. Most had combined with others for protection. Some were able to retain a land base and their particular
identities. Others, often defined by outsiders as "free people of color,"
over time lost some of their specific national traditions, languages,

and identities, even as they retained their own clear community identity as Indians. Their white neighbors' ignorance about their being Native may have helped to protect them from removal. One of the largest peoples to remain in place was the Lumbees, who managed to stay in their eastern North Carolina homes because, as Lumbee historian Malinda Maynor Lowery explains, they "owned their land individually, like other settlers—they did not possess their land collectively, as a nation—and so neither the United States nor the state of North Carolina had a legal means of seizing it." In South Carolina, the Catawbas avoided nineteenth-century removal in part by putting land in the name of one of their prominent women, Sally New River, but continuing to live and farm on it communally. In many of these communities, women made and sold pottery or baskets using methods and styles that their ancestors had developed, thereby both making a living and keeping a community culture alive.[47]

These peoples remained, despite great odds against them and repeated assaults on their livelihood and safety. As Ojibwe historian Brenda J. Child explains, "Their efforts to survive and remain on their lands, fishing grounds, forests, hills, and mountains—and especially their sacred places—countered newly established US legal regimes and enabled their descendants to maintain indigenous communities into the present day."[48]

THE GREAT PEACE

As Native easterners succeeded or failed in remaining on their homelands, some of those in the West worked together to create a place many Native nations could preserve together. In the past, Delawares and Shawnees had fought Cherokees, Cherokees had fought Haudenosaunee and Muscogees, Shawnees and Cherokees had fought Osages, and all had fought Kiowas and Comanches. But by the time of the gathering at the great Wichita town in the summer of 1834, mentioned at the start of this chapter, Native nations east of the Mississippi and in the regions just west of it had come to the conclusion that the United States was an enemy too powerful to

LEFT: *Tuch-ee* [Tahchee], *A Celebrated War Chief of the Cherokees,*
by George Catlin, 1834.
VIRGINIA MUSEUM OF FINE ARTS, PAUL MELLON COLLECTION, 85.628.
PHOTOGRAPH BY KATHERINE WETZEL

RIGHT: Jesse Chisholm, photograph taken between 1865 and 1868.
KANSAS STATE HISTORICAL SOCIETY

fight militarily or even to stand against diplomatically on their own. This gathering took place before the Cherokee Trail of Tears, but already many realized that their future was in the West. People from the East and those just west of the Mississippi needed to get along with one another and to persuade people of the Plains that peace with them was better than war.

Not surprisingly, Shawnees were involved in these peace efforts. Back in 1823, when Shawnee Chief Captain Lewis went west from Lewistown, in the Ohio Valley, to see available lands west of the Mississippi, he met with peoples who had already moved west, including other Shawnees, Delawares, Cherokees, and Peorias. On his return trip, a delegation from the West came too, meeting at Wapakoneta with Black Hoof and other Shawnees and all of their allies remaining in the Ohio Valley "to propose a general peace among all the Indians." At the time, before the Indian Removal Act, Black Hoof and others were still resisting removal, but groups that moved early laid the foundation for peace when the rest had to move too.[49]

The Quapaws had allied with the Shawnees, the Cherokees, and

other immigrants from the East, while the Osages fought the Native immigrants early on. But gradually the Osages made peace. As
the United States carved up Osage country to form Indian Territory,
the Osages realized that they could not continue to fight all of these
enemies. They already generally got along with the Muscogees and
Choctaws who had moved nearby because Kiowas, Comanches, and
Pawnees targeted all of them, and by the early 1820s they were meeting with Delawares to discuss ways to peacefully share hunting
lands. At a major peace conference in St. Louis in September 1826,
Osage diplomats officially made peace with Delawares, Shawnees,
Piankeshaws, Peorias, Miamis, Ohio Senecas, and Kickapoos, a
peace that the Cherokees, Choctaws, and Muscogees in the West
soon joined as well.[50]

The peace agreements of the 1820s set the stage for the 1834
meeting at the Wichita town. The meteor shower of 1833 may have
helped persuade some that it was time for this Great Peace effort,
which involved peoples speaking languages from at least seven different language *families*. Two thousand miles lay between Comanche country, in the West, and the original Haudenosaunee homeland
of the Ohio Senecas. They would have to learn foreign histories and
new diplomatic forms and phrases and overcome past prejudices.

A delegation of relatively young, though respected and multilingual, delegates made the preliminary steps at the Wichita town in
July 1834. The head of the Cherokee delegation was one of the oldest,
a man named Tahchee (**Wह**) or Dutch, who was born in Turkeytown and moved west as a child with some of the first Cherokees to
do so. He had fought in the Osage–Cherokee War and would later
serve in the Cherokee National Council. Another was Jesse Chisholm, a Cherokee in his late twenties whose father was a trader at
Arkansas Post. Surrounded by many kinds of people at the trading
post, Chisholm learned Caddo, English, French, and a little Spanish, to go along with his native Cherokee. After the Civil War, he
would pioneer the cattle drives across Texas and Oklahoma along
what would be named the Chisholm Trail, for him. Attending for
the Osages, Monpisha was a young man, the son of a deceased chief,
who had learned to speak, read, and write English at the missionary

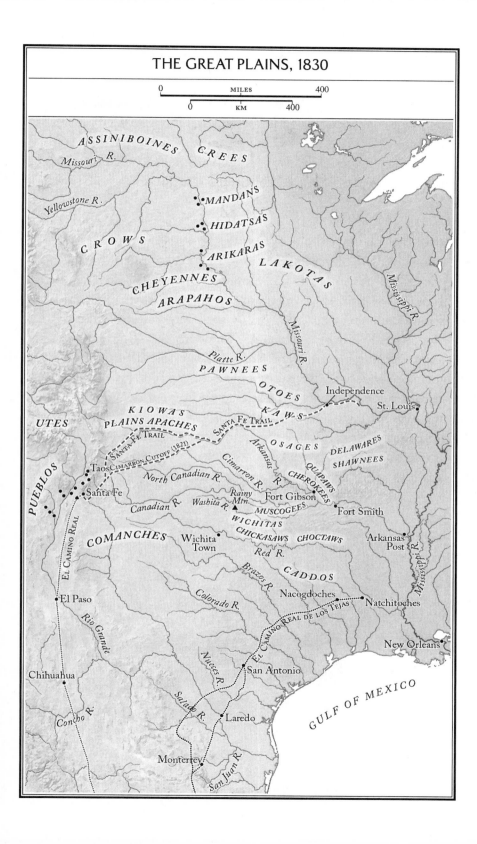

THE GREAT PLAINS, 1830

MILES
0   400
KM
0   400

ASSINIBOINES

CREES

Missouri R.

Yellowstone R.

MANDANS

HIDATSAS

CROWS

ARIKARAS

LAKOTAS

CHEYENNES

Mississippi R.

ARAPAHOS

Missouri R.

Platte R.

PAWNEES

OTOES

Independence

KIOWAS

KAWS

St. Louis

PLAINS APACHES

SANTA FE TRAIL

SANTA FE TRAIL

UTES

OSAGES

DELAWARES

SHAWNEES

SANTA FE TRAIL
CIMARRON CUTOFF (1821)

Arkansas R.

Cimarron R.

QUAPAWS

PUEBLOS

Taos

North Canadian R.

CHEROKEES

Santa Fe

Rainy
Mtn.

Fort Gibson

Canadian R.

Washita R.

MUSCOGEES

Fort Smith

WICHITAS

CHICKASAWS

CHOCTAWS

Arkansas
Post

COMANCHES

Wichita
Town

Red R.

CADDOS

EL CAMINO REAL

Brazos R.

Nacogdoches

El Paso

Colorado R.

Natchitoches

EL CAMINO REAL DE LOS TEJAS

Rio Grande

New Orleans

Chihuahua

Nueces R.

San Antonio

Concho R.

Salado R.

Laredo

GULF OF MEXICO

Monterrey

San Juan R.

school recently founded among the Osages. Also with the Osage delegation was Pierre Beatte, in his late thirties, who had grown up in Osage country, although his parents seem to have been French or perhaps Quapaw. Beatte had guided the famous author Washington Irving on a western tour two years earlier. George Bullet (Pondoxy), who headed the Delaware delegation, later would be a Delaware leader.[51]

As part of their peace overtures, the Osages would return captives they had taken: one or two Wichita girls and White Weasel, the Kiowa girl whom the Osages took along with her little brother, the Thunderer, in 1833, the Summer That They Cut Off Their Heads. The painter George Catlin painted a portrait of the two Kiowa children at Fort Gibson, on their way to the Wichita town. But just as White Weasel and the Thunderer had their hopes raised about returning home, a ram had struck the Thunderer in the abdomen and knocked him against a fence, killing him. So White Weasel had ridden out onto the Plains, deep in mourning, hoping to be reunited with her Kiowa family.[52]

Along with the Native delegates came a contingent of U.S. sol-

Túnk-aht-óh-ye, Thunderer, a Boy, and Wun-pán-to-mee,
White Weasel, a Girl, by George Catlin, 1834.
SMITHSONIAN AMERICAN ART MUSEUM

diers. They were recruited to impress Plains peoples with the might of the United States but encountered the same difficulties that earlier U.S. expeditions had. Initially there were between four and five hundred U.S. troops, but their numbers thinned rapidly as many of them caught what Catlin, himself sick with it, described as "a slow and distressing bilious fever."[53] It was probably malaria, or perhaps dengue or yellow fever, all of which can quickly destroy the liver. Heatstroke and thirst added to their suffering, as did the supposed cures for fevers: bleeding and large doses of calomel powder (mercurous chloride), a poison that causes diarrhea and dehydration, exactly the opposite of what they needed.[54]

Soon half of them, including the expedition's leader, General Henry Leavenworth, were so incapacitated that they had to halt while Colonel Henry Dodge led a much smaller contingent of between 200 and 250 onward, also leaving behind the supply wagons, which were entirely unsuited for the horse road they were traveling on. By the time about 180 of them reached the Wichita town, they were, Catlin admitted, "all in a state of dependence and almost literal starvation," almost half of them "too sick to have made a successful resistance if we were to have been attacked." Another noted that "we were on the brink of starvation having nothing to eat save what we got from those Indians."[55]

In 1834, the Wichita town was an impressive place, with several hundred large, thatch-roofed houses. Rock cliffs and the Red River protected the town on three sides, while its front side had a long view of the Plains. Wichita women's fields of corn, pumpkins, melons, beans, and squash were, one of the U.S. men noted, "well cultivated, neatly enclosed, and very extensive, reaching, in some instances, several miles." Wichita women fed their guests corn and beans, with watermelons and plums for dessert, and walked through the visitors' camp selling dried meat, corn, pumpkins, melons, and occasionally a horse, in exchange for vermilion paint, buttons, ribbons, strips of cloth, and blankets.[56]

When the Kiowas heard that the Osages had brought White Weasel, her relatives quickly raised a party of twenty or thirty men who rode into the Wichita town with their weapons at the ready, not knowing whether the mission was one of peace or war. The U.S. contingent was impressed; they found the Kiowas "a bold, warlike-looking Indian. Some of their horses are very fine; they ride well, and were admirably equipped to-day for fight or flight; their bows strung, and quivers filled with arrows." As the rest of them remained on their horses with weapons ready, one of White Weasel's relations dismounted his horse and "shed tears of joy" as he embraced her.[57] By then the captive Wichita girls had already been exchanged for a nine-year-old U.S. boy who had been captured a few weeks earlier. Their negotiations were helped by a man of African descent who was living with the Wichitas and spoke English and apparently had run away from a U.S. settlement on the Arkansas River. The return of White Weasel was essential for Kiowa–Osage peace, as was the promise of the Osage delegation to return the Kiowa Táiñmé medicine bundle.[58]

Return of Gunpa'ndama (White Weasel), Little Bear's calendar, summer 1834, in James Mooney, *Calendar History of the Kiowa Indians*.
DAVIS LIBRARY, UNIVERSITY OF NORTH CAROLINA AT CHAPEL HILL

The Native ambassadors explained why they were there. The Osage Monpisha declared, "We wish to be your brothers," and invited them to the Osage towns for further negotiations and the return of the Táiñmé. Tahchee relayed a message from the Cherokee chief that "his people wish to come to you without fear, and that you should visit them without fear."[59] The easterners also said strange things that didn't seem to fit with the feckless impression that U.S. explorers had thus far made. Because "your buffalo will be gone in a few years," Monpisha advised the Kiowas, Wichitas, and Comanches, "your Great Father, the President, will give you cattle, and teach you how to live without buffalo." The Plains attendees must have puzzled over these words, as well as the U.S. visitors' repeated insistence that they accompany them to Washington to meet with the president "where the great American chief lives."[60]

Of course, the easterners were right with their warnings about the United States. The whole reason they were living on lands that had once belonged solely to the Osages and Quapaws and venturing onto the hunting lands of the Kiowas and the Comanches was U.S. pressure. But it was also true that the United States could not yet impose its will on the West. The United States needed peace in the West. Native peoples who had agreed to leave the East had made legally binding treaties that granted them land for farming and hunting in the West. In 1834, most still had relatives in the East whom U.S. officials and eastern constituents hoped to persuade to move, people less likely to move if western lands were contested and dangerous. There were also white settlers west of the Mississippi— voters now, in their own states of Louisiana and Missouri, with full representation in Congress—who wanted protection from Plains Indians. Large-scale Native diplomacy could bring the peace that U.S. officials needed. Yet a grand alliance of eastern and western Native nations also was worrisome, too reminiscent of earlier threats like that of Tenskwatawa and Tecumseh.[61]

Therefore, the U.S soldiers had come with two goals: to make peace among these peoples whom they defined as living within the United States and to prove to them that the United States had power over them, that they actually did live in the United States. The U.S. secretary of war had told Congress the previous November that it was "indispensable to the peace and security of the frontiers that a respectable force should be displayed in that quarter, and that the wandering and restless tribes who roam through it should be impressed with the power of the United States by the exhibition of a corps so well qualified to excite their respect."[62] A Baltimore newspaper explained to its readers that the object of the 1834 expedition was "to give the wild Indians some idea of our power, and to endeavor, under such an imposing force, to enter into conference with them, to warn those Indians who have been in the habit of robbing and murdering our people who trade among them, of the dangers to which they will be exposed in case they continue their depredations and massacres." The expedition also hoped, the newspaper continued, in what reads like an afterthought, to "perhaps, enlighten the Indians generally as to the humane policy of the United States toward them, and also as to their own true interests."[63]

By that point, two previous U.S. attempts at large-scale diplomacy on the Plains had failed. One had searched and searched and not found Plains Indians at all. The other resulted in a popular book for Washington Irving but no real negotiations. This 1834 expedition was intended to be an elite regiment of mounted soldiers, the First Dragoon Regiment, veterans of the War of 1812 and men whose names came to be associated with American might in various ways, through their actions and the forts and towns that were later named for them. Henry Leavenworth had been promoted to brigadier general for leading U.S. troops against Arikaras in 1823. Henry Dodge had fought in the 1832 Black Hawk War. Other officers included Stephen Kearny, who would later be at the forefront of U.S. expansion all the way to California; a son of Daniel Boone; and twenty-six-year-old Jefferson Davis, future president of the Confederacy. The original plan was to recruit eight hundred men, outfit them with newly designed uniforms, mount each company on a different color of horse to make them especially impressive, and have them start out in the cool of the spring. Instead, several months delayed, a much smaller number—fewer than two hundred—found themselves in the heat of summer, sick and needing water and food in a place they did not understand, surrounded by thousands of Comanches, Kiowas, and Wichitas in what was clearly their country, whatever U.S. maps said.[64]

So it was that on the morning of July 24, 1834, a large council of two thousand gathered at a clearing in the woods prepared by the Wichitas. The first to speak was White Weasel's father, who described his joy in getting his daughter back. She came with him to the council, and each of the Kiowa and Comanche leaders embraced her. Kiowa women then processed past, each embracing her, as the peace pipe circulated among the men of the various nations. Just as Henry Dodge thought it was his chance to speak for the United

States, another Kiowa band of about sixty rode in. In the ethnocentric words of the official U.S. report, the latest arrivals "shook hands all round, and seated themselves with a dignity and grace that would well become senators of a more civilized society."[65] After more than three centuries of interactions with Native nations, Europeans and their descendants should not have been surprised by well-established Native politics and diplomacy, but U.S. stereotypes about Native backwardness were more extreme than ever in 1834.

When it was finally Dodge's turn, he described U.S. intentions, with the Comanche leader Tawequenah interpreting into Kiowa. At the same time, Jesse Chisholm interpreted Dodge's English into Caddo for another interpreter to translate into Wichita. There was surely a fair amount of Plains Indian sign language going on as well. Dodge promised that the United States would send more traders. He encouraged Kiowas and Comanches to cease their nomadic ways and "plant your corn and cultivate the soil, as the Cherokees and other Indians do," thereby using less land, a refrain the Osages were accustomed to hearing directed at them. And he reiterated his hope that Native representatives from the West would visit U.S. centers of population and power.[66]

One of the Kiowas responded, ignoring the nonsensical parts of Dodge's speech: "The American captain has spoken well to-day; the white men have shown themselves our friends. If a white man ever comes to my country, he shall be kindly treated; if he wants a horse, or anything that I have, he shall not pay for it; I will give him what he wants." What the English-speaking translator interpreted as "white man" was surely the Kiowa word T'ó:T'áukâui. The Kiowas agreed to accompany the visitors back to the towns of the Native delegations just west of the Mississippi River, but not to Washington. It was Native diplomacy that mattered to them.

The Native delegates repeatedly turned the conversation back to what they wanted to discuss. As one of the Wichita leaders explained to Dodge, "We have been at war with the nations which we see around us to-day; we wish now to make peace with them." Indeed, he had practically told Dodge to stop talking, saying bluntly, "We want now to hear those Indians who came with you speak to us." A Wichita would recall in 1894 that "the white people and the Osage" met with the Wichitas at "that old village, where they lived and brought that girl." They talked and "made a feast among themselves, and the soldiers had fired their guns around there. The meaning of that was a peace."[67]

The kind of peacemaking that the Kiowas were embarking on—with both Native and U.S. powers—prompted a centralization of leadership similar to what the Shawnees, Cherokees, and Quapaws had done earlier in the nineteenth century. The man who would become the Kiowas' first true principal chief was Little Bluff (Dohausen). In the past, there had been band leaders who were more influential than others, but none was a chief for all the Kiowas in the same way Little Bluff would be. There had been a lot of blame to go around after the deaths at the hands of the Osages in 1833, and some leaders had been deposed. It was logical that Little Bluff should rise to leadership. His father was a Kiowa band leader, and Little Bluff was a renowned warrior who belonged to one of the more respected military societies. But it was Little Bluff's peacemaking that made him into the man Kiowas remember as the greatest chief in their history. He also was a calendar keeper and artist, who recorded an-

Téh-tóot-sah (better known as Tohausen, Little Bluff, First Chief),
by George Catlin, 1834.
SMITHSONIAN AMERICAN ART MUSEUM

nual events and passed the calendar on to his nephew after his death. Because of George Catlin, we have a portrait of Little Bluff in 1834. He impressed Catlin as "a very gentlemanly and high minded man," who treated the Americans "with great kindness while in his country." He wore silver ornaments in his long hair and around his arms, wrists, and neck. He and the other Kiowa men had beadwork and fringe on their leggings, moccasins, and hunting shirts and wore striking red or blue cloth mantles over their shoulders.[68]

Little Bluff, along with other Kiowas, Comanches, and Wichitas, agreed to the Native and U.S. invitation that they ride east for further diplomacy at Fort Gibson, on the Arkansas River in western Cherokee country, fifty miles southeast of today's city of Tulsa. On the ride east, the Plains delegations entertained the camps nightly with jovial songs in their various languages. After two and a half days of riding, they arrived at the closest sick camps that the U.S. soldiers had left behind. Two dozen men lay incapacitated, and they soon learned that many had died, including General Leavenworth. The Comanches decided to abandon the journey, with its obvious sickness, and the other Native delegations kept their distance from the U.S. camp. As they continued riding east, some of the soldiers were pulled on horse-drawn stretchers, "and sighs and groaning are heard in all directions."[69] Some were left behind with an attendant and a horse, in the hope that they would recover enough to make their way to Fort Gibson. Every time a soldier died, he was lifted off his litter and buried beside the road. One hundred fifty men died of the 450 to 500 that started from Fort Gibson.[70]

The Kiowas and Wichitas continued on with the U.S. and other Native riders. At the Muscogee towns on the north fork of the Canadian River, Kiowas met Muscogees for the first time in peace. And when they reached Fort Gibson, the Kiowas and Wichitas met with Cherokee, Shawnee, Delaware, Choctaw, Ohio Seneca, and Osage delegates for a grand council on September 2. Little Bluff signaled friendship "by placing his hands alternately on the left then the right shoulder" of each of the Native diplomats except the Osages. He placed his hands on his heart, then the hearts of the other men, then did the same with their foreheads, saying something to each. The Kiowa and Osage delegates at first were slow to speak to one another, but finally Little Bluff "arose and hugged the Osage chief as he had the others."[71] Most important, the Osages returned the Kiowa Táiñmé medicine bundle. Little Bluff brought the matter up, offering to pay many horses for its return. Knowing the vital role it played in forging peace, the Osages returned it without payment, accepting only one horse as an acknowledgment.[72]

Over the next three weeks, they met in smaller groups, doing the slow and serious work of diplomacy as the leaders got to know one another and their histories, what brought them there, and what they wanted now. The Kiowas heard of how the United States had driven the Cherokees, Shawnees, and other eastern peoples from their homes and even restricted the powerful Osages from some of the places they had once lived and hunted. It must have been hard to believe that sick and feckless men like these could cause such wholesale horrors. Diplomacy continued over the coming years, including with the Quapaws and Haudenosaunee. At one diplomatic meeting, Seneca Chief Thomas Brant said that, although "you live far to the West, and we to the East, we are glad to see you." The Haudenosaunee, he said, "are like friends and Brothers" to "the Cherokee, Muscogee, Choctaw, Osage and Quapaw Nations." The Haudenosaunee wanted to extend the Covenant Chain out onto the Plains: "We have made a white road from your towns to ours, and we and all our people will travel it without danger." His people, including "our women and children" sent him with the message that "we must have one heart and not two, we must all think alike."[73]

In his 1834 address to Congress that December, Andrew Jackson was less grandiose in his claims than four years earlier, in the glow of passing the Indian Removal Act. Not only were the Cherokees still holding out against Georgia in 1834, Americans now understood power on the Plains a bit better than they had in 1830. Jackson admitted there had been trouble with "the wandering and predatory tribes inhabiting the western frontier" who committed "attacks upon our own citizens and upon other Indians entitled to the protection of the United States." He was happy to report, though, about Leavenworth's and Dodge's mission, which he hoped had established the

Kiowas' and Comanches' "permanent pacific relations with the United States and the other tribes of Indians upon that border," though he did have to admit that "the prevalence of sickness in that quarter has deprived the country of a number of valuable lives, and particularly that of General Leavenworth."[74]

In fact, a tremendously important peace had been made on the Plains by Native peoples, and it would hold surprisingly well. In the future, if a young Kiowa or Osage stole a horse or killed someone, there were reciprocal systems between their nations to handle it and keep it from becoming war. The peace immediately benefited the Kiowas and their allies. U.S. traders were now more willing to come to the southern Plains. A large contingent left soon after the delegates did, carrying "a large stock of goods," and Americans soon began to build trading posts accessible to the Kiowas, the Comanches, and the Wichitas.[75]

Indeed, the 1834 peace brought more prosperity to all of the Native nations who were party to it. The Osages became merchants, bringing rifles, ammunition, cloth, and other U.S. goods west up the Arkansas River when they came on their summer hunts each year and returning with what they hunted as well as bison robes, captives, and horses they had bought from the Kiowas and Comanches. Muscogee, Shawnee, Delaware, and Cherokee traders, including Jesse Chisholm, began traveling to Kiowa and Comanche country to sell guns and other goods, and a group of Shawnees, Delawares, and Kickapoos settled on the Canadian River to hunt and work as intermediaries between Plains peoples and Native communities in Indian Territory, who had manufactured goods to sell because the U.S. government paid most of their annuities in merchandise. They, in return, sold Plains products to St. Louis merchants and Native and U.S. farmers and hunters. At one trade fair in the summer of 1847, Kiowas and Comanches traded an estimated fifteen hundred horses for $24,000 worth of guns, blankets, and other goods from the Osages.[76]

While the United States had created "Indian Territory," it was Native nations that made it a workable space for one another in a time of increasing dispossession, in part through the Great Peace of 1834 and subsequent diplomacy. At a diplomatic meeting in 1835,

Quapaw Chief Heckaton explained that after the U.S.–Quapaw Treaty of 1824 took the last of their lands, Native peacemaking had created for them a home among "my Old Brothers, the Muscogees, Choctaws, Osages and Senecas" in Indian Territory. They had finally been able to establish a new homeland carved out of formerly Osage land. Although most of the splintered Quapaw bands would wander for another half century, that homeland remains the Quapaw Nation today, tucked into the northeastern corner of Oklahoma.[77]

In 1837, Little Bluff and other Kiowa leaders signed a treaty with the United States and Native nations agreeing that all of the Native parties to the peace begun in 1834 and added thereafter would "have free permission to hunt and trap" on the southern Plains, but the treaty did not give those rights to U.S. hunters or trappers, guaranteeing only that U.S. traders would have free passage to trade with Mexico and Texas. In 1840, the Kiowas negotiated another great peace with the Cheyennes and Arapahos, bringing them into the alliance. Both sides had made peace with the Lakotas by then, so now there was a monumental peace and system of alliances across nearly all of the Plains.[78]

Exchange of gifts between the Kiowas and the Cheyennes in 1840.
Howling Wolf (Southern Cheyenne, 1840–1927), Drawing Book,
c. 1875, ink and watercolor on paper.

JOSLYN ART MUSEUM, OMAHA, NEBRASKA, GIFT OF ALEXANDER M. MAISH
IN MEMORY OF ANNA BOURKE RICHARDSON, 1991

The epic peace agreements between 1834 and 1840 would spell war and destruction for people to their south. Kiowa and Comanche fighters now could safely leave their families and horse herds in their camps and increase their raids on Texas and Chihuahua and even Coahuila, Nuevo León, and Tamaulipas. Over the coming years, war parties in the hundreds—at times as many as a thousand—rode south, not only raiding but systematically making war on entire Mexican settlements, especially ones that had killed any of their relatives in a previous battle.[79] Kiowa calendars record some of these expeditions, such as one in the summer of 1843 against the A:T'áukâui (Tamaulipas) when "a great many Mexicans were killed and their houses burned." Mexican records tell of destruction and fear, year after year. Spanish supply networks had never been impressive this far north, but the tumult of Mexico's independence period brought them nearly to a standstill; therefore, the northern Mexican states were weak on defense, despite being wealthy in horses—in short, excellent targets for raiding.[80]

Texas was particularly vulnerable during its rebellion against Mexico in 1835 and 1836, and there was brutal fighting back and forth in the following years, especially during the Texas presidency of Mirabeau Lamar. He sent rangers against the Comanches and Kiowas and united with Lipan Apaches who had suffered from Comanche raids. Some Texans who did pass through learned to wave U.S. flags and pass unharmed as T'ó:T'áukâui, although the Kiowas soon caught on to that trick. Even after the United States annexed Texas in 1845, the Kiowas continued to see Texas as its own entity, not covered by their peace agreements with the United States. A U.S. party sent to explore the border with Mexico in 1845 was saved by Kiowas who, having surrounded the party and drawn their bows to shoot, suddenly realized they might be Americans instead of Texans. As one Texan remarked, "The whole country was swarming with Comanche and Kiowa Indians."[81]

In the same years, Texans debated whether to continue the alliances made when the region was under Spanish and Mexican rule, particularly with the Cherokees, Shawnees, Delawares, and others who had moved into the region earlier in the century as the places they lived in earlier filled with settlers. When Sam Houston was president of Texas, he offered them a permanent territory, as a buffer against the Comanches and the Kiowas. But Lamar, by contrast, saw all Indians as enemies and obstacles and during his presidency encouraged Texans to kill them or force them over the border into the United States. In a mass removal in 1839, Texas troops forced almost three hundred Shawnees north across the U.S. border. Together with other Shawnees, they settled to the west of the Muscogee Nation, where they could serve as peacekeepers between the Muscogees and the Kiowas and Comanches.[82]

Most Kiowa and Comanche raids targeted Mexico, and their range in these years is astounding, reportedly as far south as San Luis Potosí and as far west as the Gulf of California. Historian Brian DeLay estimates that for the eight years between 1840 and 1847, twice as many Kiowa and Comanche raiding parties traveled south as in the eight years before. He counted at least forty-four Kiowa and Comanche campaigns of at least one hundred men between 1834 and 1847 and estimates that they probably took more than a hundred thousand horses and mules from northern Mexico, and certainly tens of thousands.[83] They also captured many Mexicans and Texans, whom they adopted or sold to New Mexican or western U.S. ranches and trading operations. As with the Mohawks two centuries earlier, the Kiowas adopted captives into their families. Nearly every family had one or two captives or children of captives, and many Kiowas descend from these captives, including N. Scott Momaday and photographer Horace Poolaw. A U.S. official noted, "It is somewhat difficult to distinguish them. They sit in council with them, hunt with them, go to war with them, and partake of their perils and profits, and but few have any desire to leave them."[84]

Not all post-1840 warfare was against Mexicans and Texans—peace with all other Native former enemies allowed targeted fighting. Arapahos and Cheyennes, for example, now increased their raids on Utes to their west, sometimes with Kiowa allies. And the Kiowas and Plains Apaches joined a large number of Native nations against the Pawnees, whom Plains Apaches probably blamed for driving them south from their former homes in the early 1700s.[85]

Peace in the North and East gave Kiowas and Comanches U.S. markets for the bounty of these wars and raids. Trade also continued with Santa Fe, even though technically it was part of Mexico and really shouldn't have been buying the products of warfare on other Mexican towns. The Shawnees living between the Kiowas and the Muscogees became intermediaries in the trade, and Texans' punishment for forcing the Shawnees out was more Kiowa and Comanche raiding for this market. Strategic peacemaking—with the Comanches at the beginning of the nineteenth century and more recently with the Osages, Native newcomers from the East, and Cheyennes and Arapahos—enabled Kiowa and Comanche dominance on the southern Plains and allowed all of the allied Native nations to believe that the West might be theirs forever.[86]

THE NATIVE WEST FACES THE T'Ó:T'ÁUKÂUI

And yet, by making the Plains safer while weakening Mexico, the great western peace and Kiowa and Comanche raiding would end up facilitating the westward march of the United States. In 1845, John O'Sullivan, a New York magazine editor, gave a slogan to the growing U.S. determination to have the entire continent, proclaiming that it was "our manifest destiny to overspread the continent allotted by Providence for the free development of our yearly multiplying millions."[87] The United States was able to win the 1848 U.S.–Mexico War and add five hundred thousand square miles of territory—including California and most of New Mexico and Arizona—largely because Kiowa and Comanche attacks had both weakened Mexico's northern defenses and persuaded many Mexicans that it was good riddance to lose this Native-dominated frontier. Indeed, U.S. policymakers chose to attack through northern Mexico because they knew it was vulnerable as a result of its Indian wars. At first, northern Mexicans actually thought the U.S. troops

might have come to help them against the Comanches and Kiowas.[88]

And peace on the Plains facilitated U.S. expansion farther west,
at first via the Santa Fe Trail and related roads. Because the Plains
were not the kind of farming country that U.S. citizens wanted,
when they began to migrate west of the Mississippi Valley (having
filled the fertile lands previously farmed by Quapaw and Osage
women), they passed over the Plains and headed for Oregon and
then, after the U.S.–Mexico War, California. At first, the people of
the Plains saw the Santa Fe Trail as serving their own purposes.
Widened to accommodate wagons full of goods, it connected the
Plains to global trade in the East, through St. Louis, as well as to the
south, on El Camino Real to Mexico City. Treaties giving U.S. traders the right of passage on their way to trade with Mexico and Texas
did not seem like a concession. They merely formalized the Kiowas'
existing policy toward the T'ó:T'áukâui.[89]

The roads across the Plains brought white Americans to O'odham
country for the first time, where they also initially seemed like more
of an opportunity than a threat. U.S. trappers started coming in the
1820s, when Mexico still claimed all of O'odham country. These first
U.S. visitors marveled at the abundant corn, wheat, squash, and melons in the midst of a desert that to them seemed uninhabitable. In
1846, the Akimel O'odham and the Piipaash welcomed an expedition led by Stephen Kearny, who when we last saw him was one of
Henry Leavenworth's officers stumbling through Kiowa country in
1834. Relieved to see that the riders they spotted in the distance
weren't Apaches, a "great crowd of Indians," in the words of the expedition's report, ran out at an astonishing speed to greet the Americans. Once at the rancheria, Akimel O'odham and Piipaash men,
women, and children came to them with baskets of corn, beans, and
cornmeal and jars of saguaro syrup. In exchange, they asked for
beads, red and white cloth, and blankets. The visitors were "at once
impressed with the beauty, order, and disposition of the arrangements for irrigating and draining the land."[90]

After Americans discovered gold in 1849, the Akimel O'odham
towns became regular stops on the southern route to California. The

treaty ending the U.S.–Mexico War put the towns on the Mexico side of the border, but westward-bound U.S. citizens swung south, because the Akimel O'odham towns were a better place for food, water, and rest than anywhere else in the western United States. The Akimel O'odham made these travelers—more than twenty thousand in 1849 alone—part of the diversified economy they had built centuries earlier, in the aftermath of the Huhugam, and had shared with Spaniards and Mexicans, as well as Piipash and Sobaipuri, Tohono, and Hia-Ced O'odham. As with the Spanish, they assumed people from the United States were travelers needing hospitality, not settlers, and they welcomed their reciprocal gifts.[91]

In the Gadsden Purchase of 1854, the United States bought the part of the state of Sonora that included the Akimel O'odham Gila River towns and much of Tohono O'odham country from Mexico. When the Akimel O'odham heard about the Gadsden Purchase, they sent one of their leaders, Antonio Azul, to meet with the U.S. boundary commissioner. Azul reported back that the commissioner had expressed gratitude for Akimel O'odham support of U.S. immigrants passing through and promised to send agricultural tools in payment, seeing that the Akimel O'odham and the Piipaash, in the spirit of reciprocity, provided food and water to migrants regardless of their ability to pay. For the Tohono O'odham, the new U.S.–Mexico border crossing right through their land would have profound results in the future, but in the short run, sovereignty did not change.[92]

The Akimel O'odham increased food production to meet increasing demand from travelers. In 1858, they sold 250,000 pounds of wheat to the Overland Mail Line, not counting other foods and other buyers. Farms on the Gila irrigated tens of thousands of acres, and, as in the past, Tohono O'odham families came to help at harvest time. In the 1850s, some U.S. immigrants stayed, building ranches where the Sobaipuri O'odham had once lived on the upper Santa Cruz River, near the old site of Tumacácori and present-day Nogales, Arizona. They bought Akimel O'odham agricultural products and, like the Spanish and Mexican missions before them, provided a target that deflected Apache raids from the O'odham, which had restarted in the early 1830s after several decades of peace. The

U.S. military was a useful ally, sending soldiers in larger numbers than Mexico had and fighting alongside the O'odham against their common enemies. If anything, it was Mexican ranchers coming north who threatened O'odham lands. The United States provided weapons and ammunition, and some Akimel O'odham formed companies within the Arizona Battalion.[93]

O'odham calendar sticks give insight into how they saw these years. The O'odham have long kept saguaro-rib calendar sticks in their communities, but none from before the 1830s are publicly available. Like Kiowa calendars, they have mnemonic images that the calendar's keeper uses to recall that year's history. O'odham calendars in the 1830s and '40s consistently focus on battles in which O'odham and Piipash fought the Apaches and other enemies, sometimes alongside soldiers from the United States or Mexico.[94]

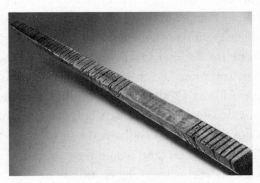

Calendar stick documenting events from 1833 to 1921, made by Joseph Head (Rattlesnake Head, Akimel O'odham).
NATIONAL MUSEUM OF THE AMERICAN INDIAN, SMITHSONIAN INSTITUTION (10/4878). PHOTOGRAPH BY NMAI PHOTO SERVICES

But eventually the O'odham, the Kiowas, and other westerners would see signs that the United States might cause the kind of trouble that Quapaws, Osages, Cherokees, Shawnees, and Haudenosaunee warned about. In 1848 and 1849, the traffic on the Plains became more alarming. During the U.S.–Mexico War, troops and supplies barreled past, the first direct evidence that the United States actually was a military power, and Kiowas had occasional skirmishes with them. Though traffic from the gold rush benefited the O'odham, it devastated Native communities in California. Over the three years after the discovery of gold in 1849, some three hundred thousand gold seekers rushed there to try to make their fortune. In their frenzied search for wealth, they violently took over land, destroyed forests and streams, forced thousands of California's Native people into slavery, and killed many more. In the continent's fastest and most purposeful genocide, of a population of some 150,000 Native Californians, after seven years, only around thirty thousand remained.[95]

Most previous immigrants had taken the Oregon Trail to the north, leaving the Santa Fe Trail mostly to traders, but migrants had so stripped the Oregon Trail of grass, wood, and bison by the late 1840s that many travelers in this new and larger rush took the Santa Fe route, doing the same damage in Kiowa country. Disease made matters worse. Pathogens from Europe weren't new to the Plains—Kiowas had suffered smallpox epidemics in 1781, 1816, and 1818—but smallpox killed a great many in the winter of 1839–40, followed by a measles outbreak in 1846 and, three years later, a bout of cholera that inflicted vomiting and diarrhea, which caused dehydration and led to death within a few hours for hundreds of Kiowas, including many medicine men. Whole families were wiped out. Kiowas later recounted it as "the most terrible experience in their history."[96]

Yet still, through the 1850s, wagon trains that wanted to go west often had to pay Kiowas, Comanches, Pawnees, Cheyennes, or Arapahos hundreds of dollars in flour, sugar, and bacon to pass. As one migrant wrote, "The Indians regarded the things we were giving them, as a sort of tribute we were under obligations to pay for the privilege of passing through their country unmolested."[97] Whereas traders were of use, these immigrant wagon trains took natural resources, so Plains people reasonably required them to pay for passage across their land. Officials assigned to guard the Santa Fe Trail complained that, as one put it in 1848, the "efforts of late (at considerable expense)" that the government had made to protect travelers had no effect "other than to exhibit a weakness and want of power to chastise the Indians." The road was "beset and continually ravaged by roaming and hostile bands of Indians." The six hundred soldiers the United States stationed on the Platte River could do little to protect the vast region, and the same was true of the five hundred placed on the Arkansas River, some of whom became victims themselves, "as the Indians took by force many of their horses." The official acknowledged that attacks seemed to have slowed recently but figured that was only because "the Indians having, in '46 and '47, secured so much booty by their daring outrages upon travelers, are now . . . luxuriating in and enjoying the spoils."[98] With raids accelerating again in 1850, the U.S. official wrote his superiors to suggest either taking Kiowas and other western Indians to Washington or "giving some one of the most unruly tribes a good flogging," because "they have not the slightest idea whatever of the strength and power of the United States." But all he could actually do was hand out presents, which he did by the wagonful.[99]

The United States employed the same measures they had in the East to begin taking the West before they had the military might to do it by force: written agreements that promised annuities and trade while inserting language that flipped assumptions of ownership from one in which Native land had U.S. posts carved out of it to one where "Indian reservations" were carved out of the United States. At every treaty negotiation, Native diplomats had to fight off new concessions, and U.S. diplomats often inserted them anyway. Sometimes they put the legal language of "reservation" into a treaty that seemed to confirm Native possession of land, setting up a process to force them onto smaller pieces of land with the next treaty once the United States had more military power and settlers in the region.

In an 1853 treaty with the United States, Little Bluff, Sitting Bear, and other Kiowas agreed to U.S. trading posts and "a right of way through their country"—with even the U.S. documents acknowledging that this was "their country," land still belonging to the Kiowas. But the Kiowas strongly objected to proposed provisions that had not been in their 1830s treaties: allowing the United States to establish military posts, forbidding fighting Mexico, and promising to return captives who had been adopted. Yet it had become the U.S. practice to prepare treaties ahead of time and declare those the official version regardless of the negotiations. Therefore, the text attached to their signatures acknowledged "the right of the United

States . . . to establish military and other posts within the territories inhabited by the said tribes" (note the use of "inhabited" rather than "their country") and their agreement "to refrain in future from war-like incursions into the Mexican provinces" and "to restore all captives that may hereafter be taken." In return, the Kiowas, Comanches, and Plains Apaches were to be paid an annuity of $18,000 per year in goods, similar to those paid to Native nations to the east when they had their land taken.[100]

The text of the treaty was not what Kiowas had actually agreed to orally, so, not surprisingly, the next year the U.S. Indian agent had to report that Kiowas "deny ever having consented not to war on Mexicans." They continued to "think that Uncle Sam is a weak old fellow, and could be easily overcome, and they have good reasons for coming to that conclusion. Nearly every party of emigrants that pass through their country have to pay their way with sugar and coffee."[101] Officials stationed in the West knew there was little the United States could do other than launch what one called "a war of extermination," which would be both "opposed to all dictates of humanity" and, in any case, "an utter impossibility" in these "regions where footsteps leave no trace, and where no fixed habitations afford an object of attack"—a description of the Plains that is strikingly similar to that recorded by the Francisco de Coronado expedition three centuries earlier.[102]

In the absence of real power, the United States kept changing the rules. When the U.S. Indian agent met with Comanches and Kiowas at Fort Atkinson in 1854 to pay them their annuity goods, he called a council of the chiefs and told them that Congress had amended their most recent treaty to allow the president to provide their annuity in the form of help establishing farms in their country. The sarcasm in Little Bluff's reply comes through in the account that the U.S. commissioners wrote: Farms were "just what he wanted," and if their "Great Father," President James Buchanan, "was going to take pity on them and send them farmers," he should "also send them land that would produce corn, as they had none that would." The agent had to write his superior acknowledging that "I fully agree with Tohansen [Little Bluff], that the entire country occupied by the Kiowas is worthless for agricultural purposes."[103]

Four years later, in 1858, U.S. officials were still writing back to Washington that, despite immigrants passing through and despite declining bison numbers, the Plains Indian "may well be pardoned his egotism in believing his people more than a match for the white man; for it is seldom you can find one who is not fully satisfied of their superiority. Having no adequate knowledge of the extent of our possessions, or the number of our people, and meeting only year after year the same faces of those trading with New Mexico, they naturally fall into the belief that we are few in number."[104] A U.S. official warned Little Bluff that if Kiowas continued to attack westward caravans, Buchanan "would not only withhold their presents, but would send his soldiers against them to burn their villages and take captive their women and children."

Little Bluff listened until the official had finished, then rose to his feet, pointing to the vast number of Kiowa and Comanche tipis spread across the valley below, and said,

> The white chief is a fool; he is a coward; his heart is small—not larger than a pebble stone; his men are not strong—too few to contend against my warriors; they are women. There are three chiefs—the white chief, the Spanish chief, and myself. The Spanish and myself are men; we do bad towards each other sometimes, stealing horses and taking scalps, but we do not get mad and act the fool. The white chief is a child, and like a child gets mad quick. When my young men, to keep their women and children from starving, take from the white man passing through our country, killing and driving away our buffalo, a cup of sugar or coffee, the white chief is angry and threatens to send his soldiers. I have looked for them a long time, but they have not come; he is a coward; his heart is a woman's. I have spoken. Tell the "great chief" what I have said.[105]

Little Bluff's speech to the blustering U.S. official is strikingly similar to scenes throughout the previous centuries and throughout this book, in which would-be colonizers crash into places they do not understand, only to have locals explain, using words or violence, how power and ownership actually work there. U.S. reports from the

1850s reveal that Native Americans still held power over the vast territory between the Mississippi Valley and the Pacific coast. Yet these officials retained a confidence in their own superiority that their European predecessors, in most cases, quickly dropped. The difference was that they had seen one mighty Native nation after another fall before their young country: Algonquian and Haudenosaunee nations, Cherokees, Quapaws, and hundreds of others were struggling to continue in a world dramatically changed by U.S. power and numbers. Officials' reports to Washington about their encounters with Plains Indians contain, along with their frustrations, a confidence about the future and a genocidal edge. In 1854, one Indian agent wrote to his superior that it was "evident to every man who has travelled over the plains recently, that the time is not very far distant when the buffalo will cease to furnish a support for the immense number of Indians that now rely entirely on them for subsistence; and as soon as this is the case, starvation is inevitable."[106] These officials endured their frustrations in the belief that "at no distant day the whole country over which those Indians now roam must be peopled by another and more enterprising race."[107]

In O'odham country, the United States used its by now well-honed methods to undermine Native people's way of life. When Antonio Azul asked the U.S. agent when the Akimel O'odham were going to receive the farming tools promised to them as a reciprocal thank-you for aiding U.S. immigrants (tools that they, unlike the Kiowas, could use), the agent replied that they would be coming soon, because Congress had appropriated $10,000 to pay for them and for a survey of the region that would mark the boundaries of a sixty-four-thousand-acre O'odham reservation. Not knowing the legal ramifications of a "reservation" within U.S. law, the O'odham figured that well-defined borders would be in their best interest against settlers in the region from both the United States and Mexico. Yet when the tools arrived, the agent had changed the proposal. He suggested a much smaller reservation that would take the Akimel O'odham resource-gathering and grazing areas and leave them with only the land around their farms and towns. It was an outrageous request from an ally and dependent trading partner.[108]

For the time being, U.S. officials could not persuade the O'odham to accept a reservation or restrict their ways of living. A few years later, in 1865, when a U.S. agent tried to get the more than six thousand Tohono O'odham who seasonally migrated around their large desert region to move in with the two hundred O'odham who lived at Bac on the Santa Cruz River, he had no success at all. By then the Catholic Church in the United States had taken over jurisdiction of the church there, begun repairs, and sent a priest. But the priest stayed only eight months and was not replaced for another decade. This was still O'odham country, but, as on the Plains, there was evidence of U.S. encroachment that anyone who had experienced it in the East could have interpreted as a very bad sign. Looking back, we know that the U.S. immigrants passing through and the officials and soldiers tasked with protecting them very soon would become the biggest threats to Native ways of life all across the Plains.[109]

THE UNITED STATES COMES APART

In the late 1800s, the United States would expand its dominance beyond the Mississippi Valley and across the continent, yet from 1861 to 1865 it appeared that history might go quite a different way. The U.S. Civil War temporarily put a stop to U.S. expansion and almost ended the United States itself. Nations and civilizations had fallen in the past, and, for a few years, it appeared that this one might have run its course.

During the Civil War, Kiowas mostly continued the kinds of raiding they had done in the past, taking advantage of growing opportunities as U.S. forces were busy fighting in the Civil War and against the Cheyennes and Dakotas, who took advantage of the war to strike at the United States. Kiowas and Comanches wreaked havoc on towns in Texas and Mexico as well as on U.S. migrants crossing the Plains to California and Oregon, now that the U.S. troops who had attempted to protect the Santa Fe Trail were occupied with fighting the Confederacy.[110]

Some Native nations geographically closer to the Civil War saw opportunity in joining the Confederacy. Both the Confederacy and the Union recruited Cherokee, Chickasaw, Choctaw, Muscogee, and Seminole assistance in the war. The governor of the seceded state of Arkansas wrote to Cherokee Principal Chief John Ross, whose post-removal nation bordered Arkansas on the west, appealing to his economic interests as a slaveholder: "Your people in their institutions, productions, latitude and Natural sympathies are allied to the common Brotherhood of the Slave holding States," whereas Abraham Lincoln saw Indian Territory "as fruitful fields, ripe for the harvest of Abolishionism, free soils, and northern montebanks."[111]

Indeed, President Lincoln's secretary of state, in an 1860 speech, had advocated appropriating lands of the Cherokees, Choctaws, Chickasaws, Muscogees, and Seminoles to give to white homesteaders, the main constituency of his Republican Party. When the U.S. commissioner for Indian affairs found out about the Confederate recruitment efforts, he wrote to promise the Cherokees and others in Indian Territory that "the government would under no circumstances permit the smallest interference with their tribal or domestic institutions," that is, their sovereignty, including the right to enslave. John Ross at first tried to keep the Cherokees neutral in the war, but Stand Watie raised a regiment for the Confederacy, the Cherokee Mounted Rifles, and ultimately became a Confederate brigadier general. After early victories by Watie's Cherokees and Chickasaw and Choctaw fighters, all three nations signed treaties with the Confederacy.[112]

It may seem strange that Cherokees who had been dispossessed by Georgia plantations would support the Confederacy, but many believed that allying with the South would advance Cherokee sovereignty, protect individual Native men's rights including the right to own slaves, and provide new arenas in which young men could fight. One of the greatest proponents was E. C. Boudinot, son of Elias and Harriett Boudinot and nephew of Stand Watie. After his father was killed, orphaned three-year-old E. C. was sent to his mother's family in Connecticut for his safety and education. At eighteen, he left New England for Fayetteville, Arkansas, where Sarah Ridge had fled with her children. E. C. Boudinot and John

Rollin Ridge (son of Sarah and John Ridge) studied law under Fayetteville's first mayor. Like his father, E. C. Boudinot published a newspaper. Started in 1859, *The Arkansian* was a pro-South and pro-slavery paper and soon also pro-secession. He served as a delegate and secretary to the Arkansas secession convention, an officer under Stand Watie, and the delegate to the Confederate Congress for the Cherokee Nation. John Rollin Ridge started a similar paper in California and in 1856 wrote to Democratic U.S. Senator Stephen Douglas to air his disappointment that, in a speech, "you seem to put Indians and Negroes upon an equality," when Indians were "vastly superior, in every respect, to any portion of the Negro race."[113]

In addition to the racist and pro-slavery sentiments that some Cherokees held, there were reasons to believe that Cherokees would be better off in the Confederacy than in the Union. Most obviously, the Confederacy needed them more, and so they had leverage. The state constitution that Arkansas adopted during the Civil War guaranteed rights to Native men right alongside white men. It declared that "the right of trial by jury shall remain inviolate to free white men and Indians," "the free white men and Indians of this State have the right to keep and bear arms for their individual or common defence," and "no free white man or Indian shall be taken, or imprisoned, or disseized of his freehold, liberties, or privileges, or outlawed, or exiled, or in any manner destroyed or deprived of his life, liberty or property, but by the judgment of his peers, or the law of the land." In the protections against "exile," it's particularly easy to see the pen of E. C. Boudinot in his role as delegate to the Arkansas convention, remembering how his family had been thrust into exile at the beginning of his young life. This state constitution offered no such protections for Black men, instead explicitly legalizing their enslavement and complete disfranchisement.[114]

The Quapaws and the Shawnees found themselves trapped between sides in the Civil War. By the mid-1850s, crop failures and hard times had persuaded many Quapaws to try living elsewhere, so there were only around 350 Quapaws on their reservation in Indian Territory when the war broke out. When the U.S. troops who had been stationed nearby left to fight elsewhere and neighboring Confederates put pressure on the Quapaws, they signed a treaty with the Confederacy. In 1862, though, Civil War violence in northeastern Oklahoma grew so intense that Quapaws there sought protection on the Ottawa reservation, in Kansas, where other Quapaws had moved previously. There, the Quapaws joined the Ottawas in supporting the Union, and at least sixty Quapaw men fought on the Union side in the Civil War.[115]

With some Shawnees in Kansas and some in Indian Territory, Shawnees likewise ended up on both sides in the Civil War. Originally, Kansas had been part of Indian Territory, but in the 1854 Kansas–Nebraska Act, Congress had created the Territory of Kansas. Pro-slavery and anti-slavery partisans rushed into "bleeding Kansas" to shoot each other and stuff ballot boxes for their side. As in the Ohio Valley, Shawnees found livestock illegally grazing on their growing crops and cabins popping up nearby. U.S. settlers stole horses and pigs and raided women's food storage. The Shawnees had to cede most of their land, shrinking their Kansas reservation from 1.6 million acres to around two hundred thousand non-contiguous acres, surrounded by one hundred thousand settlers. During the war, many Shawnees became refugees as violence continued to cross their land. Shawnee men in Kansas volunteered to fight for the Union in hopes of benefiting from their loyalty, while some of those who had moved to Indian Territory fought for the Confederacy.[116]

In the East, a Seneca man named Hasanoanda would use the opportunities of the Civil War to build a prominent career in the United States and to try to help Native people more generally. He grew up on a Seneca reservation in western New York with his Seneca parents, who were Baptists and baptized him Ely Parker, in addition to his Haudenosaunee name. He attended missionary school and college and studied law in New York State but was forbidden from taking the bar exam because he wasn't a U.S. citizen, so he served as an interpreter for the Haudenosaunee and earned a graduate degree in engineering. When the Civil War broke out, Parker offered to raise a Haudenosaunee regiment for the Union but was turned down. He instead worked as an engineer on the staff of General Ulysses S.

Grant and eventually became Grant's military secretary and adjutant general. In that role, Parker drafted the Confederate surrender agreement at Appomattox and the treaty agreements with the Cherokees and other surrendering Native nations in the West.

General Grant's staff, with Ely Parker on the far left and Grant in the middle, photograph by Matthew Brady.
LIBRARY OF CONGRESS

When Grant became president, in 1869, he chose Parker to be his commissioner of Indian affairs, the first Native American to hold that post. They implemented a "peace policy" to cease fighting Native nations and recognize their treaty rights and semi-autonomy on their reservations. Parker and Grant believed that Native Americans should be protected from incursions on their reservations and that, as for African Americans and immigrants, becoming U.S. citizens with full citizenship rights would help them to protect themselves and promote their own interests. They were opposed, though, by Americans who thought the policy too generous, especially in its insistence that reservations not be further reduced in size. Grant's own Board of Indian Commissioners worked against Parker, its chair demanding that the "savage" be stripped of his position and persuading Congress to pass legislation putting the board in charge. Without Parker's leadership, Grant succumbed to pressure to fight Native Americans in the West, including Kiowas, as we shall see.

There would not be another Native American at the head of U.S. Indian Affairs until nearly a century later, when another Haudenosaunee, Oneida Robert Bennett, was appointed in 1966.[117]

The Civil War forced Native nations into new relationships with the United States, especially as it emerged as a more powerful and unified nation after Reconstruction. For the rest of the nineteenth and twentieth centuries, U.S. policy would fluctuate between brutal violence against American Indians and attempts to incorporate them into the United States, whether on an equal basis, as Parker wanted, or as second-class citizens. Both kinds of policies sought to erode Native sovereignty. The United States treated the Cherokees, Chickasaws, and Choctaws like surrendered secessionists, even though they could hardly have seceded when they had never agreed to be part of the United States. The Cherokees and the other nations who had sided with the Confederacy were forced to surrender half of their lands in Indian Territory. Like the Southern states, Native nations had to free their slaves and grant citizenship rights to Black men in their nations. Slaveholding Native nations fought this forced equality just as hard as the former Confederate states did. They argued that their own sovereignty continued to allow them to enslave people. When the U.S. government rejected that argument, they, like the Southern states, created systems of inequality that kept people of African descent from their full citizenship rights for generations, rights that are still incomplete today.[118]

Cherokees Stand Watie and E. C. Boudinot continued to try to advance both their own interests and those of Cherokee sovereignty. When the U.S. Congress passed a national tax on tobacco in 1868, Boudinot and Watie refused to pay, arguing in the *Cherokee Tobacco* case that Cherokees should be exempt because the postwar treaty that their nation had signed with the United States exempted Cherokee citizens (as well as former slaves living in the Cherokee Nation) from paying taxes on farm products. In 1870, the U.S. Supreme Court ruled against them, deciding that the federal government could impose a tax on the Cherokees because the Cherokee Nation was not a foreign nation but, in the words of *Cherokee Nation v. Georgia* and *Worcester v. Georgia*, a "domestic dependent nation." The opinion that U.S. laws could unilaterally override treaties would have implications far into the future.[119]

RESURGENCE OF U.S. POWER

Even during the Civil War, people from the United States had fought Native people in the West, and the war's end would intensify U.S. attacks on Native land and sovereignty and put the full force of a strong nation-state behind them. From 31.5 million in 1860 (more than eight times its 1790 population), the United States grew to fifty million in 1880 and seventy-six million by 1900. In the late years of the war, the U.S. reaction to Dakota and Cheyenne military victories and continued Kiowa and Comanche raiding was brutal. Tens of thousands of troops came west, armed with repeating rifles, the rapid-fire Gatling gun, and a new purpose in fighting together after a bitter civil war. At the end of the Dakota War, the U.S. Army hanged thirty-eight Dakota men, the largest number of people executed in a single day in the United States. In 1863, the United States destroyed Navajo farms and grazing lands in a method reminiscent of Sullivan's destruction of Mohawk country during the American Revolution, and the following year the U.S. Army put Navajos on a forced march four hundred miles from their homeland to a prison camp at Bosque Redondo, in New Mexico. That same year, in what became known as the Sand Creek Massacre, a Colorado cavalry unit rode into a camp filled with Cheyenne and Arapaho women and children. Ignoring the white flag and the U.S. flag the Cheyennes and Arapahos were flying, the cavalrymen killed a large number of people, probably several hundred, in one of the worst atrocities of the Plains Wars.[120]

During the Civil War, the Republican Congress passed the Homestead Act of 1862, granting western land to poor easterners. By 1900, nearly six hundred thousand families—white and Black Americans and European immigrants—moved west under the auspices of the Homestead Act. In the 1840s and '50s, it had seemed possible that the United States would be content to take the fertile

Forty thousand bison hides, Dodge City, Kansas, 1878.
U.S. NATIONAL ARCHIVES

lands of the Mississippi Valley and leave the arid Plains mostly alone, merely crossing them to get to the Pacific coast. But extensive agriculture on the Plains became economically viable when steel plows and other technologies enabled farming in large parts of Kansas, Nebraska, and Oklahoma (which would lead to the ecological catastrophe of the Dust Bowl in the 1930s), and the construction of the transcontinental railroad allowed cattle as well as wheat to be shipped from the Plains to U.S. cities. Knowing that the Plains were Native hunting lands, U.S. farmers, ranchers, and military leaders encouraged the slaughter of the bison to destroy the long-established Native Plains economy.

The objective now was to condense all American Indians east of the Rocky Mountains into Indian Territory, shoehorning Plains peoples into the space already occupied by those removed from the East. The U.S. Congress tried to legislate Native nations out of existence by passing an 1871 law that "hereafter no Indian nation or tribe within the territory of the United States shall be acknowledged or recognized as an independent nation, tribe, or power with whom the United States may contract by treaty." The new law did not invalidate previous treaties, and in practice the United States continued to make "agreements" with Native nations, but, as legal scholar and Turtle Mountain Band of Chippewa Indians tribal judge Keith

Richotte points out, the change was part of a long "move from thinking about Native peoples in the international sphere to the domestic realm."[121]

Some Native Americans, including Ely Parker, believed that, in the face of so much deliberate destruction, the best path was to become U.S. citizens and fight for political and economic rights as Americans. E. C. Boudinot, having lost the *Cherokee Tobacco* case against federal taxation, decided on that course. More Native Americans, though, agreed instead with Cherokee National Council Senator Walter Adair Duncan, whose letter to the editor of the *Cherokee Advocate* in 1893 declared that "for my part I am not prepared for citizenship in the United States. I do not want it." Like E. C. Boudinot, Duncan wrote in English, but he did not want to be made a citizen of a foreign country.[122]

Despite Quapaws having fought for the Union, at the end of the war the U.S. Office of Indian Affairs declared that, because some Quapaws had made a treaty with the Confederacy, the United States was ending its treaty-obligated annuity payments and land agreements. Describing the circumstances of the treaty with the Confederacy, Quapaw leaders persuaded the U.S. officials that it did not reflect true Quapaw sentiment. As the Union Army retook Oklahoma, the Quapaws took the opportunity to move back to their reservation. They found their fields, houses, fences, and livestock plundered and destroyed by war and the cows of white cattlemen grazing on their shrunken farmlands. The Quapaws sold some of their remaining land to obtain the money to rebuild, but they were able to insist that some of that land go to the Peorias, who also needed a land base to start again.[123]

Even when they lived in other nations, Quapaws retained not only their tribal identity but also their affiliation with their traditional town-based political structure, despite the fact that they had lost those Quapaw towns long before. After several years of hardship, starvation, the ravages of disease, and demands by the U.S. Indian Agent that they stop living and farming communally and instead live on individual homesteads with men doing the farming, many Quapaw families decamped to take refuge with the Osages.

Almost all of the Quapaws who moved to the Osage reservation in the 1870s were members of two of the old towns. Despite U.S. government attempts to change them, women continued to farm, and Quapaws remained organized as three groups aligned with the three traditional towns, each with its own chief. They held annual dances in the summer to bring the whole nation together.[124]

Despite Shawnee service in the war, Kansans pushed them out of their state entirely by 1871. As part of the punishment of the Cherokees, the United States in 1869 forced that nation to carve lands out of its reservation for Shawnees and even allow Shawnees to become Cherokee citizens. They told the Shawnees that they had to leave their Kansas reservation and accept either Cherokee or U.S. citizenship. Most of the Shawnees still in Kansas moved in with the Cherokees, but others made different choices, including U.S. citizenship in Kansas, moving in with the Potawatomis in Indian Territory, and returning to lands some of them had previously lived on in Indian Territory at the forks of the Canadian River. The Shawnees who moved to the Cherokee Nation still tended to live in their own towns, as they had during other diasporas.[125]

In the East, Native peoples who had evaded removal continued to try to stay under the radar, to avoid violence or expulsion. In 1866, under pressure from the federal government during Reconstruction, North Carolina finally acknowledged the Eastern Band of Cherokee Indians' right to their tribal lands as a reservation. After Reconstruction, as Jim Crow descended on the postwar South, many Native people who had voting and other political and economic rights as free people of color even during the period of slavery now were the targets of discriminatory laws, segregation, and racial violence. Lumbee Henry Berry Lowry led a fight into the postwar years against the Confederate Home Guard. Lowry and his men armed themselves and robbed the wealthy to redistribute food to the poor, especially Lumbees and other people of Native and African descent (portrayed in the Lumbee play *Strike at the Wind!*). Throughout the subsequent decades, Native nations from Florida to Virginia would find various ways to carve out a Native space within the increasingly segregated South.[126]

The post–Civil War years increased U.S. power over the Kiowas. In the fall of 1865, Kiowas, Comanches, and Plains Apaches agreed to the Little Arkansas Treaty, in which they promised to stay south of the Arkansas River and away from the Santa Fe Trail. The text of the treaty assigned them reservation lands in the Texas and Oklahoma panhandles, but it was such a large region that it did not really function as a reservation, and Kiowas continued raiding to the south. Yet in retrospect, it is easy to see the rise of U.S. power on the Plains. Cheyennes and Arapahos were already being pressured onto reservations, and the Little Arkansas Treaty reflects the U.S. tactic of inserting the language of reservations into treaties. Over the following two years, Texans complained to the federal government about Indian raids, and U.S. will and power to step in on their side grew.[127]

Kiowas had little reason to consider Texas part of the United States, seeing that, as they explained to U.S. commissioners, the United States "had been at war with the people of Texas," but with the Civil War in the past and Texans back in the fold, the U.S. government in 1867 acted to protect Texas by forcing the Kiowas, Comanches, and Plains Apaches into their first major concessions. Along with their Cheyenne and Arapaho allies, Kiowas, Comanches, and Plains Apaches signed the Treaty of Medicine Lodge and were assigned as a reservation a section of their lands in what's now southwestern Oklahoma, north of the Red River and south of the Washita, with hunting rights up the Arkansas River. In return, U.S. officials agreed that any additional cessions would require the approval of three-fourths of adult men in the Kiowa, Comanche, and Plains Apache nations.[128]

The Treaty of Medicine Lodge reflected growing U.S. power, and it is the first treaty to appear as a significant event in Kiowa calendars, but it was during the Red River War of the 1870s that U.S. forces killed and captured enough men, women, and children to persuade the Kiowas to confine themselves to the reservation the written treaty had outlined. By the summer of 1879, military losses and an inability to hunt had left Kiowas eating their horses for sustenance. N. Scott Momaday writes of how his Kiowa ancestors "came in, a few at a time, to surrender at Fort Sill. Their horses and weapons were confiscated, and they were imprisoned. In a field just west of the post, the Indian ponies were destroyed. Nearly eight hundred horses were killed outright; two thousand more were sold, stolen, given away." Compressed onto only part of their former vast lands and stripped of their livelihood, the Kiowas were on a true reservation. By that time, many Kiowa war leaders had been captured and forced onto trains carrying them far from home. Most of them were imprisoned at Fort Marion, in Florida, over a thousand miles from home.[129]

Horse-Eating Sun Dance, Silver Horn's calendar, summer 1879.
MANUSCRIPT 2531, NATIONAL MUSEUM OF NATURAL HISTORY,
SMITHSONIAN INSTITUTION

It was after the Civil War that thousands of Americans appeared in Akimel, Tohono, and Hia-Ced O'odham country. They, as well as some Mexican settlers, illegally built farms and ranches just east of the Akimel O'odham towns on the Gila. Because they were upriver, they took water that Akimel O'odham farms needed. For the time being, Akimel O'odham farmers adapted by growing more oats and barley, which need less irrigation than corn.[130]

Tohono and Hia-Ced O'odham saw newcomers establish copper, silver, and lead mines in their country, then abandon them when the ore ran dry. Tohono men sometimes worked in the short-lived mining camps as part of their seasonal employment, which continued to include working on Akimel farms on the Gila River and Mexican farms on the Altar. Ranchers appeared at Tohono and Hia-Ced O'odham reservoirs with their thirsty and messy animals, but ranching, like mining, had its booms and busts, and the ranchers and their cattle didn't stay long. Conflicts with more numerous ranchers and miners were more serious for the O'odham who still lived on the Mexican side of the border, and over time many families moved north to live closer to the Tohono O'odham and establish their own cattle ranches. Together they made annual pilgrimages every fall to Magdalena, on the Altar (today an hour's drive south of the U.S. border), to celebrate O'odham rituals that had incorporated elements of Catholicism.[131]

CONCLUSION

In the fall of 1873, Antonio Azul and four other Akimel O'odham and Piipaash representatives traveled to see lands in Indian Territory, a thousand miles from their home. U.S. officials, hoping to finish the job of Indian Removal and move all Native people to Indian Territory, told them that there was plenty of water, and no white settlers. It was a long journey by horseback and the Kansas Pacific Railway across the Plains. Those who made the trip apparently were impressed with the possibility of a new start in a new place, but back home no one was for it, neither liking the idea of leaving their desert homes nor trusting the U.S. government's promises. Instead, the Akimel O'odham and the Piipaash spread their farms out to stretch their water resources further, some families leaving the Gila River entirely to farm on the Salt River or on springs, remaining in places where their Huhugam ancestors had farmed centuries earlier.[132]

In the nineteenth century, many Native nations were deported from their homelands and had to rebuild in an alien place. Others, like the descendants of the Huhugam in the West and of Ossomocomuck in the East, were squeezed into smaller and smaller parts of the land that once was theirs. The next chapter will trace the devastating changes of the late nineteenth and twentieth centuries for the peoples we've been following in this book and show how they managed to survive into the renaissance and possibilities of the present.

CHAPTER 12

THE SURVIVAL OF NATIONS

SOMETIME IN THE 1930S, MEMBERS OF THE MAU-TAME CLUB posed for a picture. They arranged themselves so that each woman's buckskin dress and headband, with their distinctive beadwork, were visible. Like most Kiowas, these women lived on what was left of their reservation in Oklahoma, but the picture was taken in Gallup, New Mexico. Mau-Tame means "Showing the Way" in Kiowa, and the club had been started in 1921 by the U.S. Office of Indian Affairs to encourage Kiowa women to learn how to keep house like white women. But by the 1930s the Mau-Tame Club was showing a more Kiowa way, promoting the sale of Native art by its Kiowa members and women from nearby Native nations in Oklahoma. Club members like the ones in the picture traveled to the annual Gallup Intertribal Ceremonial to dance and to sell their beadwork purses, moccasins, and cradleboards.

The Kiowa art historian Jenny Tone-Pah-Hote explains that when women wore their own beadwork in intertribal gatherings such as the Gallup ceremonial, non-Native customers and observers might have assumed they were displaying a generic Indianness, but in fact a woman's beadwork reflected her individual and family Kiowa style. In Oklahoma, when Kiowas gave a pair of beaded moccasins away or traded them for a horse to another Kiowa or someone from a different Native nation, they confirmed networks of community. They established a distinct southern Plains identity within Indian Territory with their longtime allies the Comanches and Plains Apaches and also the Cheyennes, Arapahos, Wichitas, and

Mau-Tame Club, Gallup, New Mexico, 1930s.
ALICE JONES LITTLEMAN COLLECTION, #9, WESTERN HISTORY
COLLECTION, UNIVERSITY OF OKLAHOMA

Caddos, based on parallel histories as well as artistic traditions, in-cluding beadwork and silverwork. Along with Native peoples throughout the continent, they worked for Native rights. And at the same time, they resolutely remained Kiowa, even as the United States continued to try to destroy them.[1]

Between the 1850s, when most of North America still belonged to Native nations, and the time these Kiowa women posed for their picture in the 1930s, much had changed. Kiowas and other Native peoples in the West experienced wars and dispossessions as geno-cidal as those that the descendants of Ossomocomuck and the Mo-hawks, Quapaws, Shawnees, and Cherokees had already faced. And, just when Native Americans were rebuilding their political and eco-nomic structures after removal and dispossession, the United States, Canada, and Mexico in the late nineteenth and early twentieth cen-turies launched new initiatives to force them to stop being Indians. These assaults on tribal sovereignty and Native families encom-passed everything from banning self-government and Indigenous religious ceremonies and language to taking their children away to faraway boarding schools. A series of court cases, laws, wars, and civilian violence made the decades from the end of the Civil War through the 1920s what Professor Keith Richotte calls "the darkest period in American history for Native peoples." In these years, Native nations truly might have disappeared if not for people's dedication to their nations and their absolute determination to remain Quapaws, Cherokees, Mohawks, Lumbees, Coharies, Saponis, Kiowas, Tohono O'odham, Akimel O'odham, and hundreds of other distinct nations.[2]

In the 1910s, Seneca archaeologist Arthur Parker marveled that his Haudenosaunee people had survived at all. The existence of more than sixteen thousand Haudenosaunee at the start of the twentieth century was, he reflected, "a remarkable fact when it is considered that they are entirely surrounded by a dominant culture whose encroachments are persistent and unrelenting."[3] Fifty years later, anthropologist William Fenton put the same sentiment in the form of a question:

> Why has Iroquois culture survived into the present century? In three hundred years of continuous contact with aggressive white people in the country's most populous state, several Iroquoian languages are still spoken from Brooklyn to Niagara. The voices of Seneca drummers rise from the swamps of Tonawanda and echo on the Allegheny hills. Masks are still carved in response to dreams, and the Falseface Society makes its spring and fall rounds. . . . The kettle endures as a symbol of hospitality, although corn soup is cooked in aluminum ware instead of iron kettles hung over the fire, or in stone-propped earthen pots. The Seneca Nation is a republic, but at Tonawanda and Onondaga chiefs are elected by clan matrons and raised with the Condolence Council.[4]

In the twenty-first century, well over a hundred thousand citizens of the Haudenosaunee nations live on and off Haudenosaunee territory on both sides of the U.S.–Canada border.[5]

In 2003, Tohono O'odham elders and scholars Daniel Lopez, Joseph T. Joaquin, Stanley Cruz, and Angelo J. Joaquin Jr. similarly reflected on the centuries in which "we have struggled to maintain himdag in the face of change." Spaniards, Mexicans, white Americans, and ongoing conflict on the U.S.–Mexico border "each challenged our culture and our connection to the land. In each case, we adapted by making choices that fit our way of life." In previous generations and still today, they wrote, "we are 'desert people.'"[6] Jenny Tone-Pah-Hote puzzled as she looked at the photograph of the Mau-Tame Club and held a silver cup made by her grandfather, etched all around with a warrior on horseback chasing a bison: "Was this part of how Kiowa people remained, well, Kiowa people?"[7]

Native Americans today live with the loss and trauma echoing from nineteenth- and twentieth-century attempts to destroy them, through both physical violence and repeated messages that being Native was backward and wrong. Rates of missing and murdered Indigenous women are so high that they are recognized as an epidemic. Many Native Americans live in poverty because economic damage from being robbed of their sources of wealth and sustenance has compounded over the years. Their stolen lands and African Americans' stolen labor subsidized white landownership and economic development, creating inequality in wealth and opportunity that today still advantages white Americans over Native and Black Americans. Tribes spend precious resources in U.S. and state courts defending their remaining sovereignty and property against perpetual attacks and buying back land that once was theirs. Yet they are still here, as individuals, as families, as communities, and as nations.[8]

Against the odds, Native America is experiencing a renaissance today as more young people are learning the languages, arts and crafts, and ceremonies of their ancestors and publicly asserting their tribal identities. If you watched the state roll call during the 2020 Democratic National Convention, you heard several delegates speaking their Native languages, a small sign of a sea change as Indigenous languages and cultures come out of concealment and take their rightful place in the American tapestry.

The first ten chapters in this book provided snapshots of a few Native nations in eras when they undeniably had the military and demographic power to protect their sovereignty. That power eroded in the East in the eighteenth century and in the West in the nineteenth with U.S. military and demographic growth. Native nations used what power they had within U.S. institutions to argue in Congress and the courts that the United States must follow its own laws and treaties. This chapter follows these nations through the era when, as Quapaw Tribal Historic Preservation Officer Everett Bandy reflects, Native nations faced the greatest threats to their nationhood. I have been inspired and informed by Native scholars of the nineteenth and twentieth centuries, including Bandy, Cherokee historian Julie Reed, and Lumbee historian Malinda Maynor Lowery, to retell even this worst era as transformation and survival rather than just victimization and erasure. As Professor Lowery explains, "We are not only victims; not just a collection of myths, legends, and stories. American Indians are the cocreators of this nation of 'one, yet many,' on which rests so much of the world's hope."[9]

This chapter provides but a quick overview of this long and complicated history, paying particular attention to the Native nations highlighted in earlier chapters. I hope readers will check out the books in my "Further Reading" suggestions, many of which are written by Native authors focusing on their own nations in the twentieth and twenty-first centuries.[10]

Because their ancestors fought so hard to survive, Native Americans are now able to reassert new kinds of power, having forced U.S. institutions back toward recognizing the legal and treaty rights of Native nations as well as the civil rights of individual Native Americans. Native nations have combined economic and cultural development to build economies that reinvigorate traditions while creating jobs and bringing in tribal revenue. As in the past, mutual support among Native nations has helped them to survive and thrive.

RESERVATIONS

By the 1880s, there wasn't a Native nation that hadn't been touched by U.S. aggression. They had been forced from their homes and crowded into places with former enemies and complete strangers or had managed to stay on small fractions of their original homelands, often cut off from the ways they had made their living before. White Americans crowded tens of thousands of Native Americans onto smaller and smaller spaces in Indian Territory and the other places where Native communities remained on the continent. Yet these reservations, large and small, became new homelands where Native nations rebuilt, painfully but necessarily. Reservations were Native places, and people kept their communities alive there.

On the Plains, the process of dispossession had happened especially fast. In less than fifty years, the Kiowas went from controlling the Plains to being confined to reservations and dependent on U.S. Indian agents. They no longer could hunt, and the land was lousy for farming. The agents distributed food, undermining the authority of leaders and parents and leaving no means for men or women to make their own living. Quarantine was more difficult on the reservation; an 1896 measles outbreak killed an estimated 15 percent of the Kiowa population. Crow woman Pretty Shield reflected that she was "trying to live a life that I do not understand."[11]

On reservations, Native people in the late nineteenth century faced extreme efforts to destroy their cultures, their histories, and their national pride. Indian agents were charged with rooting out ceremonies and dances. Fearing both the religious and military threats of the Sun Dance, which convened large numbers of Plains nations and reaffirmed their alliances, the United States outlawed it, sent troops to prevent summer gatherings, and set up courts to prosecute offenders. The Kiowas and the Plains Apaches performed their last Sun Dance in 1887. The lack of bison had undermined the ceremony by then anyway.[12]

Even though Native Americans didn't want reservations in the first place, they shifted to trying to preserve reservations rather than give up that land to continuing U.S. pressure. A nation forced from its homeland and crowded into a smaller piece of land could still be a nation, could still speak its own language, hold its own ceremonies, conduct its own affairs domestically, and tell its own history. Even as they were places of confinement, reservations became vital spaces where tribal governments maintained some authority and where

Native people continued to exist as autonomous communities. Preserving reservations meant not only stopping land loss but saving a land base as a national space that was the basis of continuing tribal sovereignty. On these slivers of land, Native nations rebuilt government institutions, schools, and networks that spanned beyond their territories. The Cherokees, Shawnees, and Choctaws all had printing presses in Indian Territory by the 1840s and published newspapers and books in their languages and those of neighboring Native nations.[13]

In the 1870s, Native nations with reservations in Indian Territory went even further. They tried to establish a General Council of the Indian Territory to govern it themselves in perpetuity, partly to ward off what the United States would do one day: make the region into a U.S. territory and eventually the state of Oklahoma. From 1870 to 1875, representatives of nearly thirty Native nations—including Quapaws, Shawnees, Cherokees, and Kiowas—met as a General Council of the Indian Territory at Okmulgee, the capital of the Muscogee Nation, with the support of Ely Parker, then commissioner of Indian affairs. Through a large number of interpreters, they discussed various concerns. Stand Watie shared his exasperation over how the U.S. Supreme Court ruling in the *Cherokee Tobacco* case violated "the sanctity and supremacy of treaties." The Kiowas sought help persuading the United States to free the prisoners held at Fort Marion. Together the delegates drafted a constitution for the governance of Indian Territory as "a free and independent Nation, not inconsistent with the Constitution, Treaties and Laws of the United States." It would have a bicameral legislature, a judiciary, and a president, and all of the representatives would be citizens of one of the Native nations of Indian Territory and elected by those nations according to their own methods. It would be a confederacy of those nations, which would retain their separate sovereignties, the constitution affirming "that the rights of each of these nations to its lands, funds and all other property, shall remain the sole and distinct property of such nation."[14]

The plan for a self-governed Indian Territory never materialized, but treaties that created reservations had embedded Native nations in U.S. treaty law, which U.S. courts recognize as binding. These treaties also form the basis for federal recognition, which became tremendously important for retaining and rebuilding sovereignty in the twentieth and twenty-first centuries. Federal recognition means that a tribe has a government-to-government relationship with the United States. While Native nations were, of course, sovereign before there even was a United States, having federal support for and acknowledgment of their inherent tribal sovereignty can be essential for tribes so that they can enact their authority over their lands, peoples, and resources. For example, federal recognition provides support for tribal nations in their relations with states and towns on their borders and ensures that they have legal standing in U.S. courts to pursue remediation for past damages.[15]

THE NADIR

At the end of the nineteenth century, a new round of federal laws and actions in the United States as well as Canada and Mexico began to wage, in Ojibwe scholar Anton Treuer's apt words, a "war on Indian culture." Part of the impetus came from the ending of the Reconstruction era in the late 1870s, when southern state after southern state overturned Reconstruction's extension of political rights and educational and economic opportunities to Black Americans and implemented harsh systems of segregation and reprisal, in violation of the postwar amendments to the U.S. Constitution. The post-Reconstruction backlash ushered in a new era of white supremacy in the late nineteenth and early twentieth centuries, with disastrous consequences for nonwhite people in North America and beyond. The eighteenth-century belief that all men could become equal was ethnocentric in its insistence that equal meant becoming like Europeans, but the "scientific" racism of this later era was even more insidious, insisting on the permanent inferiority of nonwhites. For Native Americans, as for Black and Asian Americans, the late nineteenth century and the first few decades of the twentieth century would be what historian Rayford Logan labeled the "nadir" and

Comanche scholar Paul Chaat Smith calls "our darkest hour." The attempt to force Native peoples all across the continent to end Native governance, language, and culture—to stop being nations—had two major prongs. The policy of "allotment" required nations to surrender their communal lands, the basis of their existence as nations. And boarding schools attempted to strip children from their cultures and make them into English-speaking Americans.[16]

As Reconstruction faltered, some white reformers who had been abolitionists and advocates of Black equality turned their attention to Native Americans, hoping to right injustices done to them by the United States. In 1881, Helen Hunt Jackson published *A Century of Dishonor*, a powerful condemnation of "the United States Government's repeated violations of faith with the Indians" and the poverty and lack of opportunity on reservations. Unfortunately, the solution proposed by her book, and taken up by the U.S. government, was to abolish reservations, assign Native Americans individual land title, and make them full citizens of the United States.[17] Osage anthropologist Jean Dennison states the change succinctly: "In the late nineteenth century, the federal government moved from a policy of removal, which opened up land for white settlement but left American Indian nations mostly intact, to a policy of allotment, where the hope was to eventually do away with Indians, particularly in the form of Indian nations."[18] In one of the awful ironies of U.S. history, as white southerners were robbing Black Americans of the citizenship rights and individual farms they and their allies had fought for, the white Americans who had tried and failed to help them applied the same good intentions to the wrong people and nearly destroyed Native nations.

Right away, allotment meant land loss. Embodied in the General Allotment Act, passed by the U.S. Congress in 1887, was a plan for each Native family to be allotted 160 acres from that nation's reservation and for all remaining reservation land to be sold. The resulting land loss was staggering. Native landholdings fell from around 150 million acres when the Allotment Act was passed to less than 60 million acres by the 1930s, when the policy of allotment ended. As Chickasaw scholar Jodi Byrd explains, "we Chickasaws lost our country twice," first through removal "and then through allotment and the creation of the state of Oklahoma."[19]

Native Americans accurately predicted the ramifications of allotment. Not only would it lead to land loss immediately in the sale of supposedly excess land, but individual ownership would make it easier for white people to chip away at Native land by buying small parcels from individuals rather than dealing with governments. While Congress was debating the Allotment Act in March 1886, delegates from thirteen Indian Territory nations gathered in the Muscogee Nation once again, this time to oppose allotment and defend their nationhood and their reservation land base together. They were many of the nations that had made peace half a century earlier and continued to meet in council at times of crisis, including the Kiowas, Comanches, Southern Cheyennes, Osages, Muscogees, Cherokees, Choctaws, Chickasaws, and Seminoles. Echoing agreements going back to the Ohio Valley Confederacy, the representatives agreed that "no Nation . . . shall, without the consent of all the other parties, cede or in any manner alienate to the United States any part of their present territory."[20] Nonetheless, Congress passed the Allotment Act in February 1887 and began sending government officials to each reservation to work out the details. Although there were some protections in the form of land trusts, in general it would be much more difficult to keep all *individuals* from selling land on their own. Allotment was an enormous blow to collective ownership and to self-governance.

In a skillful tactic that echoes their long-standing diplomacy, the Quapaws got out ahead of the Allotment Act. By the 1880s, fewer than fifty Quapaws lived on their reservation. Other Quapaw bands were living on the Osage reservation and in other parts of Oklahoma and Kansas, and one band had returned to the old homeland in Arkansas. These bands had retained connections and a shared Quapaw identity despite their geographic distance. Charley Quapaw was the elected chief on their reservation, and Tallchief was the hereditary Quapaw chief, based among their people who were living on the Osage reservation. Only the hereditary leader can perform certain functions, including naming children, so Tallchief regularly traveled to the Quapaw reservation. The Quapaws living in the Pine Bluff region of Arkansas made trips to the reservation to see their kin and participate in ceremonies, and economic development was beginning on the reservation. In the 1870s, the Quapaw Nation had started leasing agricultural land to white farmers and receiving a third of the crop as payment. Because the reservation lay on the cattle route up from Texas, the nation started charging the cattle drivers to fatten their animals on Quapaw prairies toward the end of the trail before selling in Kansas.[21]

But Allotment threatened the Quapaws with losing most of their reservation, because 160 acres times the around fifty people living on the reservation totals only eight thousand acres. So they began attracting more population. Chief Charley Quapaw sent delegations to the dispersed bands, inviting them to move to the reservation to prevent the U.S. government from dissolving the tribe and taking their reservation. Those living on Osage land hesitated to move to a reservation where the U.S. agent would have more oversight, but most of the Arkansas Band packed up their belongings and moved north to the reservation. The Quapaws also increased tribal numbers by adopting individual neighboring families whose ancestors had been welcomed by Quapaw ancestors, including a family of Shawnee and Cherokee descent; Miami, Peoria, and Potawatomi women and their children, and refugees from the Northeast. It wasn't just a smart strategy—adoption and inclusion were traditional Quapaw values. U.S. officials were appalled. After all, they were trying to decrease the number of Indians, not increase them.[22]

A council meeting in 1893 unanimously agreed to divide their reservation themselves before the Allotment Act could be implemented in their territory. They assigned each Quapaw man, woman, and child two hundred acres, and gave some land to a school and the Catholic Church. They proposed that any unallotted acres remain with individual Quapaws rather than being sold. They allotted the two-hundred-acre plots mostly in places each family was already farming, with adjacent plots for their children. When Senator Henry Dawes came to Indian Territory to promote allotment, they presented him with the fait accompli, and he could do nothing but agree. With his support, the Quapaws successfully lobbied Congress, which passed their version of allotment in 1897, with each Quapaw being assigned two hundred acres plus another forty out of the extra.[23]

The Quapaws tried to maintain a government that could make collective decisions. They officially created a three-chief system, with the hereditary chief and two elected chiefs representing those who had moved away and those who had stayed on the Quapaw reservation throughout the preceding era. In 1897, lead deposits were discovered on Quapaw land, and they made profits from lead and zinc mining, though the mines also brought environmental damage, exploitation by ruthless companies, and increasing U.S. government involvement in Quapaw affairs.[24]

When the United States tried to inflict allotment on the Kiowas, the Comanches, and the Plains Apaches in 1892 and take two-thirds of their remaining three million acres, those peoples took the matter to court, on the basis of the provision in the Medicine Lodge Treaty that a supermajority of 75 percent of adult men was required for any further land cessions. Kiowa leader Lone Wolf, a veteran of the Red River War against the U.S. military who had lived through the move to the reservation, led the court case, *Lone Wolf v. Hitchcock*. But they lost. In 1903, the U.S. Supreme Court ruled that their argument "ignores the status of the contracting Indians and the relation of dependency they bore and continue to bear towards the government of the United States." Not able to refute the treaty's clear 75 percent requirement, the court ruled that the Kiowas, Comanches, and Plains Apaches were dependents, more like children than like a nation with whom the United States had to keep agreements. Putting aside the recognition of nationhood from the *Worcester v. Georgia* precedent of "domestic dependent nations," the U.S. Supreme Court emphasized the "dependent" part, declaring Native Americans wards of the state. When one of the U.S. supporters of Lone Wolf heard the decision, he remarked, with only a little exaggeration, that the decision "practically inculcates the doctrine that the red man has no rights which the white man is bound to respect."[25]

Lone Wolf's goal was to confirm U.S. treaty obligations, but the court's decision in *Lone Wolf v. Hitchcock* did the opposite and pushed aside both the treaty and Native sovereignty. The Kiowas, Comanches, and Plains Apaches lost all but about 510,000 acres, and their lost lands now filled with white settlers who had flooded in as the last remaining part of Indian Territory became the state of Oklahoma.[26]

Allotment was a full-fledged attack on Native governance structures. Individual landowners were supposed to gradually come to see themselves as part of the United States and of Oklahoma or whatever state they lived in, not as citizens of tribes. The federal and state governments took over institutions that Native nations had founded and funded. One thousand schools that had been run by their nations fell into the hands of whites, who changed the curricula and instituted English-only instruction. The literacy rate in the Cherokee Nation fell from nearly 100 percent to, by 1969, 60 percent. It was a deep and terrible destruction of Native traditional ways of governing and dividing and sharing power among divisions, clans,

Etla and Lone Wolf (Kiowas), photograph taken between 1855 and 1865, Brady-Handy photograph collection.
LIBRARY OF CONGRESS, PRINTS AND PHOTOGRAPHS DIVISION

and genders. Within many tribes, political conflicts broke out over the little power they had left.[27]

Besides allotment, the era's other major assault on Native nations was sending Native children to boarding schools. It was too late, U.S. reformers feared, to assimilate adult Indians, so they targeted the children. They took them away from the supposedly terrible reservations and placed them in boarding schools, often purposefully far from home. Richard Pratt, the founder of Carlisle Indian School, in Pennsylvania, declared that his school's purpose was to "kill the Indian in him, and save the man." Reformers separated children as young as five from their parents and grandparents and made them take new names and wear strange clothes. They forbade them from speaking their own languages or practicing their own religions.[28]

As boarding school survivors remembered and later investigations and hearings exposed, many children were taken by force and, once in schools, faced horrific mental and physical abuse at the hands of people with far too much unregulated power. Former students recalled being starved and beaten. Countless children died at school, never to return home. Most Native families were affected—in 1926, for example, more than 80 percent of school-age Native American children were in boarding schools, and the schools lasted for many decades, over two full generations of children. The goal of boarding schools was to assimilate Native Americans into white American culture, yet because this era was the height of white supremacy, the place within white American society designated for Indians, like other nonwhite Americans, was not an equal one. President Theodore Roosevelt in 1901 advised that "in the schools the education should be elementary and largely industrial. The need of higher education among the Indians is very, very limited."[29]

Mohawk scholar Tom Sakokweniónkwas Porter calls Carlisle and the other boarding schools "almost a knockout blow to our Native religion, language, community based lifestyle and our Indian pride." Reservations could be places of preserving language, culture, identity, and community; boarding schools were designed to take those things away, leaving generations separated from the knowl-

edge and ways of their peoples and repeatedly told that those ways—
and their family members—were backward and doomed.[30]

Allotment and boarding schools brought tremendous loss and
trauma, yet they did not destroy Native people or their nations.
Ojibwe historian Brenda J. Child noted that her grandmother returned home from boarding school to "re-embrace her culture, language, and community." Reading letters and other accounts by
children who attended the schools, Child concluded that they were
not broken or assimilated but instead that the "deep and abiding
commitment to children, demonstrated time and time again by parents and others at home . . . outlasted and outmaneuvered a failed
educational idea." Boarding schools tried to make non-Indian children, but their families and communities "refused to allow government boarding schools to supplant their essential roles in child
rearing."[31]

Native communities had always educated their children, and
they continued to do so as best they could. Shawnee Robert "Bobby"
Bluejacket recalled seeing his brothers leave for school and then
having to go himself when he was six years old: "That was eighty-
three years ago, but I remember the day that the bus came for me."
It was a hot August day, and he knew even then that the chill he felt
"was the loss within my soul, the crying of my people, the voice of
the old ones shattered by that tortured ride." Yet every summer back
home, his grandmother would give the boys lessons in being Shawnee. "She said that we are to prepare ourselves to live in the white
world, to be like the white people. 'But don't believe their words. You
are Shawnee. Your heart will always be Shawnee,' she said." Native
families and communities were at times able to influence school
conditions and curricula, especially in the day schools and boarding
schools that were on reservations rather than far away. Some graduates became teachers and staff in the Indian schools, gradually and
quietly changing their emphases. After Carlisle, Rosa Skakah returned home to raise children and grandchildren who have held important political positions within the Eastern Shawnee Tribe. Her
daughter Dorma Hollis became head clerk of the Seneca Indian

School, in Oklahoma, and, along with other Native staff and parents, reversed the policy that forbade students from visiting their families often and started the Grandmother and Grandfather Program, in which education by tribal elders became part of students' school-sanctioned learning. Boarding schools did a great deal of damage and became a particularly poignant symbol of white supremacy, but they failed to end Native families or Native nations.[32]

Still, the era of allotment and boarding schools brought unprecedented U.S. government involvement to the lives of Native Americans, an involvement for the most part intended to destroy what U.S. officials deemed backward "tribalism." In an attempt to undermine the communal identity of Native nations, U.S. officials set up tribal police and courts to enforce U.S. laws banning traditional religion, ceremonies, and dances and regulating marriage and sexuality. Native Americans fought back in a variety of ways. On many reservations, beginning in 1882, prophets preached to restore the old ways. In 1889 and 1890, the Northern Paiute prophet Wovoka led a religious movement known as the Ghost Dance that spread across the West, including among the Kiowas. It was a new and visible religious practice that combined Native traditions for the purpose of bringing back the Plains ways of life, with plentiful bison and horses. But it was also forward-looking, advising the people of Native nations to give up war and find ways to remain Native even as they might work for wages and send their kids to U.S. schools. U.S. officials panicked and tried to stomp it out. They sent troops to reservations, including the Lakotas' Standing Rock and Pine Ridge. In December 1890, in what became known as the Wounded Knee Massacre, U.S. Army troops fired on a Lakota camp at Wounded Knee Creek, on the Pine Ridge Reservation, first on men who were surrendering to them and then on their families in the camp, ultimately killing or wounding some three hundred Lakota men, women, and children.[33]

It was only in this era that the United States began to intrude deeply into the lives of the O'odham. Farming had become more difficult in the late nineteenth century as white farmers east of the Akimel O'odham towns built an irrigation canal that diverted all of the Gila River, leaving no water to flow on to the O'odham. The diversion of the Gila opened the way to dependence on rations handed out by government agents. Instead of a reservation, Akimel O'odham lands were allotted in very small plots with no clear water rights. In 1918, the federal government assigned an Indian agent to the Tohono O'odham and outlined a two-million-acre reservation that included almost all of their lands north of the U.S.–Mexico border. To keep such a large area, they had to surrender the mineral rights.[34]

Despite reformers' intentions and Native peoples' arguments, the United States in the nineteenth and early twentieth centuries eroded Native sovereignty while not granting Native individuals true citizenship rights. As Keith Richotte explains, "tribal political autonomy was seriously diminished, tribal cultures and understandings were under constant assault, and Native peoples themselves were at their nadir, as the population was at its lowest since contact."[35] The 1900 U.S. census counted fewer than 250,000 Native Americans in the mainland United States. That is certainly an undercount—less than twenty-five years earlier, U.S. officials had counted 300,000, a number they said had been stable for many decades. What the undercount suggests is that fewer people than ever were willing to identify themselves as Native American to a U.S. census taker. Opposition to Native sovereignty and predictions of Native demise had long been at the heart of U.S. actions toward Native Americans, from the early U.S. "civilization policy" through removal and allotment.[36]

As best they could, and under damaging and demoralizing circumstances, Native nations retained their sense of themselves as sovereign communities. Native women and men quietly continued older ways of speaking, healing, working, eating, and making art, preserving the seeds of the coming resurgence of sovereignty and renaissance in language and culture that would begin in the 1930s. Kiowa linguist and University of Kansas professor Andrew McKenzie explains that Kiowas kept practicing inclusivism even in these hardest times: "For the most part Kiowas were interested in taking what they thought was helpful and blending it into their own traditional ways. As a result, Kiowas never fully lost those old ways." And Native nations continued efforts like the attempted General Council of the Indian Territory, recognizing one another as nations even when the United States did not. They sent tribal diplomatic delegations and used written English and the U.S. Postal Service to communicate with other Indigenous nations across the continent and beyond. The Muscogee Nation's official history explains it in terms that could fit all of the Native nations that made it through this period: "The end of the Muscogee Nation as envisioned by those within the United States Congress did not occur."[37]

SELF-DETERMINATION

Over the course of the twentieth century, more and more Native Americans would see themselves as U.S. citizens, but they would not stop being American Indians or citizens of their own Native nations. Indeed, boarding schools, U.S. military service, including in two world wars, and other off-reservation activities that brought together people from multiple Native nations increased the sense of an American Indian identity while spurring Native action for both self-determination as nations and civil rights as Americans.

The first generation of this kind of Native activists arose in the 1910s and '20s. They were familiar with the ways and the language of non–Native Americans and advocated for Native participation in U.S. Indian policy. Charles Eastman was a Dakota who, he later reflected, had always thought of the Ojibwe as completely foreign people whom the Dakotas had fought, people with whom he had little in common and in fact whom the Creator had intended to be different from the Dakotas. But at boarding school he met Ojibwe students and discussed what they had in common, including their histories of dealing with white American aggression. Because boarding schools taught English, the students gained a language to communicate with people of completely separate language families (in this case Siouan and Algonquian). As David Martínez explains, students like Eastman began to develop both a concept of Native

Americans as a race and "a political identity" of "the American Indian, which also did not exist before but around which Indian people, however tangentially, could identify their individual and tribal needs."[38]

Eastman and a group of boarding school graduates and others they had met founded the Society of American Indians in 1911. The "of" (rather than "for") in their organization's name was important: They were American Indians working together for the benefit of their peoples. As Arapaho Sherman Coolidge, another of the founders, put it, the Society of American Indians was to be "managed solely for and by the Indians."[39] One of the SAI's founders was Arthur Parker, the great-nephew of Seneca Commissioner of Indian Affairs Ely Parker. Born on a Seneca reservation, Arthur Parker became an archaeologist, focusing on the long history of the Haudenosaunee, working at museums to make them better reflect true Native history, serving as president of the SAI, and directing the WPA's Indian Arts Project.[40]

Art was a realm in which Native nations marked out a place that was widely recognized as Native, within and beyond their communities. At the Catholic St. Patrick's Mission School, in Anadarko, Oklahoma, a group of young Kiowas together became internationally recognized artists, known eventually as the Kiowa Six. One was Stephen Mopope, great-nephew of the calendar artist Silver Horn,

Kiowa Flute Player, by Stephen Mopope.
GILCREASE MUSEUM, TULSA, OKLAHOMA

whose art we saw earlier in this book. Mopope received art training at home and in school and went on, with his fellow young Kiowa artists, to the University of Oklahoma. Later, they exhibited their work in art shows in the United States and Europe. Their depictions of Kiowa life and dress and their Plains style, inherited from calendar art, would have a tremendous influence on later Native artists.[41]

Unlike most past American Indian leaders, those in the SAI believed that U.S. citizenship was essential for protecting and advancing Native rights. Some Native Americans had been U.S. citizens since the American Revolution, because they lived within U.S. communities (such as the Lumbees and the Occaneechis). Others had become citizens by marrying U.S. citizens or, like some Cherokees and Shawnees, by accepting treaty-based offers of citizenship and private property rights. Many people whose lands were allotted, including the Quapaws, became U.S. citizens through that process. There were also many Native Americans who still had no desire for U.S. citizenship.

In World War I, those who already were U.S. citizens could be drafted, while non-citizens volunteered. Well over twelve thousand Native American men served in the war. Unlike Black soldiers, Native men were integrated into units with white soldiers. For some men in these generations, the U.S. military was an opportunity to be warriors like their fathers and grandfathers. Half of Quapaw men of military age served in the war. Mohawk William Newell was General John Pershing's French interpreter. Native women served as nurses. Choctaw code talkers transmitted encoded messages in their own language for the U.S. military. After World War I, Congress allowed Native veterans to petition for citizenship.[42]

Native Americans remained divided over both U.S. citizenship and being part of the U.S. military. Arthur Parker wrote in praise of Native soldiers that "the Indian fights because he loves freedom and because humanity needs the defense of the freedom loving man. The Indian fights because his country, his liberties, his ideals and his manhood are assailed by the brutal hypocrisy of Prussianism. Challenged, the Indian has responded and shown himself a citizen of the world."[43] Others, though, asserted their Native sovereign rights to resist the U.S. draft and oppose U.S. foreign policy. The Haudenosaunee Confederacy itself declared war on Germany in 1917, encouraging young Haudenosaunee men to enlist in the U.S. Army but as part of the Haudenosaunee war on Germany. And it's important to note that even Parker phrased Native military service in terms larger than the United States.[44]

In 1924, in part because of Native military service in World War I and advocacy by the Society of American Indians, the U.S. Congress passed the Indian Citizenship Act, which granted citizenship rights, including the vote, to all Native Americans. Many applauded the act, which, unlike most earlier attempts to make Indians into U.S. citizens, included a provision that "the granting of such citizenship shall not in any manner impair or otherwise affect the right of any Indian to tribal or other property."[45] But some Native Americans continued to reject U.S. citizenship. They pointed out that the United States once again had not consulted Native nations before making policy affecting them. Many agreed with Mohawk Ernest Benedict, who said that the Indian Citizenship Act could not apply to the Haudenosaunee, "since they are independent Nations. Congress may as well pass a law making Mexicans citizens."[46] And in much of the South and the Southwest, Native Americans, like other nonwhite people, were still often kept from exercising their right to vote. When Akimel O'odham voters tried to cast their ballots in the U.S. presidential election of 1928, Arizona election officials denied them. The men took their case to the Arizona Supreme Court, which denied their right to vote because, it ruled, Indians were "persons under guardianship" and therefore ineligible to vote according to Arizona's state constitution. That decision was not overturned until 1948.[47]

Members of the SAI who worked for the U.S. Office of Indian Affairs turned U.S. Indian policy around in the late 1920s and '30s. As Choctaw anthropologist Valerie Lambert puts it, they managed to "leverage the power of the settler state toward their own ends." Henry Roe Cloud (Ho-Chunk) was a member of the commission that wrote the 1928 Meriam Report, which was scathing in its criticism of allotment. The report charged that "it almost seems as if the government assumed that some magic in individual ownership of property would in itself prove an educational civilizing factor, but unfortunately this policy has for the most part operated in the opposite direction." Like Helen Hunt Jackson's *A Century of Dishonor,* three and a half decades earlier, the Meriam Report detailed poverty and despair on reservations, but because of Native involvement in the report, it recommended ending allotment and instead encouraging tribal self-government and tribally directed economic development. As a Yale graduate, Henry Roe Cloud certainly rejected the assumption that Native education should be only for manual labor. The report recommended instead that "the Indian Service should encourage promising Indian youths to continue their education beyond the boarding schools and to fit themselves for professional, scientific, and technical callings," and it should "aid them in meeting the costs."[48]

The Meriam Report helped to change U.S. policy in the coming decades, but slowly. Charles Curtis, who won the vice presidency in 1928 on the ticket with Herbert Hoover, was both a supporter of allotment and a Kaw, the first and thus far only Native American to hold the office of president or vice president of the United States. Curtis grew up on the Kaw reservation, in what's now Kansas. He became a U.S. citizen, and Kansas voters elected him to the House of Representatives and subsequently the Senate, where he rose to Republican majority leader. In Congress, Curtis authored the 1898 Curtis Act, which added the Cherokees, Chickasaws, Choctaws, Muscogees, and Seminoles to the provisions of the Allotment Act.[49]

Hoover and Curtis lost reelection in 1932, and the Franklin Roosevelt administration would ultimately implement the reforms of the Native activists of the SAI. The Meriam Report helped persuade Roosevelt's commissioner of Indian affairs, John Collier, to reverse allotment and to include Native people in federal policy-making. Collier went on listening tours to reservations, and he took advice from the growing number of Native employees in his department. Arthur Parker's Indian Arts Project, under the auspices of the WPA, encouraged the production, certification, and sale of Native arts and crafts. In the Great Depression, Native people were hardly the only ones suffering from poverty and despair, and when the U.S. electorate chose Roosevelt as president, on a pledge to help the people help themselves, for once Native Americans were included, as individuals and as nations within the United States. Congress passed, and President Roosevelt signed, the 1934 Indian Reorganization Act—the centerpiece of the "Indian New Deal"—which allowed tribes to reconstitute their governments and communal landholdings, including returning some lands that had not yet been sold and allowing nations to buy back lost reservation lands and add them back to their tribal lands. Unlike reforms in the past, the Indian Reorganization Act allowed nations to vote on whether to follow it or not.[50]

Sometimes the Indian New Deal is criticized for not moving far enough from the paternalism of the past as well as for assuming that majority rule was how tribes would decide, rather than using their own ways of decision making. Still, given how disastrous U.S. policy had been for generations, it was a sea change in U.S. thinking about Native nations. As Professor Richotte explains, "No longer was the federal government seeking to destroy tribal governance and limit sovereignty." The U.S. government moved back toward the "domestic dependent nations" of *Worcester v. Georgia*. In the spirit of the New Deal's giving people a helping hand with respect rather than paternalism, the Indian New Deal emphasized self-determination for Native nations. It repealed the Allotment Act and ended the requirement of boarding schools and other official attempts to destroy Native cultures. Its 1934 Indian Religious Freedom and Indian Culture Act guaranteed Native Americans' right to practice their religions, allowing religions that had gone underground to reemerge.[51]

Under the Indian Reorganization Act, the Tohono O'odham wrote a constitution and created a tribal council with representatives from eleven districts. Many people who had sought work in Tucson or Phoenix returned home, because now those cities had high unemployment, and yet there was work at home with the Civilian Conservation Corps, building reservoirs and other public works projects. Many Tohono O'odham continued to work seasonally on farms on the Gila and Salt rivers in Arizona and the Altar River in

Sonora, even though many of those farms now were owned by non-O'odham. Although seasonal migrations continued, having work and a central government on the reservation brought the Tohono O'odham together as a nation as they had not been when their politics and economics rested in smaller bands. With their tribal standing reestablished by New Deal legislation, the Tohono O'odham now had a say in Franciscans' decisions about churches in the region. The Gila River Indian Community also wrote a constitution that included a tribal council and got some of its water back with the construction of the Coolidge Dam and the San Carlos Reservoir, although it would be decades before farming began to revive. In 2004 the U.S. government finally agreed to return water rights to the Gila River Indian Community, in the largest Indian water rights settlement in U.S. history. Day schools in the community gradually took the place of the boarding school and incorporated teaching of O'odham himdag into the curriculum.[52]

As in O'odham country, Cherokees in North Carolina found employment in the New Deal. Leonard Carson Lambert Jr. remembers that "for the first time almost everyone could find work," his father doing so with the Civilian Conservation Corps, "working on roads and trails and guarding against forest fires." Starting in the 1880s, Native people in North Carolina had petitioned for a college to train Native teachers, which ultimately resulted in the Robeson County university that today is the University of North Carolina at Pembroke. In 1957, the Haliwa-Saponis founded the Haliwa Indian School (today the Haliwa-Saponi Tribal School). Although part of the impetus was segregation in North Carolina schools that forced Native children into grossly underfunded Black schools, the Haliwa Indian School was a community endeavor, and Haliwa-Saponis remember its founding as a fundamental event in their modern nationhood.[53]

Other tribes, though, rejected the Indian Reorganization Act as pushing them backward. Quapaws called moving allotted lands back into communal tribal property "a flagrant slap at Indian intelligence." By then some Quapaws had made considerable profits on mining and other economic development and saw these moves as threatening that progress. The Quapaws declined reorganization, but they did use New Deal programs to buy back land for their tribal grounds, and they stopped sending their children to boarding schools.[54]

In these early decades of the twentieth century, the Native population reversed its long decline and began to rebound. After a low point in the first decade of the twentieth century, the Native population in the United States grew at twice the rate of the overall U.S. population. In 1917, American Indian births finally exceeded deaths, which had not been the case for decades.[55]

Because of the Indian Citizenship Act of 1924, Native men were drafted in large numbers for World War II. Some twenty-five thousand men and women served. Like the Choctaw code talkers in World War I, Navajos and others built successful code systems using Native languages. Many veterans used their reputations as heroes to help their nations when they returned home. But others resisted fighting for the United States. As in World War I, Haudenosaunee leaders declared war on Germany. Their spokesperson proclaimed from the steps of the U.S. Capitol,

> We represent the oldest, though smallest, democracy in the world today. It is the unanimous sentiment among Indian people that the atrocities of the Axis nations are violently repulsive to all sense of righteousness of our people, and that this merciless slaughter of mankind can no longer be tolerated. Now we do resolve that it is the sentiment of this council that the Six Nations of Indians declare that a state of war exists between our Confederacy of Six Nations on the one part and Germany, Italy, Japan and their allies against whom the United States has declared war, on the other part.[56]

The most famous Native American World War II soldier was Ira Hayes, an Akimel O'odham who enlisted in the U.S. Marines in August 1942, when he was nineteen years old. The Gila River Indian Community had an O'odham ceremony for him before he left for war, as they had for warriors going to battle in the past. A paratrooper, Hayes landed on the island of Iwo Jima in February 1945. For five weeks, the Marines fought to take the island, and around twenty-five thousand men were killed in some of the bloodiest fighting of the war. Hayes and five other soldiers raised the U.S. flag on the highest point of the island, high enough to be seen by Marines fighting across the island. The Pulitzer Prize–winning photograph, in which Hayes is the man in the back on the far left, became a much-needed symbol of victory finally coming in the Pacific and the model for the Marine Corps War Memorial, at the edge of Arlington National Cemetery. Three of the six men in the photograph died in action on Iwo Jima, but Hayes survived, and the Marines sent him and the other two survivors to a celebration with President Harry Truman at the White House and on a war bonds tour around the United States.

After the war, Hayes returned to the Gila River Indian Community. The U.S. government had built a Japanese internment camp on the reservation, adding insult to the injury of the water theft that had ruined the Akimel O'odham economy. Suffering from what we would now call PTSD, Hayes described how he felt: "I was sick. . . . I guess I was about to crack up thinking about all my good buddies. They were better men than me and they're not coming back. Much

Iwo Jima, February 23, 1945, photograph by Joseph Rosenthal.
ASSOCIATED PRESS

less back to the White House, like me." Hayes was dead by the age of thirty-three.[57]

There were other Native veterans, less famous to Americans generally but well known at home. John Horse was a Kiowa soldier who earned the Bronze Star and the Purple Heart from the U.S. Army. Like Ira Hayes, John Horse got a traditional ceremony at home, which included a war bonnet, recalling the military glory of his Plains warrior ancestors. Upon returning home, gunner Gus Palmer revived a Kiowa military society so that twentieth-century Kiowa veterans would be recognized as Kiowa warriors had been in the past. He went on to be chairman of the Kiowa Tribe and testified before Congress on Native religious freedom. Kiowa aerial photographer Horace (Big Horse) Poolaw became one of the most important photographers of the twentieth century. Unlike non-Native photographers, he depicted Native people not as sad and disappearing but as very much alive, people who were part of their specific cultures and communities and also modern people.[58]

Quapaw Veteran's Wall, in front of the Quapaw Tribal Museum, dedicated July 2009, Quapaw, Oklahoma.
PHOTOGRAPH COURTESY QUAPAW NATION

Native Americans also participated in the growing urbanization and industrialization of the United States. Many thousands of Native Americans worked in wartime industries, including twelve thousand Native women who left reservations to work in munitions factories and other jobs. By the 1950s, 20 percent of Native Americans lived in cities, in contrast to only 5 percent before the war. Many reservations also saw new job opportunities during and after the war, with some men becoming police or judges and women becoming teachers in the increasingly community-based schools. Mohawk men found employment and renown as ironworkers both on and off their reservations. In the 1880s, a railroad bridge was being built across the St. Lawrence River onto Mohawk land, and in return the Mohawks required the builders to hire Mohawk workers. Since that beginning, workers from Akwesasne and other Mohawk communities have worked on countless bridges and skyscrapers, including the George Washington Bridge, the Empire State Building, and the Chrysler Building.[59]

Mohawk ironworkers building the Chrysler Building, New York City, 1929, photograph by Charles Rivers.
NATIONAL MUSEUM OF AMERICAN HISTORY, SMITHSONIAN INSTITUTION

After World War II, Native American activism accelerated, with an emphasis on the self-determination of Native nations within the United States. In 1944, citizens of more than fifty nations, including Seneca Arthur Parker, founded the National Congress of American Indians (NCAI). While organizations like the NAACP worked for civil rights, the NCAI promoted the dual goals of individual civil rights within the United States and the tribal sovereign rights of Native nations. The NCAI persuaded Congress to establish the Indian Claims Commission (ICC) in 1946, a federal commission to which tribes could file cases regarding unpaid treaty obligations. Among other decisions, the ICC awarded more than $2 million to the Kiowas, Comanches, and Plains Apaches for lands taken during the allotment era and $927,668 to the Quapaw Nation in unpaid debts from their 1824 treaty.[60]

Today the NCAI is still an important voice for Native Americans, housed in the Embassy of Tribal Nations in Washington, D.C. For many of its early years, its offices were squeezed into the D.C. home of Ruth Muskrat, a Cherokee woman who grew up in the Cherokee Nation. As a young schoolteacher, she accepted a teaching position on the Mescalero Apache reservation and was a delegate to the World Student Christian Federation Conference in Beijing in

Ruth Muskrat (Cherokee) and Sherman Coolidge (Arapaho) presenting a book of Native American history to U.S. President Calvin Coolidge (no relation), 1923.
LIBRARY OF CONGRESS

1922. With this international experience, Muskrat became a Native leader who worked for Native civil rights and sovereign rights. In meeting with President Calvin Coolidge in 1923, shortly before he signed the Indian Citizenship Act, she explained that "we want to become citizens of the United States and to share in the building of this great nation that we love" but was quick to add, "We want also to preserve the best that is in our own civilization. We want to make our own unique contribution to the civilizations of the world." Like Arthur Parker, Muskrat linked her people's history to the world.[61]

By the 1950s Native Americans were still on average the poorest group in the United States, suffering from chronic diseases, shorter life expectancies, alcoholism, and poor healthcare and housing. The genocidal attempts of the nineteenth and early twentieth centuries had done great damage. But their emerging identity as Native Americans and citizens of the United States, while continuing to be members of individual nations, formed a foundation from which they fought the next attempt to destroy their nations.

In the 1950s, anti-communism and backlash against the New Deal persuaded some Americans to target the communal aspects of Native nations and again push to end reservations. With the "termination policy," the U.S. government (as well as the Canadian and Mexican governments) attempted to terminate its responsibilities to tribes—despite the fact that many of those responsibilities were guaranteed by treaties—and place individual Native Americans under the jurisdiction of states and counties. Like Georgia in the early nineteenth century, states moved to seize land, tax, and legislate within reservations and override the gains that tribal governments had made in the 1930s and '40s. In a speech to the Institute of Race Relations, delivered at Nashville's Fisk University in 1949, Ruth Muskrat accused the proponents of termination of simply wanting "Indian grazing lands, Indian oil, Indian fishing rights and Indian possessions." They "cloak their aggressive actions behind a lot of high-sounding moral phrases," she charged. "They want to set Indians free. They want to emancipate the Indians, say they. They want to help the Indian become a first-class citizen. But behind it all, when you trace it down, the forces really will say, 'Well, the Indians should not have this property.'"[62] Eventually most tribes either avoided termination or got it overturned, but not before significant land loss. Some are still fighting to reverse their terminated status and reestablish federal recognition.[63]

Also in the postwar era, many young people left their reservations for cities under the simultaneous federal Indian Relocation Act, which encouraged American Indians to leave reservations and move to cities. In some cases, the U.S. relocation policy literally gave Native participants a one-way bus ticket to a city purposefully far from home. At the age of thirteen, Wilma Mankiller, who would go on to be principal chief of the Cherokee Nation, moved with her family more than fifteen hundred miles away from the Cherokee Nation to San Francisco. In her autobiography, she compared their migration to her ancestors' Trail of Tears: "Our ordeal was not nearly as harsh or painful as the problems encountered by the Cherokee people who had been forced to take the Trail of Tears in the late 1830s. At least we did not have to walk hundreds of miles through snow and sleet. We did not worry about getting bayoneted or shot by some soldier. . . . Our relocation was voluntary and not by federal mandate." Yet, as they moved into their apartment, "we still felt as alienated as our ancestors must have felt when they finally arrived in those unfamiliar surroundings that became their new home."[64]

Sometimes non–Native Americans have assumed an incongruity between cities and Native Americans, whom they imagine as living timelessly in tipis and on horseback, despite the long history of urban North America. And indeed, as Cherokee scholar Sean Kicummah Teuton points out, poverty and alienation could be part of urban living, as for "all poor people." Native Americans did not necessarily find work or good housing in the city, and about a third went back home fairly soon. But others stayed, in what David Treuer calls "the single largest demographic and cultural shift in Indian country in a century and arguably more pervasive and transformative than the reservation system." By 1970 half of Native Americans lived in urban areas.[65]

Native people from many nations who came together in cities

forged an urban Indigenous identity. Often Native Americans lived in the same parts of town, where they founded Indian centers and self-help organizations. In cities, David Treuer explains, "they found they had much more in common with one another: a shared historical experience if not shared cultures, the same class values, the same struggles. Networks among tribes—forged through marriage, school, city living, and service in the armed forces—were strengthened."[66] For example, World War II defense work and subsequent employment opportunities drew Native Americans from North Carolina to northern cities. Lumbee historian Jessica Locklear has conducted oral interviews that tell of how Lumbees, Haliwa-Saponis, and Cherokees in Philadelphia founded the United American Indians of the Delaware Valley. Jenny Tone-Pah-Hote, whose father was sent off to boarding school as a young boy, describes her upbringing as many Native Americans do today:

> I am a citizen of the Kiowa Tribe of Oklahoma, and I grew up near Orrick, Missouri, a small town near Kansas City. In Kansas City, my family participated in an urban American Indian community. Like many others, it was intertribal, and it included folks from American Indian nations in Oklahoma, individuals who stayed in the area after attending what is now Haskell Indian Nations University, and people from the reservations in the Midwest. My family and I attended American Indian events in Kansas City, danced at powwows in the area, and visited relatives in Oklahoma, often making summer trips for the American Indian Exposition held in August in Anadarko, Oklahoma, [one of the] two major hubs of the Kiowa community.[67]

CONNECTIONS

As Tone-Pah-Hote's travel between Kansas City and Anadarko reveals, urban American Indians kept their connections to their nations. She and countless other Native children in the late twentieth and twenty-first centuries spent summers on reservations, learning lessons from their grandparents and extended kin that the United States had tried over and over to make impossible and unwanted. Perhaps the lessons are not as complete as they would have been without the attempted genocide that hit earlier generations, and most of the time the conversations happen in English, but they began to correct the damage done to the generations that had been told that being Native was a doomed and irrelevant way of the past.[68]

John Berrey was born in Denver and grew up in California but often visited his Quapaw grandparents and other relatives in Oklahoma. He got a naming ceremony from "Grandma Supernaw, who at the time when I was very young, held the right within the Quapaw Tribe to give me my Quapaw name." As a young adult, Berrey moved to his grandmother's allotment to farm hay and cattle. He studied at the University of Arkansas and eventually became chair of the Quapaw Business Committee, leading his nation's economic development in the early twenty-first century.[69] Marvin Richardson grew up in Baltimore and recalls being asked, "What are you man?" He would reply, "I'm American Indian." When they asked, "What tribe are you?" and they hadn't heard of the Haliwa-Saponis, he didn't know what to say, even though his father was the director of the Baltimore American Indian Center. Richardson recalls that "I'd been dancing and singing since I was young, and I had connections to home and came home for powwow and other holidays, but these questions inspired me to learn more and to make connections." He did research in Washington archives on Saponi history and language and, back in North Carolina, earned a B.A. in American Indian studies at UNC-Pembroke and a Ph.D. in history at UNC–Chapel Hill. He brought all this knowledge back home to help with language revitalization and to serve as the Haliwa-Saponi director of planning and development.[70]

Tommy Orange, a citizen of the Cheyenne and Arapaho tribes who grew up in Oakland, California, writes in his novel *There There*,

Getting us to cities was supposed to be the final, necessary step in our assimilation, absorption, erasure, the completion of a five-hundred-year-old genocidal campaign. But the city made us new, and we made it ours. We didn't get lost amid the sprawl of tall buildings, the stream of anonymous masses, the ceaseless din of traffic. We found one another, started up Indian Centers, brought out our families and powwows, our dances, our songs, our bead-work. . . . We made art and we made babies and we made way for our people to go back and forth between reservation and city. We did not move to cities to die.

Ojibwe historian Brenda J. Child writes of how Native women created networks in cities across tribal lines, through such activities as baby showers and raffles and through activism for educational and employment opportunities and child welfare, while they also helped their families stay connected to relatives on their reservations.[71]

Urban American Indian communities were key to the late-twentieth-century development of Native American identities as citizens of their own nations, U.S. citizens, and American Indians. In 1961, the NCAI sponsored the American Indian Chicago Conference, which brought together Native Americans young and old, from reservations and cities and from nearly one hundred nations of various sizes and regions, to talk about self-determination. North Carolina's eastern tribes played an important role. In the lead-up to the Chicago Conference, there were regional conferences around the country. Lumbee organizers asked UNC–Chapel Hill if they could hold one of the regional conferences on campus, but administrators decided that a conference on race was too controversial. So Judge Lacy Maynor organized it instead at UNC-Pembroke (then called Pembroke State College), in Robeson County, the heart of Lumbee country.[72]

A few years earlier, it would have been more dangerous to hold a conference on race in Pembroke than in Chapel Hill, but in 1958 the Lumbees had thrown the Ku Klux Klan out of Robeson County. As part of its campaign of terror on Black and Native Americans, the KKK had burned crosses in Lumbee families' yards, and that January the Klan organized a meeting to be held at a cornfield outside Maxton, in Robeson County. Around fifty Klansmen drove there that night, armed with guns and anticipating a celebratory rally. They were surprised to see a line of cars already parked along the street on the edge of the cornfield. Lumbee men—outnumbering the KKK by about five to one—began getting out of those cars, also carrying rifles and shotguns. Many of them were World War II veterans, including Simeon Oxendine, who had been a bomber on the European front. Two of the Lumbees shut off the power to the lights illuminating the field, and the Lumbees began firing into the air. The frightened Klansmen fled into the woods.[73]

Lumbees Charlie Warriax and Simeon Oxendine
(wearing his Veterans of Foreign Wars cap), 1958, photograph
by Maurie Rosen for the *Charlotte Observer*.
DAVIS LIBRARY, UNIVERSITY OF NORTH CAROLINA AT CHAPEL HILL

Through their interactions at the Chicago Conference, many delegates realized that part of self-determination was recognizing one another. When Lumbees, Haliwa-Saponis, and other Native communities that weren't officially recognized by the federal government traveled to the Chicago Conference, their major goal was to teach their histories and explain their present challenges to Native Americans who were less familiar with eastern nations' early, intensive interactions with settler colonialism and their struggles to be identified by outsiders as Indigenous. Recognition by other Native nations could be powerful. Haliwa delegate W. R. Richardson talked to Tuscaroras whose eighteenth-century ancestors had moved north from North Carolina to become the sixth Haudenosaunee nation. In the years after the Chicago Conference, Haliwas and Tuscaroras visited one another, saw similar traditions, heard similar oral histories, and began to put together their past history as close allies or perhaps members of the same nation. The Tuscaroras granted the Haliwa-Saponis official recognition as a Native nation, and that recognition helped the Haliwa-Saponis to get North Carolina state recognition in 1965.[74]

Powwows became an important expression of both individual tribal and Native American identity and culture. The Quapaws have been hosting an annual powwow in northeastern Oklahoma since the late nineteenth century, with Quapaw dances as well as dances they learned from the Shawnees and the Delawares starting when they were together in Kansas. Interviewed in 1938, Quapaw Ethel Brotherton recalled going to stomp dances her whole life, from the time she was a little girl. Shawnees interviewed in the twenty-first century recalled Quapaws coming in trucks to pick them up and passing out beef and pork to the visiting families to cook in their own camps for the nights they spent there. The Quapaw powwow has been a model for tribes in the region and an inspiration to others to host their own versions and to practice their own traditions. Similarly, on the other side of Oklahoma, late-nineteenth-century Kiowas and other southern Plains Indians visited one another's celebrations, building on the long tradition of Comanches attending Kiowa and Plains Apache sun dances.[75]

As reservations revived dances and other traditions, urban dwellers would return home for their nations' powwows. Many tribes refer to their powwow as a "homecoming," a time when people reassemble and reaffirm who they are and where they come from. A Shawnee ceremonial chief explained that "what we do here" on the ceremonial ground "makes us Shawnee."[76] The Haliwa-Saponis started a powwow in 1966, after W. R. Richardson's discussions with the Haudenosaunee. Other North Carolina Native communities did soon thereafter. In the 1980s, the Native community of Alamance, Orange, and Caswell counties, in North Carolina, reorganized as the Eno-Occaneechi Indian Association and began holding an annual powwow, which as it grew helped them to become the state-recognized Occaneechi Band of the Saponi Nation. Native American communities also began hosting their own multitribal powwows in cities and on college campuses, forging a new tradition across nations. Indigenous studies scholar Meredith McCoy (Turtle Mountain Band of Chippewa descent) explains that UNC–Chapel Hill's annual Carolina Indian Circle Powwow, started in the 1980s, "serves as both a teaching tool and a community gathering space for Native youth who often feel overlooked at a predominantly white institution."[77]

Another institution that combined individual tribal traditions is the Native American Church. Reflecting traditional religious inclusivism, the Native American Church valued the incorporation of new religious beliefs and practices and combined elements of Christianity with peyote ceremonies from the Southwest and a community's own religious traditions. Not as public as outdoor ceremonies and dances, including the Ghost Dance, Native American Church services were both out of the sight of Indian agents and more familiar-seeming to Christians. The Quapaws adopted the Native American Church as their nation's official religion in the 1880s. It was brought to the Quapaws, as well as the Osages, Caddos, and Delawares (all Quapaw neighbors in northeastern Oklahoma by this time), by the Caddo prophet Moon Head (John Wilson), who had been a leader in the Ghost Dance movement before the U.S. government cracked down on it. Many Quapaws converted, including chiefs, and Quapaws credit it for helping to hold them together as a people. Quapaw Tribal Historic Preservation Officer Everett Bandy points out that Quapaws resisted Christianity through nearly two centuries of French and U.S. missionary efforts but purposefully adopted the Native American Church, with its combination of old and new, specifically Quapaw and more generally Native. Quapaw elder William Kugee Supernaw explains that the up and down pitch of songs in their church reflects life's ups and downs, that "you have to take the bitter with the sweet." Similarly, among the Kiowas, after crackdowns against the Ghost Dance, the Native American Church survived and grew, combining Kiowa religious traditions, including the Táiñmé and men's military societies, with peyote ceremonies.[78]

Multinational Native urban communities also spawned activism, most prominently the American Indian Movement (AIM). In 1968, Ojibwe men and women living in Minneapolis founded AIM in response to urban problems, including police violence and unemployment, but they also fought for sovereignty and against poverty on reservations and the removal of Native children from their families. Mohawk Richard Oakes, who had moved across the continent from the Akwesasne Mohawk reservation to San Francisco, became part of that city's Indian community and one of the leaders of activists' 1969 takeover of Alcatraz Island, in San Francisco Bay, in the name of "Indians of all tribes." In the late 1970s, Native women founded Women of All Red Nations (WARN) to work together against the practices of forced sterilization and removing Native children from their homes and communities. As the scholars Brooke Bauer and Elizabeth Ellis observe, organizations like AIM and WARN defined themselves as broadly Native "to articulate a shared struggle against the United States and to unify people of many different nations in their fights for self-determination and sovereignty."[79]

Activism stressed sovereign rights. In 1968 Canada began charging Mohawks a bridge toll and customs fees when they brought in goods from the United States. Mohawks pointed to Jay's Treaty of 1794, between the new United States and Britain (of which Canada had still been part), which stated that "the Indians dwelling on either side of the said boundary line" had the right "freely to pass and repass, by land or inland navigation into the respective territories and countries of the two parties on the continent of America . . . and freely carry on trade and commerce with each other." Mohawk activists blockaded the bridge between Canada and the United States for months, until, in February 1969, the Canadian government gave in and stopped charging Mohawks. Forty years later, in 2009, the Canadian government decided to arm border guards with handguns, including at the border checkpoint on Mohawk land, within a residential neighborhood near a bus stop and a playground. Mohawks feared errant gunfire and asserted their sovereign rights. After several standoffs, the Canadian government stuck to its decision about guns but moved the checkpoint north, off of Mohawk land. As Mohawk scholar Scott Manning Stevens explains, Mohawks successfully argued that the "guns of someone else's nation" can't be "on our land."[80]

Because of activism of various kinds in the second half of the twentieth century, court decisions and legislation began to swing back toward recognizing Native sovereignty. In the 1959 *Williams v. Lee* case, a non-Native owner of a store on the Navajo reservation sued Navajo citizens Paul and Lorena Williams in Arizona court for overdue bills. The store owner won in the state court, but the Navajo Nation appealed in federal court, and the U.S. Supreme Court ruled that the store owner should have sued in Navajo court, not an Arizona court. Citing *Worcester v. Georgia,* from more than a century earlier, the Supreme Court ruled that Arizona had no jurisdiction over businesses on tribal lands.[81]

In 1974, Congress passed the Indian Self-Determination Act, recognizing exactly what many Native people had been fighting for: individual rights *and* tribal sovereignty. The federal government was still financially responsible for treaty obligations, yet the tribes would get control of federal aid programs and schools on reservations. The Indian Self-Determination Act paved the way for tribal economic development, and the 1988 Indian Gaming Regulatory Act recognized the right of tribes to have gaming facilities and required states to come to agreements with tribes that wanted casinos for the jobs and revenue they could bring. In an important recognition of sovereign powers, the 1978 Indian Child Welfare Act (ICWA) said that tribal governments and tribal courts have exclusive jurisdiction over child custody proceedings involving Native children living on that tribe's reservation. Such proceedings must either be held in tribal courts or include the participation of the child's tribal government.

Economic development, cultural preservation and promotion, and self-determination can be mutually reinforcing, in what Cherokee anthropologist Courtney Lewis calls "economic sovereignty." The Quapaw Business Committee negotiated a better agricultural lease on some of the land that the Quapaws had bought back in the 1930s and used that money to improve their council grounds and infrastructure for their powwow and other tribal gatherings when the nation would come together every summer. They used some of the money to pay NCAI membership dues to join in national actions and lobbying. At their first NCAI meeting, the Business Committee members joined the decision to oppose termination. Quapaws increased participation in old and new customs, including dances and naming ceremonies. Later in the twentieth and twenty-first centuries, the Quapaw Nation would build a casino, an industrial park, a large ranching business, a coffee roasting plant, and more, with employment opportunities and economic benefits going to the Quapaws and to the region. The Eastern Shawnee Tribe of Oklahoma, who in the 1920s had no assets and a reservation of only fifty-eight acres after repeated dispossessions and allotment, now has a casino that employs hundreds of locals and has allowed the tribe to reinvest in diversified businesses, including a bank, as well as fund social services, education, and research. Tribes can provide the same kinds of small-business loans and incentives to tribal members that other governments do for their citizens.[82]

The United Nations Declaration on the Rights of Indigenous Peoples, adopted by the UN General Assembly in 2007, over the objection of the United States (which subsequently reversed its position), reflects much of this activism, including the right to self-determination and self-government, the right to "not be forcibly removed from their lands," "the right to practise and revitalize their cultural traditions and customs," "the right to manifest, practise, develop and teach their spiritual and religious traditions, customs and ceremonies," "the right to maintain, protect, and have access in privacy to their religious and cultural sites," "the right to the use and control of their ceremonial objects," and the right to repatriation of ceremonial objects and human remains and restitution for "any cultural, intellectual, religious and spiritual property taken without their free, prior and informed consent or in violation of their laws, traditions and customs." Importantly, it states that "Indigenous peoples have the right to revitalize, use, develop and transmit to future

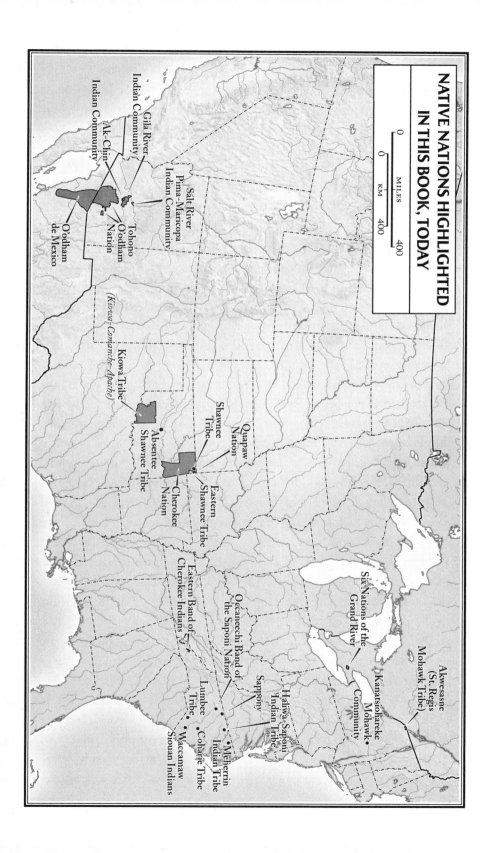

NATIVE NATIONS HIGHLIGHTED
IN THIS BOOK, TODAY

Gila River
Indian Community

Ak-Chin
Indian Community

Salt River
Pima-Maricopa
Indian Community

Tohono
O'odham
Nation

O'odham
de Mexico

(Kiowa-Comanche-Apache)

Kiowa Tribe

Absentee
Shawnee Tribe

Shawnee
Tribe

Quapaw
Nation

Cherokee
Nation

Eastern
Shawnee Tribe

Eastern Band of
Cherokee Indians

Occaneechi Band of
the Saponi Nation

Saponi

Haliwa-Saponi
Indian Tribe

Meherrin
Indian Tribe

Lumbee
Tribe

Coharie Tribe

Waccamaw
Siouan Indians

Six Nations of the
Grand River

Kanatsiohareke
Mohawk
Community

Akwesasne
(St. Regis
Mohawk Tribe)

MILES
0   400

KM
0   400

generations their histories, languages, oral traditions, philosophies, writing systems and literatures, and to designate and retain their own names for communities, places and persons."[83]

CONCLUSION

Tohono O'odham elder Mary Jane Juan-Moore recalls how one year her grandmother returned to her family's saguaro camp for the season, as she had for her entire life and her ancestors had before her. Yet when she got to the camp, her pots for boiling the saguaro syrup were gone. Someone had come upon this place—her family's property—and taken them. So when Juan-Moore sees a Tohono O'odham pot in a museum, she often thinks, "That pot is probably my grandmother's."[84] In 1983, the UNC Research Laboratories of Archaeology began excavating the Occaneechi village on the banks of the Eno River near Hillsborough, North Carolina, not knowing that Native people whose ancestors had likely lived at that town were living just a few miles away. Today, collaborations between tribes and academic researchers, including UNC archaeologists, provide information about the past that was impossible to re-create when scholars didn't acknowledge Native people in their midst. And the American Indian designers, curators, and administrators of the National Museum of the American Indian on the National Mall, in Washington, D.C., have built, in large part with funding from Native nations, not a museum focused on colonization and loss, but a monument to the Native present in all its diversity, with connections to the past and the future.[85]

And new crafts based in old traditions are being made. Quapaw potter Betty Gaedtke regularly gives demonstrations of her pottery-making at schools and events around Oklahoma, Missouri, and Arkansas. At one, a member of the audience asked if her beautiful pots were "reproductions." It was a reasonable question—they have the same off-white and muddy-red swirls as the ancient pots under glass in the exhibits at the Quapaws' Downstream Casino. But they are not reproductions, Gaedtke explained; they are real twenty-first-century Quapaw pottery, designed and made by a modern Quapaw woman who has researched and experimented to recover and honor ancient traditions of tempering, glazing, and decorating. After Gaedtke's pottery demonstration that I saw in 2017 came Virginia Mouse, with her niece and her tiny granddaughter, who showed us how to make traditional pecan butter with pecans and roasted corn, mixing it in a food processor. Back home in Quapaw, Oklahoma, Billy Joe Proctor reconstructs and revives the Quapaw language by poring through old documents trying to figure out what Quapaw sounds French and Spanish speakers were trying to record in their transcriptions. Gaedtke, Mouse, and Proctor are twenty-first-century Americans and twenty-first-century Quapaws, connecting their past and present in order to build a Quapaw future for their children. It's because of revitalization efforts like these, says Tom Sakokweniónkwas Porter, who does similar work as a Mohawk, that today you can find fifteen-year-olds who can tell you more "about

Hidden in Plain Sight, beaded bandolier bag by
Martha Berry (Cherokee). In the nineteenth and twentieth
centuries, Cherokee women put traditional symbols in their
beadwork, unnoticed by missionaries and U.S. officials.
COURTESY OF MARTHA BERRY. PHOTOGRAPH BY DAVE BERRY

tradition and about history" than most Mohawks who grew up a century ago.[86]

Despite the tremendous losses of the past two centuries, Native nations have survived, not only as the descendants of once powerful peoples but as nations within the nation-states of the United States, Mexico, and Canada. Since 2000, the U.S. Census has counted more and more Native Americans, with the 2020 census reporting an astounding 9.7 million. Not all of them are actual citizens of Native nations, but the vast majority do report a specific tribal affiliation, so there is some truth in the number. Of course, Native nations determine their own citizenship. Indeed, one of Native nations' most obvious ways of asserting sovereignty today is by deciding who is a tribal citizen and who is not, a power that each tribe holds for itself. U.S. policies did unfathomable damage, but Native Americans repeatedly rebuilt their nations and figured out how to continue being their own distinct peoples within a vastly changed continent.[87]

Comanche scholar Paul Chaat Smith notes, "Our survival against desperate odds is worthy of a celebration, one that embraces every aspect of our bizarre and fantastic lives, the tremendous sacrifices made on our behalf by our parents and grandparents and their parents." Richard West (Southern Cheyenne), founding director of the National Museum of the American Indian, says, "In the United States, all of us who call ourselves native peoples have a profound feeling that a powerful renascence is sweeping Indian America. The worst, which was very bad indeed, is over, and our confidence in our sense of cultural time and place is growing with each day." Joy Harjo (Muscogee), who was U.S. poet laureate from 2019 to 2022, closes her poem "Anchorage" with the bittersweet message of surviving genocide: "Who would believe the fantastic and terrible story of all of our survival those who were never meant to survive?"[88]

SOVEREIGNTY TODAY

I N THE SUMMER OF 2018, I PICKED UP TRIBAL HISTORIC PRESER-
vation Officer Everett Bandy at his office at the headquarters of
the Quapaw Nation. We drove around Quapaw country, Bandy
telling me where to go and occasionally reminding me to slow down
on the tight corners of narrow country roads. One of the places he
took me was their new roundhouse, which Bandy helped build. It's
all wood, gorgeous, and built on the dimensions of the old Quapaw
roundhouse that burned down before Bandy was born. They modeled the altar on the old one, with all of the sacred components of
the Quapaw Native American Church, pulling together Quapaw,
more general Native, and Christian elements. The altar has a cross
through the middle that also represents the crossroads, with east-to-
west being the road of life, symbols that go back to the Mississippian period of Quapaw ancestors at least eight centuries ago.

When Bandy showed me the roundhouse, he said to me, "I want
you to tell this in your book." Bandy and I have talked a lot about
this book, and a lot about Quapaw history, but our visit to the
roundhouse was the only time he said that. Twenty-first-century
Quapaws built this roundhouse for themselves and future Quapaws
to worship in. Bandy explained that, in the second half of the twentieth century, Quapaw participation in the Native American Church
declined, and for a while the only ceremonies his people commonly
performed were dances and burials. With today's revival in Quapaw
culture, history, and religion, Quapaws need this roundhouse, along
with their language and pottery revivals, their bison and cattle op-

erations, and their governing structures. They are people living in the present who inherited identities from their ancestors, who kept being Quapaw through the hardest times.[1]

TODAY, ALL ACROSS Indian country, Native nations are committing to reviving and expanding cultural opportunities, especially for their youth. In recent decades, the Haudenosaunee have built new longhouses for their ceremonies that can hold hundreds of people. In 1979, Mohawks founded the Akwesasne Freedom School to teach the community's children through Mohawk language and culture, and similar efforts take place among the Six Nations of the Grand River. In the 1990s, a group of Mohawks returned to the Mohawk Valley to found the community of Kanatsiohareke to reignite Mohawk language, religion, and lifeways in their ancestral homeland, "for the seeking, restoring and maintaining of the Great Peace."[2]

White settlers who took Native land wrote a new history that hid Native nationhood and power and made their own rise seem inevitable and justified. That is why textbooks rewrote the earlier centuries and told us that Christopher Columbus had "discovered" a new land and the Pilgrims had settled in a "wilderness." Nineteenth-century white Americans knew the reality of Native power and presence, and they hid it on purpose, to justify themselves. They didn't merely expel Native people from their land; they pretended it had never really been theirs at all. By ignoring Native farming and resource management, they claimed that Native Americans didn't really have a right to the land. By calling them primitive and unorganized, they persuaded themselves that these weren't sovereign nations and that they were inevitably, if sadly, doomed out of existence in the modern world. And once they were mostly out of the sight of most Americans, too many came to think they didn't exist anymore at all. In 1986, a group of Yosemite (Miwok) Indians visited the National Museum of Natural History, in Washington, D.C. They were surprised to read in one of the exhibits that their tribe had gone extinct in the nineteenth century.[3]

The Yosemite Indians' tale is not a harmless anecdote about a museum getting some history wrong; it's a horror story in which people looked their own genocide in the face and were told they aren't here. Deborah A. Miranda tells of spotting a fourth grader recording a video report in Mission Dolores, in San Francisco. Miranda told her, "Guess what? I'm a member of the Ohlone/Costanoan–Esselen Nation myself! Some of my ancestors lived in this mission." The girl's "face drained, her body went stiff, and she stared at me as if I had risen, an Indigenous skeleton clad in decrepit rags, from beneath the clay bricks of the courtyard." Miranda realized that "having me suddenly appear in the middle of her video project must have been a lot like turning the corner to find the (dead) person you were talking about suddenly in your face, talking back."[4]

Lumbee students at the University of North Carolina report finding themselves exhausted from repeatedly explaining who they are. Most of them grew up in Robeson County and went to K–12 schools in which the majority of students were Lumbee, so they rarely had to explain what it meant to be Lumbee or Native. In Chapel Hill, only a hundred miles north of home and in a state where Lumbees are the largest Indigenous population, they are shocked at the widespread ignorance of Native history and nationhood. These young people face the unreasonable choice between constantly explaining and defending their identities and simply hiding them to make their everyday lives easier.[5]

Yet once you are paying attention, you can see the Native past and present all around us, in the ways in which plants, animals, and landscapes connect contemporary Native Americans to the continent's Indigenous past. My Cherokee colleague Benjamin Frey told me about the tall yaupon holly bush that grows between his building on campus and the building right next door. Mississippians and their Cherokee and other southeastern descendants roasted its leaves and shoots to make black drink, the strong caffeinated tea that renewed them for clearheaded discussions and wise decision-making. Once Professor Frey showed me that yaupon bush, I began noticing them all over campus and in my neighbors' yards. I have walked past these bushes countless times, sometimes on my way to teach Native history, without knowing that I could have grabbed a leaf to use as a prop in class. Professor Frey points out that the yaupon are "hiding in plain sight," just as he himself walks to his office, a twenty-first-century professor and a Cherokee.

Like Ben Frey and Everett Bandy, David Martínez takes time to explain to outsiders the connections between the O'odham past and present. Standing at S'edav Va'aki (Pueblo Grande), he notes that "the remains, the ruins of our ancestors are places that you really don't want to visit. They're sacred enough where you have to respect that boundary around that location because these things, this place belongs to them," yet he also acknowledges the need to show them and explain them. As one of their descendants, he links what to outsiders might look like mysterious ruins to the O'odham communities of today. As Professor Martínez explains,

> I think persons like myself, speaking for myself, are willing to come here and talk about this place, to tell you the story that I've told precisely because I want others to learn about why this place is special to us and about how they can approach this location from a point of humbleness, from a point of wanting to learn, to understand, to appreciate this place as being a part of their sacred geography too. It's not just a tourist attraction.[6]

Still, teaching this lesson over and over can be frustrating, even for a professor as patient as Martínez. "As an educator," he says, "I do not mind adding to the public's knowledge of Indians. Nonetheless, in a nation that was once entirely Indian Country, it is nothing short of astounding the amount of ignorance I face regularly, even among Americans who grew up in the middle of ancient Indian homelands yet do not know what tribes once lived where their own homes now stand." Catawba scholar Brooke Bauer echoes Martínez's point, noting that "it's disturbing and tiring that Native people and scholars of Native America still have to emphasize" Native people's place in the past, present, and future of this continent. "Until Indian components become a standard part of every American's educational experience," Professor Martínez concludes, "the peoples, nations, and events in Indian history, a crucial part of this country's story that everyone ought to know, will remain lacunae in the collective consciousness."[7]

All across the continent, Native people are researching and teaching their languages and reviving and reinventing traditional arts, crafts, dances, and ceremonies. They assert their sovereignty in their tribal governments, their schools, U.S. federal court, public demonstrations, and countless family homes, where they tell their children true histories of their nations. This work has birthed a new era of Indigenous pride and cultural revitalization all across the continent.

Native historians have transformed how non-Native scholars see the long history of the Americas and the ways in which the present is connected to the past. Opportunities made available by the Native American Graves Protection and Repatriation Act, revenue from casinos and other tribal businesses, and increasing numbers of Native students going to college and graduate school have enabled tribes to direct and fund research into their own history, conducted by both Indigenous and non-Indigenous researchers. Tribal historic preservation officers like Everett Bandy and other scholars within Native nations are collecting historical knowledge from their communities and preserving it for the future. The Osage Nation Museum, founded by Osage scholar John Joseph Mathews in 1938, has been a model for the approximately two hundred museums and cultural centers that today present each nation's history on its own terms, places where, as Scott Manning Stevens puts it, "living cultures are as much a part of the fabric of the institution as the artifacts still displayed in exhibits." The Native American and Indigenous Studies Association (NAISA) was started by Indigenous scholars and encourages scholars' involvement with Native nations today, both for the knowledge they can add to what academic historians write and teach and for the importance of including the questions and concerns of Native nations today in what and how we study.[8]

The Shawnee Tribe, for example, encourages the practice of Nikani' kapawe ("Stand in front"), "science led by communities." As they explain, "researchers have a history of studying Native American people without their involvement or consent, treating Indigenous communities as research subjects rather than partners. Such studies often present skewed or incorrect results, findings that do not take into consideration the knowledge, values, or worldview of Native people." Chief Benjamin Barnes explains, "Only by participating with universities and other institutions," including those based in homelands from which Native nations were removed, "can we express our needs and guide future research projects, which in turn will lead to better research outcomes for the students, universities, and more importantly, our tribal citizens. When we create relationships of mutual collaboration and both sides are willing to listen to each other, a more complete truth of our Shawnee people can be told." This book reflects the influence and involvement of Indigenous scholars—both in academic institutions and in Native nations. It certainly would not be possible without them.[9]

TODAY'S INDIGENOUS RENAISSANCE is threatened by the continued invisibility of Native pasts and present in American culture and politics. There are politicians and policymakers who ignore or attack tribal sovereignty or assume that Native religion isn't protected by the U.S. Constitution. Tribal governments asserting their jurisdictions and buying back land can find themselves in fights against non-Native neighbors who fear coming under Native jurisdictions. In a 2022 article, *The New York Times* cast a fishing rights dispute between New York State and a Shinnecock fisherman as "a clash between contemporary rules and ancient customs" rather than, as the judge ruling for the fisherman recognized, a jurisdictional clash between two present-day sovereignties. In the 2023 U.S. Supreme Court case *Haaland v. Brackeen,* the states of Texas, Louisiana, and Indiana, along with several non-Native prospective parents, challenged the Indian Child Welfare Act of 1978 (ICWA), under which tribal governments have jurisdiction over Native children's foster care placement and adoption. The plaintiffs argued that

ICWA is unconstitutionally based on race. Tribal governments, along with the U.S. government in defending the law, had to explain once again that being Native American "is tied to membership in Indian tribes—which is about politics, not race."[10]

Forgetting that Native nations predated the United States also imperils the sovereignty of Native nations. The U.S. borders across Mohawk and Tohono O'odham land literally sever autonomous Native territory. Haudenosaunee sovereign communities are spread across the U.S. states of New York, Wisconsin, and Oklahoma and the Canadian provinces of Ontario and Quebec. U.S. opposition to immigration from Mexico puts the Tohono O'odham in a particularly fraught position. The Tohono reservation is the second largest in the United States at 2.7 million acres, more than three-quarters the size of Connecticut, and within it is a seventy-five-mile border between the United States and Mexico. Most Tohono O'odham, around thirty-four thousand, are U.S. citizens, but about two thousand live in Mexico. Those who live on the reservation are supposed to be able to go back and forth by showing their tribal identification cards to U.S. and Mexican authorities on what is all Tohono O'odham land. But the fact that some are U.S. citizens and some are Mexican citizens creates difficulties, including preventing some families from living together. George Ignacio pointed out the absurdity that his father was chairman of the Tohono O'odham Nation and yet, because he was born on the Mexican side of the border, was called an "illegal alien." Mexican O'odham who are the descendants of Himuri O'odham from the Altar and Magdalena river valleys live mostly in Mexican towns and have no Indigenous rights north of the border. In the face of proposals to build a wall along that border, Tohono O'odham Nation chairman Edward D. Manuel repeatedly reminded Americans, "We are a sovereign nation and they have to talk to us before they make a decision." The Tohono O'odham Nation Police Department has an enforcement partnership with the U.S. Border Patrol, and the nation spends an estimated $3 million each year on border-related expenses, including medical care for migrants.[11]

The task of reminding other Americans of Native sovereignty is particularly difficult for Native communities that are not officially recognized by the federal government, such as the Lumbees, the Haliwa-Saponis, the Occaneechis, and the Coharies in North Carolina. Particularly in states on the Atlantic coast, colonists had greatly reduced their autonomy and land base even before the United States was created, so, as Ojibwe historian Jean O'Brien explains, they "lack a treaty relationship with the United States" and therefore the kind of evidence that the federal government generally requires for official recognition. Without federal recognition, it's hard to access the protections of the NAGPRA, the ICWA, and the Indian Gaming Regulatory Act.[12]

It was in part the 1930s shift away from damaging U.S. Indian policy that slowly made room for the current renaissance, and sliding backward could too easily reverse that progress, as termination did for many tribes in the 1950s. In 2007, the Mashpee Wampanoag Tribe gained federal recognition, and in 2015 the U.S. government designated their lands in Massachusetts as a reservation, with the protections from local and state encroachment that reservation status gives. But in 2020, the Trump administration revoked that reservation status, the president himself once having said in testimony to Congress that "some of the reservations that you have approved . . . they don't look like Indians to me." It is exactly that kind of ignorance of Native history, identity, and sovereignty that still threatens Native nations. Yet the continued existence of small nations, many without federal recognition, in New England, North Carolina, Virginia, Louisiana, California, and many other places, through centuries of pressure to incorporate into either white or Black communities or other Native nations, is striking proof of the depth of their identities. A few months later a judge reversed the 2020 decision, but it is a real reminder of the continued threats faced by Native nations.[13]

The 2020 U.S. Supreme Court ruling in *McGirt v. Oklahoma* was a win for tribal sovereignty, in a case regarding jurisdiction over criminal cases. The court ruled that the treaty-defined boundaries of the Muscogee, Cherokee, Quapaw, Choctaw, Chickasaw, and Seminole nations still remain in full force, because Congress never disestablished their reservations. One result is that Google Maps has added clear borders around these nations and others with similar legal status. Yet less than two years after *McGirt*, the U.S. Supreme Court ruled in *Oklahoma v. Castro-Huerta* that the state does have some jurisdiction in crimes in which the accused is non-Native. The majority opinion, written by Justice Brett Kavanaugh, held that *Worcester v. Georgia* has been so eroded as to allow for state involvement in tribal matters. Justice Neil Gorsuch's dissent in the *Castro-Huerta* case detailed the history of Cherokees and Georgia, blasted the State of Oklahoma for portraying reservations as "lawless dystopias," and accused the majority of coming to its decision "as if by oracle, without any sense of the history . . . and unattached to any . . . legal authority. Truly, a more ahistorical and mistaken statement of Indian law would be hard to fathom."[14]

The Akimel O'odham poet Natalie Diaz writes in her poem "The Beauty of a Busted Fruit" of the "sad red-blue scab marking us both victim and survivor." Diaz reminds readers that it's important not to let Native survival obscure Native victimhood, the history of trauma, the scab that could still too easily be pulled off to expose the wound that lies below. Ojibwe historian Brenda J. Child echoes Diaz's sentiment: "It is impossible to overemphasize the personal toll of dispossession and reservation poverty on American Indian lives. 'Survival' rarely felt like freedom or sovereignty to Indigenous people." The Chickasaw scholar Jodi Byrd similarly cautions that "though the Chickasaw Nation has certainly rebuilt and is today just as unconquerable and unconquered as it ever was, there is a difference between recovered and having never lost in the first place." Ho-Chunk scholar Amy Lonetree cautions that "we did survive a holocaust in North America, and even though the U.S. government refuses to take responsibility for this act, we as Indigenous people must name this history for what it was: genocide." Scholar Nick Estes, of the Lower Brule Sioux (Kul Wicasa/Oceti Sakowin Oyate), points out that self-determination is only the beginning of the "decolonization, the repatriation of stolen lands and stolen lives," necessary to "undo centuries of settler colonialism." Ojibwe scholar Anton Treuer explains in his *Everything You Wanted to Know About Indians but Were Afraid to Ask:*

> It's kind of like this. Someone was hitting the Indian in the head with a hammer for decades, and it did a lot of damage. Now the government is (for the most part) done hitting the Indian in the head with a hammer. But there is still all this damage that takes a very long time to repair. And the government is not interested in repairing the damage—it all happened in the past. So Indians are left to heal themselves. Language and culture loss, many health issues, substance abuse, the educational opportunity gap, systemic racism, and many other problems in Indian country can be directly attributed to specific government policies. It's easy to push people into a pit, but it can be very hard for them to climb back out.[15]

The American Indian unemployment and poverty rates are consistently higher than the national average and are especially high on reservations. Native Americans have a life expectancy that is a shocking eleven years shorter than that of the average American. They disproportionately suffer from heart disease, diabetes, respiratory disease, alcoholism, suicide, and homicide—all of which tend to accompany poverty and trauma, compounded by inadequate access to healthcare in many places, even though health services are treaty-obligated to many Native nations. Covid-19 hit reservations with high rates of chronic disease and homes without running water or electricity particularly hard. In the early months of the pandemic, tribal communities had the nation's highest per capita infection and hospital rates and devastating death rates in some places. In 2020, Native Americans made up 5 percent of Arizona's population but 11 percent of its deaths from Covid-19.[16]

A S IN THE past, solutions lie with Native people themselves and the determination of the rest of us to listen to them. Because in the past few decades many tribes had taken over the management of their public health systems from the Bureau of Indian Affairs and strengthened their governments' capabilities and authority, tribal governments were in a better position than many cities, counties, school systems, and states to respond to the public health crisis of Covid-19. They were able to move quickly to convey vital information about the pandemic, institute lockdowns and mask mandates, move services online, and implement testing programs and vaccination rollouts. Many tribal governments have ultimately had better outcomes than their neighboring non-Native-majority counties, in part because Native Americans trusted their own chosen officials and health professionals.[17]

In part because of pressure from Native groups, tribal governments are now included along with state and local entities as government partners in receiving funds for Covid relief, the 2021 infrastructure bill, and the 2022 Inflation Reduction Act, and they are represented in America250, the official planning body for the 250-year anniversary of 1776. As Paul DeMain (Oneida Nation of Wisconsin) explains, decades of "filing lawsuits and challenging government directives" have led to "greater power in the hands of the tribes and ushered in a period of greater consultation and cooperation." Tribal governments have modernized and developed new powers and responsibilities. Although poverty rates remain high, they have been dropping, average income has risen, and the numbers of Native-owned businesses and Native students in college have grown dramatically.[18]

Tribes are working on preventive health, exercise programs, and community gardens. The Eastern Shawnee Tribe has built greenhouses as part of "decolonizing people's diet," as Eastern Shawnee Tribe land use coordinator Andrew Gourd explains. The Quapaw Nation operates an Indigenous seed bank to which it invites other Native nations to contribute. An official delegation from the Eastern Band of Cherokee Indians traveled to London in 2019—the first time in 255 years—dressing in traditional Cherokee regalia for the London New Year's Day Parade and in their usual twenty-first-century clothes for the delegation's meetings. David Treuer reflects, "I can't help feeling we are using modernity in the best possible way:

to work together and to heal what was broken." Comanche author and NMAI curator Paul Chaat Smith puts it starkly: "I'm glad to be here. Better than the alternative."[19]

Native artists, scholars, and teachers use many means of conveying this combination of victimhood and survival. Most of the paintings of Mohawk artist David Kanietakeron Fadden are colorful and full of life, with men and women dancing, singing, beating drums, and throwing their heads back in joyful laughter. Probably his best-known work is *"Kill the Indian, Save the Man."* On the left side of the piece are black-and-white images of Native children dressed in boarding school clothes, their faces serious. But as the viewer's eye moves to the right, the children begin to smile and take on vibrant colors, each one dressed in a different way, in the traditions of their Native nations. Then, if you look back at the boarding school children on the left, you may notice that, even in their drab uniforms and haircuts, they are individuals, each with his or her own face, and self. Fadden explains, "A lot of the young people are wearing traditional outfits again. That's representative of today where we no longer have to go to these residential schools, but we can practice our spiritual beliefs out in the open. We are emerging from that dark time."[20]

ACKNOWLEDGMENTS

I DEDICATE THIS BOOK TO MY UNC AMERICAN INDIAN AND IN-digenous Studies (AIIS) students. Without them and several key colleagues, I literally could not have written it. While this book focuses on Native nations, I also discuss other kinds of Native communities that preserve and build Indigenous knowledge and identities. Working alongside UNC's Native community for twenty years has changed how I work as a scholar and made this book possible. I particularly want to thank two decades of AIIS graduate students for what they have taught me: Mikaela Adams, Brooke Bauer, Frankie Bauer, Marissa Carmi, Patricia Dawson, David Dry, Elizabeth Ellis, Duane Esarey, Nathan Gill, Jonathan Hancock, Stark Harbour, Lucas Kelley, Aubrey Lauersdorf, Courtney Lewis, Jessica Locklear, Meredith McCoy, Warren Milteer, José Manuel Moreno Vega, Jami Powell, Gabrielle Purcell, Sebastián Quiñones, Julie Reed, Marty Richardson, Gracie Riehm, Sierra Roark, Katy Simpson Smith, Christina Snyder, Rose Stremlau, Daniel Velásquez, and Garrett Wright, as well as Nikki Locklear at Duke. A key group of American Indian and Indigenous Studies colleagues was fundamental to this project: Malinda Maynor Lowery, Danny Bell, Ben Frey, Keith Richotte, Jenny Tone-Pah-Hote, and Theda Perdue. I have also learned a great deal from AIIS colleagues past and present, including Qua Lynch Adkins, Juliana Barr, Brandon Bayne, Brandi Brooks, Randi Byrd, Larry Chavis, Daniel Cobb, Amanda Cobb-Greetham, Marcus Collins, Andrew Curley, Stephen Davis, Jean Dennison, Clyde Ellis, Raquel Escobar, Mary Beth

Fitts, Tol Foster, Michael Green, Stephen Greetham, Amy Locklear Hertel, Danielle Hiraldo, Jesalyn Keziah, Michael Lambert, Valerie Lambert, Heather Lapham, Miguel La Serna, Wayne Lee, Patricia McAnany, Jillian Ransom McNeill, Cynthia Radding, Brett Riggs, John Scarry, Margie Scarry, Erika Serrato, Vincas Steponaitis, and Chris Teuton.

The book also would never have come to be without a particular lunch with my agents, Jill Kneerim and Lucy Cleland. We had spent the lunch discussing a different book I was considering writing, but as we were leaving we suddenly thought of this idea, sat back down, ordered coffee, and sketched out what became this book. They and my amazing editor, Molly Turpin, have shaped the book from its beginnings. As she did on my previous book, Molly has proved the best of editors—encouraging, querying, pushing, supporting, and adding both brilliant insights and well-placed pencil edits and deletions, all at just the right times and with just the right tone. Many, many thanks to Molly, Lucy, and Jill, as well as to Monica Rae Brown, Marni Folkman, and the rest of the Random House team. A Guggenheim Fellowship in U.S. history, a fellowship from UNC's Institute for Arts and Humanities, and multiple other funding sources at UNC assisted my research and gave me precious time to write.

Marty Smith, John DuVal, Alexa Chambers, Randy Chambers, and my amazing writing group, Carolyn Eastman and Jocelyn Olcott, read every word of the manuscript, adding to both its quality and my joy in writing and revising it. I am very grateful to those who read and greatly improved parts of the manuscript: Everett Bandy, Brooke Bauer, Frankie Bauer, Brandon Bayne, Barry Bienstock, Marissa Carmi, Patricia Dawson, Brian DeLay, Kay DuVal, Elizabeth Ellis, Eric Foner, Jonathan Hancock, Karen Kupperman, Jacob Lee, Wayne Lee, David Martínez, Malinda Maynor Lowery, Andrew McKenzie, Warren Milteer, Julie Reed, Keith Richotte, Daniel Richter, John Scarry, Margie Scarry, Christina Snyder, Vincas Steponaitis, Scott Manning Stevens, Stephen Warren, and the undergraduate students in Marissa Carmi's spring 2023 Approaches to American Indian Studies course. For comments that broadened and deepened my thinking in various seminars (and hallways, restaurants, and bars),

I thank Cemil Aydin, Michael Blaakman, Chad Bryant, Melissa Bullard, Kathryn Burns, Jack Callaghan, Megan Cherry, Laurent Corbeil, H. M. Cushman, Laura Edwards, Oswaldo Estrada, Emma Flatt, Kevin Fogg, Blake Grindon, Glenn Hinson, Reeve Huston, Kenneth Janken, Konrad Jarausch, John Kasson, Joy Kasson, Michelle King, Richard Kohn, Lloyd Kramer, Shayne Legassie, Lisa Lindsay, Daniel Maher, Tim Marr, Terence McIntosh, Hugo Méndez, Alyssa Mt. Pleasant, Philip Otterness, Rosa Perelmuter, Elena Telles Ryan, George Sabo, Eunice Sahle, Ana María Silva Campo, Kumi Silva, Keely Smith, William Sturkey, Sean Kicummah Teuton, Wendy Warren, Benjamin Waterhouse, Harry Watson, Brett Whalen, Tomasz Wicherkiewicz, Molly Worthen, and Karin Wulf. Students Nancy Andoh, Elizabeth Carbone, Ila Chilberg, Lacey Hunter, Kate Miller, Julia Short, and Sydney Simmons provided valuable assistance and delightful interactions, and I learned from working with Elina Carpen on her honors thesis on Ossomocomuck. For help with illustrations and maps, I thank Morris Arnold, Jennifer Baker, Brandon Bayne, Lori Belknap, Jennifer Belt, Martha Berry, Elizabeth Bray, Tamira Brennan, Amanda Bulger, Aaron Carapella, Patricia Dawson, Ross Frank, Garrett Gibson, Megan Green, Beau Harris, Tim Hodgdon, Linda Jacobson, Kenny Jones, Lisa Keys, J. Laroche, Wayne Lee, Jon May, Howell Perkins, Linda Poolaw, Pat Rivera, Dario Scarinci, Neal Shipe, Nathan Sowry, Vin Steponaitis, and Lindsey Vogel-Teeter.

Finally, as always, I am tremendously grateful for my family and friends. None of us wanted to be quarantined, but hunkering down with Marty, Quentin, and Calvin brought unexpected joys. Our little locked-down world was enriched by the Bernhardt-Wrights, Chambers, Crupi-Makarushkas, La Sernas, Lees, Lentz-Smiths, McLeod-Whalens, Michelmans, Murray-Moores, and Virdins, and by family trips with Niell, Anjana, and Carol and weekly remote gatherings with those three plus Kay, John, Anne, and sometimes Steve and Dan. Thanks to Marybeth, Gene, Jane, Stacy, and John for their cheerful inquiries about the book whenever we passed on the sidewalks of Trinity Park. (It's done!) Wonderful colleagues in the UNC History Department kept me happy at work, even when through a screen—particular thanks, in addition to those mentioned above, to Matt Andrews, Karen Auerbach, Bill Barney, Claude Clegg, Erik Gellman, Antwain Hunter, Jerma Jackson, Lauren Jarvis, Louise McReynolds, Mike Morgan, Morgan Pitelka, Don Raleigh, Don Reid, Eren Tasar, and Katie Turk. Thanks especially to Department Chair Lisa Lindsay for her support and constant good cheer. With much love to Stephen, Mary Kay, Dave, Linda, Mary Lou, Len, Vanessa, and their families, and in loving remembrance of Frank. And, yet again, love and gratitude beyond words to Marty, my chef, bartender, best reader, and partner in all things.

FURTHER READING

Barker, Joanne. *Sovereignty Matters: Locations of Contestation and Possibility in Indigenous Struggles for Self-Determination.* Lincoln, 2005.

Bates, Denise E., ed. *We Will Always Be Here: Native Peoples on Living and Thriving in the South.* Gainesville, 2016.

Bauer, Brooke M. *Becoming Catawba: Catawba Indian Women and Nation-Building, 1540–1840.* Tuscaloosa, 2022.

Bauer, William J., Jr. *We Were All Like Migrant Workers Here: Work, Community, and Memory on California's Round Valley Reservation, 1850–1941.* Chapel Hill, 2009.

Blackhawk, Ned. *The Rediscovery of America: Native Peoples and the Unmaking of U.S. History.* New Haven, 2023.

———. *Violence over the Land: Indians and Empires in the Early American West.* Cambridge, Mass., 2006.

Blansett, Kent. *A Journey to Freedom: Richard Oakes, Alcatraz, and the Red Power Movement.* New Haven, 2018.

Blee, Lisa, and Jean M. O'Brien. *Monumental Mobility: The Memory Work of Massasoit.* Chapel Hill, 2019.

Bonaparte, Darren. *Creation and Confederation: The Living History of the Iroquois.* New York, 2006.

Brooks, Lisa. *Our Beloved Kin: A New History of King Philip's War.* New Haven, 2018.

Byrd, Jodi A. *The Transit of Empire: Indigenous Critiques of Colonialism.* Minneapolis, 2011.

Champagne, Duane. *Notes from the Center of Turtle Island.* Lanham, Md., 2010.

Chang, David. *The World and All the Things Upon It: Native Hawaiian Geographies of Exploration.* Minneapolis, 2016.

Cherokee Phoenix (newspaper). https://www.cherokeephoenix.org/, https://www.wcu.edu/library/digitalcollections/cherokeephoenix/.

Chickasaw TV. https://www.chickasaw.tv/.

Child, Brenda J. *Boarding School Seasons: American Indian Families, 1900–1940.* Lincoln, 1981.

———. *Holding Our World Together: Ojibwe Women and the Survival of Community.* New York, 2010.

———. *My Grandfather's Knocking Sticks: Ojibwe Family Life and Labor on the Reservation.* Minneapolis, 2014.

Child, Brenda J., and Brian Klopotek. *Indian Subjects: Hemispheric Perspectives on the History of Indigenous Education.* Santa Fe, 2014.

Crandall, Maurice S. *These People Have Always Been a Republic: Indigenous Electorates in the U.S.-Mexico Borderlands, 1598–1912.* Chapel Hill, 2019.

DeLay, Brian. *War of a Thousand Deserts: Indian Raids and the U.S.-Mexican War.* New Haven, 2008.

Deloria, Philip J. *Indians in Unexpected Places.* Lawrence, 2004.

———. *Playing Indian.* New Haven, 1998.

Deloria, Vine, Jr. *Custer Died for Your Sins: An Indian Manifesto.* New York, 1969.

Denetdale, Jennifer Nez. *Reclaiming Diné History: The Legacies of Navajo Chief Manuelito and Juanita.* Tucson, 2007.

Dennison, Jean. *Colonial Entanglement: Constituting a Twenty-First-Century Osage Nation.* Chapel Hill, 2012.

Dunbar-Ortiz, Roxanne. *"All the Real Indians Died Off": And 20 Other Myths About Native Americans.* Boston, 2016.

———. *An Indigenous Peoples' History of the United States.* Boston, 2014.

Duthu, N. Bruce. *American Indians and the Law.* New York, 2009.

———. *Shadow Nations: Tribal Sovereignty and the Limits of Legal Pluralism.* New York, 2013.

Ellis, Elizabeth N. *The Great Power of Small Nations: Indigenous Diplomacy in the Gulf South.* Philadelphia, 2022.

Estes, Nick. *Our History Is the Future: Standing Rock Versus the Dakota Access Pipeline, and the Long Tradition of Indigenous Resistance.* New York, 2019.

Estes, Nick, and Jaskiran Dhillo. *Standing with Standing Rock: Voices from the #NoDAPL Movement.* Minneapolis, 2019.

Fenn, Elizabeth A. *Encounters at the Heart of the World: A History of the Mandan People.* New York, 2014.

Fixico, Donald L. *Termination and Relocation: Federal Indian Policy, 1945–1960.* Albuquerque, 1986.

Fry, Laura F., Peter H. Hassrick, and Scott Manning Stevens. *Art of the American West: The Haub Family Collection at Tacoma.* New Haven, 2014.

Genetin-Pilawa, C. Joseph. *Crooked Paths to Allotment: The Fight over Federal Indian Policy After the Civil War.* Chapel Hill, 2014.

Greene, Candace S. *One Hundred Summers: A Kiowa Calendar Record.* Lincoln, 2009.

Greer, Allan. *Property and Dispossession: Natives, Empires and Land in Early Modern North America.* Cambridge, 2017.

Hancock, Jonathan Todd. *Convulsed States: Earthquakes, Prophecy, and the Remaking of Early America.* Chapel Hill, 2021.

Hill, Susan M. *The Clay We Are Made Of: Haudenosaunee Land Tenure on the Grand River.* Winnipeg, 2017.

Hoxie, Fredrick. *A Final Promise: The Campaign to Assimilate the Indians, 1880–1920.* Lincoln, 1984, 2001.

Jensen, Toni. *Carry: A Memoir of Survival on Stolen Land.* New York, 2020.

Kelman, Ari. *A Misplaced Massacre: Struggling over the Memory of Sand Creek.* Cambridge, Mass., 2013.

Kelton, Paul. *Cherokee Medicine, Colonial Germs: An Indigenous Nation's Fight Against Smallpox, 1518–1824.* Norman, 2015.

Klopotek, Brian. *Recognition Odysseys: Indigeneity, Race, and Federal Tribal Recognition Policy in Three Louisiana Indian Communities.* Durham, 2011.

Lambert, Leonard Carson, Jr., and Michael Lambert. *Up from These Hills: Memories of a Cherokee Boyhood.* Lincoln, 2011.

Lambert, Valerie. *Choctaw Nation: A Story of American Indian Resurgence.* Lincoln, 2007.

———. *Native Agency: Indians in the Bureau of Indian Affairs.* Minneapolis, 2022.

Lomawaima, K. Tsianina. *They Called It Prairie Light: The Story of Chilocco Indian School.* Lincoln, 1994.

Lonetree, Amy. *Decolonizing Museums: Representing Native America in National and Tribal Museums.* Chapel Hill, 2012.

Lowery, Malinda Maynor. *The Lumbee Indians: An American Struggle.* Chapel Hill, 2018.

Mankiller, Wilma, and Michael Wallis. *Mankiller: A Chief and Her People.* New York, 1993.

Marshall, Ann E., and Diana F. Pardue, eds. *Of God and Mortal Men: T.C. Cannon.* Santa Fe, 2017.

Martínez, David. *The American Indian Intellectual Tradition: An Anthology of Writings from 1772 to 1972.* Ithaca, 2011.

Mathews, John Joseph. *The Osages, Children of the Middle Waters.* Norman, 1961.

McCarthy, Theresa. *In Divided Unity: Haudenosaunee Reclamation at Grand River.* Tucson, 2016.

Milteer, Warren Eugene, Jr. *Beyond Slavery's Shadow: Free People of Color in the South.* Chapel Hill, 2021.

Miranda, Deborah A. *Bad Indians: A Tribal Memoir.* Berkeley, 2013.

Momaday, N. Scott. *The Way to Rainy Mountain.* Santa Fe, 1969.

Navajo Times (newspaper). https://navajotimes.com/.

Oberg, Michael. *The Head in Edward Nugent's Hand: Roanoke's Forgotten Indians.* Philadelphia, 2013.

O'Brien, Jean. *Dispossession by Degrees: Indian Land and Identity in Natick, Massachusetts, 1650–1790.* Lincoln, 1997.

———. *Firsting and Lasting: Writing Indians out of Existence in New England.* Minneapolis, 2010.

Ostler, Jeffrey. *Surviving Genocide: Native Nations and the United States from the American Revolution to Bleeding Kansas.* New Haven, 2019.

Pauketat, Timothy R. *Cahokia: Ancient America's Great City on the Mississippi*. New York, 2009.

Perdue, Theda, and Michael D. Green. *North American Indians: A Very Short Introduction*. New York, 2010.

Phillips, Katrina M. *Staging Indigeneity: Salvage Tourism and the Performance of Native American History*. Chapel Hill, 2021.

Porter, Tom Sakokwenionkwas. *And Grandma Said . . . Iroquois Teachings as Passed Down Through the Oral Tradition*. Bloomington, 2008.

Reed, Julie. *Serving the Nation: Cherokee Sovereignty and Social Welfare, 1800–1907*. Norman, 2016.

Reid, Joshua. *The Sea Is My Country: The Maritime World of the Makahs, an Indigenous Borderlands People*. New Haven, 2015.

Reséndez, Andrés. *The Other Slavery: The Uncovered Story of Indian Enslavement in America*. Boston, 2016.

Richotte, Keith, Jr. *Claiming Turtle Mountain's Constitution: The History, Legacy, and Future of a Tribal Nation's Founding Documents*. Chapel Hill, 2017.

———. *Federal Indian Law and Policy: An Introduction*. St. Paul, Minn., 2020.

Richter, Daniel K. *Facing East from Indian Country: A Native History of Early America*. Cambridge, Mass., 2001.

———. *The Ordeal of the Longhouse: The Peoples of the Iroquois League in the Era of European Colonization*. Chapel Hill, 1992.

Saunt, Claudio. *Unworthy Republic: The Dispossession of Native Americans and the Road to Indian Territory*. New York, 2020.

Silva, Noenoe. *The Power of the Steel-tipped Pen: Reconstructing Native Hawaiian Intellectual History*. Durham, 2017.

Simpson, Audra. *Mohawk Interruptus: Political Life Across the Borders of Settler States*. Durham, 2014.

Sleeper-Smith, Susan. *Indigenous Prosperity and American Conquest: Indian Women of the Ohio River Valley, 1690–1792*. Chapel Hill, 2018.

Smith, Paul Chaat. *Everything You Know About Indians Is Wrong*. Minneapolis, 2009.

Smith, Paul Chaat, and Robert Allen Warrior. *Like a Hurricane: The Indian Movement from Alcatraz to Wounded Knee*. New York, 1996.

Snyder, Christina. *Great Crossings: Indians, Settlers, and Slaves in the Age of Jackson*. New York, 2017.

Spector, Janet D. *What This Awl Means: Feminist Archaeology at a Wahpeton Dakota Village*. St. Paul, Minn., 1993.

Tallbear, Kim. *Native American DNA: Tribal Belonging and the False Promise of Genetic Science*. Minneapolis, 2013.

Teuton, Christopher B. *Deep Waters: The Textual Continuum in American Indian Literature*. Lincoln, 2010.

Teuton, Christopher B., Hastings Shade, Sammy Still, Sequoyah Guess, and Woody Hansen. *Cherokee Stories of the Turtle Island Liars' Club*. Chapel Hill, 2012.

Teuton, Sean Kicummah. *Native American Literature: A Very Short Introduction*. New York, 2018.

———. *Red Land, Red Power: Grounding Knowledge in the American Indian Novel.* Durham, 2008.

Teuton, Sean Kicummah, Daniel Justice, Christopher B. Teuton, and Craig Womack. *Reasoning Together: Native Critics in Dialogue.* Norman, 2008.

Tohono O'odham Community Action (TOCA), with Mary Paganelli Votto and Frances Manuel. *From I'itoi's Garden: Tohono O'odham Food Traditions.* Tohono O'odham Community, 2010.

Tone-Pah-Hote, Jenny. *Crafting an Indigenous Nation: Kiowa Expressive Culture in the Progressive Era.* Chapel Hill, 2019.

Treuer, Anton. *Everything You Wanted to Know About Indians but Were Afraid to Ask.* St. Paul, Minn., 2012.

Treuer, David. *The Heartbeat of Wounded Knee: Native America from 1890 to the Present.* New York, 2019.

Usner, Daniel H., Jr. *Indian Work: Language and Livelihood in Native American History.* Cambridge, Mass., 2009.

Warren, Louis S. *God's Red Son: The Ghost Dance Religion and the Making of Modern America.* New York, 2017.

Warren, Stephen. *The Shawnees and Their Neighbors, 1795–1870.* Urbana, 2005.

Warren, Stephen, ed., with the Eastern Shawnee Tribe of Oklahoma. *The Eastern Shawnee Tribe of Oklahoma: Resilience Through Adversity.* Norman, 2017.

Warrior, Robert. *The People and the Word: Reading Native Nonfiction.* Minneapolis, 2005.

———. *Tribal Secrets: Recovering American Indian Intellectual Traditions.* Minneapolis, 1994.

Wilkins, David E., and Heidi Kiiwetinepinesiik Stark. *American Indian Politics and the American Political System,* 3rd ed. Lanham, Md., 2011.

Williams, Kayanesenh Paul. *Kayanerenkó:wa: The Great Law of Peace.* Winnipeg, 2018.

Witgen, Michael John. *An Infinity of Nations: How the Native New World Shaped Early North America.* Philadelphia, 2011.

———. *Seeing Red: Indigenous Land, American Expansion, and the Political Economy of Plunder in North America.* Chapel Hill, 2022.

NOTES

FOREWORD: MANY NATIONS

1. Nick Estes, *Our History Is the Future: Standing Rock Versus the Dakota Access Pipeline, and the Long Tradition of Indigenous Resistance* (New York, 2019), 1–3; *Standing with Standing Rock: Voices from the #NoDAPL Movement,* ed. Nick Estes and Jaskiran Dhillo (Minneapolis, 2019); "Grande Ronde Sends More Members, Supplies to N.D. Protest," KGW8 News, Sept. 16, 2016, http://www.kgw.com/article/news /local/grande-ronde-sends-more-members-supplies-to-nd-protest/283-319384086; Alyssa Schukar and Jack Healy, "From 280 Tribes, a Protest on the Plains Speaks Out Against an Oil Pipeline," *New York Times,* Sept. 12, 2016, https://www.nytimes .com/interactive/2016/09/12/us/12tribes.html.

2. Sierra Teller Ornelas, "Donald Trump Would Make a Terrible Navajo," *New York Times,* Dec. 3, 2017, https://www.nytimes.com/2017/12/02/opinion/sunday/donald -trump-navajo-pocahontas.html; "Standing Rock Sioux Tribal Chairman Dave Archambault Says Dakota Access Pipeline Conflict Is About Respect," KFYR, Sept. 6, 2016, http://www.kfyrtv.com/content/news/Standing-Rock-Sioux-Tribal -Chairman-Dave-Archambault-says-Dakota-Access-Pipeline-conflict-is-about -respect-392525001.html; Resolution of the Saint Regis Mohawk Tribe to Support the Standing Rock Sioux Tribe in Their Opposition to the Dakota Access Pipeline, Aug. 22, 2016, Tribal Council Resolution 2016–64, https://www.srmt-nsn.gov /publications; Keith Richotte Jr., *Federal Indian Law and Policy: An Introduction* (St. Paul, Minn., 2020), 3.

3. Oscar Handlin, "The Significance of the Seventeenth Century," in *Seventeenth-Century America: Essays in Colonial History,* ed. James Morton Smith (Chapel Hill, 1959), 6.

4. Howard Zinn, *A People's History of the United States* (New York, 1980), 1; Dee Brown, *Bury My Heart at Wounded Knee: An Indian History of the American West* (New York, 1970), xi; Jared Diamond, *Guns, Germs, and Steel: The Fates of Human Societies* (New York, 1997); Charles C. Mann, *1491: New Revelations of the Americas Before Columbus* (New York, 2005); Charles C. Mann, *1493: Uncovering the New World Columbus Created* (New York, 2011).

5. *Surviving Columbus,* directed by Diane Reyna, produced by Larry Walsh (PBS, 1992); David Treuer, *The Heartbeat of Wounded Knee: Native America from 1890 to the Present* (New York, 2019), 8–11; Sarah B. Shear, Ryan T. Knowles, Gregory J.

Soden, and Antonio J. Castro, "Manifesting Destiny: Re/presentations of Indigenous Peoples in K-12 History Standards," *Theory and Research in Social Education* 43 (2015), 68–101; Kristofer Ray and Brady DeSanti, introduction to *Understanding and Teaching Native American History* (Madison, 2022), 3–7.

6. Gerald Vizenor, "Aesthetics of Survivance: Literary Theory and Practice," in *Survivance: Narratives of Native Presence* (Lincoln, 2008), 1; Brenda J. Child, *Holding Our World Together: Ojibwe Women and the Survival of Community* (New York, 2012); Brooke M. Bauer, *Becoming Catawba: Catawba Indian Women and Nation-Building, 1540–1840* (Tuscaloosa, 2022); Treuer, *Heartbeat of Wounded Knee*.

7. Scholars keep finding evidence of earlier and earlier human residence in the Americas. See, e.g., Matthew R. Bennett et al., "Evidence of Humans in North America During the Last Glacial Maximum," *Science* 373 (Sept. 23, 2021), 1528–31.

8. Throughout the book you will find citations to the tremendous body of scholarship that in recent decades has upended academic understandings of the Native (and thus also the non-Native) past in North America. For overviews, see Colin G. Calloway, *First Peoples: A Documentary Survey of American Indian History*, 6th ed. (New York, 2019); Michael Leroy Oberg, *Native America: A History*, 2nd ed. (Hoboken, N.J., 2017); R. David Edmunds, Frederick E. Hoxie, and Neal Salisbury, *The People: A History of Native America* (Boston, 2007); Daniel K. Richter, *Facing East from Indian Country: A Native History of Early America* (Cambridge, Mass., 2001); Roxanne Dunbar-Ortiz, *An Indigenous Peoples' History of the United States* (Boston, 2014); Paul Chaat Smith, *Everything You Know About Indians Is Wrong* (Minneapolis, 2009); Ned Blackhawk, *The Rediscovery of America: Native Peoples and the Unmaking of U.S. History* (New Haven, 2023); Pekka Hämäläinen, *Indigenous Continent: The Epic Contest for North America* (New York, 2022); Michael Witgen, "The Native New World and Western North America," *Western Historical Quarterly* 43 (2012), 292–99.

9. William Cothren, *History of Ancient Woodbury, Connecticut, from the First Indian Deed in 1659 to 1854* (Waterbury, Conn., 1854), 9; Jean M. O'Brien, *Firsting and Lasting: Writing Indians Out of Existence in New England* (Minneapolis, 2010), xiii; Scott Manning Stevens, "Collectors and Museums: From Cabinets of Curiosities to Indigenous Cultural Centers," *The Oxford Handbook of American Indian History*, ed. Frederick E. Hoxie (New York, 2016), 476–85; Scott Manning Stevens, "Reclaiming Our Narratives of Place: Haudenosaunee History on the Ground" (lecture), Nov. 5, 2019, University of North Carolina, Chapel Hill; Smith, *Everything You Know About Indians Is Wrong*, 24; Amy Lonetree, *Decolonizing Museums: Representing Native America in National and Tribal Museums* (Chapel Hill, 2012), 14–16, 97–98; Colin G. Calloway, ed., *After King Philip's War: Presence and Persistence in Indian New England* (Hanover, N.H., 1997); Ned Blackhawk, "The Iron Cage of Erasure: American Indian Sovereignty" in Jill Lepore's *These Truths*," *American Historical Review* 125 (2020), 1752–63; Warren E. Milteer Jr., "From Indians to Colored People: The Problem of Racial Categories and the Persistence of the Chowans in North Carolina," *North Carolina Historical Review* (2016), 28–57; Annie H. Abel, "Proposals for an Indian State, 1778–1878," *Annual Report of the American Historical Association for the Year 1907* (Washington, D.C., 1908), 1: 90; Michael Witgen, *An Infinity of Nations: How the Native New World Shaped Early North America* (Philadelphia, 2013), 14, 28; Gregory Evans Dowd, "Wag the Imperial Dog: Indians and Overseas Empires in North America, 1650–1776," in *A Com-*

panion to American Indian History, ed. Philip J. Deloria and Neal Salisbury (Oxford, 2002), 55–56; Robert Michael Morrissey, *Empire by Collaboration: Indians, Colonists, and Governments in Colonial Illinois Country* (Philadelphia, 2015); Patrick Wolfe, "Settler Colonialism and the Elimination of the Native," *Journal of Genocide Research* 8 (2006), 389–94; Eric Wolf, *Europe and the People Without History* (Berkeley, 1982); Stephen H. Lekson, *A History of the Ancient Southwest* (Santa Fe, 2008), 2.

10. Spencer Phips, Proclamation, Feb. 25, 1757, https://www.loc.gov/resource/rbpe .03502000/?st=text; Penobscot Nation Cultural and Historic Preservation Department, "Native American Veterans," http://www.penobscotculture.com/index .php/native-american-vetrans; Penobscot Nation home page, https://www .penobscotnation.org/; Dunbar-Ortiz, *An Indigenous Peoples' History of the United States,* xiii; Jeffrey Ostler, *Surviving Genocide: Native Nations and the United States from the American Revolution to Bleeding Kansas* (New Haven, 2019).

11. Dana Hedgpeth, "A 25-Foot Native American Totem Pole Arrives in D.C. After a Journey to Sacred Lands Across U.S.," *Washington Post,* July 29, 2021; Ned Blackhawk, "A New History of Native Americans Responds to 'Bury My Heart at Wounded Knee,'" *New York Times,* Jan. 20, 2019; Treuer, *Heartbeat of Wounded Knee,* 443; Jeffrey Gibson, artist talk, Nasher Museum of Art, Nov. 21, 2019; Robert Warrior, "The Indian Renaissance, 1960–2000: Stumbling to Victory, or Anecdotes of Persistence?," *Oxford Handbook of American Indian History,* 130; Shawnee Tribe Cultural Center, "About the Shawnee Tribe," https://www.shawneeculture .org/about-shawnee-tribe/. For continuing anti-sovereignty efforts, see the discussion in Doug Kiel, "Nation v. Municipality: Indigenous Land Recovery, Settler Resentment, and Taxation on the Oneida Reservation," *Native American and Indigenous Studies* 6 (2019), 58, as well as examples: Naomi Schaefer Riley, *The New Trail of Tears: How Washington Is Destroying American Indians* (New York, 2016); House Concurrent Resolution No. 3017, Sixty-fifth Legislative Assembly of North Dakota, https://www.ndlegis.gov/assembly/65-2017/documents/17-3014-03000 .pdf; *Oklahoma v. Castro-Huerta,* 597 U.S. (2022); Curtis Killman, "ICYMI: Supreme Court to Huddle Tomorrow on Whether to Take on Oklahoma's 40-plus McGirt Appeals," Jan. 16, 2023, *Tulsa World,* https://tulsaworld.com/news/state -and-regional/supreme-court-sets-date-with-oklahoma-to-respond-to-40-plus -mcgirt-appeals/article_714b62a4-59db-11ec-99d5-eb2ab6f4da01.html.

12. For the Inter-American Indian Institute, see Raquel L. Cárdenas Escobar, "Reconcile the Indian, Reconcile the Nation: Transnational Indian Reform in the Era of Inter-American Politics, 1930–1960" (Ph.D. diss., University of Illinois, 2020).

13. For retaining power and identity under colonialism in other parts of the Americas, see Charles Gibson, *The Aztecs Under Spanish Rule: A History of the Indians of the Valley of Mexico* (Stanford, 1964); James Lockhart, *The Nahuas After the Conquest: A Social and Cultural History of the Indians of Central Mexico, Sixteenth Through Eighteenth Centuries* (Stanford, 1992); Brooke Larson, *Cochabamba, 1550–1900: Colonialism and Agrarian Transformation in Bolivia,* expanded ed. (Durham, 1998); Kenneth J. Andrien, *Andean Worlds: Indigenous History, Culture, and Consciousness Under Spanish Rule, 1532–1825* (Albuquerque, 2001). For the long history of sovereignty and diplomacy in the Atlantic world, see Herman L. Bennett, *African Kings and Black Slaves: Sovereignty and Dispossession in the Early Modern Atlantic* (Philadelphia, 2019).

14. Roger C. Echo-Hawk, "Ancient History in the New World: Integrating Oral Traditions and the Archaeological Record in Deep Time," *American Antiquity* 65

(2000), 268; Joshua L. Reid, *The Sea Is My Country: The Maritime World of the Makahs, an Indigenous Borderlands People* (New Haven, 2015), 8; Richter, *Facing East from Indian Country*, 44; Philip J. Deloria, *Playing Indian* (New Haven, 1998); Michael Witgen, "American Indians in World History," *The Oxford Handbook of American Indian History*, ed. Frederick E. Hoxie (New York, 2016), 592. For an example of how the narrative can change when North America is included, see David Graeber and David Wengrow, *The Dawn of Everything: A New History of Humanity* (New York, 2021). For more on the spiritual as well as practical importance of keeping coals burning, see Christopher B. Rodning, *Center Places and Cherokee Towns: Archaeological Perspectives on Native American Architecture and Landscape in the Southern Appalachians* (Tuscaloosa, 2015), 49–54. Thanks to Brooke Bauer and Patricia Dawson for our conversations on many aspects of material culture.

15. Patrick Wolfe, *Traces of History: Elementary Structures of Race* (London, 2016).

16. Joseph J. Ellis, *The Cause: The American Revolution and Its Discontents, 1773–1783* (New York, 2021), 313; Alfred W. Crosby, "Virgin Soil Epidemics as a Factor in the Aboriginal Depopulation in America," *William and Mary Quarterly* 33 (1976), 289–99; Henry F. Dobyns, *Their Numbers Become Thinned: Native American Population Dynamics in Eastern North America* (Knoxville, 1983); Diamond, *Guns, Germs, and Steel*. Even scholarship more attuned to local histories and Indian survival at times puts too much emphasis on European-driven change and can exaggerate the disjuncture between sixteenth-century Native Americans and their descendants.

17. Karen Ordahl Kupperman, *Pocahontas and the English Boys: Caught Between Cultures in Early Virginia* (New York, 2019), ix–x; Patricia Galloway, *Choctaw Genesis, 1500–1700* (Lincoln, 1995), 128–38, 142–43, 157, 159, 163; Colin G. Calloway, *The Indian World of George Washington: The First President, the First Americans, and the Birth of the Nation* (New York, 2018), 2.

18. Paul Kelton, *Cherokee Medicine, Colonial Germs: An Indigenous Nation's Fight Against Smallpox, 1518–1824* (Norman, 2015), 10; David Henige, *Numbers from Nowhere: The American Indian Contact Population Debate* (Norman, 1998); Paul Kelton, Alan C. Swedlund, and Catherine M. Cameron, introduction to *Beyond Germs: Native Depopulation in North America* (Tucson, 2015), 3–8, 13; David S. Jones, "Death, Uncertainty, and Rhetoric," in *Beyond Germs*, 16–44; David S. Jones, "Population, Health, and Public Welfare," in *Oxford Handbook of American Indian History* (Oxford, 2016), 413–26; David S. Jones, "Virgin Soils Revisited," *William and Mary Quarterly* 60 (2003), 703–42; Suzanne Austin Alchon, *A Pest in the Land: New World Epidemics in a Global Perspective* (Albuquerque, 2003); George R. Milner, "Population Decline and Culture Change in the American Midcontinent," in *Beyond Germs*, 50–67; Tai S. Edwards, "The 'Virgin' Soil Thesis Cover-Up: Teaching Indigenous Demographic Collapse," in *Understanding and Teaching Native American History*, 29–43; Galloway, *Choctaw Genesis*, 128–38, 142–43, 157, 159; Michael Wilcox, "Marketing Conquest and the Vanishing Indian: An Indigenous Response to Jared Diamond's Archaeology of the American Southwest," in *Questioning Collapse: Human Resilience, Ecological Vulnerability and the Aftermath of Empire*, ed. Patricia A. McAnany and Norman Yoffee (New York, 2010), 136–37; Andrés Reséndez, *The Other Slavery: The Uncovered Story of Indian Enslavement in America* (Boston, 2016), 16–17; Richter, *Facing East from Indian Country: A Native*

History of Early America, 35; James Ring Adams, "The Plague Apocalypse Is Us," *American Indian Magazine* 22 (2021), 8–9. Even for the island of Hispaniola (today's Haiti and Dominican Republic), where we know European colonizers brought slavery and death early, the numbers have probably been exaggerated. High counters claimed that Hispaniola's population in 1492 was nearly eight million and that it had fallen to sixty thousand by 1508. Yet there was no island-wide census in either of these periods, and it's a big island, which the Spanish did not control. We don't know how many people lived there on either date, and certainly some people's response to Spaniards' violence and disease was to get as far from them as possible and, as a result, not be around when Spaniards were counting. High-counting scholars relied heavily on the writings of Bartolomé de las Casas, who was an important voice against real destruction in Hispaniola but whose motive of making the conquistadors look as bad as possible makes him a questionable source for statistics. Massimo Livi Bacci, "Return to Hispaniola: Reassessing a Demographic Catastrophe," *Hispanic American Historical Review* 83 (2003), 3–51; Massimo Livi Bacci, *Conquest: The Destruction of the American Indios,* trans. Carl Ipsen (Cambridge, UK, 2008); Tai S. Edwards and Paul Kelton, "Germs, Genocides, and America's Indigenous Peoples," *Journal of American History* 107 (2020), 52–76.

19. Ben Barnes, "Collaborative Research in Ethnohistory" (panel), American Society for Ethnohistory Annual Conference (remote), Nov. 7, 2020; Stephen Warren and Ben Barnes, "Salvaging the Salvage Anthropologists: Erminie Wheeler-Voegelin, Carl Voegelin, and the Future of Ethnohistory," *Ethnohistory* 65 (2018), 189–214.

20. Alyssa Mt. Pleasant, Caroline Wigginton, and Kelly Wisecup, "Materials and Methods in Native American and Indigenous Studies: Completing the Turn," *William and Mary Quarterly* 75 (2018), 207–36.

21. Brooke Bauer and Elizabeth Ellis, "Indigenous, Native American, or American Indian? The Limitations of Broad Terms," *Journal of the Early Republic* (forthcoming); Anton Treuer, *Everything You Wanted to Know About Indians but Were Afraid to Ask* (St. Paul, Minn., 2012), 7–8; Roxanne Dunbar-Ortiz and Dina Gilio-Whitaker, *"All the Real Indians Died Off" and 20 Other Myths About Native Americans* (Boston, 2016), xi, 145–49; Peter d'Errico, "Native American Indian Studies: A Note on Names," https://people.umass.edu/derrico/name.html; Amanda Blackhorse, "Do You Prefer 'Native American' or 'American Indian'? 6 Prominent Voices Respond," *Indian Country Today,* May 22, 2015, https://newsmaven.io/indiancountrytoday/archive/blackhorse-do-you-prefer-native-american-or-american-indian-kHWRPJqIGU6X3FTVdMi9EQ/.

22. Mikaëla M. Adams, *Who Belongs? Race, Resources, and Tribal Citizenship in the Native South* (New York, 2015); Benjamin Martin, *Lingua Britannica Reformata: Or, a New English Dictionary* (London, 1749); Bauer and Ellis, "Indigenous, Native American, or American Indian?"; David Martínez, *Dakota Philosopher: Charles Eastman and American Indian Thought* (Minneapolis, 2009), 52–53; Cynthia Radding, *Wandering Peoples: Colonialism, Ethnic Spaces, and Ecological Frontiers in Northwestern Mexico, 1700–1850* (Durham, 1997), 9–10; O'Brien, *Firsting and Lasting,* 202. For the changing European definition of nationhood, see Lloyd S. Kramer, *Nationalism in Europe and America: Politics, Cultures, and Identities Since 1775* (Chapel Hill, 2011).

23. The definition of "nation" given by legal scholars David E. Wilkins (Lumbee) and

Heidi Kiiwetinepinesiik Stark (Ojibwe) is "a social group that shares a common ideology, common institutions and customs, and a sense of homogeneity; controls a territory viewed as a national homeland; and has a belief in a common ancestry." David E. Wilkins and Heidi Kiiwetinepinesiik Stark, *American Indian Politics and the American Political System*, 3rd ed. (Lanham, Md., 2011), 310–11; David E. Wilkins and K. Tsianina Lomawaima, *Uneven Ground: American Indian Sovereignty and Federal Law* (Norman, 2001); Nancy Shoemaker, *A Strange Likeness: Becoming Red and White in Eighteenth-Century North America* (New York, 2004), 6–7; Witgen, *Infinity of Nations*, 75–77; Jeffrey P. Shepherd, *We Are an Indian Nation: A History of the Hualapai People* (Tucson, 2010), 11; Juliana Barr, *Peace Came in the Form of a Woman: Indians and Spaniards in the Texas Borderlands* (Chapel Hill, 2007), 8–9; Juliana Barr, "There's No Such Thing as 'Prehistory': What the Longue Durée of Caddo and Pueblo History Tells Us About Colonial America," *William and Mary Quarterly* 74 (2017), 5–46; Jeffrey M. Schulze, *Are We Not Foreigners Here? Indigenous Nationalism in the U.S.-Mexico Borderlands* (Chapel Hill, 2018), 12–16; Robin Beck, *Chiefdoms, Collapse, and Coalescence in the Early American South* (New York, 2013), 231–32.

24. Barbara Collier, "Tribe or Nation?," *Quapaw Tribal News*, 2018, 8; Treuer, *Everything You Wanted to Know About Indians*, 13.

PART I: THE INDIGENOUS PEOPLES OF NORTH AMERICA, 1000S TO 1750

1. See, e.g., the work of Ruth Wallis Herndon and Ella Wilcox Sekatau, Brooke Bauer, Lisa Brooks, David A. Chang, Patricia Dawson, Christine M. DeLucia, Elizabeth Ellis, Joseph Hall, Malinda Maynor Lowery, Warren Eugene Milteer Jr., Alyssa Mt. Pleasant, Julie L. Reed, Joshua L. Reid, and Stephen Warren.

2. Despite the general absence of North America from world history books, the big themes of early world history fit it well. The first three chapters of Cambridge's *A Concise History of the World* are "Foraging and Farming Families (to 3000 BCE)," "Cities and Classical Societies (3000 BCE–500 CE)," and "Expanding Networks of Interaction (500 CE–1500 CE)." Merry E. Wiesner-Hanks, *A Concise History of the World* (Cambridge, 2015), 45–48; J. R. McNeill, *The Webs of Humankind: A World History* (New York, 2021); Michael Balter, "Seeking Agriculture's Ancient Roots," *Science* 316 (2007), 1830–35.

3. David Graeber and David Wengrow, *The Dawn of Everything: A New History of Humanity* (New York, 2021).

4. Robert A. Williams, *Linking Arms Together: American Indian Treaty Visions of Law and Peace, 1600–1800* (New York, 1997), 5, 21.

CHAPTER 1: ANCIENT CITIES IN ARIZONA, ILLINOIS, AND ALABAMA

1. F. Richard Stephenson and David A. Green, *Historical Supernovae and Their Remnants* (New York, 2002), 150–74.

2. Stephenson and Green, *Historical Supernovae*, 151–52, 163; Gregory E. Munson, Todd W. Bostwick, and Tony Hull, *Astronomy and Ceremony in the Prehistoric Southwest: Revisited* (Albuquerque, 2014), 3; Timothy R. Pauketat, *Cahokia: Ancient America's Great City on the Mississippi* (New York, 2009), 2, 20; Stephen H. Lekson, *A History of the Ancient Southwest* (Santa Fe, 2008), 234; Michael A. Gomez, *African Dominion: A New History of Empire in Early and Medieval West*

Africa (Princeton, 2018), 36–38; Thomas N. Bisson, *The Crisis of the Twelfth Century: Power, Lordship, and the Origins of European Government* (Princeton, 2015), 1.

3. William Iseminger, *Cahokia Mounds: America's First City* (Charleston, 2010), 129.

4. Warren K. Moorehead, *The Cahokia Mounds*, ed. John E. Kelly (Tuscaloosa, 2000), 72; Biloine Whiting Young and Melvin L. Fowler, *Cahokia: The Great Native American Metropolis* (Urbana, 2000), 24.

5. Edmund Flagg, *The Far West, or, A Tour Beyond the Mountains: Embracing Outlines of Western Life and Scenery, Sketches of the Prairies, Rivers, Ancient Mounds* (New York, 1838), 1:166; G. W. Featherstonehaugh, *Excursion Through the Slave States* (London, 1844), 268.

6. Frank Hamilton Cushing, *The Lost Itinerary of Frank Hamilton Cushing*, ed. Curtis M. Hinsley and David R. Wilcox (Tucson, 2002), 239. See also A. F. Bandelier, *Hemenway Southwestern Archaeological Expedition: Contributions to the History of the Southwestern Portion of the United States* (Cambridge, Mass., 1890).

7. Kelly, introduction to *The Cahokia Mounds*, by Warren K. Moorehead (Tuscaloosa, 2000), 6; Young and Fowler, *Cahokia*, 30; Jacob F. Lee, *Masters of the Middle Waters: Indian Nations and Colonial Ambitions Along the Mississippi* (Cambridge, Mass., 2019), 1–2.

8. Beliefs in cultural evolution influenced archaeological models through much of the twentieth century; moving away from an evolutionary framework enables more attention to smaller-scale change and diversity. Thomas Maxwell, *Tuskaloosa, the Origin of Its Name, Its History, etc.: A Paper Read Before the Alabama Historical Society, by Thomas Maxwell, July 1, 1876* (Tuscaloosa, 1876), 71; David Martínez, "Whither the Huhugam? Decolonizing the Discourse on O'odham Cultural History," in J. Brett Hill, *From Huhugam to Hohokam: Heritage and Archaeology in the American Southwest* (Lanham, Md., 2019), 189; John F. Scarry, "Looking for and at Mississippian Political Change," in *Political Structure and Change in the Prehistoric Southeastern United States* (Gainesville, 1996), 4–5, 11; Michael Wilcox, "Marketing Conquest and the Vanishing Indian: An Indigenous Response to Jared Diamond's Archaeology of the American Southwest," in *Questioning Collapse: Human Resilience, Ecological Vulnerability and the Aftermath of Empire*, ed. Patricia A. McAnany and Norman Yoffee (New York, 2010), 124–25; Jean M. O'Brien, *Firsting and Lasting: Writing Indians Out of Existence in New England* (Minneapolis, 2010); Robin Beck, *Chiefdoms, Collapse, and Coalescence in the Early American South* (New York, 2013), 27–29.

9. Andrew Jackson, Second Annual Message to Congress, Dec. 6, 1830, in *A Compilation of the Messages and Papers of the Presidents* (New York, 1897), 3:1084; Noah Webster to Ezra Stiles, Oct. 22, 1787, *The American Magazine* 1 (Dec. 1787), 15–19; Webster to Stiles, Dec. 15, 1787, *American Magazine* 2 (Jan. 1788), 87–93; Webster to Stiles, Jan. 20, 1788, *American Magazine* 3 (Feb. 1788), 146–56; Webster to Stiles, July 4, 1788, *American Magazine* 7 (July 1788), 537–41; Terry A. Barnhart, *American Antiquities: Revisiting the Origins of American Archaeology* (Lincoln, 2015), 128–37; Kelly, introduction to *Cahokia Mounds*, 7–9, 16; Maxwell, *Tuskaloosa*, 71–72, 76; Young and Fowler, *Cahokia*, 29–31; John H. Blitz, *Moundville* (Tuscaloosa, 2008), 8; Robert Silverberg, *Mound Builders of Ancient America: The Archaeology of a Myth* (Greenwich, N.Y., 1968); Jason Colavito, *The Mound Builder Myth: Fake History and the Hunt for a "Lost White Race"* (Norman, 2020).

10. Pauketat, *Cahokia*, 54; Young and Fowler, *Cahokia*, 32; John Doddridge, *Notes on the Settlement and Indian Wars* (1824; repr., Pittsburgh, 1912), 36–38; Silverberg, *Mound Builders*, 62. Many thanks to Stacy Murphy for alerting me to Doddridge's memoir.

11. Edward S. Curtis, "Village Tribes of the Desert Land," *Scribner's Magazine* 45 (1909), 284; Christopher R. Loendorf, *The Hohokam-Akimel O'odham Continuum: Sociocultural Dynamics and Projectile Point Design in the Phoenix Basin, Arizona* (Sacaton, Ariz., 2012), 118. Similarly, John Mix Stanley wrote on the back of his 1847 painting *Ruins of the Casa Grande* (currently held at Buffalo Bill Center of the West, Cody, Wyoming), "The founders of which are unknown," despite having met and painted O'odham chief Juan Antonio Llunas; *Painted Journeys: The Art of John Mix Stanley*, ed. Peter H. Hassrick and Mindy N. Besaw (Norman, 2015).

12. T. J. Ferguson and Chip Colwell-Chanthaphonh, *History Is in the Land: Multivocal Tribal Traditions in Arizona's San Pedro Valley* (Tucson, 2006), 81–82, 88; Hill, *From Huhugam to Hohokam*, 4.

13. Daniel Lopez, "Huhugam," in *The Hohokam Millennium*, ed. Suzanne K. Fish and Paul R. Fish (Santa Fe, 2007), 118–20; Hill, *From Huhugam to Hohokam*; Daniel Anna Moore Shaw, *A Pima Past* (Tucson, 1974), 2; Angela D. Garcia-Lewis (Cultural Preservation Compliance Officer, Salt River Pima-Maricopa Indian Community), quoted in film shown at Casa Grande Ruins National Monument. Today, O'odham historians and other scholars generally use the name Huhugam to refer to that era's people, while Hohokam is considered a misleading term created to stand for a vanished civilization.

14. Nicolas de Finiels, "Notice sur la Louisiane Supérieure," John Francis McDermott Collection, Southern Illinois University, Edwardsville, Ill., available at http://collections.carli.illinois.edu/cdm/landingpage/collection/sie_finiels, 154.

15. George Rogers Clark to Matthew Carey, printed in Henry Rowe Schoolcraft, *Historical and Statistical Information Respecting the History, Condition, and Prospects of the Indian Tribes of the United States* (Philadelphia, 1854), 4:135–36.

16. Horatio B. Cushman, *History of the Choctaw, Chickasaw, and Natchez Indians*, ed. Angie Debo (Norman, 1999), 473–74; Christina Snyder, "The Once and Future Moundbuilders," *Southern Cultures* 26 (2020), 108.

17. David Martínez, "Huhugam Homeland to Phoenix and Back Again," Steven Yazzie, Indigenous Tours Project, 2014, https://vimeo.com/95179964.

18. Echo-Hawk, *American Antiquity* 65, 267–90; Chip Colwell-Chanthaphonh, *Living Histories: Native Americans and Southwestern Archaeology* (Lanham, Md., 2010), 123–31; Chip Colwell-Chanthaphonh, *Plundered Skulls and Stolen Spirits: Inside the Fight to Reclaim Native America's Culture* (Chicago, 2017); Michael Wilcox, "NAGPRA and Indigenous Peoples: The Social Context and Controversies, and the Transformation of American Archaeology," in *Voices in American Archaeology*, ed. Wendy Ashmore, Dorothy T. Lippert, and Barbara J. Mills (Washington, D.C., 2010), 178–92.

19. "Chickasaw Explorers 2018," *Winter Fire*, Chickasaw.tv, https://www.chickasaw.tv/episodes/winter-fire-season-2-episode-3-chickasaw-explorers-2018; "Mississippi Period 900–1400 AD," Chickasaw.tv, https://www.chickasaw.tv/events/mississippi-period. For another example, see *The Eastern Shawnee Tribe of Oklahoma: Resilience Through Adversity*, ed. Stephen Warren with the Eastern Shawnee Tribe of

Oklahoma (Norman, 2017), including that book's chapter by Benjamin J. Barnes, "Becoming Our Own Storytellers: Tribal Nations Engaging with Academia," 222–25.

20. James C. Scott, *Against the Grain: A Deep History of the Earliest States* (New Haven, 2017), 7, 11–12; Amber M. VanDerwarker, Dana N. Bardolph, and C. Margaret Scarry, "Maize and Mississippian Beginnings," in *Mississippian Beginnings,* ed. Gregory D. Wilson (Gainesville, 2017), 30–31, 34–35; Merry E. Wiesner-Hanks, *A Concise History of the World* (Cambridge, 2015), 76–77; Roderick J. McIntosh, "Different Cities: Jenne-Jeno and African Urbanism," in *Early Cities in Comparative Perspective, 4000 BCE–1200 CE,* ed. Norman Yoffee (Cambridge, U.K., 2015), 364–80.

21. Sam White, *A Cold Welcome: The Little Ice Age and Europe's Encounter with North America* (Cambridge, Mass., 2017), 2–3; Brian Fagan, *The Great Warming: Climate Change and the Rise and Fall of Civilizations* (New York, 2008), xiv, 12, 20–21, 38–41, 88; Daniel K. Richter, *Before the Revolution: America's Ancient Pasts* (Cambridge, Mass., 2011), 12–13.

22. VanDerwarker, Bardolph, and Scarry, "Maize and Mississippian Beginnings," 33–35; C. Warren Hollister, *Medieval Europe: A Short History* (New York, 1964), 156; Janet L. Abu-Lughod, *Before European Hegemony: The World System A.D. 1250–1350* (New York, 1989), 4, 8.

23. R. R. Palmer, Joel Colton, and Lloyd Kramer, *A History of Europe in the Modern World,* 11th ed. (New York, 2014), 12.

24. Abu-Lughod, *Before European Hegemony;* Wiesner-Hanks, *Concise History of the World,* 136, 177–83; Gustav Milne, *The Port of Medieval London* (Stroud, U.K., 2003), 31–32; Hollister, *Medieval Europe,* 156; Gayle J. Fritz, *Feeding Cahokia: Early Agriculture in the North American Heartland* (Tuscaloosa, 2019), 129–30.

25. Eusebio Kino, "Favores Celestiales," in *Las misiones de Sonora y Arizona, comprendiendo: La crónica titulada: "Favores Celestiales" y la "Relación diaria de la entrada al noroeste,"* ed. Francisco Fernández del Castillo and Emilio Bose (Mexico City, 1922), 29; Lieutenant Cristóbal Martín Bernal, diary, Nov. 1697, trans. Fay Jackson Smith, in *Father Kino in Arizona,* ed. Fay Jackson Smith, John L. Kessell, and Francis J. Fox (Phoenix, 1966), 41; Juan Mateo Manje, Nov. 17 or 18, 1697, "Del viaje que hice con el reverend Padre Eusebio Francisco Kino y 22 soldados," in appendix, *Kino and Manje: Explorers of Sonora and Arizona: Their Vision of the Future,* ed. Ernest J. Burrus (St. Louis, 1971), 342–43; Lopez, "Huhugam," 119–20; Douglas B. Craig and T. Kathleen Henderson, "Houses, Households, and Household Organization," in *Hohokam Millennium,* 31.

26. Suzanne K. Fish, "Hohokam Impacts on Sonoran Desert Environment," in *Imperfect Balance: Landscape Transformations in the Pre-Columbian Americas,* ed. David L. Lentz (New York, 2000), 256; Brian Fagan, *Elixir: A History of Water and Humankind* (New York, 2011), 56.

27. Suzanne K. Fish and Paul R. Fish, "The Hohokam Millennium," in *Hohokam Millennium,* 7.

28. Hill, *From Huhugam to Hohokam,* 168–69.

29. Randall H. McGuire and Elisa Villalpando C., "The Hohokam and Mesoamerica," in *Hohokam Millennium,* 57–62; Carroll L. Riley, "Early Spanish-Indian Communication in the Greater Southwest," *New Mexico Historical Review* 46

(1971), 286; Michael E. Whalen and Paul E. Minnis, "The Casas Grandes Regional System: A Late Prehistoric Polity of Northwestern Mexico," *Journal of World Prehistory* 15 (2001), 313–64; Andrew D. Somerville, Ben A. Nelson, and Kelly J. Knudson, "Isotopic Investigation of Pre-Hispanic Macaw Breeding in Northwest Mexico," *Journal of Anthropological Archaeology* 29 (2010), 125–35; Randall H. McGuire, Maria Elisa Villalpando C., Victoria D. Vargas, and Emiliano Gallaga M., "Cerro de Trincheras and the Casas Grandes World," in *The Casas Grandes World*, ed. Curtis F. Schaafsma and Carroll L. Riley (Salt Lake City, 1999), 134–46; Emil W. Haury, *The Hohokam, Desert Farmers and Craftsmen: Excavations at Snaketown, 1964–1965* (Tucson, 1976), 343–48; Lekson, *History of the Ancient Southwest*, 31–33; Charles Di Peso, *Casas Grandes: A Fallen Trading Center of the Gran Chichimeca* (Dragoon, Ariz., 1974–77).

30. Donald Bahr, Juan Smith, William Smith Allison, and Julian Hayden, *The Short, Swift Time of Gods on Earth: The Hohokam Chronicles* (Berkeley, 1994), 124, 131–36; Martínez, "Huhugam Homeland to Phoenix and Back Again," https://vimeo.com /95179964; M. Kyle Woodson, *The Social Organization of Hohokam Irrigation in the Middle Gila River Valley, Arizona* (Sacaton, Ariz., 2016), 139; Henry D. Wallace, "Hohokam Beginnings," in *Hohokam Millennium*, 14–15; Alice Beck Kehoe, *America Before the European Invasions* (London, 2002), 140; Aaron M. Wright, *Religion on the Rocks: Hohokam Rock Art, Ritual Practice, and Social Transformation* (Salt Lake City, 2014), 32–33; Tohono O'odham Nation Cultural Center and Museum exhibits; Tohono O'odham Community Action (TOCA), with Mary Paganelli Votto and Frances Manuel, *From I'itoi's Garden: Tohono O'odham Food Traditions* (Tohono O'odham Community, 2010), 316.

31. Wright, *Religion on the Rocks*, 32–33; William E. Doolittle, foreword, in M. Kyle Woodson, *The Social Organization of Hohokam Irrigation in the Middle Gila River Valley, Arizona* (Sacaton, Ariz., 2016), xi; Wiesner-Hanks, *Concise History of the World*, 73, 171.

32. Woodson, *Social Organization of Hohokam Irrigation*, 7, 137, 139; Wright, *Religion on the Rocks*, 33, 35–36; Paul R. Fish and Suzanne K. Fish, "Community, Territory, and Polity," in *Hohokam Millennium*, 45–46; Fish and Fish, "Hohokam Millennium," 5; McGuire and Villalpando, "The Hohokam and Mesoamerica," 58; George J. Gumerman, "The Hohokam: The Who and the Why," in *Hohokam Millennium*, 145; James M. Bayman, "Artisans and Their Crafts in Hohokam Society," in *Hohokam Millennium*, 77, 81.

33. Fish and Fish, "Hohokam Millennium," 5.

34. John C. Ravesloot, "Changing Views of Snaketown in a Larger Landscape," in *Hohokam Millennium*, 91; Emil W. Haury, *The Hohokam: Desert Farmers and Craftsmen, Excavations at Snaketown, 1964–1965* (Tucson, 1976); Craig and Henderson, "Houses, Households, and Household Organization," 32–37; Gumerman, "The Hohokam," 143–44; Fish and Fish, "Hohokam Millennium," 6, 9; David E. Doyel, "Irrigation, Production, and Power in Phoenix Basin Hohokam Society," in *Hohokam Millennium*, 84–86; Bayman, "Artisans and Their Crafts in Hohokam Society," 78–79; David R. Wilcox, Thomas R. McGuire, and Charles Sternberg, *Snaketown Revisited: A Partial Cultural Resource Survey, Analysis of Site Structure and an Ethnohistoric Study of the Proposed Hohokam-Pima National Monument* (Tucson, 1981); Stephanie M. Whittlesey, "Hohokam Ceramics, Hohokam Beliefs," in *Hohokam Millennium*, 66–68, 71–72; Patricia L. Crown, "Growing Up

Hohokam," 23, 25–26; David R. Abbott, "The Politics of Decline in Canal System 2," in *Centuries of Decline During the Hohokam Classic Period at Pueblo Grande,* ed. David R. Abbott (Tucson, 2016), 203–8; Wallace, "Hohokam Beginnings," 17. Scholars hypothesize about gendered divisions of labor for Huhugam based on what tools people were buried with, the few images of Huhugam people at work, and later gendered patterns among descendants.

35. Fish, "Hohokam Impacts," in *Imperfect Balance,* 258, 266–67; Ferguson and Colwell-Chanthaphonh, *History Is in the Land,* 44–46, 83; Mark D. Elson, "Into the Earth, Up to the Sky: Hohokam Ritual Architecture," in *Hohokam Millennium,* 50–52; Doyel, "Irrigation, Production, and Power," 84–86; Fish and Fish, "Community, Territory, and Polity," 41; Gumerman, "The Hohokam," 144; Paul R. Fish and Suzanne K. Fish, "Reflections on the Casas Grandes Regional System from the Northwestern Periphery," in *The Casas Grandes World,* ed. Curtis F. Schaafsma and Carroll L. Riley (Salt Lake City, 1999), 40–42; Haury, *Hohokam,* 78–79; David R. Wilcox, "The Mesoamerican Ballgame in the American Southwest," in *The Mesoamerican Ballgame,* ed. Vernon L. Scarborough and David R. Wilcox (Tucson, 1991), 101–25.

36. Fish and Fish, "Community, Territory, and Polity," 40–41; Doyel, "Irrigation, Production, and Power," 86; Gumerman, "The Hohokam," 143–44; Ravesloot, "Changing Views of Snaketown," 94–95; Lekson, *History of the Ancient Southwest,* 232.

37. Loendorf, *Hohokam-Akimel O'odham Continuum,* 119–20; Ravesloot, "Changing Views of Snaketown," 95–96; Gumerman, "The Hohokam," 145.

38. Wilcox, McGuire, and Sternberg, *Snaketown Revisited,* 223; Woodson, *Social Organization of Hohokam Irrigation,* 2–4, 7–8, 137–39; David R. Abbott and Michael S. Foster, "Site Structure, Chronology, and Population," in *Centuries of Decline,* 46; David R. Abbott, Cory Dale Breternitz, and Christine K. Robinson, "Challenging Conventional Conceptions," in *Centuries of Decline,* 10; David R. Wilcox, Gerald Robertson Jr., and J. Scott Wood, "Organized for War: The Perry Mesa Settlement System and Its Central Arizona Neighbors," in *Deadly Landscapes,* 141–68; Abbott, "Politics of Decline," 201–2, 208–9, 222; David A. Gregory, "Form and Variation in Hohokam Settlement Patterns," in *Chaco and Hohokam: Prehistoric Regional Systems in the American Southwest,* ed. Patricia L. Crown and W. James Judge (Santa Fe, 1991), 170–73, 184–87; Scott E. Ingram, "Streamflow and Population Change in the Lower Salt River Valley of Central Arizona, ca. A.D. 775 to 1450," *American Antiquity* 73 (2008), 136–65. For climatic stress and centralizing states, see Scott, *Against the Grain.*

39. Richter, *Before the Revolution,* 37–38; Gregory, "Form and Variation," 166–68; Mark D. Elson, *Expanding the View of Hohokam Platform Mounds: An Ethnographic Perspective* (Tucson, 1998); Elson, "Into the Earth, Up to the Sky," 52–54.

40. Lekson, *History of the Ancient Southwest,* 240–41; Fish, "Hohokam Impacts," in *Imperfect Balance,* 254–55; Abbott, Breternitz, and Robinson, "Challenging Conventional Conceptions," 8, 13; Abbott, "Politics of Decline," 216; Glen E. Rice, *Sending the Spirits Home: The Archaeology of Hohokam Mortuary Practices* (Salt Lake City, 2016), 1; Christian E. Downum and Todd W. Bostwick, "The Platform Mound," in *Centuries of Decline,* 166–200.

41. Elson, "Into the Earth, Up to the Sky," 49, 54; Doyel, "Irrigation, Production, and Power," 88–89; Ravesloot, "Changing Views of Snaketown," 94–95; Fish and Fish, "Community, Territory, and Polity," 44; Loendorf, *Hohokam-Akimel O'odham Con-*

tinuum, 123; Abbott, Breternitz, and Robinson, "Challenging Conventional Conceptions," 5; exhibits, Casa Grande Ruins National Monument and S'edav Va'aki Museum.

42. Wiesner-Hanks, *Concise History of the World,* 202–3.

43. Pauketat, *Cahokia,* 13–15; Megan C. Kassabaum, *A History of Platform Mound Ceremonialism: Finding Meaning in Elevated Ground* (Gainesville, 2021), 47–86, 159.

44. Pauketat, *Cahokia,* 2, 21–23, 35.

45. Gideon Lincecum, "Choctaw Traditions About Their Settlement in Mississippi and the Origin of Their Mounds," *Publication of the Mississippi Historical Society* 8 (1904), 521–42, transcription in Vernon James Knight Jr., "Symbolism of Mississippian Mounds," in *Powhatan's Mantle: Indians in the Colonial Southeast,* ed. Peter H. Wood, Gregory A. Waselkov, and M. Thomas Hatley, rev. ed. (Lincoln, 2006), 288.

46. Richter, *Before the Revolution,* 19–22, 37–38; Milne, *Port of Medieval London,* 94; Sarah Baires, "Cahokia's Rattlesnake Causeway," *Midcontinental Journal of Archaeology,* 39 (2014), 155; Brian M. Fagan, *Ancient North America: The Archaeology of a Continent,* 4th ed. (New York, 2005), 472–73.

47. Pauketat, *Cahokia,* 9–10, 16, 22; Thomas E. Emerson, "Reflections from the Countryside on Cahokian Hegemony," in *Cahokia: Domination and Ideology in the Mississippian World,* ed. Timothy R. Pauketat and Thomas E. Emerson (Lincoln, 1997), 186–87; Peter H. Wood, "Missing the Boat: Ancient Dugout Canoes in the Mississippi-Missouri Watershed," *Early American Studies* 16 (2018), 215, 221–23; Amber M. VanDerwarker, "Mississippians and Maize," *Medieval Mississippians: The Cahokian World,* ed. Timothy R. Pauketat and Susan M. Alt (Santa Fe, 2015), 49–53, 75–79.

48. Timothy R. Pauketat, Thomas E. Emerson, Michael G. Farkas, and Sarah E. Baires, "An American Indian City," *Medieval Mississippians,* 27–28; Baires, "Cahokia's Rattlesnake Causeway," 145–62.

49. Young and Fowler, *Cahokia,* 36, 123, 130–35; Melvin L. Fowler, Jerome Rose, Barbara Vander Leest, and Steven R. Ahler, *The Mound 72 Area: Dedicated and Sacred Space in Early Cahokia* (Springfield, Ill., 1999), 63–77; Thomas E. Emerson, Kristin M. Hedman, Eve A. Hargrave, Dawn E. Cobb, and Andrew R. Thompson, "Paradigms Lost: Reconfiguring Cahokia's Mound 72 Beaded Burial," *American Antiquity* 81 (2016), 405–25; Andrew R. Thompson, "Odontometric Determination of Sex at Mound 72, Cahokia," *American Journal of Physical Anthropology* 151 (2013), 408–19.

50. Emerson, Hedman, Hargrave, Cobb, and Thompson, "Paradigms Lost," 405–25; Pauketat, *Cahokia,* 73–78, 83, 132–34.

51. John Charles Chasteen, *Born in Blood and Fire: A Concise History of Latin America,* 2nd ed. (New York, 2006), 27–28, 47; Richter, *Before the Revolution,* 19–22, 37–38; Christina Snyder, *Slavery in Indian Country: The Changing Face of Captivity in Early America* (Cambridge, Mass., 2010), 27–28; Alice B. Kehoe, "Cahokia, America's Great City," *Indian Country Today* (Feb. 22, 2017); Baires, "Cahokia's Rattlesnake Causeway," 145–62; Pauketat, *Cahokia,* 73–78, 80–83, 110–12; Fowler, Rose, Vander Leest, and Ahler, *The Mound 72 Area,* 64, 69–70, 78–82; Thomas E. Emerson and Kristin M. Hedman, "The Dangers of Diversity: The Consolidation and Dissolution of Cahokia, Native North America's First Urban Polity," in *Beyond Collapse: Archaeological Perspectives on Resilience, Revitalization, and Transformation in Complex Societies,* ed. Ronald K. Faulseit (Carbondale, Ill., 2016), 166.

52. Richter, *Before the Revolution*, 30; VanDerwarker, "Mississippians and Maize," 51; Vernon James Knight Jr., "The Institutional Organization of Mississippian Religion," *American Antiquity* 51 (1986), 675–87.

53. Antony Michal Krus, "Bridging History and Prehistory: The Possible Antiquity of a Native American Ballgame," *Native South* 4 (2011), 136–45; Pauketat, *Cahokia*, 39–50, 165–68; Richter, *Before the Revolution*, 27.

54. Marc Bloch, "The Rise of Dependent Cultivation and Seigniorial Institutions," in *The Cambridge Economic History of Europe from the Decline of the Roman Empire: The Agrarian Life of the Middle Ages*, ed. J. H. Clapham and Eileen Power (Cambridge, U.K., 1941), 1: 252–56; Wiesner-Hanks, *Concise History of the World*, 149–54; Benjamin C. Waterhouse, *The Land of Enterprise: A Business History of the United States* (New York, 2017), 10–11; Susan M. Alt, "The Fabric of Mississippian Society," in *Medieval Mississippians*, 77–78. Richter, *Before the Revolution*, 41; Roy S. Dickens, ed., *Of Sky and Earth: Art of the Early Southeastern Indians* (Dalton, Ga., 1982), 20.

55. Wiesner-Hanks, *A Concise History of the World*, 45–48; J. R. McNeill, *The Webs of Humankind: A World History* (New York, 2021), 36–45; VanDerwarker, Bardolph, and Scarry, "Maize and Mississippian Beginnings," 39–40; Richter, *Before the Revolution*, 20; Fritz, *Feeding Cahokia*, 128, 141, 146; Susan M. Alt, "Cahokian Change and the Authority of Tradition," in *The Archaeology of Traditions: Agency and History Before and After Columbus*, ed. Timothy R. Pauketat (Gainesville, 2001), 141–56; Timothy R. Pauketat, "Resettled Farmers and the Making of a Mississippian Polity," *American Antiquity* 68 (2003), 39–66; Pauketat, *Cahokia*, 119–23; Susan M. Alt, "Identities, Traditions, and Diversity in Cahokia's Uplands," *Midcontinental Journal of Archaeology* 27 (2002), 217–36; Susan M. Alt, "Spindle Whorls and Fiber Production at Early Cahokian Settlements," *Southeastern Archaeology* 18 (1999), 124–33; Snyder, *Slavery in Indian Country*, 25–26.

56. Lee, *Masters of the Middle Waters*, 18–21.

57. H. Edwin Jackson, C. Margaret Scarry, and Susan Scott, "Domestic and Ritual Meals in the Moundville Chiefdom," in *Rethinking Moundville and Its Hinterland*, ed. Vincas P. Steponaitis and C. Margaret Scarry (Gainesville, 2016), 195; C. Margaret Scarry, "Domestic Life on the Northwest Riverbank at Moundville," in *Archaeology of the Moundville Chiefdom*, ed. Vernon James Knight Jr. and Vincas P. Steponaitis (Tuscaloosa, 1998), 88–89, 100; Scott W. Hammerstedt, Mintcy D. Maxham, and Jennifer L. Myer, "Rural Settlement in the Black Warrior Valley," in *Rethinking Moundville and Its Hinterland*, ed. Vincas P. Steponaitis and C. Margaret Scarry (Gainesville, 2016), 159.

58. Scarry, "Domestic Life on the Northwest Riverbank," 89–90; Vernon James Knight Jr. and Vincas P. Steponaitis, "A New History of Moundville," in *Archaeology of the Moundville Chiefdom*, 10–11; Margaret J. Schoeninger and Mark R. Schurr, "Human Subsistence at Moundville: The Stable-Isotope Data," in *Archaeology of the Moundville Chiefdom*, 128–29.

59. Vincas P. Steponaitis, "Contrasting Patterns of Mississippian Development," in *Chiefdoms: Power, Economy, and Ideology*, ed. Timothy K. Earle (Cambridge, U.K., 1991), 193–228; Knight and Steponaitis, "A New History of Moundville," 13–16; Vernon James Knight Jr., *Mound Excavations at Moundville: Architecture, Elites, and Social Order* (Tuscaloosa, 2010).

60. Garcilaso de la Vega, the Inca, "La Florida," trans. Charmion Shelby, in *The De Soto Chronicles: The Expedition of Hernando de Soto to North America in 1539–1543,* ed. Lawrence A. Clayton, Vernon James Knight Jr., and Edward C. Moore (Tuscaloosa, 1993), 2:331; John H. Blitz, "Mound X and Selective Forgetting at Early Moundville," in *Rethinking Moundville and Its Hinterland,* 68–69; Knight and Steponaitis, "A New History of Moundville," 4, 15–16; Vincas P. Steponaitis and C. Margaret Scarry, "New Directions in Moundville Research," in *Rethinking Moundville and Its Hinterland,* 1–2.

61. Vincas P. Steponaitis, "Population Trends at Moundville," in *Archaeology of the Moundville Chiefdom,* 42–43; Hammerstedt, Maxham, and Myer, "Rural Settlement in the Black Warrior Valley," 159; Knight and Steponaitis, "A New History of Moundville," 15; C. Margaret Scarry and Vincas P. Steponaitis, "Between Farmstead and Center: The Natural and Social Landscape of Moundville," in *People, Plants, and Landscapes: Studies in Paleoethnobotany,* ed. Kristen J. Gremillion (Tuscaloosa, 1997), 122; Christine Folch, "Ceremony, Medicine, Caffeinated Tea: Unearthing the Forgotten Faces of the North American Stimulant Yaupon (Ilex vomitoria)," *Comparative Studies in Society and History* 63 (2021), 464–98; Scarry, "Domestic Life on the Northwest Riverbank," 94–96; Vernon James Knight Jr., "Social Archaeology of Monumental Spaces at Moundville," in *Rethinking Moundville and Its Hinterland,* 32–34; Knight and Steponaitis, "A New History of Moundville," 16–17; Cynthia Whitney, Vincas P. Steponaitis, and John J. W. Rogers, "A Petrographic Study of Moundville Palettes," *Southeastern Archaeology* 21 (2002), 227–35; Daniel G. Gall and Vincas P. Steponaitis, "Composition and Provenance of Greenstone Artifacts from Moundville," *Southeastern Archaeology* 20 (2001), 99–118.

62. Vincas P. Steponaitis, "Mississippian Effigy Pipes: Provenance, Style, and Iconography," talk to American Indian and Indigenous Studies Colloquium, UNC, September 28, 2017; Vincas P. Steponaitis and David T. Dockery III, "A Tale of Two Pipes," *Gilcrease Journal* 21 (2014), 36–45; Vincas P. Steponaitis, "Moundville Palettes—Prestige Goods or Inalienable Possessions?," in *Rethinking Moundville and Its Hinterland,* 131–33.

63. Vernon James Knight Jr., "Characterizing Elite Midden Deposits at Moundville," *American Antiquity* 69 (2004), 304–21; Knight, "Social Archaeology of Monumental Spaces at Moundville," 32–34; Jackson, Scarry, and Scott, "Domestic and Ritual Meals in the Moundville Chiefdom," 225–29; Knight, *Mound Excavations at Moundville,* 3–4.

64. Knight and Steponaitis, "A New History of Moundville," 5, 18; Steponaitis and Scarry, "New Directions in Moundville Research," 3.

65. Fritz, *Feeding Cahokia,* 117; Mary Lucas Powell, "Of Time and the River: Perspectives on Health During the Moundville Chiefdom," in *Archaeology of the Moundville Chiefdom,* 118; Steponaitis, "Moundville Palettes," 121–22; permanent exhibit, Museum of the Cherokee Indian.

66. Jackson, Scarry, and Scott, "Domestic and Ritual Meals in the Moundville Chiefdom," 195–96, 202–3, 207–9, 229–31; Knight, "Social Archaeology of Monumental Spaces at Moundville," 36–37; Schoeninger and Schurr, "Human Subsistence at Moundville," 129; Powell, "Of Time and the River," 112, 118; Jane E. Buikstra and Della C. Cook, "Pre-Columbian Tuberculosis in West-Central Illinois: Prehistoric Disease in Biocultural Perspective," in *Prehistoric Tuberculosis in the Americas*

(Evanston, 1981), 115–40; Rachel V. Briggs, "The Civil Cooking Pot: Hominy and the Mississippian Standard Jar in the Black Warrior Valley, Alabama," *American Antiquity* (2016), 316–32; John F. Scarry, H. Edwin Jackson, and Mintcy D. Maxham, "Late Prehistoric Social Practice in the Rural Black Warrior River Valley," in *Rethinking Moundville and Its Hinterland*, 165, 177–81; Steponaitis and Scarry, "New Directions in Moundville Research," 17–18; Knight, "Characterizing Elite Midden Deposits at Moundville," 304–21.

67. Scarry, "Domestic Life on the Northwest Riverbank," 90; Paul D. Welch, "Outlying Sites Within the Moundville Chiefdom," *Archaeology of the Moundville Chiefdom*, 136–38; Tandy K. Bozeman, "Moundville Phase Communities in the Black Warrior River Valley, Alabama" (Ph.D. diss., University of California, Santa Barbara, 1982), 157–58; Hammerstedt, Maxham, and Myer, "Rural Settlement in the Black Warrior Valley," 136–37; Steponaitis and Scarry, "New Directions in Moundville Research," 17–18.

68. Welch, "Outlying Sites Within the Moundville Chiefdom," 134, 162; Jackson, Scarry, and Scott, "Domestic and Ritual Meals in the Moundville Chiefdom," 194; Knight and Steponaitis, "A New History of Moundville," 2, 15; Steponaitis and Scarry, "New Directions in Moundville Research," 3, 17–18.

69. C. Margaret Scarry and Vincas P. Steponaitis, "Moundville as a Ceremonial Ground," in *Rethinking Moundville and Its Hinterland*, 256; Scarry and Steponaitis, "Between Farmstead and Center," 118–19; Steponaitis, "Population Trends at Moundville," *Archaeology of the Moundville Chiefdom*, 42–43; Gregory D. Wilson, "Long-Term Trends in the Making and Materialization of Social Groups at Moundville," in *Rethinking Moundville and Its Hinterland*, 44, 47; Scarry, "Domestic Life on the Northwest Riverbank," 91–93; Knight and Steponaitis, "A New History of Moundville," 15; Gregory D. Wilson, *The Archaeology of Everyday Life at Early Moundville* (Tuscaloosa, 2008), 52–54, 57, 59, 62, 65–67, 69, 74–75, 77–79, 90.

70. Wilson, *Archaeology of Everyday Life at Early Moundville*, 119, 129–30; Vernon James Knight Jr., "Moundville as a Diagrammatic Ceremonial Center," in *Archaeology of the Moundville Chiefdom*, 47, 59–60; Scarry and Steponaitis, "Moundville as a Ceremonial Ground," 255–68; Wilson, "Long-Term Trends in the Making and Materialization of Social Groups at Moundville," 47; Jackson, Scarry, and Scott, "Domestic and Ritual Meals in the Moundville Chiefdom," 202–3, 207–9; Scarry, Jackson, and Maxham, "Late Prehistoric Social Practice," 167–68, 172–75.

71. Scarry, Jackson, and Maxham, "Late Prehistoric Social Practice in the Rural Black Warrior River Valley," 162–63; Scarry, "Domestic Life on the Northwest Riverbank," 94; Steponaitis, "Contrasting Patterns of Mississippian Development," in *Chiefdoms*, 193–228.

72. "ᏏᎣ ᎠᏕᎶᎢ, ᏅᎯᏳᏓ?" ("Hi friends, things going well?")

73. "ii, ᏅᎣᎵ, ᎭᏗᎾ?" ("Yeah, good, and you?")

CHAPTER 2: THE "FALL" OF CITIES AND THE RISE
OF A MORE EGALITARIAN ORDER

1. Siwani or Sivan is also known as the Bitter Man (the literal translation) or Morning Green Chief, and O'odham in the early eighteenth century called Casa Grande Sivuni. T. J. Ferguson and Chip Colwell-Chanthaphonh, *History Is in the Land: Multivocal Tribal Traditions in Arizona's San Pedro Valley* (Tucson, 2006),

79–80; Juan Mateo Manje, Nov. 2, 1697, "Del viaje que hice con el reverend Padre Eusebio Francisco Kino y 22 soldados," in appendix, *Kino and Manje, Explorers of Sonora and Arizona: Their Vision of the Future*, ed. Ernest J. Burrus (St. Louis, 1971), 343; Luis Xavier Velarde, "Descripción" (1716), in appendix, *Kino and Manje*, 627; Frank Russell, *The Pima Indians* (Washington, D.C., 1908), 227–28; Donald Bahr, Juan Smith, William Smith Allison, and Julian Hayden, *The Short, Swift Time of Gods on Earth: The Hohokam Chronicles* (Berkeley, 1994), 6, 204–33; Jesse Walter Fewkes, "Casa Grande, Arizona," in *Twenty-Eighth Annual Report of the Bureau of American Ethnology, 1906–1907* (Washington, D.C., 1912), 33, 43, 55–56; David E. Doyel, "Irrigation, Production, and Power in Phoenix Basin Hohokam Society," in *The Hohokam Millennium*, ed. Suzanne K. Fish and Paul R. Fish (Santa Fe, 2007), 88–89; Christopher R. Loendorf, *The Hohokam-Akimel O'odham Continuum: Sociocultural Dynamics and Projectile Point Design in the Phoenix Basin, Arizona* (Sacaton, Ariz., 2012), 119; Glen E. Rice, *Sending the Spirits Home: The Archaeology of Hohokam Mortuary Practices* (Salt Lake City, 2016), 10.

2. Brian Fagan, *The Great Warming: Climate Change and the Rise and Fall of Civilizations* (New York, 2008), ix, 42–43, 69–71, 107–8, 112, 208–12; Hubert Lamb, *Climate Change and the Modern World* (London, 1982), xii, 48, 134–39; Daniel K. Richter, *Before the Revolution: America's Ancient Pasts* (Cambridge, Mass., 2011), 31.

3. Gonzalo Fernández de Oviedo y Valdés, *Historia General y Natural de las Indias, Islas y Tierra-Firme del Mar Océano* (Madrid, 1853), 2:592; Luis Hernández de Biedma, "Relation," trans. John E. Worth, *The De Soto Chronicles: The Expedition of Hernando de Soto to North America in 1539–1543*, ed. Lawrence A. Clayton, Vernon James Knight Jr., and Edward C. Moore (Tuscaloosa, 1993), 1:236, 243; Rodrigo Rangel, "Account and Discovery of Hernando De Soto," trans. John E. Worth, *De Soto Chronicles*, 1:297; A Gentleman of Elvas, "True Relation of the Hardships Suffered by Governor Don Hernando de Soto," trans. James Alexander Robertson, *De Soto Chronicles*, 1:130; Fagan, *Great Warming*, ix; Richter, *Before the Revolution*, 12; Broxton W. Bird, Jeremy J. Wilson, William P. Gilhooly III, Byron A. Steinman, and Lucas Stamps, "Midcontinental Native American Population Dynamics and Late Holocene Hydroclimate Extremes," *Scientific Reports* 7 (2017); Charles R. Cobb and Adam King, "Re-Inventing Mississippian Tradition at Etowah, Georgia," *Journal of Archaeological Method and Theory*, 12 (2005), 183; Brian Fagan, *The Little Ice Age: How Climate Made History, 1300–1850* (New York, 2000), xv–xvi, 28–50, 65–66, 113; Sam White, *A Cold Welcome: The Little Ice Age and Europe's Encounter with North America* (Cambridge, 1980), 41; J. R. McNeill, *The Webs of Humankind: A World History* (New York, 2021), 353–54, 553, 580, 675.

4. David Martínez, "Whither the Huhugam? Decolonizing the Discourse on O'odham Cultural History," in J. Brett Hill, *From Huhugam to Hohokam: Heritage and Archaeology in the American Southwest* (Lanham, Md., 2019), 190; Ferguson and Colwell-Chanthaphonh, *History Is in the Land*, 82–83; Megan C. Kassabaum, *A History of Platform Mound Ceremonialism: Finding Meaning in Elevated Ground* (Gainesville, 2021), 178; Robin Beck, *Chiefdoms, Collapse, and Coalescence in the Early American South* (New York, 2013), 237.

5. Merry E. Wiesner-Hanks, *A Concise History of the World* (Cambridge, 2015), 69–70; Paul Kelton, *Cherokee Medicine, Colonial Germs: An Indigenous Nation's Fight*

Against Smallpox, 1518–1824 (Norman, 2015), 18; Pierre Clastres, *Society Against the State: Essays in Political Anthropology* (New York, 1987), 9, 12.

6. James C. Scott, *The Art of Not Being Governed: An Anarchist History of Upland Southeast Asia* (New Haven, 2009), x–xi; James C. Scott, *Against the Grain: A Deep History of the Earliest States* (New Haven, 2017), 1–2, 7–10.

7. Horace, "The Country Mouse and the Town Mouse," *The Satires*, trans. A. S. Kline, https://www.poetryintranslation.com/PITBR/Latin/HoraceSatiresBkIISatVI .php.

8. McNeill, *The Webs of Humankind,* 674.

9. Richter, *Before the Revolution,* 27; Biloine Whiting Young and Melvin L. Fowler, *Cahokia: The Great Native American Metropolis* (Urbana, 2000), 313–14.

10. Gayle J. Fritz, *Feeding Cahokia: Early Agriculture in the North American Heartland* (Tuscaloosa, 2019), 127–28, 151–52; Stephen Williams, "The Vacant Quarter and Other Late Events in the Lower Valley," in *Towns and Temples Along the Mississippi,* ed. David H. Dye (Tuscaloosa, 1990), 170–80; White, *Cold Welcome,* 32–33; Stephen H. Lekson, *A History of the Ancient Southwest* (Santa Fe, 2008), 243; Scott M. Kwiatkowski, "Evidence for Subsistence Problems," in *Centuries of Decline During the Hohokam Classic Period at Pueblo Grande,* ed. David R. Abbott (Tucson, 2016), 48, 57, 63–68; David R. Abbott and Michael S. Foster, "Site Structure, Chronology, and Population," in *Centuries of Decline,* 46–47; David R. Abbott, "The Politics of Decline in Canal System 2," in *Centuries of Decline,* 214–15; Suzanne K. Fish, "Hohokam Impacts on Sonoran Desert Environment," in *Imperfect Balance: Landscape Transformations in the Pre-Columbian Americas,* ed. David L. Lentz (New York, 2000), 252, 275.

11. Kwiatkowski, "Evidence for Subsistence Problems," 48, 58–63, 67; Steven R. James, "Hunting and Fishing Patterns Leading to Resource Depletion," in *Centuries of Decline,* 70–81; David R. Abbott, "The Politics of Decline," in *Centuries of Decline,* 213–14; Susan Guise Sheridan, "Childhood Health as an Indicator of Biological Stress," in *Centuries of Decline,* 82–106.

12. Steven A. LeBlanc and Glen E. Rice, eds., "Southwestern Warfare: The Value of Case Studies," in *Deadly Landscapes: Case Studies in Prehistoric Southwestern Warfare* (Salt Lake City, 2001), 1–18; Ferguson and Colwell-Chanthaphonh, *History Is in the Land,* 46–48, 50; Henry D. Wallace and William H. Doelle, "Classic Period Warfare in Southern Arizona," in *Deadly Landscapes,* 239–86; Abbott and Foster, "Site Structure, Chronology, and Population," 28, 33, 46–47; Loendorf, *Hohokam-Akimel O'odham Continuum,* 6, 123, 128–29; exhibits, S'edav Va'aki Museum; Patricia L. Crown and Suzanne K. Fish, "Gender and Status in the Hohokam Pre-Classic to Classic Tradition," *American Anthropologist* 98 (1996), 807; Fish and Fish, "Hohokam Millennium," in *Hohokam Millennium,* 9; James Bayman, "Artisans and Their Crafts in Hohokam Society," in *Hohokam Millennium,* 79; Abbott, "Politics of Decline," 208–10; Barbara J. Mills, "Intermarriage, Technological Diffusion, and Boundary Objects in the U.S. Southwest," *Journal of Archaeological Method and Theory* 25 (2018), 1051–86.

13. Abbott, "Politics of Decline," 221–23; Rice, *Sending the Spirits Home;* Douglas R. Mitchell, "Burial and Society," in *Centuries of Decline,* 122–24; Crown and Fish, "Gender and Status in the Hohokam Pre-Classic to Classic Tradition," 808;

Crown, "Growing up Hohokam," 29; Bayman, "Artisans and Their Crafts in Hohokam Society," 77, 81; Doyel, "Irrigation, Production, and Power," 86; Loendorf, *Hohokam-Akimel O'odham Continuum*, 129; Aaron M. Wright, *Religion on the Rocks: Hohokam Rock Art, Ritual Practice, and Social Transformation* (Salt Lake City, 2014), 34–36.

14. Timothy R. Pauketat, *Cahokia: Ancient America's Great City on the Mississippi* (New York, 2009), 122–23; Fritz, *Feeding Cahokia*, 154–59; Young and Fowler, *Cahokia*, 310, 312; J. R. McNeill, *The Webs of Humankind: A World History* (New York, 2021), 353–55.

15. Young and Fowler, *Cahokia*, 310, 313–14; Thomas E. Emerson and Kristin M. Hedman, "The Dangers of Diversity: The Consolidation and Dissolution of Cahokia, Native North America's First Urban Polity," in *Beyond Collapse: Archaeological Perspectives on Resilience, Revitalization, and Transformation in Complex Societies*, ed. Ronald K. Faulseit (Carbondale, Ill., 2016), 147–75; Brian M. Fagan, *Ancient North America: The Archaeology of a Continent*, 4th ed. (New York, 2005), 475; Williams, "Vacant Quarter," 170–80.

16. David Martínez, "Whither the Huhugam? Decolonizing the Discourse on O'odham Cultural History," in Hill, *From Huhugam to Hohokam*, 190, 194; Hill, *From Huhugam to Hohokam*, 79–85; David Martínez, "Huhugam Homeland to Phoenix and Back Again," Steven Yazzie, Indigenous Tours Project, 2014, https://vimeo.com/95179964; Ferguson and Colwell-Chanthaphonh, *History Is in the Land*, 4–14, 27–28, 79–81; Bahr, et al., *Short, Swift Time of Gods on Earth*, 209–10, 245, 247–62; Rice, *Sending the Spirits Home*, 7, 10; Donald M. Bahr, "O'odham Traditions About the Hohokam," in *Hohokam Millennium*, 125–26; Thomas E. Sheridan, *Landscapes of Fraud: Mission Tumacácori, the Baca Float, and the Betrayal of the O'odham* (Tucson, 2006), 20–21; Ruth M. Underhill, *Papago Indian Religion* (New York, 1946), 8–12; Mark E. Harlan and Deni J. Seymour, "Sobaipuri O'odham and Mobile Group Relevance to Late Prehistoric Social Networks in the San Pedro Valley," in *Fierce and Indomitable: The Protohistoric Non-Pueblo World* (Salt Lake City, 2017), 173, 176, 185; Randall H. McGuire, Maria Elisa Villalpando C., Victoria D. Vargas, and Emiliano Gallaga M., "Cerro de Trincheras and the Casas Grandes World," in *The Casas Grandes World*, ed. Curtis F. Schaafsma and Carroll L. Riley (Salt Lake City, 1999), 134–46; "Culture History of Southern Arizona: Trincheras Culture," Arizona State Museum, https://statemuseum.arizona.edu/online-exhibit/culture-history-southern-arizona/trincheras; James S. Griffith, *Beliefs and Holy Places: A Spiritual Geography of the Pimería Alta* (Tucson, 1992), 15.

17. Williams, "Vacant Quarter," 170–80.

18. Vernon James Knight Jr. and Vincas P. Steponaitis, preface to *Archaeology of the Moundville Chiefdom*, ed. Vernon James Knight Jr. and Vincas P. Steponaitis (Tuscaloosa, 1998), xix; Knight and Steponaitis, "A New History of Moundville," 17–18; Shannon Chappell Hodge, "Population Dispersal and Human Health at Moundville," *Southeastern Archaeology* 30 (2011), 226–41.

19. Steponaitis, "Population Trends at Moundville," in *Archaeology of the Moundville Chiefdom*, 42–43; Vincas P. Steponaitis and C. Margaret Scarry, "New Directions in Moundville Research," in *Rethinking Moundville and Its Hinterland*, ed. Vincas P. Steponaitis and C. Margaret Scarry (Gainesville, 2016), 2–3; H. Edwin Jackson, C. Margaret Scarry, and Susan Scott, "Domestic and Ritual Meals in the

Moundville Chiefdom," in *Rethinking Moundville and Its Hinterland,* 194–95, 213, 215; John F. Scarry, H. Edwin Jackson, and Mintcy D. Maxham, "Late Prehistoric Social Practice in the Rural Black Warrior River Valley," in *Rethinking Moundville and Its Hinterland,* 179; Knight and Steponaitis, "A New History of Moundville," 19–22; Steponaitis, "Population Trends at Moundville," *Archaeology of the Moundville Chiefdom,* 39–40; Gregory D. Wilson, "Long-Term Trends in the Making and Materialization of Social Groups at Moundville," in *Rethinking Moundville and Its Hinterland,* 50–52; Gregory D. Wilson, *Archaeology of Everyday Life at Early Moundville* (Tuscaloosa, 2008), 56, 62, 86–87; Paul D. Welch, "Outlying Sites Within the Moundville Chiefdom," in *Archaeology of the Moundville Chiefdom,* 136, 148–65.

20. Williams, "Vacant Quarter," 170–80; Beck, *Chiefdoms, Collapse, and Coalescence,* 49–58; Mark Williams, "Busk Sites of the Oconee Valley," *Early Georgia* 44 (2016), 109–10, 123.

21. Their name is spelled varous ways, including Anikutani and Unanti. Permanent exhibit, Museum of the Cherokee Indian, Cherokee, N.C.; James Mooney, "Myths of the Cherokee," *Smithsonian Institution Bureau of American Ethnology Annual Report* 19 (1902), 392–93; Robert J. Conley, *The Cherokee* (New York, 2011), 20–21; Sequoyah Guess, "The Cherokee Migration Story," in Christopher B. Teuton, Hastings Shade, Sammy Still, Sequoyah Guess, and Woody Hansen, *Cherokee Stories of the Turtle Island Liars' Club* (Chapel Hill, 2012), 74–75; Raymond D. Fogelson, "Who Were the Aní-Kutáni? An Excursion into Cherokee Historical Thought," *Ethnohistory* 31 (1984), 255–63 (including Fogelson's transcriptions of: D. J. MacGowan, "Indian Secret Societies," *The Historical Magazine* 10 (1866), 139–40; Carl F. Klinck and James J. Talman, eds., *The Journal of Major John Norton, 1816* (Toronto, 1970), 80; Charles R. Hicks to John Ross, Mar. 1, 1826, Ayer collection, Newberry Library).

22. Sequoyah Guess, *Kholvn* (Kansas, Okla., 1992), iii, quoted in Joshua B. Nelson, *Progressive Traditions: Identity in Cherokee Literature and Culture* (Norman, 2014), 40, 132–33.

23. Matthew W. Stirling, "Origin Myth of Acoma and Other Records," *Smithsonian Institution Bureau of American Ethnology Bulletin* 135 (Washington, D.C., 1942), 71–75; Richter, *Before the Revolution,* 11; Leslie A. White, "The World of the Keresan Pueblo Indians," in *Primitive Views of the World,* ed. Stanley Diamond (New York, 1964), 89–90.

24. Stephen H. Lekson, *A History of the Ancient Southwest* (Santa Fe, 2008), 234–35, 242–46; Juliana Barr, "There's No Such Thing as 'Prehistory': What the Longue Durée of Caddo and Pueblo History Tells Us About Colonial America," *William and Mary Quarterly* 74 (2017), 206, 223, 226–29; Stephen H. Lekson, "Chaco Matters: An Introduction," in *The Archaeology of Chaco Canyon: An Eleventh-Century Pueblo Regional Center* (Santa Fe, 2006), 29; Wilcox, "Marketing Conquest," in *Questioning Collapse: Human Resilience, Ecological Vulnerability and the Aftermath of Empire,* ed. Patricia A. McAnany and Norman Yoffee (New York, 2010), 134.

25. McAnany and Yoffee, "Why We Question Collapse and Study Human Resilience, Ecological Vulnerability, and the Aftermath of Empire," in *Questioning Collapse;* Hill, *From Huhugam to Hohokam,* 3–4; Loendorf, *Hohokam-Akimel O'odham Continuum,* 130–33; Pauketat, *Cahokia,* 124–25; Williams, "Vacant Quarter,"

170–80; Martínez, "Whither the Huhugam?," 194; Abbott, "Politics of Decline," 202, 226; E. Christian Wells, *From Hohokam to O'odham: The Protohistoric Occupation of the Middle Gila River Valley, Central Arizona* (Sacaton, Ariz., 2006), 43–45.

26. Martínez, "Whither the Huhugam?," 194; "Fray Marcos de Niza, Relación (1539)," ed. Jerry R. Craddock, *Romance Philology* 53 (1999), 89. Translations of Niza documents are by John DuVal.

27. Rangel, "Account and Discovery of Hernando De Soto," 1:296; Elvas, "True Relation of the Hardships Suffered by Governor Don Hernando de Soto," 1:105; Biedma, "Relation," 1:236; Charles Hudson, Marvin T. Smith, and Chester B. De-Pratter, "The Hernando de Soto Expedition: From Mabila to the Mississippi River," in *Towns and Temples Along the Mississippi*, 183–88; Knight and Steponaitis, "A New History of Moundville," 23–24; Patricia Galloway, *Choctaw Genesis, 1500–1700* (Lincoln, 1995), 134; Beck, *Chiefdoms, Collapse, and Coalescence*, 15, 62–95.

28. Galloway, *Choctaw Genesis*, 152–53.

29. Daniel T. Reff, "Sympathy for the Devil: Devil Sickness and Lore Among the Tohono O'odham," *Journal of the Southwest* 50 (2008), 359; Cary Miller, *Ogimaag: Anishinaabeg Leadership, 1760–1845* (Lincoln, 2010), 4.

30. Thomas Hatley, "Cherokee Women Farmers Hold Their Ground," in *Appalachian Frontiers: Settlement, Society, and Development in the Preindustrial Era*, ed. Robert D. Mitchell (Lexington, 1991), 39–40; Jane Mt. Pleasant, "The Paradox of Plows and Productivity: An Agronomic Comparison of Cereal Grain Production Under Iroquois Hoe Culture and European Plow Culture in the Seventeenth and Eighteenth Centuries," *Agricultural History* 85 (2011), 460–92; Jane Mt. Pleasant, "A New Paradigm for Pre-Columbian Agriculture in North America," *Early American Studies* 13 (2015), 374–412; Jessica Diemer-Eaton, "Hominy: An Original Native American Dish," Woodland Indian Educational Programs, 2011, http://www.woodlandindianedu.com/hominy.html; R. Douglas Hurt, *Indian Agriculture in America: Prehistory to the Present* (Lawrence, Kan., 1987), 34–35; Brian Fagan, *The Little Ice Age* (New York, 2019), 106–7; William E. Doolittle "Agriculture in North America on the Eve of Contact: A Reassessment," *Annals of the Association of American Geographers* 82 (1992), 386–401.

31. Peter H. Wood, "Missing the Boat: Ancient Dugout Canoes in the Mississippi-Missouri Watershed," *Early American Studies* 16 (2018), 197–254; Daniel K. Richter, *Ordeal of the Longhouse: The Peoples of the Iroquois League in the Era of European Colonization* (Chapel Hill, 1992), 22; Mary Lucas Powell, "Of Time and the River: Perspectives on Health During the Moundville Chiefdom," in *Archaeology of the Moundville Chiefdom*, 102–3, 118; Margaret J. Schoeninger and Mark R. Schurr, "Human Subsistence at Moundville: The Stable-Isotope Data," in *Archaeology of the Moundville Chiefdom*, 128, 130, 132; Jackson, Scarry, and Scott, "Domestic and Ritual Meals in the Moundville Chiefdom," 195; LeBlanc and Rice, "Southwestern Warfare," 14; Kwiatkowski, "Evidence for Subsistence Problems," 59; Loendorf, *Hohokam-Akimel O'odham Continuum*, 5–6, 130–32.

32. Conversation with David Martínez, Mar. 15, 2019, Tempe, Ariz.; David Martínez, "Whither the Huhugam? Decolonizing the Discourse on O'odham Cultural History," in Hill, *From Huhugam to Hohokam*, 191, 194; Ferguson and Colwell-Chanthaphonh, *History Is in the Land*, 51.

33. Conversation with David Martínez, Mar. 15, 2019, Tempe, Ariz.; John C. Ravesloot, "Changing Views of Snaketown in a Larger Landscape," in *Hohokam Millennium*, 96; Daniel T. Reff, "Anthropological Analysis of Exploration Texts: Cultural Discourse and the Ethnological Import of Fray Marcos de Niza's Journey to Cibola," *American Anthropologist* 93 (1991), 645–47; Carroll L. Riley, "Early Spanish-Indian Communication in the Greater Southwest," *New Mexico Historical Review* 46 (1971), 294; Loendorf, *Hohokam-Akimel O'odham Continuum*.

34. Himdag Ki Tohono O'odham Nation Cultural Center and Museum exhibit, Topawa, Arizona; David Martínez, "Hiding in the Shadows of History: Revitalizing Hia-Ced O'odham Peoplehood," *Journal of the Southwest* 55 (2013), 158; Dean Saxton, Lucille Saxton, and Susie Enos, *Dictionary: Papago/Pima-English, O'othham-Mil-gahn; English-Papago/Pima, Mil-gahn-O'othham*, ed. R. L. Cherry, 2nd ed. (Tucson, 1983), 22; Tohono O'odham Community Action (TOCA), with Mary Paganelli Votto and Frances Manuel, *From I'itoi's Garden: Tohono O'odham Food Traditions* (Tohono O'odham Community, 2010), 8; Ruth Murray Underhill, *Social Organization of the Papago Indians* (1939; repr., New York, 1969), 20.

35. Winston P. Erickson, *Sharing the Desert: The Tohono O'odham in History* (Tucson, 2003), 12; Papago Tribe of Arizona, *Tohono O'odham: History of the Desert People* (Tohono O'odham, Ariz., 1985), 3; Underhill, *Social Organization*, 10, 90; Bahr, Smith, Allison, and Hayden, *Short, Swift Time of Gods on Earth*, 277.

36. Bahr, Smith, Allison, and Hayden, *The Short, Swift Time of Gods on Earth*, 276 (in this version, I'itoi has the alternative name Siuuhu); Underhill, *Social Organization*, 90, 95, 104–5; Donald M. Bahr, "Pima and Papago Social Organization," in *Handbook of North American Indians: Southwest*, ed. Alfonso Ortiz (Washington, D.C., 1983), 189; David Rich Lewis, *Neither Wolf nor Dog: American Indians, Environment, and Agrarian Change* (New York, 1994), 124.

37. TOCA, Votto, and Manuel, *From I'itoi's Garden*, 228–29, 232–40; Ferguson and Colwell-Chanthaphonh, *History Is in the Land*, 70, 88; Underhill, *Papago Woman*, 34–35; Underhill, *Social Organization*, 102–3; Eusebio Kino, "Favores Celestiales," in *Las misiones de Sonora y Arizona, comprendiendo: La crónica titulada: "Favores Celestiales" y la "Relación diaria de la entrada al noroeste,"* ed. Francisco Fernández del Castillo and Emilio Bose (Mexico City, 1922), 131; Velarde, "Descripción," 642–43, 646; Pfefferkorn, *Sonora*, 192; R. Douglas Hurt, *Indian Agriculture in America: Prehistory to the Present* (Lawrence, 1988), 42–43.

38. Richard S. Felger and Gary Paul Nabhan, "Deceptive Barrenness," *Ceres* (1976), 34; Paul R. Fish, "1,000 Years of Prehistory in the Sonoran Desert," in *Dynamics of Southwest Prehistory*, ed. Linda S. Cordell and George J. Gumerman (Tuscaloosa, 2006), 21–22; Kwiatkowski, "Evidence for Subsistence Problems," 59; Cynthia Radding, *Wandering Peoples: Colonialism, Ethnic Spaces, and Ecological Frontiers in Northwestern Mexico, 1700–1850* (Durham, 1997), 22, 48, 55; Dean and Lucille Saxton, *O'othham Hoho'ok A'agitha: Legends and Lore of the Papago and Pima Indians* (Tucson, 1973), 167; Lewis, *Neither Wolf nor Dog*, 123–28; James C. Scott, *Against the Grain: A Deep History of the Earliest States* (New Haven, 2017), 10; Wild Horse Pass exhibits, Gila River Indian Community; TOCA, Votto, and Manuel, *From I'itoi's Garden*, 252–62.

39. Robert A. Williams Jr., *Linking Arms Together: American Indian Treaty Visions of Law and Peace, 1600–1800* (New York, 1997), 62–63; Jenny Hale Pulsipher, "Gaining the Diplomatic Edge: Kinship, Trade, Ritual, and Religion in Amerindian Alliances in Early North America," in *Empires and Indigenes: Intercultural Alliance,*

Imperial Expansion, and Warfare in the Early Modern World, ed. Wayne E. Lee (New York, 2011), 22–24.

40. Daniel K. Richter, *Ordeal of the Longhouse: The Peoples of the Iroquois League in the Era of European Colonization* (Chapel Hill, 1992), 22, 47.

41. Gus Palmer Jr., *Telling Stories the Kiowa Way* (Tucson, 2003), xviii–xix; R. David Edmunds, Frederick E. Hoxie, and Neal Salisbury, *The People: A History of Native America* (Boston, 2007), 2, 12, 28.

42. "History of Events Leading to the Salt River Pima-Maricopa Indian Community (SRPMIC)" brochure, Huhugam Ki Museum, Salt River Pima-Maricopa Indian Community; Underhill, *Papago Woman*, 63, 67; George Webb, *A Pima Remembers* (Tucson, 1959), 29; Hurt, *Indian Agriculture in America*, 45; Erickson, *Sharing the Desert*, 11–12; Seymour, *Where the Earth and Sky Are Sewn Together*, 2; J. Andrew Darling and Barnaby V. Lewis, "Songscapes and Calendar Sticks," in *Hohokam Millennium*, 133–35; Juan Mateo Manje, Feb. 21, 1699, "Relación itineraria diaria que hice con los reverendos Padres Eusebio Francisco Kino y Adamo Gilg," in appendix, *Kino and Manje*, 393.

43. Underhill, *Papago Woman*, 64, 67, 68.

44. Velarde, "Descripción," 649; Erickson, *Sharing the Desert*, 12; Maurice Crandall, *These People Have Always Been a Republic: Indigenous Electorates in the U.S.-Mexico Borderlands, 1598–1912* (Chapel Hill, 2019), 6; Daniel K. Richter, "Stratification and Class in Eastern Native America," in *Class Matters: Early North America and the Atlantic World*, ed. Simon Middleton and Billy G. Smith (Philadelphia, 2008), 42; Shoemaker, *Strange Likeness*, 47; Young and Fowler, *Cahokia*, 314; Thomas E. Emerson, "Reflections from the Countryside on Cahokian Hegemony," *Midcontinental Journal of Archaeology* 27 (2002), 188; Loendorf, *Hohokam-Akimel O'odham Continuum*, 130–32; Donald M. Bahr, "O'odham Traditions About the Hohokam," in *Hohokam Millennium*, 123–29; Bahr et al., *Short, Swift Time of Gods on Earth*, 32–33; Beck, *Chiefdoms, Collapse, and Coalescence*, 140; Reff, "Sympathy for the Devil," 358.

45. Francis La Flesche, "The Osage Tribe: Rite of the Chiefs; Sayings of the Ancient Men," in *Annual Report of the Bureau of American Ethnology to the Secretary of the Smithsonian Institution* 36 (1914–1915), (Washington, D.C., 1921), 59–60, 67–68; Louis F. Burns, *Osage Indian Customs and Myths* (Fallbrook, Calif., 1984), 3–4, 29; Mathews, *The Osages*, 31–52, 103–8, 141–48; W. David Baird, *The Osage People* (Phoenix, 1972), 6; Nancy Shoemaker, *A Strange Likeness: Becoming Red and White in Eighteenth-Century North America* (New York, 2004), 47.

46. Miller, *Ogimaag*, 1–3, 65; Vernon James Knight Jr., "The Institutional Organization of Mississippian Religion," *American Antiquity* 51 (1986), 682–83; Reff, "Sympathy for the Devil," 359, 369; Clastres, *Society Against the State*, 15–16, 22, 29–32; William Bartram, *Travels Through North and South Carolina, Georgia, East & West Florida, the Cherokee Country, the Extensive Territories of the Muscogulges, or Creek Confederacy, and the Country of the Chactaws* (Philadelphia, 1791), 454–56; John Howard Payne to a relative in New York, 1835, printed in *Continental Monthly* 1 (1862), 19.

47. Loendorf, *Hohokam-Akimel O'odham Continuum*, 6, 132–33; Christopher B. Rodning, "Native American Public Architecture in the Southern Appalachians," in *Archaeological Perspectives on the Southern Appalachians: A Multiscalar Approach*, ed. Ramie A. Gougeon and Maureen S. Meyers (Knoxville, 2015), 122–24; Himdag Ki

Tohono O'odham Nation Cultural Center and Museum exhibit; Webb, *A Pima Remembers*, 43–44; *A Dictionary of Creek/Muskogee*, comps. Jack B. Martin and Margaret McKane Mauldin (Lincoln, 2000), 336; *Chickasaw: An Analytical Dictionary*, comps. Pamela Munro and Catherine Willmond (Norman, 1994), 524; *A Dictionary of the Choctaw Language*, comp. Cyrus Byington, ed. John R. Swanton and Henry S. Halbert (Washington, D.C., 1915), 586; Peter Nabokov, *A Forest of Time: American Indian Ways of History* (New York, 2002), 133–34; Joshua Piker, *Okfuskee: A Creek Town in Colonial America* (Cambridge, Mass., 2004), 1–10; Joseph M. Hall Jr., *Zamumo's Gifts: Indian-European Exchange in the Colonial Southeast* (Philadelphia, 2009), 15–16.

48. The Shawnee divisions, in varying spellings, were Chalagawtha and Thawegila (which usually provided the political leaders for the nation as a whole), Kispokothas (which provided the war chiefs), Piquas (responsible for religious ceremonies), and Maykujays (in charge of health and medicine). Robert J. Miller, "Treaties Between the Eastern Shawnee Tribe and the United States: Contracts Between Sovereign Governments," in *The Eastern Shawnee Tribe of Oklahoma: Resilience Through Adversity*, ed. Stephen Warren with the Eastern Shawnee Tribe of Oklahoma (Norman, 2017), 149; R. David Edmunds, *Tecumseh and the Quest for Indian Leadership* (Boston, 1984), 44; Bernard Mishkin, *Rank and Warfare Among the Plains Indians* (New York, 1940), 35–42, 47, 52–56.

49. Kayanesenh Paul Williams, *Kayanerenkó:wa: The Great Law of Peace* (Winnipeg, 2018), ix, xi, 1–2, 300–301; Barbara A. Mann, "The Lynx in Time: Haudenosaunee Women's Traditions and History," *American Indian Quarterly* 21 (1997), 439–40; Horatio Hale, *The Iroquois Book of Rites* (Philadelphia, 1883), 33; Doug George-Kanentiio, "Appendix: The Haudenosaunee Confederacy, 1774–1777," in *Kanatsiohareke: Traditional Mohawk Indians Return to Their Ancestral Homeland*, ed. Tom Sakokweniónkwas Porter (Greenfield Center, N.Y., 2006), 141; Porter, *And Grandma Said*, 423; Seth Newhouse (Mohawk), with assistance from Albert Cusick (Onondaga-Tuscarora), "The Dekanawida Legend," in Arthur C. Parker, *The Constitution of the Five Nations* (Albany, 1916), 42; Committee of the Chiefs, "Code of Dekanahwideh," 105, 107; Parker, *Constitution of the Five Nations*, 11; Daniel K. Richter, *Facing East from Indian Country: A Native History of Early America* (Cambridge, Mass., 2001), 145–46; Richter, "Stratification and Class in Eastern Native America," 36.

50. Shoemaker, *Strange Likeness*, 35–39.

51. Underhill, *Papago Woman*, 42, 47–54, 61, 67, 80–82; Underhill, *Social Organization*, 72–74, 78, 94; Seymour, *Where the Earth and Sky Are Sewn Together*, 240.

52. Permanent exhibit, Museum of the Cherokee Indian, Cherokee, N.C.; Mooney, "Myths of the Cherokee," 392–93.

53. Young and Fowler, *Cahokia*, 314; Emerson, "Reflections from the Countryside on Cahokian Hegemony," 188; Richter, *Before the Revolution*, 33; Wilson, "Long-Term Trends in the Making and Materialization of Social Groups at Moundville," 44, 46.

54. C. Margaret Scarry and Vincas P. Steponaitis, "Moundville as a Ceremonial Ground," in *Rethinking Moundville and Its Hinterland*, 256, 261–64; Jason Baird Jackson, "The Opposite of Powwow: Ignoring and Incorporating the Intertribal War Dance in the Oklahoma Stomp Dance Community," *Plains Anthropologist* 48 (2003), 238–39.

55. Mississippi Band of Choctaw Indians, "Nanih Waiya," www.choctaw.org/culture
/mound.html; Gideon Lincecum, "Choctaw Traditions About Their Settlement
in Mississippi and the Origin of Their Mounds," *Publications of the Mississippi
Historical Society* 8 (1904), 521–42, transcription in Vernon James Knight Jr., "Symbolism of Mississippian Mounds," in *Powhatan's Mantle: Indians in the Colonial
Southeast,* ed. Peter H. Wood, Gregory A. Waselkov, and M. Thomas Hatley, rev.
ed. (Lincoln, 2006), 288–89; H. S. Halbert, "Nanih Waiya, The Sacred Mound of
the Choctaws," *Publications of the Mississippi Historical Society* 2 (1899), 223–34;
Snyder, "Once and Future Moundbuilders," 108, 110–13; Jay Miller, *Ancestral
Mounds: Vitality and Volatility of Native America* (Lincoln, 2015), 9, 81–88; Scott
Mckie, "Tribe to Purchase Land Adjacent to Nikwasi Mound," *Cherokee One
Feather,* Aug. 3, 2017, https://theonefeather.com/2017/08/tribe-to-purchase-land
-adjacent-to-nikwasi-mound/; Conley, *The Cherokee,* 20; Robert J. Conley, *The Way
of the Priests* (Norman, 1992); Alfred Berryhill, foreword to Miller, *Ancestral
Mounds,* ix; John Howard Payne to a relative in New York, 1835, printed in *Continental Monthly* 1 (1862), 19–29; Albert S. Gatschet, *A Migration Legend of the Creek
Indians* (Philadelphia, 1884), 176–80; Snyder, "Once and Future Moundbuilders,"
97–99, 105, 112; John R. Swanton, "The Green Corn Dance," *Chronicles of Oklahoma*
10 (1932), 170–95; Frank T. Schnell, Vernon J. Knight Jr., and Gail S. Schnell, *Ce-
mochechobee: Archaeology of a Mississippian Ceremonial Center on the Chattahoochee
River* (Gainesville, 1981), 144–45; Knight, "Institutional Organization," 683; Vernon James Knight Jr., "Symbolism of Mississippian Mounds," in *Powhatan's Mantle: Indians in the Colonial Southeast,* ed. Peter H. Wood, Gregory A. Waselkov, and
M. Thomas Hatley, rev. ed. (Lincoln, 2006), 425–26; Kassabaum, *History of Platform Mound Ceremonialism,* 178–81; Jackson, "Opposite of Powwow," 242; Hall,
Zamumo's Gifts, 15. English explorers saw seven hundred people from several
towns gather in Weapemeoc, on the Albemarle Sound, for their 1585 Green Corn
Ceremony. Ralph Lane to Francis Walsingham, Sept. 8, 1585, in *The Roanoke Voyages, 1584–1590: Documents to Illustrate the English Voyages to North America Under
the Patent Granted to Walter Raleigh in 1584,* ed. David Beers Quinn (London,
1955), 1:213.

56. Steponaitis and Scarry, "New Directions in Moundville Research," 15–16; George
E. Lankford, "The Great Serpent in Eastern North America" and "The 'Path of
Souls': Some Death Imagery in the Southeastern Ceremonial Complex," in *An-
cient Objects and Sacred Realms: Interpretations of Mississippian Iconography,* ed.
F. Kent Reilly and James F. Garber (Austin, Tex., 2007), 107–35, 174–212; Erin E.
Phillips, "The Distribution of Hemphill-Style Artifacts at Moundville," in *Re-
thinking Moundville and Its Hinterland,* 100–106; Knight and Steponaitis, "A New
History of Moundville," 19–20; Vincas P. Steponaitis and Vernon J. Knight, Jr.,
"Moundville Art in Historical and Social Context," in *Hero, Hawk, and Open
Hand: American Indian Art of the Ancient Midwest and South,* ed Richard F.
Townsend and Robert V. Sharp (Chicago and New Haven, 2004), 166–81.

57. Richter, *Facing East,* 14, 84; James Axtell, *The Invasion Within: The Contest of Cultures in Colonial North America* (New York, 1985), 285; Gregory Evans Dowd, *A
Spirited Resistance: The North American Indian Struggle for Unity, 1745–1815* (Baltimore, 1992), 18; Anton Treuer, *Everything You Wanted to Know About Indians but
Were Afraid to Ask* (St. Paul, Minn., 2012), 52–53.

58. Williams, "Vacant Quarter," 170–80; Kathleen DuVal, *The Native Ground: Indians
and Colonists in the Heart of the Continent* (Philadelphia, 2006), 20, 29–31; Chris-

tina Snyder, *Slavery in Indian Country: The Changing Face of Captivity in Early America* (Cambridge, Mass., 2010), 1–2, 24–25, 116–17.

59. Knight, "Institutional Organization," 682; Hall, *Zamumo's Gifts*, 25; Patricia Galloway, "'The Chief Who Is Your Father': Choctaw and French Views of the Diplomatic Relation," in *Powhatan's Mantle*, 348.

60. Vernon James Knight Jr., "The Formation of the Creeks," in *The Forgotten Centuries: Indians and Europeans in the American South, 1521–1704*, ed. Charles Hudson and Carmen Chaves Tesser (Athens, Ga., 1994), 374, 385–86; Patricia Galloway, "Confederacy as a Solution to Chiefdom Dissolution: Historical Evidence in the Choctaw Case," in *Forgotten Centuries*, 393, 395, 399, 407–8; Galloway, *Choctaw Genesis*, 2, 140, 142; Williams, *Linking Arms Together*, 33.

61. Wayne E. Lee, *The Cutting-Off Way: Indigenous Warfare in Eastern North America, 1500–1800* (Chapel Hill, 2023); Wayne E. Lee, *Barbarians and Brothers: Anglo-American Warfare, 1500–1865* (New York, 2011), 134–35; Wayne E. Lee, "The Military Revolution of Native North America: Firearms, Forts, and Polities," in *Empires and Indigenes: Intercultural Alliance, Imperial Expansion, and Warfare in the Early Modern World*, ed. Wayne E. Lee (New York, 2011), 49–55; Daniel K. Richter, "War and Culture: The Iroquois Experience," *William and Mary Quarterly* 40 (1983), 535–36; Samuel de Champlain, *Des Sauvages, ou, Voyage de Samuel Champlain, de Brouage, fait en la France nouvelle, l'an 1603* (Paris, 1603), 5–5v; Louis Armand de Lom d'Arce, baron de Lahontan, *Nouveaux voyages de Mr. le baron de Lahontan dans l'Amérique Septentrionale* (The Hague, 1703), 2:176.

62. Hall, *Zamumo's Gifts*, 13, 20–25, 32; Williams, *Linking Arms Together*, 70–73; Shoemaker, *Strange Likeness*, 117–19; John P. Bowes, *Exiles and Pioneers: Eastern Indians in the Trans-Mississippi West* (New York, 2007), 125–26.

63. Williams, *Linking Arms Together*, 34–36, 38; Bernard L. Fontana, *Of Earth and Little Rain: The Papago Indians* (Flagstaff, 1981), 101, 107; Griffith, *Beliefs and Holy Places*, 78–79; Donald J. Blakeslee, "The Origin and Spread of the Calumet Ceremony," *American Antiquity* 46 (1981), 759–68; Ian W. Brown, "The Calumet Ceremony in the Southeast as Observed Archaeologically," *Powhatan's Mantle: Indians in the Colonial Southeast*, ed. Gregory A. Waselkov, Peter H. Wood, and M. Thomas Hatley, rev. ed. (Lincoln, 2006), 371–420; Tracy Neal Leavelle, *The Catholic Calumet: Colonial Conversions in French and Indian North America* (Philadelphia, 2011).

64. *Algonquian* refers to a large linguistic and cultural group stretching from today's eastern Canada to the Carolinas, which included many separate polities. Newhouse, "Dekanawida Legend," 20; George R. Hamell, "Wampum: Light, White and Bright Things Are Good to Think," in *"One Man's Trash Is Another Man's Treasure": The Metamorphosis of the European Utensil in the New World* (Rotterdam and Williamsburg, 1996), 41–45; Richter, *Facing East*, 137.

65. Ryan DeCaire, Thanksgiving Address and Condolence Ceremony, Native American and Indigenous Studies Association, June 17, 2021; Mary Druke Becker, "Linking Arms: The Structure of Iroquois Intertribal Diplomacy," in *Beyond the Covenant Chain: The Iroquois and Their Neighbors in Indian North America, 1600–1800*, ed. Daniel K. Richter and James H. Merrell (1987; University Park, Pa., 2003), 36–38. For published recent examples, see Clayton Logan (Seneca), "The Thanksgiving Address" and Chief Jake Swamp (Mohawk), "The Edge of the Woods," given in 1994 and transcribed in *Treaty of Canandaigua*, 7–14.

66. David R. Abbott, Cory Dale Breternitz, and Christine K. Robinson, "Challenging Conventional Conceptions," in *Centuries of Decline*, 4.

67. A. F. Bandelier to the president of the Archaeological Institute of America, "Reports by A. F. Bandelier on his Investigations in New Mexico During the Years 1883–84," appendix, Archaeological Institute of America Annual Report (Boston, 1884), 85–86.

68. Martínez, "Whither the Huhugam?," 190; Loendorf, *Hohokam-Akimel O'odham Continuum*, 118, 135; Bahr, et al., *Short, Swift Time of Gods on Earth*, 1–2; Rice, *Sending the Spirits Home*, 10.

69. Richter, *Before the Revolution*, 55–57; Miller, *Ogimaag*, 2–4; R. R. Palmer, Joel Colton, and Lloyd Kramer, *A History of Europe in the Modern World*, 11th ed. (New York, 2014), 36; Thomas N. Bisson, *The Crisis of the Twelfth Century: Power, Lordship, and the Origins of European Government* (Princeton, 2015), 3, 6; Benjamin C. Waterhouse, *The Land of Enterprise: A Business History of the United States* (New York, 2017), 12.

70. J. R. McNeill, *The Webs of Humankind: A World History* (New York, 2021), 545–74; Palmer, Colton, and Kramer, *History of Europe in the Modern World*, 51.

71. David Graeber and David Wengrow, *The Dawn of Everything: A New History of Humanity* (New York, 2021), 31–67.

72. Galloway, *Choctaw Genesis*, 131, 143; Schoeninger and Schurr, "Human Subsistence at Moundville," 131; White, *Cold Welcome*, 26; Paul W. Mapp, *The Elusive West and the Contest for Empire, 1713–1763* (Chapel Hill, 2011), 71–98; Kelton, *Cherokee Medicine*, 22–24, 27–30, 39, 48; Paul Kelton, *Epidemics and Enslavement: Biological Catastrophe in the Native Southeast, 1492–1715* (Lincoln, 2007); Williams, "Vacant Quarter," 170–80; Richter, "Stratification and Class in Eastern Native America," 43; Beck, *Chiefdoms, Collapse, and Coalescence*, 93, 124, 134–36.

CHAPTER 3: OSSOMOCOMUCK AND ROANOKE ISLAND

1. Arthur Barlowe, "Discourse of the First Voyage," in *The Roanoke Voyages, 1584–1590: Documents to Illustrate the English Voyages to North America Under the Patent Granted to Walter Raleigh in 1584*, ed. David Beers Quinn (London, 1955), 1:98. Most of the Roanoke documents are available online at https://docsouth.unc.edu /nc/. I have standardized the spellings in quotations from sixteenth-century English accounts. Throughout this chapter, I owe a debt to Quinn's editorial work and historical notes in *Roanoke Voyages* and the tremendous scholarship of Karen Ordahl Kupperman, *Roanoke: The Abandoned Colony*, 2nd ed. (Lanham, Md., 2007), and Michael Leroy Oberg, *The Head in Edward Nugent's Hand: Roanoke's Forgotten Indians* (Philadelphia, 2008).

2. Barlowe, "Discourse of the First Voyage," 1:100–101.

3. Karen Ordahl Kupperman, *Indians and English: Facing Off in Early America* (Ithaca, 2000), 12.

4. Charles Hudson, *The Juan Pardo Expeditions: Explorations of the Carolinas and Tennessee, 1566–1568*, rev. ed. (Tuscaloosa, 2005); Michael Leroy Oberg and David Moore, "Voyages to Carolina: Europeans in the Indians' Old World," *New Voyages to Carolina: Reinterpreting North Carolina History*, ed. Larry E. Tise and Jeffrey J. Crow (Chapel Hill, 2017), 42–48.

5. Barlowe, "Discourse of the First Voyage," 1:94.

6. People referred to themselves mostly by town, even if they were confederated with other towns, and it's not clear what, if any, collective names they had, so I refer to the polity that included Roanoke as Wingina's people and to the inhabitants of the broader region as the people of Ossomocomuck. Oberg, *Head in Edward Nugent's Hand*, 3.

7. The stretch of sound between Roanoke and the mainland was shallower and narrower than it is today. One colonist said it was possible to wade across. Pedro Diaz, "The Relation of Pedro Diaz," in *Roanoke Voyages*, 2:789; Michael P. O'Connor, Stanley R. Riggs, and Don Winston, "Recent Estuarine Sediment History of the Roanoke Island Area, North Carolina," *Geological Society of America Memoir* 133 (1972), 453–63; Kupperman, *Roanoke*, 19, 31; Coll Thrush, *Indigenous London: Native Travelers at the Heart of Empire* (New Haven, 2016), 35; Malinda Maynor Lowery, *The Lumbee Indians: An American Struggle* (Chapel Hill, 2018), 22; Edward Clay Swindell, "Archaeology of the North Carolina Algonkians: Colington Phase Summary and Research Framework," in *Deciphering the Roanoke Mystery: Archaeology and Document Research and On-Stage in Paul Green's the Lost Colony*, ed. Lebam Houston and Douglas Stover (Manteo, N.C., 2015), 173, 180; David Sutton Phillips, *Archaeology of the Tillett Site: The First Fishing Community at Wanchese, Roanoke Island* (Greenville, N.C., 1984), 2–8, 23–30.

8. James Horn, *A Kingdom Strange: The Brief and Tragic History of the Lost Colony of Roanoke* (New York, 2010), 47; Peter H. Wood, "The Changing Population of the Colonial South: An Overview by Race and Region, 1685–1790," in *Powhatan's Mantle: Indians in the Colonial Southeast*, ed. Gregory A. Waselkov, Peter H. Wood, and Tom Hatley, rev. ed. (Lincoln, 2006), 60; Patrick H. Garrow, *The Mattamuskeet Documents: A Study in Social History* (Raleigh, 1975), 4–5. For more on the environmental history of Ossomocomuck and the Roanoke colony, see Elina Carpen, "Nature's Lost Colony: Peace and Power in Roanoke, 1585–1590" (honors thesis, University of North Carolina, Chapel Hill, 2022).

9. Barlowe, "Discourse of the First Voyage," 1:98–99. For the probable archaeological site of this town, see David S. Phelps, "Archaeology of the Native Americans: The Carolina Algonkians," in *Deciphering the Roanoke Mystery*, 201.

10. Barlowe, "Discourse of the First Voyage," 1:107–9; Thrush, *Indigenous London*, 35.

11. Kupperman, *Indians and English*; Peter C. Mancall, *Nature and Culture in the Early Modern Atlantic* (Philadelphia, 2018), xi, 40–41; Brian Fagan, *The Little Ice Age: How Climate Made History, 1300–1850* (New York, 2000), 34; Merry E. Wiesner-Hanks, *A Concise History of the World* (Cambridge, 2015), 85; Helen Rountree, *Manteo's World: Native American Life in Carolina's Sound Country Before and After the Lost Colony* (Chapel Hill, 2021), 106–7; Jacob F. Lee, *Masters of the Middle Waters: Indian Nations and Colonial Ambitions Along the Mississippi* (Cambridge, Mass., 2019), 4, 7; Karen Ordahl Kupperman, *Pocahontas and the English Boys: Caught Between Cultures in Early Virginia* (New York, 2019), 30–31.

12. Thomas Harriot, "A Brief and True Report," in *Roanoke Voyages*, 1:372–75; Daniel K. Richter, *Facing East from Indian Country: A Native History of Early America* (Cambridge, Mass., 2001), 39; Oberg, *Head in Edward Nugent's Hand*, 71–75.

13. Christopher Columbus, *Book of Prophecies*, in *The Libro de las profecías of Christopher Columbus: An en face edition*, trans. and ed. Delno C. West and August Kling

(Gainesville, 1991), 105, 110–11, 233, 255; Karen Ordahl Kupperman, "Roanoke's Achievement," *European Visions: American Voices* (London, 2009), 9.

14. Kupperman, *Indians and English*, 51; Mancall, *Nature and Culture in the Early Modern Atlantic*, 90; Peter C. Mancall, *Hakluyt's Promise: An Elizabethan's Obsession for an English America* (New Haven, 2007), 160; Carpen, "Nature's Lost Colony," chap. 3; Richter, *Facing East*, 14, 84; James Axtell, *The Invasion Within: The Contest of Cultures in Colonial North America* (New York, 1985), 285.

15. Barlowe, "Discourse of the First Voyage," 1:100–101; Mary W. Helms, *Ulysses' Sail: An Ethnographic Odyssey of Power, Knowledge, and Geographical Distance* (Princeton, 1988); Cary Miller, *Ogimaag: Anishinaabeg Leadership, 1760–1845* (Lincoln, 2010), 2.

16. *The Song of Roland,* trans. John DuVal (Indianapolis, 2012), laisses 3, 7; Daniel K. Richter, *Before the Revolution: America's Ancient Pasts* (Cambridge, Mass., 2011), 26.

17. *Beowulf: An Illustrated Edition,* trans. Seamus Heaney (New York, 2008), 3–5; Wiesner-Hanks, *Concise History of the World*, 152.

18. Joaneath Spicer, "The Renaissance Elbow," in *A Cultural History of Gesture*, ed. Jan Bremmer and Herman Roodenburg (Ithaca, 1991), 93–100. Thanks to Karen Kupperman for this insightful comparison.

19. Kupperman, *Roanoke*, 50; Pauline Turner Strong, *Captive Selves, Captivating Others: The Politics and Poetics of Colonial American Captivity* (Boulder, 1999), 47, 72.

20. Pierre Clastres, *Society Against the State: Essays in Political Anthropology* (New York, 1987), 15–16, 22, 29–32.

21. Richter, *Before the Revolution*, 46–47; Susan M. Hill, *The Clay We Are Made Of: Haudenosaunee Land Tenure on the Grand River* (Winnipeg, 2017), 2. Female werowances show up in Croatoan, in Powhatan's Tsenacomoco, and presumably at a Weapemeoc town that English maps labeled "the woman's town."

22. Kathleen M. Brown, *Good Wives, Nasty Wenches, and Anxious Patriarchs: Gender, Race, and Power in Colonial Virginia* (Chapel Hill, 1996); Nancy Shoemaker, "An Alliance Between Men: Gender Metaphors in Eighteenth-Century American Indian Diplomacy East of the Mississippi," *Ethnohistory* (1999), 239–63.

23. Louis Armand de Lom d'Arce, baron de Lahontan, *Nouveaux voyages de Mr. le baron de Lahontan dans l'Amérique Septentrionale* (The Hague, 1703), 2:175 (the second volume of *Nouveaux voyages* is also known by a separate title, *Memoires de l'Amerique Septentrionale*); Allan Greer, *Property and Dispossession: Natives, Empires and Land in Early Modern North America* (New York, 2018), 12–18 ("les limites sont réglées. Chaque Nation connoit les bornes de son Païs").

24. Oberg, *Head in Edward Nugent's Hand*, 18; Swindell, "Archaeology of the North Carolina Algonkians," 176–78.

25. Thomas N. Bisson, *The Crisis of the Twelfth Century: Power, Lordship, and the Origins of European Government* (Princeton, 2015), 8.

26. Bill to Confirm Raleigh's Patent, December 1584, in *Roanoke Voyages*, 1:127.

27. Barlowe, "Discourse of the First Voyage," 94, 98–99.

28. Keith Richotte Jr., *Federal Indian Law and Policy: An Introduction* (St. Paul, Minn., 2020), 51.

29. Philip Deloria, "The Invention of Thanksgiving: Massacres, Myths, and the Making of the Great November Holiday," *New Yorker*, Nov. 25, 2019, 74; Wayne E. Lee,

Empires and Indigenes: Intercultural Alliance, Imperial Expansion, and Warfare in the Early Modern World (New York, 2011), 50–51; Alan Gallay, *Walter Ralegh: Architect of Empire* (New York, 2019), 18–19; Francis Jennings, *The Invasion of America: Indians, Colonialism, and the Cant of Conquest* (Chapel Hill, 1975), 3–5; Wayne E. Lee, *Barbarians and Brothers: Anglo-American Warfare, 1500–1865* (New York, 2011), 17–25, 35–38, 59–60, 123; Kupperman, *Roanoke*, 63, 66–67.

30. John White, "John White's Narrative of his Voyage" (1587), in *Roanoke Voyages*, 2:526; John White, "John White's Narrative of the 1590 Voyage," in *Roanoke Voyages*, 2:616; Quinn, *Roanoke Voyages*, 2:616n2; Charles R. Ewen and Erik Farrell, "'All That Glitters': A Reassessment of a 'Lost Colony' Artifact," *North Carolina Historical Review* 96 (2019), 409; Rountree, *Manteo's World*, 22–25.

31. David B. Quinn, "Thomas Harriot and the Problem of America," in *Thomas Harriot: An Elizabethan Man of Science*, ed. Robert Fox (New York, 2017), 14–15; Kupperman, *Roanoke*, 108; Richard Butler, deposition, n.d. (c. 1594), *New American World: A Documentary History of North America to 1612*, ed. David B. Quinn, Alison M. Quinn, and Susan Hillier (New York, 1979), 3:330.

32. *The Journal of the Earl of Egmont: Abstract of the Trustees Proceedings for Establishing the Colony of Georgia, 1732–1738*, ed. Robert G. McPherson (Athens, Ga., 1962), 60–61; Nancy Shoemaker, *A Strange Likeness: Becoming Red and White in Eighteenth-Century North America* (New York, 2004), 35–39; Horn, *Kingdom Strange*, 24–25, 121–23, 129; Kupperman, *Roanoke*, 37; Liza Picard, *Elizabeth's London: Everyday Life in Elizabethan London* (New York, 2003), xxii, xxiv, 9, 33–34; Oberg, *Head in Edward Nugent's Hand*, 51–55; Jace Weaver, *The Red Atlantic: American Indigenes and the Making of the Modern World, 1000–1927* (Chapel Hill, 2014), 140; Giles Milton, *Big Chief Elizabeth: The Adventures and Fate of the First Colonists in America* (New York, 2000), 62–64; John W. Shirley, *Thomas Harriot: A Biography* (Oxford, 1983), 81–82; Brian Fagan, *The Great Warming: Climate Change and the Rise and Fall of Civilizations* (New York, 2008), 33, 36–37. See also Garrett Wright, "'To the Other Side of the Sun': Indigenous Diplomacy and Power in the Midcontinent," *Kansas History: A Journal of the Central Plains* 41 (2018), 197–209.

33. Thrush, *Indigenous London*, 34–36; Lowery, *The Lumbee Indians*, 23.

34. Diego Hernández de Quiñones to King Philip II, June 22, 1585, in *Roanoke Voyages*, 2:735; "The Relation of Hernando de Altamirano," June 1585, in *Roanoke Voyages*, 2:741; Kupperman, *Roanoke*, 18, 24.

35. Journal of the *Tiger*, June 26–Aug. 25, 1585, in *Roanoke Voyages*, 1:178–79; Kupperman, *Roanoke*, 16.

36. Butler, deposition, n.d. (c. 1594), 3:330.

37. Harriot, "Brief and True Report," 1:417; Peter Stallybrass, "*Admiranda narratio*: A European Best Seller," in Thomas Harriot, *A Briefe and True Report of the New Found Land of Virginia* (Charlottesville, 2007), 9–30; Kupperman, *Roanoke*, 39; Kupperman, *Indians and English*, 41–45; Mancall, *Nature and Culture in the Early Modern Atlantic*, 92–107.

38. Harriot, "Brief and True Report," 1:421–22.

39. Shirley, *Thomas Harriot*, 119; Kupperman, *Roanoke*, 17, 20–22.

40. Kupperman, *Roanoke*, 63, 66–67; Lee, *Barbarians and Brothers*, 125, 128.

41. Alfred W. Crosby, "Virgin Soil Epidemics as a Factor in the Aboriginal Depopu-

lation in America," *William and Mary Quarterly* 33 (1976), 290; Paul Kelton, "Avoiding the Smallpox Spirits: Colonial Epidemics and Southeastern Indian Survival," *Ethnohistory* 51 (2004) 45–71; Harriot, "Brief and True Report," 1:378; Quinn, *Roanoke Voyages,* 1:381n1.

42. R. R. Palmer, Joel Colton, and Lloyd Kramer, *A History of Europe in the Modern World,* 11th ed. (New York, 2014), 50; Fagan, *Great Warming,* 42–44, 82–83, 129–31; Fagan, *Little Ice Age,* 82–83, 129–31; Sam White, *A Cold Welcome: The Little Ice Age and Europe's Encounter with North America* (Cambridge, Mass., 2017), 22–23, 28–33, 73–76; Daniel K. Richter, *Before the Revolution: America's Ancient Pasts* (Cambridge, Mass., 2011), 51–52; J. R. McNeill, *The Webs of Humankind: A World History* (New York, 2021), 674.

43. Paul Kelton, *Cherokee Medicine, Colonial Germs: An Indigenous Nation's Fight Against Smallpox, 1518–1824* (Norman, 2015), 62, 88–91, 95–96.

44. Harriot, "Brief and True Report," 1:377–79.

45. Harriot, "Brief and True Report," 1:377.

46. Harriot, "Brief and True Report," 1:379–81.

47. Harriot, "Brief and True Report," 1:381; Butler, deposition, n.d. (c. 1594), 3:330.

48. Ralph Lane's account covers the period from August 1585 through June 1586, and Thomas Harriot's report summarizes these events as well. Ralph Lane, "Discourse on the First Colony," in *Roanoke Voyages,* 1:255–94; Harriot, "Brief and True Report," 1:372–81, Quinn, *Roanoke Voyages,* 1:246–48.

49. Paul Green, *The Lost Colony: A Symphonic Drama of American History* (Chapel Hill, 2001), act 1, scene 5 (this UNC Press edition reprints the original script).

50. This kind of placing youths within another culture to understand it and interpret it was very common. Kupperman, *Pocahontas and the English Boys.* Muskogean peoples in the Southeast developed a diplomat called a fanemingo ("squirrel king"), whose job was to speak for the allies. Thomas Nairne, *Nairne's Muskhogean Journals: The 1708 Expedition to the Mississippi River* (Jackson, Miss., 1988), 40–41; Nancy Shoemaker, *A Strange Likeness: Becoming Red and White in Eighteenth-Century North America* (New York, 2004), 40.

51. Lane to Richard Hakluyt the Elder and Master H. of the Middle Temple, Sept. 3, 1585, in *Roanoke Voyages,* 1:207–8; Lane to Walsingham, Sept. 8, 1585, in *Roanoke Voyages,* 1:213; Butler, deposition, n.d. (c. 1594), 3:330; Quinn, *Roanoke Voyages,* 1:244–45.

52. Swindell, "Archaeology of the North Carolina Algonkians," 172–73. Chowan is also referred to as Chowanoac.

53. Lane, "Discourse on the First Colony," 1:259.

54. Kupperman, *Roanoke,* 14; Frederic W. Gleach, *Powhatan's World and Colonial Virginia: A Conflict of Cultures* (Lincoln, 1997), 22–26; James Horn, *1619: Jamestown and the Forging of American Democracy* (New York, 2018), 31–33.

55. Lane, "Discourse on the First Colony," 1:259–61.

56. Lee, *Barbarians and Brothers,* 126–27.

57. Archaeologists have found Ganz's lab on Roanoke Island. Quinn, *Roanoke Voyages,* 1:196n1; Shirley, *Thomas Harriot,* 121–22; Kupperman, *Roanoke,* 172.

58. Lane, "Discourse on the First Colony," 1:268–70; Paul W. Mapp, *The Elusive West and the Contest for Empire, 1713–1763* (Chapel Hill, 2011), 101.

59. Lane, "Discourse on the First Colony," 1:270.

60. Thrush, *Indigenous London*, 35. Europeans believed sassafras might be able to cure syphilis.

61. Lane claims that all of his men survived, although a Spanish man who was with the colony testified that four of them were killed in a skirmish on the mainland. Diaz, "Relation," 2:789–90.

62. Lane, "Discourse on the First Colony," 1:278.

63. Harriot, "Brief and True Report," 1:377.

64. Some scholars have suggested that Ossomocomuck was running out of corn because of drought, which can be observed in tree rings, but the heaviest years of drought didn't start until 1587, and Roanoke had never been a site for much farming because its soil was so inferior to inland fields.

65. Lee, *Barbarians and Brothers*, 128–29.

66. Lane, "Discourse on the First Colony," 1:283, 288–89; Francis Drake, "Sir Francis Drake's Expedition: His Visit to Florida and Virginia," in *Roanoke Voyages*, 1:300–301; Kupperman, *Roanoke*, 89; Dennis B. Blanton, "If It's Not One Thing It's Another: The Added Challenges of Weather and Climate for the Roanoke Colony," in *Searching for the Roanoke Colonies*, 173–74.

67. Latin version of Drake's account, in Quinn, *Roanoke Voyages*, 1:300, 131n11.

68. Drake, "Sir Francis Drake's Expedition," 1:301–2; Richard Hakluyt, "Principall Navigations" (1589), in *Roanoke Voyages*, 1:477; Quinn, *Roanoke Voyages*, 253–55.

69. Quinn, *Roanoke Voyages*, 2:790n5; Hakluyt, "Principall Navigations," 1:477–80; Diaz, "Relation," 2:790–91.

70. White, "Narrative" (1587), 2:528–29.

71. Kupperman, *Roanoke*, 91.

72. White, "Narrative" (1587), 2:524.

73. White, "Narrative" (1587), 2:522–23.

74. White, "Narrative" (1587), 2:523; Kupperman, *Roanoke*, 107.

75. White, "Narrative" (1587), 2:525.

76. Shirley, *Thomas Harriot*, 119; Kupperman, *Roanoke*, 82.

77. White, "Narrative" (1587), 2:526–29.

78. White, "Narrative" (1587), 2:529–31.

79. White, "Narrative" (1587), 2:531.

80. Kupperman, *Roanoke*, 131–32.

81. Blanton, "If It's Not One Thing It's Another," 169–73; Fagan, *Little Ice Age*, 96.

82. White, "John White's Narrative of the 1590 Voyage," 2:608–18; Quinn, *Roanoke Voyages*, 2:594; Kupperman, *Roanoke*, 128–29. Rumors at Jamestown two decades later suggesting that they went to the lower Chowan River between Chowan and Moratuc gained some support when investigations of Raleigh's copy of White's map recently revealed a drawing of a fort. That was not what they wrote on the

sign, however, so I suspect it was just a marking of what Lane thought would be a good site for a fort. Janet Ambers, Joanna Russell, David Saunders, and Kim Sloan, "Hidden History? Examination of Two Patches on John White's Map of 'Virginia,'" *The British Museum Technical Research Bulletin* 6 (2012), 47–54; Kupperman, *Roanoke*, 133–34.

83. Early in the eighteenth century, Native people living on Hatteras Island told Europeans that they had white ancestors, although it's hard to tell whether these Indians were descendants of the Croatoans or had moved there more recently. John Lawson, *A New Voyage to Carolina; Containing the Exact Description and Natural History of That Country* (London, 1709), 62; Kupperman, *Roanoke*, 91, 173; Gary S. Dunbar, "The Hatteras Indians of North Carolina," *Ethnohistory* (1960), 410–18; Kupperman, *Pocahontas and the English Boys*, 10; Rountree, *Manteo's World*, 102, 108. In June or July 1588, a Spanish expedition apparently discovered evidence of the Roanoke settlement, including wells made out of barrels and "other debris indicating that a considerable number of people had been here." The Spaniards apparently were out of eyesight of the main Roanoke settlement, so the European colonists may have still been there. Luis Jerónimo de Oré, "Relation of the Martyrs of Florida," in *Roanoke Voyages*, 2:810–13; Joseph Hall, "Glimpses of Roanoke, Visions of New Mexico, and Dreams of Empire in the Mixed-Up Memories of Gerónimo de la Cruz," *William and Mary Quarterly* 72 (2015), 321–50. For more on various theories of what happened to the Roanoke colonists, informed by Native American history, see Oberg, *Head in Edward Nugent's Hand*, chap. 6; Hiroyuki Tsukada, "Powhatan and the Fate of the Lost Colonists of Roanoke: Decoding William Strachey's Imaginary Geography," *North Carolina Historical Review* 98 (2021), 42–64.

84. Katrina M. Phillips, *Staging Indigeneity: Salvage Tourism and the Performance of Native American History* (Chapel Hill, 2021), 15–19, 21. I use the most familiar spelling of Raleigh, which was used among many other spellings by Sir Walter and his contemporaries. H. G. Jones, "Sir Walter's Surname," in *Raleigh and Quinn: The Explorer and His Boswell*, ed. H. G. Jones (Chapel Hill, 1987), 269–70.

85. Green, *Lost Colony*, act 1, scene 5.

86. *Strike at the Wind!*, performed at the Lumbee Tribe Cultural Center, Maxton, N.C., July 13, 2019; Lowery, *The Lumbee Indians*, 41, 75–88, 200–201, 237–39; James Bass, "Play Part of UNCP Effort to Preserve History," *The Robesonian*, May 24, 2017.

87. Advertisement for *Strike at the Wind!*, 2017, https://www.youtube.com/watch?v=qeXioKv6FS4.

88. Willie French Lowery, interviewed by Michael C. Taylor, "Hello, America: The Life and Work of Willie French Lowery," *Southern Cultures* 16 (2010), 96–100.

89. Jeff Whiting, Sam Davis, and Nicholas Mahon, "History and Highballs: The Lost Colony," North Carolina Museum of History, https://www.ncmuseumofhistory.org/history-and-highballs/lost-colony; Tomeka Sinclair, "Eight Members of the Lumbee Tribe Make History by Being Part of 'The Lost Colony' Cast," *The Robesonian*, June 4, 2021; Fred Wasser, "Chapel Hill Playwright Paul Green's Drama Has a Long, Complicated History. Now It's Time for a New Act," *Indy Week*, May 26, 2021; Heidi L. Nees, "'Indian' Summers: Querying Representations of Native American Cultures in Outdoor Historical Drama" (Ph.D. diss., Bowling Green State University, 2012), 75–78; Cherokee Historical Association, "Unto These

Hills," https://www.cherokeehistorical.org/unto-these-hills/; Phillips, *Staging Indigeneity*, 76–132.

90. Kupperman, *Indians and English*, 13–14; Kathleen Donegan, *Seasons of Misery: Catastrophe and Colonial Settlement in Early America* (Philadelphia, 2014), 68.

91. Peter C. Mancall, "The Age of Failure," *Early American Literature* 56 (2021), 23–73.

92. Harriot, "Brief and True Report," 1:378; Kelton, *Cherokee Medicine*, 10, 27–30; Ewen and Farrell, "All That Glitters," 412; Rountree, *Manteo's World*, 118–20. The Muscogee town of Coosa, e.g., renamed itself after it was flooded. Joseph M. Hall Jr., *Zamumo's Gifts: Indian-European Exchange in the Colonial Southeast* (Philadelphia, 2009), 39; Robert A. Williams Jr., *Linking Arms Together: American Indian Treaty Visions of Law and Peace, 1600–1800* (New York, 1997), 24.

CHAPTER 4: MOHAWK PEACE AND WAR

1. Onondaga Nation, "Hiawatha Belt," *Onondaga Nation People of the Hills*, https://www.onondaganation.org/culture/wampum/hiawatha-belt/; Darren Bonaparte, *Creation and Confederation: The Living History of the Iroquois* (Mohawk Territory of Akwesasne, 2006), 116–20; Seth Newhouse (Mohawk), with assistance from Albert Cusick (Onondaga-Tuscarora), "The Dekanawida Legend," in *The Constitution of the Five Nations*, ed. Arthur C. Parker (Albany, 1916), 46–47; David Cusick, *David Cusick's Sketches of Ancient History of the Six Nations* (Lockport, N.Y., 1848), 23; *Kaianerekowa Hotinonsionne / The Great Law of Peace of the Longhouse People*, trans. *Akwesasne Notes*, with assistance of Ray Tehanetorens Fadden (Akwesasne, 1970; repr. Berkeley, 1999), 29, 31; Susan M. Hill, *The Clay We Are Made Of: Haudenosaunee Land Tenure on the Grand River* (Winnipeg, 2017), 33.

2. George R. Hamell, "Wampum: Light, White and Bright Things Are Good to Think," in *"One Man's Trash Is Another Man's Treasure": The Metamorphosis of the European Utensil in the New World* (Rotterdam and Williamsburg, 1996), 41–45; Jaap Jacobs, "Beavers for Drink, Land for Arms: Some Aspects of the Dutch-Indian Trade in New Netherland," in *One Man's Trash*, 107; Daniel K. Richter, *Facing East from Indian Country: A Native History of Early America* (Cambridge, Mass., 2001), 137; Susanah Shaw Romney, *New Netherland Connections: Intimate Networks and Atlantic Ties in Seventeenth-Century America* (Chapel Hill, 2014), 141–42; Lisa Brooks, *The Common Pot: The Recovery of Native Space in the Northeast* (Minneapolis, 2008), 54–57; Robert A. Williams, *Linking Arms Together: American Indian Treaty Visions of Law and Peace, 1600–1800* (New York, 1997), 51, 62; Daniel K. Richter, *The Ordeal of the Longhouse: The Peoples of the Iroquois League in the Era of European Colonization* (Chapel Hill, 1992), 47; Jenny Hale Pulsipher, "Gaining the Diplomatic Edge: Kinship, Trade, Ritual, and Religion in Amerindian Alliances in Early North America," in *Empires and Indigenes: Intercultural Alliance, Imperial Expansion, and Warfare in the Early Modern World*, ed. Wayne E. Lee (New York, 2011), 22–24.

3. Peter Francis Jr., "The Beads That Did *Not* Buy Manhattan Island," in *One Man's Trash*, 55; Neal Salisbury, "Toward the Covenant Chain: Iroquois and Southern New England Algonquians, 1637–1684," in *Beyond the Covenant Chain: The Iroquois and Their Neighbors in Indian North America, 1600–1800*, ed. Daniel K. Richter and James H. Merrell (1987; University Park, Pa., 2003), 61–62, 65–66; Richter, *Ordeal of the Longhouse*, 85; Jacobs, "Beavers for Drink," 107; Andrew Lipman, *The Saltwater Frontier: Indians and the Contest for the American Coast* (New Haven, 2015), 110;

Peter C. Mancall, *The Trials of Thomas Morton: An Anglican Lawyer, His Puritan Foes, and the Battle for a New England* (New Haven, 2019), 32.

4. Issack de Rasière to My Lords, Sept. 23, 1626, in *Documents Relating to New Netherland, 1624–1626, in the Henry E. Huntington Library,* ed. and trans. A.J.F. van Laer (San Marino, 1924), 232; Francis, "Beads That Did *Not* Buy Manhattan Island," 54–55; Andrew Lipman, *The Saltwater Frontier,* 105–9; Margriet de Roever, "Merchandises for New Netherland: A Look at Dutch Articles for Barter with the Native American Population," in *One Man's Trash,* 92; Neal Salisbury, *Manitou and Providence: Indians, Europeans, and the Making of New England, 1500–1643* (New York, 1982), 147–49.

5. Lisa Brooks, *Our Beloved Kin: A New History of King Philip's War* (New Haven, 2018), 21–23; Francis, "Beads That Did *Not* Buy Manhattan Island," 60–62; Amy C. Schutt, *Peoples of the River Valleys: The Odyssey of the Delaware Indians* (Philadelphia, 2007), 3–4; Stuart Banner, *How the Indians Lost Their Land: Law and Power on the Frontier* (Cambridge, Mass., 2005), 69–77; Lipman, *Saltwater Frontier,* 129; Paul Otto, "Real Estate or Political Sovereignty? The Dutch, Munsees, and the Purchase of Manhattan Island," in *Opening Statements: Law, Jurisprudence, and the History of Dutch New York,* ed. Albert M. Rosenblatt and Julia C. Rosenblatt (Albany, 2013), 67–81; Gunlög Fur, *A Nation of Women: Gender and Colonial Encounters Among the Delaware Indians* (Philadelphia, 2009), 5–6; Neal Salisbury, "The Indians' Old World: Native Americans and the Coming of Europeans," *William and Mary Quarterly* 53 (1996), 435–58, was an early and influential correction of historians' primitivist belief.

6. Newhouse, "Dekanawida Legend," 16–17; Baptist Thomas (Sa ha whi) (Onondaga, Turtle Clan), "The Hiawatha Tradition," in Parker, *Constitution of the Five Nations,* 119; John Arthur Gibson and Hanni Woodbury, *Concerning the League: The Iroquois League Tradition as Dictated in Onondaga by John Arthur Gibson* (Winnipeg, 1992), 1; Henry R. Schoolcraft, *Notes on the Iroquois, or, Contributions to the Statistics, Aboriginal History, Antiquities and General Ethnology of Western New York* (New York, 1846), 29.

7. Tom Sakokweniónkwas Porter, *Clanology: Clan System of the Iroquois* (Akwesasne, 1993), 4, 22–23.

8. Porter, *Clanology,* 24; Tom Sakokweniónkwas Porter, *And Grandma Said . . . Iroquois Teachings as Passed Down Through the Oral Tradition,* ed. Lesley Forrester (Mohawk Territory of Akwesasne, 2008), 273; Kayanesenh Paul Williams, *Kayanerenkó:wa: The Great Law of Peace* (Winnipeg, 2018), 78–82; Bonaparte, *Creation and Confederation,* 47–52; *Kaianerekowa Hotinonsionne,* dedication page; Cusick, *David Cusick's Sketches,* 23; Barbara A. Mann and Jerry L. Fields, "A Sign in the Sky: Dating the League of the Haudenosaunee," *American Indian Culture and Research Journal* 21 (1997), 105, 111.

9. Gayanashagowa is spelled various ways, including starting with an *R* or a *K,* in the different Haudenosaunee orthographies (conventional spellings). The Roman alphabet was designed for writing down the sounds of Latin and thus imperfectly fits unrelated languages. Hill, *Clay We Are Made Of,* Table 1; Cusick, *David Cusick's Sketches,* 19–23; Paul A. W. Wallace, *The White Roots of Peace* (Philadelphia, 1946), 7–8; Gibson and Woodbury, *Concerning the League,* 38; Porter, *Clanology,* 24; Alyssa Mt. Pleasant, "Independence for Whom? Expansion and Conflict in the Northeast and Northwest," in *The World of the Revolutionary American Republic:*

Land, Labor, and the Conflict for a Continent, ed. Andrew Shankman (New York, 2014), 119–20.

10. Committee of the Chiefs appointed by the Six Nations' Council of Grand River, Canada, "The Code of Dekanahwideh Together with the Tradition of the Origin of the Five Nations' League" (1900), in Parker, *Constitution of the Five Nations,* 70–72, 76–90; Gibson and Woodbury, *Concerning the League,* 8–31, 38, 65–74, 90–93, 101–39, 164–226, 232; Parker, *Constitution of the Five Nations,* 8; Porter, *And Grandma Said,* 272–307; Barbara A. Mann, "The Lynx in Time: Haudenosaunee Women's Traditions and History," *American Indian Quarterly* 21 (1997), 431–37; Hill, *Clay We Are Made Of,* 28–30; Newhouse, "Dekanawida Legend," 24–26; Karihwakeron Tim Thompson, "Celebrating TransIndigenous Diplomacy" panel, Native American and Indigenous Studies Association, June 17, 2021.

11. Newhouse, "Dekanawida Legend," 30–31; Porter, *And Grandma Said,* 298–306; Cusick, *David Cusick's Sketches,* 23; Gibson and Woodbury, *Concerning the League,* 227–35, 238, 297–98; *Kaianerekowa Hotinonsionne,* 1–2; Chief Irving Powless Jr., "Treaty Making," in *Treaty of Canandaigua, 1794: 200 Years of Treaty Relations Between the Iroquois and the United States,* ed. G. Peter Jemison and Anna M. Schein (Santa Fe, 2000), 15–19.

12. Literally, "they made the house" or "the whole house." The word has various spellings and slight differences in pronunciation in the different languages. I'll use the most common, Haudenosaunee. The Mohawk spelling is Rotinonhsón:ni or Rotinonshonni. In other Haudenosaunee orthography, the first letter is often represented by a *K* or a *G.* Frenchmen wrote it down in 1654 as "Hotinnonchiendi, c'est a dire la Cabane achevée; Comme s'ils n'estoient qu'un famille" ("Hotinnonchiendi, that is to say the whole house; as if they were all one family"). François le Mercier, "Relation de ce qui s'est passé en la mission des peres de la Compagnie de Jesus, en la Nouvelle France, les annees 1653 & 1654," in *The Jesuit Relations and Allied Documents: Travels and Explorations of the Jesuit Missionaries in New France, 1610–1791,* ed. Reuben Gold Thwaites (Cleveland, 1898), 41:86 (the *Jesuit Relations* collection includes French and English; I have made my own translations); Porter, *Clanology;* Elias Johnson, *Legends, Traditions and Laws, of the Iroquois, or Six Nations, and History of the Tuscarora Indians* (Lockport, N.Y., 1881), 51–52; Alyssa Mt. Pleasant, "After the Whirlwind: Maintaining a Haudenosaunee Place at Buffalo Creek, 1780–1825" (Ph.D. diss., Cornell, 2007), 1, 54–56, 156; Schoolcraft, *Notes on the Iroquois,* 27.

13. Mercier, *Relation,* 41:86; Gibson and Woodbury, *Concerning the League,* 310.

14. Kayanesenh Paul Williams, "The Mohawk Valley: Yesterday, Today and Tomorrow," in *Kanatsiohareke: Traditional Mohawk Indians Return to Their Ancestral Homeland,* ed. Tom Sakokweniónkwas Porter (Kanatsiohareke and Greenfield Center, N.Y., 2006), 4.

15. Newhouse, "Dekanawida Legend," 45; Committee of the Chiefs, "Code of Dekanahwideh," 101–3; Gibson and Woodbury, *Concerning the League,* 300–307, 458–60, 613–14; Williams, *Kayanerenkó:wa,* 339–44; Hill, *Clay We Are Made Of,* 35, 42–43; William Starna, "The Oneida Homeland in the Seventeenth Century," in *The Oneida Indian Experience,* ed. Jack Campisi and Laurence M. Hauptman (Syracuse, 1988), 20; Brooks, *Common Pot,* 3–7; Nancy Shoemaker, *A Strange Likeness: Becoming Red and White in Eighteenth-Century North America* (New York, 2004), 86–87.

16. Kayanesenh Paul Williams notes that the balances are more important than the checks. Williams, *Kayanerenkó:wa*, ix, xi, 1–4, 300–301; Horatio Hale, *The Iroquois Book of Rites* (Philadelphia, 1883), 33; Doug George-Kanentiio, "Appendix: The Haudenosaunee Confederacy, 1774–1777," in *Kanatsiohareke*, 141; Porter, *And Grandma Said*, 423; Newhouse, "Dekanawida Legend," 42; Committee of the Chiefs, "Code of Dekanahwideh," 105, 107; Parker, *Constitution of the Five Nations*, 11; Richter, *Facing East*, 145–46; Daniel K. Richter, "Stratification and Class in Eastern Native America," *Class Matters: Early North America and the Atlantic World*, ed. Simon Middleton and Billy G. Smith (Philadelphia, 2008), 36.

17. Newhouse, "Dekanawida Legend," 37; Williams, *Kayanerenkó:wa*, 294–96; *Kaianerekowa Hotinonsionne*, 13.

18. Williams, "Mohawk Valley," 7.

19. Newhouse, "Dekanawida Legend," 33, 37–39; Committee of the Chiefs, "Code of Dekanahwideh," 104.

20. René-Robert Cavelier, Sieur de La Salle, to a Friend of L'Abbé de Gallinée, 1678, in *Découvertes et établissements des français dans l'ouest et dans le sud de l'Amérique Septentrionale (1614–1754)*, ed. Pierre Magry (Paris, 1876), 350; Mary Druke Becker, "Linking Arms: The Structure of Iroquois Intertribal Diplomacy," in *Beyond the Covenant Chain*, 36–38; William N. Fenton, *The Great Law and the Longhouse: A Political History of the Iroquois Confederacy* (Norman, 1998), 254–55.

21. Ryan DeCaire, Thanksgiving Address and Condolence Ceremony, Native American and Indigenous Studies Association, June 17, 2021; Becker, "Linking Arms," 36–38; Clayton Logan (Seneca), "The Thanksgiving Address" and Chief Jake Swamp (Mohawk), "The Edge of the Woods," given in 1994 and transcribed in *Treaty of Canandaigua*, 7–14.

22. Newhouse, "Dekanawida Legend," 34–39, 42–47; Committee of the Chiefs, "Code of Dekanahwideh," 61, 93–97, 106–7; Porter, *Clanology*, 1–4, 16–19, 36; *Kaianerekowa Hotinonsionne*, 9; "Confederacy Structure," Haudenosaunee Confederacy website, https://www.haudenosauneeconfederacy.com/government/; Joseph-François Lafitau, *Mœurs des sauvages ameriquains: comparées aux moeurs des premiers temps* (Paris, 1724), 2:165–66, 178. For more on matrilineages and clans, see Becker, "Linking Arms," 30–34.

23. Johannes Megapolensis Jr., "A Short Account of the Mohawk Indians," in *Narratives of New Netherland, 1609–1664*, ed. J. Franklin Jameson (New York, 1909), 174; Hill, *Clay We Are Made Of*, 53–54, 63.

24. Thomas Procter to Henry Knox, 1791, in *American State Papers: Indian Affairs*, ed. Walter Lowrie (Washington, D.C., 1832), 1:160.

25. Mann, "The Lynx in Time," 439–40; Newhouse, "Dekanawida Legend," 34–37, 42–44, 46–47; George-Kanetio, "Appendix: The Haudenosaunee Confederacy," 141–42; Committee of the Chiefs, "Code of Dekanahwideh," 106–7; Porter, *Clanology*, 16–19, 36; Hill, *Clay We Are Made Of*, 30, 35, 58–62, 67; Mann and Fields, "Sign in the Sky," 123; Becker, "Linking Arms," 34; Daniel K. Richter, "War and Culture: The Iroquois Experience," *William and Mary Quarterly* 40 (1983), 530.

26. Megapolensis, "Short Account," 179–80.

27. Scott Manning Stevens, "Reclaiming Our Narratives of Place: Haudenosaunee History on the Ground," Nov. 5, 2019, University of North Carolina, Chapel Hill. The phrase "Shé:kon ken skennen'kó:wa" is made up of Shé:kon (still), ken (a yes/

no question marker), and *skennen'kó:wa* (the Great Peace). Many thanks to Scott Stevens for his careful explanations.

28. Porter, *Clanology,* 29; Megapolensis, "Short Account," 174; Louis Armand de Lom d'Arce, baron de Lahontan, *Nouveaux voyages de Mr. le baron de Lahontan dans l'Amérique Septentrionale* (The Hague, 1703), 2:181 (the second volume of Lahontan's *Nouveaux voyages* is also known by a separate title, *Memoires de l'Amerique Septentrionale*); Gabriel Sagard, *Le Grand Voyage du Pays des Hurons* (Paris, 1632), 203–4; Cusick, *David Cusick's Sketches,* 23–35; Richter, *Ordeal of the Longhouse,* 53, 56; *Kiowa Recipes* (Anadarko, 1934; repr. Excelsior, Minn., 1985), 2; Wayne E. Lee, *The Cutting-Off Way: Indigenous Warfare in Eastern North America, 1500–1800* (Chapel Hill, 2023), 41, 68–69. Making hominy goes back at least as far as the Mississippian period. See Rachel V. Briggs, "The Civil Cooking Pot: Hominy and the Mississippian Standard Jar in the Black Warrior Valley, Alabama," *American Antiquity* 81 (2016), 316–32.

29. Harmen Meyndertsz van den Bogaert, *A Journey into the Mohawk and Oneida Country, 1634–1635,* ed. and trans. Charles T. Gehring and William A. Starna (Syracuse, 1988), 4, 27n17; Minutes, Extraordinary Session, June 16, 1657, in *Fort Orange Court Minutes, 1652–1660,* ed. and trans. Charles T. Gehring (Syracuse, 1990), 304.

30. Samuel de Champlain, *Les Voyages faits au grand fleuve Saint Laurens par le sieur de Champlain Capitaine ordinaire pour le Roy en la marine, depuis l'année 1608 jusques en 1612* (printed as the second book in *Les voyages du sieur de Champlain, xaintongeois, capitaine ordinaire pour le roy, en la marine, divisez en deux livres,* Paris, 1613), 226; Matthew Dennis, *Cultivating a Landscape of Peace: Iroquois-European Encounters in Seventeenth-Century America* (Ithaca, 1993), 35–36; Karonhí:io Delaronde and Jordan Engel, "Haudenosaunee Country in Mohawk," *The Decolonial Atlas,* Feb. 4, 2015, https://decolonialatlas.wordpress.com/2015/02/04/haudenosaunee-country-in-mohawk-2/; Cusick, *David Cusick's Sketches,* 34–35; Janny Venema, *Beverwijck: A Dutch Village on the American Frontier, 1652–1664* (Albany, 2003), 178.

31. Kathryn Magee Labelle, *Dispersed but Not Destroyed: A History of the Seventeenth-Century Wendat People* (Vancouver, 2013), 1–2; "The History of the Huron-Wendat Nation," http://www.wendake.com/history.html.

32. Champlain, *Les Voyages faits au grand fleuve Saint Laurens,* 223–24, 228. The Innu of eastern Canada should not be confused with the Inuit peoples of the Arctic. "Montagnais" is the French word for mountain people.

33. Champlain, *Les Voyages faits au grand fleuve Saint Laurens,* 229.

34. Van den Bogaert, *Journey into the Mohawk and Oneida Country,* 9–10; Champlain, *Les Voyages faits au grand fleuve Saint Laurens,* 229.

35. Champlain, *Les Voyages faits au grand fleuve Saint Laurens,* 230–31.

36. Samuel de Champlain, *Des Sauvages, ou, Voyage de Samuel Champlain, de Brouage, fait en la France nouvelle, l'an 1603* (Paris, 1603), 5–5v; Lahontan, *Nouveaux voyages,* 2:176; Samuel de Champlain, *Second Voyage du Sieur de Champlain, fait en la Nouvelle France en l'annee 1610* (Paris, 1613), 250–54; Wayne E. Lee, *Barbarians and Brothers: Anglo-American Warfare, 1500–1865* (New York, 2011), 134–35; Wayne E. Lee, "The Military Revolution of Native North America: Firearms, Forts, and Polities," in *Empires and Indigenes,* 49–55; Richter, "War and Culture," 535–36; Peter C. Mancall, *Fatal Journey: The Final Expedition of Henry Hudson* (New York, 2009), 71.

37. Richter, *Ordeal of the Longhouse,* 51–54; Neal Salisbury, "Spiritual Giants, Worldly Empires: Indigenous People and New England to the 1680s," in *World of Colonial America: An Atlantic Handbook,* ed. Ignacio Gallup-Diaz (New York, 2017), 154–55; Richter, *Facing East,* 42–43; Alexandra van Dongen, "'The Inexhaustible Kettle': The Metamorphosis of a European Utensil in the World of the North American Indians," in *One Man's Trash,* 139–42; William Engelbrecht, *Iroquoia: The Development of a Native World* (Syracuse, 2003), 133–35.

38. Salisbury, "Spiritual Giants," 155–56; Bruce G. Trigger, *The Children of Aataentsic: A History of the Huron People to 1660* (Montreal, 1976), 209, 228–29; Richter, *Facing East,* 26–33.

39. Jaap Jacobs, *The Colony of New Netherland: A Dutch Settlement in Seventeenth-Century America* (Ithaca, 2009), 19–22; Mancall, *Fatal Journey,* 62–72; Romney, *New Netherland Connections,* 124, 128–29; Richter, *Ordeal of the Longhouse,* 54.

40. Champlain, *Les Voyages faits au grand fleuve Saint Laurens,* 209–10.

41. Champlain, *Second Voyage,* 249.

42. Samuel de Champlain, *Les Voyages de la Nouvelle France Occidentale dicte Canada, faits par le Sr. de Champlain, Saintongeois, Capitane pour le Roy en la Marine du Ponant, & toutes les Découvertes qu'il a faites en ce païs depuis l'an 1603 jusques en l'an 1629* (Paris, 1632), part 2, 41; Williams, *Linking Arms Together,* 5, 21.

43. Champlain, *Des Sauvages,* 3v–4; Trigger, *Children of Aataentsic,* 230.

44. Champlain, *Des Sauvages,* 4v.

45. Samuel de Champlain, *Voyages et Descouvertures Faites en La Nouvelle France, depuis l'année 1615 jusques a la fin de l'année 1618, par le Sieur de Champlain, Capitain ordinaire pour le Roy en la Mer du Ponant* (Paris, 1619), 13v; Ned Blackhawk, *The Rediscovery of America: Native Peoples and the Unmaking of U.S. History* (New Haven, 2023), 76–84; Jon Parmenter, *The Edge of the Woods: Iroquoia, 1534–1701* (East Lansing, Mich., 2010), 25–27.

46. Champlain, *Les Voyages de la Nouvelle France Occidentale dicte Canada,* part 2, 166–70; Trigger, *Children of Aataentsic,* 456–57.

47. Champlain, *Des Sauvages,* 8; Champlain, *Voyages et Descouvertures Faites en La Nouvelle France, depuis l'année 1615 jusques a la fin de l'année 1618,* 14; *Dictionary of Canadian Biography,* www.biographi.ca.

48. Richter, *Ordeal of the Longhouse,* 52; Mt. Pleasant, "Paradox of Plows," 470–71.

49. Richter, *Ordeal of the Longhouse,* 54–55; Bruce G. Trigger, "The Mohawk-Mahican War (1624–28): The Establishment of a Pattern," *Canadian Historical Review* 52 (1971), 277–78; George-Kanentiio, "Appendix: The Haudenosaunee Confederacy," 141–43.

50. Salisbury, *Manitou and Providence,* 147.

51. Johan de Laet, *New World, or Description of West-India,* 1625, in *Narratives of New Netherland, 1609–1664,* ed. J. Franklin Jameson (New York, 1909), 47.

52. Donna Merwick, *The Shame and the Sorrow: Dutch-Amerindian Encounters in New Netherland* (Philadelphia, 2006), 7; Jacobs, "Beavers for Drink," 95.

53. Champlain, *Les Voyages de la Nouvelle France Occidentale dicte Canada,* part 2, 41–44, 73; Salisbury, *Manitou and Providence,* 82; Richter, *Ordeal of the Longhouse,*

55, 58; Trigger, "Mohawk-Mahican War," 277–79; David Hackett Fischer, *Champlain's Dream* (New York, 2008), 382–83.

54. Nicolaes van Wassenaer, *Historisch Verhael*, Nov. 1626, in *Narratives of New Netherland, 1609–1664*, ed. J. Franklin Jameson (New York, 1909), 84–85; de Rasière to My Lords, Sept. 23, 1626, in *Documents Relating to New Netherland*, 212.

55. Isaac Jogues, "Novum Belgium and an Account of René Goupil," 1644, *In Mohawk Country: Early Narratives About a Native People*, ed. Dean R. Snow, Charles T. Gehring, and William A. Starna (Syracuse, 1996), 31.

56. Van Wassenaer, *Historisch Verhael*, Nov. 1626, 84–85.

57. Megapolensis, "Short Account," 172; van Wassenaer, *Historisch Verhael*, Nov. 1626, 84; Jonas Michaëlius to Adrianus Smoutius, 1628, in *Narratives of New Netherland, 1609–1664*, 131; Account of the Jurisdictions, Management and Condition of the Territories Named Rensselaerswyck, July 20, 1634, trans. Mrs. Alan H. Strong, *Van Rensselaer-Bowier Manuscripts, Being the Letters of Kiliaen van Rensselaer, 1630–1643*, ed. and trans. A.J.F. van Laer (New York, 1908), 306–8; Richter, *Ordeal of the Longhouse*, 55–56; Trigger, "Mohawk-Mahican War," 276, 281. Mohawk-Mahican conflict would break out again in 1669. Lee, *Cutting-Off Way*, 25–30.

58. Jonas Michaëlius to Adrianus Smoutius, 1628, in *Narratives of New Netherland, 1609–1664*, ed. J. Franklin Jameson (New York, 1909), 131; William Deepinge, sworn statement, Nov. 6, 1633, in *Documents Relative to the Colonial History of the State of New York*, ed. E. B. O'Callaghan (Albany, 1856), 1:78.

59. David J. Silverman, *Thundersticks: Firearms and the Violent Transformation of Native America* (Cambridge, Mass., 2016), 25–28.

60. Starna, "Oneida Homeland in the Seventeenth Century," 20; "Relation de ce qui s'est passé en la Mission des Peres de la Compagnie de Jesus aux païs de la Nouvelle France, depuis l'Esté de l'année 1657 jusques à l'Esté de l'année 1658," in *Jesuit Relations*, 44:140.

61. Minutes, Oct. 6, 1656, in *Fort Orange Court Minutes*, 252.

62. Magistrates' Statement, Aug. 15, 1657, in *Fort Orange Court Minutes*, 323–25; Interrogatory of Marten Bierkaecker, Aug. 15, 1657, in *Fort Orange Court Minutes*, 324–25; Minutes, Extraordinary Session, Aug. 20, 1657, in *Fort Orange Court Minutes*, 327–28.

63. Minutes, Extraordinary Session to Hear the Propositions Made by the Maquas, Sept. 6, 1659, in *Fort Orange Court Minutes*, 453; Minutes, Extraordinary Session, Jan. 12, 1658, in *Fort Orange Court Minutes*, 346–47; Minutes, Extraordinary Session, Jan. 12, 1658, in *Fort Orange Court Minutes*, 347–48; Minutes, Mar. 11, 1658, in *Fort Orange Court Minutes*, 357–58. Maqua, or Mingo, was a Lenape word for Iroquoian speakers.

64. For more on the fraught history of alcohol and attempts to control its use, see Peter C. Mancall, *Deadly Medicine: Indians and Alcohol in Early America* (Ithaca, 1995); Sami Lakomäki, Ritva Kylli, and Timo Ylimaunu, "Drinking Colonialism: Alcohol, Indigenous Status, and Native Space on Shawnee and Sámi Homelands, 1600–1850," *Native American and Indigenous Studies* 4 (2017), 1–29.

65. "Journal of New Netherland," 1647, in *Narratives of New Netherland, 1609–1664*, ed. J. Franklin Jameson (New York, 1909), 244, 274; Jacobs, "Beavers for Drink," 95–97; Jaap, *Colony of New Netherland*, 115–16; Merwick, *Shame and the Sorrow*, 115; Ven-

ema, *Beverwijck,* 181–82, 254–63; Silverman, *Thundersticks,* 32. In Europe, a pelt was generally worth around six guilders and a gun twelve guilders.

66. Minutes, Feb. 25, 1654, *Council Minutes, 1652–1654,* ed. and trans. Charles T. Gehring (Baltimore, 1983), 116; Jacobs, "Beavers for Drink," 99.

67. Silverman, *Thundersticks,* 31.

68. "Journal of New Netherland," 1647, 271, 273; Jogues, "Novum Belgium," 1644, 32; Jacobs, *Colony of New Netherland,* 45–46, 97–99; Venema, *Beverwijck,* 22–23.

69. Merwick, *Shame and the Sorrow,* 69–70.

70. Romney, *New Netherland Connections,* 155–57; Simon Middleton, "'How It Came That the Bakers Bake No Bread': A Struggle for Trade Privileges in Seventeenth-Century New Amsterdam," *William and Mary Quarterly* 58 (2001), 353; Engelbrecht, *Iroquoia,* 80; Jaap, *Colony of New Netherland,* 115, 134–35.

71. "Ordinance of the Director and Council of New Netherland Prohibiting the Exportation of Grain and Bread from New Netherland," passed Nov. 8, 1649, in *Laws and Ordinances of New Netherland,* 112; Minutes, Ordinary Session, Feb. 11, 1653, in *Fort Orange Court Minutes,* 41; Minutes, Ordinary Session, Mar. 4, 1653, in *Fort Orange Court Minutes,* 45; Petition by Joannes Dijckman and the Magistrates of the Court of Fort Orange and Beverwijck to the Hon. Director General Peter Stuyvesant, Mar. 16, 1654, in *Fort Orange Court Minutes,* 109–10; Romney, *New Netherland Connections,* 155–57.

72. Venema, *Beverwijck,* 24, 61, 176–78; Jaap, *Colony of New Netherland,* 116–17; Richter, *Ordeal of the Longhouse,* 76.

73. "Journal of New Netherland," 1647, 273; Jogues, "Novum Belgium," 1644, 32; Jacobs, "Beavers for Drink," 101, 104–5; Merwick, *Shame and the Sorrow,* 220; Venema, *Beverwijck,* 91–92, 100, 178, 187; Romney, *New Netherland Connections,* 12, 14, 155, 164–67; Dennis, *Cultivating a Landscape of Peace,* 121.

74. Megapolensis, "Short Account," 177; Romney, *New Netherland Connections,* 124, 150; *Fort Orange Court Minutes,* 252; Paul Otto, *The Dutch-Munsee Encounter: The Struggle for Sovereignty in the Hudson Valley* (New York, 2006), 138; de Roever, "Merchandises for New Netherland," 77, 88, 92; Dennis, *Cultivating a Landscape of Peace,* 125; van Dongen, "Inexhaustible Kettle," 135; Venema, *Beverwijck,* 180.

75. Megapolensis, "Short Account," 169–72; "Journal of New Netherland," 1647, 272; Romney, *New Netherland Connections,* 11, 13–14, 147–50; Venema, *Beverwijck,* 19–20, 101, 165–67; Jacobs, *Colony of New Netherland,* 55–56.

76. Megapolensis, "Short Account," 177–78.

77. Deborah Rosen, "Women and Property Across Colonial America: A Comparison of Legal Systems in New Mexico and New York," *William and Mary Quarterly* 60 (2003), 355–82; Jacobs, "Beavers for Drink," 104–5; Romney, *New Netherland Connections,* 141–45, 185–87; Venema, *Beverwijck,* 82, 100–102, 187–88; Richter, *Ordeal of the Longhouse,* 84.

78. Richter, *Ordeal of the Longhouse,* 75, 79–80; Megapolensis, "Short Account," 178; Van den Bogaert, *Journey into the Mohawk and Oneida Country,* 4. For more on how Native languages incorporated foreign concepts, see Sean P. Harvey and Sarah Rivett, "Colonial-Indigenous Language Encounters in North America and the Intellectual History of the Atlantic World," *Early American Studies* 15 (2017), 442–73; David J. Silverman, "Indians, Missionaries, and Religious Translation:

Creating Wampanoag Christianity in Seventeenth-Century Martha's Vineyard," *William and Mary Quarterly* 62 (2005), 141–74.

79. Lahontan, *Nouveaux voyages,* 2:180; Barthélemy Vimont, "Relation de ce qui s'est passé en la Nouvelle France, en l'année 1642 et 1643," in *Jesuit Relations,* 24:270; Father Isaac Jogues to the Governor of New France, June 30, 1643, in *Jesuit Relations,* 24:294; "Journal of New Netherland," 1647, 274; John Warner and the Sha-womet (Rhode Island) Commissioners to the Massachusetts General Court, June 20, 1644, in *Records of the Colony of Rhode Island and Providence Plantations in New England,* ed. John Russell Bartlett (Providence, 1856), 1:140; Meeting of the Commissioners for the United Colonies of New England, Sept. 12, 1648, in *Records of the Colony of New Plymouth, in New England,* ed. David Pulsifer (Boston, 1859), (vol. 1 of *Acts of the Commissioners of the United Colonies of New England, 1643–1679),* 116; Daniel Gookin, "Historical Collections of the Indians in New England," 1674, *Massachusetts Historical Society Collections* (1792), 164; Catherine Cangany, "Fashioning Moccasins: Detroit, the Manufacturing Frontier, and the Empire of Consumption, 1701–1835," *William and Mary Quarterly* 69 (2012), 265–304; Richter, *Ordeal of the Longhouse,* 62, 79–80; Craig S. Keener, "An Ethnohistorical Analysis of Iroquois Assault Tactics Used Against Fortified Settlements of the Northeast in the Seventeenth Century," *Ethnohistory* 46 (1999), 777–807.

80. Van den Bogaert, *Journey into the Mohawk and Oneida Country,* 4; Richter, *Facing East,* 43–44; Richter, *Ordeal of the Longhouse,* 79–80; van Dongen, "Inexhaustible Kettle," 127, 129.

81. Richter, *Ordeal of the Longhouse,* 76; Venema, *Beverwijck,* 178.

82. De Rasière to My Lords, September 23, 1626, in *Documents Relating to New Netherland,* 228–31; Scott Manning Stevens, "Tomahawk: Materiality and Depictions of the Haudenosaunee," *Early American Literature* 53 (2018), 475–511.

83. De Roever, "Merchandises for New Netherland," 88; Silverman, *Thundersticks,* 12–13, 27–28.

84. Newhouse, "Dekanawida Legend," 51–52.

85. Newhouse, "Dekanawida Legend," 53–54; Parker, *Constitution of the Five Nations,* 9–10; *Kaianerekowa Hotinonsionne,* 43–44.

86. *Kaianerekowa Hotinonsionne,* 40.

87. *Kaianerekowa Hotinonsionne,* 42–44; Newhouse, "Dekanawida Legend," 30, 53–54; Parker, *Constitution of the Five Nations,* 9–10; Williams, *Kayanerenkó:wa,* 398–400.

88. *Kaianerekowa Hotinonsionne,* 25.

89. *Kaianerekowa Hotinonsionne,* 34–35; Richter, "War and Culture," 528–59; Richter, *Ordeal of the Longhouse,* 65–73; Hill, *Clay We Are Made Of,* 62–63; Lahontan, *Nouveaux voyages,* 2:185; Porter, *Clanology,* 33; Porter, *And Grandma Said,* 423; Newhouse, "Dekanawida Legend," 49–52.

90. Francis Jennings, *Ambiguous Iroquois Empire: The Covenant Chain Confederation of Indian Tribes with English Colonies from Its Beginnings to the Lancaster Treaty of 1744* (New York, 1984), 10–11, 18–19; Daniel K. Richter and James H. Merrell, preface to *Beyond the Covenant Chain* (2003).

91. Richter, "War and Culture," 530–36.

92. Richter, "War and Culture," 536–37; Van den Bogaert, *Journey into the Mohawk and Oneida Country,* 4; Richter, *Ordeal of the Longhouse,* 58–59; Hill, *Clay We Are Made*

Of, 88; Paul Kelton, *Cherokee Medicine, Colonial Germs: An Indigenous Nation's Fight Against Smallpox, 1518–1824* (Norman, 2015), 22, 39–40; Dean R. Snow and Kim M. Lanphear, "European Contact and Indian Depopulation in the Northeast: The Timing of the First Epidemics," *Ethnohistory* 35 (1988), 15–33; Tai S. Edwards and Paul Kelton, "Germs, Genocides, and America's Indigenous Peoples," *Journal of American History* 107 (2020), 69; Michael Leroy Oberg, *Native America: A History,* 2nd ed. (Hoboken, N.J., 2018), 40–41. For an outline of evidence of disease outbreaks, see José António Brandão, *"Your Fyre Shall Burn No More": Iroquois Policy Toward New France and Its Native Allies to 1701* (Lincoln, 1997), 145–51. Brandão's book also contains appendices listing the (spotty) evidence for Haudenosaunee population numbers in the seventeenth century.

93. Williams, *Kayanerenkó:wa,* 3, 401.

94. Vimont, "Relation de ce qui s'est passé en la Nouvelle France, en l'année 1642 et 1643," 24:272, 276, 278, 290, 292; Isaac Jogues to the Governor of New France, June 30, 1643, in *Jesuit Relations,* 24:294; Lahontan, *Nouveaux voyages,* 2:176; Gookin, "Historical Collections," 162–63; Trigger, *Children of Aataentsic,* 634–40; Richter, *Ordeal of the Longhouse,* 57, 61–64; Silverman, *Thundersticks,* 28–30, 35–36.

95. Vimont, "Relation de ce qui s'est passé en la Nouvelle France, en l'année 1642 et 1643," 24:274, 276.

96. Vimont, "Relation de ce qui s'est passé en la Nouvelle France, en l'année 1642 et 1643," 25:24; Lee, *Cutting-Off Way,* 23–24, 68–69.

97. Vimont, "Relation de ce qui s'est passé en la Nouvelle France, en l'année 1642 et 1643," 25:24.

98. Kiliaen van Rensselaer, Memorial to the Assembly of the Nineteen of the West India Company, Nov. 25, 1633, *Van Rensselaer-Bowier Manuscripts,* 248.

99. Salisbury, *Manitou and Providence,* 204–6; Brooks, *Common Pot,* 58–59; Katherine A. Grandjean, "New World Tempests: Environment, Scarcity, and the Coming of the Pequot War," *William and Mary Quarterly* 68 (2011), 75–100.

100. Roger Williams to John Winthrop, July 3, 1637, in *Winthrop Papers* (Boston, 1929), 3:438; Williams to Winthrop, July 10, 1637, in *Winthrop Papers,* 3:446; Williams to Winthrop, July 15, 1637, in *Winthrop Papers,* 3:451; Williams to Winthrop, July 21, 1637, in *Winthrop Papers,* 3:456. Currency equivalents estimated using tool created by the British National Archives: www.nationalarchives.gov.uk/currency-converter.

101. John Winthrop to William Bradford, July 28, 1637, in *Winthrop Papers,* 3:456; John Winthrop, entry for Aug. 5, 1637, *Winthrop's Journal: "History of New England," 1630–1649,* ed. James K. Hosmer (New York, 1908), 1:229–30; Richard Davenport to John Winthrop, August 23, 1637, in *Winthrop Papers,* 3:490–91; William Bradford, *Of Plymouth Plantation,* ed. Samuel Eliot Morison (New York, 1959), 297; Salisbury, "Toward the Covenant Chain," 62–65; Lipman, *Saltwater Frontier,* 140–41.

102. Jacobs, *Colony of New Netherland,* 76–77; Lipman, *Saltwater Frontier,* 142–64.

103. William Bradford to John Winthrop, June 29, 1640, in *Winthrop Papers* (Boston, 1944), 4:258–59; John Winthrop, entry for Sept. 7, 1640, in *Winthrop's Journal: "History of New England," 1630–1649,* ed. James K. Hosmer (New York, 1908), 2:6–7.

104. John Mason to John Winthrop, Dec. 1, 1643, in *Winthrop Papers,* 4:419; Meeting of

the Commissioners for the United Colonies of New England, Sept. 7, 1643, *Records of the Colony of New Plymouth,* 9:11; John Haynes to John Winthrop, Dec. 1, 1643, in *Winthrop Papers,* 4:418; Edward Winslow to John Winthrop, Jan. 7, 1644, in *Winthrop Papers,* 4:427–28; Meeting of the Commissioners for the United Colonies of New England, Sept. 12, 1648, *Records of the Colony of New Plymouth,* 9:116; Haynes to Winthrop, Sept. 20, 1648, in *Winthrop Papers,* 5:257.

105. Salisbury, "Spiritual Giants," 157–60.

106. Bradford, *Of Plymouth Plantation,* 339–41.

107. Minutes of the Meeting of the Inhabitants Regarding the Rumors of War, Sept. 21, 1650, *Minutes of the Court of Rensselaerswyck, 1648–1652* (Albany, 1922), 127–28; Commission for Arent van Curler et al., Sept. 23, 1650, *Minutes of the Court of Rensselaerswyck,* 128–29.

108. Today they are the Stockbridge-Munsee Community or Mohican Nation Stockbridge-Munsee Band.

109. Paul le Jeune, "Relation de ce qui s'est passé en la Nouvelle France, les années 1640 et 1641," in *Jesuit Relations,* 21:32–40, 54–56; Trigger, *Children of Aataentsic,* 634–37.

110. Barthélemy Vimont, "Relation de ce qui s'est passé en la Nouvelle France, en l'année 1644 et 1645," in *Jesuit Relations,* 27:246–72; Trigger, *Children of Aataentsic,* 655–63; William N. Fenton, Francis Jennings, and Mary A. Druke, "The Earliest Recorded Description: The Mohawk Treaty with New France at Three Rivers, 1645," in *The History and Culture of Iroquois Diplomacy: An Interdisciplinary Guide to the Treaties of the Six Nations and Their League,* ed. Francis Jennings, William N. Fenton, Mary A. Druke, and David R. Miller (Syracuse, 1985), 127–30, 133–36; Williams, *Kayanerenkó:wa,* 2; Trigger, *Children of Aataentsic,* 647–50.

111. Father Isaac Jogues to the Governor of New France, June 30, 1643, in *Jesuit Relations,* 24:294, 296; Hierosme Lalemant, "Relation de ce qui s'est passé . . . en la Nouvelle France, sur le Grand Fleuve de S. Laurens en l'année 1647," in *Jesuit Relations,* 31:114–20; Schoolcraft, *Notes on the Iroquois,* 29; Newhouse, "Dekanawida Legend," 14–15; Wallace, *White Roots of Peace,* 13; Trigger, *Children of Aataentsic,* 726–29, 740–42; Jennings, *Ambiguous Iroquois Empire,* 92–93, 96–97; Richter, *Ordeal of the Longhouse,* 60–64; Richter, "War and Culture," 541; Labelle, *Dispersed but Not Destroyed,* 120–21.

112. Oneiotchronon (Oneida) ambassador speech, Nov. 3, 1656, Jean de Quen, Journal des Pères Jésuites, in *Jesuit Relations,* 42:252.

113. Jennings, *Ambiguous Iroquois Empire,* 99; Lee, *Cutting-Off Way,* 31–32; Wayne E. Lee, "Peace Chiefs and Blood Revenge: Patterns of Restraint in Native American Warfare in the Contact and Colonial Eras," *Journal of Military History* 71 (2007), 707–9; Keener, "An Ethnohistorical Analysis of Iroquois Assault Tactics," 785, 788; Labelle, *Dispersed but Not Destroyed,* 49, 122–40.

114. Jesuit Journal, 1651, in *Jesuit Relations,* 36:118–36; Sagard, *Grand Voyage,* 208; "Our History," *Wyandotte Nation,* https://wyandotte-nation.org/culture/our-history; "The History of the Huron-Wendat Nation," http://www.wendake.com/history .html; Labelle, *Dispersed but Not Destroyed,* 47–59, 77–80, 84–85; Jacob F. Lee, *Masters of the Middle Waters: Indian Nations and Colonial Ambitions Along the Mississippi* (Cambridge, Mass., 2019), 43; Silverman, *Thundersticks,* 37–79.

115. Jean de Quen, Journal des Jésuites, 1656–57, in *Jesuit Relations,* 43:264; Lallemant, Relation de ce qui s'est passé en la Nouvelle France en l'année 1660, 45:204–8;

Parker, *Constitution of the Five Nations*, 10; Richter, "War and Culture," 541; Hill, *Clay We Are Made Of*, 91; Williams, *Kayanerenkó:wa*, 326; Jennings, *Ambiguous Iroquois Empire*, 102. Lallemant said no more than 1,200 were born Haudenosaunee out of a population with nearly 2,200 men of fighting age, so the total population would have been around 6,000.

116. "Our History," *Wyandotte Nation*, https://wyandotte-nation.org/culture/our-history.

117. Brandão, *"Your Fyre Shall Burn No More,"* 92.

118. Lahontan, *New Voyages*, 2:177; Vimont, "Relation de ce qui s'est passé en la Nouvelle France, en l'année 1642 et 1643," 24:290.

119. Anastasius Douay, Relation, *First Establishment of the Faith in New France*, ed. Christian Le Clerq, trans. John Gilmary Shea (New York, 1881), 2:271–72.

120. Scott Manning Stevens, session no. 142 at AHA 2018.

121. Native North American Indian Traveling College, *Traditional Mohawk Clothing* (Akwesasne, n.d.), 3–4, 14; Megapolensis, "Short Account," 173.

122. Megapolensis, "Short Account," 174–75; Vimont, "Relation de ce qui s'est passé en la Nouvelle France, en l'année 1642 et 1643," 24:280; Richter, "War and Culture," 533.

123. Champlain, *Les Voyages de la Nouvelle France Occidentale dicte Canada*, part 2, 174, 176.

124. William Wood, *New England's Prospect: A True, Lively and Experimental Description of That Part of America Commonly Called New England* (London, 1634), 57.

125. Roger Williams to John Winthrop, October 24, 1636, in *Winthrop Papers*, 3:318; Williams to Winthrop, July 3, 1637, in *Winthrop Papers*, 3:438; Stevens, "Tomahawk," 476; "Mohawk (Kanien'keha)," *Kanien'kéha: An Open Source Endangered Language Initiative*, https://kanienkeha.net/about/; Thomas S. Abler, "Scalping, Torture, Cannibalism and Rape: An Ethnohistorical Analysis of Conflicting Cultural Values in War," *Anthropologica* 34 (1992), 13–15.

126. John Lothrop Motley, *The Rise of the Dutch Republic: A History* (London, 1861), 2:41–42; Sagard, *Grand Voyage*, 203; Stevens, "Tomahawk," 482–83; A Gentleman of Elvas, "True Relation of the Hardships Suffered by Governor Don Hernando de Soto," trans. James Alexander Robertson, in *The De Soto Chronicles: The Expedition of Hernando de Soto to North America in 1539–1543*, ed. Lawrence A. Clayton, Vernon James Knight Jr., and Edward C. Moore (Tuscaloosa, 1993), 1:152; *Narratives of the Coronado Expedition, 1540–1542*, ed. George Hammond and Agapito Rey (Albuquerque, 1940), 217, 326–28; "A Transcription of the Testimony, 8th de Oficio Witness (Juan Troyano)," in Richard Flint, "Great Cruelties Have Been Reported: The 1544 Investigation of the Coronado Expedition" (Ph.D. diss., University of New Mexico, 1999), 186–87; Abler, "Scalping, Torture, Cannibalism and Rape," 11–12; *The Song of Roland*, trans. John DuVal (Indianapolis, 2012), laisses 3880–90; John DuVal, "Three Laisses from the Franco-Italian Song of Roland," *Transference* 6 (2018), 49–53; Thomas N. Bisson, *The Crisis of the Twelfth Century: Power, Lordship, and the Origins of European Government* (Princeton, 2015), 6; Merwick, *Shame and the Sorrow*, 162–63.

127. Vimont, "Relation de ce qui s'est passé en la Nouvelle France, en l'année 1642 et 1643," 24:271, 26:175.

128. Relation, 1650–1651, in *Jesuit Relations*, 36:166.

129. New Netherland Council to the States General of the United Netherlands, Oct. or Nov. 1655, *Council Minutes, 1655–1656,* 122; Romney, *New Netherland Connections,* 15–16, 126, 160–61, 192; Gabriel Dreuillette to John Winthrop, n.d. (c. 1651), in *Jesuit Relations,* 36:78–81; Gabriel Dreuillette, "Narrative of the Journey Made in Behalf of the Mission of the Abnaquiois, and of the Information Obtained in New England, and of the Disposition of the Magistrates of That Commonwealth in Regard to Aid Against the Iroquois," 1651, in *Jesuit Relations,* 36:92, 104; Salisbury, "Toward the Covenant Chain," 63–64; Salisbury, "Spiritual Giants," 160–61.

130. Propositions Made by Certain Sachems of the Mohawks, Nov. 19, 1655, in *Fort Orange Records, 1654–1679,* ed. and trans. Charles T. Gehring and Janny Venema (Syracuse, 2009), 84.

131. Proposal Made by the Maquas in Fort Orange, June 26, 1660, in *Fort Orange Court Minutes,* 503–4.

132. Jerome Lallemant, Relation de ce qui s'est passé en la Nouvelle France en l'année 1660, in *Jesuit Relations,* 45:204–8; Richter, "His Own, Their Own," 210.

133. Richter, "War and Culture," 538; Richter, *Ordeal of the Longhouse,* 61–62; Silverman, *Thundersticks,* 39–43; Michael McConnell, *A Country Between: The Upper Ohio Valley and Its Peoples, 1724–1774* (Lincoln, 1997), 62; Michael A. McDonnell, *Masters of Empire: Great Lakes Indians and the Making of America* (New York, 2015), 35–36; Jennings, *Ambiguous Iroquois Empire,* 102; Silverman, *Thundersticks,* 44–45; Labelle, *Dispersed but Not Destroyed,* 68–71, 74; Matthew Kruer, *Time of Anarchy: Indigenous Power and the Crisis of Colonialism in Early America* (Cambridge, Mass., 2021).

134. Hill, *Clay We Are Made Of,* 89–90; Loren Michael Mortimer, "Kaniatarowanenneh Crossings: Indigenous Power and Presence in the St. Lawrence River Watershed, 1534–1842" (Ph.D. diss., University of California, Davis, 2019); Lee, *Masters of the Middle Waters,* 42; David Andrew Nichols, *Peoples of the Inland Sea: Native Americans and Newcomers in the Great Lakes Region, 1600–1870* (Athens, Ohio, 2018), 43–44.

135. "Journal of New Netherland," 1647, 274; Propositions Made by the Chiefs of the Savages Living in the Neighborhood of the Manhattans, July 19, 1649, in *Documents Relating to the Colonial History of the State of New York,* ed. and trans. Berthold Fernow, F. B. O'Callaghan, and John Brodhead (Albany, 1881), 13:25; Merwick, *Shame and the Sorrow,* 131, 199, 226–27; Becker, "Linking Arms," 33–34; Shoemaker, *Strange Likeness,* 91–92, 118; Richter, *Facing East,* 147–48; Jennings, *Ambiguous Iroquois Empire,* 112, 115, 123.

136. According to Haudenosaunee oral tradition, the Two-Row Wampum belt began with their first treaty with the Dutch in 1613. "Two Row Wampum—Guswenta," https://www.onondaganation.org/culture/wampum/two-row-wampum-belt -guswenta/; Guswenta Two-Row Wampum belt description, National Museum of the American Indian, Washington, D.C.; Powless, "Treaty Making," 23; Mt. Pleasant, "Independence for Whom?," 120; Hill, *Clay We Are Made Of,* 85–86, 95–98; Williams, *Linking Arms Together,* 4; Richter, *Ordeal of the Longhouse,* 136–45, 210–13; Silverman, *Thundersticks,* 46–48; Richter, "War and Culture," 540–41. See also "Special Issue: Early Iroquoian-European Contacts: The Kaswentha Tradition, the Two Row Wampum Belt, and the Tawagonshi Document," ed. Paul Otto and Jaap Jacobs, *Journal of Early American History* 3 (2013).

137. Williams, "Mohawk Valley," 4–5.

138. Salisbury, "Toward the Covenant Chain," 66–67.

139. Venema, *Beverwijck*, 172.

140. Scott Manning Stevens, session no. 142 at AHA 2018; Onondaga Nation, "Hiawatha Belt Returns to Onondaga Lake," October 24, 2016, *Onondaga Nation*, https://www.onondaganation.org/news/2016/hiawatha-belt-returns-to-onondaga-lake; Chief Irving Powless Jr., "The Day That 12 Wampum Belts Returned to Onondaga," Oct. 21, 1989, *Onondaga Nation*, https://www.onondaganation.org/culture/the-day-that-12-wampum-belts-returned-to-onondaga/; Porter, *And Grandma Said*, 33, 36.

CHAPTER 5: THE O'ODHAM HIMDAG

1. Eusebio Kino, "Favores Celestiales," in *Las misiones de Sonora y Arizona, comprendiendo: La crónica titulada: "Favores Celestiales" y la "Relación diaria de la entrada al noroeste,"* ed. Francisco Fernández del Castillo and Emilio Bose (Mexico City, 1922), 24; John L. Kessell, "Peaceful Conquest in Southern Arizona," in *Father Kino in Arizona*, ed. Fay Jackson Smith, John L. Kessell, and Francis J. Fox (Phoenix, 1966), 55, 60–63; Deni J. Seymour, *Where the Earth and Sky Are Sewn Together: Sobaipuri-O'odham Contexts of Contact and Colonialism* (Salt Lake City, 2011), 1–2, 52–70, 281; E. Christian Wells, *From Hohokam to O'odham: The Protohistoric Occupation of the Middle Gila River Valley, Central Arizona* (Sacaton, Ariz., 2006), 8; Charles C. Di Peso, *The Upper Pima of San Cayetano del Tumacacori* (1956; repr., Millwood, N.Y., 1974); Wild Horse Pass exhibits, Gila River Indian Community; Marian Betancourt with Michael O'Dowd and Jack Strong, *The New Native American Cuisine: Five-Star Recipes from the Chefs of Arizona's Kai Restaurant* (Guilford, Conn., 2009), 5; Dean Saxton, Lucille Saxton, and Susie Enos, *Dictionary: Papago/Pima-English, O'othham-Mil-gahn; English-Papago/Pima, Mil-gahn-O'othham*, ed. R. L. Cherry (Tucson, 1983), 99; George Webb, *A Pima Remembers* (Tucson, 1959), 65.

2. Smith, *Father Kino in Arizona*, 14n47; Saxton, Saxton, and Enos, *Dictionary: Papago/Pima-English*, 138; Ronald Geronimo, "Establishing Connections to Place: Identifying O'odham Place Names in Early Spanish Documents," *Journal of the Southwest* 56 (2014), 222; Ruth M. Underhill, *Papago Woman* (New York, 1979), 7.

3. Eusebio Kino, "Relación Diaria," in *Las misiones de Sonora*, 405; Underhill, *Papago Woman*, 65–66; Winston P. Erickson, *Sharing the Desert: The Tohono O'odham in History* (Tucson, 1994), 16–17; Cynthia Radding, *Wandering Peoples: Colonialism, Ethnic Spaces, and Ecological Frontiers in Northwestern Mexico, 1700–1850* (Durham, 1997), 10, 59, 267; R. Douglas Hurt, *Indian Agriculture in America: Prehistory to the Present* (Lawrence, Kan., 1987), 47; Ruth M. Underhill, *Papago Indian Religion* (New York, 1946), 211–12.

4. I am focusing on the region outlined in the Tohono O'odham textbook used in the nation's schools, *Sharing the Desert*, which includes the Hia-Ced, Sobaipuri, and Himuri O'odham as part of connected O'odham peoples, plus the Akimel O'odham as "very closely related, not only linguistically but also economically and socially." The name Sobaipuri may have been given by outsiders, with no meaning in O'odham language, but it is usually used for the O'odham on the Santa Cruz

and San Pedro rivers in the seventeenth century. I follow *Sharing the Desert* in using the term Himuri for the rancherias on the Altar, Magdalena, and Concepción rivers. Himuri was the name of one of their towns (Ímuris, Mexico, today). They composed a cohesive O'odham region with strong ties to the Tohono O'odham and continue to be connected to one another and the Tohono O'odham today. Readers should take these categories as approximations, though. As *Sharing the Desert* notes, divisions both in the past and today are "somewhat a matter of opinion." Erickson, *Sharing the Desert*, 9–10, 13–17, 24; Kino, "Favores Celestiales," 24, 58–59; Juan Mateo Manje, Feb. 21, 1699, "Relación itineraria diaria que hice con los reverendos Padres Eusebio Francisco Kino y Adamo Gilg," in appendix, *Kino and Manje, Explorers of Sonora and Arizona: Their Vision of the Future*, ed. Ernest J. Burrus (St. Louis, 1971), 393; Kino, "Relación Diara," 411–12; Bernard L. Fontana, *Of Earth and Little Rain: The Papago Indians* (Flagstaff, 1981), 33–35; T. J. Ferguson and Chip Colwell-Chanthaphonh, *History Is in the Land: Multivocal Tribal Traditions in Arizona's San Pedro Valley* (Tucson, 2006), 54–56, 62; Seymour, *Where the Earth and Sky Are Sewn Together*, 47, 80, 127, 284, 294; Radding, *Wandering Peoples*, 154; Wells, *From Hohokam to O'odham*, 8; Luis Navarro Garcia, *Sonora y Sinaloa en el Siglo XVII* (Sevilla, 1967), 253; Webb, *A Pima Remembers*, 22, 53, 71; Dale S. Brenneman, "Bringing O'odham into the 'Pimería Alta': Introduction," *Journal of the Southwest* 56 (2014), 205–7; Edward H. Spicer, *Cycles of Conquest: The Impact of Spain, Mexico, and the United States on the Indians of the Southwest, 1533–1960* (Tucson, 1962), 119; Saxton, Saxton, and Enos, *Dictionary: Papago/Pima-English*, 3, 21, 59; David Martínez, "Hiding in the Shadows of History: Revitalizing Hia-Ced O'odham Peoplehood," *Journal of the Southwest* 55 (2013), 132, 147–49; David Rich Lewis, *Neither Wolf nor Dog: American Indians, Environment, and Agrarian Change* (New York, 1994), 120–23, Seth Schermerhorn, *Walking to Magdalena: Personhood and Place in Tohono O'odham Songs, Sticks, and Stories* (Lincoln, 2019), 3. On Europeans struggling to name Native ways of living, see Michael Witgen, *An Infinity of Nations: How the Native New World Shaped Early North America* (Philadelphia, 2013), 19–20, 27.

5. Erickson, *Sharing the Desert*, 8–10; Papago Tribe of Arizona, *Tohono O'odham: History of the Desert People* (Tohono O'odham, Ariz., 1985), 4; Fontana, *Of Earth and Little Rain*, 37–38.

6. In current O'odham orthography, pim means "not" and maic, or mahch, means "to know." Brenneman, "Bringing O'odham into the 'Pimería Alta,'" 216n3; Saxton, Saxton, and Enos, *Dictionary: Papago/Pima-English*, 50, 72, 81, 90, 108; Michael Wilcox, "Marketing Conquest and the Vanishing Indian: An Indigenous Response to Jared Diamond's Archaeology of the American Southwest," in *Questioning Collapse: Human Resilience, Ecological Vulnerability and the Aftermath of Empire*, ed. Patricia A. McAnany and Norman Yoffee (New York, 2010), 116–17; Luis Xavier Velarde, "Descripción del sitio, longitud y latitud de las naciones y sus adyacentes septentrionales y seno Californio y otras noticias y observaciones, por el R. Padre Luis Velarde, de la Compañía de Jesús, rector y ministro de dicha Pimería," in appendix, *Kino and Manje*, 622, 641; Ruth M. Underhill, *A Papago Calendar Record* (Albuquerque, 1938), 5; Underhill, *Papago Woman*, 3; Juan Mateo Manje, "Viaje que hicieron los reverendos Padres visitador Antonio Leal, Eusebio Francisco Kino y Francisco Gonzalvo," in appendix, *Kino and Manje*, 453.

7. The Spanish divided the region into Pímeria Alta and Pímeria Baja, but the O'odham define themselves more locally by kinship, community, and economy. For today's districts within the Tohono O'odham Nation, see http://www.tonation-nsn.gov/districts/.

8. Velarde, "Descripción," 647, 649; Daniel K. Richter, *Before the Revolution: America's Ancient Pasts* (Cambridge, Mass., 2011), 31; Steven A. LeBlanc and Glen E. Rice, "Southwestern Warfare: The Value of Case Studies," in *Deadly Landscapes: Case Studies in Prehistoric Southwestern Warfare*, ed. Glen E. Rice and Steven A. LeBlanc (Salt Lake City, 2001), 14; Scott M. Kwiatkowski, "Evidence for Subsistence Problems," in *Centuries of Decline During the Hohokam Classic Period at Pueblo Grande*, ed. David R. Abbott (Tucson, 2016), 59; Chris Loendorf, *Hohokam-Akimel O'odham Continuum: Sociocultural Dynamics and Projectile Point Design in the Phoenix Basin, Arizona* (Tucson, 2013), 5–6, 130–32.

9. Kino, "Favores Celestiales," 24, 58–59, 131, 148; Kino, "Relación Diara," 411–12; Manje, Feb. 21, 1699, "Relación itineraria diaria que hice con los reverendos Padres Eusebio Francisco Kino y Adamo Gilg," 393; Luis Xavier Velarde, "Descripción," 1716, in Appendix, *Kino and Manje*, 642–43, 646; Pfefferkorn, *Sonora*, 57, 192; Tohono O'odham Community Action, with Mary Paganelli Votto and Frances Manuel, *From I'itoi's Garden: Tohono O'odham Food Traditions* (Tohono O'odham Community, 2010), 228–29, 232–40; Underhill, *Papago Woman*, 34–35; Underhill, *Social Organization*, 102–3; George Webb, *A Pima Remembers*, 16, 20; "'House of the Ancestors': Cultural Heritage" brochure, Huhugam Ki Museum, Salt River Pima-Maricopa Indian Community; "Woven Through Time" exhibit, Arizona State Museum, Tucson; Loendorf, *Hohokam-Akimel O'odham Continuum*; Ferguson and Colwell-Chanthaphonh, *History Is in the Land*, 54–56; Seymour, *Where the Earth and Sky Are Sewn Together*, 47, 97–98; Radding, *Wandering Peoples*, 154; E. Christian Wells, *From Hohokam to O'odham: The Protohistoric Occupation of the Middle Gila River Valley, Central Arizona* (Sacaton, Ariz., 2006), 8; Hurt, *Indian Agriculture in America*, 42–43.

10. TOCA, Votto, and Manuel, *From I'itoi's Garden*, 72, 150–76; Richard S. Felger and Gary Paul Nabhan, "Deceptive Barrenness," *Ceres* (1976), 34–37; Ferguson and Colwell-Chanthaphonh, *History Is in the Land*, 70; Edward F. Castetter and Willis H. Bell, *Pima and Papago Indian Agriculture* (Albuquerque, 1942), 63; Erickson, *Sharing the Desert*, 10; Manje, Feb. 22, 1699, "Relación itineraria diaria que hice con los reverendos Padres Eusebio Francisco Kino y Adamo Gilg," 394; Pfefferkorn, *Sonora*, 71; *Kiowa Recipes* (1934; Excelsior, Minn., 1985), 3; Hatley, "Cherokee Women Farmers Hold Their Ground," 39.

11. Ruth Murray Underhill, *Social Organization of the Papago Indians* (1939; repr. New York, 1969), 57, 70, 91; Underhill, *Papago Woman*, 9, 39; Wild Horse Pass exhibits, Gila River Indian Community; TOCA, Votto, and Manuel, *From I'itoi's Garden*, 252–62. See also Rebecca Crocker, "Healing on the Edge: The Construction of Medicine on the Jesuit Frontier of Northern New Spain," *Journal of the Southwest* 56 (2014), 293–318.

12. Tohono O'odham Nation Cultural Center and Museum exhibit; Kino, "Favores Celestiales," 314–15; Underhill, *Papago Woman*, 18–19, 39–40, 67, 69, 73, 78, 98–99; Underhill, *Social Organization*, 124–25; TOCA, Votto, and Manuel, *From I'itoi's Garden*, 68–87; Ferguson and Colwell-Chanthaphonh, *History Is in the Land*, 88.

13. TOCA, Votto, and Manuel, *From I'itoi's Garden*, 104, 106–7, 112–13, 116; Underhill, *Papago Woman*, 17, 22, 40, 97–98; Radding, *Wandering Peoples*, 58–59; Ruth M. Un-

derhill, Donald M. Bahr, Baptisto Lopez, Jose Pancho, and David Lopez, *Rainhouse and Ocean: Speeches for the Papago Year* (Flagstaff, 1979), 21–22.

14. Ofelia Zepeda, *Ocean Power: Poems from the Desert* (Tucson, 1995), 87; Felger and Nabhan, "Deceptive Barrenness," 36; Erickson, *Sharing the Desert,* 4–5.

15. TOCA, Votto, and Manuel, *From I'itoi's Garden,* 104–5, 118–21, 126–27, 329; Underhill, *Papago Calendar Record,* 7.

16. TOCA, Votto, and Manuel, *From I'itoi's Garden,* 8, 16, 21–23, 277–78, 355–57; Underhill, *Social Organization,* 94; Underhill, *Papago Woman,* 23–27, 40, 52–53, 94; Underhill, Bahr, B. Lopez, Pancho, and D. Lopez, *Rainhouse and Ocean,* 17, 24; Zepeda, "Wind," in *Ocean Power,* 17; Cory Dale Breternitz, et al., "Archaeology of the Ak-Chin Indian Community West Side Farms Project," prepared for the Ak-Chin Indian Community, vol. 3 of *Soil Systems Publications in Archaeology* (1986–1990); Castetter and Bell, *Pima and Papago Indian Agriculture,* 48; Tohono O'odham Nation Cultural Center and Museum exhibit; Erickson, *Sharing the Desert,* 11; Gary Paul Nabhan, *The Desert Smells Like Rain: A Naturalist in O'odham Country* (Tucson, 1982), 5, 41–45.

17. TOCA, Votto, and Manuel, *From I'itoi's Garden,* 316–18, 321–31, 337; Felger and Nabhan, "Deceptive Barrenness," 34, 38; Radding, *Wandering Peoples,* 48, 55, 58.

18. Underhill, *Papago Woman,* 68.

19. Manje, Mar. 19, 1701, "Relación itineraria diaria del viaje que hice con los reverendos Padres rector Juan María de Salvatierra y Eusebio Francisco Kino," 475; Martínez, "Hiding in the Shadows of History," 157–59.

20. Juan Nentvig, *Descripción Geográfica de Sonora,* ed. Germán Viveros (México, 1971), 120; Martínez, "Hiding in the Shadows of History," 132, 140.

21. Indeed, an old spelling of their name was "Hiatit Ootam" or "Hi a tak o'otam." Martínez, "Hiding in the Shadows of History," 131, 144–49; Manje, Mar. 20, 1694, "Del Segundo viaje," 303.

22. Martínez, "Hiding in the Shadows of History," 144–45, 149, 157–59; Ferguson and Colwell-Chanthaphonh, *History Is in the Land,* 45, 82; Underhill, Bahr, B. Lopez, Pancho, and D. Lopez, *Rainhouse and Ocean,* 37; Himdag Ki Tohono O'odham Nation Cultural Center and Museum exhibit; Underhill, *Papago Indian Religion,* 211–42; J. Andrew Darling and Barnaby V. Lewis, "Songscapes and Calendar Sticks," in *The Hohokam Millennium,* ed. Suzanne K. Fish and Paul R. Fish (Santa Fe, 2007), 131–39.

23. Manje, Feb. 16, 1699, "Relación itineraria diaria que hice con los reverendos Padres Eusebio Francisco Kino y Adamo Gilg," 390; Martínez, "Hiding in the Shadows of History," 149; Kino, "Relación Diaria," 404; Kino, "Favores Celestiales," 108; Castetter and Bell, *Pima and Papago Indian Agriculture,* 48. I have standardized the spelling of Sonoyta, on the Río Sonoyta, which flows into the north end of the Gulf of California (which the Spanish call with various spellings, San Marcelo del Sonoyta or Sonoydag), and the Sobaipuri town of Sonoita, on Sonoita Creek, a tributary of the Santa Cruz River in present-day Arizona (which the Spanish call, variously, San Ignacio de Sonoita or Sonoitac).

24. Kino, "Favores Celestiales," 159; Manje, Feb. 7–Mar. 14, 1699, "Relación itineraria diaria que hice con los reverendos Padres Eusebio Francisco Kino y Adamo Gilg," 390–91; Kino, "Relación Diaria," 400; Manje, Mar. 18, 1701, "Relación itineraria

diaria del viaje que hice con los reverendos Padres rector Juan María de Salvatierra y Eusebio Francisco Kino," 474; Martínez, "Hiding in the Shadows of History," 134–35, 149; Bernard L. Fontana, "A Man in Arid Lands: The Piman Indians of the Sonoran Desert," in *Desert Biology: Special Topics on the Physical and Biological Aspects of Arid Regions,* ed. G. W. Brown Jr. (New York, 1974), 2:501–2; Underhill, *Social Organization,* 57, 91, 95.

25. Manje, Mar. 12, 1701, "Relación itineraria diaria del viaje que hice con los reverendos Padres rector Juan María de Salvatierra y Eusebio Francisco Kino," in appendix, *Kino and Manje,* 472–73; Erickson, *Sharing the Desert,* 4, 14; Martínez, "Hiding in the Shadows of History," 138–39.

26. Underhill, *Papago Woman,* 36–37, 52–53, 56, 64–65, 94.

27. Kino, "Favores Celestiales," 64 ("gente de muy distinto traje, semblante y lengua"); Ignaz Pfefferkorn, *Sonora: A Description of the Province,* 1794–95, ed. and trans. Theodore E. Treutlein (Albuquerque, 1949), 29; Paul H. Ezell and Bernard L. Fontana, "Plants Without Water: The Pima-Maricopa Experience," *Journal of the Southwest* 36 (1994), 315–16.

28. "History of Events Leading to the Salt River Pima-Maricopa Indian Community (SRPMIC)" brochure, Huhugam Ki Museum, Salt River Pima-Maricopa Indian Community; Anna Moore Shaw, *A Pima Past* (Tucson, 1974), 6; Webb, *A Pima Remembers,* 22–25; Natale A. Zappia, *Traders and Raiders: The Indigenous World of the Colorado Basin, 1540–1859* (Chapel Hill, 2014), 42–47, 56. Piipaash is the spelling in the orthography used by the Tohono O'odham Nation and the Salt River Pima-Maricopa Indian Community, while the orthography used by the Gila River Indian Community spells it Pee Posh. For more on O'odham orthographic systems, grammar, and pronunciation, see Ofelia Zepeda, *A Tohono O'odham Grammar* (Tucson, 1983).

29. "'House of the Ancestors': Cultural Heritage" brochure, Huhugam Ki Museum, Salt River Pima-Maricopa Indian Community; Wild Horse Pass exhibits, Gila River Indian Community; Kino, "Favores Celestiales," 103, 106; Kino, "Relación Diaria," 401; Paul H. Ezell and Bernard L. Fontana, "Plants Without Water: The Pima-Maricopa Experience," *Journal of the Southwest* 36 (1994), 318; Frank Russell, *The Pima Indians* (Washington, D.C., 1908), 196.

30. Peter Gerhard, *The North Frontier of New Spain,* rev. ed. (1982; Norman, 1993), 281; Hurt, *Indian Agriculture in America,* 44. It's usually general histories that make these mistakes; historians who focus on this region tend to figure out the shallowness of Kino's claims.

31. "History of Events Leading to the Salt River Pima-Maricopa Indian Community (SRPMIC)" brochure, Huhugam Ki Museum, Salt River Pima-Maricopa Indian Community. An official history of the Tohono O'odham similarly writes, "The traditional history of the Spanish 'conquest' of the New World describes how wherever the Spaniards found the Indians, they crushed native institutions and killed great numbers of Indians. This is an accurate portrayal of the Spanish-Indian experience in many places. In the Pimería Alta, however, events differ from this pattern." Papago Tribe of Arizona, *Tohono O'odham: History of the Desert People* (Tohono O'odham, Ariz., 1985), 8–14, 17.

32. Kino, "Favores Celestiales," 57, 95. On Native Californians' use of priests' bestowal of staffs and similar signs of leadership, see Steven W. Hackel, "The Staff of Leadership: Indian Authority in the Missions of Alta California," *William and Mary Quarterly* 54 (1997), 347–76.

33. "Fray Marcos de Niza, Relación (1539)," ed. Jerry R. Craddock, *Romance Philology* 53 (1999), 87–88, 90; Gerónimo de Zárate Salmerón, "Relaciones de todas las cosas que en el Nuevo-México se han visto y sabido, así por mar como por tierra, desde el año de 1538 hasta el de 1626," in *Documentos para Servir a la Historia del Nuevo México, 1538–1778* (Madrid, 1962), 169–71; Seymour, *Where the Earth and Sky Are Sewn Together*, 4, 42–43, 74, 127; Mark E. Harlan and Deni J. Seymour, "Sobaipuri O'odham and Mobile Group Relevance to Late Prehistoric Social Networks in the San Pedro Valley," in *Fierce and Indomitable: The Protohistoric Non-Pueblo World in the American Southwest*, ed. Deni J. Seymour (Salt Lake City, 2017), 172; Daniel T. Reff, "Anthropological Analysis of Exploration Texts: Cultural Discourse and the Ethnological Import of Fray Marcos de Niza's Journey to Cibola," *American Anthropologist* 93 (1991), 637, 640–43; George J. Undreiner, "Fray Marcos de Niza and His Journey to Cibola," *Americas* 3 (1947), 433; Erickson, *Sharing the Desert*, 21.

34. Carlos II, Royal Cédula, May 14, 1686, in Kino, *Las Misiones de Sonora*, 17; *The Laws of Burgos of 1512–1513: Royal Ordinance for the Good Government and Treatment of the Indians*, ed. and trans. Lesley Byrd Simpson (San Francisco, 1960), 45; Maurice S. Crandall, *These People Have Always Been a Republic: Indigenous Electorates in the U.S.-Mexico Borderlands, 1598–1912* (Chapel Hill, 2019), 7, 16–18; Radding, *Wandering Peoples*, 12.

35. Radding, *Wandering Peoples*, 25; Brian R. Hamnett, *A Concise History of Mexico*, 2nd ed. (New York, 2006), 105.

36. Kino to the Duchess of Aveiro, Dec. 15, 1683, Oct. 25, 1684, and Dec. 8, 1684 (two letters of that date), in *Kino Escribe a la Duquesa: Correspondencia del P. Eusebio Francisco Kino con la Duquesa de Aveiro*, ed. Ernest J. Burrus (Madrid, 1964), 228–29, 231, 277, 284–85, 289 (English translations available in *Kino Writes to the Duchess: Letters of Eusebio Francisco Kino, S.J., to the Duchess of Aveiro*, ed. and trans. Ernest J. Burrus [Rome and St. Louis, 1965]); Kessell, *Spain in the Southwest*, 130–34; Gerhard, *North Frontier of New Spain*, 292; Spicer, *Cycles of Conquest*, 123. For similar baptizing in a different place and time, see Michelle T. King, *Between Birth and Death: Female Infanticide in Nineteenth-Century China* (Palo Alto, 2014), 116–17.

37. Carlos II, Royal Cédula, May 14, 1686, in Kino, "Favores Celestiales," 17; Herbert Eugene Bolton, *Rim of Christendom: A Biography of Eusebio Francisco Kino, Pacific Coast Pioneer* (New York, 1936), 249–51; Spicer, *Cycles of Conquest*, 121, 126; Brandon Bayne, "Willy-Nilly Baptisms and *Chichimeca* Freedoms: Missionary Disputes, Indigenous Desires and the 1695 O'odham Revolt," *Journal of Early Modern History* 21 (2017), 15, 20.

38. Kino, "Favores Celestiales," 26, 342; Mission San Xavier del Bac exhibits.

39. Kino, *Kino's Biography of Francisco Javier Saeta*, 89; Kino, "Favores Celestiales," 19–20; Papago Tribe of Arizona, *Tohono O'odham*, 8; Lewis, *Neither Wolf nor Dog*, 134; Underhill, *Social Organization*, 102–3; Erickson, *Sharing the Desert*, 13–14; Seymour, *Where the Earth and Sky Are Sewn Together*, 9–11, 42.

40. Erickson, *Sharing the Desert*, 33–34.

41. Radding, *Wandering Peoples*, 282.

42. Geronimo, "Establishing Connections to Place," 222, 228; Manje, "Viaje que hicieron los reverendos Padres visitador Antonio Leal, Eusebio Francisco Kino y Francisco Gonzalvo," 453; Kino, "Favores Celestiales," 21, 23–26, 31–32; Kino, *Kino's Biography of Francisco Javier Saeta*, 46; Juan Mateo Manje, Nov. 24 and 26, 1697, "Del viaje que hice con el reverendo Padre Eusebio Francisco Kino y 22 soldados," in appendix, *Kino and Manje*, 348–49; Saxton, Saxton, and Enos, *Dictionary: Papago/Pima-English*, 138; Underhill, *Papago Woman*, 7; Kessell, "Peaceful Conquest in Southern Arizona," 73, 80; Smith, *Father Kino in Arizona*, 14n47; Seymour, *Where the Earth and Sky Are Sewn Together*, 55, 241; Erickson, *Sharing the Desert*, 31. These priests (Pedro de San Doval, Luys Pineli, Antonio Arias, and Juan de Castillegjo for Ímuris, Tubutama, Magdalena, and Cabórica) were soon withdrawn (or, in the case of Castillejo, perhaps never arrived). Agustin de Campos was sent in 1693, and then in 1694, three more were sent: Fernando Bayerca for the Magdalena River, Daniel Januske for Tubutama on the Altar River, and Francisco Javier Saeta downriver at Caborca. For more on Baicatcan, see https://www.archaeologysouthwest.org/2016/12/21/new-site-protection-acquisition-the-taylor-site/.

43. Juan Mateo Manje, Mar. 20, 1694, "Del Segundo viaje que hice con el R. P. Eusebio Francisco Kino, para el poniente, hasta el brazo del mar Californio y Pímico, con fin de hacer un barco para pasar el mar y descubrir la tierra incógnita de esta Septentrional América y las regiones y naciones de California, año 1694," in appendix, *Kino and Manje*, 303.

44. Pope Paul III, *Sublimus Dei*, May 29, 1537, www.papalencyclicals.net; Flint and Flint, *Documents of the Coronado Expedition*, 45, 59; John Charles Chasteen, *Born in Blood and Fire: A Concise History of Latin America*, 2nd ed. (New York, 2006), 56; Ian W. Record, *Big Sycamore Stands Alone: The Western Apaches, Aravaipa, and the Struggle for Place* (Norman, 2008), 38–42, 73–76; James F. Brooks, *Captives and Cousins: Slavery, Kinship, and Community in the Southwest Borderlands* (Chapel Hill, 2001). Spain would extend these regulations in the New Laws of 1542. Reséndez, *The Other Slavery*, 46–47, 70–75.

45. Pfefferkorn, *Sonora*, 146–47; Jack D. Forbes, *Apache, Navajo, and Spaniard*, 2nd ed. (Norman, 1994), 148–49, 190–209, 228.

46. Forbes, *Apache, Navajo, and Spaniard*, xvii; Jack D. Forbes, "Unknown Athapaskans: The Identification of the Jano, Jocome, Jumano, Manso, Suma, and Other Indian Tribes of the Southwest," *Ethnohistory* 6 (1959), 97–159; Paul Conrad, *The Apache Diaspora: Four Centuries of Displacement and Survival* (Philadelphia, 2021), 45–46, 89–92, 120–21; Karl Jacoby, *Shadows at Dawn: A Borderlands Massacre and the Violence of History* (New York, 2008), 20–23; Deni J. Seymour, "The Canutillo Complex: Evidence of Protohistoric Mobile Occupants in the Southern Southwest," *Kiva* 74 (2009), 421–46; Deni J. Seymour, "Jano and Jocome: Canutillo Complex," https://www.deni-seymour.com/; Saxton, Saxton, and Enos, *Dictionary: Papago/Pima-English*, 47.

47. Eusebio Francisco Kino, *Kino's Biography of Francisco Javier Saeta, S. J.*, trans. Charles W. Polzer, ed. Ernest J. Burrus (St. Louis, 1971), 132. Burris's volume includes Spanish and English versions. I have cited the Spanish and made my own translations; Radding, *Wandering Peoples*, 25; David J. Weber, *The Spanish Frontier in North America* (New Haven, 1992), 137; Colin G. Calloway, *One Vast Winter Count: The Native American West Before Lewis and Clark* (Lincoln, 2003), 181–82; Conrad, *Apache Diaspora*, 88.

48. Lucero Radonic, "The Mototícachi Massacre: Authorized Pimas and the Specter of the Insurrectionary Indian," *Journal of the Southwest* 56 (2014), 253–68.

49. Manje, Mar. 16–Apr. 4, 1694, "Del Segundo viaje," 313–15; Spicer, *Cycles of Conquest,* 124; Bayne, "Willy-Nilly Baptisms," 28–29; Radding, *Wandering Peoples,* 281–62.

50. Manje, Feb. 22, 1699, "Relación itineraria diaria que hice con los reverendos Padres Eusebio Francisco Kino y Adamo Gilg," 394; Erickson, *Sharing the Desert,* 34, 48.

51. Radding, *Wandering Peoples,* 282.

52. Saxton, Saxton, and Enos, *Dictionary: Papago/Pima-English,* 47; Radding, *Wandering Peoples,* 24.

53. Hamnett, *Concise History of Mexico,* 104.

54. Juan Mateo Manje, "Diario del tercer viaje que, para el poniente, hice con el reverendo Padre Francisco Kino, jesuita, y 15 indios sirvientes, a fin de proseguir la fábrica del barco y descubrir las demás rancherías de la nación pima; desde 6 hasta 26 de junio de 1694 años," June 6–26, 1694, in appendix, *Kino and Manje,* 313–14 ("les han hecho extraordinarios castigos," "en Cabeza y costados," "por haber comido un pedazo del trigo del Padre"); Kino, *Kino's Biography of Francisco Javier Saeta,* 80, 84–87; Bayne, "Willy-Nilly Baptisms," 21–23, 28–29, 33–35; Juan Fernández de la Fuente, journal, June 7–Oct. 3, 1695, in *The Presidio and Militia on the Northern Frontier of New Spain: A Documentary History,* ed. Thomas H. Naylor and Charles W. Polzer (Tucson, 1986), 1:677–86 ("por quitarse de vexaciones de extrañeros").

55. Kino, *Kino's Biography of Francisco Javier Saeta,* 88–92; Kino, "Favores Celestiales," 38–39; Bayne, "Willy-Nilly Baptisms," 11–13; Radding, *Wandering Peoples,* 282.

56. Kino, "Favores Celestiales," 40; Kino, *Kino's Biography of Francisco Javier Saeta,* 136–40; Bayne, "Willy-Nilly Baptisms," 13; Radding, *Wandering Peoples,* 283.

57. "De paz y sin armas": Kino, *Kino's Biography of Francisco Javier Saeta,* 132; Fernández de la Fuente, journal, 1:616, 618.

58. Kino, *Kino's Biography of Francisco Javier Saeta,* 134–36; Fernández de la Fuente, journal, 1:636; Tohono O'odham Nation Cultural Center and Museum; Bayne, "Willy-Nilly Baptisms," 13; Erickson, *Sharing the Desert,* 29–30; Radding, *Wandering Peoples,* 283.

59. Kino, *Kino's Biography of Francisco Javier Saeta,* 136–38; Bayne, "Willy-Nilly Baptisms," 13, 30; Kino, "Favores Celestiales," 40–41.

60. Fernández de la Fuente, journal, June 7, 1695, in *Presidio and Militia on the Northern Frontier of New Spain,* 1:585–86, 623, 628. This collection includes a Spanish transcription and an excellent English translation, which I use.

61. Fernández de la Fuente, journal, July 16, 1695, 1:597; Kino, *Kino's Biography of Francisco Javier Saeta,* 142–44.

62. Fernández de la Fuente, journal, July–August, 1695, 1:599, 605–6, 627; Kino, "Favores Celestiales," 43–44; Kino, *Kino's Biography of Francisco Javier Saeta,* 140, 142–44; Fernandez de la Fuente, journal, Aug. 14, 1695, 1:622, 628.

63. Kino, *Kino's Biography of Francisco Javier Saeta,* 94.

64. Kino, "Favores Celestiales," 52, 55; Erickson, *Sharing the Desert,* 13; Calloway, *One Vast Winter Count,* 183–84; Underhill, *Social Organization,* 23; Forbes, *Apache, Navajo, and Spaniard,* 247–49, 261, 277–78. This priest was Father Pedro Ruis de Contreras for Cocóspera.

65. Juan Mateo Manje, Nov. 2–Dec. 2, 1697, "Relación de la entrade que hize con el Padre Eusebio Francisco Kino y con 22 soldados, est año 1697," in appendix, *Kino and Manje*, 366; Lieutenant Cristóbal Martín Bernal, diary, Nov. 1697, trans. Fay Jackson Smith, in *Father Kino in Arizona*, 39–40.

66. Manje, Nov. 1697, "Del viaje que hice con el reverendo Padre Eusebio Francisco Kino y 22 soldados," 334, 338, 344; Kino, "Favores Celestiales," 55–58, 316; Bolton, *Rim of Christendom*, 357; Spicer, *Cycles of Conquest*, 126; Kessell, "Peaceful Conquest in Southern Arizona," 68; Bernal, diary, Nov. 1697, 41.

67. Kino, "Favores Celestiales," 57–58, 103; Bernal, diary, Nov. 1697, 36–40; Manje, Nov. 1697, "Del viaje que hice con el reverendo Padre Eusebio Francisco Kino y 22 soldados," 336–38.

68. Manje, Nov. 13 or 14, 1697, "Del viaje que hice con el reverendo Padre Eusebio Francisco Kino y 22 soldados," 339.

69. Manje, Nov. 15, 1697, "Del viaje que hice con el reverendo Padre Eusebio Francisco Kino y 22 soldados," 340.

70. Bernal, Diary, Nov. 1697, 36–38.

71. Eusebio Francisco Kino, "The Remarkable Victory Which the Pima-Sobaípuris Have Won Against the Enemies of the Province of Sonora," May 3, 1698, trans. Fay Jackson Smith, in *Father Kino in Arizona*, 49; Manje, Nov. 1697, "Del viaje que hice con el reverendo Padre Eusebio Francisco Kino y 22 soldados," 338.

72. Kino, "Favores Celestiales," 94, 96–97, 290–92.

73. Kino, "Favores Celestiales," 99.

74. Frances Manuel and Deborah Neff, *Desert Indian Woman: Stories and Dreams* (Tucson, 2001), 107–9, 119–20; Schermerhorn, *Walking to Magdalena*, 6; Thomas E. Sheridan, *Landscapes of Fraud: Mission Tumacácori, the Baca Float, and the Betrayal of the O'odham* (Tucson, 2008), 75; Daniel T. Reff, "Sympathy for the Devil: Devil Sickness and Lore Among the Tohono O'odham," *Journal of the Southwest* 50 (2008), 356; Radding, *Wandering Peoples*, 297–98, 301–5; James S. Griffith, *Beliefs and Holy Places: A Spiritual Geography of the Pimería Alta* (Tucson, 1992), 76–78; Crandall, *These People Have Always Been a Republic*, 99–105; Spicer, *Cycles of Conquest*, 132.

75. Juan Mateo Manje, Feb. 18, 1694, "Itinerario, diario del descubrimiento que hicieron los RR. Padres Eusebio Francisco Kino y Marcos Antonio Kappus, jesuitas, y el alférez Juan Mateo Manje, teniente de alcalde mayor y capitán a guerra de la nación pima, hacia el poniente y cación soba y brazo de mar de California, desde 7 hasta 23 de febrero de este año de 1694," in appendix, *Kino and Manje*, 296–97; Kessell, "Peaceful Conquest in Southern Arizona," 62–63.

76. Underhill, *Papago Indian Religion*, 9–10; Webb, *A Pima Remembers*, 104–8.

77. William H. Doelle and Bernard Siquieros, foreword to J. Brett Hill, *From Huhugam to Hohokam: Heritage and Archaeology in the American Southwest* (Lanham, Md., 2019), xii; Cynthia Radding, *Landscapes of Power and Identity: Comparative Histories in the Sonoran Desert and the Forests of Amazonia from Colony to Republic* (Durham, 2005), 204–10, 227–28; Reff, "Sympathy for the Devil," 355–76; Schermerhorn, *Walking to Magdalena*, 6; David L. Kozak and David I. Lopez, *Devil Sickness and Devil Songs: Tohono O'odham Poetics* (Washington, D.C., 1999), 3–4.

78. Kino, "Favores Celestiales," 316–17.

79. Kino, "Favores Celestiales."

80. Bernal, diary, Nov. 1697, 46; Erickson, *Sharing the Desert*, 24–25.

81. Kino, "Favores Celestiales," 59–60.

82. The Tohono O'odham were from Coati and Sibuoidag, north of today's town of Sells in the Tohono O'odham nation. The attack was at Gaybanipitea, also called Santa Cruz de Cuervo. Kino, "Relación Diaria," 402; Eusebio Francisco Kino, "The Remarkable Victory Which the Pima-Sobaípuris Have Won Against the Enemies of the Province of Sonora," May 3, 1698, trans. Smith, 47–49; Kino, "Favores Celestiales," 62; Deni J. Seymour, *A Fateful Day in 1698: The Remarkable Sobaipuri-O'odham Victory over the Apaches and Their Allies* (Salt Lake City, 2014); Erickson, *Sharing the Desert*, 32; Seymour, *Where the Earth and Sky Are Sewn Together*, 59.

83. In 1705, some of them moved back to the San Pedro to rebuild, but by the 1760s they had returned to the Santa Cruz permanently. Kino, "Favores Celestiales," 95; Kino, "Relación Diaria," 399; Manje, Mar. 7, 1699, "Relación itineraria diaria que hice con los reverendos Padres Eusebio Francisco Kino y Adamo Gilg," 402; Manje, Mar. 7, 1699, "Relación ytineraria del Nuevo descubrimiento," 415, 430–31; Ferguson and Colwell-Chanthaphonh, *History Is in the Land*, 84; Seymour, *Where the Earth and Sky Are Sewn Together*, 286, 289; Erickson, *Sharing the Desert*, 32; Record, *Big Sycamore Stands Alone*, 79.

84. Manje, Mar. 6, 1699, "Relación itineraria diaria que hice con los reverendos Padres Eusebio Francisco Kino y Adamo Gilg," 402; Manje, Mar. 6, 1699, "Relación ytineraria del Nuevo descubrimiento," 430; Kino, "Favores Celestiales," 74; Antonio Leal to Kino, Aug. 29, 1699, in Kino, "Favores Celestiales," 75.

85. Himdag Ki Tohono O'odham Nation Cultural Center and Museum exhibit; Spicer, *Cycles of Conquest*, 127; Radding, *Wandering Peoples*, 252; Calloway, *One Vast Winter Count*, 206.

86. Cristoval Granillo Salazar to Kino, Feb. 28, 1703, in Kino, "Favores Celestiales," 192; Kino, "Favores Celestiales," 190, 232; Underhill, *Social Organization*, 23.

87. Manje, "Itinerario, diario del descubrimiento que hicieron los RR. Padres Eusebio Francisco Kino y Marcos Antonio Kappus," 285.

88. Pfefferkorn, *Sonora*, 150–51.

89. Kino, "Relación Diaria," 399; Kino, "Favores Celestiales," 76; Manje, Mar. 7, 1699, "Relación itineraria diaria que hice con los reverendos Padres Eusebio Francisco Kino y Adamo Gilg," 402; Manje, Mar. 7, 1699, "Relación ytineraria del Nuevo descubrimiento," 430–31.

90. Manje, Oct. 29, 1699, "Viaje que hicieron los reverendos Padres visitador Antonio Leal, Eusebio Francisco Kino y Francisco Gonzalvo," 450–51.

91. Kino, "Favores Celestiales," 131.

92. Kino, "Favores Celestiales," 145–47.

93. Pfefferkorn, *Sonora*, 28, 30; Manje, Mar. 1694, "Del Segundo viaje," 302–3; Manje, Feb. 1699, "Relación itineraria diaria que hice con los reverendos Padres Eusebio Francisco Kino y Adamo Gilg," 390–91; Kino, "Favores Celestiales," 124; Hurt, *Indian Agriculture in America*, 43; Martínez, "Hiding in the Shadows of History," 136–37.

94. Kino, "Favores Celestiales," 59, 140, 142, 268, 302; Kessell, "Peaceful Conquest in Southern Arizona," 89–92; "Los Santos Ángeles de Guevavi," National Park Service, www.nps.gov/tuma/historyculture/guevavi.htm; Seymour, *Where the Earth and Sky Are Sewn Together*, 46, 52; John L. Kessell, *Mission of Sorrows: Jesuit Guevavi and the Pimas, 1691–1767* (Tucson, 1970), 49. These were Ignacio de Iturmendi, then Gerónimo Minutuli, at Tubutama; Gaspar de las Barillas, then Domingo Crescoli, at Caborca; Francisco Gonzalvo at Bac; and Juan de San Martin to serve Tumacácori and Guevavi.

95. Ginny Sphar, "Agustín de Campos," Tumacácori National Historical Park, National Park Service, https://www.nps.gov/tuma/learn/historyculture/agustin-de-campos.htm; Spicer, *Cycles of Conquest*, 128–29; Kessell, "Peaceful Conquest in Southern Arizona," 92–95; Kessell, *Mission of Sorrows*, chap. 3; Ginny Sphar, "History and Culture," Tumacácori National Historical Park, https://www.nps.gov/tuma/learn/historyculture/. Kino's replacement at Cosari was Luis Xavier Velarde. The new priests who didn't last long in Sobaipuri country were Johann Baptist Grazhoffer and Felipe Segesser. Ignacio Xavier Keller remained to serve Suamca, Guevavi, and Bac. The priests in Himuri country were Gaspar Stiger, as Campos's replacement at Cabórica, Jacobo Sedelmayr, and Joseph Garrucho.

96. Radding, *Wandering Peoples*, 252, 285–86; Erickson, *Sharing the Desert*, 39; Kessell, *Mission of Sorrows*, chap. 3.

97. Radding, *Wandering Peoples*, 267; Martínez, "Hiding in the Shadows of History," 140; Juan Nentvig, *Rudo Ensayo: A Description of Sonora and Arizona in 1764*, translated, clarified, and annotated by Alberto Francisco Pradeau and Robert R. Rasmussen (Tucson, 1980), 71n12; Erickson, *Sharing the Desert*, 40–46; Pfefferkorn, *Sonora*, 259; Sheridan, *Landscapes of Fraud*, 43–49.

98. Pfefferkorn, *Sonora*, 212–20, 254–55.

99. Erickson, *Sharing the Desert*, 34–37, 50; Gerhard, *North Frontier of New Spain*, 283; Sphar, "Agustín de Campos."

100. Kino, "Favores Celestiales," 121–22, 131–33; Velarde, "Descripción," 627; Castetter and Bell, *Pima and Papago Indian Agriculture*, 8; Seymour, *Where the Earth and Sky Are Sewn Together*, 285–89; Ferguson and Colwell-Chanthaphonh, *History Is in the Land*, 81; Kessell, *Spain in the Southwest*, 230; Radding, *Wandering Peoples*, 155.

101. Bernard L. Fontana, report before the Indian Claims Commission, published in William H. Kelly and Bernard L. Fontana, *Papago Indians III* (New York, 1974), 165 (p. 10 of Fontana report); Ferguson and Colwell-Chanthaphonh, *History Is in the Land*, 61; Pfefferkorn, *Sonora*, 262; Underhill, *Social Organization*, 17; Erickson, *Sharing the Desert*, 50–51; Kenneth D. Madsen, "A Basis for Bordering: Land, Migration, and Inter-Tohono O'odham Distinction Along the US-Mexico Line," in *Placing the Border in Everyday Life*, ed. Reece Jones and Corey Johnson (New York, 2014), 102–3.

102. "Statement of Don Agustin de Vildosola," 1735, in Donald Rowland, "The Sonora Frontier of New Spain, 1735–1745," *New Spain and the Anglo-American West*, ed. George P. Hammond (1932; New York, 1969), 1:155; Hamnett, *Concise History of Mexico*, 107; Radding, *Wandering Peoples*, 267, 283; Conrad, *Apache Diaspora*, 109, 117, 120–23; Paul W. Mapp, *The Elusive West and the Contest for Empire, 1713–1763* (Chapel Hill, 2011), 48.

103. Underhill, *Social Organization,* 26; Pfefferkorn, *Sonora,* 265, 285.

104. Radding, *Wandering Peoples,* 153, 253.

105. Elizabeth A. H. John, *Storms Brewed in Other Men's Worlds: The Confrontation of Indians, Spanish, and French in the Southwest, 1540–1795* (Norman, 1996), 388, 499, 569–70.

106. Shaw, *A Pima Past,* 5–6; Papago Tribe of Arizona, *Tohono O'odham,* 12.

107. Wells, *From Hohokam to O'odham,* 10; Record, *Big Sycamore Stands Alone,* 43; Gerhard, *North Frontier of New Spain,* 284; Erickson, *Sharing the Desert,* 47; Kessell, "Peaceful Conquest in Southern Arizona," 55.

108. Reff, "Sympathy for the Devil," 356; Manuel and Neff, *Desert Indian Woman,* 182; Griffith, *Beliefs and Holy Places,* xiv, 34, 44; Nick Phillips, "Pilgrims Have Many Motives to Trek to Magdalena," Oct. 4, 2019, *Nogales International,* https://www .nogalesinternational.com/news/pilgrims-have-many-motives-to-trek-to -magdalena/article_855feaoc-e6co-11e9-8ace-9fdao4bc9820.html; Kendal Blust, "'Nothing Will Deter' Catholic Pilgrims Walking to Magdalena, Mexico," Oct. 4, 2018, Arizona Public Media, https://www.azpm.org/p/home-articles-news/2018/10 /4/138397-nothing-will-deter-catholic-pilgrims-walking-to-magdalena-mexico/.

109. Webb, *A Pima Remembers,* 17, 64–65.

CHAPTER 6: QUAPAW DIPLOMACY

1. This chapter draws on my book *The Native Ground: Indians and Colonists in the Heart of the Continent* (Philadelphia, 2006), especially chap. 3, and owes a great deal to Morris S. Arnold, *The Rumble of a Distant Drum: The Quapaws and Old World Newcomers, 1673–1804* (Fayetteville, Ark., 2000); W. David Baird, *The Quapaw Indians: A History of the Downstream People* (Norman, 1980); several articles by Joseph Key cited in these notes, including "The Calumet and the Cross: Religious Encounters in the Lower Mississippi Valley," *Arkansas Historical Quarterly* 61 (2002), 152–68; and most of all to the Quapaw people, especially Everett Bandy, John Berrey, Carrie V. Wilson, Risë Supernaw Proctor, and Billy Joe Proctor.

2. "Welcome to Ogapah," Quapaw Nation, http://www.quapawtribe.com/; conversation with Carrie V. Wilson, Feb. 2017; multiple conversations with Everett Bandy; Marisa Miakonda Cummings, "An Umonhon Perspective," in *Medieval Mississippians: The Cahokian World,* ed. Timothy R. Pauketat and Susan M. Alt (Santa Fe, 2015), 43–44; Timothy R. Pauketat, *Cahokia: Ancient America's Great City on the Mississippi* (New York, 2009), 37–38, 158; Jacques de la Métairie, "Procèsverbal de cette prise de possession au pays des Akansas," Mar. 13 and 14, 1682, *Découvertes et établissements des Français dans l'ouest et dans le sud de l'Amérique Septentrionale, 1614–1698, mémoires et documents inédits,* ed. Pierre Margry (New York: AMS Press, 1974), 2:189; John Joseph Mathews, *The Osages, Children of the Middle Waters* (Norman, 1961), 171.

3. Joseph P. Key, "An Environmental History of the Quapaws, 1673–1803," *Arkansas Historical Quarterly* 79 (2020), 297–316.

4. Christina Snyder, *Slavery in Indian Country: The Changing Face of Captivity in Early America* (Cambridge, Mass., 2010), 46–79; Alan Gallay, *The Indian Slavery Trade: The Rise of the English Empire in the American South, 1670–1717* (New Haven, 2003); Robin Beck, *Chiefdoms, Collapse, and Coalescence in the Early American South* (New York, 2013), 124, 134–36.

5. David J. Silverman, *Thundersticks: Firearms and the Violent Transformation of Native America* (Cambridge, Mass., 2016), 57–58.

6. Jacques Marquette, *Recit des Voyages et des Decouvertes du R. Père Jacques Marquette de la Compagnie de Jesus, en l'année 1673 et aux Suivantes* (Albany, 1855), 81–87.

7. Marquette, *Recit des Voyages,* 84.

8. R. P. Louis Hennepin, *Description de la Louisiane, nouvellement découverte au sud'oüest de la nouvelle France* (Paris, 1683), 180–81.

9. Jacob F. Lee, *Masters of the Middle Waters: Indian Nations and Colonial Ambitions Along the Mississippi* (Cambridge, Mass., 2019), 5, 27; Donald J. Blakeslee, "The Origin and Spread of the Calumet Ceremony," *American Antiquity* 46 (1981), 759–68; Ian W. Brown, "The Calumet Ceremony in the Southeast as Observed Archaeologically," in *Powhatan's Mantle: Indians in the Colonial Southeast,* ed. Gregory A. Waselkov, Peter H. Wood, and M. Thomas Hatley, rev. ed. (Lincoln, 2006), 371–420; Tracy Neal Leavelle, *The Catholic Calumet: Colonial Conversions in French and Indian North America* (Philadelphia, 2011).

10. Métairie, "Procès-verbal," 2:183–84.

11. Métairie, "Procès-verbal," 2:189.

12. Minet, journal, 30. For Quapaw-Koroa fighting, see, e.g., Jean-Baptiste Le Moyne, Sieur de Bienville, to Jérôme de Pontchartrain, Sept. 6, 1704, *Mississippi Provincial Archives: French Dominion,* ed. and trans. Dunbar Rowland and A. G. Sanders (vols. 1–3 Jackson, 1927; vols. 4–5 ed. Patricia Kay Galloway, Baton Rouge, 1984) 3:22–23.

13. Jean-Baptiste Bénard de La Harpe, Mar. 1, 1722, *Journal historique de l'établissement des Francais à la Louisiane* (Paris, 1831), 313; George Izard, Jan. 10, 1827, "A Report on the Quapaw: The Letters of Governor George Izard to the American Philosophical Society, 1825–1827," ed. David W. Bizzell, *Pulaski County Historical Review* 29 (1981), 27.

14. Etienne Veniard de Bourgmont, "Etienne Veniard De Bourgmont's 'Exact Description of Louisiana,'" c. 1714, trans. Mrs. Max W. Myer, ed. Marcel Giraud, *Missouri Historical Society Bulletin* 15 (1958), 13.

15. Nancy Shoemaker, *A Strange Likeness: Becoming Red and White in Eighteenth-Century North America* (New York, 2004), 40, 43.

16. Antoin E. Murphy, *John Law: Economic Theorist and Policy-maker* (Oxford, 1997), 128–30, 165, 188, 213–15, 308–11; Paul Du Poisson to Louis Patouillet, 1726, *The Jesuit Relations and Allied Documents: Travels and Explorations of the Jesuit Missionaries in New France, 1610–1791,* ed. Reuben Gold Thwaites (New York, 1959), 67:259–61; Bienville, order, Nov. 26, 1721, fol. 148, roll 9, C13A6, Louisiana Colonial Records Project, Historic New Orleans Collection, New Orleans, microfilmed from the Archives Nationales Colonies, Paris; Bienville, order, Dec. 12, 1721, fol. 148, roll 9, C13A6, Louisiana Colonial Records Project.

17. Many thanks to Everett Bandy for sharing his research on seventeenth- and early-eighteenth-century Quapaw towns.

18. O-zo-ti-o-we (ozó ttiowé), Quapaw Tribal Ancestry website, "Quapaw Dictionary," http://www.quapawtribalancestry.com/quapawdictionary/05.htm.

19. See, e.g., James H. Merrell, *The Indians' New World: Catawbas and Their Neighbors from European Contact Through the Era of Removal* (New York, 1989).

20. Antoine Simon Le Page Du Pratz, *Histoire de la Louisiane, Contenant la Décou-verte de ce vaste Pays* (Paris, 1758), 2:291; La Harpe, *Journal historique*, 313, 315–16.

21. Harry Gordon, "Journal of Captain Harry Gordon's Journey from Pittsburg down the Ohio and the Mississippi to New Orleans, Mobile, and Pensacola, 1766," *Travels in the American Colonies*, ed. Newton D. Mereness (New York, 1916), 480; Jean François Buisson de St. Cosme to the Bishop of Quebec, 1699, *Early Voyages Up and Down the Mississippi by Cavelier, St. Cosme, Le Sueur, Gravier, and Guignas*, ed. and trans. John Gilmary Shea (Albany, N.Y., 1861), 72.

22. Guedetonguay, speech, June 20, 1756, *Mississippi Provincial Archives: French Dominion*, 5:174.

23. La Harpe, *Journal historique*, 306–7, 313–14; Bernard Diron d'Artaguiette, journal, 1722–1723, *Travels in the American Colonies*, 56.

24. Diron d'Artaguiette to Jean Frédéric Phélypeaux, Count de Maurepas, Mar. 20, 1730, *Découvertes et établissements*, 1:76; Daniel H. Usner Jr., *American Indians in the Lower Mississippi Valley: Social and Economic Histories* (Lincoln, 1998), 15–32; Patricia Dillon Woods, *French-Indian Relations on the Southern Frontier, 1699–1762* (Ann Arbor, 1979), 73–74.

25. Étienne de Périer to Maurepas, roll 19, folio 300, C13A12, Louisiana Colonial Records Project; Périer to Philibert Ory, Dec. 18, 1730, *Mississippi Provincial Archives: French Dominion*, 4:39; Le Page Du Pratz, *Histoire de la Louisiane*, 3:255–57; James F. Barnett, *Natchez Indians: A History to 1735* (Jackson, 2007), 104–6.

26. Périer to Maurepas, Aug. 1, 1730, *Mississippi Provincial Archives: French Dominion*, 4:35; Périer to Maurepas, Dec. 10, 1731, *Mississippi Provincial Archives: French Dominion*, 4:104–5.

27. Mathurin Le Petit to Louis d'Avaugour, July 12, 1730, *Jesuit Relations*, 67:377; Watrin, "Banishment of the Jesuits from Louisiana," Sept. 3, 1764, *Jesuit Relations*, 70:247.

28. Pierre de Charlevoix, *Histoire et Description de la Nouvelle France* (Paris, 1744), 2:489–90; Périer, Mar. 25, 1731, "Governor Perier's Expedition Against the Natchez Indians," ed. and trans. John A. Green, *Louisiana Historical Quarterly* 19 (1936), 553; Le Page du Pratz, *Histoire de la Louisiane*, 3:267–76.

29. Périer to Maurepas, Apr. 10, 1730, *Mississippi Provincial Archives: French Dominion*, 1:121; Périer to Ory, Dec. 18, 1730, *Mississippi Provincial Archives: French Dominion*, 4:41; François de Marchand to Périer, abstract, Sept. 15, 1732, *Mississippi Provincial Archives: French Dominion*, 4:124; Périer to Maurepas, Jan. 25, 1733, *Mississippi Provincial Archives: French Dominion*, 1:167–68.

30. Bienville to Maurepas, Apr. 23, 1734, *Mississippi Provincial Archives: French Dominion*, 1:228; "Interconnectedness and Diversity in 'French Louisiana,'" in *Powhatan's Mantle*, 133–62.

31. Diron d'Artaguiette to Maurepas, Feb. 9, 1730, *Mississippi Provincial Archives: French Dominion*, 1:59; Jadart de Beauchamp to Maurepas, Nov. 5, 1731, *Mississippi Provincial Archives: French Dominion*, 4:81.

32. Périer to Ory, Dec. 18, 1730, *Mississippi Provincial Archives: French Dominion*, 4:41.

33. Le Page du Pratz, *Histoire de la Louisiane*, 3:403–5.

34. Wendy Cegielski and Brad R. Lieb, "*Hina' Falaa*, 'The Long Path': An Analysis of Chickasaw Settlement Using GIS in Northeast Mississippi, 1650–1840," *Native*

South 4 (2011), 32–34, 40; John W. Wright, "Notes on the Siege of Yorktown in 1781 with Special Reference to the Conduct of a Siege in the Eighteenth Century," *William and Mary Quarterly* 12 (1932), 231–35; Kathleen DuVal, *Independence Lost: Lives on the Edge of the American Revolution* (New York, 2015), 191–92.

35. Le Page du Pratz, *Histoire de la Louisiane*, 3:405–16, 419.

36. Bienville and Edme Gatien Salmon to Maurepas, Dec. 22, 1737, *Mississippi Provincial Archives: French Dominion*, 1:357–59.

37. Le Page du Pratz, *Histoire de la Louisiane*, 3:419–20.

38. Le Page du Pratz, *Histoire de la Louisiane*, 3:421–24; Salmon to Maurepas, May 4, 1740, *Mississippi Provincial Archives: French Dominion*, 1:441–45; Bienville to Maurepas, May 6, 1740, *Mississippi Provincial Archives: French Dominion*, 1:449–61; Daniel H. Usner Jr., *Indians, Settlers, and Slaves in a Frontier Exchange Economy: The Lower Mississippi Valley Before 1783* (Chapel Hill, 1992), 84.

39. Pierre François de Rigaud, Marquis de Vaudreuil, to Pierre Henri d'Erneville, Nov. 11, 1744, 3:144, LO 9, Vaudreuil Letterbook, Loudoun Collection, Huntington Library, San Marino, Calif.; Vaudreuil to Maurepas, Dec. 24, 1744, 1:44v, LO 9, Vaudreuil Letterbook; Vaudreuil to Maurepas, Mar. 15, 1747, LO 89, box 2, Vaudreuil Papers, Loudoun Collection; Vaudreuil to Maurepas, Nov. 5, 1748, LO 147, box 3, Vaudreuil Papers; Vaudreuil to Antoine Louis Rouillé, Sept. 22, 1749, LO 185, box 4, Vaudreuil Papers.

40. Silverman, *Thundersticks*, 16.

41. Sam Eveleigh to Herman Verelst, Oct. 16, 1736, *Colonial Records of the State of Georgia*, 21:214; Silverman, *Thundersticks*, 32, 85.

42. Paul Augustin Le Pelletier de La Houssaye to Vaudreuil, Dec. 1, 1752, box 8, LO 410, Vaudreuil Papers; Henri d'Orgon to Vaudreuil, Oct. 7, 1752, box 8, LO 399, Vaudreuil Papers.

43. Louis Billouart, Chevalier de Kerlérec, to Rouillé, Aug. 20, 1753, *Mississippi Provincial Archives: French Dominion*, 5:131.

44. "Harrangues faites dans l'assemblée tenue á l'hôtel du government cejourdhui," June 20, 1756, and Nicholas René Berryer to Louis de Kerlérec and Bobé Descl0-seaux, July 14, 1769, both quoted in Morris S. Arnold, *Colonial Arkansas, 1686–1804: A Social and Cultural History* (Fayetteville, Ark., 1991), 132–34.

45. D'Orgon to Vaudreuil, Oct. 7, 1752, LO 399, box 8, Vaudreuil Papers.

46. La Houssaye to Vaudreuil, Dec. 1, 1752, box 8, LO 410, Vaudreuil Papers.

47. Jean-Baptiste Bénard de la Harpe, "Relation du voyage de Bénard de la Harpe, découverte faite par lui de plusieurs nations situées a l'ouest," 1719, *Découvertes et établissements*, 6:289–93; George H. Odell, *La Harpe's Post: A Tale of French-Wichita Contact on the Eastern Plains* (Tuscaloosa, 2002).

48. La Harpe to the Directors of the Company of the Indies, Dec. 25, 1720, fol. 99, roll 9, C13A6, Louisiana Colonial Records Project.

49. La Harpe, *Journal historique*, 284.

50. La Harpe, *Journal historique*, 314–19; Jean-Baptiste Bénard de La Harpe, "Exploration of the Arkansas River by Benard de La Harpe, 1721–1722: Extracts from His Journal and Instructions," ed. and trans. Ralph A. Smith, *Arkansas Historical Quarterly* 10 (1951), 348–51.

51. Périer to Ory, Dec. 18, 1730, *Mississippi Provincial Archives: French Dominion*, 4:39–40.

52. Vaudreuil to Maurepas, Oct. 30, 1745, 1:65, LO 9, Vaudreuil Letterbook.

53. My 2006 book put too much faith in European observations of Quapaw numbers, but for what's it's worth, see DuVal, *Native Ground*, 78, 128, 190.

54. Philip Pittman, *The Present State of the European Settlements on the Mississippi* (London, 1770), 40; Kristen J. Gremillion, "Adoption of Old World Crops and Processes of Cultural Change in the Historic Southeast," *Southeastern Archaeology* 12 (1993), 15–20; John H. House, "Wallace Bottom: A Colonial-Era Archaeological Site in the Menard Locality, Eastern Arkansas," *Southeastern Archaeology* 21 (2002), 257–68.

55. Périer to La Chaise, Mar. 30, 1728, fol. 66, roll 17, C13A11, Louisiana Colonial Records Project.

56. Guedetonguay, speech, June 20, 1756, *Mississippi Provincial Archives: French Dominion*, 5:174.

57. Guedetonguay, speech, June 20, 1756, *Mississippi Provincial Archives: French Dominion*, 5:173–75.

58. Marc de Villiers du Terrage, *Les dernières années de la Louisiane française* (Paris, 1904), 30–38.

59. Villiers du Terrage, *Les dernières années de la Louisiane française*, 30–38.

60. Jean-Jacques-Blaise d'Abbadie, journal, in *A Comparative View of French Louisiana, 1699 and 1762: The Journals of Pierre Le Moyne d'Iberville and Jean-Jacques-Blaise d'Abbadie*, ed. and trans. Carl A. Brasseaux, rev. ed. (Lafayette, 1981), 122.

61. Vaudreuil to Rouillé, Comte de Jouy, Sept. 22, 1749, box 4, LO 185, Vaudreuil Papers.

62. Henry A. Gemery, "The White Population of the Colonial United States, 1607–1790," in *A Population History of the United States*, ed. Michael R. Haines and Richard H. Steckel (New York, 2000), 150; Elizabeth Ellis, "Dismantling the Dream of 'France's Peru': Indian and African Influence on the Development of Early Colonial Louisiana," *The World of Colonial America: An Atlantic Handbook*, ed. Ignacio Gallup-Diaz (New York, 2017), 355–72.

63. Vaudreuil, to Rouillé, Feb. 1, 1750, LO 203, box 5, Vaudreuil Papers.

64. Périer to Maurepas, Apr. 10, 1730, *Mississippi Provincial Archives: French Dominion*, 1:119, 121.

PART II: CONFRONTING SETTLER POWER, 1750 AND BEYOND

1. Francisco Cruzat to Esteban Miró, Aug. 23, 1784, in *Spain in the Mississippi Valley, 1765–1794*, ed. and trans. Lawrence Kinnaird (Washington, D.C., 1946–49), 2:117–19; John Shy, *A People Numerous and Armed: Reflections on the Military Struggle for American Independence*, rev. ed. (Ann Arbor, 1990), 4.

2. Emerson W. Baker and John G. Reid, "Amerindian Power in the Early Modern Northeast: A Reappraisal," *William and Mary Quarterly* 61 (2004), 77–106; Mary Beth Norton, *In the Devil's Snare: The Salem Witchcraft Crisis of 1692* (New York, 2002); Christopher Bilodeau, "The Economy of War: Violence, Religion, and the Wabanaki Indians in the Maine Borderlands" (Ph.D. diss., Cornell University,

2006); Colin G. Calloway, *The Indian World of George Washington: The First President, the First Americans, and the Birth of the Nation* (New York, 2018), 20–21, 31, 186.

3. David Andrew Nichols, *Red Gentlemen and White Savages: Indians, Federalists, and the Search for Order on the American Frontier* (Charlottesville, 2008), 199; Sarah Knott, *Mother Is a Verb: An Unconventional History* (New York, 2019), 12–13.

4. Brian DeLay, "Indian Polities, Empire, and the History of American Foreign Relations," *Diplomatic History* 39 (2015), 932–33.

5. Warren Eugene Milteer Jr., *North Carolina's Free People of Color, 1715–1885* (Baton Rouge, 2020); Warren E. Milteer Jr., "From Indians to Colored People: The Problem of Racial Categories and the Persistence of the Chowans in North Carolina," *North Carolina Historical Review* (2016), 39–40; Jean M. O'Brien, *Firsting and Lasting: Writing Indians Out of Existence in New England* (Minneapolis, 2010); Jack D. Forbes, *Africans and Native Americans: The Language of Race and the Evolution of Red-Black Peoples*, 2nd ed. (Urbana, 1993); Daniel R. Mandell, *Tribe, Race, History: Native Americans in Southern New England, 1780–1880* (Baltimore, 2011); Ruth Wallis Herndon and Ella Wilcox Sekatau, "The Right to a Name: The Narragansett People and Rhode Island Officials in the Revolutionary Era," Thomas L. Doughton, "Unseen Neighbors: Native Americans of Central Massachusetts, A People Who Had 'Vanished,'" and other chapters in the pathbreaking *After King Philip's War: Presence and Persistence in Indian New England*, ed. Colin G. Calloway (Hanover, N.H., 1997), 114–43, 207–30; Juliana Barr and Edward Countryman, eds., "Maps and Spaces, Paths to Connect, and Lines to Divide," in *Contested Spaces of Early America* (Philadelphia, 2014), 20.

6. For the two paragraphs on North Carolina, see Milteer, "From Indians to Colored People," 28–57; Patrick H. Garrow, *The Mattamuskeet Documents: A Study in Social History* (Raleigh, 1975), 17–29; Lawrence A. Dunmore III, foreword to *Excavating Occaneechi Town: Archaeology of an Eighteenth-Century Indian Village in North Carolina*, ed. R. P. Stephen Davis Jr., Patrick C. Livingood, H. Trawick Ward, and Vincas P. Steponaitis (web edition, 2003), https://eotonline.org; Roy S. Dickens Jr., H. Trawick Ward, and R. P. Stephen Davis Jr., "Archaeological Background," *Excavating Occaneechi Town;* H. Trawick Ward and R. P. Stephen Davis Jr., "Occaneechi Town: A Summary of Archaeological Findings," *Excavating Occaneechi Town;* Forest Hazel, "Occaneechi-Saponi Descendants in the Texas Community of the North Carolina Piedmont," *Excavating Occaneechi Town;* Occaneechi Band of the Saponi Nation, "A Brief History of the Occaneechi Band of the Saponi Nation," https://obsn.org/a-brief-history-of-the-occaneechi-band-of-the-saponi -nation/; Warren E. Milteer Jr., "Life in a Great Dismal Swamp Community: Free People of Color in Pre–Civil War Gates County, North Carolina," *North Carolina Historical Review* 91 (2014), 147–49, 153; Michael Leroy Oberg, *The Head in Edward Nugent's Hand: Roanoke's Forgotten Indians* (Philadelphia, 2008), 147–52; Bradley J. Dixon, "'His one Neteve ples': The Chowans and the Politics of Native Petitions in the Colonial South," *William and Mary Quarterly* 26 (2019), 41–74; Lars C. Adams, "'Sundry Murders and Depredations': A Closer Look at the Chowan River War, 1676–1677," *North Carolina Historical Review* 90 (2013), 149–72; Marvin T. Jones, "A Rebirth on the Chowan," in *We Will Always Be Here: Native Peoples on Living and Thriving in the South*, ed. Denise E. Bates (Gainesville, 2016), 57; Shoshone Peguese-Elmardi, "Speaking for My Ancestors," in *We Will Always Be*

Here, 61–65; Doug Patterson, "The Chowanoke Indian Resurgence," in *We Will Always Be Here,* 72–78; Kristalyn Marie Shefveland, *Anglo-Native Virginia: Trade, Conversion, and Indian Slavery in the Old Dominion, 1646–1722* (Athens, Ga., 2016); Robin Beck, *Chiefdoms, Collapse, and Coalescence in the Early American South* (New York, 2013), 144–46, 171–72; Marvin Richardson, "Find Your Path to Help Your People," Nov. 25, 2019, University of North Carolina, Chapel Hill, N.C.; Brooke M. Bauer, *Becoming Catawba: Catawba Indian Women and Nation-Building, 1540–1840* (Tuscaloosa, 2022); James H. Merrell, "'This Western World': The Evolution of the Piedmont, 1525–1725," *Excavating Occaneechi Town;* James H. Merrell, *The Indians' New World: Catawbas and Their Neighbors from European Contact Through the Era of Removal* (Chapel Hill, 1989); Malinda Maynor Lowery, *The Lumbee Indians: An American Struggle* (Chapel Hill, 2018), 64; Ryan E. Emanuel, "Water in the Lumbee World: A River and Its People in a Time of Change," *Environmental History* 24 (2019), 25–51.

7. Lawrence A. Dunmore III, foreword to *Excavating Occaneechi Town;* Dickens Jr., Ward, and Davis Jr., "Archaeological Background"; Ward and Davis Jr., "Occaneechi Town: A Summary of Archaeological Findings"; Hazel, "Occaneechi-Saponi Descendants in the Texas Community of the North Carolina Piedmont"; Occaneechi Band of the Saponi Nation, "A Brief History of the Occaneechi Band of the Saponi Nation"; Milteer Jr., "Life in a Great Dismal Swamp Community," 147–49, 153; Oberg, *The Head in Edward Nugent's Hand,* 147–52; Dixon, "'His one Neteve ples,'" 41–74; Adams, "Sundry Murders and Depredations," 149–72; Kristalyn Marie Shefveland, *Anglo-Native Virginia: Trade, Conversion, and Indian Slavery in the Old Dominion, 1646–1722* (Athens, Ga., 2016); Beck, *Chiefdoms, Collapse, and Coalescence in the Early American South,* 144–46, 171–72; Richardson, "Find Your Path to Help Your People"; Bauer, *Becoming Catawba;* Merrell, "'This Western World'"; Lowery, *The Lumbee Indians,* 64; Malinda Maynor Lowery, "On the Antebellum Fringe: Lumbee Indians, Slavery, and Removal," *Native South* 10 (2017), 44–46; Emanuel, "Water in the Lumbee World," 25–51.

8. Peter H. Wood, "The Changing Population of the Colonial South: An Overview by Race and Region, 1685–1790," *Powhatan's Mantle: Indians in the Colonial Southeast,* rev. ed. (Lincoln, 2006), 60; Steven C. Hahn, *The Invention of the Creek Nation, 1670–1763* (Lincoln, 2004); Robert A. Williams Jr., *Linking Arms Together: American Indian Treaty Visions of Law and Peace, 1600–1800* (New York, 1997), 24.

CHAPTER 7: SHAWNEE TOWNS AND FARMS IN THE OHIO VALLEY

1. David Jones, *A Journal of Two Visits Made to Some Nations of Indians on the West Side of the River Ohio, in the Years 1772 and 1773* (Burlington, 1774), 39–43; Susan Sleeper-Smith, *Indigenous Prosperity and American Conquest: Indian Women of the Ohio River Valley, 1690–1792* (Chapel Hill, 2018).

2. Katrina M. Phillips, *Staging Indigeneity: Salvage Tourism and the Performance of Native American History* (Chapel Hill, 2021), 133–81.

3. Shawnee Tribe Cultural Center, Miami, Okla., author visit, June 21, 2019; https://www.shawneeculture.org/exhibits/; Gordon M. Sayre, *The Indian Chief as Tragic Hero: Native Resistance and the Literatures of America, from Moctezuma to Tecumseh* (Chapel Hill, 2005). In contrast to the updated *Lost Colony,* the *Tecumseh!* outdoor drama still does not have Shawnee advisers. Benjamin J. Barnes, "Becoming Our

Own Storytellers: Tribal Nations Engaging with Academia," in *The Eastern Shawnee Tribe of Oklahoma: Resilience Through Adversity*, ed. Stephen Warren with the Eastern Shawnee Tribe of Oklahoma (Norman, 2017), 219.

4. Benjamin J. Barnes, "Collaborative Research in Ethnohistory" panel, American Society for Ethnohistory Annual Conference (remote), Nov. 7, 2020; Robert J. Miller, "Treaties Between the Eastern Shawnee Tribe and the United States: Contracts Between Sovereign Governments," in *Eastern Shawnee Tribe of Oklahoma*, 114.

5. Barnes, "Becoming Our Own Storytellers," 217.

6. Shawnee speech, 1803, in *Indian Biography, or, An Historical Account of Those Individuals Who Have Been Distinguished Among the North American Natives as Orators, Warriors, Statesmen, and Other Remarkable Characters*, ed. B. B. Thatcher (New York, 1832), 190.

7. Sami Lakomäki, *Gathering Together: The Shawnee People Through Diaspora and Nationhood, 1600–1870* (New Haven, 2014), 15–16, 22; Laura Keenan Spero, "'Stout, Bold, Cunning and the Greatest Travellers in America': The Colonial Shawnee Diaspora" (Ph.D. diss., University of Pennsylvania, 2010), 54–57.

8. Colin G. Calloway, *The Shawnees and the War for America* (New York, 2007), 11; Spero, "Stout, Bold, Cunning and the Greatest Travellers in America," 74–77; Alan Gallay, *The Indian Slave Trade: The Rise of the English Empire in the American South, 1670–1717* (New Haven, 2002), 55–57; Amy C. Schutt, *Peoples of the River Valleys: The Odyssey of the Delaware Indians* (Philadelphia, 2007), 3–4, 62–70; Peter C. Mancall, *Valley of Opportunity: Economic Culture Along the Upper Susquehanna, 1700–1800* (Ithaca, 1991), 31, 35–46.

9. Arthur C. Parker, *The Constitution of the Five Nations* (Albany, 1916), 10; Francis Jennings, *Ambiguous Iroquois Empire: The Covenant Chain Confederation of Indian Tribes with English Colonies from Its Beginnings to the Lancaster Treaty of 1744* (New York, 1984), 21–24, 94–96; Calloway, *Shawnees and the War for America*, 7–12; Michael N. McConnell, *A Country Between: The Upper Ohio Valley and Its Peoples, 1724–1774* (Lincoln, 1992), 14, 16, 22; Daniel K. Richter, *The Ordeal of the Longhouse: The Peoples of the Iroquois League in the Era of European Colonization* (Chapel Hill, 1992), 241–44; Spero, "Stout, Bold, Cunning and the Greatest Travellers in America," 108–16, 129–31, 227–30; Gunlög Fur, *A Nation of Women: Gender and Colonial Encounters Among the Delaware Indians* (Philadelphia, 2009), 160–98.

10. Christina Snyder, *Slavery in Indian Country: The Changing Face of Captivity in Early America* (Cambridge, Mass., 2010), 115–18; Gallay, *Indian Slave Trade*, 60–62, 73, 210–11; Lakomäki, *Gathering Together*, 56; Spero, "Stout, Bold, Cunning and the Greatest Travellers in America," 143–56, 173–76, 180, 195–200; James H. Merrell, *The Indians' New World: Catawbas and Their Neighbors from European Contact Through the Era of Removal* (New York, 1989), 118–19.

11. Stephen Warren, *Shawnees and Their Neighbors, 1795–1870* (Urbana, 2005), 15–16; Calloway, *Shawnees and the War for America*, xv, 5; Lakomäki, *Gathering Together*, 26–32; R. David Edmunds, *Tecumseh and the Quest for Indian Leadership* (Boston, 1984), 3; Stephen Warren and Randolph Noe, "The Greatest Travelers in America," in *Mapping the Mississippi Shatter Zone: The Colonial Indian Slave Trade and Regional Instability in the American South*, ed. Robbie Ethridge and Sheri M.

Shuck-Hall (Lincoln, 2009), 167–68; McConnell, *Country Between,* 27; Miller, "Treaties Between the Eastern Shawnee Tribe and the United States," 149.

12. Meadow / gëda;yë', "English-Seneca Dictionary," comp. Wallace Chafe, https://senecalanguage.com/wp-content/uploads/2014/04/SENECA-DICTIONARY-FINAL.pdf; "Native American Tribes of Kentucky," http://www.native-languages.org/kentucky.htm; Spero, "Stout, Bold, Cunning and the Greatest Travellers in America," 7–8, 10–15; Sleeper-Smith, *Indigenous Prosperity,* 215; Lakomäki, *Gathering Together,* 45; Calloway, *Shawnees and the War for America,* 15; Paul Conrad, *The Apache Diaspora: Four Centuries of Displacement and Survival* (Philadelphia, 2021), 2–3.

13. William L. Ramsey, *The Yamasee War: A Study of Culture, Economy, and Conflict in the Colonial South* (Lincoln, 2008), 179–82; McConnell, *Country Between,* 3, 5, 20, 29–31, 229, 282; Lakomäki, *Gathering Together,* 42–45; Schutt, *Peoples of the River Valleys,* 103–6; David L. Preston, *The Texture of Contact: European and Indian Settler Communities on the Frontiers of Iroquoia, 1667–1783* (Lincoln, 2009), 218–19; Wayne E. Lee, *The Cutting-Off Way: Indigenous Warfare in Eastern North America, 1500–1800* (Chapel Hill, 2023), 10.

14. The peoples of the Wendat Confederacy and the Petuns are the ancestors of today's Huron-Wendat, Wyandotte, and Wyandot nations. "The History of the Huron-Wendat Nation," http://www.wendake.com/history.html; "Our History," Wyandotte Nation, https://wyandotte-nation.org/culture/our-history/; Heidi Kiiwetinepinesiik Stark, "Marked by Fire: Anishinaabe Articulations of Nationhood in Treaty Making with the United States and Canada," *American Indian Quarterly* 36 (2012), 121; Michael A. McDonnell, *Masters of Empire: Great Lakes Indians and the Making of America* (New York, 2015), 5–7, 40, 143; Labelle, *Dispersed but Not Destroyed,* 120; Richter, *Ordeal of the Longhouse,* 61–62; McConnell, *Country Between,* 15, 48, 52–54, 62; Heidi Bohaker, *Doodem and Council Fire: Anishinaabe Governance Through Alliance* (Toronto, 2020); David Andrew Nichols, *Peoples of the Inland Sea: Native Americans and Newcomers in the Great Lakes Region, 1600–1870* (Athens, Ohio, 2018), 24–39; Jacob F. Lee, *Masters of the Middle Waters: Indian Nations and Colonial Ambitions Along the Mississippi* (Cambridge, Mass., 2019), 43–44; Michael Witgen, *An Infinity of Nations: How the Native New World Shaped Early North America* (Philadelphia, 2013), 13–14; Brenda J. Child, *Holding Our World Together: Ojibwe Women and the Survival of Community* (New York, 2012), xiii–xiv; Helen Hornbeck Tanner, *Atlas of Great Lakes Indian History* (Norman, 1987); Edmunds, *Tecumseh,* 4; Lakomäki, *Gathering Together,* 47; Sleeper-Smith, *Indigenous Prosperity,* 95.

15. William Shirley to Shingas, Apr. 23, 1755, *Minutes of the Provincial Council of Pennsylvania,* ed. Samuel Hazard (Harrisburg, 1851), 6:370; Richter, *Ordeal of the Longhouse,* 274; Lakomäki, *Gathering Together,* 43–45; McConnell, *Country Between,* 54–59; Calloway, *Shawnees and the War for America,* 12–13; Spero, "Stout, Bold, Cunning and the Greatest Travellers in America," 131–32.

16. Spero, "Stout, Bold, Cunning and the Greatest Travellers in America," 297; Andrew Sturtevant, "'Over the Lake': The Western Wendake in the American Revolution," *From Huronia to Wendakes: Adversity, Migrations, and Resilience, 1650–1900,* ed. Thomas Peace and Kathryn Magee Labelle (Norman, 2016), 35–44; Witgen, *Infinity of Nations,* 218.

17. The English often called the Senecas and other Haudenosaunee who moved to the Ohio Valley "Mingos." Lakomäki, *Gathering Together*, 47–48; Sleeper-Smith, *Indigenous Prosperity*, 7–8; Warren and Noe, "Greatest Travelers in America," 167; Calloway, *Shawnees and the War for America*, 12–14; McConnell, *Country Between*, 16, 19, 23, 208–9; Spero, "Stout, Bold, Cunning and the Greatest Travellers in America," 322–23, 327–28.

18. Warren and Noe, "Greatest Travelers in America," 167; Alyssa Mt. Pleasant, "Independence for Whom? Expansion and Conflict in the Northeast and Northwest," in *The World of the Revolutionary American Republic: Land, Labor, and the Conflict for a Continent*, ed. Andrew Shankman (New York, 2014), 123; Witgen, *Infinity of Nations*; McConnell, *Country Between*, 22, 30, 50, 209–10; Lakomäki, *Gathering Together*, 48–49; Richard White, *The Middle Ground: Indians, Empires, and Republics in the Great Lakes Region, 1650–1815* (New York, 1991); Sleeper-Smith, *Indigenous Prosperity*, 9–10.

19. John M'Cullough, "A Narrative of the Captivity of John M'Cullough, Esq.," in *Narratives of North American Indian Captivities*, ed. Wilcomb E. Washburn (New York, 1977), 57:102; McConnell, *Country Between*, 195, 213; Sleeper-Smith, *Indigenous Prosperity*, 10–11, 15–16, 47, 126–27, 203–9, 285, 317.

20. Sleeper-Smith, *Indigenous Prosperity*, 6, 95; McConnell, *Country Between*, 211; David J. Silverman, *Thundersticks: Firearms and the Violent Transformation of Native America* (Cambridge, Mass., 2016), 82.

21. Sleeper-Smith, *Indigenous Prosperity*, 189–90, 202; Calloway, *Shawnees and the War for America*, 19–20; Sophie White, *Wild Frenchmen and Frenchified Indians: Material Culture and Race in Colonial Louisiana* (Philadelphia, 2014). See paintings of Shawnees at the National Museum of the American Indian by early-twentieth-century Shawnee artists Johnny John and Earnest L. Spybuck, for example.

22. Jones, *Journal of Two Visits*, 62–63; Sleeper-Smith, *Indigenous Prosperity*, 193–98.

23. Sleeper-Smith, *Indigenous Prosperity*, 210; McConnell, *Country Between*, 31–32.

24. McConnell, *Country Between*, 20–21, 211; Jones, *Journal of Two Visits*, 62–63; Sleeper-Smith, *Indigenous Prosperity*, 176, 178, 190–92, 202, 207; Calloway, *Shawnees and the War for America*, 88.

25. Sleeper-Smith, *Indigenous Prosperity*, 202; Warren and Noe, "Greatest Travelers in America," 168; Warren, *Shawnees and Their Neighbors*, 15; Lakomäki, *Gathering Together*, 32, 34.

26. Jones, *Journal of Two Visits*, 54.

27. Jones, *Journal of Two Visits*, 52–53; Calloway, *Shawnees and the War for America*, 19.

28. Calloway, *Shawnees and the War for America*, 23.

29. McConnell, *Country Between*, 41–82; McDonnell, *Masters of Empire*, 158–59; Spero, "Stout, Bold, Cunning and the Greatest Travellers in America," 291–92, 311.

30. Charles Stuart, "The Captivity of Charles Stuart, 1755–57," ed. Beverly W. Bond Jr., *Mississippi Valley Review* 12 (1926), 63–64; McConnell, *Country Between*, 95–96, 102–5, 110–20; Fred Anderson, *Crucible of War: The Seven Years' War and the Fate of Empire in British North America, 1754–1766* (New York, 2000), 95–96, 99; Calloway, *Shawnees and the War for America*, 25–27; Lakomäki, *Gathering Together*, 69–70; McDonnell, *Masters of Empire*, 163–70; Schutt, *Peoples of the River Valleys*, 108–9.

31. McConnell, *Country Between*, 120–29; Anderson, *Crucible of War*, 61; Edmunds,

Tecumseh, 4–5; Spero, "Stout, Bold, Cunning and the Greatest Travellers in America," 292, 313–22.

32. Brooke M. Bauer, *Becoming Catawba: Catawba Indian Women and Nation-Building, 1540–1840* (Tuscaloosa, 2022), 107–14.

33. McConnell, *Country Between,* 132, 142–43; Lakomäki, *Gathering Together,* 73; "George Croghan's Journal," May and June, 1759, *Pennsylvania Magazine of History and Biography* 71 (1947), 316–17; "Minutes of Conferences Held at Pittsburgh, in July, 1959," *Minutes of the Provincial Council of Pennsylvania,* 8:382–93; Paul Kelton, "The British and Indian War: Cherokee Power and the Fate of Empire in North America," *William and Mary Quarterly* 69 (2021), 786–87; McDonnell, *Masters of Empire,* 191.

34. Kelton, "The British and Indian War," 789–90; Edmunds, *Tecumseh,* 6–8; Calloway, *Shawnees and the War for America,* 30–31; McConnell, *Country Between,* 128–29, 181.

35. McConnell, *Country Between,* 151–52, 159–69, 176–78; Spero, "Stout, Bold, Cunning and the Greatest Travellers in America," 352–56; White, *Middle Ground;* Matthew C. Ward, "Redeeming the Captives: Pennsylvania Captives Among the Ohio Indians, 1755–1765," *Pennsylvania Magazine of History and Biography* 125 (2001), 162; McDonnell, *Masters of Empire,* 211–16. For the aftermath of the war more generally, see Colin G. Calloway, *The Scratch of a Pen: 1763 and the Transformation of North America* (New York, 2006).

36. Pontiac's Speech, May 7, 1763, trans. John DuVal, in Robert Navarre, "Journal ou dictation d'une conspiration, faite par les sauvages contre les Anglais, et du siège du fort de Detroix par quatre nations différentes le 7 mai, 1763," in *Journal of Pontiac's Conspiracy,* ed. M. Agnes Burton (Detroit, 1912), 23–33; McConnell, *Country Between,* 119; Lee, *Masters of the Middle Waters,* 130–33; Joel W. Martin, *The Land Looks After Us: A History of Native American Religion* (New York, 2001), 48–56; Gregory Evans Dowd, *War Under Heaven: Pontiac, the Indian Nations, and the British Empire* (Baltimore, 2002).

37. McConnell, *Country Between,* 182–94; Anderson, *Crucible of War,* 538–41; Calloway, *Shawnees and the War for America,* 34–35.

38. William Trent, June 24, 1763, "William Trent's Journal at Fort Pitt," ed. A. T. Volwiler, *Mississippi Valley Historical Review* 11 (1924), 400; Jeffery Amherst to Henry Bouquet, July 16, 1763, quoted in Elizabeth A. Fenn, "Biological Warfare in Eighteenth-Century North America: Beyond Jeffery Amherst," *Journal of American History* 86 (2000), 156–57; Fenn, "Biological Warfare," 154–58; McConnell, *Country Between,* 195; Edmunds, *Tecumseh,* 8–9; Anderson, *Crucible of War,* 541–43.

39. George Croghan to William Johnson, May 12, 1765, *The Papers of Sir William Johnson,* ed. James Sullivan, et al. (Albany, 1921–1965), 11:736–37; Anderson, *Crucible of War,* 565–67, 624–29; McConnell, *Country Between,* 196–205.

40. Woody Holton, *Forced Founders: Indians, Debtors, Slaves, and the Making of the American Revolution in Virginia* (Chapel Hill, 1999).

41. Robert A. Williams Jr., *Linking Arms Together: American Indian Treaty Visions of Law and Peace, 1600–1800* (New York, 1997), 24.

42. Sleeper-Smith, *Indigenous Prosperity,* 209, 317; McConnell, *Country Between,* 208–10; Lakomäki, *Gathering Together,* 76–77; Sturtevant, "Over the Lake," 49–51.

43. Guy Johnson to Thomas Gage, Oct. 21, 1774, *Papers of Sir William Johnson*, 13:688; Shawnees to John Connolly, May 21, 1774, *Documents Relative to the Colonial History of New York*, ed. Edmund B. O'Callaghan, Berthold Fernow, and John Brodhead (Albany, 1853–1887), 8:465–67; Guy Johnson to Earl of Dartmouth, July 26, 1774, *Documents Relative to the Colonial History of New York*, 8:472–74; Calloway, *Shawnees and the War for America*, 48–49; Anderson, *Crucible of War*, 731–32; Edmunds, *Tecumseh*, 10–11; McConnell, *Country Between*, 239, 260–61; Stephen Aron, *How the West Was Lost: The Transformation of Kentucky from Daniel Boone to Henry Clay* (Baltimore, 1996).

44. Michael John Witgen, "The Indian Menace in David McCullough's *The Pioneers*," *Journal of the Early Republic* 41 (2021), 228; Edmunds, *Tecumseh*, 10–11; Sleeper-Smith, *Indigenous Prosperity*, 211; Calloway, *Shawnees and the War for America*, 44–46; McConnell, *Country Between*, 255–56.

45. Red Hawk speech, 1770, *Papers of Sir William Johnson*, 7:407; Nimwha speech, in George Croghan's minutes of a conference held at Fort Pitt, April and May 1768, quoted in Dowd, *War Under Heaven*, 216; Calloway, *Shawnees and the War for America*, 43–47.

46. Cornstalk, speech to Congress, transcribed by George Morgan, fall 1776, quoted in Calloway, *Shawnees and the War for America*, 62–63.

47. George Washington, diary entry for Nov. 17, 1770, *The Diaries of George Washington, 1748–1770*, ed. Donald Jackson and Dorothy Twohig (Charlottesville, 1976–1979), 2:316.

48. Lakomäki, *Gathering Together*, 78–90.

49. Arthur St. Clair to John Penn, Aug. 25, 1774, *Pennsylvania Archives*, 4:573–75; Richard Butler, "Account of the Rise of the Indian War, 1774," *Pennsylvania Archives* (Philadelphia, 1852), 4:570; McConnell, *Country Between*, 238–41, 264–68, 274–75; Lakomäki, *Gathering Together*, 102–3; Calloway, *Shawnees and the War for America*, 48–52.

50. McConnell, *Country Between*, 278–79; Calloway, *Shawnees and the War for America*, 52–57; Edmunds, *Tecumseh*, 11–16.

51. Edmunds, *Tecumseh*, 18–22; Calloway, *Shawnees and the War for America*, 59–74.

52. Henry Stuart to John Stuart, Aug. 25, 1776, *Colonial and State Records of North Carolina*, 10:773, 778–79, available at http://docsouth.unc.edu/csr; Henry Hamilton to Frederick Haldimand, Dec. 30, 1778, *Documents of the American Revolution*, 15:291–92; Hamilton to Haldimand, Jan. 24, 1779, *Documents of the American Revolution*, 17:48; Henry Stuart to John Stuart, Aug. 25, 1776, *Documents of the American Revolution*, 12:198–203; Calloway, *Shawnees and the War for America*, 59–60; Jeffrey Ostler, *Surviving Genocide: Native Nations and the United States from the American Revolution to Bleeding Kansas* (New Haven, 2019), 105; Gregory Evans Dowd, *A Spirited Resistance: The North American Indian Struggle for Unity, 1745–1815* (Baltimore, 1992), 47–49, 52–59; Tyler Boulware, *Deconstructing the Cherokee Nation: Town, Region, and Nation Among Eighteenth-Century Cherokees* (Gainesville, 2011), 156–57; Lucas P. Kelley, "'It Is Right to Mark our Boundaries on the Map': Native Sovereignty and American Empire in the Tennessee and Cumberland Valleys, 1770–1820," 68; J. Leitch Wright Jr., *Creeks and Seminoles: The Destruction and Regeneration of the Muscogulge People* (Lincoln, 1986), 120.

53. Calloway, *Shawnees and the War for America*, 14, 70–73.

54. Sleeper-Smith, *Indigenous Prosperity*, 11, 178, 198, 200, 209, 212–14.

55. Wayne E. Lee, "Restraint and Retaliation: The North Carolina Militias and the Backcountry War of 1780–1782," in *War & Society in the American Revolution*, ed. John Resch and Walter Sargent (Dekalb, 2007), 178–79; Richter, *Facing East*, 226.

56. Colin G. Calloway, *The Victory with No Name: The Native American Defeat of the First American Army* (New York, 2015), 43–44; Calloway *Shawnees and the War for America*, 78; Dowd, *Spirited Resistance*, xviii.

57. U.S. Census (1790), https://www2.census.gov/library/publications/decennial/1790/; Witgen, *Infinity of Nations*, 20–21; Brian DeLay, "Indian Polities, Empire, and the History of American Foreign Relations," *Diplomatic History* 39 (2015), 927–42.

58. Thomas Jefferson to George Rogers Clark, Jan. 1, 1780, *The Papers of Thomas Jefferson*, ed. Julian P. Boyd (Princeton, 1951), 3:259 (and see 259n1); Jefferson to Clark, Jan. 29, 1780, *Papers of Thomas Jefferson*, 3:273–74, 276–77; Woody Holton, "The Ohio Indians and the Coming of the American Revolution in Virginia," *Journal of Southern History* 60 (1994), 453–78.

59. Clear Sky speech, reply of the Six Nations Assembled in Council at Buffalo Creek to a speech from General Henry Knox delivered by General Israel Chapin, Apr. 21, 1794, *Michigan Historical Collections* 12 (1888), 114; *Treaty of Canandaigua, 1794: 200 Years of Treaty Relations Between the Iroquois and the United States*, ed. G. Peter Jemison and Anna M. Schein (Santa Fe, 2000), viii.

60. Tai S. Edwards, *Osage Women and Empire: Gender and Power* (Lawrence, 2018), 61.

61. Edmunds, *Tecumseh*, 26–27; Sleeper-Smith, *Indigenous Prosperity*, 220; Calloway, *Shawnees and the War for America*, 84, 89; Lakomäki, *Gathering Together*, 120–21; R. David Edmunds, "'A Watchful Safeguard to Our Habitations: Black Hoof and the Loyal Shawnees," in *Native Americans and the Early Republic*, ed. Frederick E. Hoxie, Ronald Hoffman, and Peter J. Albert (Charlottesville, 1999), 173, 175.

62. Speech of the United Indian Nations at their Confederate Council, Nov. and Dec. 1786, in *American State Papers: Indian Affairs*, ed. Walter Lowrie (Washington, D.C., 1832), 1:8–9; Sleeper-Smith, *Indigenous Prosperity*, 218; Lisa Brooks, *The Common Pot: The Recovery of Native Space in the Northeast* (Minneapolis, 2008), 121–24; Mt. Pleasant, "Independence for Whom?," 123.

63. Sleeper-Smith, *Indigenous Prosperity*, 219–20; Edmunds, *Tecumseh*, 27; Patrick Griffin, *American Leviathan: Empire, Nation, and Revolutionary Frontier* (New York, 2007); Samantha Seeley, *Race, Removal, and the Right to Remain: Migration and the Making of the United States* (Chapel Hill, 2021), 68.

64. McGillivray to Miró, June 20, 1787, "Papers from the Spanish Archives Relating to Tennessee and the Old Southwest," 11:82–84; Kathleen DuVal, *Independence Lost: Lives on the Edge of the American Revolution* (New York, 2015), 295–304; Dowd, *Spirited Resistance*, 104.

65. Alexander McGillivray for the Chiefs of the Creek, Chickasaw, and Cherokee Nations, July 10, 1785, in *McGillivray of the Creeks*, ed. John Walton Caughey, 2nd ed. (Columbia, S.C., 2007), 90–93; DuVal, *Independence Lost*, 295–309, 324–32.

66. Knox, "Statement Relative to the Frontiers Northwest of Ohio," Dec. 26, 1791, in *American State Papers: Indian Affairs*, 1:197–99; Alan Taylor, *Divided Ground: Indi-*

ans, Settlers, and the Northern Borderland of the American Revolution (New York, 2007), 237–40; Miller, "Treaties Between the Eastern Shawnee Tribe and the United States," 113–14; Sleeper-Smith, *Indigenous Prosperity*, 227–30.

67. Little Turtle, speech, July 18, 1795, Treaty of Greenville minutes, in *American State Papers: Indian Affairs*, 1:567.

68. John Cleves Symmes to Jonathan Dayton, May 1789, *The Correspondence of John Cleves Symmes: Founder of the Miami Purchase*, ed. Beverly W. Bond (New York, 1926), 74–75; John Francis Hamtramck to Josiah Harmar, Aug. 31, 1788, *Outpost on the Wabash, 1787–1791*, ed. Gayle Thornbrough (Indianapolis, 1957), 19:114–16; Andrew R. L. Cayton, *Frontier Indiana* (Bloomington, 1996), 125; Edmunds, *Tecumseh*, 27; Sleeper-Smith, *Indigenous Prosperity*, 221–23, 227.

69. Knox to Benjamin Lincoln, Beverley Randolph, and Timothy Pickering, Apr. 26, 1793, in *American State Papers: Indian Affairs*, 1:341; Sleeper-Smith, *Indigenous Prosperity*, 309; Oberg, *Peacemakers*, 86.

70. Calloway, *Shawnees and the War for America*, 91–92.

71. Young King of the Six Nations, speech, May 21, 1791, in *American State Papers: Indian Affairs*, 1:165; Erastus Granger, Apr. 18, 1812, in *American State Papers: Indian Affairs*, 1:807; Brooks, *Common Pot*, 135–40; Kayeneseh Paul Williams, "The Mohawk Valley: Yesterday, Today and Tomorrow," in *Kanatsiohareke: Traditional Mohawk Indians Return to Their Ancestral Homeland*, ed. Tom Sakokweniónkwas Porter (Kanatsiohareke and Greenfield Center, N.Y., 1998), 5–6, 9–10; Mt. Pleasant, "Independence for Whom?," 118, 123–26; Alyssa Mt. Pleasant, "Debating Missionary Presence at Buffalo Creek: Haudenosaunee Perspectives on Land Cessions, Government Relations, and Christianity," in *Ethnographies and Exchanges: Native Americans, Moravians, and Catholics in Early North America*, ed. A. G. Roeber (University Park, Pa., 2008), 177; Susan M. Hill, *The Clay We Are Made Of: Haudenosaunee Land Tenure on the Grand River* (Winnipeg, 2017), 133, 136–42; Audra Simpson, *Mohawk Interruptus: Political Life Across the Borders of Settler States* (Durham, 2014), 39, 46–48; The Six Nations, *Memorandum in Support of the Position of the Six Nations That They Constitute an Independent State* (Branford, Ontario, 1924), 1; Brooks, *Common Pot*, 117–21, 131; Loren Michael Mortimer, "Kaniatarowanenneh Crossings: Indigenous Power and Presence in the St. Lawrence River Watershed, 1534–1842" (Ph.D. diss., University of California, Davis, 2019); Matthew Dennis, *Seneca Possessed: Indians, Witchcraft, and Power in the Early American Republic* (Philadelphia, 2010).

72. Edmunds, *Tecumseh*, 28; Sleeper-Smith, *Indigenous Prosperity*, 237–41.

73. Sleeper-Smith, *Indigenous Prosperity*, 275; Calloway, *Shawnees and the War for America*, 93–94.

74. Taylor, *Divided Ground*, 241, 257, 277–81.

75. Indian Council at the Glaize, 1792, *The Correspondence of Lieut. Governor John Grave Simcoe*, ed. E. A. Cruikshank (Toronto, 1923), 1:218–29; Indian Council at the Glaize, *The Collected Speeches of Sagoyewatha, or Red Jacket*, ed. Granville Ganter (Syracuse, 2006), 46–47; Hendrick Aupaumut, "A Narrative of an Embassy to the Western Indians from the Original Manuscript of Hendrick Aupaumut," ed. B. H. Coates, *Memoirs of the Historical Society of Pennsylvania* (1827), 2 (part 1), 76–77, 87–131; Calloway, *Victory with No Name*, 145–46; Calloway, *Shawnees and the War for America*, 96; Sleeper-Smith, *Indigenous Prosperity*, 303–9; Alan Taylor,

"Captain Hendrick Aupaumut," *Ethnohistory* 43 (1996), 431–57; Oberg, *Peacemakers*, 82–90; Brooks, *Common Pot*, 133, 151–55.

76. General Wayne to Henry Knox, Aug. 14, 1794, *American State Papers: Indian Affairs*, 1:490; William Clark, journal entry Aug. 22, 1794, "William Clark's Journal of General Wayne's Campaign," ed. R. C. McGrane, *Mississippi Valley Historical Review* 1 (1914), 431; letter from an officer in Wayne's army, Sept. 21, 1794, "William Clark's Journal," 431n38; Dowd, *Spirited Resistance*, 113; Sleeper-Smith, *Indigenous Prosperity*, 314; Lakomäki, *Gathering Together*, 127–28.

77. "A Treaty of Peace Between the United States of America and the Tribes of Indians, Called the Wyandots, Delawares, Shawanoes, Ottawas, Chipewas, Putawatimes, Miamis, Eel-river, Weas, Kickapoos, Piankashaws, and Kaskaskias" (Treaty of Greenville), 1795, in *Indian Affairs: Laws and Treaties*, ed. Charles J. Kappler (Washington, D.C., 1903–1971), 2:39–45; Lakomäki, *Gathering Together*, 126–29.

CHAPTER 8: DEBATES OVER RACE AND NATION

1. Tenskwatawa to William Henry Harrison, Aug. 1, 1808, in *Messages and Letters of William Henry Harrison*, ed. Logan Esarey (Indianapolis, 1922), 1:300.

2. Shawnee speech, 1803, in *Indian Biography; or, an Historical Account of Those Individuals Who Have Been Distinguished Among the North American Natives as Orators, Warriors, Statesmen, and Other Remarkable Characters*, ed. B. B. Thatcher (New York, 1832), 2:190; Gregory Evans Dowd, *A Spirited Resistance: The North American Indian Struggle for Unity, 1745–1815* (Baltimore, 1992).

3. Tenskwatawa to Harrison, Aug. 1, 1808, in *Messages and Letters of William Henry Harrison*, 1:300; Tecumseh's speech to Harrison, Aug. 20, 1810, in *Messages and Letters of William Henry Harrison*, 1:466; Adam Jortner, *The Gods of Prophetstown: The Battle of Tippecanoe and the Holy War for the American Frontier* (New York, 2012), 151–52.

4. Stephen Warren and Randolph Noe, "The Greatest Travelers in America: Shawnee Survival in the Shatter Zone," in *Mapping the Mississippian Shatter Zone: The Colonial Indian Slave Trade and Regional Instability in the American South*, ed. Robbie Ethridge and Sheri M. Shuck-Hall (Lincoln, 2009), 163–87.

5. Samantha Seeley, *Race, Removal, and the Right to Remain: Migration and the Making of the United States* (Chapel Hill, 2021).

6. Albert James Pickett, *History of Alabama, and Incidentally of Georgia and Mississippi, from the Earliest Period* (Charleston, 1851), 241; R. David Edmunds, *Tecumseh and the Quest for Indian Leadership* (Boston, 1984), 17–18; Jonathan Todd Hancock, *Convulsed States: Earthquakes, Prophecy, and the Remaking of Early America* (Chapel Hill, 2021), 92.

7. Sami Lakomäki, *Gathering Together: The Shawnee People Through Diaspora and Nationhood, 1600–1870* (New Haven, 2014), 166–75; John P. Bowes, *Land Too Good for Indians: Northern Indian Removal* (Norman, 2016), 91–96; Kathleen DuVal, *The Native Ground: Indians and Colonists in the Heart of the Continent* (Philadelphia, 2006), 160.

8. Pickett, *History of Alabama*, 241; Harrison to the Secretary of War, Aug. 7, 1811, in *Messages and Letters of William Henry Harrison*, 1:548; Benjamin Hawkins to William Eustis, Jan. 13, 1812, in *Letters, Journals and Writings of Benjamin Hawkins*, ed. Charles L. Grant (Savannah, 1980), 2:601; J. W. Whickar, "Shabonee's Account of

the Battle of Tippecanoe," *Indiana Magazine of History,* ed. Christopher Coleman (Indianapolis, 1921), 17:356; R. David Edmunds, *The Shawnee Prophet* (Lincoln, 1983), 28–31; Edmunds, *Tecumseh,* 19–25; Stephen Warren, *Shawnees and Their Neighbors, 1795–1870* (Urbana, 2005), 17; Angela Pulley Hudson, *Creek Paths and Federal Roads: Indians, Settlers, and Slaves and the Making of the American South* (Chapel Hill, 2010), 88–89; Colin G. Calloway, *The Shawnees and the War for America* (New York, 2007), 54–55, 69, 110, 126.

9. Warren, *Shawnees and Their Neighbors,* 17, 24; Edmunds, *Shawnee Prophet,* 31–37; "A Journey to the Indians," in Edward Deming Andrews, "The Shaker Mission to the Shawnees," *Winterthur Portfolio* 7 (1972), 122; Edmunds, *Tecumseh,* 69.

10. "Diary of the Little Indian Congregation on the White River for the Year 1805," Dec. 3, 1805, *Indiana Historical Collections* 23 (1939), 392; Thomas Forsyth to William Clark, Dec. 23, 1812, in Lucy Trumbull Brown, "The Writings of Thomas Forsyth on the Sauk and Fox Indians, 1812–1832" (MA thesis, The College of William and Mary, 1982), 67; Edmunds, *Shawnee Prophet,* 34–35.

11. Proceedings of the General Council held at the Glaize, Sept. 30 to Oct. 9, 1792, quoted in Lakomäki, *Gathering Together,* 123; Gregory E. Dowd, "Thinking and Believing: Nativism and Unity in the Ages of Pontiac and Tecumseh," *American Indian Quarterly* 16 (1992), 309–10.

12. "Diary of the Little Indian Congregation on the White River," Dec. 3, 1805, 392; Black Hawk, *Life of Ma-Ka-Tai-Me-She-Kia-Kiak or Black Hawk* (1834; Iowa City, 1932), 51; William Wells to William Henry Harrison, Aug. 20, 1807, in *Messages and Letters of William Henry Harrison,* 1:239–40; Richard M'Nemar, *The Kentucky Revival; or, A Short History of the Late Extraordinary Outpouring of the Spirit of God in the Western States of America* (New York, 1846), 123–32; Harrison to the Secretary of War, Sept. 1, 1808, in *Messages and Letters of William Henry Harrison,* 1:302; Edmunds, *Shawnee Prophet,* 54, 57, 59–61; R. David Edmunds, "'A Watchful Safeguard to Our Habitations': Black Hoof and the Loyal Shawnees," in *Native Americans and the Early Republic,* ed. Frederick E. Hoxie, Ronald Hoffman, and Peter J. Albert (Charlottesville, 1999), 167; Dowd, "Thinking and Believing," 311; Hancock, *Convulsed States,* 1, 27–28; Edmunds, *Tecumseh,* 80.

13. M'Nemar, *Kentucky Revival,* 128; Tecumseh's speech to Harrison, Aug. 20, 1810, in *Messages and Letters of William Henry Harrison,* 1:467; Hancock, *Convulsed States,* 2, 28; "A Journey to the Indians," in Andrews, "Shaker Mission to the Shawnees," 113–28; Red Jacket, speech, Oct. 20, 1800, "Secretary to the Directors of the Missionary Society," *Publications of the Buffalo Historical Society* (Buffalo, 1896–1960), 6:197–201; Dowd, "Thinking and Believing," 313.

14. The Trout, speech to various tribes, May 4, 1807, *Michigan Historical Collections,* 40 (1929), 127–33; J. Dunham to William Hull, May 20, 1807, *Michigan Historical Collections,* 40 (1929), 123–27; Dowd, "Thinking and Believing," 321; Dowd, *Spirited Resistance,* xxii, 21, 129, 145.

15. Harrison to the Secretary of War, Aug. 22, 1810, in *Messages and Letters of William Henry Harrison,* 1:460; Dowd, *Spirited Resistance,* 140–41; Edmunds, *Shawnee Prophet,* 80–83.

16. Isaac Brock to Lord Liverpool, Aug. 29, 1812, in *Messages and Letters of William Henry Harrison,* 2:102; Dowd, *Spirited Resistance,* 139–40.

17. Harrison to the Secretary of War, Aug. 7, 1811, in *Messages and Letters of William*

Henry Harrison, 1:549; William Wells to Henry Dearborn, Apr. 20, 1808, in *The Territorial Papers of the United States,* ed. Clarence E. Carter (Washington, D.C., 1934–1962), 7:556–57; Wells to Dearborn, Apr. 22, 1808, in *Territorial Papers,* 7:559; James W. Biddle, "Recollections of Green Bay in 1816–17," *Collections of the State Historical Society of Wisconsin, for the Year 1854* 1 (1855), 53–54; Nehemiah Matson, "Sketch of Shaubena, Pottowattamie Chief," *Collections of the State Historical Society of Wisconsin* 7 (1876), 416; Nehemiah Matson, *Pioneers of Illinois, Containing a Series of Sketches Relating to Events That Occurred Previous to 1813* (Chicago, 1882), 231–32; John Sugden, *Tecumseh: A Life* (New York, 1997), 205; Bethel Saler, *The Settlers' Empire: Colonialism and State Formation in America's Old Northwest* (Philadelphia, 2015), 83.

18. M'Nemar, *Kentucky Revival,* 127.

19. Tecumseh's speech to Harrison, Aug. 20, 1810, in *Messages and Letters of William Henry Harrison,* 1:465–66; Harrison to the War Department, June 26, 1810, in *American State Papers: Indian Affairs,* ed. Walter Lowrie (Washington, D.C., 1832), 1:799.

20. Charles Jouett to Henry Dearborn, Dec. 1, 1807, in *Territorial Papers,* 7:496; Dunham to Hull, May 20, 1807, *Michigan Historical Collections,* 40 (1929), 127; John Tanner, *Narrative of the Captivity and Adventures of John Tanner* (New York, 1830), 155–58; John Askin Jr., to John Askin Sr., Sept. 1, 1807, *The John Askin Papers,* ed. Milo M. Quaife (Detroit, 1931), 2:568–69; Theodore J. Karamanski, *Blackbird's Song: Andrew J. Blackbird and the Odawa People* (East Lansing, 2012), 14–16; Edmunds, *Shawnee Prophet,* 39–41, 49–53.

21. Shawnee speech, 1803, in *Indian Biography,* 190; "Shauwonoa Traditions—Black Hoof's Account," n.d. (c. 1825), in *Shawnese Traditions: C. C. Trowbridge's Account,* ed. Vernon Kinietz and Erminie Wheeler-Voegelin, *Occasional Contributions from the Museum of Anthropology of the University of Michigan, No. 9* (Ann Arbor, 1939), 61; R. David Edmunds, "Forgotten Allies: The Loyal Shawnees and the War of 1812," in *The Sixty Years' War for the Great Lakes, 1754–1814,* ed. D. C. Skaggs and L. L. Nelson (East Lansing, 2001), 338; Warren, *Shawnees and Their Neighbors,* 26; Jonathan Todd Hancock, "Widening the Scope on the Indians' Old Northwest," in *Warring for America: Cultural Contests in the Era of 1812,* ed. Nicole Eustace and Fredrika J. Teute (Chapel Hill, 2017), 373; Edmunds, *Shawnee Prophet,* 25–26. See also *Folk-Lore and Legends, Oriental and North American Indian* (London, 1894), 192.

22. Edmunds, "Forgotten Allies," 338; Warren, *Shawnees and Their Neighbors,* 27; John P. Bowes, *Exiles and Pioneers: Eastern Indians in the Trans-Mississippi West* (New York, 2007), 30–35; DuVal, *Native Ground,* 208–9; Matson, "Sketch of Shaubena," 416; Harrison to the Secretary of War, Aug. 6, 1811, in *Messages and Letters of William Henry Harrison,* 1:544; Sugden, *Tecumseh,* 205–7, 210, 253.

23. Treaty of Greenville, 1795, in *Indian Affairs: Laws and Treaties,* 2:41–42; Edmunds, "Forgotten Allies," 340; Edmunds, "Watchful Safeguard to Our Habitations," 162–99; Warren, *Shawnees and Their Neighbors,* 20–22, 26; Robert J. Miller, "Treaties Between the Eastern Shawnee Tribe and the United States: Contracts Between Sovereign Governments," in *The Eastern Shawnee Tribe of Oklahoma: Resilience Through Adversity,* ed. Stephen Warren with the Eastern Shawnee Tribe of Oklahoma (Norman, 2017), 116; Robert J. Miller, "Tribal, Federal, and States Laws Impacting the Eastern Shawnee Tribe, 1812 to 1945," in *Eastern Shawnee*

Tribe of Oklahoma, 150–51; R. David Edmunds, "A Patriot Defamed: Captain Lewis, Shawnee Chief," in *Eastern Shawnee Tribe of Oklahoma,* 15–18; Dowd, "Thinking and Believing," 317; Dowd, *Spirited Resistance,* 132–36; Lakomäki, *Gathering Together,* 132–34, 138–39.

24. The Prophet to Harrison, Aug. 1, 1808, in *Messages and Letters of William Henry Harrison,* 1:299.

25. Wells to Dearborn, Apr. 22, 1808, in *Territorial Papers,* 7:560; Tecumseh's speech to Harrison, Aug. 20, 1810, in *Messages and Letters of William Henry Harrison,* 1:465–66; Harrison to the War Department, June 26, 1810, in *American State Papers: Indian Affairs,* 1:799; Dowd, *Spirited Resistance,* 131.

26. See, e.g., Jedidiah Morse, *A Report to the Secretary of War of the United States, on Indian Affairs, Comprising a Narrative of a Tour Performed in the Summer of 1820* (New Haven, 1822), 79; Thomas Jefferson to John Breckenridge, Aug. 12, 1803, *State Papers and Correspondence Bearing upon the Purchase of the Territory of Louisiana* (Washington, D.C., 1903), 234–35; Jefferson to Pierre Samuel Dupont de Nemours, Nov. 1, 1803, *State Papers and Correspondence Bearing upon the Purchase,* 261–62; Jefferson to Dearborn, Apr. 8, 1804, in *Territorial Papers,* 13:19; Wilkinson to Jefferson, Nov. 6, 1805, in *Territorial Papers,* 13:266; Robert F. Berkhofer Jr., *The White Man's Indian: Images of the American Indian from Columbus to the Present* (New York, 1978), 47; Anthony F. C. Wallace, *Jefferson and the Indians: The Tragic Fate of the First Americans* (Cambridge, Mass., 2009); Bernard W. Sheehan, *Seeds of Extinction: Jeffersonian Philanthropy and the American Indian* (Chapel Hill, 1973); Reginald Horsman, "Indian Policy of an 'Empire for Liberty,'" in *Native Americans and the Early Republic,* 48–52; Alan Taylor, *The Civil War of 1812: American Citizens, British Subjects, Irish Rebels, and Indian Allies* (New York, 2010), 126.

27. Miller, "Treaties Between the Eastern Shawnee Tribe and the United States," 114; Emilie Connolly, "Strategies of Succession and the 1797 Treaty of Big Tree," paper presented at "Making a Republic Imperial" conference, Mar. 28, 2019, Philadelphia; Michael John Witgen, *Seeing Red: Indigenous Land, American Expansion, and the Political Economy of Plunder in North America* (Chapel Hill, 2021); Warren, *Shawnees and Their Neighbors,* 21.

28. Forsyth to Clark, Dec. 23, 1812, in Brown, "Writings of Thomas Forsyth," 68; The Trout, speech to various tribes, May 4, 1807, 130; Hancock, *Convulsed States,* 28; Michael McConnell, *A Country Between: The Upper Ohio Valley and Its Peoples, 1724–1774* (Lincoln, 1997), 36, 40.

29. Forsyth to Clark, Dec. 23, 1812, in Brown, "Writings of Thomas Forsyth," 67; Susan Sleeper-Smith, *Indigenous Prosperity and American Conquest: Indian Women of the Ohio River Valley, 1690–1792* (Chapel Hill, 2018), 317; Gregory A. Waselkov, *A Conquering Spirit: Fort Mims and the Redstick War of 1813–1814* (Tuscaloosa, 2006), 75–76. For the differently gendered prophecies of Seneca prophet Handsome Lake, see Matthew Dennis, *Seneca Possessed: Indians, Witchcraft, and Power in the Early American Republic* (Philadelphia, 2010), 84–89; also see Sarah M. S. Pearsall, *Polygamy: An Early American History* (New Haven, 2019).

30. M'Nemar, *Kentucky Revival,* 128.

31. Dowd, *Spirited Resistance,* xiv–xv; Hancock, *Convulsed States,* 4, 28; Cary Miller, *Ogimaag: Anishinaabeg Leadership, 1760–1845* (Lincoln, 2010), 2–3, 65.

32. Harrison to the War Department, June 26, 1810, in *American State Papers: Indian*

Affairs, 1:799; Harrison to the Delawares, 1806, in *Messages and Letters of William Henry Harrison*, 1:182–84; Hancock, "Widening the Scope," 374–75; Dowd, "Thinking and Believing," 319–20; Lakomäki, *Gathering Together*, 147; Warren, *Shawnees and Their Neighbors*, 27–28. Regarding accusations of witchcraft, see Dennis, *Seneca Possessed*.

33. William H. Keating, *Narrative of an Expedition to the Source of St. Peter's River, Lake Winnepeek, Lake of the Woods, &c. &c., Performed in the Year 1823* (Philadelphia, 1824), 1:229–30.

34. Tenskwatawa (probably), "Shauwonoa Traditions," July 24, 1824, in *Shawnese Traditions: C. C. Trowbridge's Account*, 12–13; Edmunds, "Forgotten Allies," 338–39; Lakomäki, *Gathering Together*, 139, 143, 195; Warren, *Shawnees and Their Neighbors*, 13–42; Calloway, *Shawnees and the War for America*, 16, 69–70; Edmunds, *Tecumseh*, 44–45.

35. Tecumseh's speech to Harrison, Aug. 20, 1810, in *Messages and Letters of William Henry Harrison*, 1:466; Warren, *Shawnees and Their Neighbors*, 35; McConnell, *Country Between*, 30.

36. Forsythe to Clark, Dec. 23, 1812, transcribed in Brown, "Writings of Thomas Forsyth," 67–68; Warren, *Shawnees and Their Neighbors*, 31; Hancock, "Widening the Scope," 369–70; Sleeper-Smith, *Indigenous Prosperity*, 141, 316; Edmunds, *Shawnee Prophet*, 68; R. David Edmunds, "Main Poc: Potawatomi Wabeno," *American Indian Quarterly* 9 (1985), 259, 265.

37. Sleeper-Smith, *Indigenous Prosperity*, 316.

38. Harrison to the Secretary of War, Aug. 6, 1810, in *Messages and Letters of William Henry Harrison*, 1:457; Harrison to War Department, May 19, 1808, in *American State Papers: Indian Affairs*, 1:798; General Clark to War Department, Apr. 5, 1809, in *American State Papers: Indian Affairs*, 1:798; Harrison to War Department, July 18, 1810, in *American State Papers: Indian Affairs*, 1:79; William Claus, Diary, 1808, *Michigan Historical Collections* (Lansing, 1915–1929), 23:52–56; Warren, *Shawnees and Their Neighbors*, 31–34.

39. Wells to Dearborn, Apr. 22, 1808, in *Territorial Papers*, 7:558–59; Harrison to War Department, May 19, 1808, in *American State Papers: Indian Affairs*, 1:798; Dowd, *Spirited Resistance*, 132, 138; Edmunds, *Shawnee Prophet*, 75.

40. The Prophet to Harrison, June 24, 1808, in *Messages and Letters of William Henry Harrison*, 292; Sleeper-Smith, *Indigenous Prosperity*, 317; Warren, *Shawnees and Their Neighbors*, 34–35.

41. Harrison to the Secretary of War, June 14, 1810, in *Messages and Letters of William Henry Harrison*, 1:423–24; Harrison to the Secretary of War, Aug. 22, 1810, in *Messages and Letters of William Henry Harrison*, 1:460; Treaty of Fort Wayne, in *Indian Affairs: Laws and Treaties*, 2:101–2; John Johnson to Harrison, June 24, 1810, 430–31; Edmunds, *Shawnee Prophet*, 80–83; Warren, *Shawnees and Their Neighbors*, 38; Edmunds, "Watchful Safeguard to Our Habitations," 172–73.

42. Harrison to the Secretary of War, May 15, 1810, in *Messages and Letters of William Henry Harrison*, 1:421; Harrison to the Secretary of War, Aug. 6, 1811, in *Messages and Letters of William Henry Harrison*, 1:544–45; Harrison to the Secretary of War, Aug. 7, 1811, in *Messages and Letters of William Henry Harrison*, 1:548; John Gordon to the War Department, Sept. 10, 1811, in *American State Papers: Indian Affairs*, 1:801; Matson, "Sketch of Shaubena," 416; Henry S. Halbert and T. H. Ball, *Creek War of*

1813 and 1814, ed. Frank L. Owsley Jr. (Tuscaloosa, 1969), 40, 63; George Stiggins, "A Historical Narration of the Genealogy Traditions and Downfall of the Ispocaga or Creek Tribe of Indians, Written by One of the Tribe," part 2, transcribed in Theron A. Nunez Jr., "Creek Nativism and the Creek War of 1813–1814," *Ethnohistory* 5 (1958), 145; Thomas S. Woodward, *Woodward's Reminiscences of the Creek, or Muscogee Indians, Contained in Letters to Friends in Georgia and Alabama* (Montgomery, 1859), 94; Sugden, *Tecumseh*, 237; Dowd, "Thinking and Believing," 328; Frank L. Owsley Jr., "Prophet of War: Josiah Francis and the Creek War," *American Indian Quarterly* 9 (1985), 277; Dowd, *Spirited Resistance*, 144–45.

43. Gordon to War Department, Sept. 10, 1811, in *American State Papers: Indian Affairs*, 1:801; Hawkins to Eustis, Sept. 21, 1811, in *Letters, Journals and Writings of Benjamin Hawkins*, 2:591; Hawkins to Eustis, Jan. 13, 1812, in *Letters, Journals and Writings of Benjamin Hawkins*, 2:601; Dowd, *Spirited Resistance*, 93–94, 144–45; Sugden, *Tecumseh*, 240, 243; Hudson, *Creek Paths*, 88–89; Kathleen DuVal, *Independence Lost: Lives on the Edge of the American Revolution* (New York, 2016), 300.

44. Alexander McGillivray to William Leslie, Nov. 20, 1788, in *McGillivray of the Creeks*, ed. John Walton Caughey, 2nd ed. (Columbia, S.C., 2007), 206–8.

45. McGillivray to O'Neill, May 12, 1786, "Papers from the Spanish Archives Relating to Tennessee and the Old Southwest," ed. and trans. D. C. and Roberta Corbitt, *East Tennessee Historical Society's Publications*, 10:138–39; DuVal, *Independence Lost*, chap. 16.

46. Halbert and Ball, *Creek War*, 40; Stiggins "Historical Narration," part 2, 146–47; Woodward, *Woodward's Reminiscences*, 36; Sugden, *Tecumseh*, 237, 247; Dowd, *Spirited Resistance*, 146; Waselkov, *Conquering Spirit*, 78, 296. On Tecumseh's dances, see James H. Howard, *Shawnee! The Ceremonialism of a Native American Tribe and Its Cultural Background* (Athens, Ohio, 1981), 285, 319–21.

47. Halbert and Ball, *Creek War*, 40–57; Waselkov, *Conquering Spirit*, 74, 77; Edmunds, *Tecumseh*, 146–47, 150–51.

48. Stiggins, "Historical Narration," part 2, 146–47; Pickett, *History of Alabama*, 242–43, 247n; Tustunnuggee Hopoie, paraphrased in Hawkins to Eustis, Jan. 13, 1812, in *Letters, Journals and Writings of Benjamin Hawkins*, 2:601; Hawkins to Big Warrior, Little Prince, and other Creek Chiefs, June 16, 1814, in *Letters, Journals and Writings of Benjamin Hawkins*, 2:687; Hawkins to Eustis, Sept. 21, 1811, in *Letters, Journals and Writings of Benjamin Hawkins*, 2:591; James Robertson to the War Department, Sept. 9, 1811, in *American State Papers: Indian Affairs*, 1:801; J. Neilly to War Department, Nov. 29, 1811, in *American State Papers: Indian Affairs*, 1:802; Woodward, *Woodward's Reminiscences*, 95; Thomas McKenney, *Memoirs, Official and Personal; with Sketches of Travels Among the Northern and Southern Indians* (New York, 1846), 164–65; Hudson, *Creek Paths*, 94; *Dictionary of Creek/Muskogee*, ed. Jack B. Martin and Margaret McKane Mauldin (Lincoln, 2000), 46–47; Halbert and Ball, *Creek War*, 41–52; Samuel Manac, deposition, Aug. 2, 1813, Halbert and Ball, *Creek War*, 91–93; Dowd, *Spirited Resistance*, 148; Waselkov, *Conquering Spirit*, 78–79; Sugden, *Tecumseh*, 244–46.

49. Joel W. Martin, *Sacred Revolt: The Muskogees' Struggle for a New World* (Boston, 1991), 171–86; R. David Edmunds, *Tecumseh and the Quest for Indian Leadership* (Boston, 1984), 146–47, 150–51.

50. Benjamin Hawkins to John Armstrong, July 28, 1813, in *Letters, Journals, and Writ-*

ings of Benjamin Hawkins, 2:652; Dowd, *Spirited Resistance,* 149–90; Duane Champagne, *Social Order and Political Change: Constitutional Governments Among the Cherokee, the Choctaw, the Chickasaw, and the Creek* (Stanford, 1992), 117–19; Martin, *Sacred Revolt,* 124; Edmunds, *Tecumseh,* 148–51; Waselkov, *Conquering Spirit,* 82–86; Sugden, *Tecumseh,* 247–48; Nunez, "Creek Nativism," part 1, 8–12.

51. Harrison to the War Department, Oct. 6, 1811, in *American State Papers: Indian Affairs,* 1:801; Saliene to War Department, June 2, 1811, in *American State Papers: Indian Affairs,* 1:799–800; Harrison to James Madison, Nov. 18, 1811, in *American State Papers: Indian Affairs,* 1:776; Ninian Edwards to War Department, June 20, 1811, in *American State Papers: Indian Affairs,* 1:799–800; Clark to War Department, July 3, 1811, in *American State Papers: Indian Affairs,* 1:800; William Whiteside and Samuel D. Davidson to James Madison, 1811, in *American State Papers: Indian Affairs,* 1:803–4; Harrison to the Secretary of War, Apr. 25, 1810, in *Messages and Letters of William Henry Harrison,* 1:417; Harrison to the Secretary of War, June 14, 1810, in *Messages and Letters of William Henry Harrison,* 1:422–30; Michel Brouillet to Harrison, in *Messages and Letters of William Henry Harrison,* 1:436–37; Harrison to the Secretary of War, June 19, 1811, in *Messages and Letters of William Henry Harrison,* 1:518; Harrison to the Secretary of War, July 24, 1811, in *Messages and Letters of William Henry Harrison,* 1:537–38; Hancock, "Widening the Scope," 379.

52. Harrison to the Secretary of War, Aug. 6, 1811, in *Messages and Letters of William Henry Harrison,* 1:543–44; speeches delivered by different Miami chiefs in answer to a speech from William H. Harrison, 1811, in *Messages and Letters of William Henry Harrison,* 1:577–82; Warren, *Shawnees and Their Neighbors,* 18.

53. Whickar, "Shabonee's Account of the Battle of Tippecanoe," 17:354–56; Captain Snelling to Harrison, Nov. 20, 1811, in *Messages and Letters of William Henry Harrison,* 1:643–44; Harrison to the Secretary of War, Dec. 4, 1811, in *Messages and Letters of William Henry Harrison,* 1:643–46; Eustis to Samuel McKee, Dec. 19, 1811, in *American State Papers: Indian Affairs,* 1:797; Warren, *Shawnees and Their Neighbors,* 40.

54. McKee to War Department, June 13, 1812, in *American State Papers: Indian Affairs,* 1:797; Harrison to the War Department, Oct. 13, 1811, in *American State Papers: Indian Affairs,* 1:801; Harrison to the Secretary of War, Nov. 18, 1811, in *Messages and Letters of William Henry Harrison,* 1:618–22, 628; *National Intelligencer,* Sept. 10, 1806, p. 1; Jortner, *Gods of Prophetstown,* 3; Sugden, *Tecumseh,* 22–23, 246–47.

55. Log of the Army to Tippecanoe, Sept. 26 to Nov. 18, 1811, in *Messages and Letters of William Henry Harrison,* 1:633–34; Harrison to the Secretary of War, Nov. 18, 1811, in *Messages and Letters of William Henry Harrison,* 1:622–30; Matthew Elliott to Isaac Brock, Jan. 12, 1812 [Nov. 8, 1811], in *Messages and Letters of William Henry Harrison,* 1:616–18; Warren, *Shawnees and Their Neighbors,* 40–41; Calloway, *Shawnees and the War for America,* 144–45; Jortner, *Gods of Prophetstown,* 194–99; Karen L. Marrero, "'Borders Thick and Foggy': Mobility, Community, and Nation in a Northern Indigenous Region," in *Warring for America,* 443–44.

56. Whickar, "Shabonee's Account of the Battle of Tippecanoe," 17:354–56; Snelling to Harrison, Nov. 20, 1811, in *Messages and Letters of William Henry Harrison,* 1:643–44; Harrison to the Secretary of War, Dec. 4, 1811, in *Messages and Letters of William Henry Harrison,* 1:643–46; Hancock, "Widening the Scope," 363–65, 374–75; Warren, *Shawnees and Their Neighbors,* 40–41; Hancock, *Convulsed States,* 28–29.

57. Dowd, "Thinking and Believing," 322–27; Hancock, *Convulsed States,* 82–83; Jort-

ner, *Gods of Prophetstown*, 194–99. The relevant documents are John Sergeant to Reverend Dr. March, Mar. 25, 1808, and Hendrick Aupaumut to Sergeant, Jan. 3, 1809, cited in Hancock, *Convulsed States*, 1, and Tisa Wenger, "Making Settler Religion: Missionary Benevolence in the Early Republic," paper presented at Making a Republic Imperial conference, Mar. 28, 2019, Philadelphia.

58. Hancock, *Convulsed States*, 1, 13, 83; Sugden, *Tecumseh*, 252; Hancock, "Widening the Scope," 375–77; *Virginia Argus*, Dec. 24, 1811, quoted in Hancock, *Convulsed States*, 83.

59. Pickett, *History of Alabama*, 245–46; Waselkov, *Conquering Spirit*, 78–80; Hancock, *Convulsed States*, 93, 130.

60. Hancock, *Convulsed States*, 84–86; Martin, *Sacred Revolt*, 115, 124.

61. John Hunter, a white captive raised among the Osages, recalled these words as those of Tecumseh. The speaker could instead have been one of the movement's other emissaries; however, Tecumseh told Harrison that he would visit the Osages after the Muscogees and Choctaws, and other sources agree that Tecumseh visited the Osages in 1811. Some U.S. officials claimed that Hunter did not live with the Osages at all, but John Sugden and other scholars have noted that U.S. officials at the time were trying to discredit him as a critic of U.S. Indian policies. John Dunn Hunter, *Manners and Customs of Several Indian Tribes Located West of the Mississippi* (Philadelphia, 1823), 51–56; extract of a letter from William Clark, Mar. 22, 1812, in *American State Papers: Indian Affairs*, 1:807; Waselkov, *Conquering Spirit*, 78; Sugden, *Tecumseh*, 253–55; Pierre Chouteau to John Armstrong, Mar. 5, 1813, in *The Territorial Papers of the United States*, ed. Clarence E. Carter (Washington, D.C., 1934–1962), 14:640; William Clark to the Secretary of War, Sept. 18, 1814, in *Territorial Papers*, 14:787; Harrison to the Secretary of War, Aug. 6, 1811, in *Messages and Letters of William Henry Harrison*, 1:544–45; Clark to the War Department (extract), Mar. 22, 1812, in *American State Papers: Indian Affairs*, 1:807; Sleeper-Smith, *Indigenous Prosperity*, 302.

62. Hunter, *Manners and Customs*, 51–60. It's not clear that Hunter's use of "red children" is an accurate translation of what Tecumseh said in Shawnee, not only translated through Osage into English but also dependent on Hunter's memory, but "red" was a term that southeastern Native people used for themselves by this point. See Nancy Shoemaker, "How Indians Got to Be Red," *American Historical Review* 102 (1997), 625–44.

63. Thomas Jefferson to Albert Gallatin, July 12, 1804, Series 1: General Correspondence, 1651–1827, Thomas Jefferson Papers, Library of Congress, available at https://www.loc.gov/resource/mtj1.030_1054_1054/; Tai S. Edwards, *Osage Women and Empire: Gender and Power* (Lawrence, 2018), 51–52; DuVal, *Native Ground*, chap. 4. One Kiowa name for the Osages is the "Shaved Head People." Another is a Kiowa pun on what the Osages called themselves, Wa-zha-zhe, which apparently sounds like the Kiowa words for "Smelly Feces People." William C. Meadows, "Kiowa Ethnonymy of Other Populations," *Plains Anthropologist* 58 (2013), 7, 20, 21.

64. Edwards, *Osage Women and Empire*, 51–52.

65. Hunter, *Manners and Customs*, 51, 56; Willard Hughes Rollings, *Unaffected by the Gospel: Osage Resistance to the Christian Invasion, 1673–1906: A Cultural Victory* (Albuquerque, 2004).

66. Speech of the Ottawa nation of Indians, delivered to the Secretary of War, Oct. 5, 1811, in *American State Papers: Indian Affairs*, ed. Walter Lowrie (Washington, D.C., 1832), 1:804; William Wells to Harrison, Feb. 10, 1812, in *American State Papers: Indian Affairs*, 1:805; Waselkov, *Conquering Spirit*, 92–93, 146, 173; Edmunds, "Main Poc," 262; Warren, *Shawnees and Their Neighbors*, 39.

67. Harrison to the Secretary of War, July 4, 1810, in *Messages and Letters of William Henry Harrison*, 1:439.

68. Speech by Tecumseh, June 8, 1812, in *Select British Documents of the Canadian War of 1812*, ed. William C. H. Wood (Toronto, 1920–1928), 1:313–14.

69. Extract of a letter from J. Rhea, Mar. 14, 1812, in *American State Papers: Indian Affairs*, 1:806; extract of a letter from Captain Heald, Feb. 7, 1812, in *American State Papers: Indian Affairs*, 1:806; Hancock, "Widening the Scope," 359–85; Robert M. Owens, *Red Dreams, White Nightmares: Pan-Indian Alliances in the Anglo-American Mind, 1763–1815* (Norman, 2015).

70. William Wells to the Secretary of War, Mar. 1, 1812, in *Messages and Letters of William Henry Harrison*, 2:27; H. Starke, Jan. 1, 1812, in *American State Papers: Indian Affairs*, 1:809; extract of a letter from Clark, Jan. 12, 1812, in *American State Papers: Indian Affairs*, 1:806; Little Turtle to Harrison, Jan. 25, 1812, in *American State Papers: Indian Affairs*, 1:805; extract of a letter from Clark, Feb. 13, 1812, in *American State Papers: Indian Affairs*, 1:807; Irwin, Mar. 10, 1812, in *American State Papers: Indian Affairs*, 1:808; extract from a letter from N. Heald, Mar. 11, 1812, in *American State Papers: Indian Affairs*, 1:806; extract of a letter from Clark, Mar. 15, 1812, in *American State Papers: Indian Affairs*, 1:807; extract of a letter from N. Heald, Apr. 15, 1812, in *American State Papers: Indian Affairs*, 1:806; Irwin, Apr. 16, 1812, in *American State Papers: Indian Affairs*, 1:808; Harrison to the Secretary of War, Apr. 22, 1812, in *Messages and Letters of William Henry Harrison*, 2:41; Harrison to the Secretary of War, Apr. 29, 1812, in *Messages and Letters of William Henry Harrison*, 2:41–44; Harrison to the Secretary of War, May 6, 1812, in *Messages and Letters of William Henry Harrison*, 2:44; Harrison, May 13, 1812, in *American State Papers: Indian Affairs*, 1:808; Harrison, June 3, 1812, in *American State Papers: Indian Affairs*, 1:808; Hancock, *Convulsed States*, 82.

71. Speeches, May 15, 1812, in Moses Dawson, *A Historical Narrative of the Civil and Military Services of Major-General William H. Harrison* (Cincinnati, 1824), 265–66; B. F. Stickney to Governor Hull, May 25, 1812, in *Messages and Letters of William Henry Harrison*, 53–54; William Claus to Brock, June 16, 1812, in *Messages and Letters of William Henry Harrison*, 2:61–62; Hancock, "Widening the Scope," 371.

72. Proceedings of a council, June 6, 1812, *War on the Detroit: The Chronicles of Thomas Verchères de Boucherville and the Capitulation by an Ohio Volunteer*, ed. Milo Milton Quaife (Chicago, 1940), 199, 204–5.

73. Black Hawk, *Life of Black Hawk: Ma-ka-tai-me-she-kia-kiak* (1834; Iowa City, 1932), 10; Zachary Taylor to Harrison, Aug. 9, 1812, in *Messages and Letters of William Henry Harrison*, 2:82–83; Brock to Lord Liverpool, Aug. 29, 1812, in *Messages and Letters of William Henry Harrison*, 2:102–3; Taylor, *Civil War of 1812*, 162–68; Calloway, *Shawnees and the War for America*, 146–47; Hancock, "Widening the Scope," 363–68, 377–79; Edmunds, *Tecumseh*, 150–65.

74. Tecumseh speech, Sept. 18, 1813, in *Messages and Letters of William Henry Harrison*, 2:541–43; Calloway, *Shawnees and the War for America*, 149–50.

75. John Johnston, report, May 21, 1812, in *American State Papers: Indian Affairs*, 1:808; Hancock, *Convulsed States*, 84–85, 96; Edmunds, *Tecumseh*, 152; Edmunds, "Watchful Safeguard to Our Habitations," 179, 184, 186–89, 192; Edmunds, "A Patriot Defamed," 23–27; Nichols, *Red Gentlemen and White Savages*, 198; Hancock, "Widening the Scope," 373–74; Warren, *Shawnees and Their Neighbors*, 44–45; Bowes, *Land Too Good for Indians*, 98–99.

76. Samuel Manac, deposition, Aug. 2, 1813, in Halbert and Ball, *Creek War of 1813 and 1814*, 92–93; Hancock, "Widening the Scope," 381–82; Waselkov, *Conquering Spirit*, 98.

77. Calloway, *Shawnees and the War for America*, 150–51; Edmunds, *Tecumseh*, 191–96; Taylor, *Civil War of 1812*, 244–46.

78. Henry Clay to James Monroe, Aug. 18, 1814, in *The Papers of Henry Clay*, ed. James F. Hopkins and Mary W. M. Hargreaves (Lexington, 1959), 1:964–65; Henry Goulburn to Henry Bathurst, Sept. 16, 1814, quoted in Brian Jenkins, *Henry Goulburn, 1784–1856: A Political Biography*, 86; Taylor, *Civil War of 1812*, 413–14; Lakomäki, *Gathering Together*, 151; Calloway, *Shawnees and the War for America*, 153.

79. Hancock, "Widening the Scope," 282–85.

80. Saler, *Settlers' Empire*, 196; Warren, *Shawnees and Their Neighbors*, 15, 19.

CHAPTER 9: THE NINETEENTH-CENTURY CHEROKEE NATION

1. Substance of a discourse between Col. John Lowry as a Delegate from the Cherokee Nation and His Excellency James Madison President of the U. States, Feb. 22, 1816, John Ross Papers, Gilcrease Museum, Tulsa, Oklahoma. This and other documents from the John Ross papers are available online at https://collections.gilcrease.org/.

2. William G. McLoughlin, *Cherokee Renascence in the New Republic* (Princeton, 1986), 194–95, 198–202.

3. Nanohetahee (Pathkiller), instructions to John Lowry, John Walker, Major Ridge, Richard Taylor, Cheucunsenee, and John Ross, Jan. 10, 1816, John Ross Papers, Gilcrease Museum; Lowry to Madison, Feb. 16, 1816, Letters Received by the Secretary of War, Record Group 107, National Archives, Washington, D.C., available at Founders Online, https://founders.archives.gov/documents/Madison/03-10-02-0250; *National Intelligencer*, Feb. 22, 1816, 1.

4. John Lowry, John Walker, The Ridge, Richard Taylor, John Ross, and Cheucunsenee to George Graham, Mar. 4, 1816, John Ross Papers, Gilcrease Museum; William Crawford to Return J. Meigs, Mar. 2, 1816, John Ross Papers, Gilcrease Museum; Treaty with the Cherokee, Mar. 22, 1816, in *Indian Affairs: Laws and Treaties*, ed. Charles J. Kappler (Washington, D.C., 1903–71), 2:125–26; Treaty with the Cherokee, Sept. 14, 1816, in *American State Papers: Indian Affairs*, 2:92; Jackson to William Crawford, Sept. 20, 1816, in *American State Papers: Indian Affairs*, 2:105; Thurman Wilkins, *Cherokee Tragedy: The Ridge Family and the Decimation of a People* (Norman, 1989), 87–93; McLoughlin, *Cherokee Renascence*, 209–11.

5. Theda Perdue and Michael D. Green, *The Cherokee Nation and the Trail of Tears* (New York, 2007), 59–61.

6. Annie H. Abel, "Proposals for an Indian State, 1778–1878," *Annual Report of the*

American Historical Association for 1907, 1:91; Kathleen DuVal, *The Native Ground: Indians and Colonists in the Heart of the Continent* (Philadelphia, 2006), 179–80.

7. Julie L. Reed, *Serving the Nation: Cherokee Sovereignty and Social Welfare, 1800–1907* (Norman, 2016), 24.

8. Giduwa is also spelled Kituwa or Keetoowah. Scholars today usually use *v* to indicate the "uh" sound when translitering Cherokee, but I have retained the older method of using *u,* because it will be easier for most readers to use as a pronunciation guide. Robert J. Conley, *The Cherokee* (New York, 2011), 20; Paul Kelton, *Cherokee Medicine, Colonial Germs: An Indigenous Nation's Fight Against Smallpox, 1518–1824* (Norman, 2015), 32; Rachel Caroline Eaton, *Chief John Ross and the Cherokee Indians* (Menasha, Wisc., 1914), 7; Ben Frey, Cherokee Coffee Hour, UNC; Tyler Boulware, *Deconstructing the Cherokee Nation: Town, Region, and Nation Among Eighteenth-Century Cherokees* (Gainesville, 2011). Many thanks to Ben Frey and Patricia Dawson for their Cherokee language help throughout this chapter.

9. Thomas L. McKenney and James Hall, *History of the Indian Tribes of North America, with Biographical Sketches and Anecdotes of the Principal Chiefs* (Philadelphia, 1849), 2:86; Conley, *The Cherokee,* 21; permanent exhibit, Museum of the Cherokee Indian, Cherokee, N.C.; James Mooney, "Myths of the Cherokee," *Smithsonian Institution Bureau of American Ethnology Annual Report* 19 (1902), 392–93; Jonathan Todd Hancock, *Convulsed States: Earthquakes, Prophecy, and the Remaking of Early America* (Chapel Hill, 2021), 23, 92.

10. Elias Boudinot, "Indian Clans," *Cherokee Phoenix,* February 18, 1829, 2; Perdue, *Cherokee Women,* 50–55, 135; Reed, *Serving the Nation,* 6–7, 15; Conley, *The Cherokee,* 22.

11. Speech from the Cherokee Women to the Women of the Six Nations, July 21, 1758, in *The Papers of Sir William Johnson,* ed. Almon W. Lauber (Albany, 1939), 9:950; Perdue, *Cherokee Women,* 55–56, 88, 91; Paul Kelton, "The British and Indian War: Cherokee Power and the Fate of Empire in North America," *William and Mary Quarterly* 69 (2021), 776.

12. War Woman of Chota to the U.S. Commissioners, Nov. 23, 1785, in *American State Papers, Indian Affairs,* ed. Walter Lowrie and Matthew St. Clair Clarke (Washington, D.C., 1832), 1:41; Sarah H. Hill, *Weaving New Worlds: Southeastern Cherokee Women and Their Basketry* (Chapel Hill, 1997), 29, 87–88; Perdue, *Cherokee Women,* 101.

13. Kelton, *Cherokee Medicine,* 104–5, 145; Michael N. McConnell, *A Country Between: The Upper Ohio Valley and Its Peoples, 1724–1774* (Lincoln, 1992), 240.

14. Henry Stuart to John Stuart, Aug. 25, 1776, *Colonial and State Records of North Carolina,* 10:764, available at http://docsouth.unc.edu/csr; McLoughlin, *Cherokee Renascence,* 18–20, 25–27, 33, 60, 68, 77; Theda Perdue, "The Conflict Within: Cherokees and Removal," in *Cherokee Removal: Before and After,* ed. William L. Anderson (Athens, Ga., 1991), 57; Colin G. Calloway, *The Shawnees and the War for America* (New York, 2007), 59–60; Lucas P. Kelley, "'It Is Right to Mark our Boundaries on the Map': Native Sovereignty and American Empire in the Tennessee and Cumberland Valleys, 1770–1820" (Ph.D. diss., University of North Carolina, Chapel Hill, 2021), 68, 164–65.

15. Beau Duke Carroll, Alan Cressler, Tom Belt, Julie Reed, and Jan F. Simek, "Talk-

ing Stones: Cherokee Syllabary in Manitou Cave, Alabama," *Antiquity* (2019), 521; Boulware, *Deconstructing the Cherokee Nation*, 176–77.

16. Turtle at Home to Meigs, Oct. 1, 1809, Records of the Cherokee Indian Agency in Tennessee, M208, roll 4; Douglas C. Wilms, "Cherokee Land Use in Georgia Before Removal," table 1, in *Cherokee Removal*, ed. Anderson, 7; McLoughlin, *Cherokee Renascence*, table 7, 295, 278.

17. Theda Perdue, *Cherokee Women: Gender and Culture Change, 1700–1835* (Lincoln, 1998), 9–10; Eliga H. Gould, *Among the Powers of the Earth: The American Revolution and the Making of a New World Empire* (Cambridge, Mass., 2012).

18. McKenney and Hall, *History of the Indian Tribes*, 2:93–95; Eaton, *Chief John Ross*, 25–26; Patricia Dawson, "The Weapon of Dress: Identity and Innovation in Cherokee Clothing, 1794–1838" (MA thesis, University of Oklahoma, 2017), 49–52; William G. McLoughlin, "The Cherokee Ghost Dance Movement of 1811–1813," in William G. McLoughlin, with Walter H. Conser Jr. and Virginia Duffy McLoughlin, *The Cherokee Ghost Dance: Essays on the Southeastern Indians, 1789–1861* (Macon, Ga., 1984), 111–12; McLoughlin, *Cherokee Renascence*, 179–85; Dowd, *Spirited Resistance*, 112–13; Hancock, *Convulsed States*, 24–25. Many thanks to Patricia Dawson for our conversations on Cherokee revivals.

19. Treaty with the Cherokee (Treaty of Washington), 1806, in *Indian Affairs: Laws and Treaties*, 2:90–92; John Howard Payne, notes on Doublehead, in *The Payne-Butrick Papers*, ed. William L. Anderson, Jane L. Brown, and Anne F. Rogers (Lincoln, 2010), 2:102–5; McLoughlin, *Cherokee Renascence*, 58–60, 92–93, 96–97, 100, 102–8, 120–21; Theda Perdue and Michael D. Green, *The Cherokee Removal: A Brief History with Documents*, 2nd ed. (Boston, 2005), 8–9; Reed, *Serving the Nation*, 32–33; DuVal, *Native Ground*, chap. 7; William L. Anderson, introduction to *Cherokee Removal*, ed. Anderson, ix–x.

20. National Council at Willstown to Return J. Meigs, Sept. 27, 1809, Records of the Cherokee Indian Agency in Tennessee, 1801–1835, M208, roll 4, Record Group 75, National Archives; McKenney and Hall, *History of the Indian Tribes*, 2:90–92; McLoughlin, *Cherokee Renascence*, 156–57.

21. Lloyd S. Kramer, *Nationalism in Europe and America: Politics, Cultures, and Identities Since 1775* (Chapel Hill, 2011), 1–3, 25–26, 149; Eaton, *Chief John Ross*, 12; Duane Champagne, *Social Order and Political Change: Constitutional Governments Among the Cherokee, the Choctaw, the Chickasaw, and the Creek* (Stanford, 1992), 25–26, 28–29, 92–107; McLoughlin, *Cherokee Renascence*, 8–9, 90–91.

22. Perdue, *Cherokee Women*, 105–7; Reed, *Serving the Nation*, 12–13; Eaton, *Chief John Ross*, 34.

23. National Council at Willstown to Meigs, Sept. 27, 1809, Records of the Cherokee Indian Agency in Tennessee, M208, roll 4; Perdue, "Conflict Within," 58; McLoughlin, *Cherokee Renascence*, 352–53, 404.

24. Gary E. Moulton, *John Ross: Cherokee Chief* (Athens, Ga., 1978), 31.

25. Meigs to Andrew Jackson, Aug. 6, 1816, quoted in McLoughlin, *Cherokee Renascence*, 203–4.

26. *Laws of the Cherokee Nation*, 68–72.

27. Michael D. Green, *The Politics of Indian Removal* (Lincoln, 1982), 75.

28. Petition, May 2, 1817, in Perdue and Green, *Cherokee Removal,* 131–32; Perdue and Green, *Cherokee Removal,* 130.

29. Charles Hicks to John Calhoun, 1820, transcribed in Jedidiah Morse, *A Report to the Secretary of War of the United States, on Indian Affairs, Comprising a Narrative of a Tour Performed in the Summer of 1820* (New Haven, 1822), 167–68; Harriett Boudinot to Herman Vaill, Nov. 21, 1827, in *To Marry an Indian: The Marriage of Harriett Gold and Elias Boudinot in Letters, 1823–1839,* ed. Theresa Strouth Gaul (Chapel Hill, 1996), 159; Perdue, *Cherokee Women,* 18, 25, 73, 85, 117, 130; Hill, *Weaving New Worlds,* 1–109; Thomas Hatley, "Cherokee Women Farmers Hold Their Ground," in *Appalachian Frontiers: Settlement, Society, and Development in the Preindustrial Era,* ed. Robert D. Mitchell (Lexington, 1991), 41–42; Paul Webb, "Cherokee Cabins at Hickory Log," in *Native American Log Cabins in the Southeast,* ed. Greg Waselkov (Knoxville, 2019), 89–111; Gabrielle C. Purcell, "An Analysis of Cherokee Foodways During European Colonization" (Ph.D. diss., University of North Carolina, Chapel Hill, 2022). Thanks to Patricia Dawson, Gabby Purcell, and Brett Riggs for conversations about new crops in this era.

30. Wilms, "Cherokee Land Use in Georgia Before Removal," table 1, 7; McLoughlin, *Cherokee Renascence,* table 7, 295.

31. McLoughlin, *Cherokee Renascence,* 62–63.

32. Hicks to Calhoun, 1820, transcribed in Morse, *Report to the Secretary of War,* 169; Perdue, *Cherokee Women,* 121–22; Snyder, *Slavery in Indian Country,* 192.

33. Wilms, "Cherokee Land Use in Georgia Before Removal," table 1, 7; McLoughlin, *Cherokee Renascence,* 226, 295, 327–28; Theda Perdue, *Cherokee Editor: The Writings of Elias Boudinot* (Athens, Ga., 1996), 11–12.

34. Snyder, *Slavery in Indian Country,* 182–90.

35. W. S. Lovely to Return J. Meigs, May 17, 1803, Records of the Cherokee Indian Agency in Tennessee, 1801–1835, roll 2; Lovely to Meigs, Apr. 19, 1804, Records of the Cherokee Indian Agency in Tennessee, 1801–1835, roll 2; McLoughlin, *Cherokee Renascence,* 338–39.

36. Fay A. Yarbrough, *Race and the Cherokee Nation: Sovereignty in the Nineteenth Century* (Philadelphia, 2008), 26–27.

37. McLoughlin, *Cherokee Renascence,* 31–32; Reed, *Serving the Nation,* 34.

38. Hicks to Calhoun, 1820, transcribed in Morse, *Report to the Secretary of War,* 169; *Laws of the Cherokee Nation,* 37–40; Theda Perdue, *Slavery and the Evolution of Cherokee Society, 1540–1866* (Knoxville, 1979), 57; McLoughlin, *Cherokee Renascence,* 328–30.

39. William G. McLoughlin and Walter H. Conser Jr., "The Cherokee Censuses of 1809, 1825, and 1835," in William G. McLoughlin, with Walter H. Conser Jr. and Virginia Duffy McLoughlin, *The Cherokee Ghost Dance: Essays on the Southeastern Indians, 1789–1861* (Macon, Ga., 1984), table 5, 245; Perdue, "Conflict Within," 62–63; Perdue, *Slavery and the Evolution of Cherokee Society,* 57–59.

40. McLoughlin, *Cherokee Renascence,* 329, 352–53; Colin G. Calloway, *The Indian World of George Washington: The First President, the First Americans, and the Birth of the Nation* (New York, 2018), 10; Christopher L. Hill, "Conceptual Universalization in the Transnational Nineteenth Century," in *Global Intellectual History,* ed.

Samuel Moyn and Andrew Sartori (New York, 2013), 134–58; Reed, *Serving the Nation*, 59. For more on James Vann's plantation, see Tiya Miles, *The House on Diamond Hill: A Cherokee Plantation Story* (Chapel Hill, 2010).

41. Treaties with the Cherokee, 1805, in *Indian Affairs: Laws and Treaties*, 2:82–84; McLoughlin, *Cherokee Renascence*, 104; Perdue, *Cherokee Women*, 133.

42. Perdue, *Cherokee Women*, 136–37; Snyder, *Slavery in Indian Country*, 187.

43. Ocuma Melton to Meigs, June 30, 1815, Records of the Cherokee Indian Agency in Tennessee, M208, roll 6; *Laws of the Cherokee Nation*, 4–5; McLoughlin, *Cherokee Renascence*, 224–26, 330–31; Hill, *Weaving New Worlds*, 96–97.

44. Julie Reed, "Episode 286: Elections in Early America: Native Sovereignty," Oct. 20, 2020, in *Ben Franklin's World*.

45. McLoughlin, *Cherokee Renascence*, 288–89.

46. Eaton, *Chief John Ross*, 26; Perdue, *Cherokee Women*, 55.

47. National Council to Jackson, July 2, 1817, in *American State Papers: Indian Affairs*, 2:143; "Treaty with the Cherokees," 1817, in *Indian Affairs: Laws and Treaties*, 2:140–44; McLoughlin, *Cherokee Renascence*, 229–32.

48. Perdue, "Conflict Within," 56–57. Muscogee leaders tried very hard to keep Seminoles in the Confederacy. Kathleen DuVal, *Independence Lost: Lives on the Edge of the American Revolution* (New York, 2015), 248–49.

49. *Laws of the Cherokee Nation*, 5; John Ross, George Lowery, Major Ridge, and Elijah Hicks to John Calhoun, Feb. 25, 1824, Cherokee Agency, 1824–1880: Cherokee Agency, East, 1824–1825, M234, roll 71, digital images nos. 27–46, https://catalog.archives.gov/id/163729443, Record Group 75, National Archives; Eaton, *Chief John Ross*, 30; Reed, *Serving the Nation*, 45–49; William G. McLoughlin, "Experiment in Cherokee Citizenship, 1817–1829," in *Cherokee Ghost Dance*, 153–91; Museum of the Cherokee Indian exhibits, Cherokee, N.C.; Anderson, introduction to *Cherokee Removal*, ix.

50. McKenney and Hall, *History of the Indian Tribes*, 2:77–90; Elias and Harriett Boudinot to Herman and Flora Vaill, Jan. 5, 1827, in *To Marry an Indian*, 154–56; National Council at Willstown to Return J. Meigs, Sept. 27, 1809, Records of the Cherokee Indian Agency in Tennessee, M208, roll 4.

51. McKenney and Hall, *History of the Indian Tribes*, 2:87–89; Eaton, *Chief John Ross*, 3–6, 28, 56–57; Reed, *Serving the Nation*, 29; Moulton, *John Ross*, 2–6, 30–31; Christina Snyder, *Great Crossings: Indians, Settlers, and Slaves in the Age of Jackson* (New York, 2017).

52. *National Intelligencer*, Feb. 22, 1816, p. 1.

53. Treaty with the Cherokee, 1819, in *Indian Affairs: Laws and Treaties*, 2:177–79; petition, June 30, 1818, in Perdue and Green, *Cherokee Removal*, 132–33; Perdue and Green, *Cherokee Removal*, 130; McLoughlin, "Experiment in Cherokee Citizenship," 156–57; Moulton, *John Ross*, 20–21.

54. *Laws of the Cherokee Nation: Adopted by the Council at Various Periods* (Tahlequah, C.N., 1852), 6–10.

55. Hicks to Calhoun, 1820, transcribed in Morse, *Report to the Secretary of War*, 169–70; *Laws of the Cherokee Nation*, 11–18; Reed, *Serving the Nation*, 54–55.

56. *Laws of the Cherokee Nation*, 23–24; 1823 correspondence printed in *Cherokee Phoe-*

nix, June 18, 1828, 1–2, and June 25, 1828, 2; McLoughlin, *Cherokee Renascence,* 304, 366–67, 370.

57. Journal entry for Nov. 11, 1823, *The Brainerd Journal: A Mission to the Cherokees, 1817–1823,* ed. Joyce B. Phillips and Paul Gary Phillips (Lincoln, 1998), 386–87, 543n45; McLoughlin, *Cherokee Renascence,* 304–5; Green, *Politics of Indian Removal,* 75.

58. William McIntosh to John Ross, Oct. 21, 1823, *The Papers of Chief John Ross,* ed. Moulton (Norman, 1985), 1:78; Pathkiller and Cherokee National Council to Big Warrior and Little Prince, Oct. 24, 1823, quoted in Green, *Politics of Indian Removal,* 76; McLoughlin, *Cherokee Renascence,* 304–5.

59. Chilly McIntosh to James Barbour, May 17, 1825, Cherokee Agency, 1824–1880: Cherokee Agency, East, 1826–1828, M234, https://catalog.archives.gov/id/300334; Eaton, *Chief John Ross,* 43–46; Green, *Politics of Indian Removal,* 88–97.

60. John Ross, George Lowery, Major Ridge, and Elijah Hicks to John Calhoun, Feb. 11, 1824, Cherokee Agency, 1824–1880: Cherokee Agency, East, 1824–1825, M-234, digital images nos. 8–17, roll 71, https://catalog.archives.gov/id/163729443; McLoughlin, *Cherokee Renascence,* 305–7.

61. "An Act to Regulate Trade and Intercourse with the Indian Tribes, and to Preserve Peace on the Frontiers" (Philadelphia, 1796), 2, Library of Congress, http://hdl.loc.gov/loc.rbc/rbpe.22300070a; Keith Richotte Jr., *Federal Indian Law and Policy: An Introduction* (St. Paul, Minn., 2020), 35–36.

62. *Laws of the Cherokee Nation,* 54–55; McLoughlin, *Cherokee Renascence,* 309–11.

63. Turtle at Home to Meigs, Oct. 1, 1809, Records of the Cherokee Indian Agency, M208, roll 4.

64. John Ross, George Lowery, Major Ridge, and Elijah Hicks to John Calhoun, Feb. 25, 1824, Cherokee Agency, 1824–1880: Cherokee Agency, East, 1824–1825, M234, roll 71, digital images nos. 27–46, https://catalog.archives.gov/id/163729443; McLoughlin, *Cherokee Renascence,* 319–24.

65. Charles Hicks and John Ross to Hugh Montgomery, Dec. 11, 1826, Cherokee Agency, 1824–1880: Cherokee Agency, East, 1826–1828, M234, roll 72, digital images nos. 45–62, https://catalog.archives.gov/id/163729443; McLoughlin, *Cherokee Renascence,* 324.

66. McLoughlin, *Cherokee Renascence,* 324–25.

67. Elias and Harriett Boudinot to Herman and Flora Vaill, Jan. 5, 1827, in *To Marry an Indian,* 154–56; McKenney and Hall, *History of the Indian Tribes,* 2:87–89; Eaton, *Chief John Ross,* 56–57; Salem Board Minutes, Jan. 23, 1811, *Records of the Moravians in North Carolina,* ed. Adelaide L. Fries (Raleigh, 1947), 7:3143; John F. Wheeler, "The Cherokees: Recollections of a Life of Fifty Years Among Them," *Indian Record* (Muscogee, Indian Territory) vol. 1 (Oct. 1886); Reed, *Serving the Nation,* 30–31, 54; Snyder, *Great Crossings.*

68. Perdue and Green, *Cherokee Removal,* 12; Wheeler, "Cherokees: Recollections of a Life"; Perdue, *Cherokee Women,* 115–34; McLoughlin, *Cherokee Renascence,* 383.

69. Kelton, *Cherokee Medicine,* 20, 176–77.

70. Megan Gannon, "Cave Markings Tell of Cherokee Life in the Years Before Indian Removal," *Smithsonian Magazine,* Apr. 10, 2019.

71. Reed, *Serving the Nation*, 29–30.

72. Major Lowry, "The Life of George Gist," translated into English by multiple Cherokees including Lowry and transcribed by John Howard Payne, in *Payne-Butrick Papers*, 2:136; Elias Boudinot, letter to the editor, *American Annals of Education*, Apr. 1, 1832, in *Cherokee Editor*, 49–58; Samuel L. Knapp, "See-Quay-Yah: The Cherokee Philosopher," in *Cherokee Phoenix, and Indians' Advocate*, July 29, 1829.

73. Spelled out, GWY would be *tsalagi* or *jalagi*, depending on the dialect. Lowry, "Life of George Gist," 2:137–38; Carroll, Cressler, Belt, Reed, and Simek, "Talking Stones," 521; Mary Ann Littlefield, "John Foster Wheeler of Fort Smith: Pioneer Printer and Publisher," *Arkansas Historical Quarterly* 44 (1985), 261–62.

74. Elias Boudinot, letter to the editor, *American Annals of Education*, Apr. 1, 1832, in *Cherokee Editor*, 49–58; Lowry, "Life of George Gist," 2:140; Jack Frederick Kilpatrick and Anna Gritts Kilpatrick, "Letters from an Arkansas Cherokee Chief: 1828–29," *Great Plains Journal* 5 (1965), 26–34; Perdue, *Cherokee Editor*, 61n20.

75. Wheeler, "Cherokees: Recollections of a Life"; *Laws of the Cherokee Nation*, 47; Boudinot, letter to the editor, *American Annals of Education*, Apr. 1, 1832, and "An Address to the Whites, Delivered in the First Presbyterian Church, on the 26th of May, 1826, by Elias Boudinot, a Cherokee Indian," Philadelphia, 1826, in *Cherokee Editor*, 58, 76; McLoughlin and Conser, "Cherokee Censuses of 1809, 1825, and 1835," 229; McLoughlin, *Cherokee Renascence*, 352–53; Carroll, Cressler, Belt, Reed, and Simek, "Talking Stones," 521; Perdue, *Cherokee Editor*, 63n38, 145n2.

76. *Laws of the Cherokee Nation*, 81.

77. Carroll, Cressler, Belt, Reed, and Simek, "Talking Stones," 524–36. See also Margaret Bender, *Signs of Cherokee Culture: Sequoyah's Syllabary in Eastern Cherokee Life* (Chapel Hill, 2002).

78. Ben Frey, Cherokee Coffee Hour, UNC. Spelled here in the Kituwah/Giduwa dialect used by the Eastern Band of Cherokee Indians.

79. Sean P. Harvey and Sarah Rivett, "Colonial-Indigenous Language Encounters in North America and the Intellectual History of the Atlantic World," *Early American Studies* 15 (2017), 444.

80. *Laws of the Cherokee Nation*, 118.

81. *Laws of the Cherokee Nation*, 73–77; James Mooney, *Myths of the Cherokee* (Washington, D.C., 1902), 113–14; McLoughlin, *Cherokee Renascence*, 388–93.

82. *Laws of the Cherokee Nation*, 10, 57; McLoughlin, *Cherokee Renascence*, 333.

83. *Laws of the Cherokee Nation*, 71–76, 130; McLoughlin, *Cherokee Renascence*, 394–95; Perdue, "Conflict Within," 61–62, 70.

84. McLoughlin, *Cherokee Renascence*, 394–95; Perdue, "Conflict Within," 63–66.

85. *Laws of the Cherokee Nation*, 118–30.

86. Reed, *Serving the Nation*, 58.

87. *Laws of the Cherokee Nation*, 45–46, 118–19.

88. *Laws of the Cherokee Nation*, 73, 120–21.

89. *Laws of the Cherokee Nation*, 120; Yarbrough, *Race and the Cherokee Nation*, 41–42; Snyder, *Slavery in Indian Country*, 210–11.

90. *Cherokee Phoenix,* July 1, 1829; Payne, Notes on Shoe Boots, in *Payne-Butrick Papers,* 2:108–9; Yarbrough, *Race and the Cherokee Nation,* 39–41.

91. Snyder, *Slavery in Indian Country,* 193; Perdue and Green, *Cherokee Removal,* 58; Perdue, "Conflict Within," 62–63; Perdue, *Slavery and the Evolution of Cherokee Society,* 56–57; Reed, *Serving the Nation,* 51–52.

92. Address by Hugh Montgomery to the Cherokee Chiefs, Apr. 16, 1828, Cherokee Agency, 1824–1880: Cherokee Agency, East, 1826–1828, M234, roll 72, digital images nos. 550–53, https://catalog.archives.gov/id/163729443; McLoughlin, *Cherokee Renascence,* 401, 409–10.

93. See Lisa Ford, *Settler Sovereignty: Jurisdiction and Indigenous People in America and Australia, 1788–1836* (Cambridge, Mass., 2010).

94. *Laws of the Cherokee Nation,* 62–64; Boudinot, letter to the editor, *American Annals of Education,* Apr. 1, 1832, in *Cherokee Editor,* 57–58; Wheeler, "Cherokees: Recollections of a Life"; Henry T. Malone, "New Echota—Capital of the Cherokee Nation, 1825–1830: A Report to the Georgia Historical Commission," Oct. 18, 1953, *Early Georgia* 1 (1955), 7; Perdue, *Cherokee Editor,* 57–58, 87; *Cherokee Phoenix,* https://www.cherokeephoenix.org/.

95. *Laws of the Cherokee Nation,* 84–85; Elias Boudinot to Herman and Flora Vaill, Jan. 23, 1829, in *To Marry an Indian,* 162; Constance Owl, "*Tsalagi Tsulehisanvhi:* Uncovering Cherokee Language Articles from the Cherokee Phoenix Newspaper, 1828–1834" (MA thesis, Western Carolina University, 2020), 24.

96. Elias and Harriett Boudinot to Herman and Flora Vaill, Jan. 5, 1827, in *To Marry an Indian,* 154–56; Kenny A. Franks, *Stand Watie and the Agony of the Cherokee Nation* (Memphis, 1979), 2–3; Perdue, *Cherokee Editor,* 3–6; Owl, "*Tsalagi Tsulehisanvhi,*" 25. Boudinot fired the first printer, Isaac Harris, for undermining him by publicly claiming that missionary Samuel Worcester had too much influence over the paper.

97. Benjamin Gold to Flora and Herman Vaill, Oct. 29, 1829, in *To Marry an Indian,* 166; Elias Boudinot to Benjamin and Eleanor Gold, June 3, 1830, in *To Marry an Indian,* 170; Perdue, *Cherokee Editor,* 6; The American Indian Archaeological Institute, "A Tale of Two Nations," *Artifacts* 10 (1981), 2; Susan Sleeper-Smith, *Indigenous Prosperity and American Conquest: Indian Women of the Ohio River Valley, 1690–1792* (Chapel Hill, 2018), 226–27. For the tribe-of-Israel theory held by Buck Watie's namesake, see Elias Boudinot, *A Star in the West; or, A Humble Attempt to Discover the Long Lost Ten Tribes* (Trenton, 1816).

98. Brainerd Journal, Nov. 1, 1820, *Brainerd Journal: A Mission to the Cherokees,* 195. Thanks to Patricia Dawson for giving me this quotation.

99. "Memorabilia of the Congregation in Salem and of the Other Wachovia Congregations for the Year 1818," *Records of the Moravians in North Carolina,* 7:3363; Adam Hodgson, letter of Mar. 7, 1821, *Letters from North America Written During a Tour in the United States and Canada* (London, 1824), 2:292–95; Edward C. Starr, *A History of Cornwall, Connecticut: A Typical New England Town* (New Haven, 1926), 147–48; American Indian Archaeological Institute, "Tale of Two Nations," 2; Perdue, *Cherokee Editor,* 7–8.

100. Harriett Gold to Herman and Flora Vaill and Catherine Gold, June 25, 1825, in *To Marry an Indian,* 84–85; Elias Boudinot to Herman Vaill, Nov. 21, 1827, in *To Marry an Indian,* 159; *Eighteenth Annual Report of the American Board of Commis-*

sioners for Foreign Missions (Boston, 1827), 18:150–51; American Indian Archaeo-logical Institute, "Tale of Two Nations," 1–2, 15–16; John Demos, *The Heathen School: A Story of Hope and Betrayal in the Age of the Early Republic* (New York, 2014); Perdue, *Cherokee Editor,* 9–10; McLoughlin, *Cherokee Renascence,* 367–68; Lillian Delly, "Episode at Cornwall," *Chronicles of Oklahoma* 51 (1973), 444–50.

101. Elias Boudinot, "An Address to the Whites, Delivered in the First Presbyterian Church, on the 26th of May, 1826, by Elias Boudinot, A Cherokee Indian," Phila-delphia, 1826, in *Cherokee Editor,* 69; Perdue, *Cherokee Editor,* 13, 15, 67; Sean Ki-cummah Teuton, *Red Land, Red Power: Grounding Knowledge in the American Indian Novel* (Durham, 2008), 163–64.

102. *Cherokee Phoenix,* Feb. 21, 1828; Boudinot, letter to the editor, *American Annals of Education,* April 1, 1832, in *Cherokee Editor,* 58; Perdue, *Cherokee Editor,* 15.

103. Wheeler, "Cherokees: Recollections of a Life"; Henry T. Malone, "New Echota—Capital of the Cherokee Nation, 1825–1830: A Report to the Georgia Historical Commission," Oct. 18, 1953, *Early Georgia* 1 (1955), 7; *Cherokee Phoenix,* Mar. 20, July 2, Aug. 20, Sept. 3, Sept. 17, and Oct. 8, 1828; Perdue, *Cherokee Editor,* 88, 145n3; Owl, "*Tsalagi Tsulehisanvhi,*" 26–28.

104. Elias Boudinot, "To the Public," *Cherokee Phoenix,* Feb. 21, 1828, 3; Kilpatrick and Kilpatrick, "Letters from an Arkansas Cherokee Chief," 26–34; Owl, "*Tsalagi Tsu-lehisanvhi,*" 28–30.

105. ᏚᏬᏯᎾ (Galagina), "ᏣᏫᎩ ᏙᎭᎠᎻᎤᎣᎯ" ("Cherokee Phoenix"), *Cherokee Phoenix,* Feb. 21, 1828, 3, English translation by Tom Belt and Wiggins Blackfox, appendix 1; Owl, "*Tsalagi Tsulehisanvhi,*" 86–92; Owl, "*Tsalagi Tsulehisanvhi,*" 30–32.

106. "ᏣᎭ ᏥᎠ ᎣᎬᎣᏣᎭ, ᏤᎲᏬᎩᎩ ᏣᎭ ᏗᏊ ᎭᎬᏂ ᏒᏔᎬᎢ ᎠᎠ ᏒᏍᏫ ᎣᎡᎩᎣᏫ" ("Parts of the speech to the Georgia Governor and the delegates of Georgia"), *Cherokee Phoenix,* Feb. 21, 1828, 3, English translation by Tom Belt and Wiggins Blackfox, appendix 2; Owl, "*Tsalagi Tsulehisanvhi,*" 93–97; Owl, "*Tsalagi Tsulehisanvhi,*" 39–45.

107. Elijah Hicks, "An Address to the Citizens of Coosewatee District," *Cherokee Phoe-nix,* July 21, 1828.

108. Marshall, letter to the editor, *Cherokee Phoenix,* May 6, 1828; A Cherokee, letter to the editor, *Cherokee Phoenix,* June 4, 1828.

109. Utaletah, letter to the editor, *Cherokee Phoenix,* May 6, 1828.

110. John Huss, letter to the editor, *Cherokee Phoenix,* July 2, 1828; *Cherokee Phoenix,* Oct. 17, 1828; Wheeler, "Cherokees: Recollections of a Life"; Owl, "*Tsalagi Tsule-hisanvhi,*" 47; Abel, "Proposals for an Indian State," 1:94.

111. McLoughlin, *Cherokee Renascence,* 407.

112. Malone, "New Echota," 8–9; *Laws of the Cherokee Nation,* 114–15; Wheeler, "Cher-okees: Recollections of a Life"; Benjamin Gold to Flora and Herman Vaill, Oct. 29, 1829, in *To Marry an Indian,* 166; Benjamin Gold to Flora and Herman Vaill, Apr. 14, 1830, in *To Marry an Indian,* 169; Gaul, *To Marry an Indian,* 158n12, 163n6, 170n2.

113. Harriett Boudinot to Herman Vaill, Nov. 21, 1827, in *To Marry an Indian,* 159; Wheeler, "Cherokees: Recollections of a Life"; Malone, "New Echota," 8–10; Lit-tlefield, "John Foster Wheeler," 267.

114. *Cherokee Phoenix,* Oct. 22, 1828; Eaton, *Chief John Ross,* 54–56.

115. Quotation was at http://www.aboutnorthgeorgia.com/ang/New_Echota_Historic _Site, a website that no longer exists; Andrew Denson, *Monuments to Absence: Cherokee Removal and the Contest over Southern Memory* (Chapel Hill, 2017).

116. *Speech of Mr. Frelinghuysen, of New Jersey, Delivered in the Senate of the United States,* Apr. 6, 1830 (Washington, D.C., 1830), 9; Owl, *"Tsalagi Tsulehisanvhi,"* 58–59; Perdue and Green, *Cherokee Nation,* 61–64.

CHAPTER 10: KIOWAS AND THE CREATION OF THE PLAINS INDIANS

1. James Mooney, "Calendar History of the Kiowa Indians," in *Seventeenth Annual Report of the Bureau of American Ethnology to the Secretary of the Smithsonian Institution, 1895–96* (Washington, 1898), 282; Candace S. Greene, *One Hundred Summers: A Kiowa Calendar Record* (Lincoln, 2009), 1–4. I have used Mooney's illustrations for Little Bear's calendar because they reproduce well in black and white. Little Bear's original calendar is at the National Anthropological Archives, Smithsonian Institution. For multiple calendars in color and biographies of calendar artists, see https://kiowacalendars.org, a website run by the Kiowa Tribal Museum and the University of Texas that shows all the known surviving calendars of the nineteenth century by season, with careful attribution of the artists.

2. David J. Weber, *The Spanish Frontier in North America* (New Haven, 1992); Brian DeLay, "Indian Polities, Empire, and the History of American Foreign Relations," *Diplomatic History* 39 (2015), 932.

3. N. Scott Momaday, *The Way to Rainy Mountain* (1969; Albuquerque, 2019), 47.

4. Pedro de Castañeda, *Relación de la Jornada de Cíbola,* transcribed by George Parker Winship, *Fourteenth Annual Report of the Bureau of Ethnology to the Secretary of the Smithsonian Institution, 1892–93* (Washington, D.C., 1896), 1:466.

5. François-Antoine Larocque, "Journal of an Excursion of Discovery to the Rocky Mountains by Mr. Larocque in the Year 1805 from the 2d of June to the 18th of October," in *Early Fur Trade on the Northern Plains: Canadian Traders Among the Mandan and Hidatsa Indians, 1738–1818,* ed. W. Raymond Wood and Thomas D. Thiessen (Norman, 1985), 207.

6. George Catlin, *Letters and Notes on the Manners, Customs and Condition of the North American Indians* (New York, 1841), 2:56.

7. Peter Mitchell, *Horse Nations: The Worldwide Impact of the Horse on Indigenous Societies Post-1492* (Oxford, 2015), 42–43, 79, 81, 99, 130, 194–95.

8. John C. Ewers, *The Horse in Blackfoot Indian Culture* (Washington, D.C., 1980), 332; Colin G. Calloway, *One Vast Winter Count: The Native American West Before Lewis and Clark* (Lincoln, 2003), 276.

9. "Saukamapee on the Coming of Horses, Guns, and Smallpox, 1700s," *Interpreting a Continent: Voices from Colonial America,* ed. Kathleen DuVal and John DuVal (Lanham, Md., 2009), 129, 131; Ned Blackhawk, "Toward an Indigenous Art History of the West: The Segesser Hide Paintings," in *Contested Spaces of Early America,* ed. Juliana Barr and Edward Countryman (Philadelphia, 2014), 279.

10. Elliott West, *The Contested Plains: Indians, Goldseekers, and the Rush to Colorado* (Lawrence, Kan., 1998), 49–58, 333–36; Pekka Hämäläinen, "The Rise and Fall of Plains Indian Horse Cultures," *Journal of American History* 90 (2003), 833–62; Calloway, *One Vast Winter Count,* 267–312; Frederick E. Hoxie, *The Crow* (New York,

1989), 13–31; Paul Conrad, *The Apache Diaspora: Four Centuries of Displacement and Survival* (Philadelphia, 2021); Kathleen DuVal, "Living in a Reordered World, 1680–1763," in *The Oxford Handbook of American Indian History*, ed. Frederick Hoxie (Oxford, 2016), 57–75.

11. Thomas J. Barfield, *The Nomadic Alternative* (Upper Saddle River, N.J., 1993), 3; Elliott West, "Called-Out People: The Cheyennes and the Central Plains," in *The Essential West: Collected Essays by Elliott West* (Norman, 2012), 59–60. Thanks to Andrew Curley for his advice on understanding nomadism.

12. Mitchell, *Horse Nations*.

13. Earlier than this history, the Kiowas may have moved north from the Rio Grande Valley into the Rockies. Parker McKenzie, "The Kiowa Migration to the North," in Andrew McKenzie, Daniel Harbour, and Laurel J. Watkins, eds., "Plains Life in Kiowa: Voices from a Tribe in Transition," *International Journal of Linguistics* 88 (2021), 27–34; McKenzie, Harbour, and Watkins, introduction to "Plains Life in Kiowa," 10; Momaday, *The Way to Rainy Mountain*, 1, 4; Mooney, "Calendar History," 160; George E. Hyde, *Indians of the High Plains: From the Prehistoric Period to the Coming of Europeans* (Norman, 1959), 138; Francis Haines, *The Plains Indians* (New York, 1976), 57, 93; Maurice Boyd, *Kiowa Voices: Ceremonial Dance, Ritual and Song* (Fort Worth, 1981), 1:12; Frederick E. Hoxie, *Parading Through History: The Making of the Crow Nation in America, 1805–1935* (New York, 1995), 36–42; Jerrold E. Levy, "Kiowa," in *Handbook of North American Indians: Plains*, ed. Raymond J. DeMallie (Washington, D.C., 2001), 907; Mitchell, *Horse Nations*. Nancy P. Hickerson hypothesizes that some of the Jumanos of the southern Plains became Kiowas at the end of the seventeenth century, but Kiowa oral histories unanimously trace a northern origin. Nancy P. Hickerson, "Ethnogenesis in the South Plains: Jumano to Kiowa?," in *History, Power, and Identity: Ethnogenesis in the Americas, 1492–1992* (Iowa City, 1996), 70–89.

14. Parker McKenzie, "Kiowa Migration to the North," 32–33; George W. Kendall, *Narrative of an Expedition Across the Great South-western Prairies, from Texas to Santa Fé: With an Account of the Disasters Which Befell the Expedition from Want of Food and the Attacks of Hostile Indians; The Final Capture of the Texans and Their Sufferings on a March of Two Thousand Miles as Prisoners of War, and in the Prisons and Lazarettos of Mexico* (London, 1845), 1:227–28; James William Abert, *Expedition to the Southwest: An 1845 Reconnaissance of Colorado, New Mexico, Texas, and Oklahoma*, ed. H. Bailey Carroll (Lincoln, 1999), 66–67; Boyd, *Kiowa Voices*, 1:12; Larocque, "Journal of an Excursion," 207, 213; Thomas Say account, in *James' Account of S. H. Long Expedition*, in *Early Western Travels* (Cleveland, 1905), 16:201; Calloway, *One Vast Winter Count*, 304.

15. N. Scott Momaday, *The Names: A Memoir* (New York, 1976), 28; West, *Contested Plains*, 54, 56.

16. Mitchell, *Horse Nations*, 109–10, 126–29, 173, 355; Boyd, *Kiowa Voices*, 1:14; Larocque, "Journal of an Excursion," 207; Calloway, *One Vast Winter Count*, 270; Barfield, *Nomadic Alternative*, 4, 11–12. Many thanks to Andrew McKenzie for his help with Kiowa words. Kiowa language instruction and writing today is based on the Parker McKenzie Writing System. For ease in reading, I write Kiowa words in the orthography used by tribal language programs, and I refer to most Kiowas in this chapter by the English translations of their names. For Kiowa orthography, see Gus Palmer Jr., *Telling Stories the Kiowa Way* (Tucson, 2003), xxv–xxx, 4–6, 11;

Laurel J. Watkins, with the assistance of Parker McKenzie, *A Grammar of Kiowa* (Lincoln, 1984); McKenzie, Harbour, and Watkins, introduction to "Plains Life in Kiowa," 13.

17. Today, their nation's official name is the Apache Tribe of Oklahoma. In the nineteenth century they called themselves Katakas or Naisha Diné (literally, "Our People"). Garrett Wright, "Paawaariihusuɔ: Travel and the Central Great Plains" (Ph.D. diss., University of North Carolina, Chapel Hill, 2019), 27–37; Morris W. Foster and Martha McCollough, "Plains Apache," in *Handbook of North American Indians: Plains,* 926; Conrad, *Apache Diaspora,* 80, 88–89.

18. Mooney, "Calendar History," 150, 152, 158, 159, 290–91; Momaday, *The Way to Rainy Mountain,* 15; Francis Joseph Attocknie, *The Life of Ten Bears: Comanche Historical Narratives,* ed. Thomas W. Kavanagh (Lincoln, 2016), 31; W. P. Clark, *The Indian Sign Language* (1885; Lincoln, 1982), 43–44, 132–33, 229; Pierre Antoine Tabeau, *Tabeau's Narrative of Loisel's Expedition to the Upper Missouri,* ed. Annie Heloise Abel (Norman, 1939), 155; John B. Dunbar, "The Pawnee Indians: The History and Ethnology," *Magazine of American History* 4 (1880), 245.

19. Alice Marriott and Carol K. Rachlin, *Plains Indian Mythology* (New York, 1975), 96–97; George E. Hyde, *Life of George Bent, Written from His Letters,* ed. Savoie Lottinville (Norman, 1968), 17; West, "Called-Out People," 57–75.

20. Frank B. Linderman, *Pretty-shield: Medicine Woman of the Crows* (Lincoln, 2003), 44; Palmer, *Telling Stories the Kiowa Way,* 4; Larocque, "Journal of an Excursion," 207, 209; Calloway, *One Vast Winter Count,* 273, Kay Yandell, "The Moccasin Telegraph: Sign-Talk Autobiography and *Pretty-shield, Medicine Woman of the Crows,*" *American Literature* 84 (2012), 533–61.

21. Momaday, *The Way to Rainy Mountain,* 1, 4–5, 83.

22. *Kiowa Recipes* (1934; Excelsior, Minn., 1985), 2–3, 5; Boyd, *Kiowa Voices,* 1:14; Jacki Thompson Rand, *Kiowa Humanity and the Invasion of the State* (Lincoln, 2008), 13–15, 17–20, 28; Larocque, "Journal of an Excursion," 207, 209; Mooney, "Calendar History," 273. For the relationship between polygamous marriage and the gendered work of a household, see Sarah Pearsall, *Polygamy: An Early American History* (New Haven, 2019).

23. Clark, *Indian Sign Language,* 210.

24. Rand, *Kiowa Humanity,* 20–23; Say account, in *James' Account of S. H. Long Expedition,* 16:204; Mooney, "Calendar History," 271; John H. Moore, *The Cheyenne* (Cambridge, Mass., 1996), 54, 60–65; John C. Ewers, *Murals in the Round: Painted Tipis of the Kiowa and Kiowa-Apache Indians: An Exhibition of Tipi Models Made for James Mooney of the Smithsonian Institution During His Field Studies of Indian History and Art in Southwestern Oklahoma, 1891–1904* (Washington, D.C., 1978), 16–17.

25. William Clark, "A List of the Names of the Different Nations & Tribes of Indians Inhabiting the Country on the Missouri and Its Waters, and West of the Mississippi," in *The Journals of the Lewis and Clark Expedition,* ed. Gary E. Moulton (Lincoln, 1987), 3:403, 422; Larocque, "Journal of an Excursion," 215; Hoxie, *Parading Through History,* 31–32; Mooney, "Calendar History," 158; Elizabeth A. Fenn, *Encounters at the Heart of the World: A History of the Mandan People* (New York, 2014), 234, 238–39; Calloway, *One Vast Winter Count,* 302; Hyde, *Indians of the High Plains,* 139.

26. Mooney, "Calendar History," 161; Rufus B. Sage, *Rocky Mountain Life; or, Startling Scenes and Perilous Adventures in the Far West, During an Expedition of Three Years* (Dayton, 1858), 315; Haines, *Plains Indians,* 115; Larocque, "Journal of an Excursion," 213, 215; Clark, "List of the Names of the Different Nations," 3:422; Zebulon Pike, *The Expeditions of Zebulon Pike, 1805–1807,* ed. Elliot Coues (New York, 1895, 1987), 2:743–44.

27. Clark, "List of the Names of the Different Nations," 3:401, 403, 422; Clark, undated entry (c. 1804), in *Journals of the Lewis and Clark Expedition,* ed. Moulton, 3:135–36; Larocque, "Journal of an Excursion," 213–15; Domingo Cabello y Robles to Commandant General, Apr. 30, 1786, San Antonio de Bexar, Bexar Archives, University of Texas, Austin, https://www.cah.utexas.edu/projects/bexar; Pike, *Expeditions of Zebulon Pike,* 2:757–58; Mooney, "Calendar History," 171; Fenn, *Encounters at the Heart of the World,* 79–80, 203, 142, 156, 237–39; Calloway, *One Vast Winter Count,* 302; Sylvia Van Kirk, *Many Tender Ties: Women in Fur-Trade Society, 1670–1870* (Norman, 1980); Jennifer S. H. Brown, *Strangers in Blood: Fur Trade Company Families in Indian Country* (Vancouver, 1980); Hickerson, "Ethnogenesis in the South Plains," 83; Kathleen DuVal, *The Native Ground: Indians and Colonists in the Heart of the Continent* (Philadelphia, 2006), 103–27; Forrest D. Monahan Jr., "The Kiowas and New Mexico, 1800–1845," *Journal of the West* 8 (1969), 67.

28. The term "Sun Dance" describes the ceremony in several Plains nations; Kiowas have their own names for their ceremony. Palmer, *Telling Stories the Kiowa Way,* 33–41, 122; McKenzie, "Kiowa Migration to the North," 33; Wilbur S. Nye, "The Annual Sun Dance of the Kiowa Indians: As Related by George Hunt to Lieut. Wilbur S. Nye, U.S. Army Historian," *Chronicles of Oklahoma* 12 (1934), 342–43; Mooney, "Calendar History," 156, 237–42, 280; Jenny Tone-pah-hote, *Crafting an Indigenous Nation: Kiowa Expressive Culture in the Progressive Era* (Chapel Hill, 2019), 9; Boyd, *Kiowa Voices,* 1:12, 37; Hickerson, "Ethnogenesis in the South Plains," 86; Foster and McCollough, "Plains Apache," 926; Levy, "Kiowa," 911; JoAllyn Archambault, "Sun Dance," in *Handbook of North American Indians: Plains,* 983; Boyd, *Kiowa Voices,* 1:12–13, 38.

29. Momaday, *The Way to Rainy Mountain,* 10; Jacob Fowler, *The Journal of Jacob Fowler: Narrating an Adventure from Arkansas Through the Indian Territory, Oklahoma, Kansas, Colorado, and New Mexico, to the Sources of the Rio Grande del Norte, 1821–22,* ed. Elliott Cous (New York, 1898), 56; Jennifer Graber, *The Gods of Indian Country: Religion and the Struggle for the American West* (New York, 2018), 2–3. I have standardized the creative spelling Fowler used in this journal he kept while on the journey.

30. Rand, *Kiowa Humanity,* 29; Bernard Mishkin, *Rank and Warfare Among the Plains Indians* (New York, 1940), 26–27, 35; Jane Richardson, *Law and Status Among the Kiowa Indians* (New York, 1940), 6; Levy, "Kiowa," 910–11; Kracht, *Kiowa Belief and Ritual,* 41–43; Greene, *One Hundred Summers,* 15; Palmer, *Telling Stories the Kiowa Way,* xii; Brian DeLay, *War of a Thousand Deserts: Indian Raids and the U.S.-Mexican War* (New Haven, 2008), 96–97.

31. Nye, "Annual Sun Dance," 343–44.

32. Palmer, *Telling Stories the Kiowa Way,* 40; Mooney, "Calendar History," 242, 282, 312; Boyd, *Kiowa Voices,* 1:37; Nye, "Annual Sun Dance," 341–42; Mishkin, *Rank and Warfare Among the Plains Indians,* 1; Graber, *Gods of Indian Country,* 3–8.

33. Benjamin R. Kracht, *Kiowa Belief and Ritual* (Lincoln, 2017), 44–45; Palmer, *Tell-*

ing Stories the Kiowa Way, 39–40; Nye, "Annual Sun Dance," 342; Rand, *Kiowa Humanity,* 31; Richardson, *Law and Status Among the Kiowa Indians,* 9–10. For more on military societies, see William C. Meadows, *Kiowa, Apache, and Comanche Military Societies: Enduring Veterans, 1800 to the Present* (Austin, 1999); Mishkin, *Rank and Warfare Among the Plains Indians.*

34. Say account, in *James' Account of S. H. Long Expedition,* 16:201, 209; Nye, "Annual Sun Dance," 343.

35. Fowler, *Journal,* 62–63; Kracht, *Kiowa Belief and Ritual,* 44–45; George Bird Grinnell, *The Fighting Cheyennes* (1915; Norman, 1956), 67; Hyde, *Life of George Bent,* 40. Fowler's account comes from a December hunt, but it is useful for seeing the discussions leading up to moving camp.

36. Mooney, "Calendar History," 167–68, 312; Mishkin, *Rank and Warfare Among the Plains Indians,* 28–30; Garrick Mallery, "Pictographs of the North American Indians," in *Fourth Annual Report of the Bureau of Ethnology to the Secretary of the Smithsonian Institution, 1882–83* (Washington, D.C., 1886), 135, plate XL; Candace S. Greene and Russell Thornton, eds., *The Year the Stars Fell: Lakota Winter Counts at the Smithsonian* (Lincoln, 2007), 156–57.

37. Mooney, "Calendar History," 153–58, 271; De B. Randolph Keim, *Sheridan's Troopers on the Borders: A Winter Campaign on the Plains* (Philadelphia, 1885), 183–84; Clark, "List of the Names of the Different Nations," 3:422; John, "Earlier Chapter of Kiowa History," 381; Thomas W. Kavanagh, *Comanche Political History: An Ethnohistorical Perspective, 1706–1875* (Lincoln, 1996), 201–2; Greene, *One Hundred Summers,* 222; William C. Meadows, "Kiowa Ethnonymy of Other Populations," *Plains Anthropologist* 58 (2013), 7, 21; McKenzie, Harbour, and Watkins, Appendix A, "Plains Life in Kiowa," 167; David J. Silverman, *Thundersticks: Firearms and the Violent Transformation of Native America* (Cambridge, Mass., 2016), 226–31, 235; DuVal, *Native Ground,* 121–22, 266–67n6; Hickerson, "Ethnogenesis in the South Plains," 86; Haines, *Plains Indians,* 121; Hyde, *Indians of the High Plains,* 60.

38. The Kiowas also had separate names for some Comanche bands. Meadows, "Kiowa Ethnonymy," 7, 19; McKenzie, Harbour, and Watkins, Appendix A, "Plains Life in Kiowa," 167; Pekka Hämäläinen, "The Western Comanche Trade Center: Rethinking the Plains Indian Trade System," *Western Historical Quarterly* 29 (1998), 485–513; Elizabeth A. H. John, "An Earlier Chapter of Kiowa History," *New Mexico Historical Review* 60 (1985), 380–81; John, *Storms,* 764–65; Rudolph C. Troike, "A Pawnee Visit to San Antonio in 1795," *Ethnohistory* 11 (1964), 380–88. Manuel Muñoz, Feb. 15, 1795, transcribed in Troike, "Pawnee Visit," 387–88.

39. The paragraphs on the Kiowa-Comanche peace come from Mooney, "Calendar History," 162–64; Attocknie, *Life of Ten Bears,* 31–33; Kavanagh, *Comanche Political History,* 146–47; John, "Earlier Chapter of Kiowa History," 386–87; Tone-pah-hote, *Crafting an Indigenous Nation,* 10. Wolf Lying Down (Guik'ate) was probably the leader whom the Spanish called El Ronco (the Hoarse Man). Afraid of Water's Comanche name was Patuuya. Kiowa and Comanche oral histories, using calculations based on the ages of involved leaders, place this event between 1790 and 1820.

40. Attocknie, *Life of Ten Bears,* 33–37; Kavanagh, *Comanche Political History,* 146–47. In this chapter, I usually use "Comanche" rather than the names of distinct bands. For a more complete version of Comanche history and politics, see Kavanagh, *Comanche Political History;* Comanche National Museum and Cultural Center, website, http://www.comanchemuseum.com/.

41. Joaquín Real Alencaster to Juan Salcedo, Santa Fe, Dec. 25, 1805, doc. 1937, reel 15, frame 131, Spanish Archives of New Mexico, Santa Fe, N.M., mf copy Duke University, Durham; Salcedo to Real Alencaster, Jan. 16, 1806, doc. 1953 (150), mf reel 16, frames 42–45, Spanish Archives of New Mexico; Real Alencaster to Salcedo, Aug. 30, 1806, doc. 2006 (302), mf reel 16, frames 211–12, Spanish Archives of New Mexico; John, "Earlier Chapter of Kiowa History," 386–87; Kavanagh, *Comanche Political History*, 146; Noel H. Loomis and Abram P. Nasatir, *Pedro Vial and the Roads to Santa Fe* (Norman, 1967), 450–51.

42. Abert, *Expedition to the Southwest*, 66; Kavanagh, *Comanche Political History*, 147–48; John, "Earlier Chapter of Kiowa History," 384; Pekka Hämäläinen, *The Comanche Empire* (New Haven, 2008), 110–11, 161.

43. Attocknie, *Life of Ten Bears*, 31, 37.

44. Palmer, *Telling Stories the Kiowa Way*, 4.

45. Fowler, *Journal*, 65; Kracht, *Kiowa Belief and Ritual*, 46; Rand, *Kiowa Humanity*, 13, 15.

46. Joaquín de Arrendondo to the governor, Sept. 29, 1818, Bexar Archives, University of Texas, microfilm copy at North Carolina State University, Raleigh, N.C.; T. B. Wheelock, "Journal of Colonel Dodge's Expedition from Fort Gibson to the Pawnee Pict Village," *American State Papers: Military Affairs*, 5:378, 381; John, "Earlier Chapter of Kiowa History," 383, 393–94.

47. John, *Storms*, 666–69; Kavanagh, *Comanche Political History*, 112–18; Gary Clayton Anderson, *The Indian Southwest, 1580–1830: Ethnogenesis and Reinvention* (Norman, 1999), 212; Calloway, *One Vast Winter Count*, 384–87.

48. Real Alencaster, "Extraordinary costs of expeditions and special gifts to the allies," Santa Fe, Dec. 1806 to Oct. 1807, doc. 2084, mf reel 16, frames 426–33, Spanish Archives of New Mexico; Attocknie, *Life of Ten Bears*, 32; Kendall, *Narrative of an Expedition*, 1:228; Monahan, "Kiowas and New Mexico," 67–70; Rand, *Kiowa Humanity*, 11; John, "Earlier Chapter of Kiowa History," 391–92, 389–90; Ross Frank, *From Settler to Citizen: New Mexican Economic Development and the Creation of Vecino Society, 1750–1820* (Berkeley, 2000), 119–75.

49. Paul W. Mapp, *The Elusive West and the Contest for Empire, 1713–1763* (Chapel Hill, 2011); Pike, *Expeditions of Zebulon Pike*; Jared Orsi, *Citizen Explorer: The Life of Zebulon Pike* (Oxford, 2014); *The Forgotten Expedition: The Louisiana Purchase Journals of Dunbar and Hunter, 1804–1805*, ed. Trey Berry, Pam Beasley, and Jeanne Clements (Baton Rouge, 2006); *Southern Counterpart to Lewis and Clark: The Freeman and Custis Expedition of 1806*, ed. Dan L. Flores (Norman, 1984); Kavanaugh, *Comanche Political History*, 155; R. Duffus, *The Santa Fe Trail* (1930; Albuquerque, 1972), 56–60.

50. Mooney, "Calendar History," 168, 171–72, 255, 269, 271, 281, 283, 287–88, 394–96, 400, 413, 426–27, 429–30, 435, 438–39; Meadows, "Kiowa Ethnonymy," 12–14, 26–27; McKenzie, Harbour, and Watkins, Appendix A, "Plains Life in Kiowa," 167–68; John P. Harrington, *Vocabulary of the Kiowa Language* (Washington, D.C., 1928), 222, 231; Greene, *One Hundred Summers*, 8, 66–67, 207; Fowler, *Journal*, 64; Fenn, *Encounters at the Heart of the World*, 234–36; Hämäläinen, *Comanche Empire*, 162–64; Hickerson, "Ethnogenesis in the South Plains," 87; Kavanagh, *Comanche Political History*, 155. T'áukâui is sometimes translated as "Mexican" or "white," but those translations impose European-descended self-definitions onto the word.

Thomas Say wrote the word that Kiowas and Arapahos used for northerners/ Americans as "Tabbyboo," noting that it was particularly applied to Americans as distinct from other white people and also that he had difficulty imitating and transcribing Kiowa words. Say account, in *James' Account of S. H. Long Expedition,* 16:207, 209–10.

51. Kavanagh, *Comanche Political History,* 155, 201–2; John, "Earlier Chapter of Kiowa History," 392–93.

52. Fowler, *Journal,* 55–56.

53. José Maria Ronquillo to Ayudante Inspector, June 28, 1833, letter no. 419, frames 930–31, reel 14, Mexican Archives of New Mexico, 1821–1846; Kavanagh, *Comanche Political History,* 206–7.

54. Richard Irving Dodge, *The Plains of the Great West and Their Inhabitants, Being a Description of the Plains, Game, Indians, &c. of the Great North American Desert* (New York, 1877), 322.

55. Edwin James, *James' Account of S. H. Long Expedition, 1819–20,* in *Early Western Travels,* 16:55–56.

56. Say account, in *James' Account of S. H. Long Expedition,* 16:193–97.

57. Say account, in *James' Account of S. H. Long Expedition,* 16:192–210. Say includes Kaskaskias, an Illinois people, among the encampment, which is possible—some had moved west by this point—but seems unlikely.

58. Fowler, *Journal,* 4–5, 49–72; Kavanagh, *Comanche Political History,* 211–12. Fowler used the name Ietans, which was sometimes used for Comanches, and a group of this size was surely part of the Comanches. There was also excitement in the United States about Mexico's independence. See Caitlin Fitz, *Our Sister Republics: The United States in an Age of American Revolutions* (New York, 2016).

59. Mooney, "Calendar History," 254–57; Greene, *One Hundred Summers,* 204; Josiah Gregg, *Commerce of the Prairies: Or the Journal of a Santa Fé Trader During Eight Expeditions Across the Great Western Prairies and a Residence of Nearly Nine Years in Northern Mexico* (New York, 1844), 2:49–53; *Niles Register,* Mar. 23, 1833 (Baltimore) 44:51; William Vaill, May 9, 1833, "Osages: Journal of Mr. Vaill, During a Preaching Tour," *Missionary Herald* 29 (1833), 369; Tone-Pah-Hote, *Crafting an Indigenous Nation,* 34–35; John Joseph Mathews, *The Osages, Children of the Middle Waters* (Norman, 1961), 553. Mooney writes "adal-hangya" for "hair metal."

60. Vaill, May 7, 1833, "Journal of Mr. Vaill," 367; DuVal, *Native Ground.*

61. Calloway, *Shawnees and the War for America,* 156–61.

62. Parker McKenzie, "Massacre at Cutthroat Gap," in "Plains Life in Kiowa," 35–40; Mooney, "Calendar History," 257–60; Vaill, May 10, 1833, "Journal of Mr. Vaill," 369; Mathews, *The Osages,* 556–57; Louis F. Burns, *A History of the Osage People,* 2nd ed. (Tuscaloosa, 2004), 216–17. Vaill's journal says the victims were Pawnees, but this is clearly the attack that the Kiowas remember. For divisions between the Arkansas Missouri Osages, which are important for understanding the Osage side of these conflicts, see DuVal, *Native Ground,* chaps. 6 and 7.

63. Boyd, *Kiowa Voices,* 1:33–34; Greene, *One Hundred Summers,* 46–48, 204; Momaday, *The Way to Rainy Mountain,* 83; Palmer, *Telling Stories the Kiowa Way,* 64; Rollings, *The Osage,* 269.

64. William Bradford to the Secretary of War, Mar. 28, 1818, in *The Territorial Papers*

of the United States, ed. Clarence E. Carter (Washington, D.C., 1934–1962), 19:59–60.

65. Mooney, "Calendar History," 261; Greene, *One Hundred Summers,* 50–51, 204; Momaday, *The Way to Rainy Mountain,* 83; Mallery, "Pictographs of the North American Indians," 138, plate XLIII; Greene and Thornton, *The Year the Stars Fell,* 193–95.

CHAPTER 11: REMOVALS FROM THE EAST TO A NATIVE WEST

1. Andrew Jackson, Second Annual Message to Congress, Dec. 6, 1830, *A Compilation of the Messages and Papers of the Presidents, 1789–1897,* ed. James D. Richardson (Washington, D.C., 1896), 2:520–21. On recent scholarship on the Removal era, see Christina Snyder, "Many Removals: Re-evaluating the Arc of Indigenous Dispossession," *Journal of the Early Republic* 41 (2021), 623–50.

2. Claudio Saunt, *Unworthy Republic: The Dispossession of Native Americans and the Road to Indian Territory* (New York, 2020), xiii, 318–19; Jeffrey Ostler, *Surviving Genocide: Native Nations and the United States from the American Revolution to Bleeding Kansas* (New Haven, 2019), 247–373 (for statistics, see 361–62).

3. T. B. Wheelock, "Journal of Colonel Dodge's Expedition from Fort Gibson to the Pawnee Pict Village," *American State Papers: Military Affairs,* 5:379; James Hildreth, *Dragoon Campaigns to the Rocky Mountains; Being a History of the Enlistment, Organization, and First Campaigns of the Regiment of United States Dragoons, Together with Incidents of a Soldier's Life and Sketches of Scenery and Indian Character, by a Dragoon* (New York, 1836), 172–75, 221; "The Journal of the Proceedings at Our First Treaty with the Wild Indians, 1835," ed. Grant Foreman, *Chronicles of Oklahoma* 14 (1936), 416; Brian DeLay, "Foreign Relations Between Indigenous Polities, 1820–1900," *Cambridge History of America and the World* (New York, 2021), 387–411. Many thanks to Brian DeLay for sharing his work with me before publication and helping me to think about this period of Kiowa history in new ways.

4. Thomas Jefferson to George Rogers Clark, Jan. 1, 1780, *The Papers of Thomas Jefferson,* ed. Julian P. Boyd (Princeton, 1951), 3:259.

5. Nicholas Guyatt, *Bind Us Apart: How Enlightened Americans Invented Racial Segregation* (New York, 2016), 6–7. For the evolution of U.S. removal policy from the Northwest Ordinance to 1830, see John P. Bowes, *Land Too Good for Indians: Northern Indian Removal* (Norman, 2016), 50–62.

6. Saunt, *Unworthy Republic.*

7. Ostler, *Surviving Genocide,* 383–87; Saunt, *Unworthy Republic,* 22–24; Jack Norton, *When Our Worlds Cried: Genocide in Northwestern California* (San Francisco, 1979); James Taylor Carson, "'The Obituary of Nations': Ethnic Cleansing, Memory, and the Origins of the Old South," *Southern Cultures* 14 (2008), 6–31; Roxanne Dunbar-Ortiz and Dina Gilio-Whitaker, *"All the Real Indians Died Off" and 20 Other Myths About Native Americans* (Boston, 2016), 58–66; Andrew Fitzmaurice, *Sovereignty, Property, and Empire, 1500–2000* (Cambridge, 2014), 6–7, 26–27, 171–73.

8. *Abstract of the Returns of the Fifth Census* (Washington, D.C., 1832), 41, 43.

9. William Dunbar, Jan. 10, 1805, "The Exploration of the *Red,* the *Black,* and the

Washita Rivers," in *Documents Relating to the Purchase and Exploration of Louisiana* (Boston, 1904), 167; "Treaty with the Quapaw," Aug. 24, 1818, in *Indian Affairs: Laws and Treaties, 1778–1883,* 2:160–61; Petition to Congress by Inhabitants of Arkansas County, Nov. 2, 1818, in *The Territorial Papers of the United States,* ed. Clarence E. Carter (Washington, D.C., 1934–1962), 19:11–12; Robert Crittenden to Calhoun, Sept. 28, 1823, in *Territorial Papers,* 19:549; "Treaty with the Quapaw," Nov. 15, 1824, in *Indian Affairs: Laws and Treaties, 1778–1883,* 2:210–11; Kathleen DuVal, *The Native Ground: Indians and Colonists in the Heart of the Continent* (Philadelphia, 2006), chap. 8.

10. Jean Marie Odin to M. Cholleton, n.d. (1824 trip), *Annales de la Propagation de la Foi* 2 (1827), 383; John E. Rybolt, "Vincentian Missions Among Native Americans," *Vincentian Heritage Journal* 10 (1989), 161–71; Quapaw Nation, "Who Was Saracen?," https://www.quapawtribe.com/598/Saracen. Thanks to Everett Bandy for the French source.

11. *Arkansas Gazette,* Nov. 30, 1824; W. David Baird, *The Quapaw Indians: A History of the Downstream People* (Norman, 1980), 84–86.

12. Jackson, Sixth Annual Message to Congress, Dec. 1, 1834, 3:113.

13. "An Act to add the Territory lying within the limits of this State, and occupied by the Cherokee Indians, to the counties of Carroll, DeKalb, Gwinnett, Hall and Habersham; and to extend the laws of this State over the same," Dec. 20, 1828, *Acts of the General Assembly of the State of Georgia, Passed in Milledgeville at an Annual Session in November and December, 1828* (Milledgeville, 1829), 88–99; "An Act to prevent the exercise of assumed and arbitrary power, by all persons under pretext of authority from the Cherokee Indians, and their laws, and to prevent white persons from residing within that part of the chartered limits of Georgia, occupied by the Cherokee Indians, and to provide a guard for the protection of the gold mines, and to enforce the laws of the State within the aforesaid territory," Dec. 22, 1830, *Acts of the General Assembly of the State of Georgia, Passed in Milledgeville at an Annual Session in October, November and December, 1830* (Milledgeville, 1831), 114–17; Mary Young, "The Exercise of Sovereignty in Cherokee Georgia," *Journal of the Early Republic* 10 (1990), 43–63.

14. Theda Perdue, *Cherokee Editor: The Writings of Elias Boudinot* (Athens, Ga., 1983), 21–23, 151n72; Jason Lee Edwards, "All that Glitters: Judge Clayton and a Forgotten Chapter of the Cherokee Removal in Georgia" (MA thesis, University of North Carolina, Chapel Hill, 2021); William G. McLoughlin, *Cherokee Renascence in the New Republic* (Princeton, 1986), 438–39.

15. *Cherokee Phoenix,* Feb. 10, 1830, 2.

16. Harriett Boudinot, postscript to Benjamin Gold to Flora and Herman Vaill, Apr. 1830, transcribed in Ralph Gabriel, *Elias Boudinot, Cherokee, and His America* (Norman, 1941), 119; Harriett Boudinot to Herman and Flora Vaill, Jan. 7, 1831, in *To Marry an Indian: The Marriage of Harriett Gold and Elias Boudinot in Letters, 1823–1839,* ed. Theresa Strouth Gaul (Chapel Hill, 1996), 173; Harriett Boudinot to Herman and Flora Vaill, July 1, 1831, in *To Marry an Indian,* 173.

17. *Cherokee Phoenix,* Apr. 21, 1830, 2.

18. *Cherokee Phoenix,* Mar. 26 and July 16, 1831.

19. *Cherokee Phoenix*, Mar. 26, Aug. 12, Aug. 27, and Sept. 17, 1831; Perdue, *Cherokee Editor*, 21–23, 151n72.

20. Theda Perdue and Michael D. Green, *The Cherokee Nation and the Trail of Tears* (New York, 2007), 61–62; Theda Perdue and Michael D. Green, *The Cherokee Removal: A Brief History with Documents*, 3rd ed. (Boston, 2016), 100–109.

21. Boudinot editorial, May 7, 1831, trans. Belt and Blackfox, appendix 5, in Constance Owl, "*Tsalagi Tsulehisanvhi:* Uncovering Cherokee Language Articles from the Cherokee Phoenix Newspaper, 1828–1834" (MA thesis, Western Carolina University, 2020), 111–16; Owl, "*Tsalagi Tsulehisanvhi*," 57–58, 67–69.

22. *Cherokee Nation v. Georgia*, 1831, in Keith Richotte Jr., *Federal Indian Law and Policy: An Introduction* (St. Paul, Minn., 2020), 56–64.

23. Elias Boudinot to Herman and Flora Vaill, Jan. 7, 1831, in *To Marry an Indian*, 174; *Cherokee Phoenix*, Mar. 26 and May 28, 1831; Owl, "*Tsalagi Tsulehisanvhi*," 66–67; Perdue, *Cherokee Editor*, 152n101.

24. Elias Boudinot to Stand Watie, Mar. 7, 1832, in Edward Everett Dale, "Letters of the Two Boudinots," *Chronicles of Oklahoma* 6 (1928), 332–33; Perdue, *Cherokee Editor*, ix. See also *Cherokee Cavaliers: Forty Years of Cherokee History as Told in the Correspondence of the Ridge-Watie-Boudinot Family*, ed. Edward E. Dale and Gaston Litton (Norman, 1995).

25. *Worcester v. Georgia*, 1832, in Richotte, *Federal Indian Law and Policy*, 64–70; Perdue, *Cherokee Editor*, 24–25; Jill Norgren, *The Cherokee Cases: Two Landmark Federal Decisions in the Fight for Sovereignty* (Norman, 2004).

26. *Cherokee Phoenix*, Mar. 24, 1832.

27. Boudinot, editorial, Mar. 24, 1832, *Cherokee Phoenix*, English translation by Tom Belt and Wiggins Blackfox, appendix 6, Owl, "*Tsalagi Tsulehisanvhi*," 116–20; Owl, "*Tsalagi Tsulehisanvhi*," 70–73.

28. *Cherokee Phoenix*, Dec. 21, 1831, 3; *Cherokee Phoenix*, Aug. 1, 1832; Perdue, *Cherokee Editor*, 25, 152n104, 153n105, 157, 174–75, 226n1; S. C. Stambaugh and Amos Kendall to the Secretary of War, Dec. 26, 1845, in "Message from the President of the United States Relative to the Cherokee Difficulties," Apr. 13, 1846, H.R. Doc. No. 185, 29th Cong., 1st Session (1846), 49–50; Richotte, *Federal Indian Law and Policy*, 73; Thurman Wilkins, *Cherokee Tragedy: The Ridge Family and the Decimation of a People*, rev. ed. (Norman, 1986), 236–38.

29. "An Act to add the Territory lying within the limits of this State, and occupied by the Cherokee Indians," Dec. 20, 1828, *Acts of the General Assembly of the State of Georgia*, 88–89; "An Act to declare void all contracts hereafter made with the Cherokee Indians," Dec. 23, 1830, *Acts of the General Assembly of the State of Georgia, Passed in Milledgeville at an Annual Session in October, November and December, 1830*, 118; Elias Boudinot, Aug. 4, 1832, in *Cherokee Editor*, 168; Perdue, *Cherokee Editor*, 226n22.

30. Elias Boudinot, "Letters and Other Papers Relating to Cherokee Affairs: Being a Reply to Sundry Publications Authorized by John Ross," 1837, in *Cherokee Editor*, 160.

31. Wayde Brown, *Reconstructing Historic Landmarks: Fabrication, Negotiation, and the Past* (New York, 2019), 171.

32. Cherokee Protest, 1834, Committee on Indian Affairs, 23rd Cong., SEN 23A-G6,

National Archives and Records Administration, Washington, D.C.; *Cherokee Phoenix*, Aug. 1, 1832; Perdue, *Cherokee Editor*, 25–26. Thank you to Patricia Dawson for alerting me to the 1834 petition and sharing her pictures of the amazing lists of names. Also see Memorial of John Ross and Others, Jan. 21, 1835, *Public Documents Printed by Order of the Senate of the United States, Second Session of the Twenty-Third Congress* (Washington, D.C., 1834–1835), vol. 3, document set 71.

33. Elias Boudinot to John Ross, Nov. 25, 1836, in *Cherokee Editor*, 225; Treaty with the Cherokee, 1835, in *Indian Affairs: Laws and Treaties*, 2:439–49.

34. Elias Boudinot to Benjamin and Eleanor Gold, Aug. 16, 1836, in *To Marry an Indian*, 183–90; Elias Boudinot to Benjamin and Eleanor Gold, May 20, 1837, in *To Marry an Indian*, 199–201.

35. The American Indian Archaeological Institute, "A Tale of Two Nations," *Artifacts* 10 (1981), 16; Perdue, *Cherokee Editor*, 30–31; Samuel Worcester to Daniel Brinsmade, June 27, 1839, in *To Marry an Indian*, 202–3. The National Council in October 1829 passed a resolution stating that "*whereas*, a law has been in existence for many years, but not committed to writing, that if any citizen or citizens of this Nation shall treat and dispose of any lands belonging to this Nation without special permission from the National Authorities, he or they, shall suffer death," and explicitly passed such a law. *Laws of the Cherokee Nation*, 136.

36. Nancy Hendricks, "Fayetteville Female Seminary," Encyclopedia of Arkansas, https://encyclopediaofarkansas.net/entries/fayetteville-female-seminary-2171/.

37. Julie L. Reed, *Serving the Nation: Cherokee Sovereignty and Social Welfare, 1800–1907* (Norman, 2016); Mary Ann Littlefield, "John Foster Wheeler of Fort Smith: Pioneer Printer and Publisher," *Arkansas Historical Quarterly* 44 (1985), 270–73; "History of the Cherokee Phoenix," https://www.cherokeephoenix.org/site/about.html; "*The Encyclopedia of Oklahoma History and Culture*," Oklahoma Historical Society, https://www.okhistory.org/publications/enc/entry.php?entry=CH016.

38. "Treaty with the Wyandot, Seneca, Delaware, Shawanese, Potawatomees, Ottawas, and Chippeway," 1817, in *Indian Affairs: Laws and Treaties*, ed. Charles J. Kappler (Washington, D.C., 1903–71), 2:145–55; list of Indian Tribes under the Superintendence of the Governor of Missouri Territory, Aug. 24, 1817, in *Territorial Papers*, 15:305–6; Stephen Warren, *Shawnees and Their Neighbors, 1795–1870* (Urbana, 2005), 15–16, 49–56; Calloway, *Shawnees and the War for America*, 56, 156–58; Edmunds, "Watchful Safeguard to Our Habitations," 198.

39. Henry Harvey, *History of the Shawnee Indians* (Cincinnati, 1855), 186–99; Treaty with the Shawnee, Aug. 8, 1831, in *Indian Affairs: Laws and Treaties*, 2:331–34.

40. Harvey, *History of the Shawnee Indians*, 208–13.

41. Harvey, *History of the Shawnee Indians*, 215–16, 230–32; Calloway, *Shawnees and the War for America*, 162–66; Warren, *Shawnees and Their Neighbors*, 106–7; John P. Bowes, *Exiles and Pioneers: Eastern Indians in the Trans-Mississippi West* (New York, 2007), 99–102.

42. Sami Lakomäki, *Gathering Together: The Shawnee People Through Diaspora and Nationhood, 1600–1870* (New Haven, 2014), 177–89.

43. List of Indian Tribes under the Superintendence of the Governor of Missouri Territory, Aug. 24, 1817, in *Territorial Papers*, 15:306; Richard Graham to John Calhoun, Dec. 23, 1823, in *Territorial Papers*, 19:580–82; Harvey, *History of the Shawnee Indians*, 184, 234–37; Calloway, *Shawnees and the War for America*, 156–61, 166–68; Warren,

Shawnees and Their Neighbors, 95–101; Lakomäki, *Gathering Together*, 153–64, 186–90. For similar U.S. removals of Miamis, Delawares, Wyandots, Potawatomis, and Ohio Senecas, see Bowes, *Land Too Good for Indians*, 66–76, 104–81.

44. Andrew Barnard to Edward Dudley, Apr. 6, 1840, quoted in John R. Finger, *The Eastern Band of Cherokee Indians* (Knoxville, 1984), 68; Finger, *Eastern Band*, 20–40, 67–70; Leonard Carson Lambert Jr., as told to Michael Lambert, *Up from These Hills: Memories of a Cherokee Boyhood* (Lincoln, 2011), x–xi, 3–10; Mikaëla M. Adams, *Who Belongs? Race, Resources, and Tribal Citizenship in the Native South* (New York, 2015), 96–168.

45. Claudia B. Haake, "Civilization, Law, and Customary Diplomacy: Arguments Against Removal in Cherokee and Seneca Letters to the Federal Government," *Native American and Indigenous Studies* 4 (2017), 37–38; Michael Leroy Oberg, *Peacemakers: The Iroquois, the United States, and the Treaty of Canandaigua, 1794* (New York, 2016), 132–33, 144; Mt. Pleasant, "Independence for Whom?" 127–28; *Treaty of Canandaigua, 1794: 200 Years of Treaty Relations Between the Iroquois Confederacy and the United States*, ed. G. Peter Jemison and Anna M. Schein (Santa Fe, 2000); Susan M. Hill, *The Clay We Are Made Of: Haudenosaunee Land Tenure on the Grand River* (Winnipeg, 2017), 175–90.

46. Susan Sleeper-Smith, *Indigenous Prosperity and American Conquest: Indian Women of the Ohio River Valley, 1690–1792* (Chapel Hill, 2018), 285, 319–20; Michael John Witgen, *Seeing Red: Indigenous Land, American Expansion, and the Political Economy of Plunder in North America* (Chapel Hill, 2022); Bowes, *Land Too Good for Indians*, 182–210; Brenda J. Child, *Holding Our World Together: Ojibwe Women and the Survival of Community* (New York, 2012), xix–xx; Stephen Kantrowitz, "'Not Quite Constitutionalized': The Meanings of 'Civilization' and the Limits of Native American Citizenship," in *The World the Civil War Made*, ed. Gregory P. Downs and Kate Masur (Chapel Hill, 2015), 75–105.

47. Malinda Maynor Lowery, *The Lumbee Indians: An American Struggle* (Chapel Hill, 2018), 64–65; Patrick H. Garrow, *The Mattamuskeet Documents: A Study in Social History* (Raleigh, 1975), 31–43, 46; Warren E. Milteer Jr., "From Indians to Colored People: The Problem of Racial Categories and the Persistence of the Chowans in North Carolina," *North Carolina Historical Review* 93 (2016), 28–57; Jean M. O'Brien, *Firsting and Lasting: Writing Indians Out of Existence in New England* (Minneapolis, 2010); Ann Marie Plane and Gregory Button, "The Massachusetts Indian Enfranchisement Act: Ethnic Contest in Historical Context, 1849–1869," in *After King Philip's War: Presence and Persistence in Indian New England*, ed. Colin G. Calloway (Hanover, N.H., 1997), 178–206; Helen Rountree, *Manteo's World: Native American Life in Carolina's Sound Country Before and After the Lost Colony* (Chapel Hill, 2021), 120; Michelle LeMaster, "In the 'Scolding Houses': Indians and the Law in Eastern North Carolina, 1684–1760," *North Carolina Historical Review* 83 (2006), 193–232; Brooke M. Bauer, *Becoming Catawba: Catawba Indian Women and Nation-Building, 1540–1840* (Tuscaloosa, 2022); James H. Merrell, *The Indians' New World: Catawbas and Their Neighbors from European Contact Through the Era of Removal* (New York, 1989); Daniel H. Usner, *Weaving Alliances with Other Women: Chitimacha Indian Work in the New South* (Athens, Ga., 2015); Denise E. Bates, ed., *We Will Always Be Here: Native Peoples on Living and Thriving in the South* (Gainesville, 2016).

48. Brenda J. Child, "Gender, Sexuality, and Family History: Naynaabeak's Fishing

Net," *The Oxford Handbook of American Indian History*, ed. Frederick E. Hoxie (New York, 2016), 398; Lowery, "On the Antebellum Fringe," 41–42; Ostler, *Surviving Genocide*, 368–73.

49. William Clark to John Calhoun, Sept. 5, 1823, vol. 53, box 28, Foreman Collection, Gilcrease Museum and Library, Tulsa, Okla., Eastern Shawnee Tribe of Oklahoma Digital Collection, https://ohiomemory.org/digital/collection/p16007coll27 /id/7365/; Warren, *Shawnees and Their Neighbors*, 91–94; R. David Edmunds, "A Patriot Defamed: Captain Lewis, Shawnee Chief," in *The Eastern Shawnee Tribe of Oklahoma: Resilience Through Adversity*, ed. Stephen Warren with the Eastern Shawnee Tribe of Oklahoma (Norman, 2017), 30–34.

50. Treaty of peace and friendship between the Osage nation and the Delawares, Shawanees, Kickapoos, Weas, Piankeshaws, and Peorias, Oct. 7, 1826, in *American State Papers: Indian Affairs*, 2:673–74; The Glass to the Cherokee Nation, Aug. 17, 1827, printed in *Cherokee Phoenix*, Apr. 17, 1828, English trans. in Jack Frederick Kilpatrick and Anna Gritts Kilpatrick, "Letters from an Arkansas Chief, 1828–1829," *Great Plains Journal* 1 (1965), 27–29; The Glass to the Cherokee Nation, Fall 1828, printed in the *Cherokee Phoenix*, Oct. 29, 1828, English trans. in Kilpatrick and Kilpatrick, "Letters," 29–31; Rollings, *The Osage*, 262; DuVal, *Native Ground*, chap. 7; Agnew, *Fort Gibson*, 69–70; Bowes, *Exiles and Pioneers*, 131–36; Lakomäki, *Gathering Together*, 179–81.

51. Wheelock, "Journal," 5:373, 375–76, 379; Stan Hoig, *Jesse Chisholm: Ambassador of the Plains* (1991; reissued Norman, 2005), 7–15, 39; Robert J. Conley, *A Cherokee Encyclopedia* (Albuquerque, 2007), 64, 90; William G. McLoughlin, *Cherokee Renascence in the New Republic* (Princeton, 1986), 111, 120–21, 152; C. A. Weslager, *The Delaware Indians: A History* (New Brunswick, N.J., 1990), 362. I haven't found anything about Denathdeago, the leader of the Seneca delegation.

52. Wheelock, "Journal," 5:373; Hildreth, *Dragoon Campaigns to the Rocky Mountains*, 118, 143; "A Journal of Marches by the First United States Dragoons, 1834–1835," ed. Louis Pelzer, *Iowa Journal of History and Politics* 7 (1909), 343; Catlin, *Letters and Notes*, 2:57, 71–75; James Mooney, "Calendar History of the Kiowa Indians," in *Seventeenth Annual Report of the Bureau of American Ethnology to the Secretary of the Smithsonian Institution, 1895–96* (Washington, D.C., 1898), 262–63. More Wichita women were ransomed the following year. "The Journal of the Proceedings at Our First Treaty with the Wild Indians, 1835," 400–401, 416.

53. Gregg, *Commerce of the Prairies*, 1:147.

54. Mark F. Boyd, "An Historical Sketch of the Prevalence of Malaria in North America," *American Journal of Tropical Medicine and Hygiene* s1-21 (1941), 229–30; Leonard McPhail, "The Diary of Assistant Surgeon Leonard McPhail on His Journey to the Southwest in 1835," ed. Harold W. Jones, *Chronicles of Oklahoma* 18 (1940), 285, 289–90; Thomas A. Apel, *Feverish Bodies, Enlightened Minds: Science and the Yellow Fever Controversy in the Early American Republic* (Stanford, 2016). Thanks to Carolyn Eastman for talking with me about malaria and yellow fever.

55. Hildreth, *Dragoon Campaigns to the Rocky Mountains*, 119, 147–48, 160, 175; Evans, "Journal," 181–84, 192–93; Catlin, *Letters and Notes*, 2:69, 72–73, 84; Wheelock, "Journal," 5:376–77; "Journal of Marches by the First United States Dragoons," 354; Mooney, "Calendar History," 264–68; Agnew, *Fort Gibson*, 123–25, 132, 236n26.

56. Mooney, "Calendar History," 264–68; Wheelock, "Journal," 5:377; Catlin, *Letters*

and Notes, 2:69, 76; Hugh Evans, "The Journal of Hugh Evans, Covering the First and Second Campaigns of the United States Dragoon Regiment in 1834 and 1835," ed. Fred S. Perrine and Grant Foreman, *Chronicles of Oklahoma* 3 (1925), 192–93; Hildreth, *Dragoon Campaigns to the Rocky Mountains,* 160; Agnew, *Fort Gibson,* 132; "Journal of Marches by the First United States Dragoons," 354.

57. Wheelock, "Journal," 5:380.

58. Catlin, *Letters and Notes,* 2:71–72, 75; Evans, "Journal," 194; Wheelock, "Journal," 5:378–79; Agnew, *Fort Gibson,* 128; Candace S. Greene, *One Hundred Summers: A Kiowa Calendar Record* (Lincoln, 2009), 204–5; Mooney, "Calendar History," 261–62, 269; John Joseph Mathews, *The Osages, Children of the Middle Waters* (Norman, 1961), 561.

59. Wheelock, "Journal," 5:378–80. These proceedings are also in Evans, "Journal," 195–205.

60. Wheelock, "Journal," 5:375–79.

61. Raymond J. DeMallie, "Early Kiowa and Comanche Treaties: The Treaties of 1835 and 1837," *American Indian Journal* 9 (1986), 16–17.

62. "Annual Report of the Secretary of War Showing the Condition of That Department in 1833," Nov. 29, 1833, *American State Papers: Military Affairs* (Washington, D.C., 1860), 5:170.

63. *Niles Register,* Aug. 2, 1834 (Baltimore), 46:390.

64. "The Journal of the Proceedings at Our First Treaty with the Wild Indians, 1835," 393; James Hildreth, *Dragoon Campaigns to the Rocky Mountains; Being a History of the Enlistment, Organization, and First Campaigns of the Regiment of United States Dragoons, Together with Incidents of a Soldier's Life and Sketches of Scenery and Indian Character, by a Dragoon* (New York, 1836), 119; Wheelock, "Journal," 5:373; Catlin, *Letters and Notes,* 2:84; Evans, "Journal," 190; Agnew, *Fort Gibson,* 115–16, 128, 130.

65. Wheelock, "Journal," 5:380.

66. Wheelock, "Journal," 5:380.

67. Wheelock, "Journal," 5:375–80; Mooney, "Calendar History," 268.

68. Catlin, *Letters and Notes,* 2:74; Wheelock, "Journal," 5:380; James William Abert, *Expedition to the Southwest: An 1845 Reconnaissance of Colorado, New Mexico, Texas, and Oklahoma,* ed. H. Bailey Carroll (Lincoln, 1999), 78; Mooney, "Calendar History," 259, 263; Ewers, *Murals in the Round,* 13; Greene, *One Hundred Summers,* 3, 48; Candace S. Greene, *Silver Horn: Master Illustrator of the Kiowas* (Norman, 2001), 25, 31; Candace S. Greene, "Exploring the Three 'Little Bluffs' of the Kiowa," *Plains Anthropologist* 41 (1996), 224–29; McKenzie, Harbour, and Watkins, introduction to "Plains Life in Kiowa," 13.

69. Evans, "Journal," 205–12; "Journal of Marches by the First United States Dragoons," 359; Wheelock, "Journal," 5:381; Catlin, *Letters and Notes,* 2:75–79; Agnew, *Fort Gibson,* 134–35.

70. Wheelock, "Journal," 5:382; Catlin, *Letters and Notes,* 2:82; Evans, "Journal," 212; "The Journal of the Proceedings at Our First Treaty with the Wild Indians, 1835," 394; Agnew, *Fort Gibson,* 136.

71. Evans, "Journal," 212–13; Wheelock, "Journal," 5:382.

72. Mooney, "Calendar History," 259; Rollings, *The Osage,* 271; Kathleen DuVal, "Cross-Cultural Crime and Osage Justice in the Western Mississippi Valley," *Ethnohistory* 54 (2007), 697–722.

73. "The Journal of the Proceedings at Our First Treaty with the Wild Indians, 1835," 394–416; McPhail, "Diary," 281–89; "Treaty with the Comanche and Wichetaw Indians and Their Associated Bands," Aug. 24, 1834, in *Indian Affairs: Laws and Treaties,* 2:435; DeMallie, "Early Kiowa and Comanche Treaties," 18–19; Agnew, *Fort Gibson,* 143–48.

74. Jackson, Sixth Annual Message to Congress, Dec. 1, 1834, in *Compilation of the Messages and Papers of the Presidents,* 3:112–13.

75. Catlin, *Letters and Notes,* 2:83; Mooney, "Calendar History," 171–72, 262; Gregg, *Commerce of the Prairies,* 2:18–19; Thomas W. Kavanagh, *Comanche Political History: An Ethnohistorical Perspective, 1706–1875* (Lincoln, 1996), 240.

76. Victor Tixier, *Travels on the Osage Prairies,* ed. John Francis McDermott, trans. Albert Salvan (Norman, 1940), 151; McPhail, "Diary," June 25–July 7, 284; William Armstrong to T. Hartley Crawford, n.d., in *Annual Report of the Commissioner of Indian Affairs,* 1839 (Washington, D.C., 1839), 475; "The Journal of the Proceedings at Our First Treaty with the Wild Indians, 1835," 396; Rollings, *The Osage,* 271–72; Kavanagh, *Comanche Political History,* 318; Agnew, *Fort Gibson,* 143; Brian DeLay, *War of a Thousand Deserts: Indian Raids and the U.S.-Mexican War* (New Haven, 2008), 106–8, 207; Silverman, *Thundersticks,* 241–42; Hoig, *Jesse Chisholm,* 43; David La Vere, *Contrary Neighbors: Southern Plains and Removed Indians in Indian Territory* (Norman, 2000), 118.

77. "The Journal of the Proceedings at Our First Treaty with the Wild Indians, 1835," 394–416; McPhail, "Diary," 281–89; Baird, *Quapaw Indians,* 84–86; Mathews, *The Osages,* 565–66; Rollings, *The Osage,* 271.

78. "Treaty with the Kioway, Ka-ta-ka and Ta-wa-ka-ro, Nations of Indians," in *Indian Affairs: Laws and Treaties,* 2:489; Mooney, "Calendar History," 169–72; Agnew, *Fort Gibson,* 149; Kavanagh, *Comanche Political History,* 242–43; DeMallie, "Early Kiowa and Comanche Treaties," 19–20; Greene, *One Hundred Summers,* 62–63, 206; George Bird Grinnell, *The Fighting Cheyennes* (1915; Norman, 1956), 66–69; Elliott West, *The Way to the West: Essays on the Central Plains* (Albuquerque, 1995), 14; Elliott West, *The Contested Plains: Indians, Goldseekers, and the Rush to Colorado* (Lawrence, Kan., 1998), 77; Jenny Tone-Pah-Hote, *Crafting an Indigenous Nation: Kiowa Expressive Culture in the Progressive Era* (Chapel Hill, 2019), 10; DeLay, *War of a Thousand Deserts,* 80–81; DeLay, "Foreign Relations Between Indigenous Polities," 387–411; Candace S. Greene and Thomas D. Drescher, "The Tipi with Battle Pictures: The Kiowa Tradition of Intangible Property Rights," *Trademark Reporter* 84 (1994), 420–23. Thanks to Jenny Tone-Pah-Hote for information on artwork about the Great Peace, Sitting Bear (Sa Tank'), and much else.

79. Greene, *One Hundred Summers,* 206.

80. DeLay, *War of a Thousand Deserts,* 83–85.

81. Rufus B. Sage, *Rocky Mountain Life,* 326–28; Kendall, *Narrative of an Expedition,* 1:210–25; Mooney, "Calendar History," 170, 277, 280; Abert, *Expedition to the Southwest,* 65, 77; Greene, *One Hundred Summers,* 58–59, 206; Kavanagh, *Comanche Political History,* 209–10; DeLay, *War of a Thousand Deserts,* 76–77.

82. Twenty years later, Texans removed the rest of the Shawnees and Delawares as well as Caddos and Wichitas—some fourteen hundred people. Bowes, *Land Too Good for Indians*, 214–16, 220; Lakomäki, *Gathering Together*, 187–91.

83. DeLay, *War of a Thousand Deserts*, 95, 117, 128–37; DeLay, "Foreign Relations Between Indigenous Polities," 387–411; Mooney, "Calendar History," 165, 271, 282; Kavanagh, *Comanche Political History*, 208–9; Greene, *One Hundred Summers*, 53.

84. Thomas S. Drew to George W. Manypenny, in *Annual Report of the Commissioner of Indian Affairs*, 1853 (Washington, D.C., 1853), 363; Mooney, "Calendar History," 165; Hyde, *Life of George Bent*, 69; Abert, *Expedition to the Southwest*, 67, 79; Momaday, *The Way to Rainy Mountain*, 57; Palmer, *Telling Stories the Kiowa Way*, 134n5; Alma Ahote, "Captive Woman," in "Plains Life in Kiowa," 43–50; Kavanagh, *Comanche Political History*, 208–9; DeLay, *War of a Thousand Deserts*, 93.

85. Ned Blackhawk, *Violence over the Land: Indians and Empires in the Early American West* (Cambridge, Mass., 2006), 179–81, 197–98; Garrett Wright, "Paawaariihusuɔ: Travel and the Central Great Plains" (Ph.D. diss., University of North Carolina, Chapel Hill, 2019), 27–37; Mooney, "Calendar History," 286, 297–99; John B. Dunbar, "The Pawnee Indians: The History and Ethnology," *Magazine of American History* 4 (1880), 250, 254–55; Rollings, *The Osage*, 272–75; DeLay, *War of a Thousand Deserts*, 127–28.

86. Mooney, "Calendar History," 165; Kavanagh, *Comanche Political History*, 208–9, 248, 284; George Bird Grinnell, "Bent's Old Fort and Its Builders," *Collections of the Kansas State Historical Society* 15 (1923), 42; DeLay, *War of a Thousand Deserts*, 83; Lakomäki, *Gathering Together*, 191–92.

87. John O'Sullivan, "Annexation," *United States Magazine and Democratic Review* 17 (1845), 5.

88. DeLay, *War of a Thousand Deserts*, xv, 253–54.

89. William Armstrong to T. Hartley Crawford, n.d., in *Annual Report of the Commissioner of Indian Affairs*, 1839, 475–76; Mooney, "Calendar History," 172; Hyde, *Life of George Bent*, 70.

90. William Emory, "Major Emory's Narrative," in *Notes of Travel in California; Comprising the Prominent Geographical, Agricultural, Geological, and Mineralogical Features of the Country; Also, the Route to San Diego, in California, Including Parts of the Arkansas, Del Norte, and Gila Rivers, from the Official Reports of Col. Fremont and Maj. Emory* (Dublin, 1849), 202–8; Edward H. Spicer, *Cycles of Conquest: The Impact of Spain, Mexico, and the United States on the Indians of the Southwest, 1533–1960* (Tucson, 1962), 132–33, 146–47; Winston P. Erickson, *Sharing the Desert: The Tohono O'odham in History* (Tucson, 1994), 68; Paul H. Ezell and Bernard L. Fontana, "Plants Without Water: The Pima-Maricopa Experience," *Journal of the Southwest* 36 (1994), 326.

91. Michael Wilcox, "Marketing Conquest and the Vanishing Indian: An Indigenous Response to Jared Diamond's Archaeology of the American Southwest," in *Questioning Collapse: Human Resilience, Ecological Vulnerability and the Aftermath of Empire*, ed. Patricia A. McAnany and Norman Yoffee (New York, 2010), 116; Woodson, *Social Origin of Hohokam Irrigation*; Martínez, "Hiding in the Shadows of History," 133; Ezell and Fontana, "Plants Without Water," 338.

92. Spicer, *Cycles of Conquest*, 133, 147; Erickson, *Sharing the Desert*, 69–76; David Rich Lewis, *Neither Wolf nor Dog: American Indians, Environment, and Agrarian Change* (New York, 1994), 135.

93. Ruth Murray Underhill, *Social Organization of the Papago Indians* (1939; New York, 1969), 105; Hurt, *Indian Agriculture*, 49–50; Lewis, *Neither Wolf nor Dog*, 134; Erickson, *Sharing the Desert*, 65–67; Natale A. Zappia, *Traders and Raiders: The Indigenous World of the Colorado Basin, 1540–1859* (Chapel Hill, 2014), 84–85, 126–29, 138–39; Spicer, *Cycles of Conquest*, 134–36, 147–48.

94. Akimel O'odham Oos:hikbina (calendar stick), c. 1833–1921, interpreted by Barnaby Lewis, permanent collection, National Museum of the American Indian, Washington, D.C.; Tohono O'odham calendar stick kept at San Xavier del Bac, in Ruth M. Underhill, *A Papago Calendar Record* (Albuquerque, 1938), 19–42; Webb, *A Pima Remembers*, 7–8; J. Andrew Darling and Barnaby V. Lewis, "Songscapes and Calendar Sticks," in *The Hohokam Millennium*, ed. Suzanne K. Fish and Paul R. Fish (Santa Fe, 2007), 137; Karl Jacoby, *Shadows at Dawn: A Borderlands Massacre and the Violence of History* (New York, 2008), 31–46.

95. Kavanagh, *Comanche Political History*, 317; Benjamin Madley, *An American Genocide: The United States and the California Indian Catastrophe, 1846–1873* (New Haven, 2016).

96. Mooney, "Calendar History," 168, 172–73, 274–75, 289–90; Gregg, *Commerce of the Prairies*, 1:147, 2:136–37; Larocque, "Journal of an Excursion," 206; Fitzpatrick to Mitchell, Sept. 24, 1850, in *Annual Report of the Commissioner of Indian Affairs, 1850* (Washington, D.C., 1850), 21; Hyde, *Life of George Bent*, 96; Greene, *One Hundred Summers*, 55, 64–65, 68–69, 206–7; Mallery, "Pictographs of the North American Indians," 142, plate XLVI; Greene and Thornton, *The Year the Stars Fell*, 203, 226; Fenn, *Encounters at the Heart of the World*, 84, 154–55, 317–25; DeLay, *War of a Thousand Deserts*, 305.

97. W. B. Napton, *Over the Santa Fe Trail, 1857* (Kansas City, 1905), 31–32; West, *The Way to the West*, 43–44.

98. Mooney, "Calendar History," 286–87, 290; Thomas Fitzpatrick to Thomas H. Harvey, Oct. 6, 1848, in *Annual Report of the Commissioner of Indian Affairs*, 1848 (Washington, D.C., 1848), 470–73; Greene, *One Hundred Summers*, 207; Fitzpatrick to D. D. Mitchell, Sept. 24, 1850, in *Annual Report of the Commissioner of Indian Affairs*, 1850, 19–25; Charles Redbird, "Wagon Attack," in "Plains Life in Kiowa," 51–54.

99. Fitzpatrick to Mitchell, Sept. 24, 1850, in *Annual Report of the Commissioner of Indian Affairs*, 1850, 19–25; Whitfield to Cumming, Sept. 27, 1854, in *Annual Report of the Commissioner of Indian Affairs*, 1854 (Washington, D.C., 1854), 89; Kavanagh, *Comanche Political History*, 321–22, 343–44.

100. Drew to Manypenny, in *Annual Report of the Commissioner of Indian Affairs*, 1853, 360–65; "Treaty with the Comanche, Kiowa, and Apache, 1853," in *Indian Affairs: Laws and Treaties*, 2:600–602.

101. Whitfield to Cumming, Sept. 27, 1854, in *Annual Report of the Commissioner of Indian Affairs*, 1854, 91, 95.

102. Drew to Manypenny, in *Annual Report of the Commissioner of Indian Affairs*, 1853, 360–65.

103. Whitfield to Cumming, Sept. 27, 1854, in *Annual Report of the Commissioner of Indian Affairs*, 1854, 91.

104. Robert C. Miller to A. M. Robinson, Aug. 17, 1858, *Report of the Commissioner of Indian Affairs Accompanying the Annual Report of the Secretary of the Interior for the Year 1858* (Washington, D.C., 1858), 97–98.

105. Miller to Robinson, Aug. 17, 1858, *Report of the Commissioner of Indian Affairs Accompanying the Annual Report of the Secretary of the Interior for the Year 1858*, 99.

106. John W. Whitfield to A. Cumming, Sept. 27, 1854, in *Annual Report of the Commissioner of Indian Affairs*, 1854, 95.

107. Drew to Manypenny, in *Annual Report of the Commissioner of Indian Affairs*, 1853, 360–65.

108. Spicer, *Cycles of Conquest*, 147–48.

109. Erickson, *Sharing the Desert*, 78; Spicer, *Cycles of Conquest*, 136; John L. Kessell, *Spain in the Southwest: A Narrative History of Colonial New Mexico, Arizona, Texas, and California* (Norman, 2002), 336; National Park Service San Xavier del Bac page; James S. Griffith, *Beliefs and Holy Places: A Spiritual Geography of the Pimería Alta* (Tucson, 1992), 159.

110. Scott Manning Stevens, "American Indians and the Civil War," *Why You Can't Teach United States History Without American Indians*, ed. Susan Sleeper-Smith, Juliana Barr, Jean M. O'Brien, Nancy Shoemaker, and Scott Manning Stevens (Chapel Hill, 2015), 139–40; West, *Contested Plains*; Benjamin R. Kracht, *Kiowa Belief and Ritual* (Lincoln, 2017), 49–50; Mooney, "Calendar History," 310–12. For smallpox, see the calendars for the winter of 1861–62, https://kiowacalendars.org.

111. Henry Rector to John Ross, Jan. 29, 1861, "Letters of Henry M. Rector and J. R. Kannaday to John Ross of the Cherokee Nation," ed. Harry J. Lemley, *Chronicles of Oklahoma* 42 (1964), 320.

112. *Report of the Commissioner of Indian Affairs, Accompanying the Annual Report of the Secretary of the Interior, for the Year 1861* (Washington, D.C., 1861), 9.

113. John R. Ridge to Stephen A. Douglas, Sept. 19, 1858, Stephen A. Douglas Papers, Special Collections Research Center, University of Chicago Library, Illinois; James W. Parins, *Elias Cornelius Boudinot: A Life on the Cherokee Border* (Lincoln, 2006). Many thanks to Sean Kicummah Teuton for introducing me to the career of E. C. Boudinot and to Joshua Lynn for sharing the John R. Ridge letter.

114. Arkansas State Constitution, 1861, Arkansas State Archives, Little Rock, Arkansas.

115. Baird, *Quapaw Indians*, 93–99, 103–8, 117–19.

116. Tai S. Edwards, "Disruption and Disease: The Osage Struggle to Survive in the Nineteenth-Century Trans-Missouri West," *Kansas History* 36 (2013/2014), 227; Warren, *Shawnees and Their Neighbors*, 127–29, 149–51, 155–58, 166–67.

117. C. Joseph Genetin-Pilawa, *Crooked Paths to Allotment: The Fight over Federal Indian Policy After the Civil War* (Chapel Hill, 2014); Mary Stockwell, *Interrupted Odyssey: Ulysses S. Grant and the American Indians* (Carbondale, 2018).

118. Theda Perdue, *Slavery and the Evolution of Cherokee Society, 1540–1866* (Knoxville, 1979); Fay A. Yarbrough, *Race and the Cherokee Nation: Sovereignty in the Nineteenth Century* (Philadelphia, 2008); Barbara Krauthamer, *Black Slaves, Indian Masters: Slavery, Emancipation, and Citizenship in the Native American South* (Chapel Hill, 2015); Alaina E. Roberts, *I've Been Here All the While: Black Freedom on Native Land* (Philadelphia, 2021).

119. *The Cherokee Tobacco*, 1870, in Richotte, *Federal Indian Law and Policy*, 87–91.

120. Stevens, "American Indians and the Civil War," 141–43; West, *Contested Plains*; Ari

Kelman, *A Misplaced Massacre: Struggling over the Memory of Sand Creek* (Cambridge, Mass., 2013); Heather Cox Richardson, *West from Appomattox: The Reconstruction of America After the Civil War* (New Haven, 2007).

121. "An Act to Establish Peace with Certain Hostile Indian Tribes," July 20, 1867, *U.S. Statutes at Large* 15 Stat. 17; Report to the President by the Indian Peace Commission, Jan. 7, 1868, in *Annual Report of the Commissioner of Indian Affairs, 1868* (Washington, D.C., 1868), 26; "Making appropriations for the current and contingent expenses of the Indian department, and for fulfilling treaty stipulations with various Indian tribes," Mar. 3, 1871, *U.S. Statutes at Large* 16 Stat. 566; Richotte, *Federal Indian Law and Policy,* 113–30.

122. *Cherokee Advocate,* Oct. 14, 1893, quoted in Reed, *Serving the Nation,* 3–4.

123. G. C. Snow to J. Wortham, Sept. 5, 1867, *Annual Report of the Commissioner of Indian Affairs, 1867* (Washington, D.C., 1867), 324; Baird, *Quapaw Indians,* 93–99, 103–8, 117–19.

124. Snow to Thomas Murphy, Sept. 8, 1868, *Annual Report of the Commissioner of Indian Affairs, 1868* (Washington, D.C., 1868), 272–73; Snow to Ely Parker, July 24, 1869, *Annual Report of the Commissioner of Indian Affairs, 1869* (Washington, D.C., 1869), 381–82; Risë Supernaw Proctor, "Quapaw Tribal Information," http://www.quapawtribalancestry.com/quapawtribalorder.htm; John Berrey, talk, July 5, 2018, Quapaw Tribal Museum, Quapaw, Okla.; Velma Seamster Nieberding, "St. Mary's of the Quapaws, 1894–1927," *Chronicles of Oklahoma* 31 (1953), 4–5; Velma Seamster Nieberding, *The Quapaws (Those Who Went Downstream)* (Miami, Okla., 1976), 103–13.

125. Warren, *Shawnees and Their Neighbors,* 170–71; Bowes, *Land Too Good for Indians,* 225; "History of the People," Shawnee Tribe, https://www.shawnee-nsn.gov/history.

126. Museum of the Cherokee Indian, Cherokee, N.C.; Malinda Maynor Lowery, *Lumbee Indians in the Jim Crow South: Race, Identity, and the Making of a Nation* (Chapel Hill, 2010), 15–16; Lowery, "On the Antebellum Fringe," 41; Brian Klopotek, *Recognition Odysseys: Indigeneity, Race, and Federal Tribal Recognition Policy in Three Louisiana Indian Communities* (Durham, 2011), 131–45.

127. Treaty with the Comanche and Kiowa, 1865, in *Indian Affairs: Laws and Treaties,* ed. Charles J. Kappler (Washington, D.C., 1903–71), 2:892–95; Mooney, "Calendar History," 319–20; Jerrold E. Levy, "Kiowa," in *Handbook of North American Indians: Plains,* ed. Raymond J. DeMallie (Washington, D.C., 2001), 915.

128. Report to the President by the Indian Peace Commission, Jan. 7, 1868, in *Annual Report of the Commissioner of Indian Affairs,* 1868, 27–39; Treaty with the Kiowa and Comanche, 1867, in *Indian Affairs: Laws and Treaties,* 2:977–84; Levy, "Kiowa," 915; Kracht, *Kiowa Belief and Ritual,* 52; Richotte, *Federal Indian Law and Policy,* 140–41.

129. N. Scott Momaday, *The Way to Rainy Mountain* (Albuquerque, 1969; 2019), 8; Mooney, "Calendar History," 321–45.

130. Ezell and Fontana, "Plants Without Water," 363–70.

131. Papago Tribe of Arizona, *Tohono O'odham: History of the Desert People* (Tohono O'odham, Ariz., 1985), 41–42; Tohono O'odham calendar stick kept at San Xavier del Bac, in Underhill, *Papago Calendar Record,* 20–21, 33; Erickson, *Sharing the Desert,* 82–85; Spicer, *Cycles of Conquest,* 137–39.

132. David H. Dejong, "'See the New Country': The Removal Controversy and Pima-Maricopa Water Rights, 1869–1879," *Journal of Arizona History* 33 (1992), 379–83; Spicer, *Cycles of Conquest,* 148.

CHAPTER 12: THE SURVIVAL OF NATIONS

1. Jenny Tone-Pah-Hote, *Crafting an Indigenous Nation: Kiowa Expressive Culture in the Progressive Era* (Chapel Hill, 2019), 80–84; Jacki Thompson Rand, *Kiowa Humanity and the Invasion of the State* (Lincoln, 2008).

2. Keith Richotte Jr., *Federal Indian Law and Policy: An Introduction* (St. Paul, Minn., 2020), 113; Susan M. Hill, *The Clay We Are Made Of: Haudenosaunee Land Tenure on the Grand River* (Winnipeg, 2017), 212–38.

3. Arthur C. Parker, *The Constitution of the Five Nations* (Albany, 1916), 12.

4. William N. Fenton, "This Island, the World on the Turtle's Back," *Journal of American Folklore* 75 (1962), 284.

5. Doug George Kanentiio, "Iroquois Population Update," *Indian Time,* Jan. 8, 2015, https://www.indiantime.net/story/2015/01/08/opinion/iroquois-population-update /16409.html; "The American Indian and Alaska Native Population: 2010," https:// www.census.gov/prod/cen2010/briefs/c2010br-10.pdf; Tom Sakokwenionkwas Porter, *Kanatsiohareke: Traditional Mohawk Indians Return to Their Ancestral Homeland* (Kanatsiohareke and Greenfield Center, N.Y., 2006), 21, 92–93.

6. Daniel Lopez, Joseph T. Joaquin, Stanley Cruz, and Angelo J. Joaquin Jr., 2003, Himdag Ki Tohono O'odham Nation Cultural Center and Museum exhibit.

7. Tone-Pah-Hote, *Crafting an Indigenous Nation,* xii.

8. Michael John Witgen, *Seeing Red: Indigenous Land, American Expansion, and the Political Economy of Plunder in North America* (Chapel Hill, 2022); Robert Lee, "Accounting for Conquest: The Price of the Louisiana Purchase of Indian Country," *Journal of American History* 104 (2017), 921–42.

9. Malinda Maynor Lowery, *The Lumbee Indians: An American Struggle* (Chapel Hill, 2018), xiii; Julie L. Reed, *Serving the Nation: Cherokee Sovereignty and Social Welfare, 1800–1907* (Norman, 2016); Michael Wilcox, "Marketing Conquest and the Vanishing Indian: An Indigenous Response to Jared Diamond's Archaeology of the American Southwest," in *Questioning Collapse: Human Resilience, Ecological Vulnerability and the Aftermath of Empire,* ed. Patricia A. McAnany and Norman Yoffee (New York, 2010), 135–38.

10. For a more in-depth survey of this period, see David Treuer, *The Heartbeat of Wounded Knee: Native America from 1890 to the Present* (New York, 2019).

11. Frank B. Linderman, *Pretty-shield: Medicine Woman of the Crows* (Lincoln, 2003), 44; James Mooney, "Calendar History of the Kiowa Indians," in *Seventeenth Annual Report of the Bureau of American Ethnology to the Secretary of the Smithsonian Institution, 1895–96* (Washington, D.C., 1898), 235; Tone-Pah-Hote, *Crafting an Indigenous Nation,* xi.

12. JoAllyn Archambault, "Sun Dance," in *Handbook of North American Indians: Plains,* 988; Levy, "Kiowa," 917, 988; Benjamin R. Kracht, *Kiowa Belief and Ritual* (Lincoln, 2017), 327; Momaday, *The Way to Rainy Mountain,* 65; Candace S. Greene, *One Hundred Summers: A Kiowa Calendar Record* (Lincoln, 2009), 120–21; Jennifer

Graber, *The Gods of Indian Country: Religion and the Struggle for the American West* (New York, 2018), 154–79.

13. Richotte, *Federal Indian Law and Policy*, 74, 329; Treuer, *Heartbeat of Wounded Knee*, 1; Reed, *Serving the Nation;* Christina Snyder, "The Rise and Fall and Rise of Civilizations: Indian Intellectual Culture During the Removal Era," *Journal of American History* (2017), 406.

14. *Journal of the General Council of the Indian Territory* (Lawrence, 1870); *Journal of the Second Annual Session of the General Council of the Indian Territory* (Lawrence, 1871); *Journal of the Adjourned Session of the Sixth Annual General Council of the Indian Territory* (Lawrence, 1875); Greene, *One Hundred Summers,* 100–101, 104–5; Annie H. Abel, "Proposals for an Indian State, 1778–1878," *Annual Report of the American Historical Association for the Year 1907* (Washington, D.C., 1908), 1:100–104.

15. David E. Wilkins and Heidi Kiiwetinepinesiik Stark, *American Indian Politics and the American Political System*, 3rd ed. (Lanham, Md., 2011), 4–17, 308; *Recognition, Sovereignty Struggles, and Indigenous Rights in the United States: A Sourcebook,* ed. Amy E. Den Ouden and Jean M. O'Brien (Chapel Hill, 2013), 14–15; Brian Klopotek, *Recognition Odysseys: Indigeneity, Race, and Federal Tribal Recognition Policy in Three Louisiana Indian Communities* (Durham, 2011), 2–3; Jeffrey Ostler and Nick Estes, "The Supreme Law of the Land: Standing Rock and the Dakota Access Pipeline," in *Standing with Standing Rock: Voices from the #NoDAPL Movement,* ed. Nick Estes and Jaskiran Dhillo (Minneapolis, 2019), 96–100.

16. Anton Treuer, *Everything You Wanted to Know About Indians But Were Afraid to Ask* (St. Paul, Minn., 2012), 138; Rayford W. Logan, *The Negro in American Life and Thought: The Nadir, 1877–1901* (New York, 1954); Paul Chaat Smith, *Everything You Know About Indians Is Wrong* (Minneapolis, 2009), 2; Fredrick Hoxie, *A Final Promise: The Campaign to Assimilate the Indians, 1880–1920* (1948; Lincoln, 2001); Kendra Taira Field, *Growing Up with the Country: Family, Race, and Nation After the Civil War* (New Haven, 2018), 1–4; Jeffrey M. Schulze, *Are We Not Foreigners Here? Indigenous Nationalism in the U.S.-Mexico Borderlands* (Chapel Hill, 2018), 59, 150.

17. Helen Hunt Jackson, *A Century of Dishonor: A Sketch of the United States Government's Dealings with Some of the Indian Tribes* (Boston, 1889).

18. Jean Dennison, *Colonial Entanglement: Constituting a Twenty-First-Century Osage Nation* (Chapel Hill, 2012), 56.

19. The General Allotment Act of 1887 is also called the Dawes Act for Senator Henry Dawes. Jodi A. Byrd, *The Transit of Empire: Indigenous Critiques of Colonialism* (Minneapolis, 2011), xi; Richotte, *Federal Indian Law and Policy*, 95; John P. Bowes, "Divided Lands and Dispersed People: Allotment and the Eastern Shawnees from the 1870s to the 1920s," in *The Eastern Shawnee Tribe of Oklahoma: Resilience Through Adversity,* ed. Stephen Warren with the Eastern Shawnee Tribe of Oklahoma (Norman, 2017), 58–71.

20. R. David Edmunds, Frederick E. Hoxie, and Neal Salisbury, *The People: A History of Native America* (Boston, 2007), 326.

21. Quapaw Elder Vida Valliere interview, Mar. 31, 1938, University of Oklahoma Libraries, Norman; W. David Baird, *The Quapaw Indians: A History of the Downstream People* (Norman, 1980), 119–26, 130.

22. Quapaw Nation General Council Meeting Minutes, July 17, 1886, courtesy Quapaw TPHO Everett Bandy; Quapaw Elder Irene Shafer interview, Dec. 1, 1937, University of Oklahoma Libraries, Norman; Baird, *Quapaw Indians,* 127–29; Nieberding, Quapaws, 115–29. The current enrollment roll used by the Quapaw Nation was researched and finalized in 1959 and does not include the individuals adopted in the late 1800s. Many thanks to Everett Bandy for helping me understand this complicated history.

23. Baird, *Quapaw Indians,* 131–47.

24. Baird, *Quapaw Indians,* 142, 150–75.

25. Richotte, *Federal Indian Law and Policy,* 141–46; Tone-Pah-Hote, *Crafting an Indigenous Nation,* 22–23.

26. Levy, "Kiowa," 918–19; David A. Chang, *The Color of the Land: Race, Nation, and the Politics of Landownership in Oklahoma, 1832–1929* (Chapel Hill, 2010).

27. Snyder, "The Rise and Fall and Rise of Civilizations," 409.

28. Richard H. Pratt, "The Advantages of Mingling Indians with Whites," *Americanizing the American Indians: Writings by the "Friends of the Indian" 1880–1900,* ed. Francis Paul Prucha (Cambridge, Mass., 1973), 260–71.

29. The National Native American Boarding School Healing Coalition, "Healing Voices Volume 1: A Primer on American Indian and Alaska Native Boarding Schools in the U.S.," 2nd ed., June 2020, available at https://boardingschoolhealing .org; Robin Dushane with Sarah Mohawk Dushane Longbone and Robert "Bobby" Bluejacket, "Shawnee Resilience: Eastern Shawnees and the Boarding School Experience," in *Eastern Shawnee Tribe of Oklahoma,* 91–92; K. Tsianina Lomawaima, *They Called It Prairie Light: The Story of Chilocco Indian School* (Lincoln, 1995); Brenda J. Child, *Boarding School Seasons: American Indian Families, 1900–1940* (Lincoln, 2000); Richotte, *Federal Indian Law and Policy,* 107.

30. Porter, *Kanatsiohareke,* 90–92; Nieberding, *Quapaws,* 135.

31. Brenda J. Child, "The Boarding School as Metaphor," *Journal of Indian Education* 57 (2018), 37–57; Rose Stremlau, *Sustaining the Cherokee Family: Kinship and the Allotment of an Indigenous Nation* (Chapel Hill, 2011); Leonard Carson Lambert Jr., as told to Michael Lambert, *Up from These Hills: Memories of a Cherokee Boyhood* (Lincoln, 2011), xiii, 65–67.

32. Dushane with Longbone and Bluejacket, "Shawnee Resilience," 87–100; Amanda J. Cobb, *Our Grandmothers' Stories: The Bloomfield Academy for Chickasaw Females, 1852–1949* (Lincoln, 2000).

33. Richotte, *Federal Indian Law and Policy,* 108; Louis S. Warren, *God's Red Son: The Ghost Dance Religion and the Making of Modern America* (New York, 2017); Mooney, "Calendar History," 349–50; Graber, *Gods of Indian Country,* 84–85, 162–63, 173–74.

34. Papago Tribe of Arizona, *Tohono O'odham,* 42; Spicer, *Cycles of Conquest,* 140, 149–50.

35. Richotte, *Federal Indian Law and Policy,* 113.

36. David S. Jones, "Population, Health, and Public Welfare," in *The Oxford Handbook of American Indian History,* ed. Frederick E. Hoxie (New York, 2016), 416, citing S. N. Clark, "Are the Indians Dying Out? Preliminary Observations Relating to Indian Civilization and Education" (Nov. 24, 1877), in *Annual Report of the Com-*

missioner of Indian Affairs to the Secretary of the Interior for the Year 1877 (Washington, D.C., 1877), 520.

37. Andrew McKenzie, Daniel Harbour, and Laurel J. Watkins, eds., introduction to "Plains Life in Kiowa: Voices from a Tribe in Transition," *International Journal of Linguistics* 88 (2021), 10; "Muscogee History," https://www.fivecivilizedtribes.org /Muscogee-History.html; "Tribal Histories: Muscogee (Creek) Nation Research Report," https://ftp.txdot.gov/pub/txdot-info/env/toolkit/415-08-rpt.pdf; http:// www.mcn-nsn.gov/culturehistory; Justin Gage, *We Do Not Want the Gates Closed Between Us: Native Networks and the Spread of the Ghost Dance* (Norman, 2020); Brenda J. Child, *My Grandfather's Knocking Sticks: Ojibwe Family Life and Labor on the Reservation* (Minneapolis, 2014); William J. Bauer Jr., *We Were All Like Migrant Workers Here: Work, Community, and Memory on California's Round Valley Reservation, 1850–1941* (Chapel Hill, 2009).

38. David Martínez, *Dakota Philosopher: Charles Eastman and American Indian Thought* (St. Paul, Minn., 2009), 55–56, 60.

39. Sherman Coolidge, "The Function of the Society of American Indians," *The Quarterly Journal of the Society of American Indians* 2 (1914), reprinted in *American Indian Nonfiction: An Anthology of Writings, 1760s–1930s*, ed. Bernd C. Peyer (Norman, 2007), 346.

40. Arthur C. Parker, *Parker on the Iroquois*, ed. William N. Fenton (Syracuse, 1981); Chip Colwell-Chanthaphonh, *Inheriting the Past: The Making of Arthur C. Parker and Indigenous Archaeology* (Tucson, 2016); Joy Porter, *To Be Indian: The Life of Seneca-Iroquois Arthur Caswell Parker* (Norman, 2001); Robert Warrior, "The SAI and the End(s) of Intellectual History," *American Indian Quarterly* 37 (2013), 219–35; David Martínez, "Carlos Montezuma's Fight Against 'Bureauism': An Unexpected Pima Hero," *American Indian Quarterly* 37 (2013), 311–30; K. Tsianina Lomawaima, "The Mutuality of Citizenship and Sovereignty: The Society of American Indians and the Battle to Inherit America," *American Indian Quarterly* 37 (2013), 333–51 (and other articles in this volume of the *AIQ*).

41. Tone-Pah-Hote, *Crafting an Indigenous Nation;* John W. Troutman, *Indian Blues: American Indians and the Politics of Music, 1879–1934* (Norman, 2009).

42. Russel Lawrence Barsh, "American Indians in the Great War," *Ethnohistory* 38 (1991), 277–80; Treuer, *Heartbeat of Wounded Knee,* 189, 219; Thomas A. Britten, *American Indians in World War I: At Home and at War* (Albuquerque, 1997).

43. Arthur C. Parker, "Why the Red Man Fights for Democracy," *Carlisle Arrow and Red Man,* Nov. 2, 1917.

44. Michael Leroy Oberg, "Onondaga, 1918: A Declaration of War, and Other Stories," https://michaelleroyoberg.com/teaching-native-american-history/onondaga-1917 -a-declaration-of-war-and-other-stories/; "Did You Know? Oneidas Declared War on Germany in 1918," Oneida Indian Nation, https://www.oneidaindiannation .com/did-you-know-oneidas-declared-war-on-germany-in-1918/; Treuer, *Heartbeat of Wounded Knee,* 189.

45. Indian Citizenship Act, June 2, 1924, Public Law 68-175, 43 Stat 253.

46. Ernest Benedict to the American Civil Liberties Union, Mar. 27, 1941, quoted in Laurence M. Hauptman, *Seven Generations of Iroquois Leadership: The Six Nations Since 1800* (Syracuse, 2008), 172; Laurence M. Hauptman, *Tribes and Tribulations: Misconceptions About American Indians and Their Histories* (Albuquerque, 1995),

74–75; Richotte, *Federal Indian Law and Policy,* 154–55; The Six Nations, *Memorandum in Support of the Position of the Six Nations That They Constitute an Independent State* (Branford, Ontario, 1924), 1. Thanks to Margaret Franz for alerting me to the 1924 Six Nations memorandum.

47. Hauptman, *Tribes and Tribulations,* 77; Treuer, *Heartbeat of Wounded Knee,* 200–201.

48. "The Meriam Report," http://nativeamericannetroots.net/diary/1414; Valerie Lambert, *Native Agency: Indians in the Bureau of Indian Affairs* (Minneapolis, 2022), 11, 46–47; Ned Blackhawk, *The Rediscovery of America: Native Peoples and the Unmaking of U.S. History* (New Haven, 2023), 392–98; Treuer, *Everything You Wanted to Know About Indians,* 140.

49. Alysa Landry, "Herbert Hoover: Only US President to Have Lived on Indian Reservation," Aug. 2, 2016, updated Sept. 13, 2018, *Indian Country Today,* https:// indiancountrytoday.com/archive/herbert-hoover-only-us-president-to-have -lived-on-indian-reservation.

50. Richotte, *Federal Indian Law and Policy,* 153–56, 162–66; Doug Kiel, "Nation v. Municipality: Indigenous Land Recovery, Settler Resentment, and Taxation on the Oneida Reservation," *Native American and Indigenous Studies* 6 (2019), 53; Lambert, *Native Agency.*

51. Richotte, *Federal Indian Law and Policy,* 170–72; Archambault, "Sun Dance," 988; Jacob Betz, "Beyond the Judeo-Christian Tradition? Restoring American Indian Religion to Twentieth-Century U.S. History," *Why You Can't Teach United States History Without American Indians,* 232.

52. "Landmark Indian Water Rights Settlement Fully Implemented," U.S. Department of Interior Indian Affairs, https://www.bia.gov/as-ia/opa/online-press -release/landmark-indian-water-rights-settlement-fully-implemented; "About [the] Water Settlement," Gila River Indian Community, https://www.gilariver .org/index.php/about/water-settlement; Ruth Murray Underhill, *Social Organization of the Papago Indians* (1939; New York, 1969), 105; Winston P. Erickson, *Sharing the Desert: The Tohono O'odham in History* (Tucson, 1994), 99–102, 126–28, 132–52; Spicer, *Cycles of Conquest,* 142–44, 151; James S. Griffith, *Beliefs and Holy Places: A Spiritual Geography of the Pimería Alta* (Tucson, 1992), 73; Jeffrey M. Schultz, *Are We Not Foreigners Here? Indigenous Nationalism in the U.S.-Mexico Borderlands* (Chapel Hill, 2018), 139–40, 144–45, 193–94; J. Brett Hill, *From Huhugam to Hohokam: Heritage and Archaeology in the American Southwest* (Lanham, Md., 2019), xi.

53. Lambert, as told to Lambert, *Up from These Hills,* 42; Lawrence T. Locklear, "UNCP's Founders," https://www.uncp.edu/about/history/uncps-founders; Marvin Richardson, "Find Your Path to Help Your People," Nov. 25, 2019, University of North Carolina, Chapel Hill; Marvin Richardson, "Racial Choices: The Emergence of the Haliwa-Saponi Indian Tribe, 1835–1971" (Ph.D. diss., University of North Carolina, Chapel Hill, 2016).

54. Baird, *Quapaw Indians,* 176–78, 203–5, 209–11.

55. Nancy Shoemaker, *American Indian Population Recovery in the Twentieth Century* (Albuquerque, 1999), 75.

56. Jim Windle, "Six Nations Confederacy on the Global Stage in 1942," Sept. 21, 2016, *Two Row Times,* https://tworowtimes.com/news/local/six-nations-confederacy-on

-the-global-stage-in-1942/; "The Russians Remember," *Mohawk Nation News*, http://mohawknationnews.com/blog/tag/iroquois-declare-war-on-germany-ww -1-ii/; Oberg, "Onondaga, 1918"; Hauptman, *Tribes and Tribulations*, 76; Treuer, *Heartbeat of Wounded Knee*, 218; Erickson, *Sharing the Desert*, 154–55; William C. Meadows, "The Code Talkers' Legacy: Native Languages Helped Turn the Tides in Both World Wars," *American Indian Magazine* (Fall 2020), 14–17; Kenneth William Townsend, *World War II and the American Indians* (Albuquerque, 2000), 103–24; Laurence M. Hauptman, *The Iroquois Struggle for Survival: World War II to Red Power* (Syracuse, 1986), 2–5.

57. Treuer, *Heartbeat of Wounded Knee*, 222.

58. Gus Palmer obituary, Nov. 21, 2006, Indianz.com, https://www.indianz.com/News /2006/016997.asp; Laura E. Smith, *Horace Poolaw, Photographer of American Indian Modernity* (Lincoln, 2016), xvii–xxviii; William C. Meadows, *Kiowa, Apache, and Comanche Military Societies: Enduring Veterans, 1800 to the Present* (Austin, 1999), 139–76; McKenzie, Harbour, and Watkins, eds., introduction to "Plains Life in Kiowa," 10.

59. Douglas K. Miller, *Indians on the Move: Native American Mobility and Urbanization in the Twentieth Century* (Chapel Hill, 2019); Joseph Mitchell, "The Mohawks in High Steel," Sept. 17, 1949, *New Yorker*, 38–52; https://www.wnyc.org/story /192807-sky-walking-raising-steel-mohawk-ironworker-keeps-tradition-alive/; Brenda J. Child, *Holding Our World Together: Ojibwe Women and the Survival of Community* (New York, 2010), 139–60.

60. Treuer, *Heartbeat of Wounded Knee*, 288–90; Baird, *Quapaw Indians*, 209; Jeffrey M. Schulze, *Are We Not Foreigners Here? Indigenous Nationalism in the U.S.-Mexico Borderlands* (Chapel Hill, 2018), 154.

61. Gretchen G. Harvey, "Ruth Muskrat Bronson," *Notable American Women: A Biographical Dictionary Completing the Twentieth Century*, ed. Susan Ware and Stacy Braukman (Cambridge, Mass., 2004), 80–82; Erin Binney, "The Best of Both Worlds," *Mount Holyoke Alumnae Quarterly* (Winter 2018).

62. Ruth Muskrat Bronson, "The American Indian," speech and panel discussion, 1949, Sixth Race Relations Institute, NAACP, Amistad Research Center, New Orleans; Richotte, *Federal Indian Law and Policy*, 173, 181–82; Amy E. Den Ouden and Jean M. O'Brien, eds., "Introduction: Why 'Recognition' Matters," in *Recognition, Sovereignty Struggles, & Indigenous Rights in the United States: A Sourcebook* (Chapel Hill, 2013); Kyle T. Mays, "Transnational Progressivism: African Americans, Native Americans, and the Universal Races Congress of 1911," *American Indian Quarterly* 37 (2013), 243–61.

63. Donald L. Fixico, *Termination and Relocation: Federal Indian Policy, 1945–1960* (Albuquerque, 1986); Hauptman, *Iroquois Struggle for Survival*, 45–83; Treuer, *Heartbeat of Wounded Knee*, 255–56, 277; Treuer, *Everything You Wanted to Know About Indians*, 99.

64. Wilma Mankiller, *Mankiller: A Chief and Her People*.

65. Richotte, *Federal Indian Law and Policy*, 180; Treuer, *Heartbeat of Wounded Knee*, 268, 277–78, 296; Sean Kicummah Teuton, *Red Land, Red Power: Grounding Knowledge in the American Indian Novel* (Durham, 2008), 72.

66. Treuer, *Heartbeat of Wounded Knee*, 279.

67. Tone-Pah-Hote, *Crafting an Indigenous Nation*, xi; Jessica R. Locklear, "Leaving

the Only Land I Know: A History of Lumbee Migrations to Philadelphia, Pennsylvania" (MA thesis, Temple University, 2020); Ashley Minner, "The Lumbee Community: Revisiting the Reservation of Baltimore's Fells Point," in *Baltimore Revisited: Stories of Inequality and Resistance in a U.S. City*, ed. P. Nicole King, Kate Drabinski, and Joshua Clark Davis (New Brunswick, 2019), 185–96.

68. Miller, *Indians on the Move*, 160–86.

69. John Berrey talk, Quapaw Tribal Museum, Quapaw Nation, July 5, 2018.

70. Marvin Richardson, "Find Your Path to Help Your People," Nov. 25, 2019, University of North Carolina, Chapel Hill; Marvin Richardson, "Generations Within the Circle," in *We Will Always Be Here: Native Peoples on Living and Thriving in the South*, ed. Denise E. Bates (Gainesville, 2016), 131–39; Ashley Minner, "A Tour of Baltimore's American Indian 'Reservation,'" *American Indian* (Summer 2022), 10–11.

71. Tommy Orange, *There There* (New York, 2018), 8–9; Child, *Holding Our World Together*, 148–60.

72. Donald L. Fixico, "From Tribal to Indian: American Indian Identity in the Twentieth Century," in *Native Diasporas: Indigenous Identities and Settler Colonialism in the Americas*, ed. Gregory D. Smithers and Brooke N. Newman (Lincoln, 2014), 473, 484–86; Laurence M. Hauptman and Jack Campisi, "The Voice of Eastern Indians: The American Indian Chicago Conference of 1961 and the Movement for Federal Recognition," *Proceedings of the American Philosophical Society* (1988), 316–29; Hauptman, *Tribes and Tribulations*, 95–108; Robert Warrior, "The Indian Renaissance, 1960–2000: Stumbling to Victory, or Anecdotes of Persistence?," *The Oxford Handbook of American Indian History*, ed. Frederick E. Hoxie (New York, 2016), 131–32.

73. Lowery, *Lumbee Indians in the Jim Crow South*.

74. Marvin M. Richardson, "Looking Past the Racial Classification System: Teaching Southeastern Native Survival Using the Peoplehood Model," in *Understanding and Teaching Native American History*, ed. Kristofer Ray and Brady DeSanti (Madison, 2022), 193–95; Katherine Osburn, *Choctaw Resurgence in Mississippi: Race, Class, and Nation Building in the Jim Crow South, 1830–1977* (Lincoln, 2014).

75. Jason Baird Jackson, "The Opposite of Powwow: Ignoring and Incorporating the Intertribal War Dance in the Oklahoma Stomp Dance Community," *Plains Anthropologist* 48 (2003), 237–53; Ethel Brotherton, interview, 1938, Oklahoma Federation of Labor Collection, M452, box 5, folder 2, Western History Collections, University of Oklahoma, Norman; Maude Supernaw, "Stick Dance & Stomp Dance," "Stomp Dance Grounds," and "Stomp Dance & Quapaw Dance," interviews by Bill Supernaw Jr., 1965, http://www.quapawtribalancestry.com/oralhistory/page4.htm; Baird, *Quapaw Indians*, 212; Risë Supernaw Proctor, Reservation and Removal Panel, Clinton Presidential Center, Little Rock, Ark., Feb. 13, 2017; Amy Dianne Bergseth, "'Each Band Knew Their Own Country': Land, Cooperation, and Community in Nineteenth-Century Shawnee Intertribal Interactions," in *Eastern Shawnee Tribe of Oklahoma*, 81; interviews with Larry Kropp, Winifred "Winkie" Froman, Brett Barnes, Rhonda Barnes, Shawn King, Norma Kraus, and Joe Kraus, in *Eastern Shawnee Tribe of Oklahoma*, 284–85, 300–301, 304–6, 314–21, 336–37; Clyde Ellis, *A Dancing People: Powwow Culture on the Southern Plains*

(Lawrence, 2003); Archambault, "Sun Dance," 989; Treuer, *Everything You Wanted to Know About Indians*, 68–78.

76. Andy Warrior, 2005 interview, in Stephen Warren and Randolph Noe, "The Greatest Travelers in America: Shawnee Survival in the Shatter Zone," in *Mapping the Mississippian Shatter Zone: The Colonial Indian Slave Trade and Regional Instability in the American South*, ed. Robbie Ethridge and Sheri M. Shuck-Hall (Lincoln, 2009), 179.

77. Meredith L. McCoy, "We Are Here: Powwow and Higher Education in North Carolina," *Southern Cultures* 24 (2018), 106–18; Chris Goertzen, "Powwows and Identity on the Piedmont and Coastal Plains of North Carolina," *Ethnomusicology* 45 (2001), 59–62; Levy, "Kiowa," 918–20; Marvin Richardson, "Find Your Path to Help Your People," Nov. 25, 2019; Lumbee Homecoming (website), https://www.lumbeehomecoming.com/; Locklear, "Leaving the Only Land I Know," 48; Forest Hazel, "Occaneechi-Saponi Descendants in the Texas Community of the North Carolina Piedmont," *Excavating Occaneechi Town*.

78. William Kugee Supernaw, talk, July 5, 2018, Quapaw Tribal Museum; Tone-Pah-Hote, *Crafting an Indigenous Nation*, 34–43; Betz, "Beyond the Judeo-Christian Tradition," 231–32; Baird, *Quapaw Indians*, 180–82; Nieberding, *Quapaws*, 135–46; John Berrey autobiographical statement, https://www.friendsofjohnberrey.com/meet-john-berrey; Risë Supernaw Proctor and John Berrey talks, Clinton Presidential Center, Feb. 13, 2017; Levy, "Kiowa," 917–18, 920.

79. Paul Chaat Smith and Robert Allen Warrior, *Like a Hurricane: The Indian Movement from Alcatraz to Wounded Knee* (New York, 1996); Child, *Holding Our World Together*, 156–60; Brooke Bauer and Elizabeth Ellis, "Indigenous, Native American, or American Indian? The Limitations of Broad Terms," *Journal of the Early Republic*, forthcoming; Smith, *Everything You Know About Indians Is Wrong*, 18–19; Teuton, *Red Land, Red Power;* Treuer, *Heartbeat of Wounded Knee*, 296; Treuer, *Everything You Wanted to Know About Indians*, 109–11.

80. Hauptman, *Iroquois Struggle for Survival*, 123–50; Scott Manning Stevens, session no. 142 at AHA 2018.

81. Richotte, *Federal Indian Law and Policy*, 194–98; Peter Iverson and Wade Davies, *"We Are Still Here": American Indians Since 1890* (West Sussex, UK, 2015), 149; Alexandra Harmon, "American Indians, American Law, and Modern American Foreign Relations," *Diplomatic History* 39 (2015), 943–54.

82. Courtney Lewis, *Sovereign Entrepreneurs: Cherokee Small-Business Owners and the Making of Economic Sovereignty* (Chapel Hill, 2019); Baird, *Quapaw Indians*, 211–15; John Berrey talk, Clinton Presidential Center, Feb. 13, 2017; Stephen Warren, "Introduction: The Eastern Shawnees and the Repatriation of Their History," in *Eastern Shawnee Tribe of Oklahoma*, 3; Klopotek, *Recognition Odysseys*, 97–109, 175, 240–45; Jessica Cattelino, *High Stakes: Florida Seminole Gaming and Sovereignty* (Durham, 2008).

83. "United Nations Declaration On the Rights of Indigenous Peoples," https://www.un.org/development/desa/indigenouspeoples/declaration-on-the-rights-of-indigenous-peoples.html.

84. T. J. Ferguson and Chip Colwell-Chanthaphonh, *History Is in the Land: Multivocal Tribal Traditions in Arizona's San Pedro Valley* (Tucson, 2006), 237.

85. Forest Hazel, "Occaneechi-Saponi Descendants in the Texas Community of the North Carolina Piedmont," *Excavating Occaneechi Town;* Scott Manning Stevens, "Reclaiming Our Narratives of Place: Haudenosaunee History on the Ground," Nov. 5, 2019, University of North Carolina; Smith, *Everything You Know About Indians Is Wrong,* 62–63, 99, 106–10; Anne Bolen, "Restoring Balance: A Two-Decade Effort Shepherds Dozens of Tlingit Objects Home," *American Indian Magazine* (Winter 2020), 8–17. The NMAI and other Native-designed museums and cultural centers have to try to balance the theme of survival with calling attention to genocide and the past and continuing damage of colonialism. For a careful critique of the NMAI, see Amy Lonetree, *Decolonizing Museums: Representing Native America in National and Tribal Museums* (Chapel Hill, 2012), 73–122, and for insightful context, analysis, and perspectives, see *The National Museum of the American Indian: Critical Conversations,* ed. Amy Lonetree and Amanda J. Cobb (Lincoln, 2008).

86. Betty Gaedtke and Virginia Mouse, demonstrations, Clinton Presidential Center, Feb. 13, 2017; Tom Sakokweniónkwas Porter, *And Grandma Said . . . Iroquois Teachings as Passed Down Through the Oral Tradition,* ed. Lesley Forrester (Mohawk Territory of Akwesasne, 2008), 27; Thomas Belt and Margaret Bender, "Speaking Difference to Power: The Importance of Linguistic Sovereignty," in *Foundations of First Peoples' Sovereignty,* ed. Ulrike Wiethaus (New York, 2008), 187–96. On Catawba women passing down pottery traditions, see Brooke Bauer, "In My Mother's Hands," in *We Will Always Be Here,* 109–13.

87. Nicholas Jones, Rachel Marks, Roberto Ramirez, Merarys Ríos-Vargas, "2020 Census Illuminates Racial and Ethnic Composition of the Country," U.S. Census Bureau, https://www.census.gov/library/stories/2021/08/improved-race-ethnicity -measures-reveal-united-states-population-much-more-multiracial.html; Tina Norris, Paula L. Vines, and Elizabeth M. Hoeffel, "The American Indian and Alaska Native Population: 2010," Census Brief, January 2012, https://www.census .gov/history/pdf/c2010br-10.pdf; Jean M. O'Brien, *Firsting and Lasting: Writing Indians Out of Existence in New England* (Minneapolis, 2010), 201–2; Mikaëla M. Adams, *Who Belongs? Race, Resources, and Tribal Citizenship in the Native South* (New York, 2015); Audra Simpson, *Mohawk Interruptus: Political Life Across the Borders of Settler States* (Durham, 2014), 14.

88. Smith, *Everything You Know About Indians Is Wrong,* 27; W. Richard West Jr., Preface, *Robes of Splendor: Native American Painted Buffalo Hides* (New York, 1993), 15; Joy Harjo, "Anchorage," *She Had Some Horses* (1983, New York, 2008), 4–5.

AFTERWORD: SOVEREIGNTY TODAY

1. William Kugee Supernaw, talk, July 5, 2018, Quapaw Tribal Museum, Quapaw Nation.

2. Louellyn White, *Free to Be Mohawk: Indigenous Education at the Akwesasne Freedom School* (Norman, 2015); Theresa McCarthy, *In Divided Unity: Haudenosaunee Reclamation at Grand River* (Tucson, 2016); Tom Sakokweniónkwas Porter, *Clanology: Clan System of the Iroquois* (Akwesasne, 1993), 40–47; Kayanesenh Paul Williams, "The Mohawk Valley: Yesterday, Today and Tomorrow," in *Kanatsiohareke: Traditional Mohawk Indians Return to Their Ancestral Homeland,* ed. Tom Sakokweniónkwas Porter (Kanatsiohareke and Greenfield Center, N.Y., 2006), 10–11; Kay Ionataiewas Olan, "Epilogue," in *Kanatsiohareke,* 117–25; Chris Clements,

"Between Affect and History: Sovereignty and Ordinary Life at Akwesasne, 1929–1942," *History and Theory* 54 (2015), 105–24.

3. Kathleen L. Hull, "Quality of Life: Native Communities Within and Beyond the Bounds of Colonial Institutions in California," in *Beyond Germs: Native Depopulation in North America*, ed. Catherine M. Cameron, Paul Kelton, and Alan C. Swedlund (Tucson, 2015), 222; Kathleen L. Hull, *Pestilence and Persistence: Yosemite Indian Demography and Culture in Colonial California* (Berkeley, 2009); Patrick Wolfe, "Settler Colonialism and the Elimination of the Native," *Journal of Genocide Research* 8 (2006), 389–94.

4. Deborah A. Miranda, *Bad Indians: A Tribal Memoir* (Berkeley, 2013), xviii–xix.

5. For a similar experience, see Anton Treuer, *Everything You Wanted to Know About Indians but Were Afraid to Ask* (St. Paul, Minn., 2012), 3.

6. "Huhugam Homeland to Phoenix and Back Again," Steven Yazzie, Indigenous Tours Project, 2014, https://vimeo.com/95179964.

7. David Martínez, *Dakota Philosopher: Charles Eastman and American Indian Thought* (Minneapolis, 2009), 52–53, 159; written communication from Brooke Bauer, Aug. 11, 2022.

8. Majel Boxer, "'2,229': John Joseph Mathews, the Osage Tribal Museum, and the Emergence of an Indigenous Museum Model," *Wicazo Sa Review* 31 (2016), 69–93; "Osage Nation Museum," Osage Culture website, https://www.osageculture.com/culture/museum; Scott Manning Stevens, "Collectors and Museums: From Cabinets of Curiosities to Indigenous Cultural Centers," in *The Oxford Handbook of American Indian History*, ed. Frederick E. Hoxie (New York, 2016), 485–87, 492; Joshua M. Gorman, *Building a Nation: Chickasaw Museums and the Construction of History and Heritage* (Tuscaloosa, 2011); Amy Lonetree, *Decolonizing Museums: Representing Native America in National and Tribal Museums* (Chapel Hill, 2012).

9. "Nikani' Kapawe," Shawnee Tribe Cultural Center website, https://www.shawneeculture.org/exhibits/from-ancient-hands/m.staff/89/view/9; Stephen Warren, ed., with the Eastern Shawnee Tribe of Oklahoma, "Introduction: The Eastern Shawnees and the Repatriation of Their History," in *The Eastern Shawnee Tribe of Oklahoma: Resilience Through Adversity* (Norman, 2017), 5–6; Benjamin J. Barnes, "Becoming Our Own Storytellers: Tribal Nations Engaging with Academia," in *Eastern Shawnee Tribe of Oklahoma*, 223–25; "Cherokee Scholars' Statement on Sovereignty and Identity," https://www.thinktsalagi.com/blog/2020/2/13/-cherokee-scholars-statement-on-sovereignty-and-identitynbsp.

10. Doug Kiel, "Nation v. Municipality: Indigenous Land Recovery, Settler Resentment, and Taxation on the Oneida Reservation," *Native American and Indigenous Studies* 6 (2019), 51–73; Corey Kilgannon, "Indians in the Hamptons Stake Claim to a Tiny Eel with a Big Payday," Feb. 1, 2018, *New York Times*, https://www.nytimes.com/2018/02/01/nyregion/hamptons-shinnecock-indians-eels.html?smid=url-share; Mark Harrington, "Judge Finds Shinnecock Tribe Member Guilty of Illegal Fishing," *Newsday*, June 6, 2019, https://www.newsday.com/long-island/politics/shinnecock-eels-fishing-q42633; Jennifer Solis, "Supreme Court to Hear Case Tribes Fear Is a Threat to Sovereignty," Mar. 1, 2022, *Nevada Current*, https://www.nevadacurrent.com/2022/03/01/supreme-court-to-hear-case-tribes-fear-is-a-threat-to-sovereignty/; Adam Liptak, "Supreme Court to Hear Challenge to Law on Adopting Native American Children," Feb. 28, 2022, *New York*

Times, https://www.nytimes.com/2022/02/28/us/supreme-court-native-american -children.html; Elizabeth Ellis, "Centered Sovereignty: How Standing Rock Changed the Conversation," in *Standing with Standing Rock: Voices from the #NoDAPL Movement,* ed. Nick Estes and Jaskiran Dhillo (Minneapolis, 2019); Treuer, *Everything You Wanted to Know About Indians,* 66–67, 86–89; Duane Champagne, *Notes from the Center of Turtle Island* (Lanham, Md., 2010), 147–62.

11. Ronald Geronimo, "Establishing Connections to Place: Identifying O'odham Place Names in Early Spanish Documents," *Journal of the Southwest* 56 (2014), 220; Stephanie Innes, "Tohono O'odham Leaders: Trump's Wall Won't Rise on Tribal Borderland," *Arizona Daily Star,* Feb. 21, 2017; Resolution of the Tohono O'odham Legislative Council (Border Security and Immigration Enforcement on the To-hono O'odham Nation), Resolution 17-053, Feb. 7, 2017, http://www.tonation-nsn .gov/wp-content/uploads/2017/02/17-053-Border-Security-and-Immigration -Enforcement-on-the-Tohono-Oodham-Nation.pdf; Tohono O'odham Nation, "There's No O'odham Word for Wall," 2017, https://www.youtube.com/watch?v= RQu-YEmKCN8&t=18s; Jeffrey M. Schultz, *Are We Not Foreigners Here? Indige-nous Nationalism in the U.S.-Mexico Borderlands* (Chapel Hill, 2018), 159, 194–96, 199–200; Elizabeth Ellis, "The Border(s) Crossed Us Too: The Intersections of Native American and Immigrant Fights for Justice," *Emisférica* 14 (2018); Brenden W. Rensink, *Native but Foreign: Indigenous Immigrants and Refugees in the North American Borderlands* (College Station, Tex., 2018); Joanne Barker, *Sovereignty Matters: Locations of Contestation and Possibility in Indigenous Struggles for Self-Determination* (Lincoln, 2005).

12. Keith Richotte Jr., *Federal Indian Law and Policy: An Introduction* (St. Paul, Minn., 2020), chaps. 22–25; O'Brien, *Firsting and Lasting,* 203–4; *Recognition, Sovereignty Struggles, and Indigenous Rights in the United States: A Sourcebook,* ed. Amy E. Den Ouden and Jean M. O'Brien (Chapel Hill, 2013).

13. *Boston Globe,* Apr. 1, 2020; *Implementation of Public Law 100-497, The Indian Gam-ing Regulatory Act of 1988, and Related Law Enforcement Issues: Oversight Hearing, Before the Subcomm. on Native American Affairs of the Comm. on Natural Resources,* 103rd Cong. (1993), https://turtletalk.files.wordpress.com/2016/07/1993-trump -nat-res-testimony-pdf.pdf; Elizabeth Ellis, *The Great Power of Small Nations: In-digenous Diplomacy in the Gulf South* (Philadelphia, 2022); O'Brien, *Firsting and Lasting.*

14. *McGirt v. Oklahoma,* 591 U.S. (2020); *Oklahoma v. Castro-Huerta,* 597 U.S. (2022); Curtis Killman, "ICYMI: Supreme Court to Huddle Tomorrow on Whether to Take On Oklahoma's 40-plus McGirt Appeals," Jan. 16, 2023, *Tulsa World,* https:// tulsaworld.com/news/state-and-regional/supreme-court-sets-date-with -oklahoma-to-respond-to-40-plus-mcgirt-appeals/article_714b62a4-59db-11ec -99d5-eb2ab6f4da01.html.

15. Natalie Diaz, "The Beauty of a Busted Fruit," *When My Brother Was an Aztec* (Port Townsend, 2012), 98; Brenda J. Child, *My Grandfather's Knocking Sticks: Ojibwe Family Life and Labor on the Reservation* (Minneapolis, 2014), 3; Jodi A. Byrd, *The Transit of Empire: Indigenous Critiques of Colonialism* (Minneapolis, 2011), xi; Lonetree, *Decolonizing Museums,* 119; Nick Estes, *Our History Is the Future: Stand-ing Rock Versus the Dakota Access Pipeline, and the Long Tradition of Indigenous Re-sistance* (2019), 254–56; Treuer, *Everything You Wanted to Know About Indians,* 154.

16. "U.S. Life Expectancy Falls Again in 'Historic' Setback," Aug. 31, 2022, *New York*

Times; https://www.ncai.org/policy-issues/economic-development-commerce/census; Mary Dorinda Allard and Vernon Brundage Jr., "American Indians and Alaska Natives in the U.S. Labor Force," *Monthly Labor Review,* U.S. Bureau of Labor Statistics, November 2019, https://doi.org/10.21916/mlr.2019.24; "Disparities," Fact Sheet, Indian Health Service, November 2019, https://www.ihs.gov/newsroom/factsheets/disparities/; "Addressing the COVID-19 Pandemic in Indian Country," National Congress of American Indians, 2021, https://www.ncai.org/FINAL_2021_ECWS_Days_One_Pager_-_DHS_.pdf; Mark Walker, "Pandemic Highlights Deep-Rooted Problems in Indian Health Service," *New York Times,* Sept. 29, 2020, https://www.nytimes.com/2020/09/29/us/politics/coronavirus-indian-health-service.html; Donovan Quintero, "The COVID-19 Outbreak in the Navajo Nation," Developing Stories: Native Photographers in the Field, National Museum of the American Indian, https://americanindian.si.edu/developingstories/quintero.html.

17. "American Indians Have Highest COVID Vaccine Rate," National Indian Council on Aging, Inc., September 10, 2021, https://www.nicoa.org/american-indians-have-highest-covid-vaccine-rate/; Quintero, "COVID-19 Outbreak in the Navajo Nation"; Katherine Florey, "The Tribal COVID-19 Response," *Regulatory Review,* Mar. 17, 2021, https://www.theregreview.org/2021/03/17/florey-tribal-covid-19-response/.

18. Paul DeMain, "Contemporary History: Native America in the Twenty-First Century," *The Oxford Handbook of American Indian History,* ed. Frederick E. Hoxie (New York, 2016), 153–56.

19. Autumn Bracey, "Eastern Shawnee Tribe Hopes to Teach People Gardening," Four States home page, February 15, 2019, https://www.fourstateshomepage.com/news/eastern-shawnee-tribe-hopes-to-teach-people-gardening/; Hannah Wallace, "The Quapaw Nation's Casino Farms Its Own Food," *Civil Eats,* December 10, 2020, https://civileats.com/2020/12/10/the-quapaw-nations-casino-farms-its-own-food/; Jacqueline Fear-Segal, "The Long and Enduring Relationship Between the Cherokee and British People," Beyond the Spectacle: Native North American Presence in Britain, University of Kent, February 12, 2019, https://blogs.kent.ac.uk/bts/2019/02/12/the-long-and-enduring-relationship-between-the-cherokee-and-british-people/; David Treuer, *The Heartbeat of Wounded Knee: Native America from 1890 to the Present* (New York, 2019), 443; Paul Chaat Smith, "The Invention of Thanksgiving," *Smithsonian Insider,* Jan. 10, 2018, https://insider.si.edu/2018/01/the-invention-of-thanksgiving/.

20. Robin Caudell, "Patches of Snow's Pallette," Plattsburgh *Press-Republican,* Feb. 6, 2020.

INDEX

Page numbers of illustrations appear in italics.

About the Author

Kathleen DuVal is a professor of history at the University of North Carolina at Chapel Hill, where she teaches early American and American Indian history. Her previous works include *Independence Lost* (2015), which was a finalist for the George Washington Prize, and *The Native Ground: Indians and Colonists in the Heart of the Continent* (2006). She is also a co-editor of *Interpreting a Continent: Voices from Colonial America* (2009).